THE LEGALIST REFORMATION

D1591209

STUDIES IN LEGAL HISTORY

Published by the University of North Carolina Press

in association with the American Society for Legal History

Thomas A. Green & Hendrik Hartog, editors

THE LEGALIST REFORMATION

Law, Politics, and Ideology in New York, 1920–1980

WILLIAM E. NELSON

The University of North Carolina Press *Chapel Hill & London*

© 2001

The University of North Carolina Press

All rights reserved

Set in Adobe Garamond

by Tseng Information Systems, Inc.

Manufactured in the United States of America

The paper in this book meets the guidelines

for permanence and durability of the Committee

on Production Guidelines for Book Longevity of

the Council on Library Resources.

Library of Congress

Cataloging-in-Publication Data

Nelson, William Edward, 1940–

The legalist reformation: law, politics, and ideology

in New York, 1920–1980 / William E. Nelson.

    p. cm. — (Studies in legal history)

Includes index.

ISBN 0-8078-2591-3 (cloth: alk. paper)

1. Law—New York (State)—History.   2. Social

change—New York (State)—History.   3. Law and

politics—History.   I. Title.   II. Series.

KFN5078 .N45   2001

340'.115'09747—dc21   00-060724

05   04   03   02   01   5   4   3   2   1

TO BERNARD BAILYN

CONTENTS

THE LEGALIST REFORMATION

INTRODUCTION

In the words of one commentator, the city of New York during the past century has witnessed "the coarse, yet closest, attempt of . . . [people] of all colors, skins, faiths and tongues to live together in community."[1] The thesis of this book is that the law of New York—law proclaimed largely by state court judges rather than by legislators or federal officials—has been the principal instrument facilitating this attempt. A further hypothesis, which this book will suggest but not document, is that the legal ideology adumbrated by New York judges has, at the threshold of a new millennium, become the standard of justice for all those people in the world who, like New Yorkers, are striving to coexist.

I did not begin my research on this book with my present thesis, or indeed with any hypotheses whatever, in mind. I decided to write the book, not because I knew what I wanted to say but because the literature of American legal history contained an enormous gap. While books and articles had been written about twentieth-century federal constitutional and regulatory law, no one had written a monographic, historical synthesis of the century's developments in state constitutional law or in the common law.

This book offers such a synthesis. But it also aims to do more. Resting on a foundational assumption that historians should rediscover forgotten data rather than rehash what is already familiar, I opted against generating my synthesis out of materials included for pedagogical and argumentative reasons in leading casebooks. Instead, I decided to reconstruct in all its detail and complexity the law, both public and private, of a single jurisdiction. By focusing on one state, I could give attention to the often highly revealing secondary opinions of the state's highest court, as well as the opinions of intermediate and trial court judges. Statistical analysis of the work of trial courts also became possible. Ultimately, my decision to focus on a single state enabled me, and I hope will enable my readers, to delight in the discovery of new knowledge and insight.

New York was the obvious state to investigate. It was home to many key twentieth-century legal players, such as Benjamin N. Cardozo and Karl Llewellyn. For most of the century, New York was the most populous state and the economic and cultural leader of the nation. It was in one important respect also more typical of the nation as a whole than any other single state: with its metropolitan center on the Atlantic coast, its upstate industrial cities little different from those of the Midwest, its expanding suburbs, and its rural farmlands and environmentally protected woodlands, New York contained locales similar to those in all the rest of the nation except the Deep South and the Far West. One would accordingly expect to find a wider variety of the sociopolitical forces that shape law in New York than in other jurisdictions. Of course, those forces might converge differently in New York than elsewhere; indeed, New York City's position as the world's first multicultural metropolis and as a center of world finance and commerce probably meant that legal changes occurred in New York before they did elsewhere. Of course, we cannot be certain that the law of New York either anticipated or otherwise paralleled the law of other jurisdictions. But until other scholars examine in detail California, Texas, and at least one southeastern state, the conclusions about New York law set forth in the pages that follow should serve as preliminary hypotheses about more general, nationwide developments in the law beyond those that occurred in the Supreme Court of the United States.

A second assumption I brought to my research was the common lawyer's faith that analysis of judicial opinions is key to understanding law. Accordingly, I read widely in some 620 volumes of the *New York Supplement* and in decisions from the Second Circuit Court of Appeals and the New York District Courts published in the *Federal Reporter* and in *Federal Supplement*.[2] In an effort to limit the scope of my research, I imposed some arbitrary limitations. When I began research in the mid-1980s, I decided to end the book in 1980; correspondingly, I chose to begin in 1920. I also decided not to read cases dealing with criminal procedure or with most of the substantive law of crime. I believe, however, that I have read most of the remaining cases.

My third assumption was that statistical analysis can help in understanding the impact of doctrine on society. With the aid of student research assistants, I accordingly gathered a random sample of approximately fifty thousand unreported trial court cases. The sample included about one hundred cases per year from each of the four federal district courts in the state and one hundred cases per year from trial courts in each of four counties—New York County, which comprises the island of Manhattan; Nassau, a suburban county on Long Island; Erie, an upstate industrialized county containing the city of Buffalo; and Tompkins, an upstate rural county.

It is important to emphasize that this book's focus on private-law doctrine and on cases in trial and appellate courts does not stem from a belief that law is autonomous or that legal change occurs independently of political, economic, or cultural change.[3] Indeed, my fourth assumption is precisely the opposite — that law is deeply embedded in the culture and political economy of its time. Thus I have studied New York law not for its own sake but for what it reveals about the people of the state and their economy, politics, and society.

On the basis of these four assumptions, my goal became to create a narrative, drawn initially out of legal sources, about how private and public law, politics, and ideology changed in tandem in New York between 1920 and 1980.[4] As I pursued research toward this goal, it became increasingly clear that, in the early decades of the twentieth century, the state was the scene of virulent struggle between a mainly upstate, White Anglo-Saxon Protestant (WASP), upper and middle class and an impoverished, New York City–centered, mainly Jewish and Roman Catholic, immigrant underclass. It also became clear that I would write a narrative about how people born into the underclass used the law to alter the dynamic of conflict and thereby gain admission into the mainstream of New York life.

At the outset of the century, two overlapping sets of beliefs, with roots deep in the American past, supported the status quo. One was a sort of populist localism, by which the countryside of upstate New York had governed itself for several generations. This populist paradigm locates political power in small, homogeneous, participatory communities, which govern themselves democratically and band together to prevent centralized bureaucratic institutions from interfering in their local governmental processes. Populist localism explains well how the small towns of upstate New York constructed a conservative coalition to govern themselves and the state as a whole from the mid-nineteenth well into the twentieth century.[5]

The other prop of the status quo was a set of racist beliefs that certain ethnic and religious groups, notably WASPs, were better suited than others, especially southern and eastern European Catholics and Jews, to participate in American civic and economic life. These beliefs, which also were deeply rooted, in this instance in the past of North Atlantic civilization, ultimately culminated on one side of the ocean in Nazism. Since most Americans espoused antistatist beliefs, few became Nazis. But the parallelism between and common roots of Nazism and American racism were nonetheless evident. As Hitler himself observed in 1933, the "American people were the first to draw practical and political conclusions from differences among races and from the different value of different races" and through immigration laws "prevented the entry of those races which seemed unwelcome to the American people." And as *Time* magazine added in publishing Hitler's comment, Germany as of 1933 had merely "reduce[d] her Jewish inhabitants to the social and political position occupied by Negroes in the southern U.S. and Orientals in the West."[6]

Inasmuch as American democracy was conceptualized in terms of local self-rule, and homogeneity was deemed essential to that self-rule, localist populism and ideas of ethnic and religious hierarchy overlapped. White, Protestant Americans had established self-governing communities within the territorial boundaries of the United States, whereas Catholics, Jews, and African Americans, it was thought, had not. If the existing communities were to be preserved, it seemed that the latter groups, which had never established their own communities, had to be excluded. Thus for the WASP groups on one side of the social divide in early twentieth-century New York, racially exclusionary policies and the preservation of democracy appeared to go hand in hand.

Populist localism and ideas of ethnic and religious hierarchy were doomed over time, however, as the center of population and power in the Empire State shifted away from small, upstate hamlets and gravitated increasingly to New York City and its growing suburbs. In 1860, the counties that would later constitute Greater New York, plus the adjacent counties of Nassau, Suffolk, and Westchester, constituted only 31 percent of the population of New York State. By 1890, that figure had risen to 45 percent. In 1900, the city and the three adjacent counties for the first time embraced a majority of the state's population. By 1910, they contained 56 percent and, by 1940, 64 percent.[7] Thus the small, homogeneous, participatory, WASP communities that had governed New York in the nineteenth century ineluctably became outnumbered in the twentieth.

The localist-racist ideas that had sufficed for governing upstate communities simply could not work in New York City, which was neither small nor ethnically and religiously homogeneous. Of all the cities of the world in 1900, New York had the second largest population. It also was the first place in America, if not the world, in which a multiplicity of diverse groups from Europe, Africa, the Americas, and even Asia came together in large numbers.[8] On Manhattan, native-born white Americans, African Americans, descendants of German and Catholic Irish immigrants, Italians, Jews, Chinese, and people from various parts of Latin America lived adjacent to each other within the space of a few square miles for most of the twentieth century.

At the outset of the century, intolerance, bigotry, and fear characterized relationships among these diverse peoples. Then, under the guidance of such judges as Benjamin N. Cardozo, Henry J. Friendly, Stanley H. Fuld, Learned Hand, Irving Lehman, Harlan Fiske Stone, and Edward Weinfeld, the law step-by-step created procedures to facilitate tolerance and productive interchange. Although New York has hardly achieved utopia, its strivings for community have gained increasing relevance as technology has brought the peoples of the world into closer proximity to each other and led to the emergence of demographic patterns like New York's in other cities and settings.

The law has obvious importance in regulating the interactions of diverse groups. At the turn of the century, racism against African Americans infected the South, for example, partially as a result of law, while discrimination against Asian Americans prevailed in California, where racism and the law were inextricably intertwined. As diverse groups faced each other in twentieth-century New York, innumerable legal issues involving race, ethnicity, and religion likewise arose.

In the main, courts and judges resolved the issues. In part, the judiciary assumed its role through default. Because no one group constituted a clear majority in New York, it usually was difficult to get the legislative process geared up to resolve issues of intergroup relations. Unable to build a majoritarian coalition behind any particular program, the legislature often had to take a pass. The courts, however, could not pass; litigants presented intergroup conflicts to them, and they had to decide the cases. Thus courts and judges became quite powerful.

Courts also became powerful because much social conflict manifested itself in the form of private-law litigation between individuals. For every dispute between government and a minority religious group, between an employer and a labor union, or between those who would grant the state broad regulatory powers and those who would hold it to narrow standards, there were hundreds of cases between individuals involving common-law issues of tort, contract, property, and procedure. And many of these cases, like the one brought against a German corporation by a Jewish refugee who claimed his employment contract was breached when he was fired solely on grounds of religion,[9] required courts, typically without legislative guidance, to resolve issues of social policy.

A final important reason for legislative passivity and judicial activism was ideology. Legislatures, it is suggested, resolve intergroup conflicts in accordance with prevalent ideological beliefs, and the two prevalent ideologies of the early twentieth century—localist populism and racial hierarchy—were useless in resolving the intergroup conflicts faced by the people of New York City.

Progressive reformers and others seeking fairer treatment of the underclass needed a new ideology—one that would justify government activism on behalf of the downtrodden. Some progressives accordingly embraced Marxism or its democratic socialist variants, which were the only reform ideologies in existence at the outset of the century. But Marxism failed in the main function for which Marx had designed it, as a predictive device. The difficulty was that no chance ever existed that the proletariat would seize power in New York and achieve the victory for which Marx had called. The Empire State was not Russia, where a politically active proletariat could grab power forcibly in one or two large cities and from those cities dominate a politically passive countryside.

Moreover, Marxism was not an option for most leaders of the progressive cause. First, some of them, like Herbert and Irving Lehman, were born wealthy, while others, like Alfred E. Smith, aspired to wealth and attained it before they died. Some Bolsheviks, of course, had also been born, if not to wealth, at least to comfort.[10] Unlike the Bolsheviks, though, leaders like the Lehmans did not feel guilty about being rich; they saw their wealth instead as a device for engaging in philanthropic activities and promoting social good. Second, the progressive leaders had all achieved power not by directing tightly knit radical groups but by winning democratic, majoritarian elections. Although the role of money in 1920s political campaigns was slight compared to its role today, money was not trivial, especially in urban settings. Money was an element of political success, and leaders who had won elections in the past and hoped to win more elections in the future could not deprive themselves of access to it.[11]

Third, leaders like Cardozo, Smith, and the Lehmans could not win elections or govern thereafter by appealing only to lower-class, ethnic, and religious minorities; to wield effective political power, they needed to form coalitions that included allies and supporters from the old WASP establishment, such as Franklin D. Roosevelt. Although occasional WASP patricians were attracted to Marxism, most were not.

Thus a totally new ideology was needed for governing the increasingly urban and pluralistic culture that was emerging in twentieth-century New York. But as badly as they needed new ideas, key progressive leaders as late as the 1920s and even the early 1930s had difficulty elaborating them. In part, that was because they were men of affairs and pragmatists, not ideologues. Smith, for example, won elections on grounds of honesty; Roosevelt, as a leader who would work hard, would learn, and would take new approaches in office; and Herbert Lehman, as a great administrator. At the same time, however, all three commanded deep loyalty among their followers and aroused strong hatred on the part of opponents.[12] Pragmatism, rhetorical skill, honesty, administrative skill, and an openness to new approaches did not produce the loyalties and hatreds of which Smith, Roosevelt, and Lehman were the focus. The loyalties and hatreds stemmed, instead, from what these progressive leaders symbolized in the eyes of their supporters and opponents—a new, slowly emerging, urban-based, but still inchoate ideology of social justice and reform hostile to populist localism, Nazism and racism, and Marxism.

Since progressive leaders proved unable to elaborate their new ideology during the 1920s or for most of the 1930s, a new approach to politics was constructed only in the late 1930s, when New Yorkers reacted to the flagrant violations of human rights and human dignity by Hitler's regime in Germany. Even then, the new ideology was not articulated by bookish intellectuals such as Karl Marx or scholarly political leaders such as Thomas Jefferson or James Madison. No one book like *Mein Kampf* proclaimed even an extremist version of the new ideology. Instead, the new ideology was proclaimed mainly by judges and lawyers, who then used it to transform judge-made doctrine over the course of the next three decades. Later, the ideology spread worldwide as the three alternative political paradigms that had existed in early twentieth-century New York collapsed on a global scale.

The new ideology was a product more of action than of ideas, although ideas sometimes influenced the direction of action or emerged in the aftermath of action, as explanations or justifications for what had been done. Above all, the new ideology was legalist in nature, in that it resulted from the arguments of lawyers seeking to influence judges or other government officials and from the endeavors of all three—lawyers, judges, and officials—to build support for what they had done. As we shall see in the chapters that follow, the new ideology often emerged and played itself out in common-law tort, contract, and property cases as well as in matters involving judicial resolution of public law matters.

I propose the term "legalist reformation" to characterize the new ideology because it encapsulates the two main elements of the movement I am portraying, which began in New York in the late 1930s and continued in the decades thereafter. The movement was reform-oriented: its goal was social change and the expansion of existing hierarchies to include people who had previously been made subordinate. Yet it was also legalist: it did not repudiate the commitment to the rule of law which late nineteenth-century elites, in their search for order, had adopted as an alternative political theory to democratic majoritarianism and evangelical Protestantism.[13] For legalist reformers of the twentieth century, the rule of law not only served as an established cultural norm but also offered greater promise of social change than any other political or philosophical alternative.

The legalist reformation developed in connection with and in the aftermath of the New Deal. But despite the vast scholarly literature on the New Deal,[14] the legalist reformation has never been studied in all its complexity in a theoretically sound fashion. The central goal of this book is to grasp this new approach, which came to dominate New York and American, and ultimately global, sociolegal culture, by observing its emergence, piece by piece, in the late 1930s and thereafter.

Thus this book will examine New York case law in the twentieth century as a series of cultural markers that reveal a society in which, before the late 1930s, issues of race, ethnicity, religion, and gender were virtually never mentioned in judicial decisions, conflict was conceptualized largely along class lines, and repression of underclasses was the norm. New Yorkers began to follow a path away from that repressive society in the World War II era, when, as both the public law and the common-law cases show, they began to reconceptualize social conflict in terms of the power of majorities and the rights of minorities. Along that path, the people of New York rejected ideologies that favored racist and localist government, on the one hand, and Marxist revolution, on the other. As they negotiated their new path, people also used law to elaborate in a step-by-step process that lasted several decades a new ideology in action — an ideology of liberty, equality, human dignity, and entrepreneurial opportunity that today has matured into the hope of the progressive world.

This mature ideology, it is essential to note, is not some fixed and final entity to which the world has now ultimately turned in a concluding stroke toward peace, freedom, and equality. Indeed, since the late 1960s, when African Americans, feminists, and political conservatives began demanding new ideologies, the contingency of the legalist reform legacy and its internal contradictions have become apparent. But neither those on the right and the left who attack the legalist reformation nor those in the center who continue to defend it have rejected its main aspirations for liberty, equality, human dignity, and opportunity. Accordingly, this book reflects my understanding that, just as the legalist reformation emerged gradually amid the conflicts and contradictions of the New Deal, World War II, and early Cold War eras, so today it is evolving gradually as those who have inherited it perceive new contradictions within it and differ over how to resolve them.

Nonetheless, I remain convinced that the birth and maturation of the legalist reformation represented a milestone in American legal history. Cardozo, Roosevelt, and other legalist reformers all have an enduring and deserved place in the pantheon; the most successful of today's leaders, such as William H. Rehnquist and William Jefferson Clinton, are not their equals. Leaders like Cardozo, Roosevelt, and the Lehmans earned their special place in history by participating in the genesis of something special; in contrast, today's politicians and judges, however smart, engaging, or eloquent, are merely working out details. All legal thinkers today are the heirs of mid-twentieth-century legalist reform, however much they may disagree about the meaning of their inheritance.

Although we must not fall prey to the vice of reifying legalist reform, we thus should recognize that the concept reflects a cluster of values that remain at the core of American legal and political thinking even today. These values initially emerged in New York law in the second quarter of the twentieth century and were more fully elaborated during the third quarter. It is to the emergence of those values in their full economic, social, and cultural context that this book next turns.

This context will be presented in the initial chapters of each of the three parts of this book: the first, entitled "1922," will portray life in New York in the opening decades of the twentieth century and then turn to political events beginning in 1922 that put into power new socioeconomic groups who slowly modified specific legal doctrines into rules more favorable to their interests. The second, entitled "1938," will trace changes in New York society and culture and in the global economy in the World War II era—changes that transformed the law of the state in profound ways. Finally, a chapter entitled "1968" will focus on the cataclysms of that year in the United States—cataclysms marking the commencement of a process of cultural change that ultimately would affect the course of New York and, indeed, all American law.

Interspersed among these three chapters are a series of chapters focusing on legal doctrinal developments connected with the matters described in the contextualizing chapters. For example, the three chapters that follow the "1922" chapter display New York legal doctrine in the first third of the twentieth century as a reflection of the economic, social, and cultural cleavages between conservatives and reformers that lasted into the 1930s. The six chapters following the "1938" chapter, in turn, focus on transformations of legal doctrine, especially in private law, that began in the late 1930s and, in some cases, endured throughout the rest of the century. Similarly, the four chapters following the "1968" chapter analyze changes in legal doctrine occurring in its aftermath.

Finally, the book ends with an epilogue entitled "A Golden Anniversary," which merely suggests how the legal ideology initially adumbrated by New York judges, lawyers, and officials over the course of the twentieth century became relevant to the world at large as the century ended.

PART I

Conservatives and Reformers

CHAPTER I

1922

Astounding contradictions marked the political economy of New York during the opening decades of the twentieth century. Take, for example, the matter of population density. Throughout the century, Hamilton County, located in the center of the Adirondacks, has been the most sparsely settled county in the United States east of the Mississippi and north of Florida. Some two hundred miles to the south, in contrast, lay Manhattan's Lower East Side, which during the first quarter of the century was probably the most densely populated place on earth.[1]

It also was one of the more squalid. In his classic muckraking work, *How the Other Half Lives,* Jacob A. Riis had described the Lower East Side as a place where "dirt and desolation reign[ed]" and "danger lurk[ed]." It was a place where "hundreds of men, women, and children [were] every day slowly starving to death" and where "the instinct of motherhood even was smothered by poverty and want" as the "poor abandon[ed] their children," leaving only little notes such as one that Riis had read "in a woman's trembling hand: 'Take care of Johnny, for God's sake, I cannot.'"[2]

Nobody better symbolized the plight of the Lower East Side "than the desperate peddler, his pack heavy on his back, hopelessly pleading for a customer." One peddler, for example, would get up at 5:30, go get his pushcart from the nearby pushcart stable, wheel it over to the wholesaler, and then take it over the ferry to Brooklyn, where he would peddle bananas for total earnings of $2.00 to $2.50 per day. Not surprisingly, families like those of the peddler had no apartment but "just a cellar with a wood floor and plenty of rats." As late as 1923, many tenement units still "didn't have electricity" but had "gaslight . . . iceboxes, coal stoves, turlets in the hall." "In fact," as one Lower East Side resident reported, "the outhouse they used to use was still in the yard," and there was "a stable right next" door, where children "used to play on the dead horses" which were left "layin' on the street, and then we'd play king of the hill on there. After a while, the smell didn't bother us."[3]

Of course, children, in addition to play, had jobs such as collecting coal as it fell off delivery trucks. As one reported, "I'd have a bag to put the stuff in. When I came home, I was as black as a black man. My mother would wash me and say, 'You mustn't do that no more,' but we needed the coal." Obviously, there also was little to eat: "for dinner there would be a quarter of a little chicken for three of us . . . and that was a special dinner—for Friday nights." More commonly, "my mother used to make a soup, just plain potato and onion—if she was lucky, a carrot, and if she was extra, extra lucky, some dill." Circumstances reached their nadir during the Great Depression, when people "were livin' in cardboard boxes under the Williamsburg Bridge" and were "on the street beggin' for pennies, sellin' whatever they could find—apples, a fountain pen, somethin' they picked up or stole—to get a couple of pennies. People that didn't wanna steal had to steal. Basically, they were honest people, but they stole to survive."[4]

Only three miles to the north, on Fifth Avenue, was Millionaires Row—an "extraordinarily expensive residential area that had an aggregate value estimated at seventy million dollars, unremarkable for a group of householders who controlled at least fifty million dollars each." Among the spectacles was the 130-room white granite mansion of Senator William A. King, a copper magnate from Montana. For residents of Millionaires Row, politics had "nothing to do with sympathy with the poor;" according to Claudia Hatch Stearns, a direct descendant of Priscilla Alden, she was not even "aware of the poverty of the 30's." Her family had come to New York in the mid-1800s, when her great-grandfather had "dealt in money." "His sister," it appears, had "married Lincoln's Secretary of the Treasury, so he floated all the bonds for the Civil War." Her grandparents had moved after the war to the Upper West Side, but then they "moved back to the East Side because the 'immigrants,' the Jews, came in and took over, and they couldn't very well live with them, so they moved."[5]

Daily life on Millionaires Row centered on balls and dinners, such as a special dinner of paté and chicken for a hundred of society's leading canines. Another event was a "party for toy dolls, who were seated at a sumptuous dining table while their otherwise adult owners chatted amiably in baby talk." "No wonder Mrs. O. H. P. Belmont threw up her hands in frustration one day and declared, 'I know of no profession, art or trade that women are working in today, as taxing on mental resources as being a leader of society.' "[6]

As Jacob Riis and others saw it, the gap between the classes in the early twentieth century widened day by day. Those who ruled New York displayed little tolerance toward the poor. The era was a time not of equality but of "repression along class . . . lines." Recipients of public assistance, for example, were seen as people " 'without habits of industry or thrift, improvident, usually physically or mentally deficient, who [were] unable through efforts of their own to gain a livelihood.' " It was " 'common knowledge' " that such poor persons were " 'constantly seeking, and generally receive[d] at somewhat regular intervals, public charity or assistance; they ha[d] a practically constant status as 'poor persons'; they [were] not able to maintain themselves for any long period of time even under ordinary conditions.' "[7]

Impoverished workers were not thought to be much better. Only a "very few men in every hundred or thousand," it was said, had sufficient "industry, brains *and* thrift" to get ahead. Wage workers, according to the same writer, remained employees of others because they had "not initiative enough to be employers themselves"; they remained "poor" because of "lack of brains, lack of wit to earn, thrift to save, and knowledge to use [their] savings." "No man who ha[d] endeavored to carry out an enterprise," according to a turn-of-the-century sermon, could avoid being "well-nigh appalled at times by the imbecility of the average man—the inability or unwillingness to concentrate on a thing and do it." Indeed, the "nature of man" was thought to be such that "the superior few and the inferior many scarcely appear[ed] to belong to the same species."[8]

If New York's leaders saw the poor as lazy, amoral, and worthy of suspicion, their vision of themselves stood in marked contrast. For the elite, "dishonesty and sinful behavior of any sort was considered not only ignoble but also an impractical way to make money." People in the upper classes understood that they possessed "character" — "a stiffening of the vertebrae which . . . cause[d] them to be loyal to a trust, to act promptly, concentrate their energies, [and] do the thing." They felt themselves bound by a "PHILOSOPHY OF FAIR PLAY"; as Julius H. Barnes, president of the U.S. Chamber of Commerce, explained, "In America the various sports of our youth teach the principles of team play and of fair play. . . . On every baseball diamond and football field the qualities of fortitude and courage and fair play, inspired by loyalty to club or town or college, are instilled in our young men." Elite New Yorkers ran their lives and businesses, they believed, in accordance with this creed of fortitude, hard work, loyalty, and fair play.[9]

Prejudices along religious and ethnic lines often lay beneath the social and economic inequality that was rampant in New York in the early twentieth century. These prejudices contrasted "a WASP vision of a tasteless, colorless, odorless, sweatless world" against a portrait of "ethnic minorities [who] cooked with vivid spices—even garlic!—and might neglect . . . deodorants, and regular bathing" and needed to be shown "how to cleanse themselves." There was virulent anti-Semitism on the part of prominent people such as Henry James, who expressed shock at the " 'Hebrew conquest of New York' " that was transforming the city into a " 'new Jerusalem,' " and Henry Ford, who as late as the 1920s issued repeated warnings against the " 'Jewish menace' " and who in 1938 accepted the Grand Cross of the German Eagle from the Nazi regime.[10] Anti-Semitism arguably persisted as late as the 1930s and early 1940s even in the Court of Appeals, which in one case sustained a village ordinance excluding a denominational mental hospital that had bought land and obtained a license from the State Hospital Commission before the ordinance was adopted, and in another declined to overturn the refusal of the commissioner of education to allow the former director of the Neurological Institute at the University of Vienna, who had fled the Nazis in 1938, to practice medicine in New York following his appointments as clinical professor of neurology at Columbia University and research neuropathologist at Montefiore Hospital. As Judge Charles S. Desmond noted in his dissent in the latter case, the refugee doctor was " 'unquestionably the most prominent of recent emigres' " and allowing him to practice would not "let . . . down any bars or mak[e] . . . possible any great inrush of emigre physicians." Still the state education commissioner would not permit him to practice, and the courts sustained the commissioner's refusal.[11]

Anti-Semitism, anti-Catholicism, and hostility to immigrants were hardly confined to elites. Many Americans in and out of New York City saw Jews, for instance, as "inflamed radical[s] responsible for Communist revolution in eastern Europe . . . [and] a vast conspiracy designed to enslave America." The chief institutional manifestation of such prejudices was the Ku Klux Klan (KKK). Although still predominantly a southern phenomenon, the Klan maintained a large, well-organized presence in New York State into the 1930s, with the *New York Times* estimating that two hundred thousand persons belonged to the Klan statewide in 1923.[12]

The Klan was virulently anti-Jewish, anti-Catholic, and anti-immigrant. The Klansman's Creed expressly stated that "I believe in the limitation of foreign immigration. I am a native-born American citizen and I believe my rights in this country are superior to those of foreigners." One letter sent by the KKK to Protestant pastors in the state exhorted them to form local klans and vote for "Protestants only who have no marriage affiliations with Catholics or Jews, or partners with either." The letter closed with "Save the county and your State from Jews and Catholics." At one KKK organizational meeting in 1922, a speaker for the Klan railed against Jewish control of everything from newspaper stands—he alleged that twenty-five thousand of the twenty-seven thousand newsstands in New York City were Jewish-owned—to the motion picture industry. At a later Klan rally, an unidentified minister warned that the Roman Catholic Church was a political party in disguise and that Jews in America sought only money and political influence—as if such ambition did not flourish in WASP circles.[13] When the Cure of Ars Catholic Church was established on suburban Long Island in 1926, the KKK burned a cross in its parking lot, and when the Irish-American Catholic Al Smith ran for president in 1928 on the Democratic Party ticket, flaming crosses burned on the hills of Alabama and Mississippi, and by order of the Suffolk County GOP—a Klan-dominated organization at the time—on the hills of Suffolk as well. Although many religious leaders condemned the Klan, not all did. Thus one Protestant minister, Rev. C. I. Oswald, pastor of the Freeport Presbyterian Church, vehemently defended the Klan in a sermon titled "Has the Ku Klux Klan the Right to Organize in New York State?" In Oswald's opinion, the answer was yes.[14]

Cross-burnings and rallies drawing thousands, with placards reading "No Koons, Kikes, or Katolics," reminded blacks, Jews, and Catholics alike that many New Yorkers continued to resent their presence. Although reports of Klan-organized violence were rare, they were not unheard-of. Cross-burnings occurred across Nassau County, for example, during the 1920s, scaring residents of Valley Stream, lighting the sky above Garden City, and frightening blacks in Freeport. As the Klan historian William Randel noted, "The symbolic power of the fiery cross. . . . casts a shadow on many a neighborhood to know that it harbors a potentially hostile element which at any moment may disrupt the illusion of peace."[15]

The Klan sometimes employed more direct means of intimidation. On August 14, 1924, eight men entered a suburban Long Island pharmacy owned by Ernest Louis, a Jew accused but cleared of child molestation. They informed him that "we don't want your type around here. You have eight days to get out. This is a warning from the Ku Klux Klan." Louis dismissed the threat as a joke, but a few days later as he walked along a local street with his wife, a car approached and a group of men jumped out, forcing Louis into the car. After driving around for a few hours, the kidnappers deposited the dazed druggist several miles away. Within a couple of weeks, Louis and his family moved from the suburbs back to New York City. Although he denied that the threat or kidnapping had anything to do with his decision, Louis remarked that "I haven't money enough to stay here and fight, any way, and I have lost all my business on account of the whole thing." Though a search was conducted for the kidnappers, the likelihood of their apprehension was remote: less than a week after the kidnapping, two thousand klansmen paraded through Louis's former village led by its police chief.[16]

In response to this rising activity by the Klan, New York State senator Jimmy Walker, the future mayor of New York City, introduced a bill in the state legislature that, while exempting labor and benevolent organizations, required private organizations to disclose membership lists. The bill passed by a narrow margin. In response to the new law, the Klan unsuccessfully attempted to incorporate as a benevolent organization under the name of Alpha Pi Sigma, Inc. After that effort failed, the Klan challenged the constitutionality of the legislation but again lost.[17]

The law achieved its intended effect as Klan influence began to wane in the 1930s. In 1933, the three-day "konklave" of the New York and New Jersey Klans attracted only 150 members, and the last recorded Klan session on Long Island occurred in 1937. Nonetheless, the demise of the Klan did not mean the end of xenophobia in New York. The German-American Bund, a pro-Nazi organization led by Fritz Kuhn, infiltrated the German-American Settlement League's camp near Yaphank, renamed it Camp Siegfried, and named streets after Hitler, Goering, and Goebbels. Armbands with swastikas and Nazi flags were prevalent on camp grounds. The *New York Times* reported that "on Sunday afternoons in 1938, the Long Island Rail Road ran special trains out to Camp Siegfried, in Yaphank, where as many as 50,000 people might gather to watch Nazi rituals and hear speeches describing the region as an Aryan paradise." [18]

Groups like the Klan and the Bund reflected, albeit in a virulent and organized form, a distrust and fear of immigrants that permeated New York society throughout the early decades of the twentieth century. Together with the class conflict considered earlier, this anti-immigrant prejudice set the tone of the state's politics.

On the one hand, Democrats, largely from New York City's Tammany Hall, represented the immigrant poor. On the other hand, Republicans, even those like Theodore Roosevelt styling themselves as progressives, reflected the prejudices against the urban underclasses that have just been examined. It is true that New York, often under progressive Republican leadership, enacted reforms enhancing the governor's power, streamlining the administration, and guaranteeing direct popular election of senators. The state also adopted workers' compensation and passed statutes providing for utility and insurance company regulation. Perhaps the two most important progressive reforms in which New York participated were women's suffrage and prohibition.[19]

It is essential to emphasize, however, that New York's Republican progressives were not proto–New Dealers. The rural and small-town voters from upstate New York who provided the preponderance of the Republican Party's votes showed little of the sympathy for the poor and for descendants of immigrants that New Deal Democrats would display three decades later. Thus the Republican Party tended to oppose legislation designed to assist the laboring classes — legislation that was enacted in early twentieth-century New York mainly during brief intervals of Democratic ascendancy. On issues relating to the poor, to immigrants, and to the working classes, progressive Republicans were mostly as conservative as more traditional members of the GOP and tended to accept elite assumptions that the political, legal, and business order should always act to protect "the principles of right and justice and honesty" — that is, to impede any redistribution of wealth.[20]

Throughout the first two decades of the century, Republicans generally dominated the politics of New York State and typically controlled the legislative and executive branches of state government. By virtue of their majority on the state's highest court, the Court of Appeals, Republicans also dominated the judicial branch as late as the outset of the 1920s. Although the years 1920 and 1921 were a time of rapid change of personnel on the court, there were seven judges — William S. Andrews, Benjamin N. Cardozo, Frederick E. Crane, Frank H. Hiscock, John W. Hogan, Chester B. M'Laughlin, and Cuthbert W. Pound — who had joined the court by 1920 and remained there until the end of 1921. Of the seven, two were Democrats — Cardozo, a Jew from New York City, and Hogan, a Roman Catholic who had lived and practiced in several upstate cities before joining the court. The five remaining judges were Republicans, four of them from upstate and all of them Protestants.[21] Thus as of the early 1920s, upstate, Protestant Republicans were firmly entrenched on the New York State bench.

The political culture of New York changed, however, during the course of the 1920s, beginning with the 1922 gubernatorial election.

The 1922 election marked "'the first drift in the United States toward the conception that political responsibility involve[s] a duty to improve the life of the people.'"[22] Unlike earlier victories by progressive candidates, which often were mere interludes in longer periods of conservative ascendancy, the victory of Alfred E. Smith in the 1922 election transformed the Empire State's politics over time. Indeed, Smith's victory inaugurated seventy-two years of reform-oriented rule in New York during which only two Republicans — the liberals Thomas E. Dewey and Nelson A. Rockefeller — were able to wrest the governor's chair away from Democrats.

Building on a base of immigrants and the urban working class, Smith was able in 1922 to assemble the reform coalition that kept him, his two successors, Franklin D. Roosevelt and Herbert H. Lehman, and the Democratic Party in power in New York until 1942 and in the nation until 1952. Even in his losing bid for the presidency in 1928, Smith proved so attractive to the urban masses that, for the first time in history, the Democratic Party won a plurality of the votes in the nation's twelve largest cities.[23]

Roosevelt and Lehman continued Smith's practice of courting the urban, lower-class vote. Placing his "faith . . . in the forgotten man at the bottom of the economic pyramid," Roosevelt argued that it was the "responsibility of the State" to aid "large numbers of men and women incapable of supporting either themselves or their families because of circumstances beyond their control" and that aid should be granted "not as a matter of charity but as a matter of social duty." Lehman similarly spoke on behalf of the urban, immigrant class when he urged that "group isolation" was "no longer . . . possible in a well ordered body politic" and "insisted that freedom and liberty, political and economic self-determination must never tolerate artificial barriers of race, creed, color, sex or geography."[24]

Under the leadership of Smith, Lehman, and especially FDR, state and national politics became a battleground between conservatives and reformers. Conservatives strove to develop "a discriminating defense of the [existing] social order against change and reform," while future New Dealers "push[ed] actively for reform, and dr[e]w particular support from the disinherited, dislocated and disgruntled." Roosevelt's unique rhetorical accomplishment lay in transforming the battle into a struggle not between classes but between good and evil. On the side of his good were the farmers, miners, and workers who were "part and parcel of a rounded whole" and who understood that "we all go up, or else we all go down, as one people" and "that the welfare of your family or mine cannot be bought at the sacrifice of our neighbor's family." Arrayed against the people as they strove to build "a people's Government at Washington" that would promote the common good, Roosevelt pitted "the rulers of the exchange of mankind's goods" — "the comparative few" who "speculate[d] with other people's money" — in short, "the power of concentrated wealth."[25]

The transformation of the Smith-Lehman-Roosevelt agenda into "the modern movement for social and economic progress through legislation" enabled reformers to portray conservative constitutional doctrine as protecting nothing more than the power of " 'malefactors of great wealth' " "under a private contract to exact a pound of flesh."[26] This portrait enabled the three reform governors to win elections consistently and thus retain power over time; their prolonged hold on power, in turn, made possible a long-term legislative program focusing on the enactment of regulatory and social legislation designed to prevent the continued exploitation by established elites of the reformers' lower-class constituencies.

Smith again began the process. As Smith himself noted, he and "the Democratic party believe[d] that law" should "relieve and . . . protect and care for the great mass of the people," and therefore he proposed and encouraged legislation dispensing workers' compensation, shortening the work week for men, women, and children, safeguarding working conditions, and providing for the widows and orphans of the working class. He was also a pioneer in highway construction, public housing, and the elimination of railroad grade crossings. As governor, Roosevelt continued Smith's approach by supporting old-age pensions, public power, and unemployment relief. Lehman added such items as public housing, regulation of the dairy industry, unemployment insurance, and utility regulation.[27]

The established elites and business interests that bore the brunt of this new regulatory and welfare legislation, of course, fought back. Relying on constitutional claims about private property and the limited nature of the police power, they brought a series of challenges seeking to invalidate statutes either on their face or as applied to particular litigants. As a result, the New York courts during the 1920s and 1930s faced a series of important police power cases that pitted claims of deprivation of property rights against efforts to use legislative power to prevent exploitation of the weak and the poor, to redistribute wealth and power, and thereby to achieve social justice.

The same political realities that brought new police power cases to the courts during and after the mid-1920s also produced change in the courts themselves. In part, the courts changed because of differences in judicial personnel. The makeup of the Appellate Division was altered, for instance, as Governors Smith, Roosevelt, and Lehman during the twenty years from 1923 to 1942 elevated Democrats and progressive-minded Republicans rather than conservatives from among the elected judges of the Supreme Court who were eligible to sit on the higher bench. Even more striking were the changes that gubernatorial appointments and reform-minded voters produced on the Court of Appeals.

The first important change occurred with the 1923 election to the court of Irving Lehman, a Democrat and a Jew from Manhattan who was the brother of future governor Herbert Lehman. Once on the court, Lehman became the close ally of Benjamin N. Cardozo, who had served on the court since 1914. In cases in which the Court of Appeals was not unanimous, Lehman was on the same side as Cardozo 66 percent of the time, whereas Republican stalwarts such as William S. Andrews, Frederick E. Crane, and Irving G. Hubbs were on the same side as Cardozo only 54, 49, and 51 percent of the time respectively.[28]

Three years later the 1926 election elevated Cardozo to chief judge of the Court of Appeals and soon gave him, in addition, a working majority on the court. Elected that year with Cardozo was Henry T. Kellogg, who, although a Republican from upstate, had received a bipartisan nomination for a vacant seat on the Court of Appeals. Kellogg apparently was chosen for the nomination by a bar association committee on which such leading reformers as Samuel Seabury and Louis Marshall had considerable influence.[29] Once on the court, Kellogg became another ally of Cardozo, siding with him in 56 percent of the cases on which the Court of Appeals divided—more than the Republican stalwarts though less than Cardozo's Democratic allies.

Cardozo's elevation to chief judge created yet another vacancy on the court, to which Governor Smith named John F. O'Brien, who was elected to a full term the next November. O'Brien was a Democrat and a Roman Catholic who before being named to the court had served as assistant corporation counsel of the city of New York for twenty-eight years. He sided with Cardozo in 62 percent of the cases in which the Court of Appeals divided. Meanwhile, Cuthbert Pound, a cousin of Roscoe Pound and a former professor of law at Cornell University, had become a regular ally who also voted with Cardozo in 62 percent of cases in which the Court of Appeals disagreed.[30] Thus, upon his elevation to the chief judgeship at the outset of 1927, Cardozo found himself at the head of a working majority of the Court of Appeals; in the 299 cases in which the court divided during his tenure as chief judge, Cardozo was in the majority 76 percent of the time and dissented alone only 3 percent of the time.

The transformation of the Court of Appeals involved more, however, than merely the elevation of new judges. The key development was the emergence, under Cardozo's guidance, of a new understanding of the nature of the judicial process. Since Cardozo's understanding has been absorbed into all subsequent twentieth-century analyses of the art of judging and has become intrinsic to our own thought processes, we tend to lose sight of its originality. But it was profoundly novel and original, like "an electric flash from the high heavens, clearing away the murk."[31]

The problem with which Cardozo wrestled in his two most important books, *The Nature of the Judicial Process* and *The Growth of the Law*, had plagued the American judiciary for more than a century. The problem was an excess of precedent. Cardozo agreed that precedent fixed "the point of departure from which the labor of the judge begins," that "*stare decisis* [was] at least the everyday working rule of our law," and hence that "in the main there [should] be adherence to precedent." Adherence to precedent, according to Cardozo, was supposed to serve as "a steadying force, the guarantee . . . of stability and certainty." But an avalanche of decisions by tribunals great and small"—a "fecundity of . . . case law [that] would make Malthus stand aghast" —was instead producing a "maze," in which "one line is run here; another there," with "a filigree of threads and cross-threads, radiating from the center, and dividing one another into sections and cross-sections." "The output of a multitude of minds . . . contain[ed] its proportion of vagaries," produced "perplexity" on the part of judges, and ultimately created a "situation where citation of precedent [was] tending to count for less." The excess of precedent turned the law into "a hopeless mess" and created a need "to grapple with the monster of uncertainty and slay him." [32]

What could be done, Cardozo asked, when "obscurity of statute or of precedent . . . or some collision between some or all of them . . . [left] the law unsettled?" One answer was for judges to recognize, as many had in the early nineteenth century, that their duty was not to find law but to make it. But as Cardozo fully appreciated, New York judges in the 1920s could not admit that their decision-making processes resulted in "the destruction of all rules and the substitution in every instance of the individual sense of justice" of the judge. Rhetoric that "the law is as it is, and the duty of this court is to give force and effect to the decisions as we find them" was thought to require judges to announce that, even if they had "no hesitancy in awarding . . . judgment" on the basis of "conscience," it might not be "legally possible to do so." [33]

Perhaps, Cardozo hoped, judges could dodge the problem by asking scholars to bring order out of chaos, as Cardozo believed James Kent and Joseph Story had done in their day and as he hoped the Restatements of Law would do in his.[34] But as we now know in retrospect, legal scholars were not up to such a task. Some other means of imposing order would be needed.

The technique which Cardozo primarily espoused was to approach law as a science. In doing so, he followed in the path of Christopher Columbus Langdell and the young Oliver Wendell Holmes, who in the 1870s and early 1880s had turned to science to generate legal categories and concepts under which to arrange precedent. Cardozo rejected Langdell's mechanistic jurisprudence of conceptions,[35] which in his view led "to harsh or bizarre conclusions, at war with social needs" and gave law "the aspect of a scholastic exercise, divorced from the realities of life." But he did not reject the idea of ordering the law scientifically. Cardozo simply had a different understanding of science, by which he sought to make "justice, morals, and social welfare" the "final test" of whether cases were decided scientifically. Although we now believe that Cardozo's test leaves judges with a vast "power of innovation" amounting to lawmaking freedom, Cardozo did not; in his view, "the bulk and pressure of the rules that hedge" judges "on every side" made their freedom "insignificant." [36]

The "analysis of social interests," according to Cardozo, had "developed a science of its own," with the result that, when a judge "appropriated" the science, he had to do so "subject to restrictions which limit[ed] his freedom." For instance, if "the legislature ha[d] spoken," a judge had to "subordinate his personal . . . estimate of value to the estimate thus declared." Even if the legislature had failed to speak, a judge had to regulate his judgment "by the thought and will of the community rather than by his own idiosyncrasies." Cardozo had faith that, when judges embarked on the "search for social justice," they would not find competing conceptions of justice but a single coherent, community conception opposed only by useless rules "invoked by injustice after the event to shelter and intrench itself." [37]

A summary of Cardozo's position will emphasize its originality and power. Unlike early nineteenth-century instrumentalists, Cardozo denied being a judicial policymaker. In his view, he did not make policy choices. On the contrary, he felt bound, as he thought judges should be, by precedent, and, when precedent pointed in conflicting directions, he felt bound to take the route dictated by science. In all these views, Cardozo was merely adopting the conventional jurisprudential wisdom of his time. His originality lay in his definition of science, which stacked the judicial deck in favor of progressive reform. He rejected the Langdellian idea of a science internal to the law—an idea that, in Cardozo's opinion, resulted in mechanical jurisprudence. In its place, he substituted a scientific analysis of societal needs in pursuit of law's ultimate end of achieving social justice.

The nub of Cardozo's jurisprudence lay in his image of society as a cohesive entity progressing collectively toward social justice.[38] On the assumption that the image accurately reflected reality, it followed that judges should decide cases to promote justice and the common good rather than apply precedents protecting an outmoded status quo. As long as Cardozo and his judicial colleagues could identify scientifically what society as an entity wanted—and we shall see in Chapter 3 that they often believed they could—they possessed a powerful engine for altering the law.

None of Cardozo's judicial allies elaborated the method of reform as articulately as he did, but it seems clear that they joined him in using it. Like Cardozo, Irving Lehman "hesitate[d] to overrule a previous decision," but he believed that a court could "refuse to perpetuate previous error" "when convinced that an artificial rule of practice, created by it, is erroneous and hampers the administration of justice." Lehman thus was "a human judge . . . ever astute to declare the law in the light . . . of the kaleidoscopic changes of an ever-shifting world." Similarly, Cuthbert Pound understood that there were "multitudes of situations in which judges of all sorts, finding an applicable precedent or principle or statute, [did] not feel free to enact something different," but he also "recognize[d] that within vague . . . limits their decisions [were] compelled neither by prior decisions nor by a supposed historical movement, and that within these limits they . . . must be guided by ideas of justice or of social advantage."[39]

As Chief Judge Cardozo and his allies assumed control of the New York Court of Appeals, they began to push legal doctrine in the novel directions demanded by their emerging though not yet fully developed conception of social justice. But for three reasons, they did not push doctrine either too hard or too far. First, their acceptance of the binding nature of precedent limited their capacity to create new law. The doctrine of precedent tended to freeze things in place, as they classically had been, allocating resources to a particular person as property and ensuring that judges would not alter the allocation. The Court of Appeals, indeed, said as much. Viewing its function to include "the duty uniformly to settle the law for the entire state and finally to determine its principles," the court not surprisingly held that it was not within the judiciary's "province . . . to alter a rule of property" that had "doubtless governed the conduct of buyer and seller in innumerable sales." Only "the Legislature," it was said, could provide "relief." Judges, in contrast, had "to follow the authority" of prior cases, even when doing so created "problems" from the perspective of "the student of social science," since " 'law . . . [was] a logical development' " that could "not be lightly flung aside."[40]

Second, the conflict between conservatives and reformers that had characterized the early decades of the twentieth century continued well into the 1930s. Despite the hopes of optimists like Cardozo, Americans in the 1920s and early 1930s did not constitute a single, cohesive entity progressing collectively toward a shared view of social justice. Reformers and conservatives had sharply competing visions of a just society, and they continued to battle over those visions as they had for decades. Although the year 1922 marked a turning point, in that conservatives generally won the battles before that date and frequently lost them afterward, neither the conservatives before 1922 nor the reformers thereafter enjoyed anything close to complete victory. As a result, Cardozo's conception of judges as progenitors of social justice also enjoyed only partial success, at least in his own lifetime.

The third and probably the principal reason why Cardozo and the other reform-oriented political leaders and judges of his generation did not change the law more fundamentally was their lack of ideological creativity. Of course, they rejected the classic political ideologies available to them during the 1920s and 1930s. Leading reform figures such as Cardozo, Smith, the Lehmans, and ·O'Brien were not Marxists. As representatives of Catholics and Jews who occupied a distinctively minority status, they also did not have Nazism and similar fascist ideologies available to them as a possible political alternative. And since the new leaders had an "effective sympathy with . . . underdog[s]" who needed a redistribution of wealth and power in their favor, they could not turn to Populism, with its prescription of inactive, limited government.[41] Only a powerful government could accomplish redistribution. But though reformers of Smith's and Cardozo's generation did not adopt any of the then familiar approaches to law and politics, they also failed to elaborate clearly a new approach that would have enabled them to escape fully from old conceptual limitations.

As we shall see in the next three chapters, which provide a detailed analysis of legal doctrine, all judges of the 1920s and 1930s, including reformers, rejected radicalism. Wed as they were to precedent, they moved forward to a new social vision slowly and cautiously, striving merely to avoid injustice rather than to elaborate in affirmative detail any carefully particularized conception of justice. Above all, reformers like Cardozo were not, as their successors would be later in the century, proponents of liberty and equality. The reform movement was very much an elitist, top-down movement, in which social justice meant neither liberty nor equality but merely, in Cardozo's words, "charity," " 'mercy,' " and compassion.[42]

In this spirit of doing good for others, judges in the mid-1920s began the task of undermining the classical legal order, which, as Chapter 2 will show, continued to reflect a conservative agenda of protecting property and preserving conventional morality. As they supplanted classicism, the judges modified the law to fit emerging social needs, defined in Chapter 3 as preventing exploitation and providing opportunity. Their "work of modification" took place amid continuing conservative opposition, however, and hence its progress, which will be delineated in Chapter 4, was at best "gradual" and proceeded only "inch by inch."[43]

CHAPTER 2

THE CONSERVATIVE AGENDA
Protecting Property and Preserving Morality

Judge-made law had long served in the classical legal order as one of the main bulwarks of conservatives as they strove to defend themselves against the perceived onslaughts of the immigrant poor. Two bodies of doctrine had assumed special importance. The first had protected the money and property of the rich against redistribution to the poor. The second had protected inherited Puritanical traditions with regard to sexual and other moral values. This chapter will focus on the persistence into the 1920s and 1930s of elements of this classical order with its conservative biases.

PROTECTING PROPERTY

Constitutional Rules Protecting Wealth. No decision in the early 1920s better illustrates the conservative opposition to government-induced redistribution of wealth than *People v. Westchester County Nat. Bank of Peekskill.*[1] This 5–2 decision, declaring unconstitutional a bonus granted by the state to all veterans of World War I, revealed a fundamental disagreement about the scope of government's powers of spending and taxation that transcended the narrow issue of the constitutionality of the bonus. It was a disagreement about when government could act to cure social injustice.

The majority in an opinion by Judge William S. Andrews, an upstate Republican, held that the state could not give public money to individuals in the absence of obligations akin to those arising out of tort or contract. After pointing out that the federal government had been in total control of war efforts and that "the state was not the actor," Judge Andrews continued, "Neither it nor its servants injured anyone. It received no property for which it has not paid. Nor were services rendered to it. . . . Gratitude may impel an individual to reward his benefactor. One may do as he will with his own. The state of New York may not. Its Constitution forbids. *It may not attempt to equalize among its citizens inequalities caused by federal legislation.*"[2] Stated more broadly, government in the majority's view had no legitimate role to play in redistributing wealth in the pursuit of social justice or in correcting injustice caused by anything other than its own actions; it could not even be charitable.

Judge Benjamin N. Cardozo, joined only by Judge Cuthbert Pound, began his dissent by observing "that since the beginnings of our history, a sense of the moral obligation to give aid to the returning soldier has been felt and acted on by government." More particularly, he noted that it was "the state rather than the nation—possessing as the state does the residuary powers of government—which in our federal system is to be viewed as parens patriae"; a "parent," he added, "does not listen unmoved to the necessities of her sons who have fought in her defense." But eventually Cardozo moved on to the more general issue by discussing whether government could act to alleviate burdens that were merely "incidents of life in organized society." Relying on older cases, Cardozo maintained that the Court of Appeals had "held that the Legislature might readjust the incidence of the burden, might establish a more equitable distribution between the individual and the public, through the voluntary acceptance of liability for a loss which was without remedy when suffered. . . . *The readjustment of these burdens along the lines of equality and equity is a legitimate function of the state as long as justice to its citizens remains its chief concern.*" [3] Cardozo thus made it clear that in his view government had plenary power to seek justice by redistributing wealth.

But he was in dissent. On issues of public spending and taxation, classical nineteenth-century values still held sway, even though they had come under challenge. As one lower court, quoting nineteenth-century language of the Court of Appeals, declared, "a law plainly departing from the principle of equality in the distribution of public burdens, would be justly obnoxious as contrary to natural equity, and as practical confiscation." [4] On this basis, tax exemptions, for example, were strictly limited. [5]

Nineteenth-century values hostile to redistribution of wealth also continued during the 1920s and 1930s to prohibit government from using the power of eminent domain to take "the private property of one person without his consent for the private use of another." Although it was settled that uses such as roads, parks, railroads, and utilities were sufficiently public in nature to warrant the invocation of eminent domain, it was equally clear that a purely private corporation could never be "the delegate of the state, with power to condemn when it is unable to agree." [6]

Repression of Left-Wing Political Activity. As *Gitlow v. New York* [7] made clear, the conservative agenda of protecting wealth also demanded the repression of free speech by immigrants and the laboring classes. The *Gitlow* case had arisen when, in July 1919, less than two years after the Bolshevik coup in St. Petersburg, Benjamin Gitlow published "the Left Wing Manifesto" in "the Revolutionary Age, a weekly publication devoted to the international Com-

munist struggle." The centerpiece of the manifesto was its call for "a new state
. . . in which 'the proletariat as a class alone counts.'" The new state would
be achieved by "starting with strikes of protest, developing into 'mass political strikes, and then into revolutionary mass action'" and ultimately by "the
introduction of 'the transition proletarian state, functioning as a revolutionary
dictatorship,' which [was] necessary 'to coerce and suppress the bourgeois'"
who were to be "completely expropriated 'economically and politically.'"[8]

Unless the conservative judges who sat on the courts that heard Gitlow's
case had been prepared to treat the manifesto as "a mere academic and harmless discussion," they had little choice but to fear it as "advocacy of action by
one class, which would destroy the rights of all other classes." They took seriously the call to recast America on the model of Russia, where, they noted, "the
most barbaric punishment, torture, cruelty, and suffering are inflicted upon
the bourgeois" and where those who did not submit were "either starved to
death or shot." The judges also understood that, in the minds of the revolutionaries, success in Russia depended on making "the revolutionary struggle
worldwide" and especially on extending it to Western "industrial centers,
where the proletariat greatly outnumber[ed] the bourgeois." In sum, the judges
found Gitlow and his fellow revolutionaries to be "positively dangerous men"
who "intend[ed] to destroy the state, murder whole classes of citizens, [and]
rob them of their property."[9]

We need to treat this judicial rhetoric seriously, but at the same time we
must remain aware of its indistinguishable anti-Semitic and anti-immigrant
subtext. The fact is that *Gitlow* and other cases from the period involved overlapping discrimination on both class and religious grounds. In a context in
which many saw Jews as "inflamed radical[s] responsible for Communist revolution in eastern Europe," it is not surprising that the Appellate Division observed that radical "doctrines [were] principally advocated by those who come
from Russia and bordering countries and their descendants," as did Gitlow
himself. Because the United States and New York, in particular, had become
"'the abiding place of foreigners who, without understanding our institutions,
had brought with them views and prejudices . . . and doctrines which, if
put into effect, would subvert . . . organized government,'" strong action was
needed.[10]

The Supreme Court of the United States was not much different from the
wasp elite of New York and the rest of the country. Feeling as threatened as
their brethren below, a seven-justice majority in *Gitlow* agreed that a "single
revolutionary spark [could] kindle a fire that, smoldering for a time, [could]
burst into a sweeping and destructive conflagration." The majority also agreed

that it was necessary and appropriate for government "to extinguish the spark without waiting until it has enkindled the flame or blazed into the conflagration." Even the future liberal, Harlan F. Stone, who would author *Carolene Products* and a lone dissent in *Gobitis,* could join in an opinion focused like *Gitlow* on the repression of class conflict.[11] Indeed, only four of the twenty-four judges who sat in the *Gitlow* case at all levels—Louis D. Brandeis, Cardozo, Holmes, and Pound—were sufficiently unafraid to dissent and thereby challenge the conservative agenda. For most judges close to the class struggles of 1919, the Communist hope of immediate success, on the one hand, and the fear of it, on the other, threatened class violence and made repression of the lower classes seem essential.

Gitlow was no isolated case.[12] An earlier case in a somewhat like fashion had involved a "threatening crowd" of perhaps as many as two thousand strikers and sympathizers, who were hurling "stones, bricks, and other missiles" at about seventy-five policemen and National Guard troops, who opened fire and wounded two innocent bystanders. Several years later, another case sustained the conviction of a defendant who had distributed a circular urging workers to "speak to our ruling class the only language they understand," "disregard, disobey, break every injunction," and "treat every injunction as a scrap of paper." Radical action was needed because

> deadly blows [were] now being struck against every working man and working class family . . . by the capitalist dictatorship. . . . The same capitalist courts and judges who murdered Sacco and Vanzetti, who [were] keeping Mooney and Billings in the California jails, [were] now handing down injunction orders to jail the miners of Colorado, to evict the miners of Ohio, to starve the miners of Pennsylvania, to terrorize and smash the union ranks of the New York traction workers.

In the face of this call for disobedience to court orders, the Appellate Division quoted the language of the *Gitlow* majority which outlawed " 'action by mass strike, whereby government is crippled, the administration of justice paralyzed, and the health, morals, and welfare of a community endangered . . . for the purpose of bringing about a revolution in the state' " and affirmed the defendant's conviction.[13]

Similarly, the Court of Appeals approved a New York City ordinance requiring a permit to expound atheism in public streets, out of fear that the "passion, rancor, and malice sometimes aroused by sectarian religious controversies and attacks on religion seem[ed] to justify especial supervision." It also upheld a Mount Vernon ordinance prohibiting any assemblies on city streets—an ordinance that the mayor planned to enforce by "grant[ing] no further permits for Socialists' meeting[s]," while the Appellate Division sustained a judgment against another defendant for "addressing . . . [an] assemblage in favor of Socialism." And even somewhat innocuous picketing in support of a "Rent Strike against Fire Trap Conditions" led in 1934 to a conviction of a woman for disorderly conduct, since "the lawful and orderly manner of the tenants was to file their complaints with" an appropriate city agency rather than picket.[14] For judges of the 1920s and early 1930s, polite presentation of grievances was the only appropriate way for an underclass to make its case.

The courts in a series of noncriminal cases similarly repressed speech that threatened the peace and security of elites. Thus they sustained the refusal of the secretary of state to amend the certificate of incorporation of the Lithuanian Workers' Literature Society when they found it to consist of socialists who favored "the attainment of the desired revolution by forcible means." Likewise, they sustained an injunction against the American Socialist Society's operation of the Rand School of Social Science on the ground that it was "within the power of the Legislature to enact statutes . . . to prevent the teaching of doctrines advocating the destruction of the state by force." Finally, they sustained censorship of radical newspapers such as Benjamin Gitlow's *Revolutionary Age* and even of motion picture newsreels.[15]

Private Law Rules Protecting the Distribution of Wealth. In four areas of private law—trespass, conversion, fraud, and privacy—the conservative agenda similarly called for protection of the existing distribution of wealth. Judges have long protected and continue to this day to protect basic property rights in the first three of these areas, and, during the 1920s and 1930s, they also elaborated an explicitly conservative bias on the fourth.

The law of trespass has served for centuries to prevent redistribution of wealth. As late as the 1930s, protection of landed wealth was of such great moment that, "when one citizen trespasse[d] upon the real property of another," the trespasser was required to "answer in damages for the injury committed." In trespass, "the owner [was] supreme[,] his house [was] his castle, and his estate his exclusive domain." "No intrusion [was] so trifling as to be overlooked" but was "at the peril of the intruder."[16]

Analogous to trespass was the tort of conversion, which dealt primarily with personal property, whereas trespass dealt primarily with real estate. "Conversion [was] any distinct act of dominion wrongfully exerted over another's personal property in denial of or inconsistent with his rights therein," even if the "interference" was only "very slight." " 'A wrongful intent [was] not an essential element of . . . conversion.' " [17] Conversion, like trespass, thus had real bite as a strict liability tort preventing redistribution of wealth.

Also protective of the existing distribution of wealth was the law of fraud, which did "not suffer deceit to be practiced by any trick or device" and which outlawed any "breach" of "trust or confidence justly reposed" or any "gain of an advantage to another's detriment by deceitful or unfair means." [18] No particular class bias in the application of fraud doctrine emerges from the reported cases, which nonetheless generally tended to protect those with wealth from those who were attempting to take it away.

A fourth area of early twentieth-century New York law protecting property was the cause of action for invasion of privacy, which developed an explicit conservative bias in protecting only rights of a commercial nature and not rights in personhood. This was because, under the law of New York, no right of privacy existed except to the limited extent provided by sections 50 and 51 of the Civil Rights Law, which did not protect personal privacy but merely prohibited exploitation of the commercial value of an individual's name or likeness. [19]

Procedural Rules Protecting the Existing Distribution of Wealth. Conservatives in the early 1920s also manipulated the rules of civil procedure in aid of their agenda of protecting the existing distribution of wealth, typically by placing obstacles in the path of lawsuits against deep-pocket defendants. In 1920, they even induced the legislature to promulgate procedural rules that openly furthered the interests of established wealth holders, in this instance both defendants and creditor plaintiffs seeking to recover debts. In an irony of history, many procedural rules first promulgated by conservatives in the early 1920s ultimately took on a more progressive cast when, a decade and a half later, they became a basis for the new reform-oriented Federal Rules of Civil Procedure. Other rules, however, retained their conservative orientation well into the 1930s and, in some instances, even beyond.

The proclivity of the conservative legal agenda to help the rich emerged with unusual transparency in some new procedural mechanisms enacted in 1920 pursuant to a legislative directive to the Board of Statutory Consolidation to draft a civil practice act, rules of court, and forms and a later authorization of "a convention, representing the judiciary and the bar to consider and adopt rules of civil practice." [20]

The Board of Statutory Consolidation that drafted the Civil Practice Act consisted of four men—Adolph J. Rodenbeck, John G. Milburn, Adelbert

Moot, and Charles A. Collin. The four were conservative, mainly Republican, and largely lawyers from elite firms. Rodenbeck, an upstate Supreme Court judge who sat until 1931, was undoubtedly a Republican, as was Moot, an attorney from Buffalo. Milburn was a founding partner of the New York City firm of Carter, Ledyard & Milburn and president of the Association of the Bar of the City of New York; his clients included Standard Oil of New Jersey, and he was a director of the American Express Company, the New York Life Insurance Company, and other prominent corporate entities. Collin, the only Democrat on the board, had been counsel to Governor David B. Hill and a professor of law at Cornell, but he later pursued a practice in New York City that specialized "largely in railroad and other corporation law" and provided "counsel for a number of important corporations."[21] Men of this sort not surprisingly promulgated rules that advanced the interests of their upper-class clients and constituents.

Summary judgment was one new procedure emerging out of the 1920 reforms. Unlike the summary judgment remedy later included in the Federal Rules, however, the early New York procedure had a limited goal: it aimed only to eliminate the delay that a debtor could impose on a creditor by interposing frivolous defensive pleas to the creditor's suit to recover a debt. Before the Field Code in 1848, the common-law rule in New York was that a debtor was entitled to plead the general issue and thereby put a creditor to proof of his or her claim before a jury but that a false or sham special plea would be stricken by the court. Arguably, the Field Code, with its provision that "sham and irrelevant answers and defenses may be stricken out on motion," altered the common-law rule by allowing a court to strike a sham plea of the general issue as well as a special plea. The Court of Appeals initially ruled that the code did give courts authority to strike any sham plea, but then the court changed its mind and held that the code merely codified the common-law rule.[22] As a result, a defendant who lacked a bona fide defense nonetheless was free, as late as 1920, to interpose a false general denial to a complaint and thereby postpone the rendition of judgment against him or herself for a potentially significant period of time.

To put an end to such dilatory tactics, the 1920 Convention included Rule 113 allowing summary judgment in the Rules of Civil Practice. The convention, however, did not make its rule applicable for the benefit of all litigants harmed by delay. Since the purpose of the rule was merely "to enable a creditor speedily to obtain a judgment by preventing the interposition of unmeritorious defenses for purposes of delay," the new procedure was made applicable only to "commercial cases"—that is, to actions in which a plaintiff sought damages for a liquidated sum arising out of a contract. Most judges routinely held that Rule 113 was inapplicable to other cases such as equitable actions for specific performance or injunctive relief, suits for labor and material, suits by an employee for wrongful discharge, or actions of the sort most likely to be brought by lower-class plaintiffs—those sounding in negligence or tort.[23]

Nonetheless, summary judgment was so successful and so useful to the courts that pressures almost immediately appeared to expand its availability. The courts declared that Rule 113 "should be liberally construed" because it had "worked a substantial reform in practice and greatly relieved an overburdened trial calendar." In response, one court held in 1926 that summary judgment would lie in cases of *quantum meruit* and *quantum valebat,* while another in 1931 allowed recovery of a reasonable attorney's fee authorized by a promissory note.[24] Within a little more than a decade of the adoption of summary judgment, the New York Commission on the Administration of Justice recommended that all restrictions on the remedy be removed and that it be made available "in any action," and in 1932 Rule 113 was, indeed, amended to make summary judgment available in eight specified categories of actions. But the conservative bias implicit in the rule remained in place until 1959, when Rule 113 was finally amended to make summary judgment available in all categories of cases, including actions for personal injuries arising from negligence.[25]

Another innovation in New York's 1920 procedural reforms was the action for a declaratory judgment. In English practice, from which New York's declaratory judgment procedure was derived, the declaration was "confined to the construction of a deed, will, or other written instrument." New York judges agreed that the "most fruitful field for the use of this form of relief [was] in the construction of written instruments as to the interpretation of which there [was] a dispute, to determine the relative rights of the contracting parties, or the duties and obligation of trustees under a deed of trust," and they in fact heard many cases dealing with contracts, trusts, and other written instruments, especially leases. The New York declaratory judgment law became a useful mechanism through which commercial and other elite plaintiffs could obtain vindication of their rights. Although New York's statute was not so limited on its face and "extended to any rights or other legal relations," few nonbusiness cases were brought during the 1920s; indeed, only one reported case was brought during that decade for what would later become the primary use of declaratory procedure—to determine a question of state constitutional law.[26]

Starting in 1929, however, reported cases demanding the determination of marital or other family status became common. More important was the growing use of declaratory judgments in constitutional litigation. A second constitutional case, which struck down state legislation requiring that pharmacies be owned by licensed pharmacists, was reported in 1931, and in the same year, a suit was brought to determine a town's liability on a note given for money borrowed for highway purposes. By the late 1930s, litigation of such matters of public law had become the staple of declaratory judgment proceedings. In 1937, the Court of Appeals even opened a wedge allowing declaratory judgment procedure to be used to challenge the decisions of administrative agencies. Other efforts to give broad scope to the declaratory judgment procedure were rebuffed, however, as the Court of Appeals held, for example, that declaratory judgment actions would not lie to test the constitutionality of a criminal statute or regulation.[27]

A third procedural device affected by the 1920 reforms was discovery. Although use of the procedure had antedated 1920 in New York, that year witnessed a legislative change, which some labeled "radical" or "revolutionary," that in fact wrought a significant liberalization in discovery practice.[28]

Following the 1920 legislation, New York judges frequently expressed the belief that there was "no reason why a party should not be called upon to disclose to his adversary the information he has concerning the case between them." They explained that they had no interest in assisting a litigant "to conceal" evidence "in the hope that surprise at the trial may give him advantage." Accordingly, they consistently adopted the view that legislation, which had been adopted "to simplify the practice . . . by abolishing the many technical requirements" of older law, should receive "a liberal construction," "to the end that the truth might be made to appear and the cause of justice promoted."[29]

The 1920 statute changed the law by authorizing parties to take pretrial depositions of their opponents simply on notice without the necessity of applying for a court order, as had previously been the rule. There were some limitations on discovery, however, and these limitations tended to favor elite interests, such as corporations and defendants in tort suits. For example, depositions normally could not be taken in negligence or other tort cases, where plaintiffs, who sometimes lacked even basic knowledge about master-servant relationships on the defense side, typically had greater need of pretrial information than defendants. Another restriction was that corporations could usually be deposed only through agents named by them and not through individuals selected by the examiner;[30] thus corporations retained considerable control over the outward flow of information.

Restrictive rules also applied if a litigant sought to compel the production of books and documents rather than to take a viva voce deposition. Judges, as one wrote, were simply unwilling to allow plaintiffs "limitless examination and discovery of . . . books and papers" or "the right to roam at will through the books of the defendant."[31] The effect of restrictions on the production of books and documents was, of course, to help elite individuals and large entities that routinely kept them.

Courts were freer, in contrast, in acceding to demands that one party furnish to the other a bill of particulars, which limited proof at trial to material contained in the particulars provided before trial. The courts were "quite liberal in requiring a party to furnish his adversary all necessary information, to limit the scope of the evidence on the trial, and to enable him to know definitely what he intends to claim under his pleading."[32] Judges thereby restricted the freedom of all parties, but especially plaintiffs, to alter their theory of the case during trial in response to the availability or persuasiveness of evidence.

Rules about sanctions that could be imposed on parties who failed to appear for depositions or to produce required materials also contained a pro-defendant bias. Sanctions were not particularly severe. The "power to punish [was] limited" by a concern that severe sanctions, such as holding a noncomplying party in default, would "come perilously near the denial of due process of law." As Judge Lehman declared in one opinion for the Court of Appeals, a judge could not "deny the defendant a hearing upon the charge made against him, except where, from the suppression of evidence by the defendant, an inference or presumption arises that the charge made is in fact true." For this reason, the courts frequently refused to hold defendants in default. Instead, they relied on lesser sanctions such as staying proceedings by a defaulting party—a remedy that would have overwhelming impact on a plaintiff but none typically on a defendant.[33]

A final subject on which New York by 1920 had adopted advanced rules of procedure was the law governing class actions. New York's class action procedure was radically different, however, from the pro-plaintiff one that we have come to associate with modern class actions under the Federal Rules of Civil Procedure. Statistics tell much of the story. Between 1920 and 1937, the year of the adoption of the Federal Rules, only ten reported class action cases occurred in New York, and in seven of those cases, the plaintiffs who sued were denied standing to represent others. In three of the cases, standing was denied because the plaintiff and those he was seeking to represent "each held under a different instrument" or contract.[34] In two cases, the reasons given to deny standing were the absence of any allegation in the complaint that members of the class were less than "perfectly satisfied with conditions" and "perfectly content with their investments." In the sixth case, the denial rested on the right of the defendant specifically "to know what causes of action it must answer and prepare to meet," while in the seventh the specific reason for the denial is difficult to fathom.[35]

Equally interesting are the three cases in which representative standing was granted. The first—an action by a taxpayer to recover money alleged to have been illegally paid to a public officer—might fit within current conceptions of a class action, although New York today does not allow such suits. The second was a suit by a company union, the United Cloak and Suit Designers' Mutual Aid Association of America, against the president of the International Ladies' Garment Workers' Union (ILGWU), which the Mutual Aid Association accused of threats, violence, and intimidation in connection with a strike by the ILGWU that the court enjoined. The third was a suit by the chamberlain of the city of New York against an individual chosen to represent subscribers of a fund to build an arch in memory of World War I dead; the chamberlain sought and obtained permission to use the money to build five " 'War Memorial Playgrounds' " instead—a purpose which the court concluded on a motion for a declaratory judgment on the pleadings "would meet with the approval of the donors." [36]

New York's hostility during the 1920s to class actions by the weak against the strong is perhaps best illustrated by a case in which 193 investors in a corporation sued the underwriters of its stock for misrepresenting the condition of the corporation in a prospectus; they were permitted to join together as plaintiffs, but they did not bring their suit as a class action, presumably because such a suit would not have been allowed. Instead, the 193 plaintiffs had to proceed under a cumbersome procedure in which all of them could participate, perhaps adversely to each other, in all aspects of the case.[37]

Other procedural rules in existence in the 1920s and 1930s also reflected a pro-defendant bias and thus tended to favor upper-class litigants, at least in comparison with altered versions of those rules adopted in subsequent decades. Well into the twentieth century, for example, the old case of *Pennoyer v. Neff*[38] limited the jurisdiction of New York courts to cases in which a defendant's person could be served or its property attached within the boundaries of the state; *Pennoyer* thereby circumscribed the ability of plaintiffs to select where they would commence suit. Similarly, the rules governing choice of law, which during the first half of the century were comparatively fixed and clear and applied independently of the forum in which a case was being heard, helped defendants by deterring forum shopping, since plaintiffs who found that the law of a foreign jurisdiction precluded them from obtaining justice there had little incentive to come to New York for justice when New York courts mechanically applied the same foreign law.[39]

Two relatively late cases especially illustrate how even morally reprehensible defendants were protected from suit by New York's black-letter, pro-defendant choice of law rules. *Holzer v. Deutsche Reichsbahn-Gesellschaft* was the first case. In *Holzer,* a German national who had come to reside in the United States sued a German corporation for breaching a contract made with him in Germany by discharging him from employment in Germany "upon the sole ground that he [was] a Jew." Since the contract had been made and partially performed in Germany, the Court of Appeals held unanimously that German law governed, even though German law legitimated the discharge and even though the court knew that many would be outraged by such a result. As the court explained, it was "bound to respect the independence of every other sovereign State" and could "not sit in judgment on the acts of the government of another done within its own territory."[40]

An analogous result was reached even as late as the 1943 case of *Kleve v. Basler Lebens-Versicherungs-Gesellschaft,* in which Jewish refugees from Hitler sued to recover the cash surrender value of insurance policies written in Germany on their lives while they had been German nationals. The insurance company, which was a Swiss corporation, defended on the ground that under German law the Nazi regime had confiscated the policies when the plaintiffs fled Germany. In accepting this argument that German law governed and precluded recovery on the policies, the court declared that its "judgment in such matters [could] not be affected by the obnoxious character of the foreign law." Although expressing "the hope . . . that in the after-war world justice may be done, even within Germany, to the victims of German aggression," it concluded that "governing law [was] no less controlling because it [was] bad law."[41]

The results in *Holzer* and *Kleve* could have been avoided only by recourse to the principle that the "courts of New York [would] not enforce the tax laws or penal laws of another state," nor would they "aid in enforcing in behalf of another government a penalty or forfeiture." Adhering to this principle, New York judges had refused to give effect to Soviet confiscation decrees when the effect of those decrees had been to redistribute property physically located in New York.[42] No effort was made, however, to use this principle in the Nazi cases.

In two final bodies of common-law doctrine, dealing with the right to trial by jury and the principle of *res judicata,* it also is possible to detect bias in favor of upper-class litigants, although some of that bias would begin to disappear in the late 1920s.

In the early 1920s, the courts openly interpreted the rules controlling the relationship between judge and jury to favor typically upper-class defendants and thereby to prevent use of the law, especially in tort cases, to redistribute wealth from the rich to the poor. One rule that was openly proclaimed to be for the benefit of wealthy defense interests was the prohibition on compromise verdicts, where a jury found facts on the basis of some middle ground unsupported by either the plaintiff's or the defendant's evidence. The fault with a compromise verdict was that it was "not based upon careful analysis of competent evidence" or "a determination of the actual facts in controversy after mature consideration" but on "a vague groping of the mind into irrelevant matters . . . , sympathy, or lack of resolute mental action." Such a "compromise . . . , where some of the jurors favor[ed] a verdict for the adversary," constituted "an unwarranted finding in favor of" the plaintiff, the inevitable beneficiary of the jury's sympathy, and thus a violation of the rights of "the defendant, [who was] . . . entitled to have th[e] issue determined" on the merits.[43]

The same concern that juries would sympathize with plaintiffs and thereby prejudice the rights of defendants arose in cases where large plaintiffs' "verdicts must have been the result of sympathy, prejudice, or passion" after defendants had been denied adjournments to procure additional witnesses or to obtain a competent interpreter required so that cross examination of a plaintiff could effectively proceed. Another pro-defendant rule required the jury to be instructed to find a defendant's verdict if the evidence was evenly balanced. Finally, there was the rule requiring a jury to credit the testimony of defendants' employees that they had used due care, as, for example, by blowing a train whistle, when witnesses for the plaintiff testified, for instance, only that they had not heard the whistle being blown or otherwise observed due care being taken.[44]

Change began to occur in these jury-control rules in the late 1920s, but several decades passed before the change was complete. An early sign of change came in an important 1927 case, in which the Court of Appeals gave juries greater power to decide cases contrary to judges' views on the law and hence enhanced the freedom of juries to yield to their sympathy for injured plaintiffs. More specifically, the case rejected inflexible rules about the superiority of direct, positive testimony of an agent of a defendant that he had used due care over negative evidence from a plaintiff that she had not observed due care being used. Rather the court declared that "all evidence is to be weighed according to the proof which it was in the power of one side to have produced and in the power of the other side to have contradicted."[45] Later, the Court of Appeals held that an instruction "that all who gave testimony . . . were truthful witnesses" constituted "an invasion of the right of the plaintiff to have the jury pass upon the credibility of the witnesses" and another case explicitly upheld verdicts reached through apparent compromise—verdicts that reflected little but outright sympathy for plaintiffs. The growing pro-plaintiff orientation of the court even led it to condone the practice of setting aside verdicts for plaintiffs if they gave inadequate damages and ordering new trials unless defendants agreed to pay additional amounts.[46] This trend toward allowing greater interpretive freedom to juries did not reach maturity, however, until the 1950s.

The final doctrine tending to favor the wealthy was *res judicata*. On its face, the doctrine was neutral and occasionally, as in the rules that tax assessments and criminal convictions were not binding in later litigation, even appeared to favor middle-class and lower-class litigants in contests against a large, impersonal government bureaucracy.[47] The apparent facial neutrality of *res judicata* rules misses some of the doctrine's impact, however. Strict application of the principle of *res judicata* tends to favor poorer litigants, who have adequate resources for only one trial and cannot afford the costs of relitigating a matter if they win the first time around. Exceptions to the doctrine, which permit relitigation, tend to favor wealthier parties who can bear the costs. By the frequent exceptions it sanctioned,[48] New York's law of res judicata thus may have reflected at least some inarticulate bias against the poor and in favor of the rich.

Moreover, at least one "well-recognized 'apparent exception'" favoring upper-class litigants existed to the facially neutral principles and rules, especially to the principle requiring identity of parties and mutuality of estoppel in order for a prior judgment to be binding. This key exception provided that, when a person injured by the negligence of an employee of another unsuccessfully sued either the employee or his employer, that person could not subsequently turn around and sue the other.[49] Any other rule would have given a plaintiff two chances to recover for a single injury.

In short, as late as the early 1920s, much of New York's procedural law, like much of its substantive law, continued to protect the wealth of the rich and prevent its redistribution to the poor. Although courts began in the late 1920s and continued into the 1930s to alter the rules of civil procedure somewhat, they did not transform those rules entirely. When judges reconsidered particular legal doctrines, they tended to adopt newer reform values rather than older traditional ones, and hence it seems clear that the direction of doctrinal development was away from classic nineteenth-century values that had dominated the law as late as the mid-1920s. Nonetheless, it is also clear that, as a result of the doctrine of *stare decisis,* which meant that in the absence of explicit reexamination old law remained in place, the few reforms the courts did adopt were overwhelmed in the larger picture of 1920s and 1930s by established rules. In the end, the New York courts at mid-century had still left much of the state's classical, conservative law of civil procedure in place.

THE PRESERVATION OF VICTORIAN NORMS

The erection of legal barriers to the redistribution of wealth was only one element of the conservative agenda. Another component was the imposition of conventional Puritanical moral values on immigrants and the poor[50] — oftentimes with significant support from groups in immigrant and underdog communities. On the whole, conservatives succeeded in keeping the law faithful to Puritanical norms, although, especially after the end of Prohibition in 1933, they did not achieve every legal victory they sought.

Prohibition. Recognition that the elites who constituted the backbone of the Progressive movement sought to impose Victorian standards on those whom they understood to be their inferiors is not a new observation among historians. The received wisdom has long interpreted Prohibition, for example, as an effort of old-stock Protestants to enact their moral idealism into law in order, as they perceived it, to rescue the immigrant lower classes from their evil ways and thereby uplift them to a higher level of citizenship.[51] More recently, some historians have urged that Prohibition went even further and attacked not simply drinking but rather an entire working-class lifestyle symbolized by drinking. Prohibition, they contend, constituted an effort to impose a whole set of values and behaviors that upper-class and middle-class reformers sought to promulgate and develop in themselves and in others — values of discipline, hard work, frugality, responsibility, moral correctness, and self-control that "thoroughly fused the Protestant ethic and the ethos of capitalism."[52]

It is impossible to downplay the significance of the Eighteenth Amendment and the Volstead Act in the legal history of New York during the 1920s. These legislative embodiments of temperance generated innumerable criminal prosecutions and ferocious political and social conflict.[53] One of Judge Benjamin N. Cardozo's most portentous opinions, *People v. Defore,* dealt with what has since become the most frequently litigated issue in search and seizure law — whether the fruits of a warrantless and otherwise unlawful search should be excluded from evidence in a subsequent criminal trial. This issue, which arose in numerous Prohibition cases, was not definitively decided in New York, however, until the *Defore* case, which rejected the exclusionary rule because it would have given the "pettiest peace officer . . . power, through overzeal or indiscretion, to confer immunity upon the offender for crimes the most flagitious." Although Cardozo recognized that, "unless the evidence is excluded," the statutory protection against warrantless searches could become "a form and its protection an illusion," he still declined to create a system in which the "criminal" went "free because the constable [had] blundered" or which otherwise effectively failed to enforce sovereign law.[54]

Although not a Prohibition case, *Defore* was written by Cardozo with Prohibition very much in mind, only three years after New York had partially nullified federal policy by repealing the state's laws criminalizing possession of alcoholic beverages.[55] Adoption of the exclusionary rule would have hampered even further efforts to enforce what little remained of Prohibition after the repeal legislation had been passed. *Defore* thus should be viewed as an antinullification opinion, in which the judge most closely identified with the urban, immigrant opponents of Prohibition chose not to protect traditional immigrant cultures but instead embraced the Puritan vision of discipline, order, hard work, responsibility, and self-control that lay beneath the Eighteenth Amendment. Of course, on the issue of Prohibition, the victory of moralist elites was only temporary.

Sex Crimes. New York judges similarly espoused a Victorian vision of moral rectitude in addressing issues of gender and sexuality during the 1920s and 1930s. The cases we are about to examine establish that those decades were a time of continuing, and perhaps even expanded, judicial enforcement of Puritanical sexual norms. Like Prohibition, the law dealing with pornography, prostitution, homosexuality, and gender-related violence performed two functions. First, it gave effect to a widely shared societal moral code, which was accepted by Catholic and Jewish as well as Protestant religious leaders, that directed respectable, upper-class people like judges to restrain themselves from engaging in, reading about, or even discussing sexual activities outside monogamous marriage. Second, it turned to criminal sanctions in an effort, the success of which cannot be perfectly measured, to prevent "the great lower class" from breaching sexual norms and thereby "poison[ing] society all around them."[56]

Although a loosening of sexual standards may have occurred in society at large during the 1920s, strong pressures for legal enforcement of Victorian norms remained. These pressures were connected to Prohibition, which reformers hoped would result, among other things, in a reduction of male violence against wives and children. Indeed, the advocates of Prohibition were even hopeful that it would "stimulate a vast process of national purification" that would include "the sublimation of the sex instinct upon which the next stage of progress for the human race so largely depends." The early years of the 1920s were also a time when the Committee of Fourteen, a New York antivice group, was sending private investigators out to monitor places of prostitution and seeking legislation to facilitate the arrest of the male customers of prostitutes.[57] Those years also were part of the era during which medico-legal experts were creating and imposing a new allegedly inferior status of homosexuality upon those who engaged in intimate acts with individuals of their own sex — acts that at an earlier time had been understood, like adultery, as merely sinful rather than indicative of a person's fundamental identity. Societal hostility to homosexuality continued unabated and, in the 1930s, even intensified.[58]

Societal pressure for the suppression of pornography also endured. The New York Society for the Suppression of Vice, founded by Anthony Comstock and led by him until his death in 1915, remained active into the 1930s in seeking legislation against pornography, in instituting court cases, and even in burning confiscated literature. More than sixty books were banned in Boston in 1927, while as late as 1938, new antivice organizations, like the National Organization for Decent Literature, were still being formed. Thus it is not surprising that even in the late 1930s, when one New York judge took note of a 40 percent increase in sex offenses in 1936 and a 110 percent increase in 1937, he saw a need for a "drive today against sex perverts, all forms of vice engendered by loose morals, and even positive degeneracy."[59]

The view just expressed was not unusual. As the future reform-minded senator Robert F. Wagner wrote, the struggle against vice demonstrated the need for laws for the protection of women and children similar to those that had saved them "from exploitation by the unscrupulous employer." Judges felt duty-bound to prevent any " 'lecherous swing causing a corruption of the moral tone of the[se] susceptible members' of the community"; thus they were always concerned that "those who are subject to perverted influences" — the "immature, the moron, the mentally weak, or the intellectually impoverished" — "might be aroused to lustful and lecherous practices."[60]

People v. Clark will illustrate. The *Clark* case was a prosecution for attempted rape in which the district attorney asked the following questions on recross-examination:

Q. Are you the fellow when she was up at the Hotel Niagara with another boy to a dance, that tucked under the windshield wiper of his car, a little envelope saying, 'For Mary,' with a couple of c—— (contraceptive appliances) in it? A. No, sir.

Q. Are you the fellow who did that? A. No, sir.

Q. Are you the fellow who, the night before last, appeared on her father's lawn and left a couple of c—— (contraceptive appliances) on his lawn? . . . A. No, sir.

In the court's view, the mere recital of these questions, which implied that "the defendant was guilty of the despicable conduct which they suggest," was so prejudicial that it required reversal of the defendant's conviction.[61]

The notion that the mere mention of sex was something in which such respectable people as district attorneys and judges ought not even engage was repeated again and again in judicial opinions of the 1920s and 1930s. In one case of attempted sodomy, for example, in which the court gave vent to its passion against the "abnormal perversion" and against a defendant who "had a passion toward his own sex that was unnatural," the "nature of the case preclude[d] a discussion of the facts," which alone could answer the question of "who would [possibly] commit such a crime." In this case, of course, the court was merely following the ancient common-law view about the unspeakable quality of homosexual behavior, but in other cases judicial reticence extended to a broader variety of sexual matters. Thus the most plausible reading of the text of the *Clark* case suggests that condoms were a subject unfit for judicial mention, while in two cases involving suppression of books one judge found it inappropriate "to spread upon our pages all the indecent and lascivious part[s]" of the book at issue and another judge declined even to name the book being suppressed or to describe its contents so as not "to excite the curiosity of the prurient."[62]

The sense of shock at the mere mention of sex, together with the belief that those who flouted conventional standards of sexual morality or used sex for commercial gain were degenerates and perverts, were essential to the law's efforts to repress sexual freedom during the 1920s and 1930s. The language quoted in the preceding paragraphs shows that judges during the two decades in question had no empathy for anyone who violated conventional sexual taboos; the judges believed the behavior of such people to be so different from their own that they had no difficulty condemning violators as members of an evil, lower class worthy of imprisonment. Few doubted the ultimate good and verity of the conventional standards and thus the desirability of protecting the public from anyone in the lower class who might undermine them.

One important mechanism for protecting the public was movie censorship.

No movie could be shown in New York until it received a license from the Motion Picture Division of the Board of Regents, and whenever licenses were denied to movies emphasizing sex, the denials typically were judicially affirmed. Even motion pictures with an arguably educational or polemical content were sometimes subjected to the repression of the censor. One such picture was *The Naked Truth,* which traced the lives of three individuals from boyhood to manhood, portrayed the dangers and results of "association with lewd women," and showed a male and female in the nude, along with the progress and effects of different venereal diseases. An even clearer case occurred with the censorship of *Tomorrow's Children,* described in a dissenting opinion as a forceful and dramatic argument against the enactment of statutes that, under certain circumstances, permitted forced sterilization operations. The movie portrayed, among other things, a "poverty stricken feeble-minded family" submitting to sterilization in exchange for help, a young woman sentenced to submit to the operation being released only on the sudden discovery that "there was no law permitting the mutilation of her body against her will," and a judge "discharging a frenzied, moronic, sexual pervert, upon the intervention of a 'Senator' exerting political influence on the court." On these facts, the censors and the majority of the reviewing court found that the "reproductive organs are the theme and their perversion is the topic of the picture" and hence that the picture was "illegal . . . and reprehensible according to the standards of a very large part of the citizenry of the state." [63]

Efforts to censor theatrical performances also occurred and generally met with success. The courts did "not propose to sanction indecency on the stage" or other performances "calculated to exploit the excitation of lustful and lecherous desires." [64] Similarly, books were subject to censorship throughout the 1920s and 1930s, although occasional breaks occurred in the otherwise solid wall of repression and suggested the dawning of an era of greater tolerance to come.

The most important break took place in the 1934 case of *United States v. One Book Entitled Ulysses by James Joyce,* where Augustus Hand, joined by his cousin Learned Hand, held that, with literature as with science, a book could not be judged obscene "where the presentation, when viewed objectively, is sincere, and the erotic matter . . . does not furnish the dominant note of the publication." Any other test, Hand argued, "would exclude much of the great works of literature" and prove "stifling to [artistic] progress." [65]

Nonetheless, censorship remained the dominant approach to pornographic publications. As Judge Martin Manton, who dissented in the *Ulysses* case, wrote:

Statute[s] against obscenity [exist] for the protection of the great mass of our people. . . . Literature exists for the sake of the people, to refresh the weary, to console the sad, to hearten the dull and downcast, to increase man's interest in the world, his joy of living, and his sympathy in all sorts and conditions of men. Art for art's sake is heartless. . . . The people need and deserve a moral standard; it should be a point of honor with men of letters to maintain it. Masterpieces have never been produced by men given to obscenity or lustful thoughts. . . . A refusal to imitate obscenity or to load a book with it is an author's professional chastity.

Other judges agreed, observing that the "Code of Morality or Decency . . . is as old as the World itself and does not change" and that it "would sanction the destruction of all law to give to individuals . . . the privilege of having their violations of the law adjudged by standards made by themselves and labeled 'our time.' " [66]

Nothing, however, appears to have rankled judges of the 1920s and 1930s as much as nudity, which they viewed as a species of obscenity. Thus in one case, a court found that a photograph of a woman reclining in the nude with the lighting effect so arranged that "the woman's busts and private parts were brought into prominence" was "unquestionably . . . a 'provocative picture.' " Nudity, as another judge summed up the matter, could not "but offend against all sense of public decency" since "the parading of persons . . . naked, in public places, would raise thoughts of lasciviousness and lust." [67]

The extent to which discussion of sexual matters was repressed emerges in especially sharp light in a case involving the conviction of one George Swasey for advocating repeal of the section of the Penal Law prohibiting the giving of information concerning birth control. The reviewing court had no doubt that "under certain circumstances and at certain times language may undoubtedly amount to disorderly conduct," especially "where children are present" and where "the nature of the subject-matter discussed and the impropriety of discussing it in the presence of children" may cause mere speech "to produce a breach of the peace." In the case at bar, the court reversed the conviction of Swasey only because "the police officers placed a mistaken interpretation upon the language used by the defendant, . . . did not accurately report it, . . . [and] clearly did not understand" it. In other cases where the police did their work properly, however, the courts sustained convictions of defendants who, for example, distributed advertisements about cures for venereal disease or engaged in lewd dancing.[68]

Yet another subject of intense criminal regulation during the 1920s and

1930s was prostitution. Many of the prostitution cases dealt with technical questions,[69] but others raised more trenchant issues. One case, for example, held directly that a male customer of a prostitute could not be found guilty of the crime of prostitution. But this view did not prevail easily. The judge who reached it did "not argue that this attitude was just or fair" toward women, and he also recognized that "in the interest of the public health, it would have been wiser to bring the male participant . . . under some sort of governmental supervision." Another judge held that "men caught with women in an act of prostitution are equally guilty, and should be arrested and held for trial with the women." The question whether to arrest male customers was resolved only when the legislature refused to pass a bill declaring patronage of a prostitute criminal.[70]

The need to prosecute customers in order to eliminate prostitutes nevertheless seemed obvious, given the fact that prostitution was "a system" through which men "by the use of money and other valuable considerations" become "enabled to largely coerce and control the will of unfortunate women" and thereby to "dominate" those women. Indeed, judges of the 1920s and 1930s could speak quite negatively about the role of men in prostitution in cases such as one in which a man fraudulently told women that he was a representative of a major motion picture house and offered to secure for them "lucrative employment in moving pictures." Although the defendant planned "to gratuitously gratify his lust with them" as "an incident in his general scheme" for exploiting the women, his "basic purpose was to deliver the unfortunate[s] . . . to prostitution." In the court's incensed view, a "meaner or viler form of debauching persons seeking employment [was] hard to imagine."[71]

In view of concerns such as these for protecting women and preserving high moral standards, it is necessary to ask why most judges and legislators were unwilling to allow men who used the services of prostitutes to be prosecuted criminally. The reason, we might suspect, was that criminal prosecution of a customer entailed "class[ifying] an otherwise respectable man with those 'who are vagrants.' " Elite male judges found it better to permit upper-class men to dominate, control, and ultimately coerce lower-class women for purposes of sexual gratification than to subject their "erring brothers" to criminal liability and "blackmail" and thereby place them "at the mercy" of "*those conscienceless vampires who make merchandise of the passions of men.*" The same elite judges would recoil a few years later, however, when the class tables were turned and "CCC camp boys" — "an element of young men who are transients in the community" — tried to exploit a local "girl."[72]

Analogous class biases also emerged in obscenity cases. Occasional judges saw a need to bar the upper class from viewing obscenity on the grounds that it would be wrong to allow "style, imagination, [and] learning" to "create a privileged class" and that "disgusting details . . . served up in a polished style" were "all the more dangerous and insidious." Most judges, however, believed that on special occasions members of the upper class would need privileged access to sexually explicit information. It seemed obvious, for instance, that "facts" that were "not proper subject matter" for a general audience needed to be discussed openly in "the classroom of the law school, the medical school and clinic, the research laboratory, the doctor's office, and even the theological school." And as the many cases discussed above clearly showed, the lower classes and the young were seen to be the ones most in need of protection. Only "positive measures" of censoring obscene movies and publications could "protect the minds of our growing boys and girls from this pestilence and noisome filth" and save the lower classes from lives of vice and crime.[73]

Marriage and Divorce. Traditional moral values likewise continued in the 1920s and 1930s to dominate family law, especially in regard to the state's traditional policy of "preserv[ing] the family unit" and through the family "the morality of the citizens of the state."[74] As a general matter, family preservation was not an issue that divided Protestant from Catholic and Jewish religious leaders; religious groups across New York society supported family values, and various religious organizations played an active role in assisting victims, especially child victims, of family breakdown. Not every rule discussed below enjoyed clerical support, however, and it is best to understand all the rules as a carryover from nineteenth-century legislation and common-law adjudication.

The courts possessed two mechanisms for keeping families intact. One was to presume that men and women cohabiting together were married, especially if they had children. The other, which enjoyed the strong support particularly of the Roman Catholic hierarchy, was to "promote the permanency of . . . marriage contracts" by making termination of marriage difficult.[75] By systematizing marriages and forcing couples to remain married, judges hoped to ensure that children would live in nuclear families and, as a result, receive proper economic support and moral education.

At common law, a child born out of wedlock was "nullius filius"—the child of no one, entitled to neither rights nor standing in the community and "not looked upon as [a] child . . . for any civil purposes." Bastardy was a stigma upon both a child and its parents, which was designed to deter couples from engaging in sex or, if deterrence failed, to encourage them to legitimize their relationship.[76] An important vehicle of legitimation was the doctrine of common-law marriage, which permitted a couple to marry without the formality of a ceremony. The only requisite to the creation of a common-law marriage was the consent of a man and woman to take each other at the time of the consent as husband and wife.[77] The main impact of common-law marriage was to validate otherwise invalid marriages when a couple continued to agree to live together as husband and wife at a time and place where common-law marriage was recognized.[78]

This effect is illustrated by a case in which a man and woman who erroneously believed themselves to have been validly married in Pennsylvania came to live in New York in 1903, when common-law marriage was not recognized in the state. As of December 31, 1907, they were not husband and wife, but when, on January 1, 1908, common-law marriage came back into existence in New York and the couple thereafter continued their agreement to live as husband and wife, their marriage became valid.[79]

Even after legislation effective in 1933 made it impossible to enter into a common-law marriage in New York, the state's courts continued to recognize the validity of common-law marriages entered into before 1933 or in other jurisdictions. Indeed, they even went so far as to declare that New Yorkers with an uncertain marital status who went to another state that allowed common-law marriage would be deemed to have gone there "for the express purpose of renewing their consents . . . [so as] 'to remove any doubt as to the validity of their marriage.' "[80]

Through the doctrine of common-law marriage, New York's courts did what they could to regularize illicit unions and legitimize their offspring. Men and women who went through invalid, ceremonial marriages or who simply cohabited and produced offspring would be treated as nuclear families unless they manifested a clear intent to the contrary. The law's preference for marriage could hardly have been more clear.

Not only did New York law encourage cohabiting couples to enter into marriage; it also strove to keep them there by limiting the grounds of divorce. Indeed, for the first two-thirds of the twentieth century, only a single ground for divorce—adultery—existed in New York. The fact that spouses had "acted in disregard of th[eir] marriage for a long period of time . . . [would] not destroy its validity" provided their disregard had taken a form other than adultery. Indeed, one case held that even a husband's act of homosexual sodomy would not give a wife ground for divorce; while the court was "sympathetic with plaintiff [wife's] plight," it felt "powerless to alleviate it."[81]

Nonetheless, unhappy spouses who were seeking to break their matrimonial chains constantly attempted to maneuver around these restrictions by obtaining "collusive or fraudulent divorce[s]" and "divorces by agreement." In response, the courts, "interested in preserving the marriage status," developed new strictures against easy divorce.[82] At least in the 1920s, however, the rules for appraising evidence of adultery in the context of divorce were not manipulated in a fashion suggestive of discrimination against women. On the contrary, judges expressed their awareness "of the frailties and viciousness of" men. With that awareness, they were prepared to listen seriously to an accusation, for example, that a husband had committed adultery with his mother-in-law. Given their awareness, they did not find the accusation "so inherently improbable as to be beyond belief," and they accordingly required the husband to submit evidence of his innocence.[83]

The difficulty of obtaining divorce in New York induced many unhappy spouses to seek other ways out of marriage. Two such ways existed: suing for divorce in another state or seeking an annulment of their marriage in New York.

Recognizing the threat that both devices presented to the state's policy of protecting marriage, the courts strove to make both as unavailable as possible. Central to the effort to restrict the effectiveness of out-of-state divorces was the full faith and credit clause of the federal Constitution, which determined whether New York would be free to enforce its own divorce policies. Until 1942, when the United States Supreme Court held that states were required to give full faith and credit to the divorce judgments of sister states, New York courts jealously guarded the state's freedom to ignore out-of-state divorces and thereby bind its domiciliaries to its own policies.

The key case in the 1920s was *Hubbard v. Hubbard,* in which the Court of Appeals declared the state's courts "untrammeled" by the full faith and credit clause and hence free to give divorce decrees of other states "the efficacy and effect they deem rightful and salutary in view of the public policy of the state." Observing that the policy of the state was "to promote the permanency of the marriage contracts and the morality of the citizens of the state" by allowing divorce only on grounds of adultery, the court declared itself the final judge "of the occasions on which the exercise of comity [to recognize an out-of-state divorce] will or will not make for justice or morality" and that, in light of New York's policies, it would not enforce "a divorce decree of a sister state which violates the principles of morality, or the public policy, or municipal regulations established by it." [84]

In view of the difficulty of obtaining a divorce in New York for adultery and of gaining recognition of an out-of-state divorce on grounds other than adultery, many New Yorkers seeking an end to their marriage during the 1920s and

1930s turned to the third device available to them—annulment, or judicial declaration that their marriage had never existed.[85]

An annulment could be obtained on any of three grounds—duress, fraud, or incapacity. Duress was the ground for annulment in *Fratello v. Fratello,* where the groom and his relatives threatened that if the plaintiff did not marry him, "they would kidnap her, take her to New York, disfigure her face by cutting it, and would also destroy the house of plaintiff's father by blowing it to pieces"; the plaintiff and her family "not only believed that these men would carry into execution this threat, but . . . were justified in such belief."[86] Fortunately, after the marriage ceremony, the bride was able to escape, go into hiding, and bring suit.

More important, annulments could be had for fraud. The basic rule, proclaimed by the Court of Appeals, was that a valid marriage required "consent by . . . [the] parties" thereto, that "if either party consent[ed] by reason of fraud there [was] no reality of consent," and that "hence the marriage [was] voidable." Annulments for fraud were usually difficult to obtain, however, because they would be "decreed, not for any and every kind of fraud," but only for frauds deemed by the courts " 'vital' to the marriage relationship."[87]

In determining the issue of the importance of any particular fraud, courts focused in a categorical fashion on the type of fraud perpetrated rather than on the significance of the fraud in the injured spouse's individualized hierarchy of values. One category of fraud that was always held to vitiate a marriage, but probably produced few annulments, was sexual impotence. "Capability of consummation [was] an implied term in every marriage contract; and in the case of marriages between young persons, capacity for lawful sexual indulgence [was] regarded as of especial importance to the happiness of the wedded state and to the fulfillment of the ends of matrimony, viz. a lawful indulgence of the passions in order to prevent licentiousness." Thus if a husband lacked "potentia copulandi" and was incapable of "copula vera," defined as "ordinary and complete intercourse" or "natural and perfect coition," a wife was entitled to an annulment. Similarly, if a wife was suffering from "a nervous condition, an uncontrollable tension" or from "an erratic nervous condition characterized by a contraction of the sphincter muscles of the vagina" which made her "incapable of sexual intercourse with the plaintiff, though not with other persons, if such be possible, a decree of nullity [could] be granted."[88]

A similar category of cases consisted of those in which one spouse refused to engage in sexual relations with the other. But only a few such cases provided grounds for annulment. An annulment would not be granted, for instance, if there was "an adequate excuse" for a wife's "refusal to cohabit," such as a husband's failure "to perform his marital obligations of providing a home and maintenance." Even an unjustified refusal to engage in sexual relations constituted no more than a ground for separation, unless the refusal resulted from some condition preexisting the marriage, such as homosexuality or a desire for some form of "unnatural and perverted" sex with one's spouse which a court found "disgusting and deserving of utmost condemnation." A refusal of sexual relations would otherwise constitute a ground for annulment only if an intent to refuse had been formed secretly before the marriage.[89]

Similarly, fraud occurred when an unmarried, pregnant woman coerced a man into marrying her by falsely telling him that he was the father of her child. Courts uniformly granted annulments to such husbands upon their discovery of the fraud, provided they could prove that the woman was actually pregnant and that they were not the father. But normally the courts would not grant an annulment of a marriage between the actual parents of a child conceived before marriage.[90]

Incapacity was the final basis for annulment. Two forms of incapacity were the nonage of one or both spouses or their consanguinity, but the most common form of legal incapacity was that one of the spouses was lawfully married to a third person.[91] In this last sort of case, determining which of two marriages should be recognized as valid often presented courts with difficult problems.

Consider, for example, two cases arising out of the chaos of World War I. In the first, a young woman named Anastasia in 1903 married Steve Schultz in Dubra, then in Austria-Hungary and now in Bosnia. She bore her husband a daughter in 1905 and lived with him until she came to New York in 1912, with every expectation that he would follow. The outbreak of war in 1914 prevented his coming, however, and in 1918 she learned that he had died. She thereupon married Conrad Chayka, with whom she lived until she learned in 1932 from her daughter in Austria that Steve Schultz was still alive. She immediately left Chayka, who eventually found another woman. Then in 1938 her Austrian daughter wrote from Russia that Schultz had just died in Yugoslavia. On her testimony to these facts, the court held her still to be married to Chayka.[92]

A similar case arose from Emanuel Hayden's marriages. In 1913 in Russia he had married Molly Hayden, who bore a child the next year. Emanuel was nonetheless drafted into the Russian army, captured by the Germans, and confined as a prisoner of war in Germany, where he heard that "his wife had been murdered in one of the many 'pogroms' incidental to Jewish life in Russia during the late war." At the end of the war he escaped to the Netherlands and in 1920 migrated to New York, from where he continued to try to contact his wife. In 1921, however, he received confirmation through a cousin in New York that his wife and child had indeed been murdered in the pogrom. Believing Molly dead, he married Ida Hayden in 1922, with whom he promptly had a second child in 1923. In the same year, Molly contacted him, he ceased cohabiting with Ida, and finally in 1925 he was able to bring Molly and his first child to the United States. On this evidence, the court validated his marriage with Molly and annulled his marriage with Ida, concluding that he had always acted "in good faith" and had simply been a victim "of the chaotic and disturbed social, economic, and political conditions which existed in Russia" resulting in a "dislocation of the normal channels of communication."[93]

The legislature sought to provide a remedy in cases such as these, and incidentally to make annulments more difficult to obtain, by a 1922 statute requiring a person who believed his or her spouse to be dead to conduct an investigation, present the results of the investigation to a court, and obtain a court order declaring the first marriage null before taking a new spouse in a second marriage. But the only impact of the statute was to increase legal expenses for a party seeking to remarry following the undocumented death of a first spouse and to create a possibility that court orders would be erroneously and perhaps even fraudulently procured.[94]

In all other cases, courts typically, although not invariably, denied annulments. As the Court of Appeals declared, "mere nondisclosure as to birth, social position, fortune, good health, and temperament [could] not vitiate the marriage contract." It later reiterated that annulments were available only "for fraud as to matters 'vital' to the marriage relationship. . . . Premarital falsehoods as to love and affection [were] not enough, nor disclosure that one partner 'married for money.'" In such matters, the "rule of caveat emptor still ha[d] some application to the parties contracting marriage."[95]

Judges, in short, were always aware that they could "not grant annulments solely because of sympathy." They knew that plaintiffs often "resort[ed] to the process of annulment" out of "a desire for freedom from marital bonds" rather than because of some "fundamental fraud," and therefore they were always on guard "to weigh each case to determine whether it [was] honestly within the law, or [was] a sham carefully tailored and camouflaged to circumvent and defeat law." Accordingly, judges routinely refused to grant annulments because a spouse allegedly had married for money or social status rather than love.[96]

In the end, the cases on annulment, like those on divorce and full faith and credit, reflected the judiciary's constant concern to prevent "the floodgates of litigation" from being "thrown wide open" in ways that would ease the termination of marriages and thereby produce "an extension of the legislative enactment by judicial decree." The courts were always careful to avoid "legislation by the judiciary."[97] Hence annulments, like divorces, remained difficult to obtain throughout the 1920s and 1930s.

Custody and Support. Despite the untiring efforts of judges to protect children by legitimizing cohabitation as marriage and by preventing marriages from terminating, some children nonetheless found themselves heirs to broken marriages. At that point, judges had to determine to whom custody of a child would be awarded.

In formulating the rules for custody, courts in the 1920s started from the proposition that "the rights of the husband and wife to the custody of their infant children [were] equal," although the "primary right to . . . custody . . . [was] in the father." But judges did not permit the rights of the parents to become dispositive. Their principal concern was always the moral protection of children, and hence they focused on moral fault as evidence of the fitness of each parent for custody. For example, it was "unusual to award the custody of the children to the unsuccessful party" in a divorce action on grounds of adultery, "in the absence of clear and convincing evidence that the successful party was unfit." Thus when a mother obtained a divorce on the grounds of the father's cohabitation with another woman, and a fourteen-year-old son testified "that he could no longer stay with the father, because of his open and continuous association with her," custody was granted to the mother, who was "a woman of good character, of a degree of refinement, of strict notions of the propriety of relationships, such as were being maintained by the defendant with the correspondent, having great affection for the children, and anxious to do all in her power for their well-being, education, and correct moral training."[98]

In another case, however, where the evidence showed that a mother had "sustained improper relations" with her employer, the court awarded custody of her eight-year-old daughter to the child's father, even though his "health . . . was somewhat shattered," because the court found him "a man of good habits, good reputation, and both morally and financially a fit and proper person to have the care, custody, and control of his little daughter." Similarly, in a third case, a mother addicted to morphine was denied custody of her child.[99]

Like the law of child custody, the law of support following dissolution of a marriage rested on traditional concepts of moral rectitude and male duty and privilege. Absent an agreement by a husband to make "regular, substantial, periodic payments" for the support of his wife and any minor children, it was the duty of the court in a divorce or separation action to fix the amount of support. In cases where a husband had been the guilty party responsible for the separation or divorce, or both parties had been guilty, his wife was entitled to support on the basis of her needs and his means. If a wife had been the guilty party, however, then her support would be fixed only at a minimum amount that would keep her from becoming a public charge. Of course, courts would always enforce the "natural obligation" of a father to provide appropriate support for his minor children.[100]

Abandonment and Adoption. Especially disheartening cases arose when parents proved unable to support their children and found it necessary to abandon them, typically to the custody of other relatives. Although courts sometimes declared that parents were "the natural guardian[s] of . . . [their] children, and under ordinary circumstances . . . entitled to their custody and control," judges also observed that they had the "duty, to act at all times for the best interests of the children, and, if their welfare require[d] that their custody be given to their grandparents" or other collateral relatives, the latter would retain custody.[101]

Most anguishing of all were the cases in which parents left their children with strangers who subsequently tried to adopt them. Consider, for example, a case described by the court as involving "a battle for a life with grim reality." The story begins with Margaret O'Donnell, who resided in an orphanage in Hoboken, where she attended school until the age of ten and then went to work as "a kitchen drudge" until she was sixteen. At that age, in 1912, a Miss Stinson took her from the orphanage on some charitable pretext, but she soon ended up in the arms of one William Stinson, who was then separated from his wife. Over the course of approximately a decade, Margaret and William had six children, including Russell, the subject of the case, born on May 4, 1923. William finally married Margaret on June 20, 1923, but almost immediately after the ceremony, he disappeared.

With " 'nothing in the house,' " Margaret, who " 'was sick at that time,' " placed the following advertisement in a New York newspaper: " 'Nice Baby Boy given for adoption to Catholic family.' " A middle-aged woman named Florence Davis answered the ad, to which Margaret O'Donnell Stinson replied, "I got your letter about my baby I would be glad to go over to you but I have no money to go with I would be afraid to take a tax because yow may not whant to pay for it so what wood I do, why don't yow come yourself, to my home then if yow like the baby yow can take him. . . . if yow can come now all right as I ecpest an other lady to come she sent me a telegram an is grazie to get the baby." After Mrs. Davis came, Margaret agreed to give her the child. As Margaret stated, "The baby is on the bottle and no trouble a real good baby. I am a poor woman with four other children and I cannot keep him I have all I can do to get a long. I am willing to sine him over to yow he a nice baby and I no yow will like him."

Sometime after receiving Russell, Mrs. Davis took him to Florida, where she died in 1928, when Russell was five years old. On her deathbed she directed that Russell be adopted by her married son and his wife, which was accomplished by court order in 1929 without any notice to the natural parents, who were said to be unknown to the adoptive parents. Meanwhile, William Stinson had returned and become a produce peddler. He wanted his son also to be returned, and after an unsuccessful attempt by Margaret to kidnap the boy, the adoptive parents brought an action to confirm the earlier adoption proceedings.

The legal issue in the case was whether the Stinsons had abandoned Russell, in which case the 1929 adoption proceedings were valid even in the absence of notice to them and consent. The real issue in the case, however, was social class. The adoptive parents resided "in a nicely furnished and well-kept apartment of eight rooms," and the father was "in business for himself and enjoy[ed] a good income." They had "ample means to give the child good care, attendance, and education." The natural father, in contrast, was "an admitted adulterer and seducer of an immature orphan girl" who had "demonstrated his utter insensibility to the ordinary dictates of decency or obligation by abandoning his wife and five small children in a state of utter destitution." The court concluded that the natural mother "had not seen the child for seven years" and did not want "to take him back as she could not support him." But the father "wanted him and continually beat her" because "he was now old enough to help . . . on his peddler's cart." Concluding that it could believe the testimony of the upper-class adoptive parents but not of the lower-class natural parents, the court found that Russell had been abandoned and hence that the 1929 adoption proceedings had been valid.[102]

This case was not unique. Another was quite similar. Elsa, the natural mother, had married one Phillips in 1893 and had had two children by him, including Louise, the child at issue, in July 1915. Phillips, however, died the next month, and soon thereafter Elsa "married one Lentino, a gambler by profession," who in 1919 was imprisoned on a gambling conviction. During the difficult years after her natural father's death, Louise was left in the custody of several people, the last of them being Mr. and Mrs. Feser, who wished to adopt her. After protracted negotiations, Elsa signed a document authorizing Louise "to live with, and be brought up by" the Fesers, "as I do not love or care for her." The Fesers, without giving any notice to Elsa, subsequently obtained an adoption order. As between Elsa, who was married to a professional gambler serving time in state prison and who "had no means and earned nothing," and the Fesers, who were "respectable people and ha[d] sufficient financial ability properly to care for" Louise, it was not surprising that the court affirmed the right of the latter to adopt Louise.[103]

Yet another similar case occurred when one Frances Sabo turned her ten-day-old child over to the Millers for adoption. When the Millers brought their adoption petition, Sabo contested it, but the court granted the petition over her objection. In doing so, it described her as having "deserted . . . her husband and six other children," as being "in poor financial circumstances," and as having "worked as a waitress in restaurants, and . . . as housekeeper for a man by the name of Allen at 1763 Broadway, where she was known as Mrs. Allen." The Millers, in contrast, were "reputable, orderly people" who were "well regarded in their community, . . . regular church attendants, and ha[d] taken excellent care of the child."[104]

The result changed, however, in a case with one important factual difference—namely, the natural mother's ability to earn income and thereby obtain respectability. In November 1933, a Brooklyn mother, "in dire trouble, substantially destitute, . . . abandoned by the father of the child, . . . critically ill and apprehend[ing] death," gave birth to a daughter and four days later signed a document authorizing her adoption. But soon thereafter, she recovered her health, obtained employment, and within the six month period she believed was available to reopen her surrender of her daughter, sought to regain custody of the child. This demonstration "in a reasonable, seasonable, and unmistakable manner [of] her desire to resume her parental duties," together with the court's desire to avoid "an endless struggle with the instinct of mother love," won the natural mother custody of her child. In contrast, an upstate judge in a 1932 case denied custody to a "courageous and resourceful" but nonetheless impoverished mother who along with her husband had abandoned her child when they were both gravely ill. The court acted, at least in part, because the two children whose custody the mother had retained were "underfed and underweight" and because, as a result "of adversity," the mother had had to wait six years before reclaiming her child.[105]

Other cases involved natural parents who, upon appreciating their inability to take proper care of their offspring, gave custody at least temporarily to relatives or trusted family friends, who subsequently sought to adopt the children. Typically the natural parents lost.[106] The reality of class differences surfaced in these cases as well: in one case, for example, the trial judge could not help but observe in authorizing adoption of a child by trusted friends that they were "respectable people," who "own[ed] a comfortable and commodious home, with about three acres of land, in a highly respectable country locality." They had "an annual income of $5,000 from a profitable rug business, with excess profits that are left in the business, which is of a permanent character." In contrast, the natural parents lived in a "section of New York City, which [was] populated largely by people of foreign birth or descent, who speak the English language only to a limited extent." Even without the adopted child, there remained "five children . . . in an apartment that ha[d] only two bedrooms," and the father had wages of only "$3,380 yearly for a family of seven, if he . . . [remained] steadily employed and . . . in good health." The child was ultimately saved from adoption only by the insistence of a divided Court of Appeals, in a majority opinion by Cardozo, that "such considerations . . . [were] foreign to the [sole legal] issue" in the case—whether the natural parents' "silence and inaction [had been] prolonged to such a point than an intention" to abandon the child could be found from the facts as "an inference of law."[107]

A divorced mother sought to recover a son on similar facts in still another case. "Unwilling to be burdened with the care and maintenance of" her seventeen-month-old, Mary Duffy gave him, together with "all the child's clothing and playthings," to "a respectable, prudent, industrious, well thought of young married couple . . . , substantial and respected citizens of . . . [their] community," who for five years had "so generously, humanely, and carefully administered" to the boy's needs with "painstaking devotion." Although Duffy had said "she would never claim the child," she did ultimately decide that she wanted him back. Finding in Duffy "a want of maternal instincts," the court could not view the child's future with her "with much pleasure and satisfaction," whereas his new middle-class home "promise[d] to be clean, healthful, industrious, [and] honest."[108] Hence the court refused to return him to his mother.

Nothing, perhaps, illustrates the value structure of 1920s family law more clearly than these cases on adoption, in which the conservative agenda's partiality toward the rich and suspicion of the poor reemerged in juxtaposition with its Puritanical moral concerns. In their moralistic efforts to create nuclear families and hold them intact as society's primary, if not sole, mechanism for providing sustenance and moral training to the young, judges abandoned to "grim reality" those families and children whom death, destitution, or divorce had rendered unable to live by society's dominant values. The judiciary of the 1920s and early 1930s inhabited a profoundly inegalitarian world divided between respectable, economically secure, monogamous couples and their children, who had every opportunity for success and happiness, and destitute children, typically without two parents and also without hope or security. In the conservative mind-set of the 1920s and 1930s, it was simply impossible to imagine that children could have a proper upbringing in poor, single-parent families. The best that judges could do for such children was to separate them from their natural families and place them with respectable, monogamous couples, who, it was hoped, would lift them up to the perceived moral and social heights at which respectable people lived.[109]

PUBLIC ASSISTANCE LAW

This same juxtaposition of prejudice against the poor with efforts to uplift them morally can be seen in the rules attaching strings to grants of public assistance. Before the 1960s, welfare was granted not as a right but as a matter of charity, and "in accepting charity," a recipient "consented to the provisions of the law under which charity [was] bestowed." Thus a welfare recipient who preferred living in an old barn rather than in "suitable living quarters" did not have "a right to live as he please[d] while being supported by public charity." Welfare recipients had "no right to defy the standards and conventions of civilized society while being supported at public expense . . . , even though some of those conventions [were] somewhat artificial."[110]

This was true even of a man serving during the Great Depression as "an officer of an organization composed of those receiving public aid," who refused to deposit his automobile license plates with a relief agency while he was employed on work relief. In the man's view, which he "defended with asperity," this requirement on the part of the agency was " 'unreasonable' " and would prove " 'inconvenient' for him." In the court's view, however, the man by his very asperity "placed his family in a condition of abject dependency by his arbitrary and unreasonable refusal to yield to a proper rule" and thereby "subject[ed] them to the ignominy of public relief."[111] For this reason, the court held the man's children neglected, and it threatened to deprive him and his wife of their custody.

One should not be too critical, though, of the inequities of family law and welfare law, which merely reflected more general inequities in society at large. Socioeconomic realities made it impossible for everyone to live by the moral values that the conservative agenda strove to impose; it was accordingly inevitable that some would benefit from the imposition of those values, while others would suffer harm. Only structural social change of the sort which the law began to promote following the election of Governor Alfred E. Smith in 1922 and which ultimately culminated in the Great Society could begin to correct the inequities.

A final area of law in which courts and legislatures during the 1920s and 1930s sought both to protect property rights and the existing distribution of wealth, on the one hand, and to uphold moral values, on the other, was the law of fiduciary duty. At the outset, it must be emphasized that the law of fiduciary duty did not affect the very poor; conflict in connection with issues of fiduciary duty arose not between the rich and the poor but between holders of established wealth and entrepreneurial money managers, who usually had less wealth but were striving to enhance what they had. Thus the usual political divisions between conservatives and reformers did not occur, as leading reform spokesmen, such as Chief Judge Benjamin N. Cardozo and President Franklin D. Roosevelt, called for protection of established holders of wealth and most politically savvy leaders, whether conservatives or reformers, went along.

The law of fiduciary duty initially began the 1920s as a body of doctrine enforcing traditional ethical norms about stealing and dishonesty—norms that ultimately were grounded in concerns about preserving the existing distribution of wealth. The basic doctrinal standard, as stated by the Court of Appeals, had always been that fiduciaries are "bound at all times to exercise the utmost good faith toward their principals" and to "act in accordance with the highest and truest principles of morality." In addition to liability for conflicts of interest, fiduciaries also were liable for negligent breach of the duty of care which resulted in damage—that is, for failure to use the ordinary skill and judgment of a reasonable person.[112] Like other fiduciaries, directors, officers, and other agents of corporations likewise had a duty "to act in good faith and employ such vigilance, sagacity, diligence, and prudence as in general prudent men of discretion and intelligence in like matters employ in their own affairs."[113]

As Chief Judge Cardozo eloquently summed up the law of the 1920s in *Meinhard v. Salmon,* fiduciaries were "held to something stricter than the morals of the market place. Not honesty alone, but the punctilio of an honor the most sensitive, is then the standard of behavior. As to this there has developed a tradition that is unbending and inveterate. Uncompromising rigidity has been the attitude of courts of equity. . . . Only thus has the level of conduct for fiduciaries been kept at a level higher than that trodden by the crowd."[114]

Whatever its actual applicability in the day-to-day administration of corporate law,[115] *Meinhard* reflected a prevalent ethos in Cardozo's time with regard to corporate as well as trust issues. This ethos that those in power should not exploit those they were serving was evidenced not only in the case law but also in the passage in 1933 and 1934 of the two statutes that even today constitute the centerpiece of corporate law—the Securities Act of 1933 and the Securities Exchange Act of 1934, both of which were designed to protect investors from money managers who manipulated markets for their own profit at investors' expense. One need only remember the rhetoric of Franklin Roosevelt, who in campaigning for the reform of Wall Street and in signing the 1933 act, condemned the "practices of the unscrupulous money changers," who "had shown themselves either incompetent or dishonest in their handling of the people's funds . . . had used the money entrusted to them in speculations and unwise loans," and, as a result, stood "indicted in the court of public opinion." The new legislation, the president promised, would rectify the failings of existing state fiduciary law and thereby "correct some of the evils which ha[d] been so glaringly revealed in the private exploitation of the public's money."[116]

Based on the principle of loyalty elaborated in *Meinhard* and in the 1933 and 1934 acts, courts during the 1920s and 1930s, as well as later decades, routinely held numerous fiduciaries liable for breach of duty. The high-toned rhetoric used by Cardozo in *Meinhard,* as well as other judges, appears, at least to some degree, to have affected results. "The exact limitations of . . . a [fiduciary] relationship [were] impossible of statement," but the concept "embrace[d] both technical fiduciary relations and those informal relations which exist whenever one man trusts in, and relies upon, another," including relationships "between close friends" or "based upon prior business dealings." Without referring specifically to a fiduciary relationship, other judges agreed that "where one party to a transaction has superior knowledge, or means of knowledge not open to both parties alike, he is under a legal obligation to speak and his silence constitutes fraud."[117]

For two reasons, the law of fiduciary duty is a fitting subject with which to end analysis of the conservative agenda of protecting the established distribution of wealth and preserving moral values. First, fiduciary law shows that the conservative agenda sometimes had power to attract reformers like Cardozo to its banner. Second, it explains why the agenda had such power. Although conservatives at times pursued purely partisan policies such as adopting a summary judgment remedy of benefit only to creditors, at other times, as in connection with the law of trespass, conversion, and fraud, the conservative agenda called for protecting the resources of small as well as large property owners or preserving moral values, like full and honest disclosure, on which nearly all New Yorkers agreed. Thus it is not surprising that the agenda retained much of its motive force in the law into the middle decades of the twentieth century.

CHAPTER 3

THE REFORM AGENDA
Preventing Exploitation and Providing Opportunity

As they assumed increasing power with a series of electoral victories beginning in 1922, progressives such as Alfred E. Smith and Benjamin N. Cardozo gradually articulated a reform agenda in opposition to the conservative agenda of protecting property and preserving morality. Legislators played an important initiating role in this process, when, under the leadership of Governors Smith, Roosevelt, and Lehman, they enacted protective laws on matters such as working conditions, pensions, unemployment insurance, housing, and consumer protection in order to "remedy . . . injustice," "properly protect" the "working men, women and children" of the state, and "put an end to the[ir] exploitation." State court judges then followed up, a decade earlier than did the Supreme Court of the United States, with rulings sustaining the validity of the laws against constitutional attack. Finally, judges moved beyond merely upholding legislation and began to tinker with common-law doctrine in a fashion that produced some new rules more protective of society's underdogs than previous law had been. Both the new statutes and the judge-made doctrines also had a further effect beyond their primary one of controlling exploitative behavior by the strong and rich: they created conditions that gave the weak and poor "the very best opportunity in life possible" to improve their status and well-being.[1]

It is to these newly emerging rules preventing the exploitation of society's underdogs and giving them the opportunity to improve their well-being that we must now turn.

THE POLICE POWER

The core power marshaled by the legislature to protect the lower classes from exploitation was the police power. Even in the nineteenth century, the courts had construed the police power expansively.[2] But as the center of gravity on the Court of Appeals began to shift toward reformers in the mid-1920s, the judges authored increasingly sweeping statements about its breadth. The "police power," it was said, was "'the least limitable of the powers of government'" and "extend[ed] to all the great public needs." The legislature, it was added, could "require industry and commerce to be carried on in a manner which [would] promote the public health and welfare," even when such a requirement would "increase the cost of doing business." The protection of safety was treated as akin to the regulation of health, with judges speaking conjunctively about "the protection of the public health and safety."[3]

The legislature's power to protect health and safety was further expanded in *Adamec v. Post,* where the Court of Appeals made it plain that the police power extended to the regulation of housing as well as industry and agriculture. The specific issue in *Adamec* was whether the legislature could require owners of tenement houses built before the Tenement House Law of 1901, the first general regulatory law on the subject, to make alterations in their buildings that would "make them reasonably fit for use as dwellings according to modern standards of health, safety and decency" codified in the 1901 act and subsequent acts. The court penned a ringing proclamation of the legislature's power with its statement that "where economic self-interest ceases to be a sufficiently potent force for the promotion of the general welfare, or, indeed, becomes a force which may actually injure the general welfare," the legislature could impose "minimum standards . . . essential for safe, decent, and sanitary dwelling places."[4]

Another expansive doctrine, which first had been established in *Munn v. Illinois,* legitimated regulation of any business "affected with a public interest" — that is, any business "so intimately bound up with the public interest or public welfare that the industry itself and the prices charged therein [were] subject to control for the public good." On this basis the state entered into the regulation of common carriers and utilities in an effort to require that "reasonable and adequate facilities be provided to serve, not only the necessities, but the convenience of communities which are tributary."[5]

But the police power far transcended regulation in the interests of health, safety, morals, and welfare or of businesses affected with a public interest. It was "common knowledge that an era of unprecedented industrialism [had] presented rare opportunities for the exploitation of nefarious schemes at the expense of an uninformed public," thereby necessitating laws "to protect the unwary and credulous from the allurements of false tokens in the hands of bland sharpers, plying their trade under cover of a respectable environment." Thus the courts routinely sustained legislation "designed to prevent fraud and cheating." This included statutes providing for the weighing and measuring of commodities; prohibiting the sale of food labeled kosher when in fact it was not; requiring subcontractors to maintain trust funds for payment of laborers and materialmen; regulating auction and small loan companies, banks, insurance companies, and investment firms; and dealing with fraudulent practices in the securities and real estate brokerage industries.[6]

The concept of promoting fair dealing was extended even beyond fraud to " 'extortion,' or exorbitant prices exacted by oppression, instead of fixed by free agreement." As Judge Lehman explained in an opinion for the Court of Appeals from which only Judge Andrews dissented, the legislature could invoke the police power to correct a market failure occurring when "the liberty of the individual citizen to contract freely [had] been restricted by the circumstance that a man or group of men [had] obtained control of the supply of a commodity" and was using that "control . . . to compel the individual to pay any price which may be demanded though that price be far beyond the price which would be fixed by free contract." On this rationale the court upheld legislation prohibiting the resale of theater tickets at a price higher than their face value.[7]

The "elastic" nature of the police power became even greater when it was invoked in support of legislation "passed to meet an existing emergency involving the public interest," such as the Great Depression—an "emergency . . . worse than war" calling for "legislative interference" to meet the "disorganization of industry and widespread unemployment" and "to help national industrial recovery, foster fair competition, and solve the problems of a troubled nation." Other lower court judges agreed that "a compelling emergency" justified "interference by the state" in private markets and that the legislature had the necessary "power . . . to enact measures in seasons of emergency" and adopt laws favoring citizens in employment in order "to avert a threatened pauperism."[8] More significantly, the Court of Appeals also agreed.

The first body of emergency legislation came before the court as early as 1921. As described in a majority opinion by Judge Pound and four others, World War I had halted residential construction and vastly increased New York City's population, with the result that "the demand for homes thus became in excess of the supply; the landlords took advantage of the situation to exact, under threats of eviction, whatever exorbitant rents" they could obtain; and many "tenants . . . submit[ted]." Facing judicial proceedings to dispossess more than 100,000 families, the legislature had enacted statutes prohibiting landlords from charging more than a reasonable rent and suspending for two years their right to judicial assistance in recovering possession from tenants of their housing units. In sustaining the constitutionality of this legislation, Judge Pound observed that "emergency laws in time of peace are uncommon but not unknown. Wholesale disaster, financial panic, the aftermath of war . . . , earthquake, pestilence, famine, and fire, a combination of men or the force of circumstances may, as the alternative of confusion or chaos, demand the enactment of laws that would be thought arbitrary under normal conditions."[9] In a concurring opinion, Judge Frederick Crane argued that, with one hundred thousand families potentially "on the streets of the great metropolis without shelter," the "government was not so effete as to be barren of relief." He saw the case as one in which "private property could for the emergency [have been] commandeered," but the legislature instead turned to a lesser remedy of "requiring landlords at reasonable rental to keep tenants."[10]

Only one judge dissented from these broad constructions of the police power.[11] Thus little doubt remained by the end of the 1920s that the police power authorized the legislature to protect health and safety and to regulate businesses affected with a public interest, even if regulated entities ceased earning profits as a result; to protect the public against fraud; and to cure market failures resulting from monopoly or temporary emergency conditions. The important issue at the end of the 1920s was whether the police power should be expanded even further to allow the legislature to promote its vision of social justice and the social good, if necessary through the redistribution of wealth.

An early trial court opinion written in one of the rent control cases by Judge Robert F. Wagner, soon to be elected to the United States Senate, urged that legislative power be so expanded. The opinion bears quotation at length:

> I cannot subscribe to any doctrine that hinders or restrains our legislative power from enacting a clear and reasonable design to relieve the actual distress of the thousands of tenants in this community who would otherwise be made homeless. I think their rights to homes in which to live during an emergency of the kind which now confronts us is transcendently paramount to any private rights of property. . . . Our constitutional government is not an impotent one. Not so readily can its arms of protection for those whose benefit it is imposed be bound and helpless; its scope and vision is wide; its power flexibly adaptable; its aim the protection of human rights.[12]

Wagner's rhetoric is key because he conceived of the emergency rent cases differently than did the Court of Appeals. For Wagner, the issue was not about market failure and had little to do with the power of judges to declare legislation unconstitutional. His was not an effort to transform a distressing social problem into cold legal doctrine. Wagner saw human conflict: between established, often oppressive wealth, on the one hand, and families, often impoverished and of immigrant background, who were struggling to improve their economic and moral well-being, on the other. Sensitive to politics, Wagner wanted to align himself and government on the side of human rights and social justice in what he perceived as the struggle of the majority of New Yorkers against vested property rights. He accordingly recognized that the police power, if not all law, gave government power not merely to prevent fraud and protect health, safety, morals, and common welfare but also to assist the vast majority of the people in the community to make economic and social gains at the expense of the few. His rhetoric validated use of the police power not only to cure market failure but also to redistribute wealth.

The Court of Appeals, in contrast, was not prepared to reach so far even when it validated use of the police power in the second line of emergency cases that came before it, this time in the 1930s. These cases arose when debtors, as a result of the Great Depression, became unable to make mortgage payments, and the legislature, in response, adopted two major categories of legislation. The first forbade both foreclosures for nonpayment of principal and suits to recover the principal due on mortgage bonds; the second allowed state agencies to assume control of corporate entities that had lent mortgage money and to manage them in order to preserve them.[13]

A trial judge drew the most explicit connection between this legislation and the emergency rent legislation of 1920 when he declared that the mortgage moratorium legislation could "be sustained as constitutional under those decisions . . . known as the 'emergency rent cases.'" Like the rent legislation, the mortgage laws had been adopted in response to " 'a serious public emergency, . . . resulting from the abnormal disruption in economic and financial processes . . . , the abnormal deflation of real property values and the curtailment of incomes by unemployment and other adverse conditions.'" The judge accordingly held that, if "under extreme conditions the owner" of an apartment house could "be deprived of the possession of his property," then under similar conditions the legislature could "temporarily deprive the lender of the right to maintain an action for the principal of his loan."[14]

In upholding the Mortgage Moratorium Law, the Court of Appeals agreed that the legislature could act to reduce the "suffering" of "owners," who "were caught, as it were in a trap due to conditions over which no one had control" by asking "security holders to wait a reasonable time for universal economic conditions to improve." Similarly, in sustaining legislation allowing state takeover and administration of certain mortgage lenders, the Court of Appeals noted that "extraordinary conditions may call for extraordinary remedies" and that "an individual may not justly complain of a reasonable legislative restriction of his usual liberty for the purpose of averting an immediate danger which threatens the safety and welfare of the community." In the absence of an emergency that upset normal competitive market conditions, however, courts were unwilling to alter mortgage obligations; the judges, that is, were unprepared to sanction mere legislative redistribution of wealth.[15]

The Court of Appeals began to accept Wagner's approach in favor of social justice through redistribution only when it addressed another of the state's emergency regulatory schemes—a pervasive one dealing with the production, distribution, and sale of milk. As part of a "war upon disease," New York had long required that dairy cattle be tested for tuberculosis, and the Court of Appeals, of course, had sustained the requirement.[16] But New York's system of regulation went far beyond testing of cattle for disease. The legislature also required the licensing of anyone seeking to operate a milk gathering station or plant following a showing of good character and financial responsibility—a requirement sustained by the Court of Appeals in *People v. Perretta*. According to Judge Pound's unanimous opinion, it was "'a fact . . . well known . . . that the farming community [had] suffered great damage by irresponsible persons" buying milk on credit and never paying for it. On the basis of its "wide discretion in protecting the public from the dishonest or irresponsible," the legislature had accordingly adopted the licensing scheme, which the court found appropriate to "protect the farmer from fraud arising from the peculiar conditions under which milk is . . . sold."[17]

Judge Pound, however, muddied his otherwise clear recognition that the police power properly comprehended legislation with the aim of preventing fraud. He added that the legislature, in adopting licensing, had also taken notice "of the hard and often unremunerative character of farm life," thereby implying that farmers were a class entitled to special legislative solicitude that would promote a redistribution of wealth and power in their favor. In upholding another statute, which exempted agricultural cooperatives from the antitrust laws, the Appellate Division agreed, when it affirmed a referee's opinion that "the state [could] afford to give special treatment to this class of producers," as "a question, not of technical constitutional law, but of social policy." This judgment was "no doubt partly due to the fact that these organizations [were] not money organizations."[18]

Then, in 1933, the legislature imposed price control on milk by fixing both the minimum price that could be paid to farmers and the prices at which milk could be sold to consumers. In doing so, the legislature "had before it evidence of the disastrous effect of unlimited competition" and "was attempting to stabilize the industry during a limited period only." The failure of the free market had even "given rise to scenes of violence and disorder in the attempt to organize so-called milk strikes as a protest against the low prices paid [to farmers] for milk." Declaring that the Constitution was "an efficient frame of government . . . under normal conditions or in emergencies," the Court of Appeals, in the *Nebbia* case, with only one dissent, held the 1933 price control legislation valid.[19]

The *Nebbia* case next went to the United States Supreme Court, where the opinion of Justice Owen Roberts gave the police power a broad construction. First, Roberts took note of the health and safety basis for regulation, with his brief observation that milk was "an essential item of diet" that had been regulated "in the interest of public health" since 1862. But his main emphasis was on the "destructive and demoralizing competitive conditions and unfair trade practices which resulted in retail price cutting and reduced the income of the farmer below the cost of production." In particular, he observed that the "decline in [milk] prices during 1931 and 1932 was much greater than that of prices generally." Legislation was thus called for "to prevent ruthless competition from destroying the wholesale price structure on which the farmer depend[ed] for his livelihood, and the community for an assured supply of milk." Roberts's conclusion was that, in the context of such market failure, New York was free to adopt "whatever economic policy" it wished "to curb unrestrained and harmful competition."[20]

But like Judge Pound in the *Perretta* case, Justice Roberts muddied his otherwise clear opinion about emergency conditions by adopting language that simultaneously suggested the propriety of redistributive aid to achieve social justice for a particular class. Roberts wrote that the "situation of the families of dairy producers had become desperate and called for state aid similar to that afforded the unemployed." On this basis, he was prepared to conclude that New York's regulations had "a reasonable relation to a proper legislative purpose, and [were] neither arbitrary nor discriminatory," and accordingly that "the requirements of due process [were] satisfied."[21]

The handing down of this arguably "revolutionary" opinion provided dictum from the highest court in the land, as well as from the Court of Appeals of New York, intimating that the power of legislatures extended beyond the cure of market failure and authorized the enactment of legislative visions of social justice and social good. But as yet, there was no clear holding to that effect. Doubts were not fully resolved until a series of decisions in the late 1930s addressed the issue of "the sufficiency of purely aesthetic purposes as a basis for the extension of police powers."[22]

On this issue, one trial judge at an early date was prepared to uphold legislation having as its sole aim "conserv[ing] the natural beauty of the Adirondack Park." In this judge's view, the state could surely intervene to enable "the people . . . to enjoy . . . to the utmost" their "vast investment in the Adirondack Park" by preventing highways from becoming "solidly lined with billboards, hot dog stands, and . . . gasoline selling agencies." The police power was also construed broadly enough to sustain fish and game conservation and daylight saving time. Thus, it seemed, as the Court of Appeals assumed in 1937, that the police power could be used "for cultural or aesthetic reasons alone" or otherwise to promote the legislature's vision of a good or just society.[23]

By the end of the 1930s, in short, the police power had become "the widest and most elastic power of government." It "extend[ed] to all great public needs" and could be used broadly for "the improvement of the social, moral, physical, or economic condition of the public in general" — that is, for almost any purpose. Still, "there [was] a point beyond which the Legislature [could] not go."[24]

One important constraint on the legislature was precedent. Thus in the leading case of *People ex rel. Tipaldo v. Morehead,* a divided Court of Appeals declared a statute providing minimum wages for women unconstitutional because it held the statute essentially the same as the act of Congress struck down by the Supreme Court in *Adkins v. Children's Hospital*[25] and found the Supreme Court decision "binding upon us." The majority of the Court of Appeals concluded that it had to "follow the law as given, and not speculate as to the changes which have come or are supposed to have come to economic conditions in the last decade which may move the Supreme Court to a further consideration of its ruling."[26]

The New York judiciary's willingness to sustain broad regulatory legislation on its face also did not necessarily translate into a willingness to sustain legislation as applied intrusively in the fact situations of particular cases. For example, while the judiciary was eager to enforce legislation genuinely designed to achieve regulatory ends, it was not prepared to enforce legislative or administrative acts that, under the guise of protecting health and safety, were actually designed to grant monopolistic protection to certain businesses. Thus the Court of Appeals overturned a refusal by the New York City Department of Health, which had been sustained by the lower courts, to grant a permit to operate an x-ray laboratory. In the court's view, the administrative "authorities and the [lower] courts ha[d] so concentrated their vision upon the fact that the petitioner is a chiropractor of unrecognized standing in the medical profession that they ha[d] inadvertently overlooked the other fact that he is not urging his right to a limited permit because he is a chiropractor, but simply because he is a concededly experienced and skilled X-ray photographer." Thus they had acted "arbitrarily" in "reject[ing] his application" and thereby denying him the same right to participate in a profession for which he was qualified that was granted to licensed medical doctors. In a similar case, the Appellate Division construed a Glens Falls ordinance on the licensing of master plumbers narrowly so as to preserve the right of unlicensed plumbers to practice their trade, while in another case the court refused to uphold an ordinance "intended to protect local bakers from competition" by prohibiting the peddling of baked goods within one thousand feet of an established bakery.[27]

Courts also restricted administrative freedom in the application of legislation with the rule prohibiting the legislature from delegating to administrators authority to determine substantive health or safety standards. Thus the Court of Appeals held that the New York City buildings commissioner could not in the interest of safety require the owner of a building to make structural changes not called for by statute. It was a basic principle that a delegation to an administrator of "absolute and arbitrary power in determining the standards of character, experience, financial responsibility, equipment, etc." required to remain in, "enter upon or extend lawful private business, without guide or standard to direct or restrain the exercise of that power," was unconstitutional.[28]

Another set of restrictive principles was procedural. Thus the Court of Appeals declared unconstitutional a provision in the Multiple Dwelling Law that authorized the city to make specified repairs to buildings and to impose a lien on any repaired building that would take priority over an existing mortgage lien. To make a repair in this fashion, where "the mortgagee has nothing to say about it . . . , is given no opportunity for a hearing and cannot question the reasonableness or the amount of the expense" was, in the eyes of a unanimous court, "surely . . . a taking of the plaintiff's property without due process of law."[29]

Despite these occasional examples of hesitancy in the application of the police power, though, the dominant trend in the cases dealing with health, safety, and related regulation was for courts through the 1920s and 1930s to sustain gradual expansion of legislative power. As we are about to see, governmental power to protect underdogs and provide them with opportunity also underwent growth in other areas.

LABOR LAW

Another area in which judges during the decades between World War I and World War II began to erect bulwarks both against exploitation and in favor of opportunity was the highly politicized subject of labor law. These two decades witnessed a gradual trend in doctrine in favor of employees, as political leaders supported by the labor movement gained places on the courts and in the state's political branches and used their power to assist their constituents.

Injunctions. Nowhere was the shift more clear than in the rules governing the issuance of injunctions against labor union activities. The decade of the 1920s had not started out well for organized labor. Between 1920 and 1927, there were thirty-seven reported labor injunction cases in New York, in twenty-eight of which preliminary injunctions were granted; between 1923 and 1927 there were an additional forty-eight unreported cases in New York City alone, in thirty-five of which preliminary relief was granted. There was never any doubt in the early 1920s that judges would enjoin trespasses on an employer's premises or other concerted activity that was intimidating, coercive, or violent. Relying on a United States Supreme Court opinion by Chief Justice William H. Taft, one trial judge held that the presence of as few as four to six pickets inherently "involve[d] a certain amount of intimidation," while another judge found that the "effectiveness and . . . very essence . . . [of picketing lay] in the terror it excites" and that, when "unaccompanied by threats and intimidation," it was "a useless weapon." The Appellate Division agreed that it was "a matter of common knowledge" that "pickets . . . hovering around a place . . . constitute an intimidation, especially to women patrons," and it accordingly granted an injunction that a trial judge had denied.[30]

In addition to enjoining violence and intimidation, courts in the early 1920s were also prepared to enjoin strikes that constituted "act[s] of hostility to the public weal" such as interfering with the delivery of some "vital" commodity like milk. Some even barred any concerted activity undertaken with a purpose not of raising wages but of inducing employees who were not union members to join the union or of compelling employers to rehire workers "dismissed . . . in pursuance of a policy of economy and retrenchment." Although situations of these sorts, it was said, might "very well suggest . . . problems to the student of social science," the "present state of our law, which [was] adapted to prevailing conceptions of individual rights," made the grant of injunctions appropriate.[31]

The first change in the traditional antiunion approach of the New York courts occurred with the 1927 decision of *Exchange Bakery & Restaurant, Inc. v. Rifkin,* where a divided court in a four-to-three opinion authored by Judge Andrews and joined by Cardozo, Pound, and Lehman reversed the Appellate Division's issuance of an injunction barring all picketing. In *Exchange Bakery,* there had been one trespass on the employer's premises, one threat to an officer of the employer firm, and one instance in which a customer was barred from entering the restaurant, but there was "no indication that such acts [would] be repeated" and hence, in Andrews's view, no basis for injunctive relief.[32]

This was true even though the striking union had recruited employees who had signed a pledge not to join a union and, after joining, had concealed their membership from the employer. Judge Andrews observed that injunctions had appropriately been granted in past cases, in which unions acting out of malice had induced employees to join them. But, he continued, there was "as yet no precedent in this court for the conclusion that a union may not persuade its members or others to" violate a term in their "contracts of employment where the final intent lying behind the attempt [was] to extend its influence." Nor, he concluded, did the court "need to decide" that question, since the pledge entered by each employee had been signed after they had begun work and thus "was not a contract . . . , but merely a promise based upon no consideration."[33] Thus the majority opinion in *Exchange Bakery* reopened the possibility closed off by lower court decisions that unions, without being subject to injunction, could recruit as new members employees who had promised not to join them.

A year later a unanimous Court of Appeals decided *Interborough Rapid Transit Co. v. Lavin,* where the employees had made a promise to a company union not to join a rival union. Nonetheless, the employees had joined the rival, which at the very least learned that the employees joining it had concealed the fact from the Interborough Rapid Transit and perhaps had even encouraged them to do so. On this basis, the trial court had issued a broad injunction and the Appellate Division had affirmed. But the Court of Appeals reversed and remanded so that the trial court could determine whether to issue a narrower injunction to prevent threatened trespasses and violence.

In an opinion by Irving Lehman, the court observed that "conflicting considerations of economic policy [were] not the primary concern of the courts." Lehman recognized that "combinations [could] give the workmen a power of compulsion which may work harm to their employer, the public, and even to themselves," or alternatively, that if "workmen [did] not combine they [might] be compelled by force of economic circumstances to accept unfair terms of employment." But he also recognized that "freedom of contract [gave] to workers and employers the right to fix by individual or collective bargaining the terms of employment"; the judiciary's duty was to enforce the bargain they had fixed. In the *IRT* case, according to Lehman, no contract existed between the company and its workers, who had made promises only to the company union and not to the company itself. Hence the company could not prohibit them from joining a union other than the company union, and the court was not "called upon to decide whether employees may lawfully be urged to make a choice [to join a new union] in breach of a definite contract." It could continue to "leave open [even] the question whether the defendants may be enjoined from inducing the plaintiff's employees to conceal from the plaintiff that they had joined" the rival defendant union. Nonetheless, by reversing the broad injunction granted below and remanding for reconsideration without taking into account the facts of inducement and concealment, the court appeared to legitimate such union activity.[34]

Three years later the court declared explicitly the holding to which the *Exchange Bakery* and *IRT* cases had pointed. In a unanimous opinion by Chief Judge Cardozo, it modified an injunction so as to remove prohibitions that impaired "the defendant's *indubitable right* to win converts over to its fold by recourse to peaceable persuasion, and to induce them by like methods to renounce allegiance to its rival. Recent decisions of this court," and here Cardozo cited *Exchange Bakery* and *IRT,* "have established that fundamental right too emphatically and forcefully to make further vindication needful."[35]

The next year, the court reiterated its position:

> The case of Hitchman Coal & Coke Co. v. Mitchell, 245 U.S. 229 . . . has often been cited as authority for the proposition that inducements of a breach of contract for a definite term of employment are illegal, even in the case of solicitation by groups of laborers. . . . It has never been held by this court that a labor union is without justification in fairly setting forth its claims in a controversy over terms and conditions of employment by sign, handbill, or newspaper advertisement as a *legitimate means of economic coercion.* . . . The cases cited supra disclose independence of the Hitchman doctrine and of the cases which follow and enlarge upon that doctrine. We would be departing from established precedents if we upheld this injunction. We would thereby give to one labor union an advantage over another by prohibiting the use of peaceful and honest persuasion in matters of economic and social rivalry. This might strike a death blow to legitimate labor activities. It is not within the province of the courts to restrain conduct which is within the allowable area of economic conflict.

In later cases the Court of Appeals extended its rule tolerating inducement of breach of contract in labor cases not only to union efforts to attract workers as members but also to efforts to induce customers to boycott firms with which unions were having disputes. Concerted labor activity continued to be subject to injunction, however, in cases of violence or misrepresentation or cases in which union members affiliated with the Communist Party "paraded before the plaintiff's factory, singing foreign songs."[36]

The key development, however, was the legislature's 1935 passage of an act, modeled on the 1931 Norris-LaGuardia Act, prohibiting the issuance of injunctions in cases of labor disputes. The Court of Appeals promptly sustained the constitutionality of the statute and applied it broadly so as to allow a union to picket the retail seller of goods manufactured by the employer with whom the union had a labor dispute.[37]

Internal Union Governance. Courts also assisted the labor movement, though often not the individual worker, by their practice of interfering only minimally in internal union governance. Judges, for example, would do nothing to protect workers from union orders interfering with their "right to retain a job." Thus in one case when a union ordered members not to work in a particular shop for the purpose of punishing an employer who had breached a collective bargaining agreement, the Court of Appeals held that "the plaintiffs [could] not complain," since the " 'unity of action' " needed by the union "to achieve" its "objects" could "not be attained without some harm to the individual." As long as the union acted with "legality, good faith, and freedom from malice," the particular individuals who suffered had no remedy. Nor would the state courts compel a union to accept a new member. The courts would, however, provide some protection to the "*membership rights*" of existing union members by requiring that any discipline be " 'in accordance with the constitution and by-laws of the organization' " and that " 'the member [had] received fair play.' "[38]

Labor Legislation. The legislature also acted for the "well being and protection" of "persons . . . employed in industry" by adopting statutes regulating such matters as safety conditions, Sunday closing, minimum wages, maximum hours of work, industrial homework, fees paid to employment agencies, and the time for payment of wages. Several judges had little difficulty in sustaining the constitutionality of such legislation or in declaring that an employer's "financial embarrassment" provided no basis for breaking the law.[39]

An important body of prolabor doctrine arising out of safety concerns, which was solidly in place by 1920 in New York, was workers' compensation. Although the state's initial compensation legislation in 1910 had been declared invalid on state constitutional grounds in *Ives v. South Buffalo Ry.*,[40] the state's constitution was immediately amended, and new legislation, which was unanimously upheld against federal constitutional challenge, was passed. Both substantively and procedurally, workers' compensation "[met] all the requisites of due process." [41]

Another important piece of prolabor legislation, reflective of "the growing tendency of the Legislature to protect laborers on public jobs," was a 1921 act that codified an earlier requirement that all employees engaged in publicly funded work receive, at a minimum, the prevailing rate of pay in their locale. Courts promptly sustained the constitutionality of the act on the ground that the state's constitution had been explicitly amended in 1905 to authorize such legislation. They also construed the legislation broadly to apply to municipal workers as well as employees of private contractors doing work for the state and to part-time as well as permanent, full-time workers. [42]

An even greater boon to labor was the Unemployment Insurance Law adopted in 1935 and immediately challenged on both state and federal constitutional grounds as taxation for the benefit of a special class, not the public at large. The Court of Appeals rejected "this narrow view," however, and observed that "people have to live, and when they cannot support themselves some one has to look after them." The opinion of Chief Judge Crane observed "that unemployment for the last five or six years [had] been a very acute problem for state and federal government" and had "increased enormously in every part of the country, if not throughout the world." Adding that "a situation [had thus] arisen which require[d] the exercise of the reserve power of the state," the court sustained the unemployment legislation. [43]

Like much other regulatory law, labor law had thus changed significantly by the late 1930s into a body of doctrine upholding redistributive legislation and otherwise facilitating efforts of employees to increase their wealth at the expense of their employers' profits. The nineteenth century's concerns with protecting property rights and preventing redistribution were disappearing.

But in labor law as in other regulatory law, those older concerns never died completely, as several cases that gave a narrow construction to New York's anti-injunction statute will show. In one case, for instance, a majority of the Court of Appeals held that judges still retained jurisdiction to enjoin picketing in cases in which violence was threatened, while other cases held the statute inapplicable to secondary boycotts, to strikes conducted in breach of a labor contract, or to picketing of an employer who ran his own business without any employees. The statute also did not protect a group of employees who were not duly organized as a labor union under state law, nor did it apply to a case where a factory owner "elected to discontinue his factory . . . to avoid a labor dispute," since it was "the prerogative of any business man, with or without reason, to continue or discontinue in business, to change, alter or modify the nature of his business as he sees fit without necessity of explanation or excuse to anyone."[44]

CONTRACT AND UNCONSCIONABILITY

In addition to sustaining the police power and broadening the rights of the laboring class, judges took a step toward modifying common-law business doctrine so that it too would provide underdogs with greater protection against exploitation. One subject of common-law development on which New York judges were in the forefront in the late 1920s was the modern Uniform Commercial Code (UCC) doctrine of unconscionability, which sprang, in turn, out of the ancient rule that rendered unenforceable a contract involving fraud, duress, or illegality.[45]

Unconscionability itself had a long history in probate litigation, and courts continued in the 1920s and 1930s to set aside contracts in which decedents promised money in return for services. In such cases, when the parties "did not deal on terms of equality" because of "superior knowledge, or . . . overmastering influence" on the one side or "weakness, dependence, [or] unfair advantage" on the other, probate judges typically required "the stronger party to show affirmatively that no deception nor undue influence was used, and that all was fair, open, voluntary, and well understood."[46]

In one of the earliest cases outside the probate context to apply a principle analogous to unconscionability, a judge faced complex facts involving both possible fraud and possible duress. The defendant's daughter had received a series of checks from one Mr. Paul in return for her promise to marry him, but she had breached that promise and married another while nonetheless cashing the last of Mr. Paul's checks. Mr. Paul thereupon threatened to prosecute the daughter for obtaining money under false pretenses, but he withdrew the threats when the defendant gave him a note and mortgage covering his losses. When Mr. Paul's assignee brought suit to collect the money due, the court dismissed the suit, declaring that the note and mortgage had been given under "constraint," with "the parties . . . not meeting on equal terms." Even though the daughter had been "guilty of a crime and [was] liable to criminal prosecution," the debt was uncollectible because it had been given in order "to stifle prosecution."[47]

The holding of this case is far from clear. The case did not involve duress because a threat to do a lawful act—in this case, to bring a criminal prosecution against the daughter—could not constitute duress.[48] Arguably, though, the note was void because it had been given as part of an illegal bargain aimed at stifling a prosecution. At the same time, however, the opinion suggested a new concept like unconscionability: that the note was void because it had resulted from bargaining between parties forced to deal with each other on unequal terms.

Five years later, *Anthony v. Syracuse University*[49], even though it was subsequently reversed, made the new concept of unconscionability explicit. In *Anthony,* the court held that a dismissal of a student, pursuant to a contractual provision allowing dismissals without any statement of reasons, had created an "unconscionable situation." In ordering the reinstatement of the student to the university, the court proclaimed its power to refuse enforcement to any contract containing

> an extraordinary provision, one which, as a matter of law, renders the contract obnoxious to every sense of fairness, honesty and right, and is such as to make its enforcement clearly unconscionable. . . . Where it is perfectly plain that one party has overreached the other and has gained an unjust and undeserved advantage which it would be inequitable and unrighteous to permit him to enforce, a court of equity should not hesitate to interfere.[50]

The next case that involved facts on which to predicate a finding of unconscionability came before the Court of Appeals. It involved an acceleration clause in a note and mortgage entitling a creditor to demand immediate payment of the entire principal if the debtor was late in making any quarterly payment. As a result of a clerical error by the debtor's bookkeeper, the check for the interest payment due on July 1, 1927, was written for $4,219.69 rather than the amount due, which was $4,621.56, and the remaining $401.87 was not paid until one day after the expiration of the grace period. Upon receiving this technically late payment, the creditor invoked the acceleration clause and demanded payment in full.

Writing for himself and two other judges, Chief Judge Cardozo found "no undeviating principle that equity shall enforce the covenants of a mortgage, unmoved by an appeal ad misericordiam, however urgent or affecting." Using the word "unconscionable" on three occasions in his opinion, Cardozo declared that "the hardship [was] so flagrant, the misadventure so undoubted, the oppression so apparent, as to justify a holding that only through an acceptance" of the late payment could "equity be done." Although he had "neither purpose nor desire to impair the stability of the rule" upholding acceleration clauses in cases of late payment of interest, he thought it appropriate to exercise a "dispensing power" through the doctrine of unconscionability under the special facts of the particular case. Although the four-judge majority on the court also referred to the concept of unconscionability on three occasions in its opinion, it did not find enforcement of the acceleration clause unconscionable under the particular facts of the case.[51]

Despite the majority's hesitancy, lower court judges nonetheless continued through the 1930s and 1940s to extend the range of unconscionability and the related concept of economic duress. One opinion held, for example, that "the pressure of financial circumstances" plus the threat of a debtor's agent "to take affirmative action to prevent the making of the loan which it had undertaken to procure" constituted sufficient duress to invalidate a less favorable loan agreement made with the agent under such pressure. Another case declared that an "agreement leav[ing] the defendant corporation at the mercy of the plaintiff" would not be "favored by the courts," and a third opined that, though "mere inadequacy of consideration is insufficient to avoid a contract," relief for unconscionability would be granted if the inadequacy of consideration was "so gross as to offend the conscience of the court."[52]

A major line of cases focused on when a seller of goods could disclaim warranties. Although the courts recognized that "adult persons of sound mind" could "limit . . . or exclud[e] implied warranties,"[53] they would not permit disclaimers that were concealed from buyers or were otherwise contrary to "natural justice and good morals."[54]

Still, as late as mid-century, the Court of Appeals remained hesitant. The key case was *Mandel v. Liebman*,[55] in which the Appellate Division in 1950 found "void, unconscionable and against public policy" a contract that in its view released an "attorney from any requirement to render services while it purported to retain for him substantial rights and benefits in defendant's earnings, . . . amounting to what might be called a tribute in perpetuity." The Court of Appeals agreed that there would "be some force to the claim of unconscionability . . . if the contract could properly be construed as was done by . . . the Appellate Division." So construed, the contract would be so unequal that " 'no man in his senses and not under a delusion would make' " it. Indeed, it would be so "unreasonable . . . in light of the mores and business practices of the time" that it would " 'shock the conscience and confound the judgment of any man of common sense.' " The Court of Appeals, however, refused to construe the contract as the Appellate Division had. It concluded that the attorney was under an obligation to render services in return for his right to a percentage of the defendant's earnings and hence that the contract was not unconscionable or even necessarily unequal.[56]

It was against this common-law background that section 2-302 of the Uniform Commercial Code was drafted during the 1940s and early 1950s. Arguably, the section was designed to allow courts to yield to what Cardozo had called "urgent or affecting" appeals "ad misericordiam" without the necessity of turning "by indirection" to "manipulation of the rules" of contract law or to "interpretation of language and the like." At least one court found "the conclusion . . . inescapable" that section 2-302 "simply codified the doctrine [of unconscionability], which was used by the common-law courts to invalidate contracts" that were " 'so monstrous and extravagant that it would be a reproach to the administration of justice to countenance or uphold' " them.[57]

Following its effective date in 1964, lower courts quickly began to rely on section 2-302 and made unconscionability the law of the state. Two cases that soon became leading ones—*Frostifresh Corp. v. Reynoso*[58] and *Jones v. Star Credit Corp.*[59]—held, for example, that excessively high prices were unconscionable. Other cases declared unconscionable contracts with consumers who had limited knowledge of English, contracts giving excessive rights to creditors, and contracts otherwise "placing one party at the mercy of the other."[60]

The Court of Appeals reacted similarly, although without always mentioning unconscionability or the code. Thus it reiterated the doctrines that a contract could be avoided on the ground of "economic duress or business compulsion" when a party was "forced to agree to it by means of a wrongful threat precluding the exercise of his free will" and that "a drastic provision . . . plac[ing] one party at the mercy of another . . . [would be] against the general policy of the law." In the end, the court declared that the law had "developed the concept of unconscionability so as to prevent the unjust enforcement of onerous contractual terms which one party is able to impose . . . because of a significant disparity in bargaining power," and it applied the principle to permit the estate of an eighty-five-year-old nursing home patient to recover property given to the home by the patient before her death and to test separation agreements between spouses "to see to it that they are arrived at fairly and equitably" and that they are not "manifestly unfair to a spouse because of the other's overreaching."[61]

CONTRACT AND THE BUSINESS COMMUNITY

Arguably the reform agenda had its greatest impact not on law dealing with laborers, consumers, and other underdogs but on contract doctrines affecting dealings among businesspeople. In connection with these doctrines, the conflict between conservatives and reformers focused marginally, if at all, around issues of class, religion, or ethnicity; the conflict was primarily a geographic one, between upstate communities that wanted a body of contract law suited to face-to-face dealings between inhabitants of small, homogeneous towns, on the one hand, and an urban, downstate constituency that wanted the law to address the more impersonal dealings of the metropolitan and ultimately the global economy, on the other.

Classical contract law, as abstracted by Christopher Columbus Langdell, had been about citizens keeping their word to other fellow citizens who were part of the same homogeneous community. Those who did not keep their word or otherwise settle disputes would lose their trustworthiness, with the result that others in their community would not enter into future business dealings with them and jurors drawn from the community would not believe their testimony about the terms of existing deals. We must understand at the outset, however, that the moral precepts underlying classical contract required only that citizens keep their word toward their equals. The precepts did not require that citizens keep, or even give their word, to outsiders or to their social inferiors. In the classical model, outsiders and inferiors had no credibility with juries. While outsiders with wealth and eminence might protect themselves by resorting to special commercial courts, like those with admiralty or diversity jurisdiction, those who were not equal either did not make contracts or faced the prospect that they could not enforce them.

Within these enforcement parameters, classical contract granted "men of full age and competent understanding . . . the utmost liberty of contracting." In "a free enterprise system," in which parties could "protect their own rights and interests and avoid oppressive contracts by seeking bargains elsewhere," every business entity was "entitled to carry on its affairs and adopt in connection therewith such means of encouraging its business as it . . . [saw] fit." It was simply not the function of courts "to guarantee every businessman's success in his enterprise, . . . or to relieve him from contracts freely negotiated, that prove to be onerous. . . . The vitality of our marketplace," it was thought, was "derived to a great degree from the time-honored caveat that the individual must enjoy the right of 'freedom of contract.' "[62]

These moralistic precepts underlying classical contract doctrine came under challenge, however, as early as the 1920s. First, as we have just seen, the judiciary developed the doctrine of unconscionability to prevent moneymaking through exploitation of the poor and ill-informed. Even more important, increasing numbers of outsiders and social inferiors began to enter the economic mainstream, to attain political influence, and in larger, urban counties to sit on juries. That made it clear that some juries no longer could be trusted to decide business disputes routinely according to the subjective intentions of a small clique of elite insiders. And once subjective intentions grounded in the shared moral assumptions and prejudices of a small elite ceased to provide a standard by which businesspeople could predict the meaning that others would attach to their deals, a new paradigm of contract, grounded in more objective standards, became necessary.

With the help of leading legal luminaries, contract law was transformed to accommodate this widening of the economy and society. New York played an especially important role in this transformation. Two New Yorkers, in particular, stand out: Benjamin N. Cardozo, who as a judge of the Court of Appeals in the 1920s wrote a line of pathbreaking contract decisions, and Karl Llewellyn, who as a professor of law at Columbia University drafted Article 2 of the Uniform Commercial Code during the 1940s and early 1950s.[63] Both men were committed to modernizing contract law so as to enable large-scale, urban business and not just a few people who dealt with each other on a face-to-face basis to function efficiently.

Important doctrinal changes began occurring as early as the 1920s. The first change was legislative, in the form of a statute authorizing the remedy of arbitration. The New York courts had begun the 1920s with a strong, common-law-based hostility toward arbitration, which provided an alternative to dispute resolution by local juries.[64] In 1920, however, the legislature enacted the Arbitration Law, which "declare[d] a new public policy, and abrogate[d] an ancient rule," by thereafter making agreements to arbitrate binding. In an opinion by Cardozo, the Court of Appeals not only sustained the law's constitutionality but also applied it retroactively to contracts made before the law's passage in regard to arbitration sought after its passage. Thereafter, arbitration became a routine part of New York contract law, as the courts recognized that to "permit an action at law after the parties have agreed to submit any dispute . . . would be to set at naught the underlying policy which has shaped the growth of arbitration law in this State." One case several decades later even held an American business to its agreement with an agency of the Soviet government to have disputes arbitrated in Russia, while another invalidated a provision allowing one but not both parties the option of litigating rather than arbitrating disputes.[65]

Further doctrinal changes followed as urban influence on the Court of Appeals increased. Following the election of Cardozo as chief judge in 1926, four of the seven judges on the highest court—Cardozo, Crane, Lehman, and O'Brien—came from the New York City metropolitan region, and three happened to be either Catholic or Jewish. The religion, ethnicity, and geographic origins of the judges mattered: men who represented the city and its social outcasts could no longer accept nineteenth-century Langdellian contract law, which left local juries free to interpret and enforce contracts on the basis of their prejudices against outsiders and those they deemed their social inferiors. Although Protestant, small-town, upstate New York in 1920 still resembled nineteenth-century America and could continue to do business under nineteenth-century Langdellian doctrine, New York City, with its immigrant masses and its national and even international commercial dealings, could not. The city needed a different body of contract law, and as its judges came to dominate the Court of Appeals, they began to give it that new law, including new rules for filling in essential contractual terms left open by the parties, the doctrine of substantial performance, the concept of promissory estoppel, and, finally, some miscellaneous rules dealing with parole evidence and contractual impossibility.

Filling in Missing Terms. An important set of rules derived from classic precepts of freedom of contract provided that, if the parties to a contract neglected to specify all the terms of their agreement, their contract would fail for indefiniteness. The classic concept was that judges could enforce only what the parties had stipulated and that, in the absence of key terms, there was nothing to enforce. Of course, parties typically could testify about the substance of apparently missing terms, and juries could fill in those terms on the basis of judgments about the trustworthiness of the parties.

As early as the 1920s, however, the New York courts were routinely declining to honor the classic doctrine. Thereafter, throughout the century, the courts took an approach, later codified in the Uniform Commercial Code, that filled in gaps in agreements by reference to business custom or other objective standards of reasonableness not dependent on ad hoc jury judgments. Requirements contracts, for example, were readily upheld. Other cases similarly determined that, when a contract failed to specify a time for performance, performance had to occur within a reasonable time; that, if a method of performance was unspecified, the method had to be reasonable; and that a failure to specify a rate of interest would result in interest payments at the legal rate. As Judge Cardozo declared in one early case construing a contract clause giving a buyer the " 'privilege . . . to confirm more of the above if' " the seller " 'can get more,' " the clause "was drawn by merchants," who "reading it would not be doubtful of its meaning. It was meant to accomplish something. We find no such elements of vagueness as to justify the conclusion that in reality it accomplished nothing." And as Cardozo added, invalidation of a contract for indefiniteness was "at best a last resort." A half-century later, the Court of Appeals still agreed that "practical business people [could] not be expected to govern their actions with reference to nice legal formalisms" and hence that "failure to articulate . . . [an] agreement in the precise language of a [Langdellian] lawyer . . . [would] not prevent formation of a contract."[66]

Although some early cases refused to fix uncertain price terms by reference to outside market standards, others did anticipate the UCC and take even that step.[67] The New York courts also anticipated other important rules subsequently codified in the code reflective of the fact that in "transactions[s] between laymen," people "used expressions as businessmen understand them," not as lawyers. Thus as early as the 1920s, the courts, in order to give precise meaning to ambiguous contract provisions, were prepared to receive evidence concerning trade usage and custom, as well as the parties' course of dealing, both of which were considered to reflect the parties' practical understanding of the contract's meaning. Finally, New York judges anticipated the UCC with the rule that all parties were under an obligation of good faith and fair dealing in their performance of their contracts.[68]

Substantial Performance. Another significant limitation on freedom of contract is the doctrine of substantial performance. At the outset of the 1920s, this doctrine was in a state of chaos.[69] But then, in 1921, the Court of Appeals took a key step forward when Cardozo wrote the now leading case of *Jacob & Youngs, Inc. v. Kent.* The contract for construction of a country residence called for use of pipe "of Reading manufacture," but the plaintiff had used different pipe of equal quality. Unfortunately, the deviation was not discovered until the residence was nearly completed, so that replacement of the correct pipe would have "meant the demolition at great expense of substantial parts of the completed structure."[70]

Reflecting his downstate biases, Cardozo wrote that the "margin of departure within the range of normal expectation upon a sale of common chattels," such as typically occurred in rural, upstate New York, "will vary from the margin to be expected upon a contract for the construction of a mansion or a 'skyscraper' " in New York City. He also recognized that "substitution of equivalents may not have the same significance in fields of art on the one side and in those of mere utility on the other." All his distinctions led to the conclusion that use of the wrong pipe constituted an insubstantial deviation from the terms of the contract and hence that the measure of damages should be "not the cost of replacement, which would be great, but the difference in value, which would be either nominal or nothing."[71]

Three judges dissented on grounds of freedom of contract. In their view, the "defendant had a right to contract for what he wanted . . . [and] to get what the contract called for." It was no answer that some other kind of pipe, "according to the opinion of the contractor, or experts, would have been 'just as good, better, or done just as well.' He agreed to pay only upon condition that the pipe installed were made by that company and he ought not to be compelled to pay unless that condition be performed."[72] Although Cardozo agreed that the parties were "free by apt and certain words to effectuate a purpose that performance of every term shall be a condition of recovery," he also appreciated the difficulties that ordinary businesspeople would have functioning under a standard that permitted the favoritism of juries to compel precise performance of contracts. Hence he permitted business convenience to trump freedom of contract as long as the deficiencies of businesspeople were both "trivial and innocent."[73]

Although the lower courts and, in one case even the Court of Appeals, sometimes took a more cautious attitude toward the doctrine of substantial performance during the 1920s and early 1930s, the trend of decision in cases in which contractual relationships had broken down before completion of performance was to allow those who had provided goods or labor to recover the rough value of what they had provided. Thus the lower courts began to apply a doctrine of substantial performance even in cases involving sales of goods and employment contracts. Ultimately, in sales of goods cases the Uniform Commercial Code made it clear that sellers who tendered less than perfect performance had to be given a reasonable opportunity to cure their imperfect tender. Only in cases involving "a complete failure to perform without either a valid reason for noncompliance or even an attempt to perform" or some other deliberate breach would the doctrine of substantial performance or the analogous UCC doctrine of cure be inapplicable by the second half of the century.[74]

Promissory Estoppel. A third doctrine limiting freedom of contract is promissory estoppel. Unlike doctrines dealing with unconscionability, indefinite contract terms, and substantial performance, however, which developed gradually before their codification in the UCC, promissory estoppel quickly came to as full a fruition as it ever would in New York in the leading case of *Allegheny College v. National Chautauqua County Bank,* authored by Cardozo in 1927.[75]

The case involved a written promise by Mary Yates Johnston to bequeath $5,000 to Allegheny College to fund a scholarship in her name. After she had paid the first $1,000, which the college set aside as it had promised, Johnston informed the college that she would not pay the remainder of her subscription. Following her death, the college sued for the remaining $4,000. After both the trial court and the Appellate Division had denied relief, the case came before the Court of Appeals, where Chief Judge Cardozo reversed and granted judgment for the college.

Much of Cardozo's opinion was devoted to establishing a factual basis for a finding that Johnston's promise was binding because the college had given consideration for it. But Cardozo's effort to fit the transaction "within the mould of consideration as established by tradition" was not especially successful, and he therefore turned to his alternative holding: that "there has grown up of recent days a doctrine that a substitute for consideration or an exception to its ordinary requirements can be found in what is styled 'a promissory estoppel.'" Cardozo cited two recent cases as "signposts on the road," even if not full-fledged precedents.[76]

The earlier of the two cases, *DeCicco v. Schweizer,*[77] involved a promise by a father to pay an annuity to his daughter if she married the man to whom she was already affianced. Her marriage could not be consideration for the promise, however, because she was already under a duty to perform her contract to marry, and it was settled that performance of a preexisting duty could not constitute consideration. Writing for the court, Cardozo had circumvented this difficulty by holding that the consideration for the father's promise was not the daughter's act of marriage but the couple's act. The daughter and her husband-to-be were under no duty to her father to complete their marriage, and thus their act of completing it could constitute consideration for the father's promise to pay. In executing this tour de force, Cardozo did not mention promissory estoppel.

The second case cited in *Allegheny College*—*Siegel v. Spear & Co.*[78]—was at least slightly more on point. In *Siegel,* the defendant's agent had promised to store the plaintiff's goods without compensation and, in addition, to obtain insurance on the goods. The Court of Appeals found that the plaintiff's delivery of his goods to the defendant's warehouse, after the defendant's promise to obtain insurance, constituted the consideration for the promise and therefore made it binding. Promissory estoppel was again not mentioned, although the argument for the existence of consideration, unlike the argument in *DiCicco,* was so weak that promissory estoppel might have constituted a stronger ground of decision.

Cardozo failed in *Allegheny College* to cite a third recent case, one in which an estoppel had been found. The case, *Lieberman v. Templar Motor Co.,* involved an initial written contract to deliver automobile parts over a period in excess of one year. Later the parties orally modified the contract, which the Court of Appeals, in an opinion by Cardozo, found binding because the parts in question had no market value and were to be delivered within less than a year from the date of the modification. Cardozo added, moreover, that "assent to new terms of performance, even if invalid as a contract, [would] serve as an estoppel" and, even more significantly, awarded damages for labor and material costs incurred in reliance on the modification.[79]

Directly in point was a fourth case decided before *Allegheny College—Russian Symphony Society v. Holstein,* where the defendant, desiring to help produce the plaintiff's orchestral concerts, signed a subscription agreement promising to pay $50 if the expenses of the concerts exceeded the profits. In holding the subscription enforceable, the Appellate Division declared that the "decisions relating to subscription agreements, which . . . become mutually binding when accepted and acted upon, govern in the disposition of this appeal, rather than decisions relating to . . . executory contracts for the sale or purchase of goods."[80]

Cardozo, of course, did not cite the *Holstein* case in *Allegheny College,* even though he held precisely what *Holstein* had held. After declining to "attempt to say" whether the new doctrine of promissory estoppel had "made its way in this state to such an extent as to permit us to say that the general law of consideration ha[d] been modified accordingly," Cardozo concluded, "Certain, at least, it is that we have adopted the doctrine of promissory estoppel as the equivalent of consideration in connection with our law of charitable subscriptions."[81]

In the decades following *Allegheny College,* the New York courts routinely applied the doctrine of promissory estoppel in charitable subscription cases. There could be little doubt that the "doctrine of estoppel ha[d] been carried to its greatest length" in such cases, where judges had "been zealous to find a consideration," and that "the trend of judicial decision . . . ha[d] been towards the enforcement of charitable pledges almost as a matter of public policy." At the same time, however, most judges thought that *Allegheny College* had "extended the doctrine of promissory estoppel only to the law relating to charitable subscriptions" and took the view that they "should go no further."[82]

Only a few judges took a more expansive view that the *Allegheny College* case "indicate[d] the growth of the judicial process wherein the law enforces the reasonable expectations arising out of conduct." Meanwhile, the Court of Appeals remained reticent and, in the few cases in which it mentioned either *Allegheny College* or promissory estoppel, it offered conflicting clues about its position. In one case, for example, the court held that a plaintiff who worked as a marketing agent for an association's products could recover promised sales commissions even though he had never exchanged any promise in return. The court also cited *Allegheny College,* although on an issue totally unrelated to promissory estoppel. But it did not decide the case on promissory estoppel grounds, holding instead that the plaintiff's labors constituted performance of a unilateral contract in response to the association's offer to pay.[83]

Two decades later, in another case the court again declined an opportunity to apply promissory estoppel in the context of a commercial case. Although three dissenting members of the court cited the *Allegheny College* case, the majority was not prepared so to advance doctrine. In a situation in which an insurance agent, at the request of the defendants, had submitted a plan for insurance on their business, but no insurance had been placed or contract reached, the four-judge majority refused to apply promissory estoppel in a fashion that "would open the door to an entirely new field of liability" and subject parties to contracts to which they had never manifested any agreement.[84]

The court arguably took a small step forward in a 1977 case, where the issue was whether a written contract could be modified by a subsequent oral agreement. A unanimous court held that the state's controlling legislation permitted oral modification in appropriate circumstances and in the alternative declared that under "the principle of *equitable estoppel* . . . a party to a written agreement [who] has induced another's significant and substantial reliance upon an oral modification . . . may be estopped from invoking the statute to bar proof of that oral modification." In so holding, however, the court neither mentioned the doctrine of promissory estoppel nor cited the *Allegheny College* case. It also took the view in another case that "the doctrine of equitable estoppel . . . should be applied with great caution," especially when dealing with realty.[85]

Allegheny College thus brought the doctrine of promissory estoppel to the fullest fruition it would achieve in New York. Although occasional attempts were made to extend the doctrine to commercial litigation, both the Court of Appeals and most lower court judges, concerned to protect classical notions of freedom of contract, rejected those attempts. It also should be noted that Karl Llewellyn, as was typically his wont, followed New York law, included no reference to promissory estoppel in Article Two of the UCC, and thus left Cardozo's *Allegheny College* legacy incomplete.

Miscellaneous Doctrines. Two final developments, dealing with the parole evidence rule and the doctrine of impossibilty, deserve mention. Both developments strengthened and enhanced weapons available to judges for interfering with contractual terms to which parties had agreed.

As early as the 1930s, judges in New York began to feel an "obvious . . . need" for "liberalizing the rule excluding oral testimony" and to further values other than enforcement of contract terms spelled out by one party. "Particularly in the face of high-pressure salesmanship" and of "contracts of sale . . . furnished on printed forms," it was all too easy for merchants to "safeguard" their rights "in the printed form" while consumers and others with whom they dealt were exploited because they relied on differing oral representations. Judges needed a device to facilitate modification of printed forms and the like, and hence they altered the parole evidence rule so as to permit nonmerchant parties to prove oral warranties not included in printed forms or to give testimony that they had understood a release complete on its face to be merely partial in its meaning.[86] As Judge Stanley H. Fuld ruled in the 1957 case of *Sabo v. Delman,* where a defendant sought to plead as a defense to a charge of fraud a provision in a written contract that nothing except what was contained in the writing would be binding on either party, enforcement of such clauses would put it in a defendant's "power to perpetrate a fraud with immunity, depriving the victim of all redress," simply by virtue of having the "foresight" and the bargaining power "to include a merger clause in the agreement."

A later case, however, *Danann Realty Corp. v. Harris,* held that a merger clause containing language that the seller had not made the specific representations on the basis of which the purchaser sued did bar suit, on the ground that any other result would make it "impossible for two businessmen dealing at arm's length to agree that the buyer [was] not buying in reliance on any representations of the seller as to a particular fact." With *Sabo v. Delman,* on the one hand, and *Dannan Realty,* on the other, the reform principle of good faith dealing and the classical principle of freedom of contract remained in tension with each other, as the lower courts had to decide whether to read particular merger clauses as fitting within the *Sabo* or the *Danann Realty* principle.[87]

The final important change was in the doctrine of impossibility. Well before the Uniform Commercial Code provided in section 2-615 for "Excuse by Failure of Presupposed Conditions," New York courts had also translated the traditional doctrine of impossibility of performance, which had allowed judges to void terms to which parties had agreed only in cases of "the destruction of the means of performance by an act of God, *vis major,* or by law," into the more serviceable concept of frustration of purpose, which they defined as the occurrence of "a supervening event or circumstance which was not within the contemplation of the parties." [88] The conceptual shift from impossibility to frustration gave judges a better tool with which to excuse parties from performance of contracts to which they had given their assent if performance became unusually hard. It thereby undercut, though it surely did not destroy, classic, Langdellian concepts of freedom of contract and brought doctrine more into accord with businesspeople's practical expectations.

When we look back over the changes in contract law noted in the pages above, it seems clear that businesspeople were the beneficiaries of most of them. This is especially true of the changes in remedial law, such as the authorization of arbitration, which helped businesspeople obtain the value of the contracts that they had made with other businesspeople. But it was also true of other doctrinal changes. Rules permitting judges to fill in terms omitted from contracts usually furthered businesspeople's actual expectations, while relaxation of the parole evidence rule and the doctrine of impossibility enabled judges to adjust contract terms to altered practical realities. The doctrine of substantial performance was, of course, a boon to the construction industry, while promissory estoppel, if applied to commercial transactions, favored business litigants as much as anyone. Even as limited by the Court of Appeals to charitable subscriptions, promissory estoppel usually favored corporate charities at the expense of individual charitable givers.

New York, of course, is a leading industrial and business state, and hence it is not surprising that its courts modified contract doctrine to fit business needs. What is surprising is how early New York acted. According to the received wisdom, the Uniform Commercial Code, adopted by states in the third quarter of the twentieth century, was the principal vehicle that "simplif[ied], clarif[ied], and modernize[d] the law governing commercial transactions." It appears, however, that the changes transforming New York law from classic, Langdellian doctrine focusing on freedom of contract to modern, utilitarian "machinery for expansion of commercial practices" began to occur some three decades earlier.[89]

To appreciate the reasons underlying contract law's early shift in New York to a more pro-business orientation, it is necessary to focus once more on the values associated with freedom of contract that provided the foundation for the classic, Langdellian model. Essentially they were the values of small-town America, where populist localism reigned and men who had repetitive transactions with each other worked out long-term relationships on individualized, face-to-face bases. Performing one's promises was essential in such a context: men with reputations for breaking promises they had seriously undertaken, and hence for being untrustworthy, would find themselves subject to censure by their peers and unable either to enter into new contracts or to convince local juries that they had acted properly in carrying out old ones.

Small-town America was not the world of Cardozo or Llewellyn, however, or of other New York judges who played a central role in the transformation of the state's law of contract. Their world was New York City. In the political metamorphosis following the 1922 elections, which elevated Alfred E. Smith to the governorship, progressives centered in the city seized control of the state from the small-town, conservative forces that had dominated it through most of the nineteenth century, and, for the next seventy-two years, New York, unlike most of the rest of the nation, was governed by urban reformers.

In the context of contract law, conservatism was represented by the classic, Langdellian, freedom-of-contract paradigm, which was adequately suited to the needs of the small-town, upstate economy. The reformers who opposed conservatism, we must remember, were not hostile to the idea of contract, to free enterprise, or to accumulating wealth; they could not possibly have been, given the presence in their coalition of men such as Franklin Roosevelt, the squire from Harvard and Hyde Park, and Herbert and Irving Lehman, the sons of one of the founders of the Lehman Brothers brokerage firm. What the reformers needed was contract law that would permit people who were not neighbors, who did not attend church together, and who could not engage in face-to-face dealings to enter into commercial transactions with each other. They needed a body of contract doctrine that would enable people who were separated from each other by long distances and cultural pluralism to interact through documents, the meaning of which was not dependent on interpretation by a potentially biased jury representing only one of the cultures. Ultimately, the Uniform Commercial Code would provide that doctrine, but until the legislature enacted the code into law in 1964, the New York judiciary set about to provide the needed doctrine by means of common-law, doctrinal reform.

In essence, then, the history of contract law in twentieth-century New York reflects the demise of classical, Langdellian doctrine suited to the values of small-town America. In its place, New York judges substituted the mores of an increasingly urban marketplace, where relationships were more routinized and disputes had to be resolved by recourse to objective commercial criteria rather than to jurors' knowledge of their neighbors' trustworthiness. This shift was essential for New York's economy to remain efficient and for all New Yorkers to participate in it. Both the fact of the shift and its occurrence in New York beginning in the 1920s make perfect sense—rural law was transformed by the judiciary into urban law at approximately the same time that a new, urban coalition took political control of the state from its traditional rural governors.

But the transformation was incomplete. As had been the case in regard to the rest of the reform agenda, the judges who established new law did not entirely eradicate the old. Just as expansion of the police power did not destroy property rights and empowerment of labor unions did not redistribute all management wealth and power to workers, so too codification of new business conventions did not destroy freedom of contract. While judges such as Cardozo crafted opinions that moved regulatory, labor, and contract law in reform directions, the legal system's reliance on precedent and continuing commitment to a capitalist marketplace ensured that much established law would remain in place.

CHAPTER 4

CONSERVATIVES VERSUS REFORMERS
The Ongoing Juridical Conflict

Of course, the main reason why the reform agenda did not entirely super-sede classical values during the 1920s and 1930s was the continuing opposi-tion of conservatives. Until the end of the 1930s, the conservative and reform agendas, both of which since the late nineteenth century had been gradually formulated and brought into issue with each other, remained locked in battle, without any clear-cut victory for either side. Nothing more conclusively illus-trates this ongoing battle between conservatives and reformers than the law of personal injury.

A word must be said about why I have chosen to discuss personal injury law in this rather than the preceding chapter on the reform agenda. It could have been analyzed in that chapter because reformers did have an agenda for personal injury law and did succeed in imposing much of it. Opposition also existed to the reform of personal injury law, as it did in connection with the other areas of law discussed in the preceding chapter. But the opposition to change in personal injury law was different: conservative judges such as Wil-liam S. Andrews and Learned Hand drafted creative opinions in tort cases and anticipated future developments rather than merely adhering to outworn nineteenth-century patterns. For this reason, analysis of personal injury law offers a special opportunity to emphasize how the ongoing battle between con-servatives and reformers persisted into the 1930s and provides a fitting begin-ning to this chapter.

PERSONAL INJURY LAW

Throughout the long course of human existence, death, illness, and injury were random parts of life that could strike tragically at any time. In 1900, for example, nearly 1 in every 200 people in the United States died from influ-enza and pneumonia, while another 1 in every 200 died from tuberculosis. Even more deadly was a well-recorded 1878 yellow fever epidemic in Mem-phis, Tennessee, that produced 5,150 fatalities in a total population of 38,500, while 20,000 deserted the city. As one family was starkly described, the mother was dead "with her body sprawled across the bed . . . black vomit like coffee grounds spattered all over . . . the children rolling on the floor, groaning."[1]

Accidents were even more devastating than disease. In the nineteenth century, approximately 10 percent of all coal miners died in mine accidents during the course of their careers, while at the turn of the century 1 in every 5,000 factory employees died annually from accidents. The worst victims of all were railroad employees: in 1901, 1 out of every 399 railroad employees was killed in an accident, while 1 out of every 26 was injured. For train crews in that year, 1 out of every 137 was killed, which translated into a nearly 20 percent probability of accidental death over a twenty-five-year career. These high accident rates resulted from coupling industry's "cavalier attitude" that " 'there's a dozen [new workers] waiting when one drops out' " as a result of " 'his own bad luck,' " with the real "hazards of axles, mules, stinging insects, boiling laundry kettles, tetanus-inducing rusty implements and barbed wire, impure water, and spoiled food." Given the pattern of accidents and illness, it is not surprising that as late as 1920 average life expectancy in the United States was only 54.1 years.[2]

Because of the frequency of workplace accidents and injuries involving public transportation, conflict between investors and entrepreneurs, on the one hand, and laborers and other ordinary people, on the other, was endemic to the law of torts in the early decades of the twentieth century. During this period, the core principle underlying classical tort doctrine in New York, like much other common law, was the norm outlawing redistribution of wealth or other property.

In pursuit of this norm, the law enforced the "familiar principle[s]" first, that a "violation of a legal right knowingly committed gives to the injured party a cause of action against the wrongdoer" and second, "that one who acts must exercise due care not to do damage to another's person or property." "If property [was] destroyed or other loss occasioned by a wrongful act, it [was] just that the loss should fall upon the estate of the wrongdoer rather than on that of a guiltless person."[3]

On the other hand, it stood "to reason that a person [could] not recover . . . [for] an inevitable accident. There [were] plenty of misfortunes to which people [were] subjected where they must suffer without recompense," and courts could not permit "sympathy, although one of the noblest sentiments of our nature," to "decide . . . questions of law" and thereby become a "basis of transferring the property of one party to another." As the Court of Appeals had proclaimed in one mid-nineteenth-century case, everyone in a "commercial" country "to some extent" ran the "hazard of his neighbor's conduct."[4]

In short, classical tort doctrine demanded that compensation be paid to a person whose injury was caused directly by another's wrongdoing but not for an injury, however serious, resulting from innocent conduct or from causes other than conduct of a defendant. Two early cases are illustrative.

In *Laidlaw v. Sage,* a burglar entered the business premises of defendant Russell Sage, demanded $1,200,000 and threatened to set off a bomb if he did not receive it. After he had discussed the matter with the burglar, Sage positioned another employee, the plaintiff Laidlaw, between himself and the burglar and then, in essence, refused the demand. When the burglar set off his bomb, Laidlaw was severely injured but Sage was saved. The plaintiff recovered a jury verdict against Sage, but the Court of Appeals reversed, holding that the bomber had caused Laidlaw's injury and that there was "no evidence in the case of any necessary relation of cause and effect" between Sage's words and actions "and the explosion which caused his [Laidlaw's] injury."[5]

Pardington v. Abraham was analogous. There the defendant, a department store owner, maintained a swinging door which another customer pushed open, whereupon the door ricocheted back and struck and injured Eliza Pardington. In reversing a jury verdict for Pardington, the court found that the doors were no less safe than similar doors used in like establishments and that "carelessness in the use of any form of door may inflict injury upon one who happens to be sufficiently near it." The court continued, "No doubt the plaintiff has been the victim of a lamentable accident; but it is attributable, as it seems to me, not to any fault of the defendants, but rather to the hasty carelessness of a third person, over whose movements and conduct they had no control."[6]

By the opening decades of the twentieth century, however, classical judicial doctrine could no longer claim to be the only plausible approach to issues of causation in tort. Randolph Bergstrom, whose valuable book on New York tort litigation covers a forty-year period almost immediately before the period here under study, shows that a competing "popular conception of liability" was emerging slowly in the years around and after the turn of the century. The evidence available to Bergstrom did not permit him to elaborate this popular paradigm in detail, but there can be little doubt, in view of a growing tendency of jury verdicts to diverge from judges' views and of the hostile reaction of judges and leaders of the bar to the divergence, that a competing paradigm existed and disturbed profoundly those adhering to the traditional one. In the words of Judge M. Bruce Linn, for example, the law was "menaced by those who would completely transform it," with "no regard for its history; no reverence for its traditions; no conception of its obligations; and no appreciation for its ideals," while Judge William Hornblower worried about the frequency with which juries "yield[ed] to local sentiment . . . [producing] erroneous decisions in accordance with the popular idea of the demands of justice."[7]

This new "popular conception of liability . . . was never clearly articulated" by its proponents, at least in part because the juries that administered it could speak only through general verdicts. The best efforts at definition thus came from the mouths of lawyers who opposed the new view. Clearest of all, though guilty of exaggeration, was Eli Hammond, who wrote that the new popular conception was "in favor of looting any public or quasi-public treasury in aid of private suffering or private want." The distinguished Elihu Root believed that "distorted and exaggerated conceptions [were] disseminated by men . . . overexcited by contemplating unhappiness and privation which perhaps no law or administration could prevent," and one H. T. Smith agreed that "juries are naturally sympathetic and . . . inclined to take the view that an employee should be compensated when injured no matter what the judge tells them about the law."[8]

As juries and others adopted the new paradigm holding that victims of injury should receive compensation from some source, they simultaneously rejected the older, nineteenth-century worldview that injury, death, and other sudden calamities were inevitable, random, and frequent events attributable to cosmic rather than human agency. Whereas nineteenth-century judges had not traced out complex chains of causation in an effort to identify the human agent most responsible for a disaster but had instead typically let "losses . . . lie where they fell," early twentieth-century jurors "came to assign cause differently." The newly emerging tort paradigm, to quote from the findings of Randolph Bergstrom, contained

an understanding of cause and effect that included a fuller sense of remote causation—that actors not at the site of an event could create the conditions that cause the event. . . . The scope of the search for liability was pushed beyond immediate contact to outlying areas where those who created the conditions that caused injury worked.

Understanding cause to spring from sources remote as well as immediate, New Yorkers brought suit over injuries from commonplace causes that "ordinarily were never noticed hitherto," and that had previously been considered the random working of fate. In doing so, they defined anew the "inevitable" event as a compensable injury, conceiving it as the cause and responsibility of someone else.[9]

By 1920, these newly emerging, though not uniformly accepted, ideas of causation and tort liability had begun to attain legitimacy even in judicial circles. As a result, classical doctrine no longer provided easy answers in every case, and judges began to recognize that issues of liability and causation involved policy choice. Competition between the new and old paradigms left no doubt that determining when a plaintiff had "a legal right" or when a defendant had committed "a wrongful act" required courts to consider whether there was "a relationship between the parties of such a character . . . that as a matter of good faith and general social policy" the defendant had a duty not to harm the plaintiff. More specifically, judges came to understand that they had "to harmonize the necessities of a competitive industrial system of business with the teachings of morality" — that is, they had to harmonize capitalism with "the sense of universal justice exemplified in the Golden Rule," all "without too radical a departure from recognized legal rules."[10]

The Court of Appeals sought to work out the tension between the competing paradigms of liability in the pace-setting case of *Palsgraf v. Long Island R.R.*[11] Not surprisingly, the court did not adopt either paradigm wholesale but instead strove to elaborate a compromise position entailing recognition of the reformers' demands for social justice, but only within the confines of existing precedent. Thus it adhered to the traditional doctrinal approach that "some culpability on the part of a defendant" was the key factor that rendered conduct tortious.[12] At the same time, however, it defined culpability more expansively and thereby increased the range of cases in which victims of injury could obtain compensation.

Still studied by all first-year law students under the rubric of proximate cause, the majority opinion in *Palsgraf* by Chief Judge Cardozo has never been examined by scholars in the context of the ongoing conflict between supporters of the new and supporters of the old paradigm of tort liability. Such an examination suggests that Cardozo wrote his *Palsgraf* opinion with the conflict in mind, that he embraced the new paradigm, but that he also recognized a need to limit the range of liability to which defendants might be subjected thereby.

The case arose when the plaintiff, Helen Palsgraf, who had purchased a ticket from the railroad and was waiting for a train, was injured through a fall of scales dislodged as a result of an explosion of fireworks at the other end of the station's platform. The explosion had occurred when two railroad employees had knocked a small package out of the hands of another passenger while helping him board a moving train. The package contained the fireworks, "but there was nothing in its appearance to give notice of its contents."[13]

The classical understanding of negligence and proximate cause was elaborated by Judge Andrews in a dissent that would have affirmed the opinion of the Appellate Division directing judgment for the plaintiff. In Andrews's view, "every one owe[d] to the world at large the duty of refraining from those acts that may unreasonably threaten the safety of others." Negligence consisted in breach of this duty, and the railroad had been negligent in *Palsgraf* when its employees permitted a man to board a moving train and even assisted him in doing so. But "obviously," as Judge Andrews himself had observed in another case, negligence liability had to have "its limits."[14]

The limit was the doctrine of proximate cause. By virtue of this doctrine, negligence did not invariably give rise to a cause of action for damages, unless the damages were "so connected with the negligence that the latter may be said to be the proximate cause of the former." By "proximate" Andrews meant "that, because of convenience, of public policy, of a rough sense of justice, the law arbitrarily declines to trace a series of events beyond a certain point," not as a matter of "logic" but of "practical politics." In determining proximate cause, it was necessary to ask questions such as "whether there was a natural and continuous sequence between cause and effect," whether "the one was a substantial factor in producing the other," and whether there was "a direct connection between them, without too many intervening causes." For Andrews, inquiries into proximate cause always involved "question[s] of fair judgment" and could lead at best not to a clear rule but only to "an uncertain and wavering line" that would yield "practical" results "in keeping with the general understanding of mankind."[15]

Andrews's language about "public policy," "a rough sense of justice," and "practical politics" was not the language of the nascent legal realist movement, as other scholars have suggested.[16] It surely was not the language of sociological jurisprudence—the language employed by Cardozo—out of which realism was emerging. It would be two more years before the realists would break clearly from sociological jurisprudence and receive their name and designation as an intellectual movement in Karl Llewellyn's famous article "A Realistic Jurisprudence—the Next Step."* Even then, legal realists did not often

---

Columbia Law Review 30 (1930): 431. N. E. H. Hull, *Roscoe Pound and Karl Llewellyn: Searching for an American Jurisprudence* (Chicago: University of Chicago Press, 1997), 175–76, states that realism emerged during the course of a debate between Llewellyn and Pound and their friends set off by Llewellyn's 1930 article. Laura Kalman, *Legal Realism at Yale, 1927–1960* (Chapel Hill: University of North Carolina Press, 1986), 3–44, however, sees the emergence of legal realism as a lengthier process, stretching back into the 1920s.

use the words quoted above that were used by Andrews. Andrews's language, as we shall see in Chapter 5, was more typically the language of the descendants of the realists in the aftermath of World War II, not the language of first-generation realists in the decade of the 1930s. It makes more sense, in my view, to understand Andrews, a conservative whom the realists never accepted as one of their own, to be describing conservative tort doctrine of recent decades, of which he was intimately aware, rather than a jurisprudential movement which he perhaps anticipated but which at the time of his writing was still in gestation.

In addition to the *Sage* and *Abraham* cases discussed above, a 1921 decision from the Second Circuit strongly supported Andrews's views. The plaintiff was the widow of a deceased alien who had been arrested and imprisoned on the orders of Attorney General A. Mitchell Palmer. She alleged that her husband had been subjected to physical and mental torture by his federal captors until he committed suicide as the only means of escape. Nonetheless, two out of the three judges sitting on the Second Circuit panel voted to dismiss her complaint, declaring that it would be "a most unreasonable inference . . . to say that suicidal mania can be regarded as the natural and probable consequence of either mental or physical torture." The dissenter, in contrast, thought it obvious "that the infliction of such wrongs continuously over a long period of time might naturally and probably would lead to . . . self destruction." As the dissenting judge further observed, however, the concept of "natural and probable consequence" over which the court was battling was a mere "expression . . . to explain the reason for the decision on the facts."[17]

Of course, authority also existed for the reform principle favored by Cardozo and the *Palsgraf* majority—the principle that, "where one undertakes

---

Ultimately, one's view of the time of realism's origin depends on one's definition of realism. In my view, realism involved more than the rejection of Langdellian conceptualism. The core tenet of realism was not simply that the law follows "an uncertain and wavering line" reflective of "public policy" and "a rough sense of justice." Cardozo and Andrews both knew that. So did Holmes thirty years earlier, as did most other judges. But for Cardozo and Andrews, at least, the line the law followed was one "in keeping with the general understanding of mankind." For later realists such as Judge Charles Clark, in contrast, judicial decisions on issues such as proximate cause depended not on society's but on the individual judge's "values and his notions of sound and desirable social policy." Pease v. Sinclair Refining Co., 104 F.2d 183, 185 (2d Cir. 1939).

Thus the core tenet of realism is not that law reflects social policy but that judges make policy choices. Cardozo and Andrews rejected that tenet; later realists like Clark and Justice William O. Douglas embraced it. As of 1930, no one had fully articulated it.

to do something involving a dangerous situation, he must do it with reasonable care." Cardozo himself had taken a preliminary step toward that view in *Glanzer v. Shepard,* in which a public weigher who had weighed beans at the request of a seller was held liable to the buyer for weighing them erroneously. As Cardozo explained, the "controlling circumstance" in determining whether tort liability existed was "not the character of the consequence" but "the thought and purposes of the actor," and in *Glanzer,* the possibility of harm to the buyer should have been in the thoughts of the weigher. Thus the weigher was liable.[18]

Writing for the *Palsgraf* majority, Chief Judge Cardozo expanded on his holding in *Glanzer* and further embraced the reform position as the underlying principle for the law of torts. Proclaiming that a finding of negligence "would entail liability for any and all consequences, however novel or extraordinary," the chief judge held that the doctrine of proximate cause would not limit liability as Andrews's dissent suggested it had traditionally done in New York law; in Cardozo's words, "the law of causation, remote or proximate, is thus foreign to the case before us." When this holding was added to the ruling in *Glanzer* that liability depended on the mental state of actors rather than the consequences of their actions, the reform principle was complete. Cardozo and a majority of the Court of Appeals had rendered people in positions of power responsible in damages if they foresaw harm resulting from their actions, however remote the harm might be and by whatever indirection it might be produced.[19]

But at the same time that Cardozo and his brethren brought the reform program to fruition, they also imposed limits on it. Cardozo and his colleagues were no radicals. They appreciated the uncertainties that entrepreneurs, who could always foresee harm, would face if they were liable in damages whenever harm, however remote and indirect, occurred. "Proof of negligence in the air," Cardozo thus wrote, would "not do." Defendants who were negligent would not be liable for all harms in the world but only for damages suffered by those at whom their negligence was directed. "Negligence," Cardozo continued, was not an open-ended concept but "a term of relation," pursuant to which "the plaintiff sue[d] in her own right for a wrong personal to her, and not as the vicarious beneficiary of a breach of duty to another." Cardozo concluded that no negligence had occurred toward the plaintiff and hence she could not recover damages for her injury since, at least "to the eye of ordinary vigilance," the act of helping a passenger onto a moving train was "innocent and harmless . . . with reference to her."[20]

In cases before and after *Palsgraf,* the Court of Appeals elaborated the rule that "to be negligent, a defendant must have acted or failed to act in such a way that an ordinary reasonable man would have realized that certain interests of certain persons were unreasonably subjected to a general but definite class of risks." Conversely, a person could not "be held liable in negligence for failing to provide against a danger he could not have reasonably foreseen." In a case decided in the same month as *Palsgraf*, the Court of Appeals with only Andrews in dissent wrote that "negligence is gauged by the ability to anticipate." "The risk reasonably to be perceived define[d] the duty to be obeyed." The "one fundamental rule," according to still another opinion from which only Andrews dissented, was "that the act of a party sought to be charged is not to be regarded as a proximate cause . . . unless it could have been reasonably anticipated that the consequences complained of would result from the alleged wrongful act." [21]

In light of this principle, the court decided cases such as *Wagner v. International Ry.*, where it found a railroad liable to a plaintiff who had gone on a trestle to rescue his cousin, who had fallen from a train; the reasoning, in another famous Cardozo opinion, was that "danger invites rescue." Since a rescue attempt was "within the range of the natural and probable" and hence foreseeable reactions to the possible peril of an injured man lying on railroad tracks, the court held the railroad liable when the person attempting the rescue was injured. [22]

Of course, damage remained "the very gist and essence of the plaintiff's cause," and that damage had to flow "from an infraction of a duty, to the injured party, from an invasion of his legal rights," for "legal liability" to be imposed. There could "be no actionable negligence in the absence of a legal duty to the plaintiffs." And determining the scope of citizens' duties to each other was a difficult matter that could not "be tested by pure logic." [23]

There were some matters on which the New York courts reached agreement. They agreed that citizens were under no duty to provide assistance to each other but that they came under a duty if they volunteered to provide help or entered into a contractual relationship. Indeed, a duty arising out of a contract could sometimes "inure to a third person" — someone not a party to the contract — "under certain circumstances." [24] What, however, were those circumstances? When would a water company that had made a contract with a city to provide water to its residents be liable to them for damage resulting from a failure to provide the water? When would an accountant who had audited a firm's books be liable to a person who had lent money to the firm in reliance on the audit?

Cardozo addressed these questions in two leading opinions: *H. R. Moch*

Co. v. Rensselaer Water Co. and *Ultramares Corp. v. Touche.* His concern was that the "field of obligation" not "be expanded beyond reasonable limits." Although "the assault upon the citadel of privity"—of tort upon contract—was "proceeding . . . apace," Cardozo was unwilling to expose contracting parties to "the involuntary assumption of a series of new relations, inescapably hooked together," and thus "to a liability in an indeterminate amount for an indeterminate time to an indeterminate class," all out of concern that the "hazards of a business conducted on these terms" would be too "extreme."[25] He was unwilling, in short, to permit large business entities to become vehicles for the redistribution of their shareholders' and customers' wealth to random sufferers of damage whose susceptibility thereto could not have been specifically foreseen and prevented; he was prepared to impose liability only on those who callously let others get hurt.

Keeping true to *Palsgraf,* Cardozo held that in the absence of "reckless and wanton indifference to consequences measured and *foreseen*" or of "reckless misstatement . . . or insincere profession of opinion . . . liability for negligence . . . [would be] bounded by the contract." Whether a defendant had acted insincerely or recklessly toward individuals who might be damaged by its negligent performance of a contract so as to become liable to them in tort presented a question of fact for juries and for future divisions on the Court of Appeals, the precise outcome of which could not readily be predicted.[26]

Despite the difficulties involved in its application in borderline cases such as *Moch* and *Ultramares,* the foreseeability standard elaborated by the *Palsgraf* majority and numerous other New York cases during the 1920s and 1930s had significant doctrinal consequences in comparison with the alternative articulated by the *Palsgraf* dissent.

A first consequence was to give juries less freedom than the approach of Judge Andrews in dissent might have allowed.* After allowing a jury first to inquire whether the defendant had committed an act that "unreasonably threat-

---

*Normally, as we saw in Chapter 2, Cardozo favored the empowerment of juries. His position in *Palsgraf* was not, in fact, inconsistent. He normally favored giving power to juries in contexts where jury power would assist plaintiffs; in *Palsgraf,* Andrews sought to give juries that had already decided the preliminary issue of wrongdoing in favor of plaintiffs the additional issue of proximate cause, which they could then resolve in favor of defendants. Moreover, it is not clear that Andrews, despite the language of his opinion, truly intended to let juries pass on the policy questions implicit in the proximate cause issue; given the extensive body of precedent that existed in New York, he may have expected judges to take proximate cause issues away from juries and rule on them as a matter of law. If such was Andrews's expectation, then Cardozo's *Palsgraf* approach was more empowering of juries.

en[ed] the safety of others," Andrews next required the jury to make a "fair judgment" about where to "draw an uncertain and wavering line" marking the point at which "because of convenience, of public policy, of a rough sense of justice, the law arbitrarily declines to trace a series of events beyond a certain point." In performing these tasks, juries would not have recourse to facts or "logic" but would be engaging in "practical politics." In contrast, the approach of Cardozo and most New York judges pointed juries to a coherent factual inquiry—did the defendant know or have reason to know that its activities posed a risk of injury to the plaintiff or to the class of people of which the plaintiff was a member? This standard, which did not involve any "balance of probabilities" but only "the existence of some probability of sufficient moment to induce action to avoid it," was a simple test that did not empower juries or judges to make any practical political decisions or other balancing judgments.[27]

A second consequence of the Cardozo approach was an almost total absence of mention in the cases of today's popular calculus of risk standard, detailed by Learned Hand in the 1947 case of *United States v. Carroll Towing Co.* By not encouraging juries to balance the foreseeability of injury against the utility of the defendant's conduct, New York law during the 1920s and 1930s largely avoided utilitarian cost-benefit analysis as part of the negligence determination. During the two decades in question, New York negligence law almost uniformly was not utilitarian. It remained committed only to the cause of social justice, although there were alternative views about the meaning of justice: on the one hand, a commitment that "sympathy" not become a "basis of transferring the property of one party to another," and on the other hand, a simple moral insight that it was the obligation of those who used "people . . . for gain and profit, to be vigilant in their efforts to protect such people."[28]

A federal admiralty case, *The No. 1 of New York,* uniquely emphasizes the nonutilitarian character of New York doctrine. In *The No. 1 of New York,* a New York City drawbridge operator who had opened a bridge for a tug and its tow then closed it to permit fire engines to pass, with the result that one of the barges in tow collided with the bridge. The court held that "a bridge owner" who had once opened a bridge could "not withdraw his consent to the passage, even in the exigency of a demand by fire apparatus responding to an alarm, at a time when withdrawal should be foreseen as endangering the vessel."[29] The noteworthy fact about this opinion is that the court, consisting of Judge Thomas Swan and the two Hand cousins, never asked what seemed likely—whether the harm that would have been done by not allowing the fire engines to pass outweighed the harm that occurred to the barge. All that mattered was that the bridge operator, having undertaken a duty to the tug and its tow, could not fail to perform that duty even when it could foresee that great harm would result from its performance.

Only one federal case, *Sinram v. Pennsylvania R.R.,* cannot be reconciled with the New York mainstream. On the issue whether a tug that rammed and damaged an empty barge above the waterline was liable for loss of a subsequently loaded cargo of coal that caused the barge to take on water through the damaged area and thereafter to sink, Judge Learned Hand declared that "we are not bound to take thought for all that the morrow may bring, even though we should foresee it." Although a tug operator who thought enough about "the precise train of events" that might follow a collision would have foreseen the sinking, the foreseeability "canon," according to Hand, was "more equivocal than appears on the surface" and "ignore[d] the excuses for much conduct . . . likely to involve damage to others." Duties, Hand continued, were "a resultant not only of what we should forecast, but of the propriety of disregarding so much of it as our own interests justify us in putting at risk."[30]

Since *Sinram* was decided the same day by the same unanimous three-judge panel that resolved *The No. 1 of New York,* it is difficult to interpret it as an explicit, early statement of the calculus of risk standard later put forward by Hand in *Carroll Towing.* Hand did not totally reject the *Palsgraf* principle of liability for all foreseeable harm. At most, *Sinram* implied that a tug operator's interest in getting its job done quickly and efficiently outweighed the costs of theoretically foreseeable but highly improbable accidents such as the one that had occurred when the damaged barge was loaded without any inspection for potential leaks. In any event, while *Sinram* may have anticipated the calculus of risk standard, it was a unique case before the 1940s. And its author was an unusually prescient judge who, perhaps because of his life-tenure appointment on the federal bench, did not participate in the reform effort of state judges like Cardozo, but instead agreed with the conservatives that it was "monstrous" to "ruin a man for a momentary dereliction" by "attribut[ing] to an act every consequence which is likely to result."[31]

Except for this prescient opinion by Hand, Andrews's equally prescient dissent in *Palsgraf,* and Cardozo's acquiescence in contractual limitations on tort liability, New York tort theory by the late 1920s reflected, on the whole, the reform view that people who intended harm to others or who acted toward others in ways which they foresaw would produce harm were liable for any harm they brought about. If harm to others was either intended or foreseen, no interest on the part of an actor—however strong that interest might be—

would justify a refusal to pay damages for infliction of the harm. Only if harm was neither intended nor reasonably foreseeable was it not compensable.

By so depriving those who administered tort law of the capacity to engage in balancing and instead tying them to a strict principle of moral obligation, the New York reformers sought to ensure that classes of people within the ordinary bounds of foreseeability, such as workers, consumers of most products, and people on public highways, would recover damages when they suffered injury. They thereby transformed the doctrine of proximate cause, which had been a discretionary political principle that conservative judges had used in a wide range of cases to set aside jury verdicts awarding damages against wealthy and powerful entrepreneurs, into an incomprehensible rule applicable only in weird cases. While ensuring entrepreneurs that they would not be liable in an indeterminate amount for an indeterminate time to an indeterminate class merely by conducting business, the New York reformers did their best to make tort law consistent with popular conceptions of justice, which had emerged in the early twentieth century, that victims of injury should recover damages from those who had created the conditions that had caused them to be hurt.

Much specific tort doctrine conformed during the 1920s and 1930s almost precisely to the culpability standard of *Palsgraff*. Product liability law was one such body of doctrine. The then recently decided case of *MacPherson v. Buick Motor Co.*,[32] which held a manufacturer liable to a purchaser of its product for negligent defects that had foreseeably led to injury, even when the purchaser had obtained the product through a retail dealer and thus was not in privity of contract with the manufacturer, was followed in several cases during the two decades under analysis. Indeed, in one case, which held manufacturers of component parts liable to consumers for injuries caused by defects in the final manufactured product, the *MacPherson* rule was even extended.[33]

In its adherence, however, to the culpability standard later codified in *Palsgraff*, *MacPherson* applied only to products "inherently beset with danger and ... reasonably certain to imperil life or limb if carelessly made," not to products when "injury was [merely] a possible consequence of the defective construction," but "not a probable result." A manufacturer could "not be charged with negligence where some unusual result" occurred that could not "reasonably be foreseen" and was "not within the compass of reasonable probability."[34]

Other limitations on *MacPherson* were also consistent with the underlying purposes of the Court of Appeals in *Palsgraff*. For example, the limitation that the *MacPherson* rule applied only to suits involving physical injuries and not to commercial loss fit well with the underlying goals of tort reformers, who sought to protect workers, consumers, and highway users but not business entrepreneurs. A second limitation—that the rule applied only to claims of negligence and not to suits for breach of warranty, which still required privity of contract between consumer and manufacturer—similarly reflected Cardozo's concerns in *Moch* and *Ultramares* that the "field of obligation" not "be expanded beyond reasonable limits" and that contracting parties not be exposed to "the involuntary assumption of a series of new relations, inescapably hooked together," since the "hazards of a business conducted on these terms" would be too "extreme."[35]

General negligence law was also consistent with *Palsgraff*, its controlling authority. In any negligence case, "the burden rest[ed] upon the plaintiff to show by a fair preponderance of the evidence" that an "accident was caused by the fault of defendant." The most notable exception to the ordinary requirement that plaintiffs provide evidence of fault occurred with the doctrine of *res ipsa loquitur*, which allowed negligence to be proved by less than "positive and direct evidence," when "circumstances" could be "shown" from which a "reasonable inference" could be drawn that an "injury resulted from negligent acts." Ultimately, *res ipsa loquitur* advanced the new tort paradigm advocated by reformers—namely, that a defendant not be permitted to "carry on its undertaking without making good any loss that occurs to the business or property of another" and that no one be allowed "rightly [to] levy toll upon the legal rights of others" by carelessly and callously advancing his or her own interests.[36]

Cardozo and other judges also advanced the cause of tort reformers with their holdings concerning the weight to be accorded to statutes. The basic rule, laid down by Cardozo in *Martin v. Herzog*, was that breach of a statute is "more than some evidence of negligence. It *is* negligence in itself." This rule, which was reiterated in many cases,[37] reflected the extreme deference of New York judges during the 1920s and 1930s to legislative alterations of the usually pro-business rules of the common law. The consequence of the rule was that, whenever reformers had sufficient political success to obtain enactment of legislation on their behalf, they could count on the ready translation of that success into results in individual cases.

Thus much change occurred in New York tort law during the 1920s and 1930s as judges announced their preference for an emerging reform paradigm of tort liability, which held that victims of injury should receive compensation from some source, rather than the traditional paradigm, which permitted compensation to be paid only when a person was injured directly by another's wrongful act. But we must not overestimate the extent of change. Led by Cardozo, the New York judiciary did not favor the new paradigm completely but instead strove to accommodate both paradigms. Cardozo, in particular, seems to have wanted both to preserve the fairness values underlying the traditional paradigm while simultaneously incorporating significant elements of the reform program into the body of New York case law.

Even so, it seems clear that, to the extent that courts reconsidered particular legal doctrines, they tended to favor the newer reform values rather than the older traditional ones, even if they did not adopt the new values in their entirety. The direction of doctrinal development in New York's personal injury law during the 1920s and 1930s was toward the reform program and away from classic nineteenth-century values. As a result of the doctrine of *stare decisis,* however, which meant that in the absence of explicit reexamination old law remained in place, litigants continued to confront mostly nineteenth-century rules. Whatever changes occurred as a result of the efforts of reformers were overwhelmed in the larger picture of 1920s and 1930s by established rules, dealing with assumption of risk, contributory negligence,[38] tort liability of landowners, and joint and vicarious liability,[39] which remained in place through sheer inertia. These established rules all continued to reflect the traditional paradigm's concern that people be held responsible only for harms they had directly caused.

In short, personal injury law during the era of Cardozo began to change, but it was not completely transformed. Judges with conservative sympathies, like Andrews and Hand, continued to elaborate theories of liability that, in the short term, were largely ignored but in later decades would be widely endorsed. Reformers frequently placed their imprint on specific doctrines for which they could obtain judicial reconsideration, but much old doctrine, which reflected nineteenth-century assumptions of limited liability, remained unexamined. Thus personal injury law at the end of the 1930s remained what it had been three decades earlier—a battleground between the conservative and reform agendas.

THE LAW OF BUSINESS TORTS

Another subject on which conflicting conservative and progressive crosscurrents led to confusing doctrinal change rather than coherent reform was the law of business torts, in particular the law dealing with suits against individuals accused of "procur[ing] breach of an existing contract." At the outset of the 1920s, doctrine was strongly biased in conservative directions. As the Second Circuit explained, "contract rights [were] property," and "to induce one of the parties wrongfully to repudiate a contract [was] as distinct a wrong as" any other action that "injure[d] or destroy[ed] . . . property."[40]

Indeed, judicial biases were unusually transparent in the reported cases. On the one hand, judges were typically unwilling to interfere with the freedom of businesspeople to follow their competitive instincts, and thus would not hold them liable in commercial cases in which there was no existing fixed contract but merely the probability of obtaining a contract or an agreement that was terminable at will.[41] On the other hand, the conservative principle of preventing redistribution led to the development of radically different rules when labor unions sought either to induce workers to violate pledges against joining a union or to prevent employees from hiring replacement workers during a strike.

For example, in the hotly contested 1920 case of *Michaels v. Hillman,* which arose out of efforts of the Amalgamated Clothing Workers to persuade the plaintiff's employees to join the union, the court declared that employers, who hired workers only on an at-will basis, "had the right to endeavor to keep their factory nonunion, . . . which included the right to request their employe[e]s not to join an outside organization, and to discharge them for doing so." The court also declared that, while workers had the right to strike, they could not "prevent" an employer "from filling with others the places of those who left." That would interfere with an employer's right not merely to enjoy the benefit of existing contracts but also to enter into future contracts; it also would interfere with "the right to work" enjoyed by other workers. Attempts by unions to interfere with such prospective contractual arrangements "savor[ed] of a species of domination which [did] not inspire confidence in the . . . ultimate purposes" of unions and which called for the courts to "protect the general public . . . from exaction and oppression."[42]

Cases decided in the next several months were consistent with *Michaels.* One case, for example, declared unlawful any "conspiracy to injure a person's business, by preventing persons from entering his employment by threats and intimidation." No "organization or combination of workingmen," the court continued, "had the right to debar any individual or group of workers from employment," and every employer had "the right to employ whom it sees fit" and to "make membership in . . . unions . . . a bar to employment in its factory; . . . even if it thereby makes collective bargaining impossible." A final case went even further. It held unions "responsible for all lawlessness growing out of strikes which they could have avoided by reasonable discipline imposed on their members" and every member thereof "responsible for the acts of the others, and particularly for the acts of any officer."[43]

It did labor unions little good that these expansive doctrines prohibiting interference with merely prospective contract rights applied to "combination[s] of employers" as well as those of employees "who by coercive measures seek to break contracts between employer and employee." Employers in most industries had no need to enter into combinations with each other or to use other mechanisms essential to carrying on union activity. Formalistic statements that "the law does not have one rule for the employer and another for the employee" meant nothing when judges were speaking of a rule that, in fact, harmed workers significantly but did nothing to hurt those who hired them. Even though "each case" involving interference with contract rights was "to be decided upon the same principles of law, impartially applied to the facts of the case, irrespective of the personality of the litigants,"[44] expansive rules prohibiting interference with a wide range of prospective labor contracts conferred vast power on entities like manufacturing firms possessing valuable contract rights and little power on factory workers whose only right was to labor for a pittance.

Judicial bias grew even clearer when courts refused to extend doctrine in employment cases where labor unions were not involved and hence there was no danger of redistribution of wealth between social classes. As Judge Learned Hand wrote, "It has never been thought actionable to take away another's employee, when the defendant wants to use him in his own business, however much the plaintiff may suffer." An employee "was free to resign . . . at will," and it was "difficult to see how servants could get the full value of their services on any other terms." Based on this reasoning, the Second Circuit held it legitimate for a corporation to entice away a director and officer of a competitor.[45]

Likewise, the courts would not extend doctrine in noncommercial cases, where extension also was not called for to protect existing wealth distribution. Thus parents, friends, and even rivals were not liable for inducing breach of a contract to marry, since "before entering upon that status" parties "should not be hindered in securing information and advice from all sources." Moreover, allowing such suits would "invite a deluge of like litigation." This second concern about "open[ing] our courts to a flood of litigation" also provided the basis for rejecting a suit by a child against a man who had enticed his mother to leave her home and family with whom she "had lived happily . . . for twenty-two years."[46]

Subtle policy judgments that the law concerning inducement of breach of contract should be expanded or contracted, as needed, to preserve the existing distribution of wealth also played a role in occasional commercial tort cases.

In one case, for example, a court allowed "an elderly lady . . . of high social position, great wealth, and culture" who had advanced $250,000 to finance a Broadway production to demand the firing from the lead role of a winner of the Miss America contest, "concededly . . . fair of face, form, and figure" who had once posed " 'in bathing costume' " for "a full figure statue in the nude." Finding that the beauty contest winner "was not equal to singing the theme song or dancing as the heroine's part was originally cast" and that the socialite's "investment" was "thus seriously impaired and jeopardized," the court declared that persons like the socialite "acting for the protection of contract rights of their own which are of an equal or superior interest to another's contractual rights may invade the latter with impunity."[47]

Indeed, lower courts sometimes allowed even defendants who acted with "a malicious motive" to invade contract rights of others if their invasion did not threaten redistribution. Thus in *Beardsley v. Kilmer,* a defendant who had acted to " 'get even' " for published statements made about him by the plaintiff was permitted to open a rival newspaper, to induce the plaintiff's employees to leave their jobs and go to work for him, and ultimately to drive the plaintiff's newspaper out of business. The explanation for this result was "that the right of competition [was] self-justification always" in "a land of opportunity, as well as of free competition in business," even though, as Judge Harold J. Hinman noted in dissent, the effect of the case would be to allow "a man who is wealthy enough and malicious enough" to "to shut the door of opportunity to the object of his hatred by rivaling him in business, with no other aim in view than his destruction."[48]

Judge Hinman also expressed his belief that the law would change, and in a matter of years, change did begin to occur as new reform-oriented judges joined the Court of Appeals and began to wield substantial power. But legal doctrine in borderline cases changed only slowly. While courts became more sensitive to the need for freedom of opportunity and ultimately upward mobility for the children of the immigrant masses, they also developed a concern for business efficiency. The tensions that emerged between these policies kept doctrine from moving decisively in any one clear direction.

The 1922 *Beardsley* dissent of Judge Hinman was finally vindicated by the Court of Appeals in a 1932 case, *Al Raschid v. News Syndicate Co.,* which gave rise to the doctrine of prima facie tort. Before *Al Raschid,* the lower courts had struggled with the impact of motive in rendering business conduct lawful or unlawful. It always had been clear, except in the early cases involving labor unions, that "one who act[ed] honestly" and without negligence was "free from liability"; the debatable issue was whether bad motive transformed otherwise innocent acts into tortious ones. On this question, lower courts initially held that lawful acts committed out of malice were not actionable. These holdings had been followed by the Appellate Division in *Al Raschid,* but the Court of Appeals, in contrast, modified the judgment below and ruled unanimously that "a lawful act done solely out of malice and ill will to injure another may be actionable." [49]

Most important, perhaps, the court cited with approval a Minnesota case imposing liability on a defendant who had "set up a barber shop for the sole purpose of injuring the plaintiff's business and driving him out of it—the wrongdoer being wealthy and not interested in the business itself—and diverting customers from the plaintiff solely for the accomplishment of his malevolent purpose." [50] This Minnesota case was directly contrary to the *Beardsley* case, which had allowed a moneyed individual to drive a less affluent antagonist out of business and had produced Judge Hinman's dissenting plea for greater freedom of opportunity for the downtrodden.

Nonetheless, the *Al Raschid* case represented a mixed development. On the one hand, the decision can be read as supporting a policy of requiring businesspeople to behave morally and, in the process, protecting the existing distribution of wealth. On this reading, *Al Raschid* increased the possibility of judicial interference in business rivalries where losers claimed that winners had acted for malicious rather than legitimate business reasons and judges then had to pass on the claims. The *Al Raschid* decision thus had the capacity to become anticompetitive if business entities used it to obtain frequent judicial inquiries into their rivals' activities. On the other hand, *Al Raschid* restrained the meanness of wealthy individuals bent on destroying their inferiors. On the assumption that, during the decade of the 1930s, it was the rich who were seeking to restrain competition from upwardly mobile underlings, *Al Raschid* was a procompetitive decision. The decision was also procompetitive in that it applied only to cases where a defendant had a culpable state of mind. Absent culpability, "the principles of free competition justif[ied] a man in getting business for himself." [51]

Despite, or perhaps because of, its ambiguities, the *Al Raschid* doctrine displayed "expansive tendencies" during the two decades after the Court of Appeals decided it. The doctrine of prima facie tort remained "in the process of growth," providing "the mechanism whereby in modern business dealings the zone of liability against those causing injury to others [was] gradually expanding." "New torts [were] created every day" pursuant to the "expanding doctrine." One instance of unethical business practice that was held on the pleadings to constitute a prima facie tort was a case in which a radio show, the *Hit Parade,* failed to play plaintiff's song as one of its top ten without ever conducting a survey to determine the song's actual ranking. Another lawsuit under the prima facie tort rubric was successfully initiated by a Puerto Rican husband and wife seeking to buy a house in a residential section of Long Island, who alleged that the defendant "expressed anger at 'colored persons' moving into the neighborhood, and threatened bodily harm" to the seller and to the plaintiffs in order to "frighten" them into "surrender[ing] their legal right to buy a house where they pleased." On the other hand, older values arguably endured; consider, for example, *Wilson v. Hacker,*[52] which enjoined picketing by a labor union that refused to admit women to membership and nonetheless insisted that the employer, which employed some women, enter into a union shop contract. Holding that the union was free to discriminate against women, the court nonetheless declared that that the union could not compel the employer to end its at-will, contractual relationship with existing employees who wished to continue working and were prepared to join the union.

ZONING

The law of zoning was a third subject on which crosscurrents of conservatism and reform conflicted during the 1920s and 1930s. But there was no trend in the law of zoning, as there was in the law of personal injuries and business torts, in the direction of the reform agenda. On the contrary, zoning law was perhaps more conservative at the end of the 1930s than it had been at the beginning of the 1920s.

As early as 1920, the essentials of modern zoning had come into place when, in *Lincoln Trust Co. v. Williams Building Corp.,* the Court of Appeals had upheld the zoning resolution of the city of New York. Thereafter, the "legality" of zoning ordinances was "repeatedly . . . upheld, so that there . . . [could] no longer [be] any question as to the right of municipalities to enact and enforce" them. It was simply "conceded that the regulation of the building zone resolution [came] within the recognized police power of the state." This "drastic power . . . to zone districts for various purposes [was] justified . . . upon the theory of the greatest good to the greatest number" and as "beneficial to property values and to the peace, comfort, and welfare of the people."[53]

Arguably, zoning met with such early judicial approval because its aims were not redistributional. It could be used, for example, to protect the residential districts of the rich. Residential districts designed to provide "safe, healthful, and comfortable family life" were, indeed, a special subject of judicial solicitude, as when the Court of Appeals sustained an ordinance excluding from residential zones "big apartment houses . . . whereby the enjoyment of light and air by adjoining property would be impaired, the congestion and dangers of traffic [would] be augmented . . . and the dangers of disease and fires would be increased" along with "other things such as the destruction of the character of the district as a residential one." The exclusion of attached dwellings from districts intended for single-family houses was likewise sustained, as was the exclusion of obnoxious uses from business districts. In sustaining such exclusions, judges, in their own words, were abandoning the "ancient habit of regarding statutes as 'alien intruders' in the precincts of the law." [54]

In addition to sustaining zoning as a mechanism for controlling the uses to which land was put, the courts also allowed municipalities to zone for the purpose of limiting the density of development. Zoning authorities were thus left free to determine the maximum permissible height and bulk of buildings. They could also set minimum requirements for open space in the form of front, rear, and side yards.[55]

But at the same time that courts construed the theoretical power to zone broadly, they also remained solicitous of the rights of property owners in cases involving particular applications of the zoning power. They understood that every "zoning ordinance [was] in derogation of common-law rights to the use of private property" and accordingly "should not be extended by implication." Thus they struck down spot zoning and other schemes that deprived owners of the full use of their property without corresponding benefit to neighbors. They also upheld liberal practices for the granting of variances. A third way in which judges displayed solicitude for private property rights was through the protection of nonconforming uses.[56]

Finally, the Court of Appeals protected property rights through rigid insistence that municipal authorities follow correct procedures in the administration of zoning, including the rule that "enforcement of a [zoning] statute" be "entrusted solely to a named public officer" and that "private citizens not intrude upon his functions." The author of this rule, Judge Irving Lehman, who in the late 1930s was probably the strongest proponent on the court of the regulatory state, expressed particular concern about "the injustice that may result from prosecution of a violator . . . upon the complaint of a private citizen." Urging that public enforcement of zoning sufficed "to bring adequate pressure upon a contumacious offender," Lehman feared that creation of a private remedy would "subject a person violating the ordinance to the risk and embarrassment of being haled into court" for violations "committed, perhaps, through ignorance and without even notice from the building inspector . . . that the ordinance [was] being violated." With private enforcement, zoning "might be diverted from its intended purpose" into a vehicle for "annoyance and oppression."[57]

The judiciary's pursuit of a balanced approach to zoning, simultaneously protective of the legislature's theoretical power to zone and of property owners subject to particular exactions, was reiterated in *Arverne Bay Const. Co. v. Thatcher*,[58] a leading case that came before the Court of Appeals in 1938. The plaintiff in *Arverne Bay* held land on a main thoroughfare in an undeveloped area of Brooklyn, where there were only three buildings within the space of a mile, among them a cow stable and an office used in conjunction with a dairy business. Until 1928, the land had been unzoned, but in that year the city zoned it for residential use. After failing to obtain a variance to build a gasoline station on its land,[59] the plaintiff brought suit for a declaration that the zoning ordinance was unconstitutional as applied to its land. The Appellate Division, however, sustained the city's zoning scheme. Although the court "conceded . . . that this property cannot, presently or in the immediate future, be profitably used for residential purposes," it declared that zoning did not "look only to the immediate present" but also looked "forward to aid the development of new districts, according to a comprehensive plan based upon a theory that what is best for the city as a whole must prevail over private interests."[60]

In reversing the Appellate Division's judgment and thereby invalidating the zoning ordinance, the Court of Appeals was less willing to sacrifice private property rights to the attainment of public good. Writing for a unanimous court, Judge Lehman declared that there was "little room for disagreement with the general rules and tests set forth in the opinion of the Appellate Division" and that the police power could not be defined "so narrowly that it would exclude reasonable restrictions placed upon the use of property in order to aid the development of new districts in accordance with plans calculated to advance the public welfare of the city in the future."[61] He shared the concern expressed by Justice Holmes in *Pennsylvania Coal Co. v. Mahon*[62] that "the natural tendency of human nature" would be to extend the police power "more and more until at last private property disappear[ed]." For this reason, courts had "not hesitated to declare statutes invalid whenever regulation [had] gone so far that it [was] clearly unreasonable." In *Arverne Bay* the court was clear that the zoning ordinance had gone "beyond regulation" and thus had to "be recognized as a taking" since it "*permanently* so restricted the use of property" that the property could "not be used for any reasonable purpose."[63]

As it and other New York courts had done in cases dealing with the general police power, the Court of Appeals in *Arverne Bay* thus gave an expansive reading to the zoning power while at the same time carefully policing its case-by-case application. Judges thereby acknowledged that government should have plenary power to promote social justice and the public good while at the same time continuing to exercise the power they had claimed throughout the nineteenth century of protecting individual property rights.

The law of zoning is thus a good subject on which to begin recapitulating the core argument of Part I of this book and anticipating the argument of Part II. Zoning law shows that, even as judicial doctrine changed during the first third of the twentieth century, conflict between those adhering to the traditional values of the classical legal order and those striving for legal reform continued without resolution and along familiar paths. In this regard, zoning was not unique.

More generally, as New York judges in the aftermath of the political cataclysm of 1922 legitimated an expansion of the police power, they simultaneously continued to protect private property rights so as to limit the redistribution of wealth. As they altered contract law to better protect consumers and urban business interests, they simultaneously left much of the old idea of freedom of contract intact. As judicial majorities rewrote the common law of tort to prevent exploitation of underdogs and provide them with improved opportunities for upward mobility, dissenters authored opinions that would constitute future foundations for undoing much of the work of reform. Conversely, on the subject on which conservatives enjoyed their greatest legal successes during the 1920s and 1930s—the regulation of personal morality—reformers nonetheless enjoyed occasional victories, including the substantial victory of repealing Prohibition. And in connection with the law of procedure, new devices initially created for conservative ends slowly assumed reform functions.

Thus by the end of the 1930s, reformers had begun to undermine the classical legal order that New Yorkers had inherited from the nineteenth century. Reformers also had begun to improve the lives and standing of the often immigrant underdogs whose votes had put them in power. But they had not made those underdogs free or equal. Partial achievement of the reform goals of preventing exploitation and providing opportunity had tended to narrow the gap between the rich and the poor and thereby reduced the dependence of the poor, but the reform agenda did not envision a classless world of independent, equal individuals. At the end of the 1930s, the class structure remained entrenched. Society's elite leaders had begun perhaps to behave more charitably toward those beneath them, but the underdogs still were expected to abide by the rules marking their place in the class structure.

Why were neither the conservatives nor the reformers able to sculpt the legal order in accordance with their vision during the first four decades of the twentieth century? The conservatives failed, I contend, because their rural, up-state demographic base slowly eroded and power ineluctably shifted to urban, downstate reformers, who were able routinely after 1922 to win political and judicial office. The reformers failed, in contrast, because they lacked a clear, commanding ideological vision to which to conform the law once they had gained control of lawmaking institutions. In need of an ideology for an activist government that could redistribute power and wealth, they rejected the populist vision of small, self-governing communities uninfluenced by larger state, national, and even international entities. New York reformers like Cardozo, the Lehmans, Roosevelt, and Smith also rejected Marxism, and they could not turn to emerging Nazi or fascist ideologies while still appealing to the various outcast groups that constituted the bulk of their constituency. And during the course of the 1920s and 1930s, they failed to invent any new ideology.

But events of the year 1938 and its aftermath, to which Part II will now turn, led to the birth of a new ideology. And that ideology, as we also will see, produced a dramatic reformation of legal doctrine.

PART II

The Legalist Reformation

CHAPTER 5

1938

By the late 1930s, reformers had been in control of New York's political and legal institutions for over a decade. They had done much to undermine the classical, conservative legal order and to substitute in its place rules that limited exploitation of underdogs and provided opportunity for upward mobility. The entrenched class structure may have been slightly weakened, and the public had perhaps become inured to the use of law to uplift the weak and the poor. In the hindsight of history, it may be possible even to perceive the occurrence of social change in the direction of equality.

Nonetheless, the idea of equality remained inchoate, as did nebulously related ideas about personal liberty and human dignity. More immediate was the reality that, for less favored New Yorkers, inequality still entailed deprivations of rights and liberties which more privileged citizens took for granted. As we have seen, workers were denied freedom of speech and association; homosexuals, harassed; Catholics, subjected to cross burnings; and Jews, kept or even driven out of town. Above all, we have witnessed the thirteen-year experiment of Prohibition depriving millions of ethnic New Yorkers of beverages of their choice or at least declaring them criminals when they purchased those beverages. In the late 1930s, ethnic New Yorkers and others were not yet either free or equal.

For the weak and the poor, inequality and lack of freedom often involved the imposition of indignity as well. We shall learn in this chapter, for example, of a well-dressed African American man in Harlem who was subjected to a strip-search for policy slips and of a mother of a child terrified by a warrantless police break-in and search of her apartment. Or consider the indignity suffered by those who "cooked with vivid spices—even garlic,"[1] when their cuisines, which are among the world's most exquisite, were trashed.

These deprivations of rights, liberty, and dignity did little to engender trust in authority, either public or private. On the contrary, the deprivations created a quandary, in which those who "welcomed (even expected) assistance from government" in ending exploitation and promoting equality "nonetheless remained skeptical of state power."[2] And this quandary was not fortuitous: it was an inevitable response to the conservative agenda, which called on the legal system to limit the power of government over property owners seeking to exert dominion over the economic lives of the poor, while at the same time sanctioning the use of government power to control citizens' private, moral lives.* To thwart this agenda and respond to the realities it created in the lives of the less privileged, reformers thus needed an ideology to justify enhancing government's power over the economy while at the same time restricting its power over personal choice.

Meanwhile, conservatives were growing increasingly skeptical of the power of government in the late 1930s. They had, of course, always distrusted the power of bureaucratic, centralized governments, although they had been willing to permit local institutions which they effectively dominated to dictate community moral standards. But as they watched their underlings assume power and wield it effectively for long periods of time, their fear that those underlings would behave toward them as they had behaved toward the underlings in the past increased their distrust of regulation, whether by bureaucratic, centralized entities or by local communities. Once it became clear, that is, that people with different values would be permitted to enter the cultural mainstream and wield power in at least some institutions, the danger that they might impose their differing values led to a predicament for anyone still committed to living by traditional ones. Although one response to such a predicament might have been to assimilate into newly reconstituted communities only those who accepted core values, an easier response was simply to cease insisting that government be in the business of imposing any values at all. Many conservatives took this easy approach and thus joined the chorus of citizens demanding limited government, individual liberty, personal choice, and the protection of human rights and dignity.

No one captured the prevailing distrust of government, shared by reformers and conservatives alike, better than Walter Lippmann. Lippmann wrote against "regimentation," which, he declared, inevitably occurred whenever "centralized decision . . . replace[d] distributed decisions" and "orders" from a "hierarchy of officials" replaced "argument, persuasion, bargaining, and compromise among individuals." Then, "the citizen [became] a conscript" in a society without "customs, contracts, constitutions, or ancient usages . . . [to] limit" "the will of the rulers above him."[3]

Because Lippmann understood that government power often was needed "to redress the balance of private transactions," he, like others who were begin-

---

* Note how Populism achieves this conservative goal by concentrating power in localities, which are too small to control the property of corporate entities spread over large geographic areas but quite capable of controlling the personal lives of their residents.

ning to call themselves liberals, did not advocate the preservation of laissez-faire. Instead, he advocated "a method of social control which is not laissez-faire, which is not communism, which is not fascism," but what he called "the method of free collectivism." Under Lippmann's scheme, "enterprise [was] free," as "men decide[d] for themselves . . . what they will produce; . . . at what they will work," and "what they will consume and how much they will save." "The object of the state's intervention [was] not to supplant this system but to preserve it by remedying its abuses, . . . correcting its errors," and subsidizing those who were seeking the opportunity to better their lives. As stated succinctly by another emerging liberal, John Maynard Keynes, the task of government was "to make the economic order work tolerably well, whilst preserving freedom of individual initiative and liberty of thought and criticism."[4]

Inchoate ideas of economic opportunity, individual liberty, and human dignity thus were in the air in the late 1930s, but they had not yet matured into a consistent, coherent philosophy. In the year 1938, however, as Hitler marched toward what history now knows as the Holocaust, New Yorkers stood staggering in shock. They insisted that New York must pursue a direction different from Germany's, and as they strove to elaborate why and how New York's direction would differ, they began articulating an ideology of equality, liberty, and dignity that ultimately would result in a legalist reformation—that is, in a complete transformation of New York law and, through law, a complete reconstruction of New York society and culture.

THE YEAR OF KRISTALLNACHT

Let us begin with the morning of November 11, 1938, when New Yorkers read with horror how on the previous day in Germany the "Nazis [had] smash[ed], loot[ed] and burn[ed] Jewish shops and temples," while "bands rove[d] cities," "plunderers trail[ed] wreckers in Berlin," and the "police" stood "idle." According to the *New York Times,* "a wave of destruction, looting and incendiarism unparalleled in Germany since the Thirty Years War . . . swept over Great Germany . . . as National Socialist cohorts took vengeance on Jewish shops, offices and synagogues." "Thousands of Jews . . . were taken from their homes and arrested—in particular prominent Jewish leaders, who in some cases, it is understood, were told they were being held as hostages for the good behavior of Jews outside Germany." Jews "were hunted out even in the homes of non-Jews where they might have been hiding," and foreign consulates "were besieged by frantic telephone calls and by persons, particularly weeping women and children, begging help that could not be given them."

It was "assumed that the Jews, who have now lost most of their possessions and livelihood, will either be thrown into the streets or put into ghettos and concentration camps."[5]

Similar persecution at Nazi hands had appalled New Yorkers only eight months earlier, when Germany had annexed Austria. At that time, "dissidents" and "Liberals and Socialists who ha[d] been permitted to remain at liberty even under the reactionary regimes which ha[d] prevailed in Austria" before the Nazi takeover were "herded into concentration camps." " 'Protective arrests' " were "ordered in the case of labor leaders, a Catholic editor, [and] former officials of the . . . government," and "the roads . . . to Austria's frontiers [were] crowded with pitiful refugees whose efforts to escape from a certain vengeance [were] in most cases doomed to failure." Also arrested were Baron Friedrich von Wiesner, the Legitimist leader, and Baron Karl Workmann, secretary to the last Hapsburg emperor. All Jewish organizations were dissolved, as was the Christian German Gymnastic Association, a Catholic group, and penalties were announced "for any one other than a 'pure racial German' who [made] use of the swastika emblem."[6]

New Yorkers observed these events in Germany with apprehension and indignation. Even Thomas E. Dewey, the Manhattan district attorney who had earned a reputation for antagonism to civil liberties and only a few days earlier had suffered defeat in the race for governor, commented in November 1938 that "not since the days of medieval barbarism ha[d] the world been forced to look upon a spectacle such as this," while an upstate newspaper wrote of "the indecency and brutality that is permitted in Germany" and the *Herald Tribune* in New York City expressed "the disgust of all civilized men." The *New York Times* spoke of "scenes which no man can look upon without shame for the degradation of his species." Finally, with the "shadow of the swastika . . . growing longer across the world," the Rev. Dr. Raymond C. Knox, the chaplain of Columbia University, warned that the "totalitarian State" constituted "the gravest menace to the freedom and peace of the world."[7]

New Yorkers not only lamented developments in Europe but banded together to take action against them. Thus M. Maldwin Fertig, a member of the governing council of the American Jewish Congress, urged four hundred delegates of Jewish organizations to act "for the collective defense of the Jews in Europe," while the National Unity Congress of the People's Committee against Fascism and Anti-Semitism heard calls from labor leader Michael Quill, Representative John M. Coffee, and future Representative Vito Mercantonio for people of "all creeds to unite against that canker of fascism and Nazism" and to "rally around the one standard of unity of the democracies."

The growing divergence between Nazi ideology and the new ideology of legalist reform emerging in New York was, perhaps, best captured in a letter written to the German Foreign Office in the aftermath of Kristallnacht by the German ambassador in Washington; the ambassador bemoaned that "the good prospects for a gradual spread of anti-Semitism had suffered a serious setback," as evidenced by an incident "in an old Protestant church . . . , which had a rabbi preach for the first time, departing from a 300-year-old tradition, in order to show that in a situation like the present they stand by the Jews."[8]

The spreading shadow of the swastika, in short, compelled Americans to articulate their emerging legalist reform ideology, which would focus on equality and human dignity, personal choice and individual initiative, and "liberty of thought and criticism." Confronting totalitarianism in Europe in the late 1930s and 1940s, Americans increasingly worried about "an all-powerful state that would provide security at the expense of liberty." "The rise of totalitarianism," according to the theologian Reinhold Niebuhr, "prompted the democratic world to view all collectivist answers . . . with increased apprehension" and to recognize that "a too powerful state is dangerous to our liberties."[9]

New Yorkers played a central role in the articulation of this new legalist reform ideology. As one New York contributor explained in a letter to a fellow New Yorker, he had become "deeply concerned about the increasing racial and religious intolerance which seem[ed] to bedevil the world" and which might "be augmented in this country." For this reason, Justice Harlan Fiske Stone had thought it necessary to draft what has since become one of American constitutional law's most important texts—footnote 4 of *United States v. Carolene Products Co.*—in order to further "the program of 'judicial reform'" on which the majority of the court had embarked in giving greater deference to economic regulatory legislation without diminishing judicial enforcement of "the guarantees of individual liberties." The footnote itself announced that the court would scrutinize strictly legislation "directed at particular religious, . . . or national, . . . or racial minorities," when "prejudice against discrete and insular minorities may be a special condition, which tends seriously to curtail the operation of those political processes ordinarily to be relied upon to protect minorities." On such occasions, a "correspondingly more searching judicial inquiry" was required to guarantee the legality of a majoritarian act.[10]

Justice Stone's concern for protection of minorities was neither as unprecedented nor unique as the received wisdom about the *Carolene Products* case would suggest.[11] Footnote 4 did not come out of nowhere: in the context of its time, it was an ingenious response not only to Nazi atrocities but also to the quandary in which legalist reformers were mired, as they strove to make all citizens equal through law while at the same time immunizing them from government control of their personal lives.

Nor was Justice Stone alone in his concern. Four days after Kristallnacht, Dorothy Thompson, one of America's most respected journalists, delivered a national radio broadcast from New York, in which she talked about the forthcoming trial of Herschel Grynszpan, a teenaged Jewish refugee whose murder of a German diplomat in Paris had touched off the Nazi pogrom. It was rumored, she reported, that Grynszpan, "an anaemic-looking boy with brooding black eyes," would "go to the guillotine, without a trial by jury, without the rights that any common murderer has." Why, she asked, was it necessary "to cut off the head of one more Jew without giving him an open trial?" Thompson also spoke of other "unheard-of things" which the world had recently endured, such as the confiscation of the fortunes of American citizens in Germany and the expulsion of two hundred American citizens of Jewish blood from Italy "as undesirable aliens." Why, she asked, didn't America expel "half a million non-naturalized Germans in the United States, and as many Italians" and confiscate "German and Italian fortunes in this country . . . as reprisals for the confiscated fortunes of American citizens and for unpaid debts."

> Why don't we do it? We don't do it because it isn't, according to our standards, decent. We don't do it because we refuse to hold people responsible for crimes that others commit. We don't do it because our sense of justice is still too strong to answer terror with terror. We don't do it because we do not want to add to the hatred and chaos which are already making this world intolerable. We fear that violence breeding violence will destroy us all in the long run.

Finally, Dorothy Thompson concluded her articulation of America's newly emerging ideology by condemning "the men of Munich . . . , who signed a pact without one word of protection for helpless minorities." Others agreed that Britain and France should have exacted from Hitler at Munich "pledges that he would curb racial persecution, that he would stop condoning, if not directing, lawlessness against race and religion."[12]

What is most striking about these condemnations of Nazi Germany is the manner in which they echoed another debate occurring in New York in the summer of 1938, as the state was holding a convention to draft a new constitution. On the one side at the Constitutional Convention of 1938 were the conservatives, who still understood politics in terms of the classic paradigms outlined in the introductory chapter above, however much they had become unprepared to press those paradigms to their logical limits. On the other side were the legalist reformers, who were striving to articulate a new ideology toward which the law had been pointing for the past decade.

The most passionately debated issue at the convention was whether New York should adopt the exclusionary rule and thereby prevent the use of illegally obtained evidence in criminal cases. Conducted in the shadow of the spreading swastika, the debate on the exclusionary rule induced legalist reformers to separate concerns about ethnic and cultural discrimination from older issues of class conflict. Ultimately, the debate enabled the reformers to redefine equality as requiring the protection of discrete ethnic, religious, and cultural minorities rather than dictating the redistribution of wealth from rich to poor.

The debate began when, at the behest of George Meany, president of the State Federation of Labor, a proposal was introduced on the convention floor to incorporate into the state constitution a rule excluding the fruits of any unlawful search or wiretap from evidence in a criminal case. The proposal, which was ultimately defeated on a vote of seventy-two in favor and eighty-nine opposed, was hotly debated, with both sides aware that its passage would determine whether a preexisting constitutional provision against warrantless searches and wiretaps, on which they both agreed, would be effectively enforced.[13]

Opponents of the exclusionary proposal did "not like these New Deal crackpots to write us a Constitution" and in the process to ignore their practical concerns and fears that tight-knit immigrant, especially Italian, communities would increase their capacity to nullify Puritanical law-enforcement machinery. As Hamilton Fish, a Republican elder statesman, who, in his own words, had "learned all . . . [his] political principles back in 1912 at the feet of Theodore Roosevelt" declaimed, the convention was "playing with fire" in a state that was "at war with organized crime . . . — unscrupulous, clever, backed by great wealth." To adopt the exclusionary rule would offer "a cloak" and "a hideout" for criminals and lead to "the greatest single celebration in the City of New York among the crooks and gangdom and racketeers that was ever known in that city." From "far and wide," he added, "all the other racketeers and murderers and kidnappers and embezzlers [would] all collect . . . to celebrate this famous victory of the forces of evil." Other delegates, who did not want to see the erection of new "walls of technicality" that would "form a chief defense for organized crime," gave examples of murderers and other violent criminals who might have escaped conviction but for the use of unlawfully obtained evidence. The leading opponent of the exclusionary proposal, however, was Manhattan district attorney Thomas E. Dewey, who had built his political career on his successful prosecution of organized crime and had played a leading role in securing legislation that made criminal prosecution easier and punishment more severe. He made the main point clearly and succinctly. The exclusionary proposal, according to Dewey, would "protect no one except the guilty criminal" and would "subject . . . [the people of the state] to the depredations of organized crime."[14]

Supporters of the proposal, like the opponents, also made their point by way of examples. One involved a member of President Roosevelt's cabinet who tapped the wires of his supporters; a second, wiretapping by a prosecutor investigating ambulance chasing in New York City; and a third, "political persecution" through wiretapping of a "priest who was interested in certain phases of charity, certainly not a criminal, surely an innocent man." But more was at stake for supporters of the exclusionary rule than the use of wiretapping in an investigation of ambulance chasing or even of innocent priests. They were worried about "the threats which dictatorship countries [were] making against Democratic countries" and about "the dangers which [were] threatening our people throughout the entire world today." The "working man, the American Federation of Labor, the laboring people, the honest business man, the private citizen," who would be "protected in the privacy of . . . [their] homes" and "office[s] and business[es]," supported adoption of an exclusionary rule because it would "re-affirm our faith in democracy; . . . preserve the principles upon which that democracy is found[ed]; and . . . strengthen so far as we can, the basic principles of a free people." "In a world gone mad in the direction of dictatorship" and in the "suppression of democratic rights," there was "no more important consideration facing the Constitutional Convention" than "to preserve and strengthen all the guarantees contained in the Bill of Rights."[15]

Nothing so far quoted fully captures, however, why organized labor and its urban immigrant members deemed an exclusionary rule of such "great importance" that they vowed to "press for . . . its passage."[16] Nothing yet explains why urban members of the New Deal coalition should have been so much more concerned about the "suppression of democratic rights" and protection of the Bill of Rights than their Republican opponents. Nothing yet accounts for why the debate over the exclusionary rule became such a central focus of concern at the 1938 state constitutional convention.

The debate became so important because it served as a surrogate for what one Republican delegate in his speech against the exclusionary rule labeled a struggle "of law and order against lawlessness"—between "real Americans . . . [who] stand for law and order" and "those using lawless means to seek some advantage over their fellow citizens." In particular, the Republican delegate expressed his concern about the "temporary periods of disorder and lawlessness" that "several communities" had recently experienced—"experiences" that were "distasteful and objectionable to the vast majority of our people." [17]

Although the delegate's meaning may not be entirely clear to today's reader, it was crystal clear to his listeners. His reference to "temporary periods of disorder and lawlessness" referred to the labor unrest associated with the organizational efforts of the Congress of Industrial Organizations (CIO) in basic manufacturing industries to change "the relationship between the working man . . . and the boss, for all time." [18] Unionism was, of course, one "lawless means" that "real Americans" feared others would use to "seek some advantage over their fellow citizens." But it was not thought to be the only "lawless means" used by organized labor and its immigrant supporters to attain their ends. Even more significant was the lawlessness that old-line Republicans found in the redistributive legislation of President Roosevelt's New Deal and Governor Herbert Lehman's Little New Deal.

Even as old-liners were worrying, however, the emerging legalist reformation was mutating. The redistribution of wealth and power was ceasing to be reform's main goal. Like the conservatives, the emerging reformers were beginning to excoriate lawlessness.

Especially revealing from the legalist reform perspective was the speech of the convention's delegate from Harlem, who focused on the relationship between racial discrimination and police lawlessness. He told, for example, of one innocent man who was arrested without a warrant and taken "to the 135th Street Police Station," where the police "proceeded to work on him." The delegate reported that, when the police saw "an individual of negro origin fairly well dressed and out in the day time," they would "suspect" him as "a policy collector" and would "push him into a hallway, strip him of his clothes, take off his shoes even, in quest of policy slips," and when they found none, "push him out." There was also "the case of a poor woman with a child . . . home in her bed late at night" while "her husband [was] out at work." When the police broke in, "the children [became] hysterical" and she became "sick." Even though the police found nothing, there was "no one" who was "going to pay for it." There were "thousands of other cases, thousands and thousands where illegal evidence [was] not found, where illegal searches [were] permitted day after day and no evidence [was] obtained." [19]

A report to Mayor Fiorello LaGuardia on a 1935 riot in Harlem continued the tale. It told of how "the police of Harlem" often invaded "the personal rights of its citizens . . . when white and colored people [were] seen consorting together." Although the report indicated that police interference was most likely when "a colored man [was] with a white woman," it told of one case of a man who was arrested "because he was walking with a colored woman" and held "until he could prove to the officer that he was a colored man." The report also brought out the fact that "the police attempted to impress" on whites "by words and acts of brutality that whites were not to associate with 'the black bastards in Harlem.'" Although the "citizens of Harlem" appreciated that "the slight regard . . . shown for their lives [was] due not only to the fact that they [were] Negroes, but also to the fact that they [were] poor and propertyless and therefore defenseless," they understood at the same time that something in addition to economic justice was at stake. They knew that they had to put an end not merely to their poverty but also to "the estimation of the police" that "the life of a Negro [was] cheap." [20]

This rhetoric suggests that today's conception of equality had begun to enter political discourse and to propel legalist reformers, mainly Democrats, in new ideological directions while conservatives, who were still mainly Republicans, adhered to old ideas. Republicans, who at least in New York tended to represent "real Americans" of WASP extraction, conjoined majoritarian political power, labor activism, and actual crime as forms of lawlessness that Democrats would use to deprive them of the independence, wealth, and social preeminence they had always enjoyed. They feared an egalitarian, redistributive revolution carried out under the forms of government but in the end not radically different from the violent one that Benjamin Gitlow and his fellow Bolsheviks had plotted in 1919. The Democrats, however, no longer had redistribution in mind. The new legalist reformers, who represented urban Catholic and Jewish immigrants and their descendants, feared in the year of Kristallnacht that Nazi-like repression might spread to America through police lawlessness and other comparable abuses. For them, the core issue in the 1938 debate over the exclusionary rule was whether urban Catholics and Jews and perhaps even blacks would obtain protection from arbitrary impositions of public and private power.

The entry into politics of this new conception of equality was marked even more clearly by another suggested amendment to the state's Bill of Rights. As originally proposed, the new amendment to the bill simply declared that "no person shall be denied the equal protection of the laws of this State or any subdivision thereof." This proposal was scarcely debated on its way to passage, but one extraordinary speech by Senator Robert F. Wagner served as a prophecy of the future course of the legalist reformation. Wagner declared:

> As we reflect sorrowfully on the turn in world events . . . , we pose in our own minds *the essential governmental problem of our times.* In the 18th and 19th centuries, that problem was how to establish the will of the majority in representative government. *In the world of today, the problem is how to protect the integrity and civil liberties of minority races and groups.* The humane solution of that problem is now the supreme test of democratic principles, the test indeed, of civilized government.
>
> We in America have long cherished the picture of a great melting pot. . . . That picture, we must all admit, is marred in this State . . . by certain manifestations of racial intolerance and prejudice. . . . The bestial manifestations of anti-semitism abroad are happily absent from our national scene. We cannot, however, be blind to the forms of anti-semitism prevalent at home. These manifestations have been vigorously challenged by spokesmen of all creeds, and many notorious instances have met with effective protest.
>
> Far less effective in marshaling informed public opinion and suffering from discrimination and prejudice so deep-seated as to be taken for granted by the community at large, are the half million Negroes in the State.

After describing graphically the discrimination that victimized African Americans in New York in the 1930s, Wagner concluded, "In the final analysis the so-called Negro problem, or any other minority problem, is but another aspect of man's eternal struggle for freedom and justice, a problem that solves itself when democracy is extended into every phase of our material life."[21]

No one as early as 1938 had as yet seen the future as clearly as did Wagner in this convention speech, but others ranging from Thomas E. Dewey and Harlan Fiske Stone to Dorothy Thompson and George Meany were beginning to develop a coherent vision. As the 1930s drew to a close, a modern conception of equality, liberty, and dignity as requiring an end to ethnic and cultural persecution was beginning slowly to permeate the societal fabric.[22] In response to the Holocaust, legislative policies protecting the downtrodden, common-law rules providing opportunity for the upwardly mobile, and Keynesian programs for putting money into everyone's pockets were gradually being transformed, if not into a coherent affirmative program, at least into a demand that New York, unlike Germany, should uphold liberty, human dignity, and legal and social equality for all—not only for Catholic and Jewish children of immigrants but even, perhaps, for African Americans.

As the 1930s turned into the 1940s, ongoing events in Nazi Germany, which culminated in World War II, nurtured the development of this ideology of equality, liberty, and dignity. In particular, the experiences of millions of Americans during the war and in its aftermath transformed the 1938 effort of political and intellectual leaders to explain the difference between America and Germany into the lived reality of the nation as a whole.[23]

The experiences of the World War II decade were so important that their impact must be traced in detail. In particular, it is necessary to examine four trends. We must focus on the continuing development, first, of equality, and, second, of liberty. Third, we need to analyze a seemingly contradictory trend toward increased bureaucratic regulation. This growth of bureaucracy enhanced the ability of majorities to oppress minorities and to restrict individual freedom and meant that equality and liberty could not grow naturally, as they sometimes had during the nineteenth century. Equality and liberty would require institutional protection. Finally, as we shall see, the judiciary would assume the role of protector. In that role, the judiciary would become the ultimate arbiter of public policy, the very meaning of law would be altered, and the legalist reformation would commence.

Equality. Well into the 1940s, the cancer of Nazism abroad nourished ideas of equality at home. One historian, at least, finds that a number of organizations, ranging from the Foreign Language Information Service through the National Conference of Christians and Jews to the American Jewish Committee, self-consciously took advantage in the late 1930s and early 1940s of the Nazi threat and of a growing American interest in unity and democracy to promote their own missions. By working together to explain to Americans "the true nature, implications, consequences and dangers of Nazism," these groups and others hoped to bring about "the education and assimilation of all of us" and to produce a spirit of "unity" in which "all Americans work[ed] and liv[ed] together harmoniously" with "tolerance and mutual understanding."[24]

When World War II came a few years later, government propagandists joined in the effort to achieve ethnic and religious justice, making a self-conscious attempt to "help clear up the alien problem, the negro problem, the anti-Semitic problem." The central racial doctrines espoused by Hitler made the propagandists' task easy by illustrating to Americans "where we end up if we think that the shape of the nose or the color of the skin has anything to do with human values and culture." Egalitarian propaganda efforts such as these were quite successful, and it became a commonplace that "in a common-wealth like New York, teeming with every race and creed," every effort had to be made to undo "the existence of racial or religious discrimination espe-cially . . . [during] a war being waged to defend the American principle that all men are entitled to equal opportunity." As President Roosevelt proclaimed, the goal of the war was to "conquer . . . racial arrogances," to promote "justice . . . and tolerance and good-will among all . . . people," and "to make a country in which no one is left out." [25]

The experience of the millions who served in the military reaffirmed what American propaganda was saying. With an army composed of "Yugoslavs and Frenchmen and Austrians and Czechs and Norwegians," "the battlefield . . . produce[d] a brotherhood" as the "common bond of death [drew] human beings toward each other over . . . artificial barriers." "The caldron of war," in short, tended to "dissolve . . . all ethnic, class, and racial enmities." Even for those, especially the young, who stayed at home, the values proclaimed during wartime left a permanent imprint on their collective psyche.[26]

The massive postwar American move to the suburbs ratified the war's disso-lution of ethnic and religious barriers, at least among whites. Old ethnic neigh-borhoods in New York City were depopulated as Italians, Jews, and Scandina-vians, for instance, moved to the suburbs and became each others' neighbors. Nassau County, a close-in suburb of New York City, furnishes an example. The scene of anti-Catholic and anti-Semitic activities on the part of the Ku Klux Klan in the 1920s, the county witnessed an enormous influx of Catho-lics and Jews during the late 1940s and 1950s. Whereas the foreign-born white population of Nassau County was only 21 percent of the total county popula-tion in 1920 and 16 percent in 1940, immigrants and their children constituted 39 percent of the county's population by 1960. This demographic trend is con-firmed by comparing religious populations before and after World War II.[27]

Unfortunately, census data do not provide information about religion. Comparative religious populations can be estimated, however, by looking at the number of religious institutions. Examination of the number of Roman Catholic parishes in Nassau suggests, for example, that the Catholic popula-tion, predominantly Irish and Italian, constituted a relatively small proportion of the county population before World War II. Although the first Catholic parish, St. Patrick's in Glen Cove, had been established in 1856, only four-teen parishes existed by the turn of the century. Catholic population increased somewhat in the first three decades of the twentieth century, but the 1950s wit-nessed the largest migration of Catholics into Nassau County and the establishment of twelve new parishes. Thereafter, the relocation of Catholic families into the county dropped off. Nevertheless, of the sixty-six parishes currently in existence, one-third of them were founded after 1940.[28]

Similarly but to an even more significant extent, the Jewish population in Nassau County was virtually nonexistent in the years before World War II but grew dramatically thereafter. The first synagogue, Congregation Tifereth Israel, was established in Glen Cove in 1897. In the following four decades, only twenty-one more synagogues were founded to serve the small Nassau Jewish community. For instance, at the end of World War II, of the 4,000 residents of Old Westbury, there were still only twenty-five Jewish families living in the village. As a consequence, congregations possessed small memberships with only a handful of families. During the 1940s, however, fifteen synagogues were founded, and an astounding forty-six congregations were established in the 1950s. The Jewish population county-wide doubled in the 1950s alone. In Great Neck, the Jewish population more than doubled from 4,000 in 1940 to 10,000 in 1950 and then almost doubled again during the 1950s to 18,000 by 1960. In 1960, there were an estimated 329,100 Jews residing in Nassau County, 25 percent of the county's total population of 1,300,171.[29]

Even more significantly, this inpouring of Jewish families outstripped the overall population growth rate during this same period. When two housing developments were completed in Oceanside in 1951, for instance, almost all of the new residents were Jewish. While the county population increased from 672,762 in 1950 to 1,300,171 in 1960—a 93 percent increase—the number of Jewish congregations in the county grew from thirty-seven to eighty-three—a 125 percent increase. Established congregations also expanded to accommodate this rapid population growth, and, in contrast to the early congregations, synagogues after World War II were composed of hundreds of families. Population growth somewhat stabilized as only sixteen synagogues were founded in the 1960s, ten in the 1970s, and three in the 1980s.[30]

The intermixing of people that occurred as a result of this influx of Jews and Catholics into suburban locales like Nassau County, together with earlier experiences in World War II, made ethnic and cultural discrimination appear increasingly perverse. As neighbors of mixed ethnic and religious backgrounds lived in proximity to each other, they discovered what they shared in common as well as how they differed. As children of diverse backgrounds attended public schools en masse, they learned conventional values together, assimilated a common body of knowledge, and developed shared aspirations for their own and their community's future. As Protestants, Catholics, and Jews ultimately intermarried, old hatreds and bigotries often disappeared.

Liberty. World War II and its aftermath were not, however, only about ethnic and religious assimilation. The war was a battle for liberty as well as equality—"a fight between a slave world and a free world." Thus President Franklin D. Roosevelt turned to an individualistic rhetoric of "rights" to exhort Americans to victory in World War II, which other government propagandists labeled "a 'people's' war for freedom." Roosevelt's proclamation of the Four Freedoms, in turn, had "a powerful and genuine appeal" to "the American people," who were "idealistically in favor of guaranteeing freedom of speech and religion all over the world." [31]

More important, World War II vastly accelerated fundamental socioeconomic changes that had begun with the end of the Great Depression and that would ultimately transform Americans' social and economic experiences and expectations. By 1940, the gross national product measured in constant dollars had nearly rebounded to its 1929 level, and thereafter it rose 186 percent between 1940 and 1950, another 77 percent between 1950 and 1960, and by 1980 was 930 percent greater than in 1940. [32]

The return and then the endurance of prosperity "changed . . . [people's] lifestyle and . . . outlook." The New Deal's aspiration for structural reforms that would protect underdogs from social conditions they could not control was replaced with a new faith growing out of the revival of economic opportunity that people "could do things" by and for themselves. Whereas people during the Depression had been "radicalized" and "convinced of the need for social change" because "the system as it was wasn't good enough," the return of prosperity showed them that "problems are of an individualistic nature" and that "the virtues and vices of the central" actors rather than "social forces . . . move[d] . . . events along." [33] Individual choice and individuals themselves again mattered as the 1930s turned into the 1940s.

In conjunction with continuing economic growth, the massive suburbanization of the postwar years reinforced the individualistic assumptions that the war years had brought to the fore. As nine million people migrated to the nation's newly constructed suburbs in the decade after the war and people of diverse ethnic and religious backgrounds became neighbors, they and their children became more important social influences on each other than their families, their old communities, or their churches could be. The new neighbors, however, would never have the dominant influence that the old communities had enjoyed, if for no other reason, as one observer has commented, because the suburbs were much more private and individualistic than the old neighborhoods had been. Suburban life was focused inside the home around new entertainment forms such as television, suburban homes opened outside into private backyards, and suburbanites usually traveled to the outside world enclosed in automobiles. In prewar city life, in contrast, homes had front porches opening on the street, entertainment occurred in public places like movie theaters, and people got places on foot or by public transportation, where they could not avoid meeting each other.[34]

As suburbanites pursued their individualistic economic opportunities and private recreations, in short, they no longer automatically accepted the values of the groups, especially the neighborhoods, churches, and extended families, of which they had been a part. As essentially private individuals, they had a choice of pursuing the lifestyles of their new neighbors or of their more familiar groups or of taking bits and portions from each. They could yield publicly to pressures for suburban conformity on some occasions while rejecting them privately on others. The result was that much social practice changed. Some of the most striking, best documented, and most important changes occurred in the realm of sexuality.

Dramatic changes had begun as early as 1940 with the first peacetime draft. They continued at an escalating level thereafter, as burgeoning war industries and the military did what the suburbs would later do: they removed people from established communities and from the traditional moral and social structures linked to them and transposed them into new, often transient groups where anonymity and the ever-present horrors of war encouraged young people to indulge. The war, in short, "provided an infinite variety of situations for the fulfillment . . . of male sexual desires."[35] Here are three eyewitness reports:

Many things took place then because the men were being shipped overseas. There were a lot of girls I knew in college who got caught in that— let's make his last days here happy, just in case he never comes back. I don't know how many had illegitimate children . . . simply because they felt they owed it to this man because this might be the last he'd ever have.

Another indelible scene I remember was a startling sight on a train. It was night and our train was slowly passing another. I turned and looked, and there in the dimly lit car was [sic] a GI and a woman having sex while several other GI's stood around watching or not watching. . . . I could hardly believe what I had seen. You took a deep breath and it was gone, yet it made a deep impression on me.

You knew everybody was going to get off the train at the next stop, and that was the end of that. You were passing each other in the night.

I let a sailor pick me up and go all the way with me. I had intercourse with him partly because he had a strong personal appeal for me, but mainly because I had a feeling of high adventure and because I wanted to please a member of the armed forces.

As one man named Roger Montgomery, who found himself involved in sexual activities that were "totally new to me," reported, he was not "a great lover in this situation, because . . . I was frightened to death about it a good deal of the time." Nonetheless, "for me it was quite a liberating experience." The same was undoubtedly true for a high school student who lost his virginity with a woman of thirty whose husband was overseas. "We weren't in love," he recalled, but the "times were conducive for this sort of thing." For another high school student working in a war plant "full of working girls who were 'on the make,' . . . a male war worker became the center of loose morality. It was a sex paradise." [36]

Gay women and men enjoyed similar experiences as the same social transformations that proved liberating for heterosexuals proved liberating for homosexuals as well. Gay GIs, who if they had been home could never have "stay[ed] out all night or promote[d] a serious affair" because their parents would have considered them "perverted" and kept them "in the house" had "no one to answer to" in the army as long as they "behave[d]" themselves "during the week and stay[ed] out of the way of the MP's on weekends." Since no one knew where they "might be sent tomorrow," gay GIs did what young Americans in the military "did with everything else," which "was take chances and risks and try to enjoy things." Those who wrote letters or kept diaries clearly did enjoy things, as did one young man who "spent the nite in an empty barracks . . . with the cutest thing you have ever seen . . . —and all was wonderful." Another man reported how his relationship with his lover "was developing more beautifully than I ever dreamed possible," while "it seemed so good" to a third man that he and his lover developed a lasting relationship. The war brought similar opportunities and experiences to lesbians such as Lisa Ben, who while sunbathing on a roof of a Los Angeles rooming house populated by women, "got to talking," stated that she preferred to "go out strictly with girls," and later was taken by her new friends to lesbian bars, where she "met *lots* of girls." [37]

The war years, in short, allowed the almost imperceptible changes that had been occurring in sexual mores since the beginning of the century to coalesce into a qualitatively new shape. "The net impression" on a leading contemporary sociologist was "that war with its accompanying increase in personal mobility, decrease in social controls, increase in women working, and reorientations in life philosophies did bring about an appreciable change." People who had lived through those years—and this is the important parallel between homosexual and heterosexual liberation during World War II—simply could not go back to their old lifestyles encrusted by the old traditions. Thus one veteran was "afraid to return to Maysville," a small Kentucky town, where he could have no "gay life . . . , being as well known as I am," while another remarked even more pointedly that he was "not going back to what I left" because "it took me a long, long time to figure out how to enjoy life." Likewise, heterosexuals who had engaged in "liberating" promiscuity during the war most likely became more tolerant of extramarital sex and promiscuity, whether it be on their own part or on the part of others. Indeed, parents of the 1950s and 1960s were far more tolerant of their children than their parents had been of them: they didn't keep their children "in the house" when the teens and even preteens of the 1950s developed the practice of "going steady . . .—a sort of play-marriage, a mimicry of the actual marriage of their slightly older peers," which "implied greater sexual intimacy." Perhaps they understood that their children were turning to intimate relationships for the same reason they had: as an escape from the competition, insecurity, and fear of the postwar era that "perpetuated that classic wartime desire for something stable in an unstable world." [38]

The new postwar attitudes toward sex were but part and parcel of a deeper and broader configuration of ideas about society and the individual. Closely related were new ideas about gender-related violence. The most astute student of the subject reports that social workers in the 1930s "did not accept the assumption that wives owed sexual availability to their husbands, but retained a rather Victorian suspicion of male sexual demands." In particular, social workers saw nothing wrong with wives demanding money in return for sex and refused to condone male violence on grounds of sexual deprivation. In the 1950s, in contrast, the "very complaints that had previously been recorded as allegations of 'sexual excess' were now rendered as evidence of female frigidity," and women who used refusal of intercourse as a weapon to gain control of their husbands' paychecks, or whose refusal led to violence, were condemned. [39]

When the new postwar ethic of sexual indulgence and male privilege was conjoined to the era's more general individualistic assumptions, the moral climate was transformed for everyone, including those who continued to abide by conventional standards of propriety. Picking up on the individualistic rhetoric of "rights" used by President Roosevelt to exhort Americans to victory in World War II, sexual libertines as well as political libertarians typically cast their demands in the language of "rights"; in the case of gay men and lesbians, they even tried to portray themselves as more conventional "minorities" entitled to special legal solicitude. Those searching for individual freedom of all sorts, sexual and otherwise, repeatedly advanced the argument initially formulated by John Stuart Mill a century earlier that "the only purpose for which power can be rightfully exercised over any member of a civilized community, against his will, is to prevent harm to others"; power could not be exercised over a person for his own moral good or "because in the opinions of others, to do so would be wise or even right." As reported in the popular press, the American Law Institute (ALI) agreed: in its Model Penal Code, the ALI adopted the view that the law should not " 'attempt to use the power of the state to enforce purely moral or religious standards' " because it was " 'inappropriate for the Government to attempt to control behavior that has no substantial significance except as to the morality of the actor.' " An individual's choice of sexual or other personal fulfillment, in short, was recognized by the ALI and others as a guaranteed private right and an essential part of the atmosphere of "human freedom" that distinguished life in the United States from the "monolithic totalitarian enslavement" that existed in much of the rest of the world.[40]

The Culmination of Regulatory Power. The most significant expansion of regulatory power ever to receive judicial sanction in American history occurred as a direct result of World War II, when "Congress suddenly assume[d] powers theretofore recognized as belonging exclusively to . . . State[s]." Less than two months after American entry into the war, Congress adopted the Emergency Price Control Act of 1942, which was "declared to be in the interest of national defense and security and necessary to the effective prosecution of the present war." The stated purpose of the act was

> to stabilize prices and to prevent speculative, unwarranted, and abnormal increases in prices and rents; to eliminate and prevent profiteering, hoarding, manipulation, speculation, and other destructive practices resulting from abnormal market conditions or scarcities caused by or contributing to the national emergency . . . ; to protect persons with relatively fixed and limited incomes, consumers, wage earners, investors, and persons dependent on life insurance, annuities, and pensions, from undue impairment of their standard of living.[41]

In pursuit of its goal of protecting from exploitation those weaker economic players least able to cope with the stresses of a wartime economy, the act established the Office of Price Administration (OPA), which regulated the distribution and price of virtually every commodity sold in the nation over the course of the next four years.

Shortly after passage of the federal legislation, the New York legislature created the War Council of the State of New York, which was "to cooperate with the Federal Government by promulgating regulations identical with the Federal regulations and then enforcing these regulations."[42] Pursuant to this state legislation, state authorities joined with federal officials in enforcing the OPA's multitudinous rules and regulations through minor criminal prosecutions and civil suits for injunctive relief and penalties. All told, thousands of judicial proceedings were brought under price control legislation during the war years.

Ultimately, the United States Supreme Court sustained the constitutionality of the 1942 legislation in *Yakus v. United States*.[43] During the two years in which the case was percolating upward, however, the constitutional issue came before state as well as lower federal courts in cases that, with one exception,[44] upheld both the federal and the state acts.[45] As one judge commented, he had "no doubt that Congress . . . may control prices as part of a wartime anti-inflation policy." The Constitution's framers, he added, could never have intended that the Constitution "be construed as a means to help destroy the very nation" through a program of judicial nullification of congressional war policies whereby the war would "be won by our soldiers abroad and lost at home through the destruction and collapse of our . . . economic and financial system." In upholding emergency price controls over dissenting opinions that focused on the "unusual, if not unique" denial of judicial review of agency action written into the legislation, the Supreme Court agreed about the need for "a nation-wide system of price control" to prevent "wartime inflation and the disorganization of our economy from excessive price rises." As Chief Justice Stone added, the "Constitution as a continuously operative charter of government [did] not demand the impossible or the impracticable."[46]

Complementing the system of price controls on commodities was a parallel system of rent controls on both residential and commercial leaseholds. The residential controls were authorized by the 1942 federal act, the constitutionality of which was upheld in a companion case to *Yakus* and in a line of earlier state and lower federal court cases. Controls on commercial property, which were effective only in the city of New York, were imposed by the state legislature after it found during the closing months of the war that "under stress of prevailing conditions accelerated by the present war, . . . a breakdown ha[d] taken place in normal processes of bargaining and *freedom of contract ha[d] become an illusory concept*." Judges also upheld the constitutionality of these commercial rent controls.[47]

As levies rose to finance military operations, the federal income tax became a second mechanism of bureaucratic control. In 1942, the top income tax rate rose to 88 percent on incomes over $200,000 and, in 1944, to 94 percent.[48] Of course, the Internal Revenue Code was filled with countless loopholes designed to induce investors to engage in activities the code favored. Together with high tax rates, these loopholes forced investors to allot their money as the loopholes directed or else watch their wealth dwindle.

Many forms of price and rent controls were gradually phased out in the postwar years, but many regulatory programs of the wartime era were retained.[49] Rent controls remained in place in New York City, and, under the Trading with the Enemy Act, the federal government continued to regulate foreign trade in a wide variety of commodities, including oddities such as hog bristles and postage stamps. Under the Defense Production Act of 1950, the federal government retained residual power, if needed, to set ceiling prices, regulate distribution practices, and require registration of producers. Finally, the federal income tax endured throughout the period under study, with rates remaining essentially at World War II levels until 1964, when major tax reduction legislation brought the top rate down to 70 percent.[50]

With the culmination of the regulatory state, the relationship between government and its citizens—between majorities and minorities and rulers and dissidents—was transformed. For centuries, coercion had been the principal mechanism by which government had secured obedience to its behavioral norms. Under the regulatory state, in contrast, coercion receded into the background. The Internal Revenue Service (IRS), for example, did most of its work through nearly invisible tax withholding procedures and through receipt of filed forms. Only rarely did the IRS commence a criminal prosecution. Instead of confronting its citizens with guns, administrative government offered them an opportunity, typically through collective activity with other citizens, to engage in profit-making activities, provided they obeyed specified behavioral norms. Obedience led to wealth and respect; disobedience led to economic and societal marginalization.

The federal tax laws point to one generic example: they suggest that people who conducted business activities within the confines of tax loopholes and maintained adequate records could become wealthy, whereas those who refused to adhere to the policy preferences of Congress would surrender up to 94 percent of their income. But businesspeople were not the only ones whom bureaucrats could control. Underclasses also were more susceptible to bureaucratic than they had been to police control.

Gay men provide an example of one such underclass. Prejudice, at least against men who flaunt their desire to engage in sexual activity with other men, has been of long standing, but in the early decades of the twentieth century, at least in New York City, government had virtually no resources for punishing or otherwise controlling these men. Private citizens in small towns used devices such as ostracism to constrain behavior they judged deviant, and in New York City groups like the Committee of Fourteen strove to institutionalize an urban regime of surveillance. Nonetheless, even the most flamboyant homosexuals were able to create space for themselves in early twentieth-century New York.[51]

Prohibition—the last of the reform efforts to originate in the nineteenth century—was a grand effort to wipe out sexual as well as other forms of deviance. Prohibition shared the perfectionist character of other movements of its time, like antislavery. Prohibiting the consumption of alcohol, it was thought, would put an end to a series of interconnected evils, in particular the working-class male culture of sociability connected with drinking, under the rubric of which male homosexuality was tolerated. But Prohibition did not have the desired effect, as the weakness of governmental efforts at coercion and the angry public response to those efforts brought the entire social purity agenda into disrepute. "Prohibition resulted instead in the *expansion* of the sexual underworld" and of its publicly visible homosexual aspects.[52]

The new regulatory regime that followed Prohibition succeeded, however, where Prohibition had failed. Its scheme of vesting the state alcohol "control body with genuine discretion" to revoke profitable, state-granted liquor licenses of those who "tolerated or even encouraged" patrons to engage in "gambling, prostitution, and indecent entertainment" transformed bar owners into the allies, however unwilling, of the police and other enforcement authorities. Public enforcement officials no longer had to be present to observe supposed violations of the law in order to stop them; the danger that they might learn of such violations and attempt to revoke or refuse to renew a liquor license threatened the profitability of bar owners and thereby forced the owners to stop the violations immediately. "Revocation of a license not only eliminate[d] the violator who [was] caught but also ha[d] a strong disciplinary effect upon all other licensees in the same community. 'A revocation,' remarked one able administrator, '[was] worth fifty routine inspections,'" and "'the power of revocation,'" according to the New York State Liquor Authority, was "'the most effective'" and indeed "the only law enforcement weapon needed for the elimination of violations by licensees."[53] With the repeal of Prohibition, in short, establishments serving liquor changed from places where behavior that was by definition deviant—namely, serving liquor—occurred whenever public officials were not present to stop it, to places where owners and their employees would put a halt to any behavior they were not confident bureaucrats would condone. Gay men found themselves being watched, in turn, not only when police were present but whenever they entered an establishment holding a liquor license.

Bar owners were scarcely unique in their role as private enforcers of administrative policy. The role, indeed, became a common one in the second half of the twentieth century. Consider, for example, how banks and other mortgage lenders have come to act as enforcers of zoning laws by requiring sellers of real estate to provide a currently valid certificate of occupancy at closings. Managers of regulated industries, like utilities, have similarly come to police business firms with which they do business.

Employment laws dealing with racial and sexual harassment provide yet another example. Many Americans, especially men, engage in behavior that offends women or racial and ethnic minorities. Government makes little effort to control merely offensive conduct when it occurs, for example, in the streets, because no efficient resources of coercion exist to police the conduct. But very different policies have emerged in the workplace, where legislation places liability on firms when their employees misbehave. As a result, firms police employee conduct in an effort to ensure that no one brings a harassment complaint; dealing with such complaints costs money, cuts profits, and thus readily transforms private managers into adjuncts of the administrative state.

Even the legal profession has come increasingly to serve such a police function. Lawyers today do not routinely take matters to litigation but instead settle disputes or advise clients how to avoid legal difficulties. Government plays no direct coercive role in the work of these lawyers, but the behavioral norms which government officials might decide to enforce are always in the forefront of lawyers' minds, and the lawyers take it upon themselves to enforce these bureaucratic norms.

The world of 1955, in sum, differed radically from the world of 1930 for most New Yorkers. As late as 1930, most of the state's citizens still lived in economically, ethnically, and religiously homogeneous communities that watched the behavior of residents and looked with fear and suspicion on strangers. Those tightly knit communities were effective in enforcing their own norms and equally effective in resisting norms imposed by outsiders. By 1955, in contrast, the state's communities had grown more diverse, tolerant of conflicting values, and willing to accept individual choice. But at the same time, administrative agencies and the bureaucrats staffing them had proliferated, and, with these changes in governmental institutions, the power of statewide and national majorities to control minorities and individual dissidents had leaped to new heights.

Regulation through licensing or other government authorization of business activity was simply a more "salutary means of maintaining" social control than "the penal law" had ever been. The reason was that "the mills of the law courts" tended to "grind slowly," with the result that "questionable" activity could be carried on, often at great profit, while its legality was being adjudicated. "On the other hand a word from the licensing authority," in the words of one law enforcement official, usually would "produce . . . immediate results. A warning of impending suspension or revocation of license [was] usually sufficient to secure elimination of objectionable acts or lines since a closure by the suspension or revocation of license mean[t] financial loss." "The desirability" of new bureaucratic tools as an efficient means of enforcing the will of the state was thus "manifest."[54]

Judges as Protectors of Liberty and Equality. But at the same time that bureaucracy was desirable, it also was threatening. Conservatives and reformers alike had become concerned by the late 1930s that a too powerful state posed dangers to liberty and equality. It therefore seemed apparent that, if liberty, equality, and other reformation values were to thrive, some institution of government had to protect minorities and dissidents from the power of majorities and bureaucrats. Proposals that the judiciary assume this protective role began to surface as early as 1938.

The next six chapters will show that New York's judges did, in fact, accept the role of protecting minorities and that, in this role, they finally became the progenitors of social justice that Cardozo had envisioned them to be. In the middle of the twentieth century, no other role made sense. Once America at large during the course of World War II embraced Senator Robert Wagner's view that "the essential governmental problem" of the time was not "how to establish the will of the majority in representative government" but "how to protect the integrity and civil liberties of minority races and groups," legislation no longer appeared, as it had to reformers of the 1920s and the early New Deal, as a source of beneficent social change. On the contrary, in the decade after the war, the legislature "not only lost its mantle of authority but became the very source of the evils the law must remedy, especially racial discrimination" and infringement of individual rights.[55] Only judges who were not beholden to the majority, it seemed, could protect discrete, insular, and powerless minorities and their rights.

In short, the change in the definition of social justice occurring in the midst of World War II transformed the role of judges and, with it, the nature of jurisprudence. For reformers of the 1920s and the early New Deal, social justice had entailed at least some redistribution of wealth. Legislators, especially those from impoverished constituencies, were well suited to the redistribution task, and progressive judges could do little but serve as their helpmates. For conservatives, in contrast, justice had entailed protection of property rights and traditional moral values, and the job of judges, relying on precedent, was to defend this status quo. Clearly, reformers and conservatives did not agree about the judiciary's role.

Once nearly all Americans came to define social justice in terms of protection of minorities from majoritarian power, however, some consensus about the judiciary's role became inevitable. Everyone had to agree that, at least on occasion, judges should step in to protect minority rights. They also had to agree that only judges could decide what occasions were appropriate for their intervention. Finally, they had to agree that the unprecedented task of deciding how to balance majoritarian power against minority rights required judges to determine matters of social policy. As a result, judges supplanted legislators as the main engines of social justice and progressive change. Judges became, as Cardozo had envisioned but never fully realized, progenitors of scientific social reform in the interest of the community as a whole.

Indeed, in their use of common-law adjudication as a tool of reform, mid-twentieth-century judges far exceeded anything Cardozo had imagined. The realist judges of Cardozo's generation, it will be recalled, had regarded themselves as legal craftsmen and not as legislative policymakers; for Cardozo, the duty to abide by precedent narrowly constrained the power of judges and left them with only a limited capacity to shift legal doctrine in socially just directions. In the aftermath of World War II, however, "legal culture changed," and the early realists, "who were at the cutting edge before the . . . War[,] began to look somewhat old fashioned afterwards."[56] Mid-century judges, unlike earlier realists, began to discuss policy openly when they found existing precedent inadequate to their newly assumed task of protecting minorities and rights.

This judicial turn to policymaking was facilitated by the comparative consensus of the decade of the 1950s—a time between the Marxian class conflict of the 1920s and 1930s and the racial, ethnic, and gender conflicts of the 1960s and 1970s. Few matters of social policy were hotly contested during the 1950s by equally balanced political competitors,[57] and on the matters that were not contested by major groups, judges could decide cases on the basis of policy without having to favor one significant interest in the community at the expense of another. Policy could thus serve, at least briefly, as a basis for decision that was as neutral and objective as precedent had seemed to an earlier generation.

In any event, the language and reasoning style of New York judges changed markedly in mid-century. A majority of the Court of Appeals, for example, first used language implying that the court possessed policymaking power of a legislative nature in a 1951 decision, where in response to its "duty to re-examine a question where justice demands it," the judges permitted tort recovery by a child born with injuries suffered as a fetus. The court's rhetoric was totally different from earlier rhetoric of Cardozo, Hand, Llewellyn, and other realist thinkers of their time and fully appropriate to the decade of *Brown v. Board of Education:*

> Of course, rules of law on which men rely in their business dealings should not be changed in the middle of the game, but what has that to do with bringing to justice a tort-feasor who surely has no moral or other right to rely on a decision of the New York Court of Appeals? Negligence is common law, and the common law has been molded and changed and brought up-to-date in many another case. . . . *While legislative bodies have the power to change old rules of law, nevertheless, when they fail to act, it is the duty of the court to bring the law in accordance with present day standards of wisdom and justice* rather than "with some outworn and antiquated rule of the past." [58]

Six years later, *Bing v. Thunig,* which overruled old cases applying the doctrine of charitable immunity to hospitals, broadcast equally stunning rhetoric. It declared the doctrine of charitable immunity

> out of tune with the life about us, at variance with modern-day needs and with concepts of justice and fair dealing. It should be discarded. To the suggestion that *stare decisis* compels us to perpetuate it until the legislature acts, a ready answer is at hand. It was intended, not to effect a "petrifying rigidity," but to assure that justice flows from certainty and stability. If, instead, adherence to precedent offers not justice but unfairness, not certainty but doubt and confusion, it loses its right to survive, and no principle constrains us to follow it.

Similar language continued to appear in the next decade, as the Court of Appeals declared that it was "the duty of the court to re-examine" precedent "if justice demand[ed]"; that it could "not perpetuate an erroneous interpretation of the State Constitution merely because it [was] contained in the reports of this court"; and that the "common law of evidence [was] constantly being refashioned by the courts . . . to meet the demands of modern litigation."[59]

Opinions of lower courts in personal injury, landlord-tenant, and criminal cases took a like approach. Judges wrote, for example, that it was "within the province of the courts to make changes in . . . [a] rule . . . 'itself of judicial making' "; that "courts, while recognizing the great desirability of the principle of 'stare decisis,' . . . [had to] be realistic and look upon the world as it is — and not as it was"; that "the law [was] not static"; and that the "public policy of one generation may not, under changed conditions, be the public policy of another." When "simple right and stark humanity dictate[d]" a particular result in a case but "technicalities bar[red] the way," judges came to have little doubt that the technicalities "should be summarily swept from the table of justice."[60]

By the 1960s at the latest, it had become clear from opinions such as these that the "principle of *stare decisis* rest[ed] more lightly on the shoulders of judges and lawyers . . . than formerly." In the face of "fluid" legal doctrine, many "cases thirty years old, or older, ha[d] been made inapplicable by changed conditions and views." Indeed, the principle "of *stare decisis*" no longer "demand[ed] unyielding resignation to even recent precedent" since "policy considerations" were always "inherent in the prudent, considered application of the doctrine." Since *stare decisis* did not either "enjoin departure from precedent or preclude the overruling of earlier decisions," a court faced with a question whether to depart from past practices always had to inquire whether those practices had "prove[d] unworkable or 'out of tune with the life about us, at variance with modern-day needs and with concepts of justice.' "[61]

The understanding that policy considerations were implicit in the application of precedent to every case meant that judges were inevitably "vested with the power to interpret the law" and thereby fashion it into the best it could be. For those who believed that "society and the individual [had] become enmeshed and paralyzed" in an "ultra-legalistic maze," the pressure was to "harmonize realism with legalism," to interpret "the law . . . in the light of common sense rules . . . as changed conditions and circumstances compel," and thereby to create "a dynamic jurisprudence" that did not "ignore the manner in which economic affairs are conducted" or enforce " 'technical rules' " that had " 'come to eat like rust into the substance of justice' " and led to "justice" being "smothered."[62] A judge with such a perspective could "not use the doctrine of judicial self-restraint as a cover to avoid his or her sworn obligation to enforce the Constitution" or the court's "function . . . to do justice under the law," although judges concerned, in contrast, with "considerations of institutional stability" and with not "venturing into areas" for which they were "ill-equipped to undertake the responsibility" could refuse to "depart from sound precedent simply for the sake of change."[63]

As these statements suggest, even judges who adhered to precedent in the second half of the century did so not because precedent bound them but because it reflected policies which the judges found worthy and just. The cases contain little indication that a large number of New York judges in the 1950s or 1960s adhered to the legal process jurisprudence being developed by Harvard professors Henry Hart and Albert M. Sacks as an antidote to legal realism. Although a few members of the federal bench, notably Henry J. Friendly and Edward Weinfeld, justly earned reputations as careful legal craftsmen, they were unusual judges, and craft was not at the heart of either's jurisprudence. Weinfeld, in particular, was a progressive judge who created much new law, especially on behalf of various sorts of dissidents, and even Friendly, despite his more conservative tendencies and his close tries to Harvard Law School, did not let precedent stop him from creating new law when he thought it appropriate.[64]

Thus a newer legal realism, with its perception that all law requires judges to make policy choices,[65] permeated the thinking of the New York bench after the middle of the century. Almost all judges had come by then to believe that fidelity to the past was outweighed by the prospect of a more free, prosperous, egalitarian, and just future. Most had also become willing to use their power, in an essentially political or policymaking rather than judicial or precedent-oriented fashion, to bring the brighter future to fruition.

For whatever reason, New York judges simply did not behave as the received jurisprudential wisdom would suggest. According to this received wisdom, which is grounded in analysis of academic writings and the opinions especially of Justice Felix Frankfurter on the Supreme Court of the United States, the sociological jurisprudence of the 1910s and 1920s was followed in the 1930s by a more radical realism, which, in turn, was followed by the more conservative legal process school.[66] In New York, however, the guarded progressivism of Cardozo remained dominant into the middle of the century, when, without provoking any conservative reaction whatsoever, a more radical realism recognizing that policy choice is implicit in all judicial decision making became dominant.

It would be foolhardy to attempt to explain why developments in New York differed from those in the Supreme Court and the legal academy. Without knowing more about trends elsewhere in the United States, we cannot even discern whether it was the judges of New York or Justice Frankfurter and the legal process writers who were aberrational.* All that can be said with confidence is that New Yorkers' post-1950 understanding of the nature of the judicial process constituted a complete re-formation of the concept of law. Whereas New York law at the outset of the century had been the embodiment of precedents preserving the existing distribution of wealth and established standards of morality, law after mid-century became the process by which judges decided how to balance the majority's vision of social justice against the liberty, dignity, and rights of minorities. As the next six chapters will show, this reformation of law would spawn dramatic changes in legal doctrine, which, in turn, would lead to significant social change. It is to the doctrinal details of this legalist reformation that we must now turn.

---

* It is worth suggesting, however, that the New York paradigm may provide a better model than the received wisdom for explaining changes in the jurisprudential attitudes of liberal Supreme Court justices during the 1930s and 1940s. Justices Hugo L. Black, William O. Douglas, Frank Murphy, and Wiley B. Rutledge, that is, displayed a quite different realist style than did their predecessors, Louis D. Brandeis and Benjamin N. Cardozo, and arguably the style of Harlan Fiske Stone changed in the late 1930s.

CHAPTER 6

GRADUAL ASSIMILATION AS A CONSTITUTIONAL MECHANISM FOR ENDING INEQUALITY

As we have just seen, the years immediately before, during, and after World War II witnessed new societal realities and a new ideology, in which ethnic and religious discrimination were identified as the paradigms of inequality. Elaboration of this new understanding of inequality did not, however, automatically generate new legal mechanisms for eliminating it. On the contrary, judges initially responded hesitantly to the new egalitarian impulse. They continued to protect underdogs from exploitation and to provide them with opportunity, but in the 1940s and even into the early 1950s, the New York courts, as part of a larger pattern of nonrecognition of novel claims of constitutional rights, refused to hold that individual victims of discrimination possessed any judicially enforceable right to immediate equal treatment.

Still, the courts and the legislature did take steps to assist ethnic and religious minorities and minority institutions, especially churches, synagogues, and parochial schools. The approach they used was to protect the liberty of all, majorities as well as minorities, to move into all communities in the state and thereby obtain entry into the existing mainstream of New York life. Thus, even though the law did not acknowledge the equality of minorities, it did facilitate their assimilation, albeit on condition that minority individuals abandon their own discordant lifestyles and accept mainstream culture.

EARLY JUDICIAL RESISTANCE TO THE RECOGNITION OF RIGHTS

One right that New York courts refused to expand in the 1940s and early 1950s was that of freedom of speech. Even as new attitudes were developing toward urban immigrant groups and the link between them and politically threatening speech was growing increasingly attenuated, New York's judges continued to pursue familiar patterns of repressing speech and political activity which they found even minimally threatening to the maintenance of social stability. In one 1942 case, for example, a defendant in a New York City bar asked "a uniformed sailor in the United States Navy," "What are you doing, fighting? And what are you fighting for? This is a capitalistic war. Why do you want to go out there and fight for a bunch of capitalists? Hitler wants his 'new order,' and Roosevelt has a 'New Deal.' What have you to choose from?" The sailor to whom these words were addressed immediately and without incident "walked away from the defendant," but, shortly thereafter, another man who had overheard the conversation "called a police officer, and caused the defendant's arrest."[1]

These facts created an analytical problem for the court. Since there was no evidence of any violence or threat of violence at the bar, a *Chaplinsky* rationale authorizing punishment for fighting words could not provide any basis for the defendant's conviction. The court had to find another ground on which to rest his guilt. In fact, it found one when it explained in the final paragraph of its opinion, "Courts . . . may place an injunction upon the public expression of seditious statements in a time of war and of national danger which incite or tend to incite disloyalty."[2]

In the midst of McCarthyism a decade later, a plurality of the Supreme Court in *Dennis v. United States,* another case arising out of New York, agreed. Speaking for the plurality, Chief Justice Fred M. Vinson "reject[ed] any principle of governmental helplessness in the face of preparation for revolution" and had no doubt that it was "within the power of Congress to prohibit acts intended to overthrow the Government by force and violence." In concurring opinions, Justices Felix Frankfurter and Robert H. Jackson likewise refused to "hold that the First Amendment deprive[d] Congress of what it deemed necessary for the Government's protection" or to "doubt that Congress has power to make" criminal "advocating or teaching overthrow of government by force or violence."[3]

The *Dennis* case and the case of sedition in the bar were not alone. In another case, the Court of Appeals held that, since the Communist Party had been declared illegal, it would not be permitted to pay unemployment taxes for its office staff and other workers, even though its employees could collect compensation if they found themselves unemployed. Although the United States Supreme Court ultimately modified this weird decision and held that the Communist Party was required to pay unemployment taxes,[4] it nonetheless continued to repress Communism. In a long line of well-known cases during the McCarthy era, it upheld denaturalizations and job deprivations on account of Communist affiliations or refusals to answer questions about those affiliations. Similar results had occurred earlier in regard to Nazi affiliations.[5]

Judges also upheld criminal convictions in picketing cases. In one case, a group carrying placards declaring "No American shall die for Churchill's empire" and "No American Sweat Blood and Tears for a Churchill's World War 3" had picketed City Hall during Winston Churchill's attendance at an official reception in 1946. In another case, which ultimately was reversed by the Court of Appeals, Puerto Rican demonstrators had picketed the United Nations and distributed leaflets declaring that the United States had "committed the crime of genocide" in Puerto Rico. Likewise, a lower court upheld the refusal of the Yonkers Board of Education to allow the Yonkers Committee for Peace to meet in a public school building.[6]

People v. Feiner can also be seen in the context just outlined as a case affirming the right of "the State . . . [to] protect and preserve its existence."[7] Although the Court of Appeals and the United States Supreme Court upheld Feiner's conviction on the finding that his street-corner speech was threatening to provoke violence, it has always been difficult to distinguish *Feiner* on that ground from its companion case of *People v. Kunz,* which reversed the conviction of a speaker whose street-corner antics had in, in fact, led to "trouble." Perhaps what distinguished the cases was the content of the speeches. Kunz made scurrilous statements about Catholics and Jews, whereas Feiner attacked the government. He called the mayor of Syracuse " 'a champaign [*sic*] sipping bum and President Truman a bum,' " and, even worse, he "said that the Negro people did not have equal rights and that they should rise up in arms and fight for them."[8] In addition to attacking officials, Feiner, in short, called for a form of political action that some judges, fearful of race riots, might have found threatening to public order. Such an effort to induce the most repressed of American underdogs to rise up and subvert the established structure of authority simply could not be tolerated by mid-century judges in the name of free speech values.

Judges in the 1940s and 1950s, in short, were no more prepared than their predecessors to protect the right of minorities to freedom of expression. Similarly, New York judges were unwilling to create judicially enforceable equality rights that would provide racial, religious, and ethnic underclasses with immunity from discrimination. While the judges were sympathetic to the goal of equality and would usually enforce legislation designed to bring that goal about,[9] they proved unwilling to grant individual plaintiffs specific rights of equality with others.

In one 1937 case, for example, in which a resident brought suit to keep a black purchaser out of his residential subdivision by enforcing a racially restrictive covenant running with the land, the court granted enforcement of the covenant and thereby decided against the black purchaser. It observed "that the issues in the case [did] not warrant the discussion of abstract social theories" but only "whether a contractual duty, knowingly and voluntarily assumed, [could] be enforced." The result was the same in two similar cases brought during the next decade, when paradoxically the use of restrictive covenants to exclude both racial and religious groups from new residential subdivisions was, in fact, on the rise. Although the more extensive of the two opinions recognized that " 'distinctions based on color and ancestry [were] utterly inconsistent with . . . [the] traditions and ideals' " for which Americans had just been " 'waging war,' " both judges, as late as one year before the Supreme Court decided *Shelley v. Kraemer,* relied on precedents holding that enforcement of racially restrictive covenants involved only private and not state action and therefore was not subject to the prohibitions of the Fourteenth Amendment. As one judge observed shortly before post–World War II realism overwhelmed the New York courts, he was "constrained to follow precedent" despite his own "sentiments," especially in view of the fact that bills to overturn the precedents had been introduced in the legislature but not yet enacted. The court did "not feel that it should judicially legislate by reading into the statutes something which the Legislature itself ha[d] failed to adopt." [10]

A four-to-three majority of the Court of Appeals took essentially the same view in the leading case of *Dorsey v. Stuyvesant Town Corp.,* which was decided one year after *Shelley.* Although Stuyvesant Town, a planned apartment complex, had assembled its land through use of the eminent domain power and had received tax exemptions on its buildings for twenty-five years, the court held it to be a purely private entity left free to discriminate under the state action requirement of the Fourteenth Amendment. The majority expressed its concern that "tax exemption and power of eminent domain [were] freely given to many organizations which necessarily limit[ed] their benefits to a restricted group" and worried that a "grave and delicate problem . . . would be posed if we were to characterize the rental policy of respondents as governmental action." It also noted that legislation to prohibit the discrimination occurring in the case had been introduced in the legislature and failed of passage. That fact, indeed, had led the trial judge in the case to declare that, although "from a sociological point of view, a policy of exclusion and discrimination on account of race, color, creed or religion . . . [was] undesirable," the ultimate "wisdom of the policy" was "a matter for the Legislature," and courts could "not usurp the function of the Legislature" by adding to statutes provisions "the Legislature [had] refused to enact." [11]

Judge Stanley H. Fuld in dissent noted that the tenants of Stuyvesant Town gained "tremendous advantages in modern housing . . . at rentals far below those charged in purely private developments." Since "Negroes as well as white people" had "contributed" through higher taxation to make low rents possible, they were entitled to "share in the benefits." Failure to give them their share amounted to a " 'distinction . . . between citizens solely because of their ancestry,' " which was by its " 'very nature odious to a free people whose institutions are founded upon the doctrine of equality.' "[12]

Another challenge to an allegedly discriminatory ruling of a public body occurred in *Goldstein v. Mills,* which questioned the New York City Tax Commission's grant of tax exemption to Columbia University. The suit rested on a statutory provision that prohibited discrimination by nonsectarian schools and colleges in the admission of students. Goldstein's specific charge was that the City Tax Commission had failed to find Columbia innocent of discrimination. Everyone knew, of course, that Columbia, like most other colleges and universities, did discriminate, especially against Jews and occasional other groups such as Italian Catholics.[13] Indeed, Nicholas Murray Butler, who was still president of Columbia at the time of *Goldstein,* had earlier imposed quotas that had the effect of reducing Jews from 40 percent to 20 percent of the student body. Moreover, at the time Goldstein filed the suit, a committee of the American Dental Association was accusing Columbia's Dental School of admitting too many Jewish students, and the Columbia administration had decided to merge the Dental School, which had no quota, into the Medical School, which did have one. Dental School alumni were publicly complaining that the purpose of the merger was "to establish a quota system for dental students restricting Jewish students," and the American Jewish Committee had launched a nationwide campaign against quotas that discriminated against Jewish and Catholic applicants. Meanwhile, a group of educators had asked President Roosevelt to appoint a committee to work toward the elimination of " 'quotas and other forms of racial and religious discriminations in the nation's colleges," which one member of the group had condemned as a " 'Nazi practice.' "[14] Nonetheless, the court dismissed the *Goldstein* case on various procedural grounds, among them the ground that the plaintiff had failed to allege that Columbia had a discriminatory admissions policy.

Then there was *People v. Bell,* in which four African American males were arrested at a suburban railroad station for loitering and later convicted in a municipal court on evidence that, after they had been in the station for thirty-five minutes, they falsely told the police they had just arrived. Defense counsel argued "that the defendants were denied equal protection" in that they "were selected for prosecution 'for reason of the color of their skin' and that the case ha[d] 'racial discrimination overtones,' " but the county judge hearing the initial appeal found the defense lawyers to be "consumed . . . with indignation over this fancied issue" and also found "nothing in the record" to support "these serious and startling charges." Although the defendants had plainly violated the loitering ordinance, which defined the offense as mere presence without a satisfactory explanation, the judge reversed their conviction by construing the ordinance as not applying to "those who are guilty of mere lassitude or indolence, those overcome by a normal weariness, or indeed those of our citizens who consider themselves students of human nature and who use station waiting rooms as their laboratory."[15]

The Court of Appeals agreed that the ordinance did not apply to people present in a station "in order to meet or to speed the departure of others, to obtain information concerning trains, to purchase tickets, to check or call for baggage or parcels, to buy tobacco, newspapers, magazines or other articles from concessionaires, to use the toilets for purposes for which they were intended, or to be present on other errands whose legitimacy can be decided as the case arises." On the contrary, the ordinance existed "to prevent persons from infesting subway, elevated or other railway stations who have no occasion to be there. The danger to the public is well understood which arises from the congregation of nondescript characters at such locations, particularly at night, where degenerates, or even 'boisterous, noisy cut-ups,' as they are called in the opinion of the County Court, may easily become anything from a public nuisance to a serious menace." On the basis of this bright line distinction, the court found the ordinance "not so vague or indefinite as to render [it] void" and further held that there was no evidence that the defendants had violated it.[16]

The *Bell* case strikes me as one in which judges, themselves guilty of egregious racial stereotyping in referring, for example, to those "guilty of mere lassitude or indolence," were unwilling either to condemn such racism or to allow it to serve as a basis for formal government action. Thus they invalidated particular acts of police racism while at the same time protesting that they were doing no such thing. By this behavior, the judges could achieve justice in the *Bell* case itself and perhaps even send an unspoken message to police forces to alter their practices. Notwithstanding, the New York courts explicitly refused to recognize the existence of racism and likewise refused to create an individual constitutional right to seek judicial relief if one were cast into a subordinate status or otherwise victimized as a result of racial discrimination.

In sum, the early response of the New York courts to lawsuits brought to outlaw racism and analogous ethnic and religious discrimination was not especially uplifting. Something happening immediately before and during World War II and especially during the decade thereafter induced victims of discrimination to demand judicial relief against the various mechanisms of subordination elites used to preserve their hegemony. But New York's judges turned a deaf ear to these claims for equal treatment. Obviously those judges were aware of the history of subordination suffered by African Americans, Catholics, and Jews and the continuing efforts of some to keep them subordinate. In instances in which the legislature had created a specific remedy against discrimination, the courts would dutifully give it effect, and they would also do ad hoc justice in random cases like *Bell*. But throughout the 1940s and into the 1950s the state courts consistently refused to elaborate any legally enforceable right to equality to which individuals could turn in a search for judicial relief if they found themselves victims of discrimination or subordination in the world of prejudice that still surrounded them.

PROVIDING SPACE FOR MINORITIES AND MINORITY INSTITUTIONS

Protecting Religious Liberty. New York's legal system compensated for its failure to confer a right to equality on Catholics and Jews by granting them instead the space and the opportunity to move into the state's social and cultural mainstream. Rather than create a judicially enforceable right to equality for subordinated individuals and groups, the courts adopted an alternative approach that achieved at least religious equality without explicitly proclaiming it. More specifically, the approach was to confer special rights and a special status not merely on Judaism and Catholicism but on all religion—a status that in large part rendered all religion immune from state power and thereby gave minority religions space within which to flourish.[17]

This move toward granting a special degree of liberty to religion began hesitantly and confusedly, however. In one of the earliest cases, *People ex rel. Fish v. Sandstrom*, the Court of Appeals in 1939 confronted "a young girl thirteen years of age . . . associated with, the religious order known as Jehovah's Witnesses" who persisted in coming to school every morning but, once there, refused to take part in "a simple ceremony of saluting the flag . . . with the other scholars."[18] For her refusal, her parents were convicted of violating the provision of the State Education Law requiring them to send her to school.

Before the Court of Appeals, the parents argued that requiring their daughter to salute the flag violated the free exercise clause of the state constitution. Judge Irving Lehman agreed. Although he found "it difficult to understand how any reasonable and well-disposed person can object to such a salute on religious or other grounds," the fact was that "this little child has been taught to believe otherwise." Judge Lehman then continued:

> The legitimate purpose of the salute to the flag is . . . to inculcate love of country and reverence for the things which the flag represents; it may be an aid in teaching good citizenship—but surely not where a little child is compelled in fear and trembling to join in an act which her conscience tells her is wrong. . . . She does not refuse to show love and respect for the flag. . . . She asks only that she not be compelled to incur the wrath of her God by disobedience to His commands. The flag salute would lose no dignity or worth if she were permitted to refrain from joining in it. On the contrary, that would be an impressive lesson for her and the other children that the flag salute stands for absolute freedom of conscience.[19]

The majority of the court agreed that "saluting a flag, even an American flag, [was] of little vital force to the nation unless behind it there is a love and reverence for the things it represents," and hence it wondered whether there might not be "a better way for accomplishing the purposes of this law than immediate resort to disciplinary measures." Writing for the majority, Chief Judge Crane expressed a hope that, if "our fine educational system" placed its "emphasis . . . more upon instruction than mere blind obedience," the child would develop "a reverence for our flag . . . and she will be glad that it is still here to salute."[20] Crane thereupon proceeded to reverse the conviction of the parents on the ground that they had not failed to send their daughter to school, as the lower court had found. But on behalf of the majority, he refused to declare that the legislature lacked constitutional power to enact a mandatory flag salute statute if it chose to do so.

This same hesitancy about creating constitutional rights also appeared in cases dealing with religious tax exemptions. Thus some early cases continued to adhere to the traditional principle that religious "exemptions from taxation . . . [were] to be strictly construed" and granted only if "such clearly appears to have been the intention of the Legislature." Nonetheless, without making any explicit declaration, judges began to display some awareness that denials of tax exempt status might reflect religious bias and to act accordingly. Thus one judge granted an exemption to a Christian summer camp for boys, while someone else in the late 1940s published a decision from 1920 that had accorded exemption to a Christian conference center. Likewise, an interfaith group consisting of Protestants, Catholics, and Jews associated with Hunter College, which was organized to "foster . . . religious idealism in the students and to serve the educational, spiritual, charitable and social needs of the students . . . , without discrimination," was able to obtain an exemption when it purchased the Sarah Delano Roosevelt House from President Roosevelt and devoted it to the quoted purpose.[21]

But the key case was *Williams Institutional Colored Methodist Episcopal Church v. City of New York.* In *Williams,* the city maintained its right to tax on the ground that the church property was owned by an out-of-state corporation—the parent church—and that only in-state entities could receive exemption. Suspecting, perhaps, that adoption of such a rule would penalize African American ecclesiastical groups, the Appellate Division rejected it and instead enunciated a general principle that to "exempt" all church "property from taxation [was] 'scarcely less the duty than the privilege of the enlightened legislator.'" Relying on *Williams,* another case then ruled that property held in New York for the purpose of carrying on overseas missionary work was also exempt. In the judge's view, *Williams* and other cases revealed "the modern trend of thought," which prohibited taxing authorities from reading "into the statute exempting a non-profit 'charitable corporation' their version of who are to be the objects of its bounty or where its bounty is to be dispensed." Charity, according to this judge, was "not provincial," and it knew "no boundaries or classes." [22] Coming as close as any to explicitly recognizing the existence of discrimination and the danger of subordination, this last case demanded respect for all claims of religious tax exemption.

Comparable developments also began to occur in the law of zoning. On the one hand, in occasional decisions courts still upheld zoning policies that were contrary to the interests of a religious institution. On the other hand, the facts of other cases suggested that denials of zoning requests by religious institutions had occurred in the face of discrimination; in such cases, although ethnic discrimination was neither proved nor judicially found, the courts had no difficulty declaring actions by zoning authorities invalid. In one lower court case, for example, a judge found a municipal ordinance "arbitrary and discriminatory in that it exclude[d] churches and places of public worship although permitting uses including village and municipal buildings, railroad stations, public schools and club houses which . . . entail[ed] in an equal or greater degree" the same results that might flow from "the erection of a church." Likewise, an ordinance that "precluded" a church-related college "from erecting any school building in the entire village . . . , while boardinghouses, multifamily houses, hospitals and hotels may be erected," although "schools and churches may not," was declared unconstitutional by the Court of Appeals.

As another judge observed in a suit arising out of the proposed construction of a school attached to the New Hyde Park Jewish Center, "no difference can be perceived in relation to the health, safety, morals and general welfare of the community by permitting public schools and not parochial schools."[23]

The cases culminated in two important 1956 decisions by the Court of Appeals—*Community Synagogue v. Bates*[24] and *Diocese of Rochester v. Planning Board of Town of Brighton.*[25] The significance of the cases, as well as their interconnection, is emphasized by the fact that the New York State Catholic Welfare Committee appeared as *amicus curiae* in support of the synagogue in the first case, while the American Jewish Congress appeared as *amicus* in support of the diocese in the second. Both cases involved analogous attempts by established suburban communities to which Catholics and Jews had migrated in large numbers since World War II to prevent the religious newcomers from building facilities of worship within their borders and thereby to slow the newcomers' influx. In *Bates,* the effort was to prevent a Reform congregation from purchasing and renovating a twenty-four-acre estate that had been used since 1941 as a home for French sailors, as a merchant marine rehabilitation center, and as a U.S. Navy Officer's Club. In *Brighton,* the town wished to prevent construction of a Roman Catholic church and school on "the only suitable property found to be centrally located and available" in a portion of town where the population had "been rapidly increasing" to some twenty-three thousand people, of whom about six thousand were Catholic.[26]

Anti-Catholicism and anti-Semitism were just below the surface in the two cases. In a county where Jews had been kidnapped by Klansmen, where " 'restricted' " communities with few Jewish families existed into the 1950s, and where synagogues had been burned by arsonists or defaced by swastikas, it took little imagination to find anti-Semitism in a chain of events that began when neighbors sued on alleged restrictive covenants to prevent the Community Synagogue from buying one piece of land, continued when the Village Board adopted a zoning ordinance restricting religious uses after the synagogue had decided to buy an existing estate, and ended when, after the repeal of the restrictive ordinance, village authorities still refused to issue a certificate of occupancy for the synagogue. At least one resident of the village, Averill Harriman, in the midst of his successful campaign for governor, found these actions "hasty and shocking . . . unjust, intolerable and un-American" and, although he never explicitly said so, probably prejudiced as well.[27]

In a similar vein, the Diocese of Rochester sensed a danger in the upstate town of Brighton that zoning restrictions might be used "to permit a new church of denomination A and to forbid a new church of denomination B, or to allow denomination A to build a church in a desirable residential location while denomination B was relegated to the wrong side of the tracks." In its *amicus* brief, the American Jewish Congress likewise took note of the danger that a "person or class of persons" might be "singled out as a special subject for hostile and discriminatory legislation."[28]

The Court of Appeals annulled the actions of both municipal bodies in a ruling that a zoning ordinance could "not *wholly exclude* a church or synagogue from any residential district," nor could it "exclude private or parochial schools from any residential area where public schools are permitted." The court, in particular, rejected the argument of the Brighton Planning Board that new churches should not be built in areas that were "almost completely built up" but rather should be constructed only "in areas where future residential development could accommodate itself to a church," as had been the case with the "churches in the town [which] had all previously been built."[29] Although the court did not say so, it probably recognized how such a proposal would disadvantage Catholic and Jewish institutions, which in the mid-1950s were following their people to the suburbs, while having much less impact on Protestant entities, most of which were already well established.

Just as it had in *People v. Bell,* however, the Court of Appeals refused explicitly to recognize discrimination aimed at keeping African Americans, Catholics, and Jews in positions of subordination or to decide the cases before it by granting subordinated individuals or groups an express right to equality. Instead, the court established a broad principle of religious autonomy that "terminated the interference of public authorities with free and unhandicapped exercise of religion" by making it impossible for "a municipal ordinance to be so construed that it would appear in any manner to interfere with the 'free exercise and enjoyment of religious profession and worship.'"[30]

The Court of Appeals and the lower courts reiterated this principle periodically in a long line of tax exemption and zoning cases in the years that followed. A judge who by chance possessed the surname Christ held, for example, that a village could not deny a building permit to a proposed Jewish Center because it would "tend to depreciate the value of property in the neighborhood" and "be detrimental to the neighborhood and the residents thereof." Another trial judge agreed that because "of the worthy purposes and moral value" of churches, "mere pecuniary loss to a few persons should not bar their erection and use," while the Appellate Division took the view that even "potential traffic hazards did not justify the exclusion of a proposed religious use."[31]

At the close of the 1970s, religious institutions in New York thus enjoyed "a constitutionally protected status which severely limit[ed] application of normal zoning standards" and "a legally superior religious privilege" which trumped any mere "annoyance or financial inconvenience" that they posed to a community. To protect "the constitutional right to the free exercise of religion" from any "chilling application of zoning laws," religion was given "to some extent an immunity from significant zoning regulation" and accorded an "all but conclusive presumption that considerations of public health, safety and welfare are always outweighed . . . by the policy favoring religious structures."[32]

The effect of the zoning and tax exemption cases on eliminating anti-Semitic and anti-Catholic prejudice and thereby facilitating the upward mobility of both groups is, however, unclear. On the one hand, suggestions continued to arise that unpopular sects were victimized by discrimination in cases involving zoning as well as tax exemption. Congregation Beth El of Rochester explicitly claimed discrimination. The fact that a YM and YWHA in suburban Westchester County was not granted a permit to hold music and dance classes in a building previously used for other, unidentified classes by the Veterans of Foreign Wars suggests that discrimination may have been occurring in that case as well. Similarly, the occurrence of four reported cases involving zoning and tax exemptions for Hasidic Jews during the single year of 1979 from the New York City suburban town of Ramapo, which a decade earlier had routinely granted a special permit for the construction of a Masonic Temple, is suggestive of anti-Semitism.[33]

On the other hand, those who watched the developing case law carefully— namely, municipalities and the lawyers who represented Catholics and Jews involved in litigation against them—must surely have understood that houses of worship and parochial schools could be neither excluded from town nor denied tax exempt status. At the very least, the religious zoning and tax cases constituted symbolic statements that religious and ethnic discrimination had gone out of style. Perhaps, the right to maintain religious buildings actually facilitated the construction of those buildings, which, in turn, may have facilitated the migration of white ethnics from urban ghettos into suburban communities, where they interacted with their new neighbors and the old barriers against them came down.

Education. Education was a second judicially sanctioned vehicle to facilitate the upward mobility of children of the immigrant classes and thereby provide the space within which they could move toward assimilation into the economic and cultural mainstream. Many Catholic and Orthodox Jewish children were educated in parochial schools, and those who were not often participated in release-time programs that permitted them to leave public school during class time so that they could receive religious instruction. State aid to parochial schools, together with governmental authorization of the release-time programs—programs uniformly favored by Catholics and supported by some though not all Jews [34]—contributed enormously to the upward mobility of both these children and their parents. These aids to religion, like the judicial decisions facilitating the construction of synagogues and Catholic churches in suburban communities, enabled white ethnics to pursue secular advancement without abandoning their traditional religious values.

The New York legislature regularly voted considerable sums of money in aid of religious education. State financial support was granted, and the grants were upheld by the courts after World War II, for such purposes as student transportation, provision of textbooks in secular courses, reimbursement of parochial schools for state-mandated testing and recordkeeping,[35] and remedial teaching for handicapped or disadvantaged parochial school students. Aid to religiously affiliated colleges that taught religion was also granted and upheld, as long as religion was taught "as an academic discipline" that focused on "the sources and development of the Judeo-Christian tradition and the religious heritage of the world" and "no denominational tenet or doctrine [was] taught in the manner of dogmatism or indoctrination." The New York legislature was prepared to go even further when it adopted programs to help parochial schools to maintain and repair their physical facilities and to grant tuition reimbursement and tax relief to parents who sent their children to parochial schools, but the Supreme Court held these programs unconstitutional.[36]

The state's legal system also displayed symbolic support for religion in general and for Catholics and Jews in particular. A powerful symbol of the equality of immigrant with WASP religion arose out of the judicially approved construction on public land at Kennedy International Airport of three chapels—one Catholic, one Jewish, and one Protestant. Other concessions to religious symbolism occurred when judges approved the addition of the words "under God" to the Pledge of Allegiance and the religious matching of adopted children with adoptive parents. Special concessions to Roman Catholic piety included judicial approval of the placement of nativity scenes on public property, as well as the upholding well into the 1970s of the constitutionality of Sunday closing laws. The New York Court of Appeals would also have upheld mandatory prayer in the public schools. Finally, in deference to traditional common law and constitutional doctrine, judges continued to rely on ecclesiastical law in resolving disputes between rival factions when a schism or analogous property dispute occurred within a church.[37]

The central conclusion of the two preceding sections, at this stage, bears repetition. The first section showed that New York courts were unwilling during the 1940s and 1950s to recognize the existence of a judicially enforceable right to equality. Nonetheless, as the second section has shown, those same judges decided cases in ways that protected the religious liberty of all and thereby facilitated efforts by Catholics and Jews, the two largest groups seeking equality, to push their way into the societal mainstream. The judges, we might say, thereby advanced the goal of equality even while denying the right.

On what terms, however, did the judges presuppose that egalitarian interaction would occur? It is to this question that we now turn.

As we shall see, the support the courts gave for religious liberty did not license religious or other minorities to celebrate or invigorate their cultural differences. American ideology in the post–World War II era did not envision a multicultural society in which former immigrant groups would perpetuate their distinctiveness. Rather, public discussion of intergroup relations, reflecting the nationalism and unity concerns of the war years, came to be dominated by an outlook that was tolerant but at the same time strongly assimilationist. Immigrants and their children were invited to abandon their ethnicity and move upward into society's mainstream, but only when they accepted the mainstream's lifestyle, melted into the mainstream on its terms, and became in the process "true Americans." They, in turn, eagerly accepted the invitation; as the American Jewish Committee declared, what we now call multiculturalism was "antagonistic to the basic tenets of the American Creed." The "preservation of all that we cherish," the committee continued, "all that is summed up in the word Americanism, depend[ed] upon the achievement of national unity." A leading Catholic theorist agreed that America was "an Anglo-Saxon country," and he accordingly urged all immigrants "unyieldingly to stand for" "two things at the very least, . . . a common *language,* and a universal *American Public School* for our children." Even if "conformity to American life . . . means our *racial self-effacement,*" he urged immigrants not to "begrudge our gift." In short, Protestants, Catholics, and Jews agreed, in the language of a popular song which inquired, "What is America to me?" that the proper answer was "All races, all religions, that's America to me," at least when those races and religions were blended into one.[38]

While subsidizing religion in the many ways noted above, state education law strongly endorsed this assimilationist and integrationist vision. It required that every child receive an education that met minimum state standards—

standards designed to convey skills essential for participation in the market-place but even more to inculcate the value system of a tolerant but neverthe-less deeply American America.* Most significantly, the courts would not allow any child to be exempted on grounds of religious belief from state-mandated requirements.

Thus, when a group of Jewish families sent their children to a parochial school that did not give "systematic instruction [in English] in the ten com-mon branches and other courses of study required by . . . the Education Law," they were held in violation of the law. The court declared that it was "more important . . . that all children within the realm of our democratic society shall receive a basic secular education in the English language . . . than that . . . religious convictions" be honored. "Secular law" had to "take precedence over the religious law, where the interests of a democratic society clearly re-quire[d] compliance with the secular law," as they did in the case of "secular education," which had "become a fundamental part of our system of society." As the court explained, secular education was "designed to give equality of op-portunity to all children in a society dedicated to the democratic ideal." The court added that "without equality of opportunity in education there" could be "no equality among the children of our democratic society," and some chil-dren would be prejudiced in their ability "in later life . . . to take their rightful place in civil society." [39]

Not only did the courts require that all children receive a basic secular edu-cation that would prepare them for the marketplace; they also upheld curricu-lar requirements that exposed students to established cultural canons, even when those canons reflected the discriminatory past of Anglo-American cul-ture. The key case that approved what amounted to cultural indoctrination was *Rosenberg v. Board of Education of City of New York.*[40]

Rosenberg challenged the Board of Education's adoption of Dickens's *Oliver Twist* and Shakespeare's *The Merchant of Venice* as approved reading in the city's high schools. These two works, it was urged, were "objectionable because they tend[ed] to engender hatred of the Jew as a person and as a race." Even the Board of Education had recognized this tendency and accordingly had "expressly required teachers to explain to pupils that the characters described therein [were] not typical of any nation or race, including persons of the Jew-

---

*As one educated during the late 1940s and 1950s in a series of New York public schools with a student body that was coincidentally one-third Catholic, one-third Jewish, and one-third white Protestant, I cannot attest strongly enough to the lasting impact of the State Education Department's liberal, tolerationist ideology.

ish faith," and thus were "not to be regarded as reflecting discredit on any race or national group." One wonders, however, at the effect of this explanation; like a cautionary instruction to a jury to ignore evidence it ought never to have heard, the teacher's explanation might have emphasized the very religious stereotyping in which, it was alleged, Dickens and Shakespeare were engaging and thereby further insulted and degraded the Jewish students who had to listen to it. By being stereotyped, and then by having the stereotype analyzed and discussed in their presence, Jewish students, it appears, were subjected to what was, at the very least, an unpleasant experience to which Christians were not subjected, and thereby treated less favorably than and, in a sense, subordinated to Christians. It is, indeed, difficult to "see how," especially after a teacher's admonition, "a Jew [could] read *The Merchant of Venice* without pain and indignation." [41]

Rosenberg thus was presented as a simple equal rights case, in which a victim of discrimination was seeking to enjoin the state from selecting and inculcating in the public mind symbols that were degrading and insulting to her. But the court did not so understand the case. In language as insulting as that of Dickens and Shakespeare, the judge held that the "public interest in a free and democratic society" did not warrant the suppression of a literary classic "at the whim of any unduly sensitive person or group," merely because "a particular race or religion is portrayed in a derogatory or offensive manner." "Removal from schools of these books," moreover, would "contribute nothing toward the diminution of anti-religious feeling"; according to the trial court, "public education and instruction in the home [would] remove religious and racial intolerance more effectively than censorship and suppression of . . . works of art." [42]

Three important lessons can be teased out of the *Rosenberg* opinion. First, the case unearthed an important issue—essentially today's issue of hate speech —that had been framed in the struggle between Jews striving to attain equality in the face of symbolic degradation and a WASP elite intent on maintaining at least its cultural hegemony through the schools. Second, this issue was one for which an equal rights jurisprudence provided no answer. Thus in the *Rosenberg* case, either Jewish interests, as understood by the Jewish plaintiff, had to be subordinated to the preservation of the established cultural tradition of which *Oliver Twist* and *The Merchant of Venice* were a part, or the cultural tradition had to be truncated and subordinated at the behest of Jews. No way existed for the court to honor equally the established tradition, aspects of which appeared to insult and degrade Jews, and the Jewish perception that the tradition was insulting and degrading. Third, insofar as the result in the case accurately reflected what higher courts would have done,[43] the outcome made clear what we have already observed: that the maintenance of cultural hegemony trumped the goal of uplifting the urban immigrant underclasses. The best that groups like Jews, Catholics, and African Americans could expect from the law was the removal of specific coercive barriers to their participation in the political and economic life of the society. Equality meant, at most, that they would be invited to abandon their ethnicity and move upward into society's mainstream. But they would have to accept the mainstream's existing lifestyle and cultural norms, even if those values and norms degraded and prejudiced them. For the law, as explicated in cases like *Rosenberg,* would not change culture and thereby end all racial, ethnic, and religious subordination. Prejudice could be eliminated and equality attained, it was said, only through private efforts and education and ultimately through the emergence of a new cultural tradition that did not rest on racial, ethnic, and religious hierarchies.[44]

Judges continued to promote upward mobility of religious minorities into the societal mainstream, conditioned, at times, even on their surrender of sectarian religious and cultural beliefs, in a line of cases requiring compulsory vaccinations as a prerequisite to entering public schools. As one judge declared when he rejected a mother's claim of religious conscience and ordered her child seized and vaccinated, the mother's refusal to vaccinate had made the child a ward of the court "to be helped, protected, and accorded the opportunities that an enlightened community affords—provide the child with the necessary guidance and education to fit him to adjust in society and carry forward the progress for an adequate life." In analogous cases, when parents refused to allow their children to undergo needed medical treatment, courts routinely ordered provision of the treatment. In the one reported case in which a trial judge refused to compel surgery, a minority on the Court of Appeals was prepared to reverse the judgment below in the belief that "every child [had] a right, so far as possible, to lead a normal life" and that religious scruples could not be permitted to stand in the way of that right and thereby "ruin his life and any chance for a normal and happy existence." The majority, recognizing that there were "important considerations both ways" and that it could "not be certain of being right under these circumstances," affirmed only because it thought it wisest to defer to the trial judge, who was closest to the facts. In general, though, bureaucratic regularity triumphed over religious scruples, as when a court refused to grant extra money to a welfare recipient to enable her to buy more expensive kosher food.[45]

The constitutional ideology of the 1940s and 1950s reflected in these cases —an ideology that might be labeled assimilationist equality—remained dominant as late as the 1963 decision by the Court of Appeals in *People v. Stover*. The *Stover* case had begun in 1956, when the Stovers, as a " 'peaceful protest' against the high taxes imposed by the city," hung a "clothesline, filled with old cloths and rags," in their front yard "in a pleasant and built-up residential district" of suburban Rye. As taxes were increased, so were the number of clotheslines, until by 1961 there were six, "from which there hung tattered clothing, old uniforms, underwear, rags and scarecrows." The city of Rye thereupon adopted an ordinance that prohibited clotheslines in front yards unless it issued a special permit because of " 'a practical difficulty or unnecessary hardship in drying clothes elsewhere on the premises.' " [46] After the city had refused to grant the Stovers a special permit and they had refused to remove their clotheslines, they were convicted of violating the ordinance and their conviction came before the Court of Appeals.

The lone dissent of Judge John Van Voorhis captured one view of American constitutionalism. The starting premise of Van Voorhis was that "protection of minority rights [was] as essential to democracy as majority vote. In our age of conformity it [ought] . . . not [be] . . . the instinct of our law to compel uniformity. . . . The right to be different has its place in this country. The United States has drawn strength from differences among its people in taste, experience, temperament, ideas, and ambitions as well as from differences in race, national or religious background." Wishing to protect the rights of minorities and the even more fundamental, related right to be different, Van Voorhis refused to condone "unlimited power in government to . . . compel . . . conformity" — a "power to rule" which "open[ed] the door to the invasion by majority rule of a great deal of territory that belongs to the individual human being." Seeing the Stovers as a minority that had been bested by "other residents in the area" in a "dispute . . . evidently political in nature," Van Voorhis would have overturned their conviction for their "unusual idea" and their unusual "form of protest." [47]

All the other judges on the court, in contrast, took the position that protection of the Stovers' "bizarre" conduct was inconsistent with values central to their understanding of American democracy. The vision of the majority, unlike that of Van Voorhis, was not a multicultural vision that celebrated differences in racial, national, or religious background. The majority's goal, instead, was to induce everyone to internalize the "sensibilities of the average person" and ultimately become fully equal participants in " 'an attractive, efficiently functioning, prosperous community.' " While it appreciated the value of free speech that furthered "the dissemination of ideas or opinion" resulting in prosperity or some other enhancement of community, it saw nothing inappropriate with legislation "designed to proscribe conduct which offends the sensibilities and tends to depress property values." The majority saw no "message" but only "offensiveness" in the " 'protest' " of the Stovers and therefore refused to accord it protection under the free speech clauses of the state and federal constitutions.[48]

In its approval of efforts to nurture a common sensibility and to discourage conduct by minorities that might prove offensive to majorities, the court's opinion in *Stover* powerfully encapsulated the great egalitarian event of the previous two decades, when Catholics and Jews had shed their immigrant identities, assumed the sensibility of their former WASP oppressors, and in the process become full and equal participants in political and economic life, at least in New York. *Stover* thus was deeply grounded in a constitutionalism that tolerated upward mobility by underdogs into the mainstream elite as long as the underdogs assumed the elite's values of civility and toleration.

In the end, judges in New York responded somewhat strangely to cases seeking their support in stopping discrimination against Catholics and Jews. They never took a simple approach of articulating a general constitutional or common-law right on which groups or individuals could rely to protect themselves against religious and ethnic discrimination or subordination. Instead, they issued a strong proclamation that all religious groups enjoyed rights to religious freedom that trumped ordinary police power regulations, and they approved a wide variety of state aid to religion that gave Jews and especially Catholics important tangible and symbolic support.

Meanwhile, the very meaning of equality was changing. In nineteenth-century America, equality had meant "equality of freedom" rather than "equality in the sense of achieving distributive justice."[49] The Catholics and Jews who were seeking assimilation into the New York mainstream in the mid-twentieth century did not base their efforts on this nineteenth-century conception of equality. On the contrary, their efforts began in the 1920s—a decade during which equality was not a politically robust idea—with notions of non-exploitation and opportunity. Nonexploitation and opportunity are principles of distributive justice, although they are not, as we saw in Chapter 3, principles of equality. Of course, they tend in the direction of equality, in that they demand a closing of the gap between elites and underdogs in regard to matters of power and wealth, and when the concept of equality as a prohibition against ethnic and religious discrimination came back into vogue in the years beginning in 1938, it became easy to merge nonexploitation, opportunity, and nondiscrimination into a new conception of equality demanding the elimination of gaps in wealth and power among various ethnic and religious groups.

With the merger, a new conception of equality as distributive justice entered into American legal thought, and the descendants of immigrant Catholics and Jews, in return for abandoning the freedom to adhere to their ancestors' life-styles, ceased to be victims of exploitation, took advantage of the opportunity to climb upward, and attained practical socioeconomic equality.

It is not surprising that the courts, in the face of this complexity, failed to respond directly to demands for a formal, legally enforceable right to equality. One obstacle to responding was the ambiguity inherent in the demands for equality as the concept of equality changed in response to ideological and soci-etal pressures during the 1940s and 1950s. But an even greater obstacle may have lain in the difficulty of formulating judicial remedies capable of achiev-ing an equal distribution of wealth and power. Judges find it feasible to order government to regulate groups in a nondiscriminatory fashion; they can, for example, strike down statutorily imposed racial segregation. New York judges, beginning in the 1920s, also were able to modify common-law doctrines to en-hance individual opportunity. Finally, the judges knew exploitation when they saw it, and they were able to apply doctrines like contract unconscionability to thwart it. But though it is possible to refuse to enforce occasional con-tracts that result from grossly unequal bargaining power or that strike judges as manifestly unjust, it is not possible for judges to insist that all contract-ing parties should have equal bargaining power or that all contracts should distribute resources equally. At best, judges probably can do only what mid-twentieth-century New York judges did: they continued to end exploitation when it came to their attention, they continued to mold doctrine to enhance individual opportunity, and they took steps, like freeing religion from regula-tion, that contributed to upward social mobility. But they left to society itself the task of achieving an ultimately just distribution of wealth and power.

CHAPTER 7

GRADUAL ASSIMILATION AS AN ECONOMIC MECHANISM FOR ENDING INEQUALITY

Constitutional law was not the only mechanism in the postwar era by which New York moved toward greater equality through the assimilation of Catholic and Jewish descendants of turn-of-the-century immigrants. Legislative and judicial modification of rules dealing with fundamental economic matters—educational opportunity, housing, and business relationships—also promoted assimilation and equality. As had been true with the constitutional doctrines we have just examined, legislators and courts in addressing these economic matters did not create any explicit rights to equality but merely pushed the law in the direction of equality with rules promulgated for other purposes.

FUNDING EDUCATIONAL OPPORTUNITY

Historians already are familiar with some of the developments detailed in this chapter, notably the educational opportunities created by the federal government through the GI Bill of Rights for veterans returning from World War II. Although President Roosevelt might have intended the veterans program as a device to promote equality, he made no effort to sell it to Congress in that fashion; rather, he presented it as a weapon against postwar unemployment and a mark of appreciation to the troops. There is no question, however, that the GI Bill procured education for millions of mainly white, male veterans who otherwise never would have received it and thereby brought them into the social and economic mainstream.[1]

CREATING SUBURBAN HOUSING

Arguably, an even more important step in bringing Catholic and Jewish immigrants and their descendants into the mainstream was to remove them from substandard housing in urban ghettos and place them in decent housing in ethnically and religiously integrated communities.[2] The process began when the federal government, private lenders, and real estate developers, in the aftermath of World War II, lowered the cost of mortgages and thereby made suburban housing extremely affordable, in certain instances even less expensive than renting a crowded apartment in the city.

Before World War II, mortgage financing was difficult to secure, particularly for working-class families. Private financial institutions maintained prohibitively strict lending rules, especially in regard to down payment requirements and maturity provisions. Most banks were compelled by law to require a 40 percent down payment, with the result that families seeking to purchase a home would need savings equivalent to a year or more of their wages to enter the housing market. Of course, few Americans possessed such savings. Moreover, the maximum length of conventional mortgages until the middle of the century was only fifteen years. Finally, home mortgage interest rates between 1920 and 1934 fluctuated only minimally—between 5.8 and 6.2 percent—although they declined during the course of the late 1930s to 5.0 percent.[3]

After World War II, mortgage financing became both more affordable and easier to obtain as the federal government, to stimulate residential housing construction, took an active role in the mortgage credit market. In 1944, Congress authorized the Veterans Administration (VA) to guarantee residential mortgages obtained by returning veterans, and at the end of 1945, it amended the Servicemen's Readjustment Act of 1944—that is, the GI Bill—to encourage the VA loan guarantee program. The amendment doubled the maximum guarantee amount from $2,000 to $4,000 and extended the maximum maturity on mortgage loans to twenty-five years. Moreover, qualified lenders were authorized to grant VA-guaranteed loans to eligible veterans without first receiving approval from the VA. Finally, the Veterans Administration gave mortgages without requiring any down payment to nearly half of all applicants.[4]

Similarly, the Housing Act of 1948 amended the terms of the Federal Housing Administration (FHA) mortgage insurance program to increase maximum insurable loan amounts and the length of time for repayment, while also lowering required down payments. Additionally and perhaps most important, the 1948 act increased the ability of the Federal National Mortgage Association, otherwise known as Fannie Mae, to purchase federally underwritten home mortgages. Chartered in 1938, Fannie Mae merits special attention since its secondary market operations directly subsidized the residential mortgage market, keeping conventional mortgage interest rates under 5 percent between the end of the war and 1953 and close to the 4 percent VA rate and the 4.25 to 4.5 percent FHA rate during those years.[5]

Next, the Housing Act of 1950 raised the ceiling on the maximum insurable amount of VA loans from $4,000 to $7,500 and increased the guarantee from 50 to 60 percent. Most important, the Housing Act of 1950 first authorized the thirty-year mortgage for VA-guaranteed loans. The thirty-year FHA loan was first authorized in 1954, and thirty-five-year mortgages were later authorized in some cases. In response to these liberalizing provisions in federal legislation, the average maturity for a VA or FHA mortgage on a new home increased roughly ten years during the period from 1946 to 1967. By 1965, the average maturity of a FHA mortgage was 31.7 years, compared with 21.0 years in 1946. VA mortgage maturities, which averaged 19.8 years in 1946, grew to 29.4 years in 1965.[6]

The loosening of government regulations regarding maximum maturity length also encouraged conventional mortgage lenders to grant mortgages with longer payment schedules. The average maturity of conventional loans for new homes increased from 14.3 years in 1950 to 25.4 years in 1967, although conventional mortgage maturities remained noticeably shorter than that for government-backed mortgages in every year.[7] This lengthening in average maturity significantly affected mortgage affordability because mortgage payments fall as the length of the mortgage rises.

This high degree of government participation in the mortgage market influenced both directly and indirectly the affordability and terms of private mortgages available to American families in the wake of World War II. Between 1945 and 1956, the amount of outstanding residential mortgage debt in the United States rose from $23.3 billion to $112.1 billion, an increase of 381 percent.[8] VA-guaranteed and FHA-insured mortgages became the primary method for working-class American families who otherwise would not have been able to secure mortgage financing from private lenders to escape the overcrowded cities and relocate to the suburban countryside.

The federal income tax code also helped create a dramatic preference for home ownership over rental housing. The deduction for mortgage interest payments provided a lucrative subsidy to the suburban housing market by reducing the after-tax cost of purchasing a home. Although the mortgage deduction was part of the 1916 tax code and still exists today in modified form, its importance increased when the average tax rate increased dramatically during World War II. Before the war, when even the highest marginal, much less average, tax rates were comparatively low, the deduction minimally favored home owners over renters. In 1916 the highest marginal tax rate was only 13 percent, which itself applied only to gross income over $2 million. When federal income tax rates increased in the 1940s to a top marginal rate of 94 percent on incomes in excess of $200,000, however, the importance of the deduction as a subsidy of home ownership grew.[9]

In addition to the mortgage interest deduction, homeowners received a variety of other tax benefits, such as a deduction for state and local property taxes and an exemption from including imputed rent—the "market value of the housing services produced by [their] property"—in taxable income, even though imputed rent represents income in a very real sense. In contrast, rental payments for apartments have never been deductible and thus must be paid in after-tax dollars. Today, the mortgage interest deduction, along with other provisions such as the property tax deduction and the special treatment of capital gains resulting from the sale of residential real estate, costs the federal treasury approximately $80 billion annually.[10]

The net effect of all government activity was to make the cost of owning a home comparable to the cost of renting an apartment for the great mass of postwar New Yorkers. With government activity, monthly mortgage payments compared favorably to monthly rent payments. Thus at the end of the 1940s, when ordinary apartments in New York City were renting for as much as $60 and $70 per month, the tax-deductible monthly mortgage payment on a new house in Levittown, which sold for $7,900, was only $42.66 per month with no down payment.[11] With such subsidies, city dwellers could not afford to refuse a move to suburbia, and many Catholic and Jewish immigrants and their children, in fact, did move.

Nonetheless, when they moved to the new suburbs, many Catholics and Jews faced discrimination. The earliest response to this discrimination occurred in 1945, when New York State became one of the first states in the nation to enact a modern civil rights statute prohibiting racial, ethnic, or religious discrimination in a variety of contexts. Although the 1945 act did not deal explicitly with the purchase or sale of real property, it nonetheless established a basic principle of racial, ethnic, and religious nondiscrimination. Another important development occurred in 1948, when the New York Court of Appeals, in response to the U.S. Supreme Court's decision in *Shelley v. Kraemer*, invalidated the use of restrictive covenants, thereby removing one of the principal means of excluding racial, ethnic, and religious minorities from residential communities.[12]

UPWARD MOBILITY THROUGH THE COMMON LAW

Legislative programs providing educational and suburban housing opportunities were not the only steps taken by the law in the aftermath of World War II to encourage the entry of Catholics and Jews into the social and economic mainstream of New York. Courts also modified common law doctrine in ways that facilitated economic opportunity and hence the upward mobility of New York's ethnics. This section focuses on three areas of doctrinal change—the law of contract, the law of commercial torts, and the law of fiduciary relations.

Contract. We have already seen how judges in New York, beginning with Cardozo, altered the law of contract to accommodate the needs of national and international businesses centered in New York City rather than the needs of upstate, small-town entrepreneurs. These changes continued into the post–World War II era and ultimately were codified in the Uniform Commercial Code, which became effective in New York in 1964.

Among the most important provisions of the code was section 1-203's imposition of "an obligation of good faith" in the performance of all duties governed by the code, which it defined in the case of a merchant to include the "observance of reasonable commercial standards of fair dealing in the trade." The drafters of the code assumed "that the essential purpose of a contract between commercial men is actual performance and they do not bargain merely for a promise, or a promise plus the right to win a lawsuit," and hence the statute approached matters as "practical issues between practical men" and "require[d] the reading of commercial background and intent into the language of any agreement and demand[ed] good faith in the performance of that agreement."[13] This approach was worked out in detail in many sections of Article 2, such as the series between section 2-305 and section 2-311 authorizing managers to enter contracts with open terms and to fill in the terms at a later time in a commercially reasonable fashion.

No judge ever declared that the purpose of the new law of contract was to provide Catholic and Jewish descendants of immigrants with economic opportunities that would enable them to enhance the quality of their lives and move upward economically. Nonetheless, the UCC did compel entrepreneurs to deal fairly not only with people of their own community but with those in the rest of society as well. Under the code, the people of upstate, rural New York had to deal with the people of the city on the basis of commercial standards common to both rather than the parochial norms of the one or the other. By facilitating large-scale, often downstate enterprises in which Catholics and Jews gained increasing prominence during the second half of the century, the new law of contract, in effect, subsidized the descendants of turn-of-the-century immigrants and thereby helped catapult them, as we shall see in Chapter 12, into positions of considerable wealth and power.

Commercial Torts. On other subjects, in contrast, judges strove explicitly to enhance business efficiency, freedom of opportunity, and hence upward social mobility. One such subject was the law regulating business torts. As we saw in Chapter 4, that law neither prevented exploitation nor conferred opportunity during the early 1920s. Indeed, as Judge Harold J. Hinman had noted in dissent in the 1922 case of *Beardsley v. Kilmer,* America was supposed to be "a land of opportunity, as well as of free competition in business," but it instead had become "a land of oppression" when the *Beardsley* majority allowed "a man who [was] wealthy enough and malicious enough . . . [to] shut the door of opportunity to the object of his hatred by rivaling him in business, with no other aim in view than his destruction."[14] Judge Hinman expressed his belief that the law would change, and in a matter of years, change did begin to occur, albeit only gradually, as new judges drawn from Catholic and Jewish immigrant groups, which traditional moral views grounded in hostility to coerced redistribution of wealth had effectively disadvantaged, began to focus less on protecting established wealth and more on the competing value of entrepreneurial opportunity.

Privacy was one of the first areas of law in which this change of focus occurred. So as not to impede entrepreneurial business activities, lower courts began giving a narrow interpretation to the civil rights law, from which the right to privacy was derived, as early as the late 1920s. At the end of that decade, they began ruling that the legislation did not always prohibit publication, even "in connection with advertising or trade," of "matters dealing incidentally with specific persons and concerning things of current interest." "Every unauthorized use of a name or picture in connection with trade or advertising [did] not imply a violation of the statute"; were "it otherwise, many lines of business would have to be abandoned."[15]

Concerns for freedom of opportunity and the related value of business efficiency also became manifest in the law of conversion in the 1930s and triumphant in the decades thereafter. Initially, those concerns merely limited the judiciary's willingness to hold innocent entities strictly liable in conversion. Thus, in a 1932 case, the Court of Appeals declined to hold a bank liable for a fiduciary's conversion of funds, with Judge Lehman observing that " 'the transactions of banking in a great financial center are not to be clogged, and their pace slackened, by overburdensome restrictions.' "[16]

In subsequent, mid-century cases dealing with the law of conversion, traditional values of business morality simply disappeared from the law's calculus. Two cases, which arose out of the breakup of employment relationships, involved a refusal by former law partners to allow a partner leaving the firm to take his books and office equipment with him and a former employer's breaking into the former employee's office and searching his files. Another case with an "acrimonious history" was *Merrick v. Four Star Stage Lighting, Inc.*, in which "a well-known stage producer" sought to repossess stage lighting equipment from a business that had provided and stored it. A final conversion case suggestive of how the breakdown of traditional patterns of ethical behavior brought litigants to court occurred when a bank, serving as an executor, had mistakenly delivered rings belonging to a different estate to an heir named Fries, who was unaware of the mistake, sold the rings for cash, and then spent it. Two years later, the bank discovered the mistake and demanded return of the rings, but Fries, declining to abide by a traditional ethical concept of not keeping property that was not rightfully his, refused to return them. The bank then sought reimbursement from its insurance company, which paid for the loss and then, unmindful of its insurer's duty to pay for losses that could no longer be readily undone, sued Fries to recover the cash. With the suit, the ethical dilemmas of whether an heir ought to keep a windfall to which he was not entitled but had already spent and whether an insurance company should cover a loss that had produced a windfall for another were transformed into a narrow, doctrinal problem of whether, for purposes of the statute of limitations, conversion had occurred when Fries had received the rings, sold the rings, or refused the bank's demand for their return.[17]

The doctrines that proved most sensitive to change, however, were those involving prima facie tort and interference with contractual relations. Around 1960, the judiciary's enthusiasm for these doctrines began to wane. The first clear sign of this waning enthusiasm was a 1958 Court of Appeals case, in which the organizer of the Cancer Welfare Fund had sued the well-known reporter, columnist, and commentator Walter Winchell and the New York philanthropist Elmer H. Bobst for inducing various public officials to investigate and ultimately destroy public confidence in the Cancer Fund so that it could not remain as an effective competitor for Winchell and Bobst's Damon Runyon Fund. In a decision from which no one on the court dissented, Chief Judge Albert Conway agreed that the "law [was] now settled" that an " 'act done solely out of malice and ill will to injure another *may* be actionable.' " But that was "not to say," Conway continued, "that the present state of the law is that an act . . . will, without exception, become actionable when it is done with . . . blameworthy purpose." There were always "reasons [why] a court [might be] constrained to ignore the wrongful motive of an actor," such as "the paramount consideration of the public welfare." Thus, whenever a claim was made, either in a prima facie tort or in an interference with contractual relations case, "that an otherwise lawful act ha[d] become unlawful because the actor's motives were malevolent," it was necessary "to analyze and weigh the conflicting interests of the parties and of the public." [18] Upon doing so in the case at hand, the Court of Appeals unanimously dismissed the plaintiff's suit.

In the next case that came before the Court of Appeals, the plaintiffs claimed that a prima facie tort or interference suit would " 'lie in favor of any whose contractual expectations ha[d] been indirectly injured by socially undesirable conduct' " when " 'the injury was foreseeable by defendant.' " Observing that under the plaintiff's "theory it might well be argued that, anytime a debtor refused to pay a creditor, the creditors of that creditor would have a cause of action against the debtor for interfering with the contract between the debtor's creditor and this creditor's creditor," the court concluded that " 'the law [did] not spread its protection so far' " and that "nothing but . . . confusion [could] be accomplished by allowing this suit to continue." [19]

Lower courts agreed that "the law of tortious interference with economic relations" was not always "based on sound logic" and that its "parameters" were "not . . . clearly defined." Because the scope of the tort was "limitless, there [was] danger that its unrestricted use [might] lead to grave abuse and unwarranted claims." Although courts recognized that prima facie tort and comparable doctrines had "proved useful in assisting the development of needed reforms" as "new relationships and power groupings formed, and continuously reformed, in the business world," they nevertheless thought it "unwise" to continue moving doctrine beyond "established . . . guidelines." [20]

This about-face in judicial attitude did not mean, of course, that no one recovered for prima facie tort or for interference with contractual relationships. Still the change in judicial approach produced dramatic transformations in doctrine. Thus, in several cases in the 1960s and 1970s, judges reached results that were precisely opposite those that other judges had reached a few decades earlier. [21] Far more important was the transformation that occurred in underlying policies. Whereas the classic law of the 1920s and 1930s had reflected adherence both to a policy of promoting competition and to traditional moral views grounded in hostility to coerced redistribution of wealth, the new law of the 1960s and 1970s was concerned solely with freedom of opportunity and upward social mobility.

In the 1960s and 1970s, judges spoke of "the policy of fostering free enterprise" and of a person's right "to advance his own economic self-interest." They recognized "that the mere occurrence of damage to a business resulting from competition carried on in good faith [did] not give rise to a cause of action" and looked upon a desire to increase profits as "sound economic policy when dealing with one's own property." Thus they refused to sustain prima facie tort claims and frowned on suits for interference with contract rights when a defendant " 'had a valid business interest to protect' " or believed "that an employee who sought to frustrate the decisions of the organization employing him had outlived his usefulness." One judge even went so far as to urge that " 'each business enterprise must be free to select its business relations in its own interest' " and that, under New York law, it was " 'well-settled . . . that the refusal to maintain trade relations with any individual is an inherent right which every person may exercise lawfully.' " [22]

The issues underlying the transformation of prima facie tort doctrine and the law of interference with contractual relations emerged with greatest clarity in *Guard-Life Corp. v. S. Parker Hardware Manufacturing Corp.*, a case decided by a closely divided Court of Appeals. The three dissenters in *Guard-Life* contended that "the *raison d'etre* of the law of interference with contractual relations" was " 'the ethical precept that one competitor must keep his hands off of the contracts of another.' " In their view "the law ha[d] decided, long ago, that enforcement of certain market morals [was] a societal interest worthy of protection." "If society were interested only in fostering economic competition," they added, "the tort of contractual interference would never have developed," and "the law would have allowed business entities to engage in unfettered competition." [23] It was in pursuit of moral values that the dissenters were prepared to keep teeth in the law of contractual interference.

The four-judge majority, in contrast, was hostile to classic doctrine, which it found "inconstant and mutable, drawing its substance from the circumstances of the particular situation at hand." The majority was especially hostile to making "the result hinge on the subjective . . . state of mind of the parties" or on the related "ethical considerations . . . urged by the dissenters as having a bearing." Above all, the majority was "concern[ed] that competition not be unduly hampered." [24]

By allowing concern for competition to trump ethical considerations, *Guard-Life* resolved the contradiction implicit in *Al Raschid* and its progeny. *Al Raschid,* as we have seen, was ambiguous, seeking both to protect the weak from exploitation and to provide them with competitive opportunities to improve their well-being. By the time of *Guard-Life,* nearly half a century later, however, the linkage between nonexploitation and opportunity had broken apart. Judicial imposition of business ethics to prevent exploitation had come to be at war with freedom of opportunity and upward social mobility. At that point, the Court of Appeals majority let its concerns for opportunity and mobility override established precedents calling for the enforcement of morality.

In the second half of the twentieth century, concerns for freedom of opportunity and upward mobility also triumphed over the nineteenth-century norms of personal and business morality that had lingered into the first half the century as a motive force for legal change in fraud doctrine. Thus judges refused with increasing frequency to grant relief in fraud cases between spouses and in other familial contexts. Cases outside the marital and family context also confirm the suggestion that traditional moral standards were beginning to erode and that the law was beginning to place less weight on ethical values of honesty and full disclosure. In one 1946 case, for example, where a defendant had claimed, allegedly contrary to the facts, to be "an honorable person . . . able to facilitate negotiations with" a particular foreign government, the court had refused to impose fraud liability declaring that "bare assertions of personal honor and of ability . . . [could not] constitute actionable fraud." [25] As early as mid-century, it seems, the value of advertising one's business capacities had already come to outweigh the older moral values that had underlain the classical law of fraud.

Only a few cases in the second half of the century pushed in the direction of protecting the moral and distributional values underlying classical doctrine. Judge Henry Friendly, for one, did declare "negligence sufficient for tort liability where a person supplies false information to another with the intent to influence a transaction in which he has a pecuniary interest," and a Brooklyn Civil Court judge held that a buyer of an automobile had to pay the unpaid portion of the purchase price even though the dealer thought the price had been fully paid because it was "no longer acceptable . . . to conclude[,] in knowing silence, a transaction damaging to a party who is mistaken about its basic factual assumptions." Quoting *Prosser on Torts,* one Second Circuit opinion even declared that "a representation made with an honest belief in its truth may still be" actionable "because of lack of reasonable care in ascertaining the facts . . . or absence of skill or competence required by a particular business or profession." [26]

But this policy of prohibiting dealmakers from exploiting each other went too far, and most judges, led by the Supreme Court of the United States, would not follow along. The Supreme Court, in a leading 1980 decision, reversed the Second Circuit and refused to recognize "a general duty between all participants in market transactions to forgo actions based on material, nonpublic information" because "such a broad duty . . . [would] depart radically from . . . established doctrine" as well as from the essential underpinnings of an entrepreneurial, capitalist economy. A capitalist entrepreneur having "the opportunity to obtain knowledge of the facts" simply could "not sit idly by to reap the harvest, if plentiful, but in the event of scarcity, charge fraud." [27] With this holding, the values of honesty, full disclosure, and not allowing property to be taken without the informed consent of its owner—the values on which classic fraud doctrine had rested—were trumped by concerns for business opportunity and upward socioeconomic mobility.

The Law of Fiduciary Duty. Like the law of commercial torts, the law of fiduciary duty initially began the 1920s as a body of doctrine enforcing traditional ethical norms grounded in concerns about preserving the existing distribution of wealth, then deployed those norms to protect the weak from exploitation, and finally found the policy of nonexploitation at odds with the goal of providing economic opportunity. At that point, beginning in the 1940s, the policy of providing economic opportunity and thereby facilitating upward mobility triumphed. This policy, which dominated fiduciary law thereafter, was articulated with remarkable explicitness by Jack Weinstein, an eminent federal judge, when he explained a few decades later that "many managers of large enterprises . . . [were] men of relatively limited financial resources who [had] risen quickly and recently through the technical ranks because of their skill and optimism" and that "rule[s] of law too restrictive and inflexible may overinhibit and dampen their drive without providing gain to the investor."[28] Weinstein wanted nothing to limit the upward mobility of these men of limited means—often the sons of immigrant Catholics and Jews who had started out with little capital and were working their way up the ladder of business success.

Like Weinstein, other judges in the latter part of the century gave money managers increased freedom to use and invest funds as they saw fit, subject only to the requirement that they use due care in making investment choices. Although courts did not dramatically alter the black-letter rules of fiduciary doctrine, they did begin during the course of the 1940s and thereafter to apply them in a more pragmatic fashion that was increasingly sensitive to the entrepreneurial needs both of fiduciaries and of beneficiaries. In particular, the courts grew more tolerant of higher-risk investment practices of entrepreneurial fiduciaries who were seeking to increase income or grow principal and less concerned with insuring the security of investments.

The 1947 case of *Washer v. Seager,* with its stated refusal to "exalt form over substance," set the tone of pragmatism and preference for entrepreneurship to which judges increasingly adhered in subsequent decades. For approximately two years, Washer and Seager had been the two sole shareholders and the officers and directors of a clothing manufacturing company. "Seager had furnished the business skill and ability; Washer was financier." When Seager decided in 1943 to break with Washer and enter the same business with another firm, Washer brought suit for breach of the duty of loyalty. The court, however, reasoning that Washer was "attempting to . . . establish a right to share indefinitely, as an inactive partner, in Seager's business ability, skill and enterprise," ruled that Seager was free to leave one firm and use his entrepreneurial skills to enter into competition with it on behalf of a new firm.[29] In so ruling, the court expressed its emerging preference for encouraging entrepreneurs to use their skills to promote their own upward mobility as well as the economy's growth, even at the expense of rentier capitalists seeking investment security.

Other cases agreed that an employee had "the right to leave" his employment, "establish his own business, solicit" his former employer's "customers and compete . . . in free enterprise, unless he were either contractually restricted from doing so or some fraud or unfair competition were involved." A director or employee also was free, at least in the absence of a specific agreement to the contrary, to work for another employer and even to deal in competing products. As the court said in another case of an employee opening his own business, "Plaintiff was simply pursuing the normal American dream of bettering himself by going out on his own, and he did it without harming defendant in any way. . . . Much as I sympathize with defendant's unhappiness over being deserted by his partner, together with his sole and valued salesman, the Court cannot be a party to solacing that unhappiness with plaintiff's earnings."[30]

Another doctrine which the courts in the 1940s began subtly to transform dealt with the appropriation by majority directors of business opportunities belonging to their corporation. The turning point was *Blaustein v. Pan American Petroleum & Oil Transport Co.*, where Supreme Court Justice Samuel I. Rosenman presided over a seventy-day nonjury trial. At issue was whether Standard Oil of Indiana, which owned nearly 80 percent of Pan American's shares, had deprived Pan American of profitable opportunities to drill and refine oil. Applying the traditional principles of *Meinhard v. Salmon* and the 1933 and 1934 securities acts that "equity . . . demands of a trustee undeviating loyalty to his beneficiary" and that a "fiduciary is forbidden to enter a situation where personal interest will conflict with the interest of his principal," Rosenman held that the directors of Pan American had diverted its business opportunities to Standard and thereby had breached their fiduciary duty.[31]

The Appellate Division reversed. It found that Pan American's directors had acted "in good faith and in the exercise of their honest judgment," on the advice of counsel and without profit to themselves, and thus had not breached their duty as fiduciaries. The Court of Appeals agreed. Although Judge Irving Lehman in dissent concluded that Pan American's directors, all of whom were officers or directors of Standard or its other subsidiaries, had acted at the direction of and on behalf of Standard and therefore were in breach of their duty to Pan American when they diverted its business opportunities to Standard, the majority shared the Appellate Division's view that "questions of policy of management, expediency of contracts or action, adequacy of consideration, lawful appropriation of corporate funds to advance corporate interests, are left solely to the . . . honest and unselfish decision" of directors who, provided they act "in good faith and the exercise of an honest judgment" without personal gain to themselves, fulfill their fiduciary duty.[32]

Two months after the Court of Appeals decision in *Blaustein,* the Appellate Division decided *Turner v. American Metal Co.* Like *Blaustein, Turner* was a case in which several individuals held officerships or directorships on both a parent and its subsidiary corporation and thus faced conflicts of interest. The Appellate Division declared, however, that "the mere existence of such a divided loyalty did not, of itself, warrant the imposition of liability against directors." In view of the parent's large financial stake in the subsidiary, the Appellate Division stated that the parent's officers and directors "not only had the right but were under a duty to act as directors [of the subsidiary], rendering such services as were necessary." The court continued that they "committed no wrong in entering into reciprocal arrangements for the supplying of information and technical data and for the exchange of routine services beneficial to both companies."[33]

It is noteworthy that in the *Blaustein* case two judges closely associated with the New Deal—Samuel Rosenman, who had been counsel to Franklin Roosevelt during his governorship,[34] and Irving Lehman, the brother of New Deal governor Herbert Lehman—both stood by traditional notions of fiduciary duty with their emphasis on high ethical standards, avoidance of conflict of interest, and nonexploitation of minority shareholders. In the final *Blaustein* and *Turner* decisions, in contrast, most of the New York judiciary leaned in the direction of enhancing the entrepreneurial freedom of business managers at the possible expense of fully equitable treatment of investors inactive in corporate governance. These decisions thus had a striking parallelism to cases like *Washer v. Seager.*

Another doctrine that tended to enhance entrepreneurial freedom at the expense of investor equity was the business judgment rule, which was fully elaborated only in the 1940s. In the first case of significance, the Court of Appeals held that an international union had properly chartered a new local union in rivalry with an existing local. The court reasoned unanimously that the decision to grant a new charter "was within the discretion and business judgment" of the international board, even though it "may have been discriminatory" in regard to the existing local.[35] Although this case raised labor law rather than corporate law issues, the court in its decision deployed the language of business judgment in a fashion precisely analogous to that in which future corporate cases would use it.

In the next case, a divided Court of Appeals addressed the issue whether a board of directors of a mortgage salvage corporation could sell the corporation's only asset—realty obtained pursuant to a foreclosure—without shareholder approval. Three judges, including Chief Judge Lehman, who, it will be recalled, had dissented in *Blaustein v. Pan American* out of concerns for equity to minority shareholders, voted in favor of requiring shareholder approval as the only means by which minority shareholders could protect their interests. A four-judge majority, however, applied the business judgment rule and held, on the ground that the corporation's divestiture of the asset "manifestly was a sale in the regular course of its business" that the sale required nothing other than the good faith approval of the board.[36] Again, the managerial freedom of entrepreneurs had triumphed at the expense of protecting minority shareholders.

Meanwhile, lower courts were reifying doctrine. Thus the First Department wrote in 1941 that as long as "a director exercises his business judgment in good faith on the information before him, he may not be called to account through the judicial process" and that a minority shareholder seeking to call directors to account had "to allege facts showing more than error in business judgment." Three years later, a trial judge wrote that "there [could] be no quarrel" with "the business judgment rule, so-called, and . . . [the] numerous authorities standing for the proposition that a court [would] not substitute its judgment for that of duly constituted officers and directors." By the time a trial judge refused to enjoin the departure of baseball's New York Giants to San Francisco on the ground that no one could "question the efficacy of a business judgment of the Board of Directors," the business judgment rule had become an accepted part of New York jurisprudence[37] and a Court of Appeals case, *Kalmanash v. Smith,* had been identified as its source, even though that case referred only to the concept of the rule and not to any specific language. Thereafter, the business judgment rule was cited with frequency, and it even made some appearances in trusts and estates, as distinguished from corporations, cases. Although it is difficult to be certain about the significance of attaching the label of the business judgment rule to a practice judges had been following throughout the early decades of the century, the label probably did matter by giving judges a better basis than they previously had possessed for declining to enforce the duty of loyalty, with its focus ultimately on issues of equity between shareholders, and instead deciding cases "on the practical basis" that entrepreneurs should be left free to manage corporations efficiently—an approach leading to enforcement only of the duty of care.[38]

Other cases likewise favored entrepreneurial efficiency and its attendant policy of upward mobility over protection and nonexploitation of investors. Judges fostered the upward mobility of entrepreneurs with a variety of holdings—that a corporate officer or director, if acting in good faith, may profit from dealings with the corporation if the corporation also profits; that the directors of a corporation in the process of acquiring another corporation need not disclose all their plans for using the acquired corporation to enhance the acquirer's profits; and that, in the absence of loss of corporate funds or of personal profit to itself, management could authorize a corporation to purchase its own stock in the open market in order to perpetuate management's control. The courts also bent traditional rules of fiduciary duty to facilitate the accumulation of start-up capital for new enterprises and to create new institutional arrangements, such as agents for actors, needed for particular industries to function.[39]

Thus just as the law dealing with commercial torts had grown more supportive of entrepreneurial opportunity over the course of the twentieth century, so too did the law of fiduciary duty. The change in fiduciary law, however, was less dramatic, and the resolution of the contradictions between ancient moral standards, concerns about preventing exploitation, and the policy favoring entrepreneurial freedom was more ambiguous. In large part, the ambiguity was a product of two still unrepealed statutes—the Securities Act of 1933 and the Securities Exchange Act of 1934—adopted during the early New Deal. Although federal judges came to view the antifraud provisions of the federal securities laws not as spurs to business honesty and morality but as mechanisms for "providing investors with all the facts needed to make intelligent investment decisions," the two statutes still embraced disclosure mechanisms, administrative regulations, and ultimately civil remedies designed to guard against insider manipulation of capital markets, and a massive body of law creating safeguards for investors far superior to those extant under the common law of fiduciary duty had matured under them.[40]

But, in conclusion, the main policy of the law of fiduciary duty—the policy of promoting economic opportunity, upward mobility, assimilation, and ultimately equality—must be emphasized. New Yorkers reached a judgment in the era of World War II that they were not Nazis and that New York would be different from Germany. They consciously rejected the bigotry that Hitler proclaimed and determined that all their citizens would be permitted to enter the mainstream of New York life.

This judgment was reflected in the work of legislatures and courts as they addressed issues both of constitutional law and of the law regulating economic transactions. Conceiving of discrimination mainly in religious rather than ethnic or class terms, judges laid down the constitutional principle that every religious denomination must be free to minister to the needs of its congregations. But judges and legislators both knew that religious freedom alone would not produce socioeconomic equality. When their legacy is examined in retrospect, it appears that they also understood that achieving equality among religious and ethnic groups would require education, suitable housing in non-segregated settings, and jobs generating a decent standard of living, as well as religious freedom.

Thus the legal system set out to provide education, housing, and jobs for all, but particularly for the Catholic and Jewish descendants of turn-of-the-century immigrants, who were perceived as the largest groups in New York victimized by prejudice and discrimination. Congress subsidized college education for virtually an entire generation of white men, while the state left religious groups free to provide primary and high school education for their children and, to some extent, even subsidized their efforts. State legislation and federal decisional law prohibited housing segregation, and Congress enacted massive subsidy programs that moved millions of Catholics and Jews from ethnic neighborhoods in New York City and upstate cities into newly constructed suburbs. Programs from the closing years of the New Deal, such as the Wagner Act and the Fair Labor Standards Act, helped to protect jobs.

The novel insight of this chapter, however, is the role played by state common law in promoting economic opportunity, upward mobility, and ultimately assimilation and equality. As this and earlier chapters have shown, judges often confront a choice when they address common-law issues: they can resolve a case in a fashion that will protect the established distribution of society's wealth, or they can tilt the law in the direction of enabling upwardly mobile entrepreneurs to seize some share of that wealth. In the early part of the twentieth century, as we have seen, the courts routinely favored existing wealth holders. In mid-century, in contrast, they favored the frequently Catholic and Jewish entrepreneurs striving to move upward. Relying on this favoritism, which constituted a form of judicial subsidization, and on other forms of legislative subsidization, the Catholic and Jewish descendants of turn-of-the-century immigrants to New York, over time, became equal.

CHAPTER 8

THE PREVENTION OF INJURY

As we saw in Chapter 4, accidents and physical injury were inevitable parts of life in early twentieth-century New York. However, the emphasis on ideals of human dignity and equality, which emerged in the late 1930s, transformed ancient assumptions. In particular, emerging public attitudes about the value of life and physical well-being affected how the American military establishment prepared for World War II.

SAVING SOLDIERS' LIVES

Military planners fully understood that the American public would place a high value on soldiers' lives and would not accept the high casualty rates to which the Allies and Germans had grown accustomed in World War I. Accordingly, the planners developed protocols for reducing injury and especially death in battle. War had always been an opportune occasion for illness, injury, and death, but the American military, "believ[ing] that American soldiers were sustaining avoidable casualties," changed all this in World War II, reducing deaths from approximately one in every ten men under arms during the Civil War to about one per hundred in the 1941–45 war.[1] More important for present purposes than the reality of this accomplishment was the public's awareness of it, which resulted from a comprehensive propaganda campaign focusing around two main themes: that with proper training few men would be injured, and that with proper medical treatment, death could be largely eliminated and most of the injured could be nursed back to health.

The military, believing that an "army . . . [was] most sparing of human lives when its training [was] soundest," reiterated its "determin[ation] that if combat should ever come, the soldier of today will be prepared for it, and will not be a needless casualty." It told soldiers that when they got "to the front," they would "be so well trained that" they could "count" their "chances of survival very high."[2] In addition to teaching basic skills, two objectives were an especially important part of military training.

The first was to teach every soldier to be part of a team. In particular, the army focused on "the 'buddy' relationship"—"a cohesive unit built around the minimization of risk; a buddy was a person a soldier felt he could rely on in case of danger." The second objective was to teach soldiers "to act calmly with sound judgment regardless of noise, confusion, and surprise." Military planners believed that raw "trainees" had a "tendency . . . to neglect" their duty "during the excitement" of battle, and they set out to correct the tendency through realistic training simulations and through explicit teaching of a training course entitled "Protection against Carelessness." The military knew that "Uncle Sam's soldiers must be alert" members of "an alert team" to function efficiently and avoid casualties. The twenty-two million veterans of the wartime and postwar military, along with some significant portion of the American public, accordingly were told repeatedly that, when soldiers "get careless, . . . there are tremendous . . . casualty rates." [3]

The military also made much of its efforts to reduce not only battle injuries but also the number of deaths resulting from injuries and illness. It promised that "hundreds of thousands of men, who would have died in any previous war, won't die in this one," and new medical developments, in the form of drugs such as sulfa and penicillin, of blood transfusions, of new surgical techniques, and of new methods for delivering medical help, often made the promise come true. The experience of World War II convinced most Americans that they were living "in an age and land of medical miracles" and that medicine now "offer[ed] the means for modern man to have life . . . abundantly." Thus whenever illness persisted or premature death occurred, there was reason to conclude that the "loss" could have been "either prevented, alleviated, or cured." [4]

These new attitudes about death and injury wrought a complete transformation of the law of tort in the post–World War II years. During the 1920s and 1930s, much of the law for remedying personal injuries reflected an accommodation between a traditional paradigm of tort liability, which permitted compensation to be paid only when a person was injured directly by another's wrongful act, and a newly emerging reform paradigm, which held that victims of injury should receive compensation from some source. Although personal injury law moved during the 1920s and 1930s in the direction of the reform paradigm, the totality of personal injury doctrine remained in equipoise. As the 1930s came to a close, much doctrine derived from the older paradigm thus remained in place, despite a decade of efforts by judges like Cardozo to change it.

World War II marked a watershed in tort law and ultimately in the elaboration of tort doctrine. For one thing, a statistically significant increase in tort litigation began to occur in 1946. Personal injury cases rose from 8.69 percent of all civil filings in the sample for 1945 to 14.46 percent in 1946, and from

12.71 percent of all filings in the ten-year period 1936–45 to 18.30 percent during the ten years beginning in 1946.[5] The median value of tort verdicts stated in 1955 dollars rose from $2,982 during the earlier decade to $6,000 during the later one.[6]

No equally sharp increase occurred in the number of underlying injuries. Automobile highway deaths in the United States, for example, were the same in 1948 as in 1930—about thirty-two thousand per year. Neither can the increase in the number of tort cases be explained on the theory that plaintiffs sued more often because they were more likely to win their cases after than before 1945. On the contrary, plaintiffs enjoyed greater success during the earlier decade, winning 79 percent of jury verdicts during the 1936–45 decade and only 70 percent during the 1946–55 decade. Changes in insurance law also seem not to have been a determinative variable: the key change in New York— a requirement that all operators of motor vehicles have compulsory insurance or comparable financial security—did not occur until 1956.[7]

Finally, the increase in tort litigation beginning in 1946 does not appear to have resulted from doctrinal changes beneficial to plaintiffs. The great transformation of tort doctrine resulting in a body of pro-plaintiff law occurred chiefly during the 1960s and 1970s in New York, and thus pro-plaintiff doctrinal changes surely could not have caused the post–World War II increase in tort litigation. On the contrary, the doctrinal changes occurred after the litigation rise and may even have been produced by it, as judges brought formal rules into harmony with broad public and professional attitudinal changes.

It would seem, therefore, that the experience of the war itself contributed to the increase in tort litigation, as the lessons about injury and death learned from World War II were transferred from military to civilian contexts. In short, the remarkable victories of World War II over illness, injury, and even death convinced the American people that their "destinies" were not "written in the stars and beyond mortal control" but were, "in large part, subject to [their] own volition." Americans had learned that they were "not the passive objects" of fate "but the active manipulators of . . . [the] forces" of nature and that they could control those forces if they faced them "with courage, determination, and calm intelligence." [8]

World War II recast Americans' vision of society from one where "insecurity was inherent" and perhaps even "useful, for it drove men . . . to render their best and most efficient service" by visiting "severe punishment on those who did not," to one backed by "a complete system of governmental security." "Social fatalism . . . vanished" with the war, as Americans grew "less willing to suffer hardship, . . . unemployment, pollution, or inadequate health care," and more "confident . . . that these problems can be solved and risks can be avoided." In the post–World War II period, the received societal wisdom came to be that "no individual [should be] allowed to suffer the consequences of . . . personal disaster"; if "an ever growing array of untoward events" arising from "faulty products, . . . criminals, . . . acts of nature, . . . misconcocted serums" and the like could not be prevented, they ought at least to be the subject of insurance and, if they occurred, compensation.[9]

A faith that calm intelligence could reduce personal disasters and injuries to an optimal level did not seem absurd to a generation that had entered World War II "drifting about aimlessly" in "an environment marked by hopelessness, lack of opportunities and a sense of failure" but had come out of the war convinced that it had "faced the test of mastering a historic challenge—and succeeded." Postwar Americans "felt themselves to be standing at the threshold of a promising new era" in which the "sense of wonderful possibilities ahead kept breaking into every part of living." In the language of the future Chief Justice Fred Vinson, who in 1945 was director of war mobilization and reconversion, the American people were "in the pleasant predicament of having to learn to live 50 percent better than they have ever lived before," while Chester Bowles, the last wartime director of the Office of Price Administration, promised that Americans had to "all learn to live constantly better, a lot better" with "unlimited opportunity for health, recreation and good living . . . an end to poverty and insecurity."[10] Using tort law not to make a statement about social justice but to provide people with the optimal balance of health and good living was a small part of the postwar American dream.

REFORMING TORT DOCTRINE

The New York Court of Appeals explicitly verbalized these emerging, postwar cultural values, which in many ways mirrored the goal of prewar reformers of increasing compensation for injuries. In *Philpot v. Brooklyn National League Baseball Club, Inc.,* for example, the court reiterated an old dictum that "one who collects a large number of people for gain or profit must be vigilant to protect them" and held that the Dodgers had not been sufficiently vigilant in protecting a spectator from being struck by a broken glass bottle. In later years, the court declared that "the policy of this State has been to reduce rather than increase the obstacles to the recovery of damages for negligently caused injury or death" and took note of "the broadening of tort liability concepts to reflect economic, social and political developments."[11]

Concerns that injuries be reduced and that victims of injury receive recompense also produced important changes in specific legal doctrines. Judges overruled traditional doctrines of municipal and charitable immunity and held municipalities and charities, such as hospitals, fully liable for the torts of their servants. Another change occurred when the Court of Appeals clarified previously ambiguous doctrine and held parties strictly liable for blasting and other ultrahazardous activities. The court also facilitated recovery of damages for injuries by ruling that wives as well as husbands could sue for loss of consortium and by easing the procedural process by which plaintiffs who had recovered judgments could collect them from companies that had insured defendants.[12]

Most of the doctrinal changes just noted were achieved quickly and easily, usually through the medium of a single Court of Appeals decision. Other changes in the law facilitating recovery for injuries, in contrast, occurred much more slowly and through complex processes often involving doctrinal infighting.

One subject of gradual judicial change was the law of product liability. Unlike the California Supreme Court, the New York Court of Appeals during the middle of the century did not assume a leadership role in expanding consumers' remedies for product defects. *MacPherson v. Buick Motor Co.*, authored by Cardozo in 1916, had placed New York in the forefront of remedial expansion, but during the next four decades New York courts engaged in "judicial curtailment of the . . . [*MacPherson*] doctrine" and were "shackled by meaningless technicalities."[13] As a result, little liberalization of product liability law occurred in New York until the 1960s.

Many of the old limitations on *MacPherson* were restated and reaffirmed in the leading 1950 case of *Campo v. Scofield,* where a farm worker using an onion topping machine had his hands mangled when they were drawn into steel rollers lacking any guard. In affirming the Appellate Division's dismissal of the complaint, the Court of Appeals first reiterated the rule that, in the absence of "privity of contract between the defendant manufacturer and plaintiff," suit could not "be sustained on any theory of implied warranty" but only on a theory of "negligence." It then declared that, while it might be desirable "to equip complicated modern machinery with all possible protective guards or other safety devices," failure to do so would not constitute negligence; the effectuation of "so fundamental a change," it added, was "the function of the legislature rather than of the courts."[14]

A first small sign of change occurred in 1957, however, when the Court of Appeals declared that "there is no visible reason for any distinction between the liability of one who supplies a chattel and one who erects a structure" and accordingly authorized suits even in the absence of privity against those who had designed or constructed buildings as long as negligence on their part could be shown.[15] The authorization was mere dictum, however, since the court dismissed plaintiff's complaint for failing to allege facts required to make out a claim of negligence.

A more important extension of doctrine occurred two years later, when a middleman was held liable to a plaintiff injured by an exploding soda bottle even though, as the dissent observed, the middleman "was neither the manufacturer nor the assembler of the finished product, which was not sold to the public on his name or reputation," and the operation the middleman performed "had nothing to do with the accident."[16] This decision had little precedential impact, however, because it merely affirmed without opinion an Appellate Division order,[17] which, in turn, had without opinion affirmed a trial court judgment rendered without opinion.

The causes of this judicial hesitancy emerged with sharp clarity in *Greenberg v. Lorenz,* where a fifteen-year-old girl had been injured by a metal sliver packed in canned salmon which her father had purchased for her at her request. She sued the retailer who had sold the can of salmon. Established law made it clear that the girl could not recover against the retailer on a negligence theory because the retailer was not negligent, nor for breach of implied warranty because she had no privity of contract with the retailer. Nonetheless, the "injustice of denying damages to a child because of nonprivity" seemed to the court "too plain for argument." Indeed, the "unfairness of the restriction ha[d] been argued in writings so numerous as to make a lengthy bibliography," and some "20 States ha[d] abolished . . . privity." *Greenberg v. Lorenz* was as "convincing a showing of injustice" as could be imagined. Still the court wanted to "be cautious and take one step at a time," since there were "two sides to the problem" and any broadening of liability, as the court had decided only a decade earlier in *Campo v. Scofield,* "must be left to the Legislature." It was "just as unfair to hold liable a retail groceryman . . . innocent of any negligence . . . for some defect in a canned product which he could not inspect and with the production of which he had nothing to do" as to deny relief to an innocent consumer. Only "the Legislature" could "determine the policy of accommodating those conflicting interests," and it would be inappropriate for the court to "assume their powers and change the rules," especially since the legislature had in three separate years refused to enact bills that would have extended the benefit of implied warranties to members of buyers' households.[18] All things considered, the court held only that lack of privity did not bar a child's cause of action merely because her parent had purchased the defective product on her behalf.

Further steps toward the liberalization of doctrine only produced division among judges and narrow, shifting majorities. Although two cases in 1961 and 1962 held for defendants, a third case in 1962 — *Randy Knitwear, Inc. v. American Cyanamid Co.* — declared broadly that manufacturers placed their "product[s] upon the market and, by advertising and labeling" them, represented their "quality to the public in such a way as to induce reliance," and therefore should be liable for any injuries the products caused. Three judges, however, "concur[red] in result only" and did "not agree that the so-called 'old court-made rule' should be modified to dispense with the requirement of privity without limitation."[19]

In *Goldberg v. Kollsman Instrument Corp.* a four-to-three majority took "another step toward a complete solution of the problem partially cleared up in *Greenberg v. Lorenz* . . . and *Randy Knitwear, Inc. v. American Cynamid Co.*" It was "clear," according to the majority, that a breach of warranty was "not only a violation of the sales contract out of which the warranty arises but . . . a tortious wrong suable by a noncontracting party whose use of the warranted article is within the reasonable contemplation of the vendor or manufacturer." Thus the majority held the manufacturer of an airplane strictly liable to the estate of a passenger killed in a crash, although it refused "for the present . . . to extend this rule" to the conceptual limit to which negligence liability had extended in the 1930s, so "as to hold [liable] the manufacturer . . . of a [defective] component part" which caused the crash.[20]

The three dissenters in *Kollsman Instrument* argued that "the counsel of prudence" required them "to be slow to cast aside well-established law in deference to a theory of social planning that is still much in dispute." The dissent observed that before *Kollsman* a suit could be brought for death or injury arising out of a plane crash only on a theory of negligence. It wondered whether "the additional risk" resulting from the imposition of strict liability on airplane manufacturers could "be effectively distributed as a cost of doing business" — a question that could "be intelligently resolved only by analysis of facts and figures compiled after hearings in which all interested groups have an opportunity to present economic arguments" and "classically within the special competence of the Legislature to ascertain." Any such displacement "of the law of negligence from its ancestral environment involve[d] an omniscience not shared by" the dissenters, and the decision to impose strict liability on the manufacturer of the airplane rather than either the airline or the manufacturer of the defective component part "involve[d] a principle of selection which [was] purely arbitrary."[21]

Both the *Kollsman* majority and the dissenters were advocating positions derived from World War II assumptions that human effort could reduce personal injuries. The majority was closely attuned to the postwar faith that injuries could be reduced by requiring those who could prevent them to do so. The dissenters, in contrast, favored what would soon emerge as a competing value—a desire for efficiency. As better efficiency calculators, the dissenters knew that injuries could not be eliminated entirely but only reduced to some optimal level. They recognized that court-mandated product safety would eventually increase product costs and that the increased costs, at some point, might exceed the benefits from increased safety. But the dissenters did not know how that point could be identified and, indeed, were convinced that, as judges, they were ill equipped to make the required cost-benefit analysis.

While both the majority and the dissenting judges in *Kollsman* derived their approaches from the World War II assumption that injuries could be reduced, their ideologies related differently to the prewar struggle between those who had sought to increase compensation for injuries and those who had striven to protect the existing distribution of wealth. The majority's approach of requiring manufacturers to pay for all product-related injuries overlapped the prewar reform paradigm, which required compensation by anyone even remotely causing harm. Although the prewar paradigm rested on a conception of social justice and the postwar approach grew out of concerns for efficiency, both led to the same practical result.

In contrast, there was much less overlap in the dissenters' approach. The nineteenth-century tort paradigm, which authorized compensation only if harm resulted from someone's moral fault, led to very different results from those produced by a law and economics standard, which authorizes compensation up to the point that costs begin to exceed benefits. At least in terms of the language used in *Kollsman,* the dissenters linked themselves to an efficiency rather than a wealth-protective view.

As these two camps on the Court of Appeals mobilized, even narrow holdings on insignificant issues that made little new law led to disagreement. A holding, for example, that a manufacturer of a malfunctioning oxygen mask was liable for the death of a co-worker who attempted to rescue the wearer of the mask produced an opinion by two judges concurring in result only, since they "envision[ed] a myriad of situations where the application of the doctrine [announced by the majority] would result in unjustified liability to manufacturers." [22]

Lower state court and federal judges, who took their law from the Court of Appeals, sensed its ambivalence and behaved accordingly. Occasional decisions eased the burden of plaintiffs in product liability cases. One trial judge, for example, concluded that a "monumental trilogy of cases [*Greenberg, Randy Knitwear,* and *Kollsman Instrument*] ha[d] revolutionized this area of the law," while *Bolm v. Triumph Corp.,* the first design defect case decided in New York in favor of a plaintiff, permitted a jury to consider the claim of a motorcyclist who had suffered genital injuries when he was thrown forward in an accident over a luggage rack placed several inches higher than the front seat.[23]

Most judges, however, continued to apply older, more pro-defendant rules. *Bolm,* in particular, was unusual, as most New York judges rejected design defect claims. New York and federal judges were equally hostile to the imposition of a duty to warn, observing that a manufacturer did not need to warn "against every injury which may ensue from mishap in the use of his product," especially against "common dangers."[24]

By the early 1970s, however, a new Court of Appeals majority had become dissatisfied with the laggardness of the New York judiciary in adopting modern product liability standards. In its next major foray into the field — *Codling v. Paglia*[25] — it indicated its dissatisfaction with clarity and unanimity. *Codling* differed from earlier Court of Appeals decisions in three respects. First, the court no longer believed strongly in the superiority of legislative over judicial law reform: the court had become willing to engage in social engineering. Second, the judges in *Codling* had finally come to a unanimous agreement about the efficiency policies product liability law should be advancing and were prepared to act to advance those policies.

No one in *Codling* questioned the appropriateness of a judicial imposition of strict liability standards in product cases. A second issue in the case, however, was whether the judiciary should abolish contributory negligence as a defense in product liability suits and in its place substitute the doctrine of comparative negligence. The majority was unwilling "at this time" to make such a substitution, apparently because the legislature was then considering the large issue of comparative negligence and the court did not want to get in its way. Two judges bristled at even this limited level of judicial deference, though, and observed that "examination of the record in other jurisdictions reveals that the assumption of legislative superiority is too patently a theoretical one" and that "courts are at least as well situated as Legislatures to inform themselves about the factors that should be taken into account in promulgating a rule of comparative negligence."[26]

Even more important than the new disinclination of the judges to defer to the legislature was their sense that "the erosion of the citadel of privity ha[d] been proceeding . . . even more rapidly in other jurisdictions" than in New York, "all with the enthusiastic support of text writers and the authors of law review articles." All seven judges agreed "that the time ha[d] now come when our court, instead of rationalizing broken field running, should lay down a broad principle" that would impose pressure "on the manufacturer . . . , who alone has the practical opportunity, to turn out useful, attractive, but safe products." The judges added that this imposition "on the manufacturer should encourage safety in design and production; and the diffusion of this cost in the purchase price of individual units should be acceptable to the user if thereby he is given added assurance of his own protection."[27] With this agreement on policy, a unanimous court held manufacturers strictly liable to anyone who came into contact with their products, even mere bystanders.

Codling v. Paglia also marked a turnaround in the Court of Appeals' jurisprudence in a third respect. Whereas the court after *Kollsman Instrument* had left the elaboration of product liability law to inferior courts, deciding only three cases in the decade between 1963 and 1973, the Court of Appeals after *Codling* remained an active force, deciding fourteen cases over the next seven years. To ensure that the lower courts would not subvert *Codling* as they had ignored *Kollsman Instrument,* the Court of Appeals assumed a direct supervisory role over product liability cases.

It began that role when only months after deciding *Codling* it reinstated a jury verdict against an elevator maintenance company which the Appellate Division had set aside. The court's theory was that, once the company had agreed to maintain the elevator, it had a duty to use reasonable care to discover and correct dangerous conditions and could be held to that duty even in the absence of direct evidence of negligence. In short, manufacturers of potentially dangerous instrumentalities and other comparable defendants were strictly liable for their safety. Next, the court ruled that a disclaimer of warranties would not bar a strict liability suit by users of a product who were strangers to any contract of purchase and sale. Two years later, in *Victorson v. Bock Laundry Machine Co.* the court made it clear "that strict products liability sound[ed] in tort rather than in contract" and thus that the statute of limitations began to run not when a product was placed on the market but at the subsequent date when injury occurred.[28]

The march continued with *Micallef v. Miehle Co.,* which overruled *Campo v. Scofield* and held that a manufacturer, "who stands in a superior position to recognize and cure defects," is "obligated to exercise that degree of care in his plan or design so as to avoid any unreasonable risk of harm to anyone who is likely to be exposed to . . . danger when the product is used in the manner for which the product was intended," even if the user was contributorily negligent.[29] Next, after noting that the "issue merits little discussion," the Court of Appeals held that "in a products liability case it is now established that, if plaintiff has proven that the product has not performed as intended and excluded all causes of the accident not attributable to defendant, the fact finder may, even if the particular defect has not been proven, infer that the accident could only have occurred due to some defect in the product or its packaging." With doctrine such as this " 'predicated largely on considerations of sound social policy'. . . including consumer reliance, marketing responsibility and the reasonableness of imposing loss redistribution," product manufacturers had become virtual insurers who, if they were to avoid liability, had the burden of convincing the fact-finder that something other than a defect in their product had caused the plaintiff's injury.[30]

Another area that developed gradually in the direction of increased compensation for injuries, with the development coming to final fruition in the 1970s, was the law dealing with landowners' liability to people entering on their land. Until the final fruition, many decisions continued to reiterate the traditional New York rule that a landowner was not liable for injuries inflicted on a trespasser or a licensee as a result of mere negligence, even if that trespasser was a child.[31] At the same time, however, received doctrine was slowly eroding as the courts made it incrementally easier for those injured on the land of another to recover damages.

One way in which the courts broke down traditional doctrine was by establishing special categories of people who were entitled to relief when they were injured on another's land even if they had entered without the landowner's permission and for purposes other than those of the owner. The first such special category was created for public officials. Classically officials had been seen as mere licensees to whom a landowner, at most, owed a duty first, to refrain from creating traps and second, to warn of hazards known to the owner into which the official might "unknowingly walk." With the onset of World War II, however, courts had to deal with a series of cases involving injuries to air raid wardens—civilian volunteers who at times suffered injury in their efforts to ensure "complete compliance with black-out regulations." "The protection afforded to life and property by the air raid warden service [was] a community enterprise," which had to be performed "with thoroughness and speed" and with which failure "to cooperate" was "incomprehensible." Voluntary performance of this patriotic duty transformed a warden into "more than a bare licensee on defendant's premises; his relationship bordered on that of an invitee, to whom defendant owed the duty of reasonable care under all the circumstances."[32]

After the war, the principle of the air raid warden cases was extended to the entire "class of persons privileged to enter upon the land for a public purpose," such as ambulance corps members, police officers, fire personnel, and even census takers. Another group given special treatment was laborers, mainly as a result of statute. One statute that was a subject of frequent litigation imposed on owners a nondelegable duty to furnish a safe workplace to anyone engaged in constructing, repairing, painting, or cleaning a building. The purpose of this statute was "not alone to provide remedies for laborers but more particularly to prevent accidents causing the injuries" by "compel[ling] a high standard of care." Another statute required owners of factory buildings to provide all stairways with handrails.[33]

Meanwhile, courts were developing other techniques to expand landowners' liability for injuries occurring on their premises. Observing that "the common law of this State is not an anachronism, but . . . a living law which responds to the surging reality of changed conditions," the judges, for example, expanded the liability of landowners to invitees, overruling old cases that did not require outdoor lighting on public buildings and holding that even a church had a duty to provide such lights.[34]

The most important change occurred when judges manipulated the rule that a landowner could not impose intentional or wanton injury or act in an affirmatively negligent fashion toward licensees and even trespassers. Thus one court held that leaving a car parked on an incline was active rather than merely passive negligence that rendered a landowner liable to a social guest struck by the car. Similarly, leaving a pool of oil on a driveway was held to be an act "of an affirmative nature, in the sense that the pool of oil was not a danger inherent in any defect in the property, but was placed there by an affirmative act." [35]

Comparable developments occurred in cases involving infant plaintiffs. Despite judges' awareness of "the statements contained in much of our case law . . . as to the degree of care owing to those stated to be trespassers, invitees, and bare licensees," which had grown out of "the necessities of industry and enterprise, and also perhaps the preservation of a freedom for one to do as he pleases with his own," the judges knew that "facts made the law." [36] By focusing on facts, they developed a new body of doctrine allowing children to recover from landowners on whose premises they suffered injury.

Mayer v. Temple Properties, a typical case in which a jury had returned a verdict on behalf of a child who had fallen into a fifty-five-foot-deep pit, will illustrate. In sustaining the verdict, the Court of Appeals declared that "to cover a hole . . . with 'flimsy' pieces of wood that quickly crumbled under the feet of the infant decedent, plunging him to his death in the boiler room far below, constitutes an affirmative creation of a situation pregnant with the gravest danger to life or limb, and . . . is tantamount to a reckless disregard of the safety of human life." As the Court of Appeals later summarized doctrine, "the 'trespass' theory" had with cases like *Mayer* "lost force . . . as a rigid concept by which all such cases are to be at once dismissed." Other cases decided through the course of the 1950s and 1960s continued to muddy the waters, with the result that, by the end of the 1960s, a trial judge ruled, only to be reversed, that the "classical common law distinctions as they relate to the duty owing to trespassers, licensees and invitees" had been transformed into matters "of *degree* and not of *substance!*"[37]

In *Basso v. Miller*, the Court of Appeals "pause[d] . . . to reflect" on the doctrinal transformation that had occurred in the law of landowners' duties toward trespassers, licensees, and invitees, "reconsider[ed] the necessity for such classification," and stated "that the distinctions need no longer be made." "Rather than to demand continued attempts to fit a plaintiff into one of the three rigid categories," the court "abandoned the classifications entirely and announced [its] adherence to the single standard of reasonable care under the circumstances"—a standard "no different than that applied in the usual negligence action." When the Court of Appeals reiterated "the all-embracing standard of reasonable care" and the lower courts followed along,[38] the special rules holding landowners to a lower than ordinary standard of care toward trespassers and nonbusiness guests were gone.

The law of negligence was a third area of doctrinal change, much of it facilitating easier recovery of damages. The most important developments occurred through the amelioration of the defenses of assumption of risk and contributory negligence. Assumption of risk came to be upheld as a valid defense only when a plaintiff had made " 'a thorough investigation' " and "with 'full knowledge' " made a decision to engage in activity for some economic profit. Even then, the defense became unavailable against a plaintiff who merely acted as the defendant had instructed or expected him to act.[39]

Even more striking was the judiciary's effort to ameliorate the harshness of the doctrine of contributory negligence. A long line of cases held that contributory negligence was inapplicable in cases where plaintiffs' rights were grounded in a statute making a defendant strictly liable. The courts also held that infants of tender years and others of similarly limited mental capacity could not be contributorily negligent and that when a superior directed a workman on a job "to proceed under circumstances recognizable as dangerous, the subordinate workman ha[d] little, if any, choice in the matter but to obey."[40]

These various ameliorations "of the recognized harshness of the contributory negligence doctrine" led one judge as early as 1957 to urge the legislature to "recognize the need for a rule of comparative negligence." By the early 1970s judges were suggesting more strongly "that a view of contributory negligence which makes it an absolute bar to a plaintiff's recovery cannot survive" and that "the applicability of the comparative negligence rule . . . [should] be examined" by the courts. Other judges went even further and held "that contributory negligence doctrine is no longer the law of this state," while the Appellate Division worried that trial judges might "misle[a]d the jury into employing a standard of comparative negligence." [41]

In the end, the change to comparative negligence was finalized not through common-law adjudication but by legislation. The new statute sought "to ameliorate the harsh result when a plaintiff is slightly negligent and fairly to apportion damages among the parties." Resting on a view that " 'fundamental fairness does not require an all-or-nothing rule which exonerates a very negligent defendant for even the slightest fault of his victim,' " the 1975 legislation "melded contributory negligence and assumption of risk into the term 'culpable conduct' and determined that such conduct" would not bar a plaintiff's suit but only result in "diminution of any damages a plaintiff might otherwise be entitled to recover." [42]

Parallel to the replacement of contributory negligence and assumption of risk by the less harsh doctrine of culpable conduct was a change in New York's rules regulating contribution among joint tortfeasors. At mid-century, New York's courts in the absence of a contract of indemnification severely limited a tortfeasor's ability to obtain contribution against joint tortfeasors.[43] Three cases decided in 1972 transformed doctrine, however. The first, *Dole v. Dow Chemical Co.,* held that "where a third party is found to have been responsible for a part . . . of the negligence for which a defendant is cast in damages, the responsibility for that part is recoverable by the prime defendant against the third party." Three months later, *Kelly v. Long Island Lighting Co.* held that even an active tortfeasor could recover contribution from another joint tortfeasor. The third case, *Hall v. E. I. Du Pont de Nemours & Co.,* continued the trend toward equitable apportionment of damages among potential defendants when it permitted infant plaintiffs injured by blasting caps to join fifteen manufacturers of the caps and their trade association in a single suit even though the plaintiffs did not know which manufacturer had produced the particular cap that had injured them, on the theory either that the "defendants . . . [had] exercise[d] actual collective control over a particular risk-creating product or activity" or that "liability . . . [should be] imposed on the most strategically placed participants in a risk-creating process."[44] Since each manufacturer was liable under these theories for some negligence, they were proper parties to a suit and proper contributors to a judgment under *Dole*.

Res ipsa loquitur was another subject of change in favor of plaintiffs. One development was the gradual erosion of the rule arising out of dictum in a 1938 case that, in cases involving more than one possible cause of injury for only one of which a defendant was responsible, the requirement of exclusive control prevented a plaintiff from recovering if it was equally probable that the injury resulted from one cause as from another. Over time, lower courts found "exclusive control" to be "a concept which is not 'absolutely rigid,'" and, in the end, they did not apply the requirement of exclusive control "overliterally."[45]

A second change favoring injury victims occurred in the rule that, when a plaintiff had some specific evidence about how an injury had occurred, he or she had to elect whether to rely on *res ipsa loquitur* or to present the specific evidence to the jury. The rule had never enjoyed unanimous acceptance, however, and the Court of Appeals ultimately ruled that a plaintiff could proceed simultaneously both with specific evidence of negligence and on a *res ipsa* theory.[46]

The central issue in the *res ipsa* cases was always how best to allow a party without access to evidence to present its case and to compel a party in possession of evidence to come forward with its proof. Throughout the middle decades of the century, the New York courts tended toward an increasingly "'common-sense'" approach, as, for instance, by holding that a plaintiff with amnesia as a result of the events causing an injury would be held to a lesser degree of proof than a plaintiff who could have testified.[47] Almost invariably this realist posture made it easier for victims of injury to maintain their actions for damages.

A final development generally favorable to injury victims occurred with the rejection of the traditional choice of law rule, which had provided that liability in tort depended on the substantive law of the place where the alleged tort had occurred. The traditional rule had always contained an exception against the application of foreign law contrary to the public policy of New York, and in the first case signaling a departure from the old rule, the Court of Appeals had refused to apply a $15,000 limitation on wrongful death recoveries contained in a Massachusetts statute, in a case where an airplane with a New York resident on board crashed in Massachusetts during a flight that had originated in New York. As the court observed, "Modern conditions make it unjust and anomalous to subject the traveling citizens of this State to the varying laws of other States through and over which they move. . . . The place of injury [has] become . . . entirely fortuitous. Our courts should if possible provide protection for our own State's people against unfair and anachronistic treatment of the lawsuits which result from these disasters." Two years later *Babcock v. Jackson* expanded the public policy exception into a new choice of law test, which gave "controlling effect to the law of the jurisdiction which, because of its relationship or contact with the occurrence or the parties has the greatest concern with the specific issue raised"—an approach that allowed New York courts "to apply 'the policy of the jurisdiction 'most intimately connected with the outcome of [the] particular litigation,' " including "New York's policy of requiring a tort-feasor to compensate . . . for injuries caused by his negligence."[48]

Most of the rest of New York's law of negligence—in particular, the basic definition of negligence "as the failure to employ reasonable care"—underwent little, if any, change after World War II. Despite superficial continuity, though, change nonetheless did begin to occur at a deeper level as traditional conceptions of negligence were put to new and more expansive uses. The most extensive new use for negligence doctrine occurred in the increasingly vast field of medical malpractice, which included cases of far-out claims like wrongful life. Another important extension was in the increasing number of suits against accountants, architects, surveyors, and others charged with negligence in the construction of buildings. Novel claims of negligence were also advanced by a widow against an insurance company that failed to put a policy into effect although informing her that it had, by the buyer of a horse against a racing association that failed to ascertain or list its sex, and by a seventeen-year-old minor who fell on his face against the bartender who served him thirteen drinks within the period of one hour.[49]

By 1980, tort doctrine had changed dramatically from what it had been in 1940. It also seems likely that products were safer and that people were more conscious of the likely consequences of careless behavior. Finally, it seems apparent that victims of accidents in 1980 had very different expectations about their entitlement to financial recovery and support than their ancestors had had a half-century earlier. In the closing decades of the century, New Yorkers no longer had reason to fear that misfortune would deprive them of what they had come to perceive as a right to lead their lives in dignity.

CHAPTER 9

LIBERTY AND SEXUALITY

The emergence of concepts of individual liberty in the era of World War II had a dramatic impact on legal doctrine. As we shall see in Chapter 11, the individualism of World War II and its aftermath would cast a considerable shadow on government regulatory powers that had grown to maturity in the 1930s. This chapter and the next will examine the impact of concepts of individual rights in two other areas—in this chapter, the law of sex crimes and, in the next, family law. In both, older Puritanical values of family and sexual responsibility came into conflict with newer values of individual freedom—in particular, freedom for adult men and, occasionally, adult women.

By the 1940s, new attitudes toward sexual mores began to appear in judicial opinions, even while old values remained deeply ensconced. Some judges became, in effect, leaders in an effort for the decriminalization of offenses such as homosexuality, prostitution, gender violence, and pornography. In their view, it was no longer necessary to keep up the "perennial struggle against all influences tending to corrupt and incite to vice" so as to preserve "the reservoir of social life" from becoming "poisoned" by "disorder and anarchy." Other judges, however, continued to give credence to more traditional values, observing that it was their "obligation . . . to protect weaker members of society from . . . corrupt influences." In particular, these traditionally minded judges felt a special need to protect "adolescents," who were "feeling the stress and strain of life in a world tortured by doubts."[1]

The conflict between libertarians seeking decriminalization and traditionalists who still supported criminal enforcement of conventional morality began when new sorts of fact situations first appeared in reported cases during the 1940s. Seven cases decided between 1940 and 1960, resulting in two convictions and five acquittals, will illustrate.

In one of the two cases involving only adults, Walden P. Stevens lured Anna Mae Faulkner away from her home and two minor children and spent the night with her in his car "contrary to law." In the other case of an adult, Hazel Prudhomme pleaded guilty to "being in a parked car having improper relations with a man not her husband, she being a married woman." Two other cases involved minors in their late teens. In one, the defendant used "a vulgar expression" in talking to a seventeen-year-old boy in the presence of a girl of the same age, with whom the boy had been keeping steady company for seven months and to whom he was unofficially engaged; the defendant "told the boy 'lay her as there are precautions you can take,' and 'go to bed together because there are precautions.'" In the other, an adult male sent a letter to a sixteen-year-old boy saying, "'I'll give you $5.00 or more if you let me' (engage with you in an act best defined as pederasty—ed.)." The boy's mother intercepted the letter and brought it to the attention of the authorities.[2]

The other three cases involved younger children or children of unknown age. In the first, a set of pictures constituting "a strip tease series" was on sale in a small neighborhood store serving the families of the area, where high school students could "come in, observe these pictures, purchase them and seek dark corners and privacy to snicker over its contents and pass the pictures around among their friends." In the second, the defendant, a man of "good reputation," was charged with asking two girls under twelve "'to commit an unnatural act with him.'" He admitted asking directions of the girls and produced a witness who testified that he overheard the conversation with the girls and heard no improper request. The prosecutor, in turn, produced two other girls who testified that, although they observed the first two girls talking to the defendant, they never saw the alleged witness. In the final case, where a "sharp question of fact [was] presented," the defendant was accused of exposing his private parts before a child of unknown age.[3]

Why did cases such as these first begin to be published in the New York reports during the 1940s? Surely such conduct had occurred earlier, and some individuals had undoubtedly been arrested and prosecuted for engaging in it. But if they had interposed defenses instead of merely pleading guilty, their arguments had not risen to a level that called for a published opinion in response. Beginning in the 1940s, however, at least some judges felt a need to write and publish opinions because they ceased to perceive at least some of the conduct as seriously criminal or exploitative of women or children. The boundary between legitimate and criminal sexual expression was becoming blurred, and judges felt a need to participate in the ongoing debate about where the line should be drawn.

A similar pattern, in which some judges overlooked sexual misconduct as trivial even while others still wanted to punish it as seriously criminal, emerges from examination of the reported New York cases during the quarter-century after World War II dealing with specific areas of the law, such as sodomy, prostitution, family violence, pornography, and even rape. Most of the cases involved commercialized vice, consensual sexual activity, or violence within families—matters in which judges and legislators increasingly came to believe that the criminal law ought not interfere. Of course, some cases, especially those that charged rape, did involve violence between strangers. But even in these, as well as in cases of nonviolence, judges increasingly hesitated to apply the criminal process rigorously, out of concern not to ruin the lives of men who, perhaps through circumstances beyond their control, had made what judges characterized as a single, stupid mistake. Comparable concern for the well-being of female and child victims, in contrast, or even an awareness that much sexual conduct could involve victimization, was not a hallmark of sex crime jurisprudence as it moved into the 1960s. For by then, the trend toward decriminalization of conduct occurring outside of public view had become dominant.

Decriminalization of private conduct did not mean, however, that all sexual or gender-related behavior came to fall outside the law's purview. As the conflict between decriminalizers and traditionalists played itself out on the New York Court of Appeals in the 1950s and 1960s, conduct occurring in the home or other similarly closeted places became immune from legal regulation, but activity with a locus in public or quasi-public places like bars, theaters, or bookstores still could be criminalized. Only when constitutional arguments came into the forefront, mainly in federal courts, did the law begin to deregulate conduct of the latter sort.

SODOMY

Much of the argument for and against decriminalization of sex offenses, both in learned journals and in the popular press, was addressed specifically to the crime of consensual sodomy. Here the argument for decriminalization was perhaps at its strongest. As one scholar explained:

> Laws against homosexual acts do not significantly control the proscribed behavior. . . . The most evident results of antihomosexuality laws are . . . the encouragement of police corruption and repressive enforcement procedures. . . . Law enforcement officials fall back on an amalgam of unsavory vice-squad . . . [and] spy techniques . . . abhorrent to the democratic way of life. . . . These laws, in short, make a good many individuals more unhappy than they would otherwise be, without showing any short-run signs of effectively dealing with the problem of homosexuality.[4]

Such arguments appear to have had a profound effect on the New York Court of Appeals. At a time when most institutions, especially those of the federal government, were aggressively engaged in oppression of homosexuals, the New York court took initial steps in the direction of decriminalization. Beginning with *People v. Doyle,*[5] a 1952 decision that placed procedural obstacles in the path of sodomy prosecutions, a majority of the judges on the Court of Appeals took a series of steps tending to decriminalize consensual homosexual acts carried on in private.

In *Doyle,* the Court of Appeals reversed the conviction of a defendant who had taught in schools for boys for twenty-five years for an act of sodomy with one of his twelve-year-old students. Finding insufficient evidence that the boy had been forced to participate against his will, the court in what Judge Charles Desmond in dissent labeled a "shocking conclusion" deemed him an accomplice, held that a man could not be convicted of a consensual homosexual act without evidence to corroborate an accomplice's testimony, and held that the corroborating evidence in this case, consisting of the defendant's admission to the police " 'that he was fooling with the boy,' " was insufficient.[6] Although the court implied that a victim of forcible sodomy could by himself provide the evidence needed for conviction, the effect of its evidentiary ruling was to render nearly impossible the prosecution of consensual homosexual acts committed in private.

It is not obvious at what the Court of Appeals was aiming in the *Doyle* case. The case did not make new law; the rule requiring corroboration of accomplice testimony in sodomy cases went back to the 1902 case of *People v. Deschessere* and had been applied uniformly in a series of Appellate Division cases in the decade before *Doyle,* and the jury in *Doyle* had been instructed in accordance with the rule. Probably the objective of the court was to signal its unwillingness to allow use of the state's criminal process in an otherwise emerging national pattern of oppression of homosexuals. The court could not use the favored concept of the 1980s—the constitutional right to privacy— to achieve that result because the Supreme Court had not yet set down the building blocks in *Griswold v. Connecticut* and subsequent cases from which to construct such a right.[7] Instead, it had to rely on the tools that were available to it—namely, rules of jurisdiction, procedure, and evidence that could be manipulated to make prosecution difficult or, in cases of private, consensual homosexuality, virtually impossible. As we shall see, the New York courts during the 1950s and 1960s relied on such rules in a wide variety of contexts, at least as often as later courts would turn to the right of privacy.'

The Court of Appeals' next attempt at reform occurred in *People v. Randall,* where a fifty-nine-year-old defendant had been convicted of sodomy for requesting and then voluntarily permitting a sixteen-year-old to perform an act of anal intercourse on him. One ground of the defendant's appeal was that the police had beaten him and caused his ear canal to bleed in order to extract a confession from him, and perhaps this claim elucidated sympathy from the court. It did not, however, reverse the conviction on this ground but chose instead to avoid the constitutional issue and deal with the case by giving a cramped reading to the sodomy statute. Noting that prior to 1950 New York law had declared that anyone who " 'carnally knows any male or female person by the anus or by or with the mouth; *or voluntarily submits to such carnal knowledge*' " . . . is guilty of sodomy" and that "abruptly" in 1950 the "statute was revised" to omit any reference to the person who " 'voluntarily submits to such carnal knowledge,' " the court held unanimously that only a man who inserted his penis into the anus or mouth of another could be guilty of sodomy; the other person could at most be guilty as an accomplice.[8]

Although one cannot be certain, it also may be that old-fashioned issues of class motivated the court in *Randall,* as well as other courts, to "emasculate . . . the statute" prohibiting consensual sodomy. The court merely noted in *Randall* that the defendant, who lived on a small family farm, had no prior record at the time of his arrest, while the sixteen-year-old had been picked up by the State Police for questioning in connection with the whereabouts of a boy who was wanted by probation authorities. An earlier court, in contrast, had been far more explicit when it described one sodomy defendant as "a man of education and culture, with a distinguished war record," while the "boy" with whom he had committed the offense "was unquestionably of low grade mentality" which, when "coupled with his vagrant habits, would not indicate a normal degree of responsibility." When a defendant was "charged with a serious and repulsive crime" like sodomy, he "should not be found guilty without clear and reliable testimony"; "it shock[ed] one's sense of justice that a person should be convicted, and should serve a long term in prison, upon testimony" of "this half-witted youth."[9] For these judges, it seems that, even if the weak and the poor were not exactly legitimate prey for the lusts of men of culture and education, such men at least ought not have their lives ruined by a blunder, the occurrence of which was evidenced by uncertain testimony.

The effect of these decisions was to make homosexual acts carried on in private difficult to prosecute. As long as both men consented to an act, the rule against convictions based on accomplice testimony prohibited either from testifying against the other. Conviction could be had only on the testimony of some third party observer; that is, conviction could be had only if a consensual act had not been truly private. Not even the most common type of nonconsensual sodomy—acts by older men against youths unable by virtue of age or mental infirmity to give their consent—could be readily prosecuted in view of the hesitancy of courts in the 1950s to rely on the testimony of boys to convict men of stature and standing. Thus while homosexuality did not gain formal legal legitimacy in the decades after World War II, men wishing to engage in private homosexual activity could, in practice, do so with reduced fear of the criminal law.

The same was not true, however, with respect to homosexual solicitation or to activity occurring in public or quasi-public places such as bars. Some New York judges were prepared to construe narrowly ambiguous legislation applying to homosexual behavior occurring outside the home, but the majority of the Court of Appeals was not. On the contrary, the majority gave several pieces of legislation a sweeping construction and thereby left police with broad powers to interdict whatever apparent homosexual activity they observed.[10]

PROSTITUTION

The law regulating prostitution was a second area in which change in the direction of decriminalization occurred. The argument for decriminalization, as expressed eloquently by Herbert L. Packer, was essentially the same as the argument for consensual homosexuality. Packer wrote, "There seems little reason to believe that the incidence of prostitution has been seriously reduced by criminal law enforcement. . . . The side effects on law enforcement are unfortunate. Police corruption is closely associated with this kind of vice control. . . . An equally disgusting kind of enforcement practice is the use of the police or police-employed decoy to detect solicitation."[11]

The earliest case reflecting the new culture of decriminalization was *People ex rel. Colletti v. Morehead,* where the defendant had become involved with two sixteen-year-old girls who had hitchhiked from their homes in Lancaster, Pennsylvania, to Long Island City in March 1944. They had been delivered by their driver to a restaurant in which the defendant worked. After giving them free food and offering to help them get work, possibly "in a defense" industry, the defendant introduced them to one Rubenstein, who offered an apartment, furs, clothing, and support to one of the girls " 'if she would be nice to him' " and have "no visitors." Rubenstein kept the defendant informed of "his negotiations," and when he asked the defendant for his approval, the defendant gave it with a nod and with the word " 'yes.' " Rubenstein thereupon obtained a hotel room for the girl, where, it was charged, "he committed an immoral act" with her.[12]

The court held that, as a matter of law, these facts did not constitute sufficient evidence to warrant holding the defendant for trial on charges of enticing a woman into prostitution. In its view, this exploitation of a sixteen-year-old girl amounted to nothing more than an "incidental concession . . . to lasciviousness." Prostitution, in contrast, involved "a permanent condition" that required " 'common, indiscriminate, meretricious commerce with men.' " It is difficult, though, to appreciate the court's reading of the facts. At the very least, *Colletti* was a case in which one man, Colletti, assisted another, Rubenstein, in buying sexual favors, while, if the case had been allowed to go to trial, facts might have emerged showing that Colletti anticipated Rubenstein to be merely the first customer. The *Colletti* case manifests too many aspects of sexual exploitation and is best understood as one where the court, consistent with cultural norms beginning to emerge during World War II, found what a later court would call " 'recreational sex' " an appropriate reward for hardworking men who, because of rationing, had few other ways to spend the money that their contribution to the war effort had brought. This was especially so when the women providing the recreation had voluntarily displayed their willingness to do so by uprooting themselves from protective homes in a moral community of middle America and hitchhiking to one of the main domestic centers of the war. The court's mind-set simply blinded it to certain small facts of the case, which in the aggregate, suggest that the defendant, "behind the mask of a legal-looking business, lure[d] innocent young girls into a respectable-appearing" restaurant "and there . . . procure[d] them for unlawful sexual intercourse." [13]

Three decisions by the Court of Appeals during the 1950s displayed a similar judicial mind-set. The three decisions, one taken with the support of an amicus brief from the American Civil Liberties Union (ACLU), can all be interpreted as upholding the civil liberties of call girls and the men involved with them. Viewed from another perspective, however, the three decisions deprived the police of their main weapons for putting call girls out of business and "undoubtedly hamper[ed] . . . law enforcement officers in their continued attempts to control th[e] social evil." [14] By declining to pass on significant constitutional issues and, in the alternative, construing statutes narrowly and holding evidence insufficient to sustain convictions, the Court of Appeals made it difficult to prosecute and thus to a significant degree decriminalized prostitution that was conducted in a discreet fashion.

People v. Gould reversed the conviction of a man admitted to the bar but engaged in the jewelry business. He had telephoned a policewoman working undercover who had placed an advertisement in a large New York daily seeking employment as a bookkeeper. After offering her a job as a salesperson, he had told her that she could earn a much higher income if she would have affairs with his customers. During a personal interview, he offered to set her up in an apartment, pay her $50 per week, and arrange to send her at least four men daily whom she could charge $10 each for acts of sexual intercourse. He also inquired whether she engaged in "two forms of abnormal sexual activity."[15]

The court concluded that the defendant had done nothing more than "suggest to a woman of good character, that she become a prostitute under his management, and she, of course, rejected the proposal at once." Noting that "very seldom in our criminal law . . . [does] a rejected suggestion of wrongdoing amount . . . to a substantive crime or offense," the majority concluded that the defendant had not violated the statute, which prohibited mere suggestions or, in its own language, "offers to secure the services of another for the purpose of prostitution."[16] By its headstrong misreading of the statute, a misreading which required undercover officers actually to engage in wrongdoing in order to obtain prostitution convictions, the majority effectively prevented their use.

The libertarian majority had similarly pursued a policy of substantially decriminalizing call-girl prostitution in *People v. Choremi.* There telephone conversations intercepted by the police under a court order, together with the defendant's own voluntary statements, showed that she had made dates on one night with men who were "very nice" and "for twice what . . . [she] expect[ed]." On another occasion, her codefendant, also a woman, arranged a date for her with a man who "had not been laid in a month, and so you can get paid and can enjoy yourself at the same time." On still another occasion, when the defendant had refused to meet another man because the money was insufficient, her codefendant replied that "you can't meet fellows like we had yesterday every day. They were exceptional and you can't always get that money."[17]

On these facts, which it characterized as only "suspicion and surmise," the majority of the Court of Appeals found no "evidence of a purpose to induce, entice, or procure another to commit an act of sexual intercourse" and "not the slightest bit of evidence" that the defendant had engaged in prostitution. With the support of an amicus brief from the ACLU, the court found the evidence too "thin and meager" to support a conviction, apparently demanding what could never be obtained by wiretapping—personal observations by police of the prostitutes and their customers "in compromising positions" in "bedrooms where the lights went off shortly after their entry."[18]

Relying on the court's recent unanimous decision in *People v. Feiner* as authority for a broad reading of the vagrancy statute, including its provision making prostitution a crime, the dissenters accused the majority of an unduly narrow construction of the act. The majority's decision, according to the dissent, thwarted the will of the legislature, put individuals who had committed a recognized crime "beyond the reach of the law," and made it impossible "to forbid persons from making themselves available for unlawful sexual intercourse." The majority's holding, it was said, produced an "incongruous" result, whereby a woman who solicited on a street corner could be convicted of prostitution, but a female who held herself forth in her home over the telephone became immune from punishment.[19] That "incongruous" result, however, was precisely where the jurisprudence of the majority was pushing: to immunize from the criminal process sex that was invisible to the public eye while continuing to criminalize that which drew public attention and thereby led to public ire.

The third case, *People v. Moss*, must be understood against the backdrop of a key fact about the law of prostitution—its ambiguity. It is relatively easy to know that an act of prostitution has occurred when a conspicuous streetwalker offers to engage in sex with a man in return for money and subsequently engages in sex and receives the money. New York legislation in effect at the time of *Moss* defined prostitution broadly, however, to include not only acts of women providing sex for money but also activities of men inducing women to lead lives of prostitution or to commit acts of prostitution or other lewd or indecent acts. This legislation, as Judge Van Voorhis noted for the court in another case, was "'obviously a patchwork affair'" that contained "'botchy and immaterial provisions'"; the "problem[s] in analyzing" the cases above "stem[med] in considerable part from the draftsmanship" of the New York statutes. As applied to *People v. Moss*, which involved a "housekeeper" who "was a willing participant" in acts of "sexual intercourse and other lewd and indecent acts" with the defendant, her employer, until she "became 'afraid of him,'" the statutory law seemed utterly lacking in precision and rigor.[20]

Judges, of course, found such conduct "reprehensible," but they also knew that prostitution convictions "may often be attended with the gravest consequences." It followed that, "if there is to be proper security of personal liberty," criminal statutes had to be strictly construed and that, "if the Legislature chooses to make . . . privately committed [sex] acts . . . a public offense or a crime, under whatever name, it should do so expressly."[21]

From *Moss* it was easy for lawyers to take the next step and argue that "a 'sexual revolution'" had occurred "in the past few decades" that had legitimated "sex for pleasure, [or] 'recreational sex'" and had recognized that "nonmarried individuals have a right to pursue sex drives even if they have to pay for it." On this basis, it could be urged that society could "not legislate morality" and that, as "older legislators and judges . . . raised in repressive sexual adaptations [were] replaced by younger *men* whose sexual adaptation" emerged out of "the more recent social mores of American society," the law would "be brought into line." One judge, at least, accepted such arguments and declared that, "however offensive it may be, recreational commercial sex threatens no harm to the public health, safety or welfare" and thus should "not be proscribed." [22]

The approach of most judges to prostitution from the 1950s even into the 1970s was thus parallel to their approach to consensual homosexuality. By construing legislation narrowly and holding evidence of guilt insufficient to sustain convictions, a majority of judges, in effect, pursued a policy of decriminalization. In doing so, moreover, they expressed a concern for protecting the personal liberty of men, while failing to appreciate how wealthy men could engage in sexual exploitation of less privileged women. The court in *Moss,* for example, could see only that "a young woman intelligent enough to have been graduated from high school at the age of seventeen . . . participated in sexual relations with the defendant voluntarily"—that two intelligent individuals had "voluntarily" entered a relationship that turned sour and came to the attention of the criminal courts only when, as the Court of Appeals observed five months later in another case, the woman "found herself rejected" and "became vindictive." The court thereupon construed the law so as " 'not . . . to place the erring male at the mercy of the erring female.' " Of course, the effect of this construction was to place women who were not in the least in error in perceiving their economic necessity [23] at the mercy of men who likewise did not err in appreciating the sexual liberties they desired. But until the 1970s, the courts did not perceive this victimization.

FAMILY VIOLENCE

The legal system's insensitivity to the victimization of women and children surfaced most starkly in connection with the legislature's 1962 adoption of Article 8 of the Family Court Act, entitled Family Offenses Proceedings. Before 1962, a family member who had been assaulted or otherwise victimized by another member and desired judicial assistance was compelled to commence a criminal action.[24] Article 8, in contrast, created a civil proceeding under the jurisdiction of the Family Court, which would attempt to provide conciliation and treatment to alleviate the violence.

Serious physical violence by men against women and children has had a long history and by 1870 had been made a fit subject for criminal prosecution and severe criminal sentences in most American jurisdictions. But criminal prosecution often did not adequately protect the victims of violent husbands and fathers, and its failures prompted the 1962 reforms. Although the drafters of Article 8 were not "expecting miracles," their hope was that "not punishment, but practical help," was the best device "for dealing with the underlying family difficulties" that often manifested themselves in domestic violence.[25]

Thus there began a curious attempt to decriminalize acts of domestic violence and thereby "save the potential" of men who, "trapped by circumstances over which they have no control," could not otherwise "channel" personal "qualities" in a fashion beneficial to themselves and "society" and thereby achieve their "right to self realization." Article 8 aimed for this result by giving exclusive original jurisdiction over family offense proceedings to the Family Court and requiring the criminal courts to transfer to it jurisdiction over proceedings previously begun.[26] In assuming jurisdiction over family offense proceedings, however, the family courts of the state and the appellate courts above them would need to focus on two main issues that the jurisdictional provisions raised: what constituted a family offense, and what constituted a family.

The early cases tended to construe the jurisdiction of the Family Court generously and to extend the decriminalization effort broadly. Thus the Court of Appeals ruled in 1967 that the Family Court should assume original jurisdiction over all "family assaults . . . and not simply those which were trivial." Lower courts agreed, even when the assault had been "a shocking offense—that the defendant placed his two-year-old son on a hot stove." Sex offenses also were placed within the coverage of the Family Court Act, as Family Court judges, for instance, accepted jurisdiction over a case of incest between a sixteen-year-old male and his twelve-year-old sister that led to the birth of a child; the judge argued that only the Family Court could "restor[e] the various members of this family to useful and less encumbered lives."[27]

Courts also extended the jurisdiction of the Family Court by construing the word "family" in the act to mean the extended rather than the nuclear family. In addition, most early judges also construed the concept of family broadly when they held that violence between a man and a woman who were living together was subject to family rather than criminal court jurisdiction, even if the two were not formally married. As one of these judges observed, the "countless households where men and women reside with their offspring . . . without being legally married" produced precisely the kinds of "behavior problems, support problems, [and] mental and emotional problems" for which, "from a social point of view, . . . the unique and flexible procedures and services available in the Family Court" could provide "a remedy."[28]

A somewhat different pattern emerged in the fourth area of law in which decriminalization ultimately took place during the 1950s and 1960s—the area of pornography. Initially, the majority on the New York Court of Appeals took a firm stand in favor of continued regulation of pornography, since prosecutions were brought mainly in connection with materials distributed in public or quasi-public places. In the years following World War II, many judges continued to subordinate concerns for freedom of expression to a perceived need of protecting "the young as well as all other segments of the population from the corrupt influences exerted through the lascivious literature." [29]

Postwar judges even remained offended by nudity. The "use of clothing to cover one's sexual organs," in one judge's view, had "been, throughout history, the practice of all humans except for the lowest grade of savages." Allowing nudity, he feared, would have "a libidinous effect upon the most ordinary, normal, healthy individuals," and its "effect upon the abnormal individual may be more disastrous." Another judge asked that "Heaven help our future generations" if nudity should ever come into "accord with the ethical and moral standards of our community." Still another thought that "much greater police activity in connection with pictures of female nudes and so-called art books would appear to be indicated." [30]

Arguably, the most important case in setting today's moral tastes and standards was *Joseph Burstyn, Inc. v. Wilson,* which arose when the state revoked the license it had granted for the showing of an Italian movie, *Il Miracolo.* According to the licensing authority, the picture, whose first character, Saint Joseph, caused a peasant girl named Mary to become intoxicated and later pregnant with a " 'blessed son,' " was sacrilegious, as well as filled with " 'drunkenness, seduction . . . and lewdness' " or, in the language of the script, " 'ardent affection, . . . sexual passion, gratification, [and] devotion.' " A five-to-two majority of the Court of Appeals sustained the revocation of the license. In an opinion that supported conventional morality not out of a belief in its righteousness but out of a policy against insulting those who still believed in it, the majority noted that the film's "ways of love" amounted to nothing more than "insults" "hurl[ed] . . . at the deepest and sincerest religious beliefs of others." "Insult, mockery, contempt and ridicule," the majority added, could "be a deadly form of persecution." America, it observed, was "essentially a religious nation" and "a land of religious freedom," and then the majority concluded that "it would be strange indeed if our Constitution, intended to protect that freedom, were construed as an instrument to uphold those who publicly and sacrilegiously ridicule and lampoon the most sacred beliefs of any religious denomination to provide *amusement.*"[31]

Having won the New York Film Critics award as the best foreign language film of 1950, *Il Miracolo* also won some support on the Court of Appeals in the form of a dissent from Judge Stanley Fuld. "Confronted in this case with censorship in its baldest form . . . —a prior restraint of broad and undefined limits," Fuld found that the licensing scheme "constitute[d] an attempt to legislate orthodoxy in matters of religious belief." The "unquestioned good faith" of the people who found *Il Miracolo* "offensive to their religious sensibilities" could not make it legitimate to "censor the free expression of ideas or beliefs in the field of religion." " 'No official,' " Fuld concluded, could " 'prescribe what shall be orthodox in politics, nationalism, religion, or other matters of opinion.' "[32]

When the majority of the United States Supreme Court agreed with Fuld, it reversed the judgment of the New York Court of Appeals and thereby began the process of abolishing most movie censorship.[33] The federal Supreme Court, out of the necessities of its institutional position, also began another new process that differentiated the decriminalization of pornography from the early stages, at least, of the decriminalization of homosexuality and prostitution. Unlike the state court, the federal tribunal did not construe legislation narrowly or reverse convictions on procedural or evidentiary grounds; on the contrary, it declared state legislation constitutionally invalid. Because the nature of federal jurisdiction deprived the Supreme Court of the gentle power, which state judges enjoyed, of engaging in a dialogue with state legislatures whereby the courts limited the scope of the criminal law over victimless offenses but left the ultimate judgment on total decriminalization to the political process, the federal court had to arrogate that ultimate judgment to itself. In arrogating such power, the Supreme Court effectively transformed the meaning of decriminalization from a process involving judicial suggestion, political discussion, and ultimate legislative determination, to one of judicial command.

The novelty of the step taken by the Supreme Court in *Burstyn* emerged most dramatically, perhaps, in the difficulty that traditionally minded New York judges had in absorbing the court's message. Thus, two years after *Burstyn,* in *Commercial Pictures Corp. v. Board of Regents,* the Court of Appeals was back in the censorship business. The case involved the French motion picture, *La Ronde,* which portrayed sexual encounters primarily between men and women not married to each other, including one episode between a soldier and a prostitute who "informs him," in a manner reminiscent of much World War II practice, "that 'civilians' pay, but for 'boys like you it's nothing.'" Noting that *La Ronde* "depict[ed] promiscuity as the natural and normal relation between the sexes, whether married or unmarried," the majority concluded that it "pander[ed] to base human emotions" and thereby constituted "a breeding ground for sensuality, depravity, licentiousness and sexual immorality," which was "portrayed in such manner as to invite concupiscence and condone its promiscuous satisfaction, with its evil social consequences."[34]

The two dissenters observed that *La Ronde* had been banned nowhere in the United States except New York, from which they concluded that the movie was "not inimical to the public peace, welfare and safety" and was "not offensive" to "a large segment of society." They accordingly refused to join in banning it, as did the United States Supreme Court, which reversed the Court of Appeals' judgment.[35]

Kingsley International Pictures Corp. v. Regents was yet another attempt by the Court of Appeals at movie censorship, despite Judge Fuld's warning in dissent that any system of prior administrative censorship was unconstitutional. The majority, however, was out "to protect" the people from the "abuses" that the movie, *Lady Chatterley's Lover,* would impose on them. It was astounded that the movie exalted "illicit sexual love in derogation of the restraints of marriage," presented the "complete surrender" of the leading characters "to the baser instincts . . . as a triumph over the social mores," and heralded their "decision to live in adultery . . . as a conquest of love over the 'form' of marriage." Banning *Lady Chatterley's Lover,* the court said in language reminiscent of Thomas E. Dewey's 1944 presidential campaign, was "necessary for our survival as a nation in an age of open conflict with atheistic materialism." Again, however, the federal Supreme Court disagreed.[36]

Despite emerging federal standards, a four-to-three majority of the Court of Appeals as late as 1963 reacted similarly to Henry Miller's *Tropic of Cancer.* The majority was responding in part, perhaps, to its "increased awareness of the serious problem" created by the "ever-increasing amount of printed material featuring sex and sensationalism . . . sold not only in bookstores but from open racks in candy stores and similar outlets." The result was "an alarming decline in the moral climate of our times." It found *Tropic of Cancer* to be "nothing more than a compilation of a series of sordid narrations dealing with sex"—"dirt for dirt's sake." In his concurring opinion, Chief Judge Desmond found the "whole book [to be] 'sick sensuality,'" with "no glory, no beauty, no stars—just mud." Despite the recent Supreme Court cases that he cited, he believed it "unthinkable that the practical political thinkers who wrote the Bill of Rights ever intended to protect downright foulness" and hence concluded that "something must remain of the ancient police power of the States . . . to ban stuff as filthy as 'Tropic of Cancer.'"[37] Because they remanded the case for a new trial on other grounds, however, Desmond and his colleagues in the majority never had the opportunity to learn how badly they had misread both Henry Miller's *Tropic of Cancer* and the Supreme Court's emerging case law.

Gradually, however, the New York courts heard the message and began to conform their views to the more libertarian federal standards. One year prior to the suppression of *Lady Chatterley's Lover,* the Court of Appeals in a four-to-three decision in the *Excelsior Pictures* case authorized the exhibition of "a fictionalized depiction of the activities of the members of a nudist group in a secluded private camp in Florida," in which the "pictured episodes" were "'honestly relevant to the adequate expression of innocent ideas.'" Nonetheless, three judges still dissented because, although "views of the adults' private parts [were] not shown to the audience," the "genitalia of children and girls [*sic*] and the buttocks and breasts of men and women [were] revealed," and, moreover, "the picture contain[ed] specific protracted scenes of women in unwholesome, sexually alluring postures."[38]

Even though *Excelsior Pictures* did not extend so far, the lower courts read it as placing all displays of mere nudity, which New York judges had traditionally treated as obscene, within the constitutionally protected scope of free expression. Another case held that "use of the word 'shit' . . . not in its usual connotation but as a definitive expression of the language of the narcotic" was not obscene. Meanwhile, an early case had declined to censor a movie about a teenage drug addict, despite the argument of the censors that "use of heroin and marijuana is directed to . . . people who seek sensual pleasures" and that "where drugs are used in mixed company, sexual immorality is generally the motivation and end result," while another case had licensed a movie that "portray[ed] under restrained and controlled conditions, a human birth," in the form of "a biological demonstration, scientific in level and tone."[39]

Soon a four-to-three majority of the Court of Appeals in an opinion by Judge Fuld went even farther, declaring that only the "sexually morbid, grossly perverse and bizarre" was obscene and thereby outside the scope of constitutional protection. Although "adolescents may be hurt by" such a standard and "virtuous adults will reject it (as all of us Judges would were we not restrained by the Roth-Alberts legal test)," even Chief Judge Desmond in concurrence knew that his "prepossessions" were "not the law," which "in a pluralist society" could "not regulate literary standards or give expression to the loftiest virtues." By the early 1970s the Court of Appeals had fully jumped aboard the libertarian bandwagon, when it reversed for vagueness a conviction resulting from a police raid on a Rochester bookstore, which had netted 126 separately titled books and calendars depicting " 'scenes of nude persons' " and of " 'the female and male genital organs, . . . including the male penis and the female breasts.' " Although the Court of Appeals upheld legislative attempts to apply stricter standards in regard to sales to minors, the New York courts gave adults in the 1970s access to all but what it declared to be the most hard-core materials, such as dildos; advertisements "soliciting . . . acts of sodomy, and wife-swapping orgies"; photographs of "young men," one of them "hardly more than a boy," all "in various stages of undress," engaged in "embracing, wrestling, spanking, beating, or . . . manually soap-lathering the genitalia of the other"; magazines rating motion pictures "by a 'Peter Meter,' a drawing of a penis superimposed upon a scale" which rates the picture "according to the percentage of erection" which the picture induces; and live sex shows, which "include[d] simulated heterosexual copulation by nude performers, masturbation, and three kinds of sodomy." [40]

When the practice of nude and topless dancing arose in bars and restaurants in the early 1970s, the courts leaned toward the view that it could not be prohibited. Thus although several trial court judges sustained state and local legislation prohibiting the practice, all the appellate judges who considered the issue declared the legislation invalid, as did some lower court judges, even where "a nude dancer . . . touched the area of her private parts, laid [sic] on the floor on a rug and performed dance maneuvers while lying there." It was similarly held that taking pictures of nudes in photography studios was constitutionally protected, although similar photography at a "farm outing" where guests paid $10 for the privilege of "photographing female models, some of whom posed in the nude," had earlier been held to violate the indecent exposure laws.[41]

As these cases make clear, the emergence of constitutional limitations on the criminalization of pornography had "evoked passion," with traditionalists speaking of "the poison of obscenity" and libertarians "deplor[ing] another breach in the constitutional bulwark against repression." But newly formulated doctrines did not bring "clarity" either "to the constitutional questions or to the social questions" raised by pornography. The reason for the confusion, according to a 1963 article by Louis Henkin that saw pornography law as the analogue of legislation against homosexuality and prostitution, was that the Supreme Court and the commentators had refused to examine the central issue raised by its obscenity cases—"the right of constitutional government to legislate morality which has no secular, utilitarian, or social purpose." In

Henkin's view, it was time "to define and articulate the extent to which the religious antecedents of our values may continue to motivate our governments in the enactment and enforcement of law." [42] At the time Henkin wrote, when the courts were striving to protect both individual liberty and religious liberty, his analysis of the issue at stake in pornography, as well as homosexuality and prostitution, surely seemed correct. But, as we shall next see, another issue — the exploitation of women by men — lurked beneath the surface and would soon emerge.

RAPE

No one, of course, ever proposed to decriminalize rape. At the height of the efforts to decriminalize homosexuality, prostitution, family violence, and pornography, the law treated what has been labeled " 'real rape' " — that is, cases of attacks on women by strangers — as a heinous crime. Indeed, as the Court of Appeals noted in one 1950 case, the "protection of women in a county with sparsely settled sections [was] one of the responsibilities" of courts and prosecutors, and contrary to its proclivity in other areas, the court was prepared in cases of "real rape" to construe criminal statutes broadly to achieve that end.[43]

But a different attitude existed when women claimed rape by men whom they knew, such as dates or former husbands and former lovers. As one scholar explained:

> When a woman is familiar with a man she claims has raped her there is always a question as to whether the force used in obtaining sexual intercourse was brought on by her own provocation. Many women with hysterical personality features are unusually seductive in their relationships with men. Sometimes their efforts at being charming arouse erotic reactions. . . . This suspicion can be legitimately raised when a woman has known her attacker, has accepted dates with him and has indulged in some kissing and petting.[44]

In such cases, the New York courts before the 1970s were loath indeed to subject men to the criminal process, and, in order to leave men free, they did exactly what they had done in their efforts to decriminalize homosexuality and prostitution: they altered technical legal doctrines surrounding the law of rape, in particular the rules requiring corroboration and strong proof of lack of consent, so as to increase the difficulty of obtaining criminal convictions.

The Corroboration Issue. Until the 1970s, no one questioned the requirement that a conviction could not be had for rape unless the testimony of the prosecutrix was duly corroborated. This requirement, which had been codified by statute long before 1920, was "not a mere rule of evidence, but a settled legislative declaration that such uncorroborated testimony is inherently untrustworthy." "Founded on centuries of social and legal experience," the corroboration requirement, it was said, "wisely recognize[d] that some complainants are designing or vicious" and that in the absence of the rule defendants would be at these women's "mercy." The requirement always had been a substantial one, and after 1950, it tended to become even more stringent, as courts, for example, reversed the old rule and declared that corroboration "must extend to the element of penetration."[45]

Several especially outrageous cases came before the Court of Appeals. One was *People v. Porcaro,* where a ten-year-old girl testified to her father's "having regular and frequent sexual intercourse" with her "during four years, in the usual manner as well as through her mouth." Noting that "a matrimonial dispute [was] in the background," the plurality opinion of Judge John Van Voorhis implied that the girl's testimony was unreliable without corroboration, and Judge Fuld in a separate concurrence would have reversed because, "as a matter of law, no conviction for impairing the morals of a child may validly rest on the uncorroborated testimony of the child victim." Van Voorhis in fact reversed on the narrower ground that the defendant claimed the girl was a virgin and was not permitted to have her medically examined as "common fairness require[d]."[46]

A companion case, *People v. Oyola,* where the defendant's ten-year-old daughter testified he had engaged in intercourse with her, was even more outrageous. The only corroboration offered was defendant's statement to his wife " 'that it was true what he had done' " and that " 'he was sorry for what he did to his daughter.' " Writing for the majority, Judge Van Voorhis observed that "testimony by complainants in these cases" should be distrusted since "errant young girls and women are given to 'contriving false charges of sexual offenses by men' " and " 'sinister possibilities of injustice . . . lurk[ed] in believing' " them. He accordingly reversed Oyola's conviction for want of proof beyond a reasonable doubt. Judge Charles Desmond dissented in both *Porcaro* and *Oyola,* noting in the latter that there "never has been a rule . . . requiring corroboration of the sworn testimony of . . . infant complainants, . . . [and] such a rule would be very much against the public interest."[47]

As it became increasingly difficult to satisfy the corroboration requirement, prosecutors in cases involving completed rapes sought to circumvent it by indicting defendants only for attempted rape or for assault with intent to rape. The Court of Appeals, however, promptly put a stop to such prosecutorial efforts. In *People v. LoVerde*, a teenage girl had accused a teenage boy of forcible rape, but in the absence of corroboration, the jury had found him guilty only of an act of intercourse that endangered the morals of a minor. In reversing his conviction, the court observed that under the established rules that had been applied by the jury "a prosecutor might easily circumvent the requirement of corroboration necessary for a conviction of misdemeanor rape simply by charging instead the impairment of the morals of a minor, as he did here. The law," the court added, "may not be so circumvented."[48]

The Court of Appeals continued to increase the difficulty of prosecuting cases of forced sex in *People v. English*, where in a four-to-three memorandum decision it reversed convictions for attempted rape and assault with intent to commit rape on the ground of lack of corroboration. The *English* rule, which was designed "as a matter of policy . . . to prevent the prosecutor from settling for the lesser conviction simply because of his inability to obtain the requisite corroboration,"[49] soon led, however, to outrageous results, as another case, *People v. Radunovic*, demonstrated.

Radunovic arose when a prosecutor, seeking to avoid the need for corroboration in a rape prosecution, brought only a charge of assault against a high school student who had attacked his teacher. Nonetheless, the majority of the Court of Appeals in an opinion by Judge Van Voorhis reversed the conviction. Van Voorhis held that when the only evidence of assault was the complainant's testimony of a completed rape, corroboration was required. He further held that bruises on the victim's thigh and medical testimony that her hymen was intact shortly before but not after the alleged assault was not sufficient corroboration.

This case produced vehement dissents. One by Judge John Scileppi called the majority opinion "a license to commit rape" since the crime was "hardly ever committed in the presence of others" and the necessary corroboration was therefore almost always unobtainable. He found this approval of license "an intolerable situation" when "the incidence of attacks on women . . . [was] steadily increasing." As Judge Albert Conway had declared only a few years earlier, the conservatives on the court were generally "disturbed" by "appeals . . . to the sexual appetite" and "by the increasing marks of moral laxity," and they were "unable to look upon [this] moral disintegration as a mere change in custom." Taking what would soon be seen as more of a feminist approach, Judge Francis Bergan noted in a companion dissent that, "if a man had been assaulted," the evidence of bruises "would be sufficient; it ought to be sufficient, too, if a woman is assaulted."[50]

Nonetheless, *English* and *Radunovic* were the law, and the lower courts uniformly applied the rule of the two cases to invalidate convictions both for attempted rape and for assault with intent to commit rape when the actual crime was a completed rape. Conviction could be had for an attempt or assault only if the evidence showed that the defendant tried to have intercourse but failed. Such holdings led, of course, to the absurd and anomalous result that " 'one who makes a sexual attack on a woman can be convicted without corroboration if he falls short of satisfying his lust, but not if he succeeds." Thus the law directed men who, even in ambiguous circumstances, had used only the slightest force in the service of passion to press forward to the end, while it directed women who complained to the police of a rape to assert at trial, presumably falsely, that their "condition at the time of the assault was such" that they "couldn't say that there had been a consummated rape." [51]

The Consent Issue. By definition, rape is forcible sexual intercourse. Thus a defendant can always negate his guilt by showing that the complainant consented to sexual relations. Black-letter law, which remained constant throughout this period, demanded that a woman offer her utmost resistance to the attack or at least " 'as much resistance as she possibly could under the circumstances and the facts' " of the case.[52] From the 1950s until the mid-1970s, judges applied this doctrine strictly, and men accordingly enjoyed the benefit of the doubt if a woman's reaction to a demand for intercourse was in the least ambiguous.

Two of the mid-1970s cases that failed to produce convictions were paradigmatic. In *People v. Evans,* the defendant used the pretense of being a psychologist to lure a college sophomore into his apartment, where he put her in fear by remarking that she was in " 'the apartment of a strange man' " and that he " 'could kill' " or " 'rape' " her. After he next yelled and screamed, he broke down and told the sophomore about " 'his lost love,' " who had committed suicide. When she reached out for him, he grabbed her, announcing " 'You're mine, you are mine.' " They then slept together for the night, during which there were three acts of sexual intercourse and an act of oral-genital contact.[53]

Although the complainant contended that she yielded out of fear and thus did not consent, the court found otherwise. It commented that it was "not illegal to feed a girl a line, to continue the attempt, not to take no for a final answer, at least not the first time." The court also noted that the defendant "spurned the readily available . . . [and] acquiescent women" and "got his kicks through the exercise of these techniques." As he boasted to the police, "this was a game he played with girls' heads" as well as their bodies—a game that gave him pleasure and power at the expense of women's victimization. While the court found this conduct "reprehensible," it was "not criminal"—it was only "conquest by con job."[54]

People v. Hughes, the second case, involved a runaway who was staying in the defendant Hughes's apartment. When he returned one evening at midnight and found her lying asleep nude in his bed, the defendant undressed and got into bed with her, kissed her, and fondled her, but, according to his testimony, did not have intercourse. According to the complainant, he attacked her with a knife, demanded sex, and, despite her protests, forced her to relent. Later he pulled her hair, choked her, and engaged in more intercourse. On these facts, plus the additional one that her two male friends sleeping in the room with her did not intervene because "they were afraid someone would get hurt," a jury found the defendant guilty, but the Appellate Division reversed, apparently finding the testimony of both the defendant and the two other men incredible.[55] The likely interpretation of the facts by the court was that the defendant and the complainant did have intercourse, but that despite her protests, her posture made it legitimate for him "not to take no for a final answer."

Thus it appears that, when a woman was acquainted with a man with whom she had had intercourse, mid-twentieth-century judges tended to accept the view of leading scholars and find that the woman's "hysterical personality" and "efforts at being charming" had "arouse[d] erotic reactions," that the act of intercourse was "brought on by her own provocation," and that it was therefore a product of her own consent. Judges believed that, even when a woman said *no* to a man's demand for sex, in reality she often meant *yes.* Their understanding, moreover, was merely a product of the era's popular culture—culture reflected, for example, in the lyrics of a song contained in Mitch Miller's *Sing Along with Mitch* collection declaring, "Your Lips Tell Me No! No! But There's Yes! Yes! in Your Eyes." Thus the holding of *People v. Evans,* which seems so outrageous today—that it was "not illegal" for a man seeking sex "to continue the attempt [and] not to take no for a final answer"—was only characteristic of the unbridled mores of its time.[56]

The Victimization of Women. The doctrinal developments in the law of rape that have been considered in this section occurred at high cost to women and with little regard for their right not to be compelled to engage in intercourse without their consent. The slight regard in which judges held a woman's right of refusal was perhaps best illustrated by two damage cases, one of which set aside as excessive a $66,000 jury verdict on behalf of a thirteen-year-old rape victim, while the other awarded a meager $5000 judgment for a fourteen-year-old victim. It was also reflected in the ancient rule that the doctrine of marital consent meant that a husband could not be guilty of raping his wife.[57]

In the context of the double standard whereby a woman, as the "controller of the sexual relation," [58] was supposed to "say . . . 'no' [even] when she mean[t] 'yes,' " date rape inevitably occurred in a "grey area," where there was "no clear dividing line between physical assault and sexuality." To use the criminal law in this context to protect a woman's right to say no would deprive men, as well as women who meant yes when they said no, of sexual opportunities that they felt entitled to pursue. Even worse, the commonly held, mid-twentieth century view of male and female sexuality understood that, once a couple had started to pursue the love and closeness that women craved, actual intercourse became "a *necessity* to [the] man." [59] In light of this view, the grant to women of a legal power of termination over the "ritual, . . . game, or . . . dance" to which "the consummation of sexuality [was] an integral part" [60] would painfully deprive men not merely of an opportunity but even more of a satisfaction to which, in mid-century understandings, they were entitled.

New York judges, as the cases decided before the 1970s show, would not countenance the use of criminal law either to deprive men of their sexual opportunities or to disappoint their sexual expectations. But in protecting the rights of men, the judges inevitably trampled on the rights of women. For what the mid-century law of date rape made clear was that, once a woman became close to a man who demanded intercourse and had the physical power to compel it, she could not refuse even if she did not, in fact, consent. Even if the words "No! No!" passed from a woman's lips, a man was free to assume that the woman's true desire—"Yes! Yes!"—was reflected in her eyes. Accommodating the sexist thought patterns of the 1960s, the law did nothing to obstruct men from obtaining the sex they wanted, even though women did not always give that sex freely. The protective attitude of the judiciary of the 1920s had, in short, largely disappeared by the 1960s.

CHAPTER 10

LIBERTY AND THE FAMILY

Although many of the values and attitudes that had characterized family law in the 1920s and 1930s persisted into the 1940s and 1950s and even beyond,[1] the era of World War II also witnessed signs of libertarian change, parallel to those occurring in the law of sex crimes.

INDIVIDUALISM AND THE PURSUIT OF HAPPINESS

One consequence of the war was family instability. Voicing a concern of many of his colleagues in the 1940s, for example, one judge perceived an increase in "marriage[s] . . . torn asunder by a disordered society under the stress and strain of war." He sensed that, as young men and women involved in the war left "home in a village in the mountains and strayed into a large city," they were "beguiled by false allurements of tinsel, glitter, lights and the glamour and fanfare of war," they "misbehaved," and they "disregarded the usual peacetime social conventions, with . . . tragic result[s]." They "committed sins of passion but not of evil purpose," as had "Mary Magdalen and Hester Prynne" and "countless others before and after them." It followed that it "would not be realistic" to "assume a sanctimonious or puritanical attitude." Since judges were "dealing with humans and not angels," they had to "take human frailties into account, especially when dealing with parties of Continental background." The "mission of the law," after all, was not a "blind and merciless casting of the first stone," but "justice . . . seasoned with compassion."[2] And doing justice required courts to protect rights designed, in turn, to foster individual liberty.

Child Custody. Not surprisingly, these new attitudes began in mid-century to affect family law doctrine. Acting out of mercy and compassion and out of recognition of parents' sexual and moral autonomy, judges began to rule, for example, that custody of children should not be denied for a "mild . . . vice" such as gambling or for one or two adulterous relationships that fell short of "promiscuity."[3] But if custody was not to be determined on the basis of fault, as it had been during the interwar decades, at least when the fault was minor, what new standard would replace it?

In a few cases, nationalism born of a vague, World War II confidence in American virtue[4] became the standard. Thus judges declared that American

children had "as a part of their birthright . . . a right to be raised and educated in this country," and for that reason they routinely granted custody to
a parent residing in the United States rather than to one planning to live in
a foreign country. One judge, for instance, refused to allow a father to bring
children born in the United States with him when he returned to his native
land—Soviet Armenia. "Nothing," according to this judge, "had greater value
and was more to be cherished" than American citizenship, which conferred "a
right to the full enjoyment of life, liberty and the pursuit of happiness"; indeed, "many regarded" American citizenship "as the highest hope of civilized
men."[5]

Another judge expressed a comparable reaction in *Ex parte Djurovic*.[6] Sla-
voljub Djurovic was a Yugoslav citizen assigned to work for a government-
operated company in New York. He and his wife had two sons living with
them in New York at the time they separated, either, as he claimed, because of
his fear of persecution if he returned with her to Yugoslavia or, as his wife alleged, because of his affair with another woman in New York. The sons were in
an upstate New York boarding school, when the Yugoslav vice consul in New
York, together with the mother, picked them up in a car owned by the con-
sulate and driven by its chauffeur and brought them to a secret hiding place
in New York City. Several days later they were secretly transferred to a ship
about to set sail to Yugoslavia. The father then sought a writ of habeas corpus
to remove them from the boat; the court granted the writ and gave custody
of the sons to the father.

A third case involved a seventeen-year-old child living with her mother in
Sault Ste. Marie, Canada, who petitioned the court to allow her to live with
her father in New York City. She felt "bored with small town life in Canada,"
where she had "very few friends" and was "was wasting her time in a small
town where she ha[d] little if any opportunities to meet people." She had a
"keen urge to come to live in New York," where she felt "that by education
and social contact here she will have the opportunity to better herself in every
way."[7] Of course, the judge agreed.

In most cases, though, nationalistic beliefs about the superiority of life in
America provided no basis for choosing one parent as custodian in preference
to the other. Of necessity, courts in most instances had to turn to the only other
standard in existence—the new gender-based standard of preferring mothers
over fathers.

This standard, although dating back to the nineteenth century, had begun
to emerge with a vengeance around the World War II years. The law, it was
then said, had "an almost reverential regard for mother love as an ingredient in

the sound upbringing of a child." This reverential regard, in turn, was reified into a general presumption "that when it becomes necessary to make a choice between mother and father it is to the child's best interest to be brought up and reared by his mother." "A widely held belief" thereupon emerged "that a mother [was] favored over a father in a legal custody proceeding," and that belief remained in place at least until the mid-1970s.[8]

The reported cases lent support to this belief. For example, a mother with "schizophrenia, paranoid type," was held fit to receive custody, and one 1952 decision even upheld custody in a mother who had been adjudicated guilty of neglecting her children as a result of her alleged "affiliation, or at least sympathy, with the Communist Party." Not even a mother's sexual lifestyle would cost her the preference for custody. Starting in the 1950s with adherence to the older dictum that a mother's "*single* deviation from the orbit of marital rectitude should not alone deprive" her "of the natural right to the custody of the child," courts by the 1970s had come to recognize that a mother's exercise of "the right of a divorced woman to engage in private sexual activities, which in no way involve or affect her minor children" would not result in her loss of custody, even when the activities involved "female homosexuality."[9]

Adoption. Change occurred in a more complex fashion in the law governing adoption. As we have seen, adoption during the 1920s and 1930s had often served the function of providing children of poverty with a means of livelihood and support. With the enactment of the New Deal welfare system in the mid-1930s, which guaranteed at least minimal support for destitute children, adoption was no longer needed for such a purpose and could take on a new goal, although initially not one connected with the protection of rights.[10]

The relation between welfare and adoption emerged with particular clarity in a 1936–37 case. Edna Betz had been adopted by her maternal grandparents at the age of twelve, apparently following the death of her mother. Eleven years later, her grandmother also was dead, her grandfather (i.e., her adoptive father) was "destitute and incapable of contributing to her support," and Edna was suffering from tuberculosis.[11] The issue was whether her natural father had some continuing duty to support her.

Under the traditional view that adoption did not totally terminate all ties between a child and its natural parents, the father did retain a duty. Thus the majority of the Appellate Division thought it "contrary to natural law" "to relieve the natural parents of their moral obligation to support their helpless offspring and to impose that burden upon the public in the event the adoptive parents died or became destitute." But a unanimous Court of Appeals, implicitly recognizing the primary obligation of the public to support the destitute and not to foist the obligation upon anyone who happened to be at hand in order to save public funds, took a different view. Thus the court held that adoption made "the adopted child the natural child of the adoptive parent," gave that " 'child the same legal relation to the foster parent as a child of his body,' " and totally " 'divest[ed] the natural parents of the relation which they had theretofore sustained toward the infant.' "[12]

It followed from this holding, at least for some judges, "*that a consummated adoption [was final and] unassailable*" and that the natural parents had no capacity to reopen it. Once an adoption had been consummated, the natural parents were not even entitled to information about the whereabouts of the child because courts feared that a natural mother "could be a source of great annoyance to the foster parents," who "deserve[d] every protection which the court [was] capable of giving them in their exclusive custody of . . . [their] child." Similar interests of finality dictated that adopted children not be given access to information about their natural parents.[13]

With these cases, the principal ends served by the law of adoption changed. In the context of the new welfare state that arose after World War II, judges reacted totally differently than their predecessors had a mere two decades earlier when parents unable to support children gave them for adoption; indeed, one judge reacted as if the world of the 1920s and 1930s had never existed. His own words can best convey the change that had occurred:

> There is still a further point which this Court considers to be of great moment. Here a young couple, already having two children, consent to the adoption of a third child and placed the child with the proposed adoptive parents almost immediately after birth, and the only excuse given for the adoption and placement is that they cannot afford to rear the third child. It is against the conscience of this Court to countenance such an act upon the part of the natural parents. The parents should make every effort to provide for the child and to give it the natural love and affection to which the child is entitled. This Court cannot and will not countenance an adoption of this nature based upon such a flimsy excuse and thus avoid a duty and an obligation imposed upon the parents.[14]

With adoption no longer available for the lasting placement of children whom their parents could not afford to raise, its primary end became the provision of childless couples with infants born out of wedlock—infants who would become, in every respect, the children of the adopting couple. The "development of . . . procedure[s] which [would] promote, encourage and facilitate . . . [such] adoption[s]" was explicitly recognized as "a legitimate area of state concern."[15]

In this context, the first major issue courts faced was the elaboration of standards for determining whether a natural mother had acted in a fashion that warranted depriving her of custody of her child and delivering it to another. The black-letter law was clear: a natural mother could be deprived of custody only if she had freely surrendered her child, had abandoned it, or was unfit to retain custody. In an effort to facilitate adoptions by "good people," however, judges as late as mid-century, who put themselves " 'in the position of a wise, affectionate, and careful parent' " seeking " 'to do what [was] best for the interests of the child,' " had readily found these requirements satisfied. One wise, affectionate, and careful judge, for instance, could not help but notice when adoptive parents maintained an "entirely satisfactory home in an atmosphere and an environment that [were] pleasant, cultured, religious and understanding" with a "family income . . . adequate to provide for all the needs of the child," while the natural mother was "unemployed, ha[d] been trained for no gainful occupation, and ha[d] made no serious attempt at employment." Hence he concluded that "it would be an act of cruelty to take this child out of her present happy environment and place her with those who spurned her when her need was greatest." Likewise, another judge, after finding that the adoptive parents had "nursed" the child "through a severe illness with loving care and at substantial financial expense," that the natural mother was willing to consent to the adoption if she was paid the right "price," and hence that "the moral and temporal interests of the child and his future happiness [would] be promoted" by the adoption, concluded that the natural mother had abandoned her son, even though she had hired an attorney in the effort to obtain his return.[16]

Lower court judges decided a few of the early cases in favor of natural mothers, however, when special factors made the conduct of those mothers appear as "striking example[s]" of "the basic sentiment of mother love." The first case involved a woman who during World War II had served in the military, where she had met a young soldier who, after promising to marry her, had gotten her pregnant. When he deserted her, she proved resourceful, obtained employment for $50 per week, and "paid for a considerable length of time for the care of her offspring." When she became ill, however, her employer and his wife took the child into their home, with the understanding that the mother was welcome to visit and have the child "from time to time, as she chose." Later the employer's attorney brought a document for her signature to the place of employment, and she signed it without understanding its "nature and . . . consequences." The court thereupon concluded that the document in question did not constitute a valid consent to adoption.[17]

In another case, a college student who found herself pregnant "sought out the services of a woman doctor" in an effort to avoid disclosing "her condition" to her father and her siblings. The doctor arranged for the child to be adopted, and, upon its birth, turned it over to the prospective adoptive parents. Five months later, however, the natural mother confessed her secret to her sisters, and her entire family promised to "stand by her financially and morally if she would take steps to obtain the baby." Her married brother offered her a home, she obtained a job, and she brought a writ of habeas corpus to recover the child. Declaring that " 'parents have the natural, God-given right to the control and custody of their children,' " the court concluded that the mother had neither abandoned her child nor given the final consent to adoption required by statute at the adoption proceeding, which had not yet occurred.[18] Thus the child was returned to the mother's custody.

THE EMERGENCE OF INDIVIDUAL RIGHTS

The Right of Parents to Children. Next the Court of Appeals entered the fray in the 1952 case of *People ex rel. Portnoy v. Strasser.*[19] And when it entered, it took a decisive stand on the side of the rights and thus the liberty of natural parents.

In May 1945, a young Jewish couple had become the parents of Robin Strasser, who lived in their home until they separated a year later. Robin and her mother then went to live with Robin's maternal grandmother, until Robin's mother obtained an apartment of her own two years later and took the child to live with her. There was no custody battle when Robin's mother obtained a divorce from her father and was awarded custody of the child.

Trouble began only in 1949, when Robin's mother married a second husband, an African American man "of fine character, steadily employed at a good salary." At that point, the maternal grandmother brought suit to obtain custody of Robin on grounds that Robin's mother — the petitioner's own daughter — was "a communist, without any regard for religious upbringing of the child, and that she [was] married to a second husband who [was] of a race . . . different from that of the child." A referee appointed by the Supreme Court granted custody to the grandmother "based on one or more of these considerations: first, that communistic activities occupied the mother's attention; second, that the mother went out to work and left the infant in a day nursery and nursery schools, and third, that the child was not being trained in the religion in which it was born," and the Appellate Division affirmed.[20]

A unanimous Court of Appeals, probably wishing neither to approve nor to "frown upon an interracial marriage," avoided completely the racially sensitive issues which the grandmother had raised. Nevertheless, it reversed the Appellate Division. In doing so, it relied on a rights-based rhetoric growing out of World War II. Citing only the inapposite case of *Meyer v. Nebraska,* the Court of Appeals held that "the *right* of a parent, under *natural law,* to establish a home and bring up children [was] a *fundamental one* and beyond the reach of any court." Declaring that the grandmother had "assumed the very heavy burden of proving that a little girl should, by court order, be separated from her own and her mother's home," the court further held that she had failed to sustain that burden. It found that the evidence "as to membership and work in alleged communistic 'Front' organizations" was not "such as to make the mother unfit to rear her own infant"; that "outside employment and the use of nursery schools by a mother are not such things that courts should try to control"; and that "the mother's failure to train the little girl in the faith of her fathers . . . [was] within the parent's sole control."[21]

The rights-based language of the *Portnoy* case was cited prominently the next year in *People ex rel. Kropp v. Shepsky,* involving an unwed, eighteen-year-old mother who had tried for a year to support her child, until "out of work and nearly out of funds" she "in desperation . . . entrusted her child to a lawyer . . . to be placed with a family." Although she signed a consent to adoption, "she made it plain that she 'was not giving . . . [her child] up for adoption'" and understood only that it was "to be boarded out." After an adoption order had been signed in a proceeding of which she received no notice, the natural mother brought habeas corpus. The trial judge denied the writ, and the Second Department of the Appellate Division, in pursuit of its usual preference for adoptive parents over unwed mothers, affirmed.[22]

The Court of Appeals reversed. No longer willing to assume, as judges typically had in the past, that a destitute woman's "offense against society and religion in having been the mother of an illegitimate child" made her less worthy than an economically secure, middle-class couple seeking to adopt a child, the court began instead to perceive such a woman as a victim who, having been misled, had made mistakes. Above all, the court recognized that natural mothers had rights, including the "right to the care and custody of a child, superior to that of all others"—a right that was " 'a fundamental one and beyond the reach of any court.' "[23]

Unlike many other family law decisions by the Court of Appeals, *People ex rel. Kropp v. Shepsky* had an immediate impact on lower courts. Perhaps because of the era's increasing emphasis on rights or perhaps because the unwed mothers they confronted were more often middle-class women with whom they could empathize, judges on the lower courts became increasingly protective of rights of women who, after having given up their children, sought to prevent their adoption. Especially in instances involving private placements through individual doctors and lawyers, where there was special reason to fear that young, unwed mothers were often overreached, courts usually held that mothers had not intended irrevocably to surrender their babies. As a result, it was clear by the early 1970s that a "baby born out-of-wedlock, even of a troubled mother, . . . [was] not 'up for grabs,'" nor "a waif claimable by the first finder, however highly qualified." [24]

Not even the legislature could undermine this fundamental right of natural parents to raise their own children. Concerned that adoptive parents needed the benefit of some procedure to guarantee that they could adopt a child without fear that the natural mother would revoke her consent, the legislature in 1972 adopted a statute making a consent executed in open court irrevocable. Although some cases decided after 1972 upheld consents in accordance with the spirit of the new law, most continued to hold it "fundamental to our legal and social system, that it is in the best interests of a child to be raised by his parents" and, as a result, to allow natural parents to revoke their adoption consents. Indeed, a judge who processed adoptions in Manhattan went so far as to suggest that he would carefully scrutinize future consents in private placement cases even in the absence of claims by mothers of impropriety.[25]

The Right to Divorce and Annulment. The most decisive shift from law based on traditional family values to law emphasizing individual rights occurred as the New York courts, beginning in the late 1930s, slowly retreated from the state's century-old policy of keeping marriage indissoluble. This policy, it will be recalled, rested on restricting in-state divorce only to cases involving adultery, limiting the recognition accorded to out-of-state divorce, and constraining relief in the form of annulments.

The first sign of change occurred in the old New York rule according recognition to out-of-state divorces only when they had been granted on the ground of adultery. The earliest case was *Glaser v. Glaser,* where the Court of Appeals recognized the validity of a Nevada divorce in a case where both spouses had submitted themselves to the jurisdiction of the Nevada court, even though the New York judges continued to insist that their action was not required by the federal Constitution's full faith and credit clause and that they had acted only as a matter "of state policy over which the United States Supreme Court ha[d] no jurisdiction." Next came the Supreme Court's decisions in *Williams v. North Carolina* holding that the full faith and credit clause determined the effect that one state was required to accord the divorce decrees of a sister state. Although the Court of Appeals promptly recognized its obligation to abide by at least the first *Williams* decision, it simultaneously continued to apply much old law refusing to recognize out-of-state decrees.[26]

More significantly, the lower courts held that they were free to inquire into the jurisdiction of any sister-state tribunal and that they were not required to obey a sister-state decree if they found the rendering tribunal without jurisdiction. In 1944, the Court of Appeals agreed and, as the lower courts continued to follow along, thereby nullified the opportunity that *Williams* had given New York residents to obtain out-of-state divorces which they could not obtain in-state. Indeed, one lower court judge in 1948 acted as if the *Williams* decision had never been rendered, when, citing the 1920 case of *Hubbard v. Hubbard,* he declared it "the well-settled policy of this State to refuse to recognize as binding a decree of divorce obtained in a court of a sister state . . . upon grounds insufficient for that purpose in this State, where the divorced spouse resided in this State and was not personally served with process and did not appear in the foreign action." [27]

When the Court of Appeals in a 1950 case reiterated its 1944 holding authorizing inquiry into the jurisdiction of sister state courts, the Supreme Court reversed, declaring that the "faith and credit given is not to be niggardly but generous, full" and that " 'local policy must at times be required to give way.' " Fifteen years of confusion followed, as some lower courts continued to inquire into the jurisdictional basis of and to refuse to give effect to out-of-state decrees, while others reached the opposite result.[28]

An especially nettlesome issue during the 1950s and into the 1960s concerned the validity of Mexican divorces. Of course, the full faith and credit clause did not require New York to give them effect, and many decisions, as a result, treated them as a nullity. Others, however, indicated a willingness to recognize Mexican decrees when one spouse had appeared in Mexico and the other had been represented by an attorney, or at the very least estopped spouses who had participated in obtaining Mexican divorces from challenging their validity.[29]

Rosenstiel v. Rosenstiel put the issue to rest by upholding a divorce granted in Mexico to a husband, who had spent one hour in the country signing an official book of residents and filing a petition for divorce, and a wife, whose attorney on the next day had submitted to the jurisdiction of the Mexican court and admitted the allegations of the petition. The effect of the decision, as noted by the dissent, was "to ignore the basic concepts and value judgments" of New York's divorce legislation, which for 170 years had permitted divorce only on grounds of adultery, out of "a design to restrict the availability of divorce and in so doing to preserve the family unit . . . considered vital and indispensable to the welfare and stability of the family, the ultimate goal being a climate conducive to the better development of our society." The dissent accordingly accused the majority of "sanction[ing] the casual and consensual dissolution of the marriage contract" by giving spouses, in the view of another member of the court, the power of "going to other jurisdictions to evade our laws by obtaining divorces after short sojourns and on grounds not cognizable here."[30]

The same tension between preserving traditional family values and giving individuals freedom to control their marital ties also appeared in a line of annulment cases occurring between the late 1930s and mid-1960s. In the earlier cases, judges had protected traditional values, as in one case, when they denied a marriage license to a Hindu migrant from India because he had left a wife behind there, even though under Indian law she could not stop him from remarrying, and in another case, when they declared a woman who had gone through a marriage ceremony with Samuel Levy to be his widow, even though Levy had intended only to make her his housekeeper and therefore had obtained no license for the marriage.[31]

In later cases such as *Siecht v. Siecht* the courts were more willing to relieve individuals from hard marriages. The *Siecht* case arose nearly two decades after Joseph Siecht and his wife, Eva, had both migrated to the United States, where Joseph quickly became a citizen. When they married in 1925, Eva also had promised to become a citizen but had never done so. Then, in 1939, when Joseph learned that Eva was a member of the Deutscher Bund, he left her. Two years later she persuaded him to return with a promise to become a citizen, but she failed again to honor the promise or to quit the Bund. Then, during World War II, Joseph left his wife again, after the following conversation reported in the court's opinion:

Q. About two days before that did you have a talk with your wife about her becoming a citizen?

A. I did. And she said there was no use of her trying to become a citizen because "these shitty British and stupid Americans can't win this war, because that man has prepared a long time for this and he will rule everything."

The Referee: That was Hitler?

The Witness: Yes. I said "who is the man," and she said "Hitler, he is going to be the boss, and whatever he says will go."

The court thereupon held that "the refusal of the defendant to become a citizen of the United States and her membership and activities in the Deutscher Bund, and her general attitude of disloyalty to our country" constituted "valid grounds for an annulment" of Joseph's marriage, even though Eva's 1925 promise to become a citizen must have had little, if any, materiality at that time in inducing him to marry her.[32]

The final case exhibiting the tension between traditional values and the right of an individual to be free of a harsh marriage was *Kober v. Kober.* The case arose when Jaqueline Kober sought an annulment of her marriage to Josef Kober on the ground that he had failed to inform her that he had been an officer in the Germany army during World War II and "that he was a Nazi and hated Jewish people and was fanatically anti-semitic; that he believed in, advocated, approved and applauded Hitler's 'Final Solution' of extermination of the Jewish people and that he would require plaintiff to weed out her Jewish friends and cease socializing with them." In denying Josef's motion to dismiss this claim, the trial court found his views "more than distasteful beliefs; they are absolutely repugnant and insufferable to all persons who believe in the divine nature of man."[33]

Out of concern for the competing set of values, the Appellate Division reversed. Although it took note of "the extreme and horrible character of the husband's past and present beliefs," the majority also knew that "the limited ground on which a divorce may be obtained in this State, produces pressure to extend the action for annulment to embrace more than it . . . logically should." The majority was concerned that "the extension" of doctrine needed to authorize annulments on the ground of political beliefs would "unleash an uncontrollable mass of collateral problems and effects." The Appellate Division majority, to quote an earlier case, knew that it could not "grant annulments solely because of sympathy" when to do so would constitute "an extension of the legislative enactment by judicial decree" and amount to "legislation by the judiciary"[34] that would have the capacity to undermine the state's entire law of marriage and divorce.

Three judges on the Court of Appeals adopted the view of the Appellate Division, but four judges voted to reverse. In their view, the defendant's "fanatical conviction . . . that a race or group of people living in the same community should be put to death as at Auschwitz, Belsen, Dachau or Buchenwald, evidence[d] a diseased mind" that might warrant annulment on the statutory ground of insanity or lunacy. In any event, the four-judge majority was convinced that the defendant's views would "plainly make the marital relationship unworkable in this jurisdiction,"[35] which, as we have earlier seen, had been slowly committing itself to integrating minorities like Jews into the mainstream of the community's life.

Decided in the same year by the same four-judge majority, the *Rosenstiel* and *Kober* cases nonetheless had exactly the effect that the dissenters had feared: they opened the floodgates to allow New Yorkers to obtain easy divorces out of state and easy annulments at home. Although the two cases show that traditional values of family preservation through limitation of divorce still commanded considerable adherence, they tipped the legislature's hand and forced it to enact the reforms of 1966–67, which finally brought about a "modernization and liberalization of . . . [New York's] medieval divorce law."[36]

After September 1, 1967, New York finally began to allow divorce on grounds in addition to adultery. One of the new grounds was cruelty. This upgrading of the significance of cruelty produced only one change, however, in its definition, when the Court of Appeals held that "even one beating" could constitute cruel and inhuman treatment authorizing a wife to obtain a divorce. The reform legislation also upgraded abandonment into a ground for divorce, while adultery, of course, also remained a ground for divorce.[37]

The reform legislation also added two new grounds for divorce. The first, which paid no heed to fault, allowed a divorce to parties who had lived separate and apart for two years—a period later reduced to one year, provided the parties had substantially performed all the terms of their separation agreement or judgment of separation. The second new ground authorized divorce when a defendant spouse was imprisoned for a term of three or more years.[38]

With the 1967 statutory changes, New Yorkers seeking to end their marriages rushed into their own courts.[39] With divorce readily available, plaintiffs no longer needed to turn to annulment law to circumvent the state's limited divorce law, especially since "a spouse in an annulment action [no longer had] any greater rights than in a separation or divorce action." As a result, annulment cases almost disappeared from the state's jurisprudence. The need to seek out-of-state relief similarly vanished, and as it did, issues of full faith and credit in divorce cases likewise nearly disappeared.[40]

THE NEW SEXISM

No one would claim that New York family law was without sexist underpinnings of a sort during the 1920s and 1930s. Nevertheless, the sexism of these early decades was constrained. The law countenanced the dominance of male family heads, but in return men were held to a duty to preserve the well-being of the women and children who were their dependents.

Sexism of this sort endured into the 1940s, the 1950s, and even the 1960s. But during these later decades, as the emphasis of family law shifted from family preservation to the protection of individual rights conducive to personal happiness, male privilege and judicial toleration of men's misbehavior became increasingly pronounced. Sexism of a new and arguably more virulent sort thus spread and, in conjunction with sexist doctrines inherited from earlier times, degraded women.

Paternity Cases. One area of newly rampant sexism grew up around the law dealing with proceedings to determine the paternity of illegitimate children. A striking fact about the paternity cases is the absence of judicial language critical of men who had sired these children. Men who got unmarried women pregnant were not subject to condemnation; their behavior, it appears, was regarded simply as natural. Women and children, in contrast, were condemned. At common law, an illegitimate child was "nullius filius" — the child of no one, entitled to neither rights nor standing in the community, and "not looked upon as [a] child . . . for any civil purposes." At mid-century, "a child born out of wedlock [was] still nullius filius," and "the common law conception . . . remain[ed] unchanged." [41]

Nor were mothers of illegitimate children more highly regarded, as is illustrated by a 1950 case involving two mothers of twelve illegitimate children. The case "illustrate[d] the many burdens which are imposed upon the taxpayers through the activities of immoral persons." After expressing his concern that "year after year new children had been appearing upon the scene, and no one seemed to have given any thought as to how the law might be invoked to curb activities of that kind," the judge himself conferred with welfare officials, urged them to prosecute the mothers for "immorality or depravity . . . which had caused their children to be neglected," and, when the mothers appeared before him without counsel, he found them guilty. Although reports had "come to the Court of [one of] the wom[e]n and her children stepping into a nice station wagon and starting off for the beach on a Sunday morning while the neighbors know that they are all burdens on the taxpayers," the judge nonetheless suspended the mothers' sentences and left their children in their custody. He explained, "It appeared, however, that . . . [the children] had received excellent physical care, and I had to consider the harm which might be done to the children by separating them abruptly even from mothers such as I had before me. I, therefore, left them in the care of their mothers." The judge also had to admit his inability to deal with the father of five of the twelve children, who "was a married man living with his family in the neighborhood." The mother, however, "consistently refused to give the man's name," and as a result, the court was "blocked in its efforts to bring him to account, if indeed any useful purpose would be served . . . in bringing to light a state of facts which might simply result in the breaking up of his own family." [42]

These mid-century cases represented a marked change from judicial attitudes a few decades earlier. Men then had been permitted to dominate their families, but the law had expected monogamy in return. At mid-century, in contrast, the double standard was judicially tolerated: women were criticized for giving birth to illegitimate children, while male promiscuity was presumed to be normal and natural. In recognizing such male privilege without imposing any corresponding duty, judges legitimated a new kind of sexism.

Annulment Cases. New sorts of sexist assumptions also appeared in annulment cases. In one case, for example, a "so-called patriotic wom[a]n," during World War II had married "a soldier solely for the purpose of getting an allotment and more if the soldier [was] killed" but thereafter had refused to live with the soldier after he had returned home; the court declared such conduct to be "the most brazen kind of a fraud and . . . a good ground for the annulment of the marriage." [43] However much the facts may have supported the court's holding, its stereotype of the brave soldier seeking love before departing to fight for his country and of the money-grubbing woman selling herself for a government pittance was naive in its view of men and outrageously unfair to women.

Judicial blindness to the faults of men and indifference to the difficulties faced by women became increasingly characteristic, though, as the 1940s and 1950s progressed. Similar sexism was rampant, for example, as courts applied the double standard in cases in which one spouse sought an annulment on the ground of sexual activities previous to marriage by the other. Thus judges held a man entitled to an annulment if his wife had failed to disclose a previous illegitimate pregnancy or marriage or even if she turned out not to be the virgin he had expected her to be. In contrast, wives were denied annulments on account of previous undisclosed sexual activities of their husbands, even if those activities had resulted in illegitimate births. [44]

Insofar as they denied women control over their reproductive lives, sexism was also inherent in the "fraudulent failure to procreate cases" that arose in large numbers in the aftermath of World War II. As one judge opined, "Marital intercourse, so that children may be born, [was] an obligation of the marriage contract and . . . the foundation upon which must rest the perpetuation of society and civilization." Thus an annulment was proper if either the husband or wife insisted on using contraception. Since either a husband or a wife could obtain an annulment, sexism, which was real if one understands that reproductive choice is more important to women than to men, was often hidden. In at least one case, though, it was not even hidden, when a judge went so far as to grant a husband an annulment because his wife insisted, for the first time after their marriage, that she would determine the time at which she would become pregnant.[45]

Separation Cases. Sexism became even more rampant in cases involving judicial elaboration of the grounds for separation. Before 1967, when New York permitted divorce only for adultery, its law also allowed the lesser remedy of a judicial separation on grounds of either cruelty or abandonment.

The first ground for separation—cruelty—not surprisingly encompassed physical violence by one spouse against the other. A double standard had long existed in the definition of cruelty, however, as cases held that one or two isolated acts of violence by a husband against his wife did not amount to cruel and inhuman treatment. Indeed, the courts became so tolerant of male violence that, among other things, they found a man justified in striking his wife after he had found her sitting on the lap of another man and kissing him. In another case, "The plaintiff admitted . . . that prior to the incident in which defendant held her head under the bathtub faucet she had thrown a pot of water on him and that prior to the incident in which he had tied her hands and feet, he had sought to make love to her and she had repulsed him, slapping and kicking him. *Such physical acts as defendant committed were, thus, provoked.*" In contrast, the courts were clear that a single violent act by wife against her husband amounted to wrongdoing on her part.[46]

Traditional forms of sexism also appeared in New York's "rigid" rules of separation, which failed to "take into account latter-day medical and sociological concepts" by recognizing "name calling, bickering, [and] threats" as a form of cruelty. The law was clear. As the Court of Appeals had stated in 1920, "Incompatibility of temper is no ground for separation in New York. The misery arising out of domestic quarrels does not justify a termination of the legal rights and duties of husband and wife. For such ills the patients must minister unto themselves; our courts of justice offer no cure." What the court labeled a "well-established rule" remained in place into the 1960s in response to the continuing "policy of the law to keep husband and wife together."

But the burden of remaining together fell largely on wives. "So long as the wife ha[d] demonstrated that she [could] live with her husband, despite his failings," the law would not grant her a separation, since she was simply required to "suffer the consequences of the apparent mistake, made when the marriage took place, in not discovering any temperamental defects that then existed." For like reasons, a wife could not obtain a separation because a husband was "lazy around the house," "indulge[d] in more liquor than a wise man should," or gambled for high stakes.[47]

On the other hand, a wife's "denial" of her husband's "marital rights" or her demand that he use contraceptives was "contrary to the principles and policy" of New York law and thereby constituted "a violation of her obligations under the marriage contract" in the nature of cruelty. In contrast, a husband's lack of sexual interest in his wife or other failure to have sexual relations did not constitute cruelty.[48]

Traditional forms of sexism also manifested themselves in holdings that a wife was guilty of cruelty if she refused to accompany her husband socially or to assist him in business. An unusual case arose when "a very ambitious lady" returned to college and medical school, as a result of which she failed to keep Jewish dietary laws in her home and to pay as much attention to her daughter as her husband felt she should. The court held that her husband had "no obligation . . . to provide for his wife the funds which she require[d] to attain a professional status" and that she had abandoned him by failing to provide proper meals and breached her "duty" as a mother when she failed to maintain "an atmosphere at home which [would] redound favorably to the growth emotionally, intellectually, and spiritually of the child."[49]

Traditional sexist assumptions finally pervaded the cases explicating the second of the statutory grounds for separation—abandonment. It was clear, for example, that judges would deem a husband who ceased supporting his wife to have abandoned her, while a wife would be guilty of abandonment if she refused to have sex with her husband. Another sexist rule was that a husband had the right to determine where and with whom he and his wife would reside. It was "a wife's burden to move with her husband to a location selected by him in good faith," at least when the move was related to the husband's employment; "her duty" was " 'to go with her husband to the home which he had provided.' "[50]

The Law of Support. Until 1967, as we have seen, a determination of guilt of cruelty or abandonment was significant because it determined the amount of support that a husband owed his wife. What we have yet to examine, however, is the extent to which sexist assumptions riddled the rules governing the judicial award of support.

An old sexist assumption, going back even beyond the 1920s, was based on alleged "considerations of equity and public policy"; it held that an "obligation" existed growing "out of the marriage relation that the husband must support his wife and family." Especially if there were young children, a wife, it was thought, "should not be compelled to work to the[ir] detriment" but "should be encouraged" to maintain "a normal mother and child relationship," in which she would "devote a considerable portion of her time to their care, guidance and well-being." A corollary of the requirement that husbands support their wives was the rule that alimony was a remedy available only to women and could never be recovered by men, who were deemed competent to support themselves. Indeed, were a "husband . . . [to] look to his wife for support," he would be "placed in an unnatural relationship," since he was supposed to be "the breadwinner and provid[er] for the family." [51]

In the postwar era, however, courts began to enforce the obligations of men to support their former wives in a less rigorous fashion, so as not to interfere with the practical right of men to devote their resources to the pursuit of their own happiness. Thus the courts declared that a woman who had "separated from her husband, should be encouraged, if consistent with her . . . obligations to her children and family, to . . . make herself economically useful." As another judge added, "Alimony was originally devised . . . to protect those without power of ownership or earning resources. It was never intended," he continued, "to assure a perpetual state of secured indolence. It should not be suffered to convert a host of physically and mentally competent women into an army of alimony drones." [52]

Nothing better encapsulates the sexism of the 1940s, 1950s, and 1960s than the support cases we have just discussed. That sexism grew in part out of the earlier sexism of the 1920s and 1930s, which had focused on what was "natural" in the relationship between the genders. The early sexism had found it "natural" for men to be somewhat violent and domineering but at the same time to serve their families as providers. It had been equally "natural" for women to remain in the home, nurture young children, and accept their subordination to men. The courts turned this early sexism into something even more perverse, however, when, with a post–World War II emphasis on individual rights, they translated what had been simply "natural" into a set of legal entitlements. In the new translation, much of what had been "natural" in the 1920s and 1930s — the duties that had corresponded to the rights — could find no place, and male privilege was left standing by itself.

This same postwar change in family law can also be described in an alternative fashion. In a wide variety of legal doctrines in New York, the years around World War II saw an end to traditional moral underpinnings of the law. New values emerged in place of the older moral ones. In the context of family law, the new values were cast in the language of rights which their bearers could enjoy without assuming any corresponding duties or responsibilities. In connection with children, mothers became the bearers of the new rights. More often, however, new ideas about rights became attached to older assumptions about normal and natural male behavior, whereupon the social advantages men had customarily enjoyed became reified into formal legal privileges standing apart from the social obligations with which traditional morality had encumbered them. The ultimate result was that men and occasionally women gained increased legal power, while women and children lost significant legal protections.

CHAPTER 11

THE GROWTH OF DISTRUST

Although the legal developments we have examined in the last five chapters did not transform New York into a utopia, they nonetheless constituted a logical maturation of the legalist reform impulse. Although the changes we have been studying failed to achieve liberty and equality for all, especially in the context of gender, they nonetheless tended to undercut the hierarchical values on which the classical legal order had rested. If the legalist reformation had resulted only in changes of this nature, we could easily have regarded it as a force for nothing but the remediation of ancient ills. But like all other legal ideologies, the legalist reformation was more complex and contradictory.

This chapter focuses on a conflict between two particular reform concerns — one, a concern for empowering government to regulate the economy, and the other, a concern for individual liberty. Concern for regulating the economy was an integral part of legalist reform ideology by the late 1930s. Then, "the rise of totalitarianism" led to a competing concern, "prompt[ing] . . . the democratic world" to recognize that "a too powerful state is dangerous to our liberties."[1] To deal with the emerging conflict between these two concerns, political and legal theorists needed to construct a new jurisprudence that balanced the need for government involvement in the economy against the need to keep government out of citizens' private lives.

Baddour v. City of Long Beach was an early case in which the Court of Appeals struggled to achieve the proper balance. *Baddour,* which was decided in 1938, arose when an owner of a dwelling in a district zoned for single-family residential use sought a declaratory judgment interpreting the municipality's zoning ordinance as not prohibiting her use of the premises as a rooming and boarding house. After a unanimous Appellate Division sustained the trial court's judgment that operation of a boarding house was inconsistent with single-family residential zoning, the case came before a closely divided Court of Appeals.[2] Over a three-judge dissent adopting a position, which the United States Supreme Court would take four decades later, that it would be "constitutionally invalid" to define a family as an entity in which "members must be united by particular motives or relationships," the four-judge majority held that the Long Beach ordinance prohibited only the use of plaintiff's property "as a boarding or rooming house as a business." But it then went on to declare that the "fact that the property may not be used for the business of keeping roomers and boarders does not bar the occupant from occasionally taking roomers or boarders, upon special considerations, where the practice is merely incidental and accessory to the principal use of the house as a home by the family of the occupant."[3] Faced, on the one hand, with a claim of a municipality's plenary power to regulate businesses that generated externalities within its borders and, on the other hand, with a claim of individuals to form whatever family relationships they wished, the opinion of the court strove for a fair balance accommodating both claims.

Baddour set the framework of accommodation within which the New York courts have functioned ever since. But over time the balance they have struck within that framework has shifted. Of course, judges have never doubted that government possesses wide regulatory powers. But as the concept of liberty, which lies at the core of the legalist reform impulse, gained vitality in the decades after 1938, it sapped the strength of the opposing concept of regulatory power, which had grown out of an earlier progressive impulse. Indeed, ideas of individual liberty undercut the very foundation on which the power of regulation rested.

The underlying assumption of the New Deal regulatory state had been that government action was essential to attain the public good. Concepts of individual liberty, in contrast, proved corrosive of the very idea of public good. As individuals were understood to have independent interests, which often were at loggerheads with the interests of other individuals, the idea of public good broke down. In the emerging postwar world in which only individuals and groups—and not the public—had interests, regulation came to appear as legislative favoritism of some groups at the expense of the freedom and equality of other groups.

Even before the regulatory state had reached its fullest fruition during the era of the New Deal and World War II, a few prescient thinkers had begun to articulate this new ideology of interest group politics, which would eventually send progressive ideas of regulation for the public good into retreat. Perhaps the first thinker to glimpse the new vision was Judge Learned Hand, who in a 1928 speech before the American Law Institute observed:

Sometimes . . . we speak of the judges as representing a common-will. . . . [But] they are not charged with power to decide the major conflicts. . . . We think of the legislature as the place for resolving these, and so indeed it is. But if we go further and insist that there at any rate we have an expression of a common-will . . . we should be wrong again. I will not of course deny that there are statutes of which we can say that they carry something like the assent of a majority. But most legislation is not of that kind; it represents the insistence of a compact and formidable minority.

Two years later a well-known legal academic elaborated on Hand's earlier insight:

> The task of government . . . is not to express an imaginary popular will, but to effect adjustments among the various special wills and purposes which at any given time are pressing for realization. . . . Government, from this point of view, is primarily an arbitrator, and since practically every arbitration must result in giving to one side more of what it thinks it ought to have than the other side is willing to admit, every governmental act can be viewed as favoring in some degree some particular and partial "will," or special interest.[4]

Although such thinking could not become dominant during the Great Depression, when so many people were suffering that the ill-fed, the ill-housed, and the underemployed seemed to constitute the majority rather than a series of diverse special interests, some slight movement did occur. For example, some New Dealers in the late 1930s began to perceive a need for the enactment of laws designed "to promote the organization of economically weak groups so that they might hold their own against stronger rivals." This development pointed, in turn, toward a redefinition of democracy as "a society of various groups and classes" whose "power [was] evenly spread," with "economic checks and balances to parallel the political checks and balances" and "a state of tension in society that permit[ted] no one group to dare bid for the total power." It went on from there with V. O. Key's classic, *Politics, Parties, and Pressure Groups,* which went through five editions and thirty-one printings between its first appearance in 1942 and its 1969 printing, and with Douglass Adair's 1951 article rescuing Madison's theory of factions in *Federalist No. 10* from the dustbin of history. Arguably, the trend culminated in Theodore Lowi's *End of Liberalism* in 1969. Lowi argued persuasively that the reformist, New Deal paradigm, under which the people had battled against special interests to achieve the common good, had become vacuous and that, in its place, a new paradigm of *"interest-group liberalism"* had emerged. Under that interest group paradigm, it was said, "organized interests pretty much fill up . . . most sectors of our lives, so that one organized group can be found effectively answering and checking some other organized group," and "the role of government is one of insuring access particularly to the most effectively organized, and of ratifying the agreements and adjustments worked out among the competing leaders and their claims."[5]

This new model of interest group politics played an important role in case law developments in the New York courts. It enabled judges to identify statutes passed to accommodate special interest groups and to differentiate those statutes from others adopted to further the common good. But the new model did not provide judges with a foundation for a new jurisprudence. Unlike some political theorists noted above, New York judges saw nothing affirmative in special interest legislation. Still adhering to the nineteenth-century principle of *Taylor v. Porter*[6] that outlawed legislative redistributions of property from A to B, the New York courts remained committed to the protection and preservation of rights of private property. Just as the courts had extended the regulatory state during the prewar decades, so now after World War II they expanded the protection they accorded property rights. As we shall see, they acted initially through detailed elaboration of rules of administrative procedure. But ultimately their protection of private property in fields such as zoning, landlord and tenant, utility and business regulation, eminent domain, and taxation rested on continued recognition of a constitutional right to wealth. The legalist reformation's acknowledgment of individualism and individual rights thereby came into service of the nineteenth-century value of preventing redistribution.

THE GROWTH OF PROCEDURAL PROTECTION

A central premise of regulatory law throughout the twentieth century was deference by the judiciary to the political branches of government. Judges routinely hesitated to "interfere with the exercise of discretion vested by statute in administrative officers." Nonetheless, the courts demanded that agencies adhere to due process requirements and otherwise act fairly in making decisions. Decisions of an administrative agency, it was said, must "be based upon a consideration of the relevant facts[,] and a fair opportunity must be afforded to present" the facts. Moreover, " 'no essential element of a fair trial [could] be dispensed with . . . and no vital safeguards violated' " without rendering the agency's decision " 'subject to reversal upon review.' "[7]

The trend during the two decades after World War II was to buttress due process requirements in administrative law. As a result, the massive bureaucracy that had been put into place before and during World War II to advance and enforce particular legislative policy goals matured from a set of informal policymaking entities into a sort of second-string judiciary. By the end of the 1960s, as the Court of Appeals observed in one administrative law case, "administrative inquiries" had become "endowed with many of the attributes of a legal proceeding, including notices of hearings, adjournments, amendment of charges, taking of testimony, availability of transcripts, filing of briefs, etc."[8]

The driving force behind this legalization of administrative procedure was a concern "not only that justice be done but that the appearance of justice be apparent." In the pursuit of justice, judges came to regard it as " 'the duty of the courts to set at naught arbitrary and unfounded administrative holdings' " and to set at naught "mechanical exercise[s] of administrative judgment" stemming from "internal policy and rules of thumb practice." The very fact that the bureaucracy had broad powers and discretion to favor some interests in preference to others made it "imperative that the courts exercise the necessary supervision to assure that the decisional process on the administrative level [was] free from impermissible or irrelevant considerations or unsupported conclusions" and to remind agencies of their " 'heavy responsibility' " to engage in " 'conscientious and painstaking assessment of the evidence presented.' " Even when the legislature declared administrative decisions final and not subject to judicial review, the result was not to eliminate all "judicial scrutiny whatsoever" because the courts still had "the power and the duty to make certain that the administrative official ha[d] not acted in excess of the grant of authority given him by statute or in disregard of the standard prescribed by the legislature."[9]

The linchpin upon which the legalization of the administrative process rested was a distinction that the courts created between the legislative and judicial functions of administrative agencies. When "an administrative tribunal [was] acting in a quasi-judicial capacity," the Court of Appeals held that "no essential element of a fair trial [could] be dispensed with unless waived." "The protection of basic fundamental rights . . . [was] highly important and necessary in an administrative . . . as well as in a purely judicial proceeding." This meant that a "party whose rights [were] being determined" had "to be fully apprised of the proof to be considered, with the concomitant opportunity to cross-examine witnesses, inspect documents and offer evidence in rebuttal or explanation." The "first fundamental of due process" — "notice of the charges made" — also applied in agency proceedings. One important right that the New York courts did not fully extend to administrative proceedings, however, was the right to counsel. Although they did hold that parties had a right to appear with retained counsel at administrative proceedings and that agency actions in the absence of such counsel were void, they refused to uphold a right to assignment of free counsel to indigents even though they recognized that "by reason of the present day complexities of administrative proceedings the layman who . . . represent[s] himself does so at a peril that is indeed substantial." [10]

The rule giving the right to retain counsel to people who could afford lawyers and who in zoning cases, license revocation cases, and the like had large amounts of money at stake, probably did more than anything else to legalize the administrative process in the post–World War II years and thereby weaken the bureaucracy's power to impose redistributional legislative policies on the rich. At the same time, the denial of counsel to the poor kept the administrative process informal in areas like welfare and public housing law and left bureaucrats with overwhelming power to accomplish their goals, often at the peril of the poor. [11]

The courts intruded far less into the legislative than into the adjudicative side of the administrative process. On the legislative side, their main task was to enforce the proscription that the "legislature may constitutionally delegate rule-making authority to an administrative agency only if it furnishes the agency with at least a broad outline" or set of standards "within which to act." They also enforced the corollary that "administrative agencies [could] only promulgate rules to further the implementation of the law" as it was handed to them and had "no authority to create a rule out of harmony with the statute." [12]

On the whole, however, judges showed considerable deference to administrative rule making. Recognizing that any statute, "but particularly social legislation, . . . must be enforced in a reasonable and humane manner in accordance with its manifest intent and purpose," the Court of Appeals ruled that "required standards need only be prescribed in so much detail as is reasonably practicable in light of the complexities of the area to be regulated." They also accorded administrative regulations the force of statute and allowed administrative agencies the power to alter their rules. Finally, they gave "great weight" to an agency's construction of its enabling legislation. [13]

In their efforts to hold administrative agencies to rules of due process and fair decision making in accordance with statutory standards, judges, in short, worked to attain a balance between protecting preexisting rights and allowing the legislature to advance the social policies desired by the majority. Their goal was to give deference to administrative policy judgments made in accordance with strictly applied statutory and procedural standards. Legislative views of social justice, redistributional or otherwise, would thereby be given effect, but administrators themselves would have their freedom narrowly constrained. In view of the role played in the administrative process by lawyers, who typically represented the rich and rarely represented the poor, it is not clear, however, that much scope was left for the attainment of the redistributional ends that had been at the heart of the New Deal's vision of social justice, with its goal of using the regulatory state to help poor multitudes at the expense of a wealthy few.

Even when administrative agencies had acted fairly and in pursuit of their statutory mandates, the courts did not always sustain their actions. Especially in the field of zoning, judges invalidated a number of statutes and municipal ordinances as unconstitutional takings of property violative of the Fourteenth Amendment of the Federal Constitution and comparable state protections.

More specifically, the Court of Appeals throughout the postwar period held that any zoning ordinance could "be stricken down as invalid" if it "prove[d] confiscatory." It first made that statement in 1954 in *Vernon Park Realty, Inc. v. City of Mount Vernon*,[14] where it invalidated an ordinance requiring a landowner to develop its property as a parking facility instead of downtown commercial business property. It repeated the essence of the statement in 1960, twice in 1966, in 1972, in 1973, twice in 1976, in 1977, in 1978, and in 1979.[15] Indeed, in this last case, the Court of Appeals labeled the anticonfiscation principle "black-letter law." The court also indicated that, even if an ordinance was not confiscatory, it would be held invalid if it was discriminatory or filled with "irrational *ad hocery*." Relying on these principles, lower courts struck down a goodly number of local zoning controls especially in cases such as one in which the municipality had "acted in a manner inconsistent with its own established plan of development and its own convictions as to proper land use," in response to pressures "raised by 'a large group of interested citizens.'" As the court in the case observed, "However meritorious a political approach, this [was] improper grounds for a zoning change."[16]

The difficulty with all zoning was that it inevitably grew to serve the interests of some portions of the state's population at the expense of others. One important group that zoning served were the descendants of the urban, immigrant poor whom the New Deal had championed. World War II and the GI Bill in its aftermath uplifted millions of those poor to a new middle-class status. With the help of VA and FHA mortgages and of new public policies discouraging discrimination on ethnic and religious grounds, the new middle class spent much of its newly acquired wealth during the next quarter-century moving out of tenement apartments and into single-family dwellings. The move to the suburbs was on, not only outside New York City but outside the larger upstate cities as well.

The law of zoning facilitated and protected this suburban growth. Indeed, the most important function served by the law of zoning during the decades following World War II was to prevent intrusion of nonresidential uses into the state's newly developing suburban residential neighborhoods. Zoning was then seen as "a vital tool for maintaining a civilized form of existence" and preserving " 'the peace and security of dwelling districts.' " "The 'blessings of quiet seclusion' [were] held to be a permissible goal of government," and for that reason judges were often prepared to enforce any "reasonable longstanding comprehensive plan with a basic policy to establish and maintain . . . [the] character [of a municipality] as a village of residences." As the leading case of *Village of Belle Terre v. Boraas* declared, the power to zone could be used to create "a quiet place where yards are wide, [and] people few" and "where family values, youth values, . . . and clean air make the area a sanctuary for people." [17]

One of the most important devices for protecting the quality of life in expensive suburban communities was large-lot zoning. Early cases, for example, upheld minimum lot sizes of one or two acres, although not six acres. Although the Court of Appeals began to express concern about " 'community efforts at immunization or exclusion' " through the device of "exclusionary zoning ordinances" and accordingly declared in the 1975 case of *Berenson v. Town of New Castle* that "in enacting a zoning ordinance, consideration must be given [by a municipality] to regional needs and requirements," even *Berenson* did not lead to clear-cut doctrine; it held merely that "courts must" in every case "assess the reasonableness of what a locality ha[d] done." Under the *Berenson* approach, in fact, the Court of Appeals sustained five-acre zoning for single-family residences in an exclusive Long Island suburb, with the result that exclusionary zoning remained alive and well in New York throughout the 1970s. [18]

A second device used by municipalities to control land use within their borders and thereby maintain a suburban lifestyle at the expense of potential newcomers was the law of subdivision exactions. As late as 1950, it seemed clear that a municipality could not require a developer whose land met existing zoning requirements to satisfy any conditions or pay any exactions in order to obtain a building permit. Two years later, however, in *Brous v. Smith*[19] the Court of Appeals began dramatically to change doctrine to favor established suburbanites.

The case arose pursuant to 1938 legislation that required cities, towns, and villages to deny building permits unless a road giving access to a proposed structure was suitably improved. In the *Brous* case, the town in question had interpreted the law to allow it to demand that developers construct roads at their own expense to properties on which they wished to build. The Court of

Appeals agreed with the town's interpretation, observing that "in this era of the automobile, modern living as we know it is impossible without improved highways linking people with their jobs, their sources of food and other necessities, their children's schools and their amusements and entertainments." The court also rejected a challenge that the law, as interpreted, was unconstitutional, in that it required a private individual to build a public road. In the court's unexplained view, the requirement of building a road was no different from minimum lot size, set back, and side yard requirements.[20]

Following the *Brous* case, several lower courts upheld municipal refusals to grant building permits in cases where adequate roads or sewers were not provided, but other judges, in contrast, refused to require developers to provide sewers or land for recreational purposes. This doctrinal uncertainty forced the Court of Appeals to return to the exactions question, which it did in *Jenad, Inc. v. Village of Scarsdale*. Over a dissent which forcibly protested that requiring " 'new people coming into the municipality . . . [to] bear the burden of the increased costs of their presence' " constituted a "surrender" by judges of "their function of protecting basic property rights . . . [and] basic principles of [equality of] taxation," a four-judge majority specifically upheld the legislature's "grant to villages of power to make such exactions." Indeed, the majority went even farther and declared that a municipality, instead of requiring a developer to build public facilities or allot land for community purposes, could demand " 'monies in lieu of land' " or construction.[21] *Jenad,* in short, made it clear that municipalities could impose the costs of newcomers entirely on developers and, through the developers, on the newcomers themselves.

Nonetheless, the cases subsequent to *Jenad* were again mixed. In some, judges sustained the imposition of penalties on developers who had subdivided land without the required approval, while in others exactions were struck down.[22]

An important by-product of *Jenad* emerged several years later when the Court of Appeals held in *Golden v. Planning Board of Town of Ramapo* that municipalities could constitutionally impose moratoria on development for such a reasonable period of time as was required to bring municipal services up to a level needed to accommodate the development. One factor that helped the court uphold the eighteen-year moratorium in the *Ramapo* case was that a developer could escape the moratorium at any time it wished simply by agreeing to construct the facilities needed to support its development—an agreement which absent the *Jenad* case might have been found unconstitutionally coercive.[23]

A third area in which the zoning power expanded in the post–World War II era, largely to protect the quality of suburban life, was aesthetic zoning. By the end of the 1930s, the Court of Appeals had found that aesthetic considerations were "not wholly without weight" in the zoning calculus and had assumed that regulations could be enacted solely for aesthetic reasons. But no court had ever actually upheld "a zoning ordinance which restrict[ed] the use of property for a purely aesthetic reason alone."[24]

The Court of Appeals did precisely that, however, in the 1963 case of *People v. Stover,* where in upholding an ordinance prohibiting clotheslines on front lawns it "recognize[d] that aesthetic considerations alone may warrant an exercise of the police power." Although the court observed that cases could "undoubtedly arise . . . in which the legislative body goes too far in the name of aesthetics," it also found that the " 'concept of public welfare [was] broad' " and included " 'aesthetic as well as monetary' " values. Quoting the United States Supreme Court, the Court of Appeals declared it " 'within the power of the legislature to determine that the community should be beautiful as well as healthy.' "[25]

Upholding a "general or unlimited power in government to regulate aesthetics" had the effect, as the dissenting opinion in *Stover* urged, of vastly increasing the breadth of the zoning power. As the dissent noted, "the avoidance by courts, sometimes seemingly to the point of evasion, of sustaining the constitutionality of zoning solely on aesthetic grounds ha[d] had its origin in a wholesome fear of allowing government to trespass through aesthetics on the human personality." Accordingly it "seem[ed] that extension of categories of local legislation for purely aesthetic purposes should be defined and limited, and, if they are to be enlarged, it should not be under reasoning which sets no ascertainable bounds to what can be done or attempted under this power."[26]

In the two decades following *Stover,* New York courts did, in fact, find themselves deeply involved in protecting aesthetic and related environmental values. Courts, for example, found themselves upholding legislation designed to protect aesthetic and environmental values in the Adirondack Park along with more prosaic legislative restrictions on the filling of wetlands. They also found themselves dealing with other aesthetic issues such as the height of fences.[27]

The courts also moved in two other directions on the subject of aesthetic zoning. First, they refused to hold unconstitutional a local ordinance creating a board of architectural review. Even more important was their upholding of historic preservation legislation. Indeed, the Court of Appeals even upheld the application of historic preservation legislation to churches, which until the 1970s had enjoyed virtual immunity from police power regulation.[28]

Taken together, the zoning cases point toward two conclusions. The first is that municipal legislative bodies frequently acted to advance the interests of the people who controlled them. The second conclusion is that New York's judges generally acquiesced in such legislative action. But the law was not without its contradictions, and occasionally, in dissent and even in majority opinions, the judges protested.

In particular, the courts held that municipalities could not impose regulations that explicitly discriminated against nonresidents. An early case in support of this principle was *People v. Grant,* which involved a municipal ordinance excluding " 'through or transient vehicular traffic' " from designated streets in an effort to preserve the tranquillity of a residential area from commuter traffic generated by the presence of a nearby factory. Without reaching any constitutional issue, the Court of Appeals ruled that "residents of a particular area in a town or village [did] not possess and [could not] be granted proprietary rights to the use of the highways therein, in priority to or exclusive of use by the general public." The court reiterated this holding in two other cases a few years after *Grant,* when it held that one municipality's attempt to bar transportation on its highways of garbage from other areas exceeded its power to regulate traffic and that another municipality's effort to maintain a park for residents of a single subdivision violated a legislatively imposed duty "to adapt park districts to the needs of growing communities." [29]

LANDLORD AND TENANT

Another body of postwar doctrine in which the courts generally acquiesced in the protection of interest groups possessing political clout was landlord-tenant law. Like much postwar real estate doctrine, it grew out of earlier legislation protective of the housing needs of the poor. The postwar legal system continued, for example, to protect the well-being of tenants at the expense of landlords by stringent enforcement of housing codes that ensured minimum health and safety conditions in multiple dwellings. The most important development in landlord-tenant law after World War II, however, was the substitution of state for federal rent control on May 1, 1950.[30] The substitution legislation over time became applicable only in New York City, where it came to be a permanent feature of the legal landscape. As such, it provided protection against the vagaries of the marketplace to some of the richest as well as many of the poorest inhabitants of the state.

Throughout its various incarnations, rent control was routinely held constitutional in its entirety. As the Court of Appeals noted as late as 1962, the state still faced a danger of "mass rent increases," which made "protection of the public against such increases in a time of a rental housing shortage . . . a valid legislative purpose," even if "in carrying out the scheme devised by the Legislature, a particular landlord or tenant may suffer."[31] But as rent control became permanent, courts began to face some extremely complex battles between various groups having interests in rent-controlled housing.

One set of questions arose as judges reviewed administrative decisions fixing rents. Even more complicated were the cases limiting the power of landlords to evict tenants who remained in possession of apartments under rent control after the expiration of their original lease.[32] Over time, this statutory right to remain in possession became transformed into a sort of quasi-inheritable estate through a byzantine process that none of those who had worked to establish rent control could possibly have foreseen.

Rent control was, after all, initially instituted as a temporary emergency measure, and landlords were deprived of the power to evict tenants only as part of a compromise that allowed them to increase rent when a new tenant entered into possession but prohibited them from evicting an existing tenant in order to obtain a new one. The question of how to deal with survivors of tenants who died while in possession of an apartment was not important either to the establishment of temporary emergency controls or to the compromise from which the eviction prohibitions sprang. As rent control became permanent, however, tenants did begin to die with some frequency, and the question of how to deal with those who had lived with them needed to be answered. Long before the 1980s it had been answered with a provision that upon death of a rent-control tenant, the landlord could not dispossess "either the surviving spouse of the deceased tenant or some other member of the deceased tenant's family who ha[d] been living with the tenant."[33] This restriction did not seriously limit a landlord's ability to regain possession of premises after death, however, because landlords were assumed to have power to restrict those who, except for spouses and minor children, could occupy an apartment with a tenant. By evicting those who were not signatories of leases, landlords could ensure that a tenancy would end at a time no later than the death of the signatory and his or her spouse and the attainment of maturity by their children.

The landlord's freedom to evict nonspouses was first challenged in *Hudson View Properties v. Weiss*. As of 1980, the tenant in the *Weiss* case had been living in the same apartment building for forty-six years, for much of the time with her husband. In 1976, her husband had moved out, apparently as part of a divorce proceeding, and then, at the end of 1979, "a man with whom tenant 'ha[d] a close and loving relationship' " began sharing the apartment.[34]

The landlord promptly ordered him to leave and, when he did not, began eviction proceedings on the ground that his presence constituted a violation of the terms of the lease. The tenant defended on the ground that expulsion of the tenant and/or her lover would constitute discrimination on the basis of marital status in violation of New York's Human Rights Law. The trial judge accepted this defense, but the Appellate Term reversed. The Appellate Division then reversed the Appellate Term and restored the trial court's judgment.[35]

In this posture the case arrived before the Court of Appeals, which reversed yet again and reinstated the judgment of the Appellate Term with the following brief explanation:

> In this case, the issue arises not because the tenant is unmarried, but because the lease restricts occupancy of her apartment . . . to the tenant and the tenant's immediate family. Tenant admits that an individual not part of her immediate family currently occupies the apartment as his primary residence. Whether or not he could by marriage or otherwise become a part of her immediate family is not an issue. The landlord reserved the right by virtue of the covenant in the lease to restrict the occupants and the tenant agreed to this restriction.[36]

On this basis, the court had no difficulty concluding that the tenant's lover was not a member of her family and thus that the landlord could exclude the lover from residing in the apartment while the tenant was alive and from having any potential claim to continued residence after the tenant died.

Affirming the right of landlords to evict live-in lovers had the potential to send thousands of New Yorkers into the housing market, however, and vociferous protests were heard all the way to Albany. The legislature responded with a special interest law declaring it "unlawful for a landlord to restrict occupancy of residential premises, by express lease terms or otherwise, to a tenant . . . and immediate family"; at least one other occupant and the dependent children of that occupant had to be allowed. Although the statute explicitly refused to grant mere occupants possessory rights greater in extent than those of a tenant, it nevertheless created the possibility that a live-in lover could claim a right to remain in an apartment after the tenant's death and, by taking on a new lover, extend that possibility ad infinitum.[37]

Through the mechanism of rent control, in short, the police power transformed residential rental markets in New York City. By the 1980s, tenants possessed a quasi-inheritable right to occupy rent-controlled apartments at fixed rentals subject only to minor cost-of-living adjustments granted by the city's rent control authorities. In significant ways, the legislature and the courts would thereafter be required to compromise and adjust conflicts between what had become, in effect, competing property owners.

UTILITY AND BUSINESS REGULATION

Nowhere was the new, postwar role of the judiciary as arbiter of the claims of special interests clearer than it was on the subject of utility and business regulation. In part, the judiciary found itself in this unpleasant position because of the expansion of the state's regulatory apparatus. Charged with maintaining just and reasonable rates for consumers, the Public Service Commission (PSC), for example, strove to carry out its mandate by expanding its jurisdiction into two areas in addition to rate setting itself: first, into the definition of capital, and second, into analysis of utility and carrier expenses. Operating under a formula by which return was equal to total rates charged consumers minus total expenses, a commission that could force a reduction in expenses could similarly reduce the rates charged consumers, while the utility still earned the same return. Likewise, if the commission could reduce capital expenditures, a smaller return and consequently lower charges to consumers would give the utility or carrier the same percentage return on its investment.

Early regulators on the Public Service Commission understood these basic business facts, and they therefore directed the use of specified accounting methods by regulated entities that would enable the commission to understand the realities of an entity's balance sheet. In 1930, the PSC also had obtained jurisdiction to approve and disapprove contracts into which a regulated firm entered. As the years progressed, the commission, with court approval, continued to monitor accounting practices and to intrude its authority more and more into policing the contracts and business practices of those it regulated. Among the contracts that the Public Service Commission policed were those between a regulated entity and an affiliated interest, such as a parent or subsidiary company; management contracts; contracts dealing with executive compensation and legal fees; and contracts providing dividends to shareholders or imposing indebtedness on the utility or carrier.[38]

The Public Service Commission also sought to expand its jurisdiction by regulating utility advertising. It thereby embroiled itself in controversy as the legitimate interests of the groups it was attempting to help came into conflict with the equally legitimate interests of competing groups. In one case, the commission, in an effort beginning in 1973 to promote energy conservation, sought to bar Central Hudson Gas & Electric from inserting advertisements in its bills urging customers to consume more electricity, while in another it sought to enjoin New York City's Consolidated Edison Company from inserting materials supporting increased use of nuclear power plants. Although a trial judge invalidated portions of the commission's directive, the Appellate Division reversed his ruling and affirmed the commission in its entirety, and the Court of Appeals affirmed the Appellate Division. The United States Supreme Court, however, relying on newly proclaimed commercial free speech rights under the First Amendment, reversed the Court of Appeals. Nevertheless, even after the Supreme Court's reversal, the Court of Appeals sustained the determination of the Public Service Commission that the expense of the advertising allowed under the First Amendment could not be included in a utility's rate base.[39]

Despite restrictions such as those considered above, regulated industries did not fully lose their basic property rights. "Under the settled law of the State," a franchise constituted "a property right . . . from the enjoyment of which" a carrier or utility could not "be excluded without compensation." Thus when the police commissioner of New York City turned several main avenues into one-way streets, the Court of Appeals required the city to pay just compensation to bus companies holding franchises to operate buses on the avenues in question in both directions.[40]

Meanwhile, other business fared even better as judges struck down a wide variety of regulatory legislation that interfered with property or entrepreneurial rights. The cases fell into essentially two categories: cases involving statutes that had no public purpose at all and thus reflected gratuitous hostility to a regulated entity, and those involving legislation that aided one group of individuals at the expense of another rather than the community as a whole.

Defiance Milk Products Co. v. DuMond was the leading case in the first category. The statute at issue in *DuMond,* which prohibited the sale of evaporated or condensed skimmed milk in containers weighing less than ten pounds, had the effect, according to the Court of Appeals, of prohibiting all consumer sales of "a wholesome and useful food product." The court conceded that, if any "reasonable basis [had] existed for an absolute ban against evaporated skimmed milk," the prohibition on its sale would have been valid, but "no one ha[d] been able to discover any such basis." The court therefore declared the act invalid.[41]

Lurking in *DuMond* was a related principle against overbroad legislation. The state had attempted to defend the legislation as an antifraud measure designed "to see to it that customers did not get evaporated skimmed milk when they were trying to buy evaporated whole milk." The court responded that "the Legislature could have demanded other kinds of labels or special sizes, shapes or colors of containers" to protect consumers but that an absolute "prohibition was, as a matter of law, not a reasonable way of dealing with such confusion or possibility of confusion as the legislators might have found to exist."[42] The legislature could not, that is, outlaw a broad range of legitimate activities in order to reach occasional illicit acts occurring under the umbrella of the legitimate ones.

The second category of cases in which courts regularly found unconstitutionality involved laws that assisted a single group in the community rather than protecting the health, safety, or welfare of the community as a whole. The leading case of *Trio Distributor Corp. v. City of Albany* arose in response to a municipal ordinance that required the Good Humor Corporation and its distributors to staff Good Humor trucks with two individuals if ice cream products were being sold from the trucks. The majority of the Court of Appeals suspected that the ordinance had been adopted to protect shopkeepers who sold ice cream from competition by itinerant Good Humor peddlers, and for this reason, the court found the ordinance invalid, declaring that "the police power is not designed to aid one group in a community against another, as the courts of this State have frequently had occasion to hold."[43]

Just as a statute could not be enacted for the purpose of advancing the interests of one group of individuals at the expense of another, so too it could not be administered with that purpose in mind. *Swalbach v. State Liquor Authority* involved a challenge to the authority's policy " 'of prohibiting the location of retail wine and liquor stores in modern shopping centers,' " apparently out of a "grave concern" that shopping centers were causing "the untimely demise of tens of thousands of small local retail businesses" and were "dangerously imperil[ing] the existence of the small local merchants." But, however laudable the goal of preserving small town businesses may have been, the State Liquor Authority could not legitimately act for that purpose. Its sole power was to promote the " 'public convenience and advantage,' " not to aid a group of established small town merchants at the expense of entrepreneurs seeking to exploit new developments in the economy found "to be convenient" by "the public itself."[44]

An agency like the State Liquor Authority could not act in pursuit of the interests of only one segment of the community even when that segment consisted "of community residents and political leaders." Thus letters from a state senator, assemblyman, and councilperson, together with a petition containing more than eight hundred signatures, in protest of the opening of a discotheque could not justify the authority in refusing to issue a liquor license to the new business. While the authority might have been " 'swayed by the number of objectors,' " the Court of Appeals declared it essential to " 'keep in mind that ours is a government of law and not of men; and that decisions, especially where property rights are protected by Constitutions and laws, must be based upon such laws and not upon sympathy or public opinion.' " [45]

These cases appear to point back toward the earlier effort by Judge Irving Lehman in the mid-1930s to preserve the police power from capture by special interests yet at the same time leave legislative bodies free to address the complex problems arising from the innumerable failures of the free market that were occurring in twentieth-century New York. As did Lehman, the judges of the post–World War II New York Court of Appeals frowned upon distributional decisions made solely in response to political pressures. Thus they would not sanction the closing of a junkyard in an area zoned for unrestricted use merely because local residents objected to its opening. [46] Lehman and later judges would have protected the residents, however, if zoning authorities had created legitimate expectations on their part by imposing restrictions in a comprehensive plan. As a result, established people in a community, who had used their political power to obtain a proper legislative or administrative determination that the good of the community consisted in the preservation of their rights, could have their rights protected. But individuals who had not used their political power in the proper forum could not thereafter use it elsewhere to defeat the claims of an entrepreneur striving to make a profit by exploiting the free market.

Thus a line that courts sometimes drew to distinguish legitimate regulations dealing with market failures from invalid regulations with the goal of simple redistribution came down to whether the interest groups assisted by legislation had followed proper procedures in the legislative process. As thin and amorphous as this line might be, it is at least a principled one. The only alternative is to engage in ad hoc balancing on a case-by-case basis, as did one court in holding that a county ordinance prohibiting the idling of motor vehicles for more than three minutes was "oppressive, unreasonable and arbitrary" in light of its "minuscule" effect in "combating air pollution." [47]

The way in which mid-century judges deciding regulatory cases either had to engage in ad hoc balancing or try to escape by recourse to procedure is best illustrated by the Court of Appeals' four-to-three decision in the case of *Wignall v. Fletcher*. At issue in *Wignall* was whether the commissioner of motor vehicles could revoke the license of an eighty-two-year-old man who had been driving a motor vehicle with a license since 1910. The man, George Wignall, came to the commissioner's attention when he became involved in the first accident in his driving career, which occurred when a boy ran into the street and into the rear end of Wignall's car. On one side of the scales was "the need for the . . . exercise by the commissioner of his duties in his laudable effort to prevent unsafe driving on the highways." On the other side was the fact that a "license to operate an automobile is of tremendous value to the individual . . . for the essential purposes of attending at the village stores, taking his invalid wife to church on Sundays, and the like."[48] How would the judges of the Court of Appeals resolve this conflict?

The conflict, it should be noted, is one that is resolved daily by countless officials and citizens, who make judgments whether to license and insure drivers and whether to take to the road and drive. The conflict is also one involving the most serious considerations on both sides. For most Americans in the second half of the twentieth century, the capacity to drive a car may have been the most important entitlement they had; without a car, they would have lost access to employment, shopping, entertainment, and social connection. Driving was surely one of the key symbols of freedom and empowerment in late twentieth-century America, and, in practical terms, one of the most fundamental rights that Americans possessed. At the same time, automobiles wrought more physical and social destruction than anything else in our culture. Apart from the inevitable diseases associated with aging and dying, nothing caused more deaths, accidents, destruction, pollution, and pain than automobiles, and thus their regulation lay at the core of the police power. Every time a state official authorized an individual to drive or declined to grant such an authorization, the official resolved this fundamental contradiction between freedom and safety that was inherent in regulatory law. That is, the official, or in the case of *Wignall* the fourth judge who created the one-vote majority on the Court of Appeals, determined whether safety, which along with health is one of the two core values protected by the police power, or individual freedom, which along with equality is one of the two central rights protected by the Constitution, should triumph.

This central issue of how to balance health and safety against freedom is one for which fixed legal principles cannot exist. This insight into the absence of principle is one at which the Supreme Court arrived in the late 1930s, when it decided to defer judicially to whatever balances legislatures reached. Arguably, when the New York Court of Appeals came down on the side of freedom in the *Wignall* case and ruled that the Motor Vehicle Bureau could not re-voke the octogenarian's license, it too was conscious of the insight, although it declined to follow the Supreme Court's approach.

Instead, it sought to avoid resolving the conflict between regulatory power and individual rights by relying on procedure. While recognizing that, under proper circumstances, the commissioner of motor vehicles would have power to revoke an octogenarian's license, the Court of Appeals held that the attempt at revocation failed because the commissioner had used improper procedures, in that, after giving notice of a hearing under one section of the Vehicle and Traffic Law to determine whether Wignall was physically fit to drive, the com-missioner had revoked Wignall's license under another section because he had failed to pass a new road test. The majority, in effect, interpreted the Vehicle and Traffic Law as authorizing the commissioner, upon receipt of notice of some default by a driver, to take a single action against the driver, such as requiring either a physical examination or a road test, but not both.

Ultimately, however, this effort to escape balancing by recourse to pro-cedure failed. It merely concealed the balancing operation beneath process rhetoric. For, in declaring that the commissioner had failed to follow proper procedures, the majority by implication also ruled that the statute gave the Motor Vehicle Bureau no power to demand anything from a licensed driver unless the driver gave cause for the demand. This ruling, in turn, reflected a balancing judgment that, at least in the case at hand, individual rights should be preferred over an exercise of regulatory power which the legislature had not explicitly authorized.

THE LAW OF EMINENT DOMAIN

Directional shifts parallel to those in the law of regulation also occurred after World War II in the law of eminent domain and taxation, as New York judges on increasing occasions grew suspicious that these public powers, like the power of regulation, were being used to further special interests rather than the good of the public as a whole. As was true with regard to regulation, there was no sharp doctrinal break during or immediately after the war years. Nonetheless, as government used eminent domain more extensively and taxed more heavily, judges began to see more cases in which the use of government powers raised suspicions. In response, the judges had to consider whether to alter their emphasis in deciding the cases.

The case in which the expanded use of eminent domain began was *New York City Housing Authority v. Muller.* The issue in *Muller,* on which there was "no case in this jurisdiction or elsewhere directly in point," was whether the city of New York could condemn privately held land in order to construct "apartments to be rented to a class designated as 'persons of low income.'" Rental to such a limited class, it was argued, made the taking one for a private rather than public use. At the height of the New Deal, however, the Court of Appeals rejected the argument, observing that it "disregard[ed] the primary purpose of the legislation," which was "not to benefit that class (i.e., the poor) or any class" but "to protect and safeguard the entire public from the menace of the slums." As the legislature had noted and the Court of Appeals reiterated, "Slum areas are the breeding places of disease which take toll not only from denizens, but, by spread, from the inhabitants of the entire city and state. Juvenile delinquency, crime, and immorality are there born, find protection, and flourish. . . . Concededly, these are matters of state concern." Thus public housing was not class legislation designed to benefit the poor by tapping into the pockets of the rich but legislation designed for the benefit of the people as a whole. It was, in short, a public use.[49]

The years following World War II witnessed an enormous expansion in the *Muller* doctrine. Subsequent cases declared that either the provision of housing for those in need or the elimination of slums and blighted areas gave sufficient ground for use of the takings power, even if the property taken was later turned over to private enterprise for the construction of the intended new use. As a result of these cases it became "clear" by the 1970s, when "the complexities of urban conditions became better understood," that properties subject to condemnation would include not only " 'slums' as that term was formerly applied" but also areas suffering from, "among other things, economic underdevelopment and stagnation." It also became acceptable for the private entity that would ultimately obtain condemned land to act as "sponsor" for the project; indeed, in New York's leading case, the Otis Elevator Company had threatened to move to a new location "if suitable land was not found for its needed modernization and expansion." The Court of Appeals found "nothing malevolent about that," nor was it troubled by the fact that Otis obtained "the condemned land for a price which [was] but a fraction of that paid" to the original "owners in condemnation." The court, in short, had come to view the condemnation power as a sort of "urban renewal subsid[y]," with the purpose of encouraging "the land clearing, the construction and other commitments the community desires . . . where the cost of acquiring the land privately . . . would be sufficiently expensive . . . to deter private entities."[50]

The use of eminent domain to subsidize urban renewal was merely the beginning, however, of the judiciary's expansion of the power. Condemnations were also upheld to facilitate the construction of parking facilities at business sites; to enable municipalities to gain control of rapid transit and bus facilities; and to provide land for future use of the United Nations. Three other cases allowed use of the power of eminent domain to save Carnegie Hall from destruction, to help the Museum of Modern Art finance a new wing, and to assist in the rehabilitation of New York City's Commodore Hotel into the Grand Hyatt Hotel.[51]

With the decision of each of these cases, the link between government action and the public good became increasingly attenuated. The case that displayed the private character of the eminent domain power most clearly, though, was *Courtesy Sandwich Shop, Inc. v. Port of New York Authority.*[52]

The Courtesy Sandwich Shop had been condemned by the Port Authority in order to assemble the land on which to build the World Trade Center, which, it was said, was needed as an instrument for the centralization of international trade. Building two more skyscrapers to house the offices of international trading firms was not the real purpose of the Trade Center, however. The real purpose, as Judge Van Voorhis noted in dissent, was to obtain rental income that "could be utilized to offset the deficits of operating the Hudson & Manhattan Railroad," a subway to New Jersey over which the Port Authority had been asked to assume control. The Port Authority, "traditionally jealous of its solvency," was unwilling to run the railroad without the income from the Trade Center, which it expected would exceed land acquisition and construction costs by enough to provide the requisite subsidy. It thus planned to "meet its [railroad] deficits by expropriating the good will and condemning the real estate of private property owners instead of by general taxation."[53] A six-to-one majority on the Court of Appeals authorized it to do so.

This ability to use eminent domain takings to subsidize narrow interest groups such as New Jersey commuters at the expense of the owners of condemned property depended, of course, on the ability of condemnors to acquire greater value than the price they had to pay to condemnees. Thus it followed that by reducing the damages payable on condemnation—the price paid to condemnees—judges could enhance eminent domain's subsidization effects. In the second half of the twentieth century, in pursuit of an ostensible policy that many government "interference[s]" should be "shouldered" without compensation as "inconveniences to be borne by the individual for the larger benefit of the community and the public in general," and that, when granted, "damages should not be awarded twice, once for the direct taking and then again under the guise of consequential damages," New York judges decided many cases that limited the award of consequential damages and thereby achieved enhancement of eminent domain's subsidization effects.[54]

Other rules also limited a condemnee's ability to recover full compensation. Nonetheless, there remained a few rare judges who approached takings cases from the perspective that "justice demands that the despoiler, whether individual, corporation, or government, be compelled to pay for that which he despoils."[55] While the courts in the context of eminent domain resolved these contradictions overwhelmingly in favor of the exercise of government power, the contradictions nonetheless persisted.

TAXATION

No fundamental changes occurred in formal doctrines of tax law during the second half of the twentieth century. But the enormous enhancement of government's power and its increased use for the benefit of special interests, the effects of which we have already witnessed in the law of regulation and eminent domain, proved transforming in the area of real estate taxation as well.

The key transformation—one that typified the new uses of government power after World War II—occurred when the legislature began to grant tax exemptions, which had long been available to government agencies and charities, to profit-making entities organized for public benefit purposes. This new approach to tax exemptions had emerged initially when the legislature in 1920 adopted the Emergency Housing Law, which for ten years had removed from the assessment rolls apartment buildings in New York City newly constructed and used exclusively for dwelling purposes, and the Court of Appeals in 1923 upheld the constitutionality of the legislation. This "so-called 'housing legislation,'" which contained "correlative provisions" granting "tax exemption" and imposing "control of rent," was designed to help the free market alleviate a perceived housing shortage in New York City in the aftermath of World War I and to regulate the housing market in the interim.[56]

Although the Emergency Housing Law expired in 1925 and apartments constructed after that date did not receive tax exemption, the courts continued to sustain other legislative subsidies for the construction of housing. For example, the Court of Appeals in 1930 sustained as "salutary" legislation that exempted buildings in the course of construction from assessment. A lower court similarly sustained a tax exemption for a corporation that constructed an apartment building in which subsidized lodging and food would be furnished to unmarried working women on the ground that no one could "close their eyes to conditions which every member of the community must know exists, nor to considerations which appeal to every right-thinking citizen." On this basis, the state judge took "judicial notice, that there are many working women whose moral and physical well-being will be improved through an opportunity to obtain food and lodging in proper surroundings."[57]

Even more important were the increases in taxes that occurred when government's assumption of increasing societal obligations demanded increased revenues. With the increase of taxes, the subsidization effect of tax exemptions for special interests likewise grew. As the legislature, in turn, granted a broader range of exemptions, the judiciary uniformly sustained the grants. The end result was that an issue that had been unresolved in 1920—whether government could use its fiscal power to compensate citizens for harm that it had not imposed—was dispositively resolved by 1980, by which time the government's power to compensate anyone for anything had become unquestioned.

Williams v. Walsh made this clear as early as 1942. The case arose when Henry Williams, a New York City fireman, enlisted in the marines in January 1942 and through his attorney-in-fact brought suit for the difference between his marine pay and his higher fire department salary, in reliance on state legislation providing for payment of such differential to all public employees absent in military service. Although the gratuity at issue in the *Williams* case would ultimately prove massive in comparison with the World War I veterans' bonus held unconstitutional in the 1921 *Westchester Bank* case, a unanimous Court of Appeals had no difficulty sustaining it. In the language of Chief Judge Irving Lehman, "the grant of special benefits and privileges . . . involved no arbitrary discrimination." Thereafter the constitutionality of civil service preferences and bonuses for veterans was unquestioned.[58]

Williams v. Walsh made it clear, in short, that the legislature possessed plenary power to redistribute wealth among special interests through taxation and welfare subsidies. The "inequalities which result[ed]," it was said, "infringe[d] no constitutional limitation."[59]

Even so, familiar limitations to the granting of exemptions continued to be proclaimed. Thus it was declared that any "exemption from taxation 'must clearly appear, and the party claiming it must be able to point to some provision of law plainly giving the exemption.'" Ambiguous language would "be 'construed against the taxpayer', although" it would not be interpreted in "so narrow and literal [a fashion] as to defeat its settled purpose." Also reiterated were the general rule that property held by an agency of the state for public, though not private, purposes was immune from taxation and the rule that property of the United States or of instrumentalities thereof was similarly immune unless Congress consented to its being taxed. As entities with complex relationships to the federal government proliferated during and after World War II, however, there was a growing " 'trend' " not to treat them as federal instrumentalities and " 'to reject immunizing these private parties from nondiscriminatory state taxes as a matter of constitutional law,' " especially when the federal government itself failed to assert a claim of immunity. The reason for the trend, as explained by a Court of Appeals judge who had also served New York as a United States senator, was "that the problems which face State and local governments in meeting their responsibilities in our complex society require the expenditure of vast amounts of money." To circumscribe their power of taxation "could seriously unbalance the fiscal affairs of local tax authorities, particularly in times of distress," and leave them unable to provide for "new and increased burdens" in the nature of "necessary community services" that federal programs had helped to create.[60]

Still, tax exemptions proliferated. Among charities, not-for-profit private schools and colleges became favored beneficiaries. When colleges in the aftermath of World War II purchased formerly private dwelling houses, not "as a matter of business acumen" or "convenience . . . to its students, faculty and staff" but out of necessity "in direct furtherance of an expanded program in higher education," those dwellings became tax exempt when used initially to house students and later to house faculty. Even fraternity houses were granted tax exempt status when they were completely under university control. Although judges were "mindful of . . . the policy of having all realty bear an equal share of the cost of public services . . . , as well as the pressing need for tax money," they clearly placed more weight on the policy " 'of encouraging, fostering and protecting . . . educational institutions.' "[61]

Hospitals were another favored charity entitled to tax exemptions. Exemptions also were extended into new areas. They were routinely granted, for example, to not-for-profit entities with a purpose of protecting the natural environment or enhancing the cultural one.[62]

Tax relief was extended even more broadly to people and organizations who constructed new housing during the post–World War II period, when housing was in short supply. Tax abatements were also upheld for veterans and low income elderly.[63]

The most important new extension of favorable tax treatment, however, resulted from the state's effort to "encourage business development . . . by providing tax exemptions to those who would build, expand or improve their industrial, business and commercial facilities." The state's Industrial Development Agency Act, for example, reflected a "modern view of the proper scope of governmental activity," which encompassed "the direct involvement of government in dealing with the economic problems of our state" by creating "a statewide program to maintain, expand and attract industry to our state." In other cases, the Court of Appeals sustained the exemption of motion picture admissions from the sales tax, out of concern "that the vitality of the moving picture theatre industry might be undermined" without the exemption, as well as favorable tax treatment for the New York Stock Exchange, out of concern that the preexisting stock transfer tax "was driving business from the State."[64]

The extension of exemptions in certain areas, with a consequent erosion of the tax base, led, in turn, to "significant . . . efforts to broaden the real property tax base" in other areas by restricting once traditional exemptions. Probably the most important of the restrictive cases—a case specifically cited by the Court of Appeals as one of these "efforts"[65]—was *Association of the Bar of the City of New York v. Lewisohn.*[66]

As the court observed in *Lewisohn,* tax exemptions had "proliferated at an alarming rate." By the mid-1960s, "more than 30% of the assessed value of all real property in the State was exempt from taxation for various reasons," and there were concerns that, if exemptions continued to grow at their then current rate, "one half of all real property on the tax rolls of local governments would [soon] be exempt from taxation." For this reason, the legislature authorized localities to terminate exemptions for all but a few specified sorts of not-for-profit organizations. Joining in this effort "to stem the erosion of municipal tax bases," the *Lewisohn* case upheld termination of the real estate tax exemptions of two hoary institutions—the Explorers Club of New York and the Association of the Bar of the City of New York.[67]

Lewisohn and the legislation that it construed did not, however, represent the sharp turn in policy which the Court of Appeals suggested they did. In fact, the courts had been growing increasingly hostile to upholding tax exemptions throughout the second half of the century. One judge in a suburban county even complained about the practice of assessing as farm land property that was "immediately salable . . . for development purposes," since the practice gave an "owner who retain[ed] such lands in a minimum use state . . . for speculative purposes . . . an unusual advantage over the ordinary landowner."[68]

The second case cited by the Court of Appeals as an effort to broaden municipal tax bases and render them more equal by limiting legislative freedom to sculpt tax benefits for special interests was *Hellerstein v. Assessor of Town* of *Islip*.[69] *Hellerstein* was decided by the Court of Appeals in the aftermath of a long history of inequality in real property tax assessments and of judicial unwillingness to create procedures to correct the inequality. It sought to achieve equality and simultaneously to enhance tax bases by enforcing legislation dating back beyond the nineteenth century that required all property to be assessed at full value.

The *Hellerstein* court gave municipalities approximately eighteen months to comply with its mandate, but, in fact, the mandate never was obeyed. Three years after *Hellerstein* the Court of Appeals was still lamenting the "deplorable disparity of equalization rates among the several boroughs" of New York City and how the problems it faced in a pending case would not have arisen "if the property owners of each borough had been receiving equal treatment from the taxing authorities at the time of this assessment." Nonetheless, the Appellate Division extended the time for compliance with *Hellerstein*'s mandate, and the legislature soon extended it even further. Finally, in December 1981, the legislature, over the governor's veto, passed "legislation which was designed to overrule" *Hellerstein,* and in *Colt Industries, Inc. v. Finance Administrator of City of New York,* the Court of Appeals acquiesced in the burial of its goal of equal taxation grounded on an enhanced tax base.[70]

Why did the court cave in? The answer lies in the practice by which "assessors customarily assessed residential at lower levels of assessment than commercial property," which in turn meant that implementation of *Hellerstein* would "result in a significant shift of the tax burden to residential home owners."[71] This caused homeowners, as well as many government officials, to unite against reassessment. Owners of commercial property, in contrast, were divided. Those who had constructed or renovated facilities in recent years had often been able to obtain favorable tax exemptions and abatements, whereas only those occupying structures built in the distant past paid full taxes. They probably found it easier over time to abandon their existing locations rather than to assemble the political pressure that was needed to force the legislature to comply with *Hellerstein.* Nor could the court impose pressure on the legislature, since it was incapable of issuing the one order that the legislature would have had to obey—an order prohibiting the collection of real estate taxes until such time as assessment practices had been brought into compliance with its mandate.

Other efforts to enhance the tax base, in comparison, were more successful than the Court of Appeals' initiative in *Hellerstein.* Among the revenue enhancements which the courts sustained were the imposition of an income tax on Native Americans residing on reservations in New York and a real property tax on house trailers. "Upon the heels of the fiscal crisis confronting the State" and its municipalities in the 1970s, the Court of Appeals also sustained legislation requiring businesses that had already collected sales taxes to accelerate their payment to the state. More generally, judges continued to adhere to the view that, to ensure adequate revenue collection, the "power of taxation on the local activities of large enterprises ought not to be viewed narrowly." "Fairness and equity" were secondary "criteria against which the validity of tax statutes" was to be measured, and it simply could "not be assumed that when the Legislature designed the particular statute it had either a specific or even a general desire to achieve a fair or balanced formula," as distinguished from "the production or allocation of optimum revenue."[72]

Despite such dicta, however, judges did not entirely abandon concerns about fairness and equity. In several cases, for example, they applied procedural rules facilitating taxpayer suits. In addition, the courts made certain that real estate assessments did not encompass income from the operation of a business but were based only on the value of the realty in question.[73]

THE ULTIMATE JUDICIAL BALANCE

Examination of doctrinal developments in New York's law of administrative procedure, regulatory power, eminent domain, and taxation has uncovered common issues and, to a lesser extent, a common response to those issues. In all four areas, the years after World War II witnessed issues arising out of a growing perception that government entities often used their power to benefit special interest groups rather than the public as a whole. The common response was, on occasion, to strike down government acts perceived to benefit narrow interests, although, in general, most legislative and administrative actions were judicially sustained.

The cases also reveal a change in judicial attitudes from the era of the 1920s and 1930s to the aftermath of World War II. Especially during the years of the Great Depression, it had seemed clear that the exercise of government power to benefit the ill-housed, the ill-fed, and the underemployed was in the public interest of nearly the entire community, which had every right to control the depredations of the few and thereby prevent exploitation of the many. In the end, judges, especially the democratically elected ones who occupied the state bench in New York, could not stand in the path of laws enacted by the many to provide redress for the injustices visited upon them by the few. Hence progressive judges deferred to the redistributive regulatory legislation of the Smith, Roosevelt, and Lehman administrations in Albany, and their deference made the legislation legitimate.

When the regulatory laws of the 1920s and 1930s were seen in light of the prosperity of the 1950s, 1960s, and 1970s, however, they assumed a new appearance. With the majority of New Yorkers no longer poor, the old regulatory laws no longer benefited the many; instead, they seemed to help smaller, narrower groups that readily came to be perceived as special interests. This perception, in turn, generated an enormous intellectual problem as it became clear that various strands of the legalist reformation were coming into conflict.

Although the regulatory impulse had originated at an earlier time, legalist reformers had, in large part, adopted it as their own in their egalitarian battle against elite WASP claims to the maintenance of established power relationships and to the ongoing enjoyment of customary privileges. Thus when legalist reform concepts of individual freedom began to corrode the regulatory impulse, the legalist ideology entered upon a war with itself. When the growth of distrust in the aftermath of World War II made it plain that protecting property rights was as integral a part of the legalist reformation as preserving regulatory power, the contradictions within the reform enterprise were laid bare.

The cases analyzing regulatory issues that we have examined in this chapter received virtually no public attention. They generated little, if any, political controversy. Thus the cases provided judges with an opportunity to address the emerging contradictions in the legalist reformation at their leisure, with time for thought and without fear of political backlash. And in deciding the cases, judges developed a pattern of thought which, as we shall see, they applied to future cases and tougher issues in which public attention was much greater and the political stakes much higher.

As legalist reform judges worked their way through the regulatory cases, they did not abandon legalist reform values. They remained committed to preventing exploitation, enhancing opportunity, upholding individual liberty, and respecting equality. Nor did they identify one or two values as trumps that outweighed other legalist norms when conflicts over values arose. Instead, they strove to avoid resolving conflicts either by insisting on procedural regularity or by engaging in ad hoc balancing. When facing contradictions in the legalist reformation, judges merely vacillated in response to the facts of particular cases, the arguments of lawyers, and their own predilections. The interest group nature of late twentieth-century politics, unlike the Marxian class-struggle character of the New Deal era, simply did not dictate a single, proper attitude that judges should adopt toward the regulatory, tax, and taking powers of government. Thus the legalist reformation did not die when the New Deal consensus in support of the regulatory state came to an end. But it did lose the capacity it had once had in its battles with classical nineteenth-century legalism to produce coherent social change.

PART III

The Endurance of Legalism and the End of Reform

CHAPTER 12

1968

At the opening of the twentieth century, as we have seen, New York was the focus of virulent class conflict between the poor, largely of immigrant Catholic and Jewish ancestry, who lived in its urban ghettos, and wealthier, mainly upstate, WASP New Yorkers determined to use law to preserve traditional moral values and their own wealth and power. Beginning in the 1920s, the underclasses began to get the better of the conflict, when Alfred E. Smith, Benjamin N. Cardozo, and their allies gained control of the political and judicial branches and used that control to remedy injustice and provide opportunity for the poor. But their victory remained incomplete. Although Cardozo and other realists of the 1920s and 1930s urged that judges had a duty to promote social justice, they also understood that courts were bound by the constraints of precedent. Adherence to precedent, of course, limited their capacity to modify the law. So did their failure to articulate an ideology acceptable to the people of the state as a whole explaining why wealth and power should be redistributed from the rich to the poor.

The advent of Nazi atrocities in the late 1930s and then World War II in the 1940s altered the dynamic of New York's conflict: that conflict began to appear not as one of class but of ethnicity and religion. Suddenly, a new ideology, declaring that people of all religious and ethnic backgrounds should be free, equal, and protected from discrimination, emerged. In defense of this ideology, New Yorkers, along with the rest of America, entered the war, defeated Hitler, and took on Stalin.

Meanwhile, the new ideology freed judges to transform legal doctrine in a more fundamental fashion than Cardozo and the legal realists had ever succeeded in doing. Two considerations explain the new ideology's transformative power. The first is that the goals of liberty, equality, and dignity, for which World War II and later the Cold War were fought, simply transcended concerns about judicial adherence to precedent; the new goals motivated masses of people in a way in which the doctrine of precedent can motivate, at best, an occasional lawyer. As a result, judges in the second half of the century wore the mantle of precedent far more lightly than their predecessors had worn it, and they felt free, without regard to ancient law, to effectuate social justice. The second explanation for the new ideology's power is that, by the end of World War II, nearly all New Yorkers accepted its tenets. Judges, like most other politically relevant people, had developed a coherent, unitary vision of justice and sound social policy in regard to most issues coming before the courts, and they could turn to this vision to adjudicate the cases they heard. Thus judges had only occasionally to make hard choices between policies favored by competing social groups, and they could understand that it was possible "to interpret the law in the best interest of society as a whole."[1] Even when tensions and contradictions existed, as in the regulatory cases discussed in the last chapter, they remained hidden from public awareness and interfered only minimally with judges' power to achieve legalist reform results.

Armed with their powerful ideology and freed from the fetters of precedent, New York's judges, as the previous six chapters have demonstrated, rewrote the state's common law and constitutional law. By empowering religion, they uplifted multitudes of Catholics and Jews. They also revolutionized contract law, tort law, the law of fiduciary duty, and the law regulating sexual expression and family relations. They reordered the law of obscenity and thereby facilitated the introduction of sex into popular culture. Finally, they elaborated a new paradigm of regulation, which recognized the plenary power of government while simultaneously limiting its capacity to wreak injustice in individual cases.

The legalist reformation also remade New York's economy, society, and culture. As a movement with a primary goal of assimilating the Roman Catholic and Jewish descendants of turn-of-the-century immigrants into the mainstream of New York life, it totally succeeded. In the aftermath of World War II, Catholics and Jews abandoned their urban ghettos and raced into newly developed, integrated suburbs. Government also provided them with educational opportunities of increasingly high quality, and many took advantage. Most significantly, Catholics and Jews began to obtain jobs and gradually assume positions of command at the highest levels of the American economy.

As late as the end of World War II, American business leaders had remained a remarkably homogeneous group. It was understood the "social compatibility" and "comfort in social relations" were conducive to producing business managers who "put considerably more store in adjustment and modesty and lack of troublesomeness." Homogeneity and agreeability were fostered by exclusive business clubs, in which "people who [were] all of the same mold" could forge those "primary relationships . . . between top management men" that could prove helpful to the smooth functioning of the economy. Most striking, perhaps, was the homogeneity of background that business executives shared. Managers remained overwhelmingly "of an Anglo-Saxon Protestant background . . . , with Catholics poorly represented, and Jews virtually excluded." One study found that early in the twentieth century business leaders were 90 percent Protestant, 7 percent Catholic, and 3 percent Jewish, while in the 1950s they remained 85 percent Protestant, 8.9 percent Catholic, and only 4.6 percent Jewish. Moreover, business leaders were "exclusively male and Caucasian, predominantly . . . Republican, and of eastern U.S. origin, from relatively affluent families, and educated at one of a handful of select universities." One study observed that as late as 1970 even WASP oilmen from Texas constituted a "fringe group" in the corporate power elite.[2]

By the 1960s, however, this homogeneity had begun to break down, first for Catholics and then for Jews. Although one study suggested that corporate presidents and board chairmen remained as Protestant as ever in the mid-1970s,[3] change had begun to occur in middle levels of corporate management a decade earlier. By 1979, executives just below the level of president and board chairman were only 68.4 percent Protestant, and Catholics had risen to 21.5 percent and Jews to 5.6 percent. Since the executives studied in 1979 had an average age of fifty-three, it is apparent that in 1966, when those business leaders averaged forty years of age and thus had already begun their climbs to the top, Catholics, at least, were moving in large numbers into middle management. Change continued apace over the next six years, as is shown by a 1985 study of the same category of executives in the 1979 study: this second study showed that Protestant representation had declined to 58.3 percent of those studied, while Catholic and Jewish representation had risen to 27.1 percent and 7.4 percent respectively. Jews began to enter corporate management in even larger numbers in the 1970s; the 1985 study shows that 13 percent of executives under forty in that year were Jewish.[4]

Statistics thus show that Catholic and Jewish representation in the corporate establishment increased approximately fourfold during the 1960s and 1970s, while Protestants declined from five-sixths to slightly more than half of all executives. Jews during these years, and perhaps Catholics as well, were also beginning to have significant business contacts with the Protestant establishment in another respect. Many firms founded as small businesses by Jewish entrepreneurs in the early twentieth century had prospered, and by the late 1960s and 1970s they had become corporate giants with still substantial Jewish representation in management and on their boards. Three examples are General Dynamics, the 83d largest industrial corporation in America in 1981; Levi Strauss, the 138th largest; and Witco Chemical, the 227th largest. Firms founded by Jews had also become especially prominent and successful in particular industries, such as entertainment, publishing, and the manufacture of women's clothing and related products.[5]

Impressionistic evidence confirms the statistics showing a widespread degree of Catholic and Jewish entry into the business mainstream. Thus in a 1979 article titled "U.S. Catholics Find Prejudices Waning," the *New York Times* reported that "in a cultural, educational and social explosion, Catholics have brushed aside the old barriers and made striking gains to reach the top in . . . business and industry, occupying the board rooms and other positions of power once denied to their forebears." The article mentioned several Catholic business executives and added that "many of these executives would say they have found little, if any anti-Catholic prejudices to trip them up." Similarly, a 1980 article noted that "proportionately more Jews than in the past ha[d] been taking jobs [as managers] in corporations," while a 1983 article, "Jews in the Corporate Establishment," showed "that Jews are not underrepresented on the nation's largest public corporations" and took note of many highly successful Jewish executives and entrepreneurs. A 1986 article summarized much of the earlier material in reporting on the successful careers of Catholics and Jews in New York City banks. It concluded that banks had "begun to open key jobs to Jews, Italians and others" and that "what ha[d] been happening in banking ha[d] been also occurring elsewhere," with "members of ethnic groups who had once been excluded in some heavy industries . . . beginning to move into top jobs." The article also "predict[ed] that the ethnic and religious diversity at the top levels . . . will continue to increase as . . . the system [becomes] more competitive and as more and more people from ethnic groups fill the pipelines of management's lower levels."[6]

These advances in housing, education, and job opportunities had a profound overall effect. In the first third of the century, it will be recalled, most Catholics and Jews had lived in poverty. By the mid-1970s, in contrast, Jews had become the most highly educated and wealthiest religious group in the United States, with family heads having an income 44 percent higher than the overall American average. Except for Latin Americans, Catholic family heads also had incomes above the national average, with incomes in some groups, like Irish Americans, exceeding the average by as much as 22 percent. Although high-status Protestants, such as Congregationalists, Episcopalians, and Presbyterians, on average remained as wealthy as Jews, there seems little doubt that by 1980 the Catholic and Jewish descendants of turn-of-the-century immigrants had attained the freedom, opportunity, dignity, and equality that other white Americans enjoyed.[7]

The legalist reformation did not, however, treat all groups equally well.

African Americans remained victimized by segregation, racism, and discrimination, as did other newer immigrant groups from Asia and Latin America. In giving sexual and other freedom to men, the law often oppressed women, who in many ways were treated as second-class citizens from the 1940s into the 1960s. Finally, the legal system tended to repress anyone, especially the young, who either could not or would not assimilate into the existing cultural order and wished instead to create alternative cultures.

By the late 1960s, these various groups perceived that the legalist reformation was not granting them freedom, equality, and dignity, and they burst into protest. With their protest, the unity of social and political vision that had enabled judges to stage a legal revolution in the aftermath of World War II broke apart into fragments in the closing years of the 1960s.

Events of the year 1968, in particular, tore the fabric of American society and convinced a number of socio-interest groups, which had thought they shared common aspirations for liberty, equality, and justice, that their interests conflicted. When the different groups each began to advance their own interests as just and courts had to choose between them without recourse to precedent, it became painfully clear that judges were constantly deciding "controversial matter[s] of significant policy."[8] In deciding those matters, courts could no longer think that they were simply advancing society's shared interests. The contradictions buried in the vague legalist reform agenda of liberty, equality, and opportunity then became patent, and as a result, the reform movement lost much of the moral power it had once possessed to move forward and change social reality.

In 1968, legalism's loss of moral force emerged publicly with a vengeance. For most Americans, the year was one of despair, albeit interspersed at times with hope. Indeed, hope and despair followed each other alternately in such rapid succession that the year assumed an often chaotic character and some people wondered whether social order was dissolving.

Dominating all else was the Vietnam War. As the year began, some optimism existed in regard to the war, at least within the government, and the Johnson administration was painting a bright picture for the American public. During early January, the military situation was comparatively calm, with General William Westmoreland, the U.S. commander, reporting that the Vietcong "seem to have temporarily run out of steam." Meanwhile, others in the Johnson administration were talking about "the light at the end of the tunnel." Only months before, the United States had opened its new embassy compound, a structure enclosed by a high wall, protected by an antirocket shield, and capped by a helicopter pad—"built to be impregnable."[9]

At approximately 3 p.m. Eastern time on January 30, reports began to reach New York and Washington that a squad of Vietcong commandos had breached the embassy wall, entered the compound, and were holding it against American reinforcements seeking to retake it. As Chet Huntley reported on the NBC evening news, snipers "in the buildings and on the rooftops near the embassy . . . [were] firing on American personnel."[10] It soon became clear that dozens of other Vietcong attacks were occurring within Saigon itself, that the Vietcong had entered the center of seven other cities, and that the American base at Khe Sanh was surrounded. The next day, the Communists seized the citadel at Hue, the old imperial capital of Vietnam, which they held for over three weeks. The Tet Offensive was in full swing. Nightly on TV, Americans saw much of Tet's action, including the South Vietnamese police chief's personal execution of a captured Vietcong guerilla, although other Tet events, such as the My Lai massacre, would not come to public attention for some time to come.

Tet transformed Americans' understanding of the war. True, the Vietcong suffered heavy casualties and made no permanent captures of territory. But "even the American military," according to NBC's Pentagon correspondent, "admired what the Vietcong were able to do" in launching, in the words of an ABC commentator, "by far the biggest and boldest and most sophisticated offensive of the whole war." No amount of explanation could blunt the impression of Vietcong prowess, and the country found it hard to swallow the continuing official line that the Communists were losing. Even President Lyndon Johnson's speechwriter "had the feeling that the country had just about had it."[11]

If Tet brought despair to those striving for an American victory in Vietnam, it brought hope to antiwar activists seeking an American pullout. And within three weeks of the end of Tet, the next shocking event of 1968—the New Hampshire primary—raised antiwar hopes to ecstasy, as Eugene McCarthy, the antiwar candidate, polled only 230 votes less than President Johnson in what was assumed to be one of the most prowar states in the nation. In the words of one of McCarthy's student workers, she and her fellow workers "woke up . . . after the New Hampshire primary, like it was Christmas Day." But ecstasy turned almost immediately to anger, when four days later New York senator Robert F. Kennedy announced his presidential candidacy and the McCarthy students "went down to the tree . . . [and] found Bobby Kennedy had stolen our Christmas presents."[12]

According to the chronicler of the 1968 election, "American politics became unhinged," as "the pace of events overtook the decisions of leaders." Two weeks after Kennedy entered the presidential race, President Johnson in a nationally televised plea for unity in search of peace announced that he would not accept renomination for another White House term. At this point in the story, the chronicler remembers a student at McCarthy headquarters "who could not have been more than eighteen years old, dressed in a brilliant yellow sweater, his hair thoroughly tousled, running up and down the corridors all by himself, loping and dancing and screaming, yelling in a solitary Indian dance. He had helped force the resignation not of a Dean, but of a President of the United States." [13]

With Vice President Hubert Humphrey's entry in lieu of Johnson into the three-way contest for the Democratic nomination, it is useful to pause to examine the ideological basis of each man's candidacy. For Humphrey, McCarthy, and Kennedy each represented something different, and what they represented helps explain the panorama of change sketched in this book.

Of the three, Humphrey most obviously represented the New Deal liberalism of Al Smith, Franklin Roosevelt, Benjamin Cardozo, Harlan Fiske Stone, and Herbert and Irving Lehman. Humphrey had first come to national attention at the 1948 Democratic convention as a leader for racial equality. For sixteen years thereafter, Humphrey had been the leading practitioner of a "politics of joy" that sought to assimilate everyone, especially African Americans, into the American mainstream. But Humphrey's politics was distinctively top-down in style—a politics in which elites would bring joy to the masses by allowing them to join the elite mainstream on the elite's terms. It is important to appreciate the extent to which the impetus of the Great Society, of which Humphrey was vice president, was to bring to the poor the social services which bureaucrats knew people needed to become joyous citizens.

If Humphrey adhered to the politics of the past, McCarthy introduced the politics of the future. His style was noncoercive, and he imposed a program on no one. In the words of one of his own speechwriters, he never did "identify himself with a positive vision of America." Indeed, the substance of McCarthy's program lay more in his student volunteers than in the candidate himself. According to the chronicler of the campaign, the McCarthy students were young people of "goodwill," "purity of spirit and . . . remarkable ability," yet they also possessed an "unconscious arrogance" and "distrusted America, saw only its evil." In the words of Sam Brown, one of their leaders, "the United States . . . [had become] the great imperialist-aggressor nation of the world." Most young antiwar students of the 1960s agreed that to be "American [was] to have been betrayed . . . [and] enraged." Privileged children of the upper and middle class, they had first grown politically aware in the early 1960s—

years of "rising hope." When, in the middle of the decade, they faced "the denial of hope and terror at the prospect of annihilation," antiwar students did not respond as their parents had by seeking to perfect the American system; instead, they concluded that " 'America [was] a crime' " burdened with not "simply bad policy but a wrongheaded social system, even a civilization." Their protests had " 'no 'political' meaning in the old sense . . . of changing the country purposively.' " They were "not [in] the mood to generate ideas about a reconstruction of politics." Their "only affirmative position was negation," as they strove to "shatter ordinary patterns of expectation" for the purpose "of stopping the war by stopping America in its tracks." [14]

In their distrust of America, the students had much in common with ghettoized African Americans. But the fact is that the student movement and the racial equality movement had split apart by 1968, each with its own diverging goals. The students, committed to sexual and other sorts of individual freedom, wished to create a new culture in which bureaucratic and coercive government would play only a minimal role. Moreover, the mainly privileged, upper-middle-class students rarely could comprehend the poverty and discrimination that blacks face every day and the consequent need of blacks for government action to redistribute wealth and power in their favor. Unsurprisingly, blacks, who still needed active government of the Great Society sort, gave little support to the McCarthy campaign in 1968.

But they also did not give much support to their obvious candidate, Humphrey, who was standing in for their Great Society benefactor, Johnson. By 1968, blacks were no longer in a mood for top-down, assimilationist equality. By then, the civil rights movement was decades old, *Brown v. Board of Education* had been decided for more than ten years, and little, if any, improvement had occurred in the lives of African Americans. In a widely publicized 1966 speech, Stokely Carmichael, a young militant who had just become leader of the Student Nonviolent Coordinating Committee, made this point with the declaration that, "We have been saying 'freedom' for six years and we ain't got nothing." In his view, the time had come to demand "*black power.*" Malcolm X had made the same point a few years earlier at Cornell University, where he announced that he could no longer believe in "the American dream" of assimilationist equality. He explained:

> Dark mankind wants freedom, justice, and equality. It is not a case of wanting integration or separation, it is a case of wanting freedom, justice, and equality. . . . Because we don't have any hope or confidence or faith in the American white man's ability to bring about a change in the injustices that

exist, instead of asking or seeking to integrate into the American society we want to face the facts of the problem the way they are, and separate ourselves. . . . We feel, that if integration all these years hasn't solved the problem yet, then we want to try something new, something different and something that is in accord with the conditions as they actually exist.[15]

As another radical added, his "fight" was "not to be a white man in a black skin." Blacks did not want "the right to be like" whites, but "freedom for us to be black, or brown, and you to be white and yet live together in a free and equal society." Ultimately, that meant freedom "to inject some black blood, some black intelligence into the pallid mainstream of American life."[16]

Blacks, along with Latinos, gravitated toward the third of the candidates, Robert Kennedy. There was no doubt either of Kennedy's commitment to minority causes or of minorities' appreciation of that commitment. According to Ralph Abernathy, Kennedy's presence established "that white America does have someone in it who cares," while Hosea Williams "remember[ed] telling him he had a chance to be a prophet." "He could see things," according to Cesar Chavez, "through the eyes of the poor," to which Chavez added, "he was ours." A ghetto youth agreed that "Kennedy . . . [was] on our side."[17]

What differentiated Kennedy from Humphrey, who also was committed to minority causes, was that Kennedy, like McCarthy, was "dissatisfied with our country." Also like McCarthy, Kennedy understood that elites could no longer direct a top-down reform movement and tell those beneath them what was in their interest. He knew it was essential for leaders to "listen." Above all, "Robert didn't come to us and tell us what was good for us," Dolores Huerta, a lieutenant for Cesar Chavez, noted. "He came to us and asked two questions. . . . 'What do you want? And how can I help?' That's why we loved him."[18] Unlike McCarthy, however, Kennedy knew that minorities needed activist government. Kennedy thus strove to articulate a political program for using government power to advance minority causes not with a top-down approach but by listening and respecting minority needs, demands, and aspirations.

Kennedy's entry into the presidential primaries raised the hopes of minorities and of other Americans who wished minorities well. Within three weeks, however, hope turned to despair, when on April 4, the great leader of poor minorities in general and of African Americans in particular—Martin Luther King Jr.—was assassinated.

On that night of April 4, rioting by angry blacks broke out in Washington, D.C. It ultimately spread to within two blocks of the White House, which along with the Capitol required protection by regular federal troops armed with machine guns, and to more than one hundred other cities. Some seventy-five thousand National Guardsmen and army regulars saw antiriot duty. A total of thirty-nine people, mostly black, were killed and more than twenty-five hundred injured. Arrests totaled twenty thousand, and property damage reached $45 million.[19]

The riots marking King's death ended a week after they started, but on April 23 in New York a new riot broke out when students at Columbia University occupied several campus buildings to protest a variety of issues. Probably the most important one concerned Columbia's plan to build a new gymnasium in Morningside Park—a plan said to represent further encroachment on the adjacent Harlem ghetto. Following a speech by Cicero Wilson, the president of the Student Afro-American Society, condemning white liberals and radicals for failing to take racism seriously, a student mob took off for the gym site but was turned back by police. The students then invaded Hamilton Hall, the first of five buildings that the rebel students would occupy.

Soon the student protest took two new directions, which would characterize reform, radical, and other left-wing movements in the decades to come and which ultimately would decimate them. The first occurred when, within several hours of the seizure of Hamilton Hall, the black students asked their white comrades to leave Hamilton and take over their own building. The whites did as requested and for the next week held four university buildings.[20]

At times, euphoria reigned among the protesters. In one building, there was a wedding ceremony, in which the officiating minister pronounced the bride and groom "children of the new age." Other students commented that the rebellion "was the beginning of a new vocabulary . . . of camaraderie" and of communal life "in which adult hypocrisies did not apply any longer, where people shared and shared alike." Yet simultaneously, political fragmentation continued among the white rebels, with a rift between proponents of youth culture and supporters of the Progressive Labor movement and with fistfights over ideology and tactics erupting in the building occupied by students identified as liberal.[21]

The second turn of events occurred at 2:30 A.M. on April 30, nearly a week after the first building takeover, when a thousand New York City police marched onto the campus in military formation to dislodge the protesters. There were a total of 722 arrests and 148 injuries, including innocent faculty observers and a *New York Times* reporter, as "platoons of police assaulted students wherever they found them" and "mounted policemen re-created scenes out of Selma as they charged anyone who looked as if he might be a demonstrator." The police attack united most students and even some faculty to support a general strike, which brought academic activity at the university to a halt. Three weeks later, on May 21, students again occupied a university building, but this time the police arrived on the same night, leading to 177 arrests, 68 injuries, and several fires, one of which burned the research papers of a faculty member.[22]

In the words of Professor Richard Hofstadter, the university and even the broader community had "suffered a disaster whose precise dimensions it [was] impossible to state."[23] Reformers and other advocates of change had abandoned legalism, had fomented violence, had disintegrated into factions, and had become victims of savage police repression. But there was still some reason for optimism. Perhaps Senator Robert Kennedy, who already had the support of blacks and other minorities, could build a coalition including minorities, angry students, and traditional reformers, win the Democratic presidential nomination and later the presidential election, end the Vietnam War, and return the nation to the days of legalist reformation it had enjoyed as recently as the early 1960s. With one exception, Kennedy was winning every presidential primary, including the all-important June 4 California primary. Then, immediately after delivering his victory speech, he was assassinated.

The body of Robert F. Kennedy was flown back home to New York City for a funeral mass at St. Patrick's Cathedral, where assimilationist equality enjoyed one more triumph as "Richard Tucker, trained as a synagogue cantor, sang," the "mass was read in English," and "Andy Williams sang 'The Battle Hymn of the Republic,' the original freedom song of the Protestants." The cathedral's rules, which had permitted only men to sing at mass, were even changed to permit a nuns' choir to participate in the service. Following the funeral mass, which thus symbolized "life in the world's greatest city, which is the coarse, yet closest, attempt of men of all colors, skins, faiths and tongues to live together in community," a train carried Kennedy's body to Washington for burial in Arlington National Cemetery, just as thirty-five years earlier a train had brought Franklin D. Roosevelt, the New Deal, and ultimately the legalist reformation from the governorship of New York to the presidency of the United States. And just as FDR's inaugural had promised to mobilize the power of government to help the people of America, Robert Kennedy's funeral made it plain "that there was no longer any reason to hope for anything; that the world was now just totally off its rocker, and that evil was ascendant, and was going to be."[24]

Additional events later in 1968 further confirmed that the old world was gone. The first, in August, was the "police riot" in Chicago. Thousands of students had gone there for the Democratic National Convention, some to make trouble and others to support the McCarthy candidacy. The police dealt first with the troublemakers. After several preliminary skirmishes on previous days, the National Guard fired tear gas at a crowd in Grant Park at about 6:30 P.M. on the night the Democrats planned to nominate their presidential candidate. Although the gas had even seeped into the convention hotels across Michigan Avenue from the park, the crowd had nonetheless reorganized itself an hour later on the avenue for a march on the convention itself. After the police had tightly surrounded the marchers, who had begun to chant, "Fuck You, LBJ, Fuck You, LBJ," sympathizers in the hotel rooms above began to throw bottles, bundles of documents, and other debris down on the officers. Then the police attacked as if in "a scene from a movie of the Russian revolution," clubbing and dragging youngsters. After a brief pause, the violence burst forth again. In the words of the chronicler of the election:

> The police seize two demonstrators. They resist. A commotion explodes in the front rank; one sees the clubs coming down; two demonstrators are being dragged to the patrol wagon; one falls; he is dragged by his heels to the wagon, his head bumping on the ground. A neat, smartly tailored lady is enraged, she dashes from the sidewalk, her arms flailing at the police dragging the demonstrator; the police grab her by the elbows, she is being dragged into the patrol wagon. There is much blood now—police blood and demonstrators' blood. The mob is yelling "Sieg Heil, Sieg Heil, Sieg Heil." The chant changes occasionally to "The Whole World is Watching, The Whole World is Watching, The Whole World is Watching." . . . The Whole World was indeed watching . . . through the eyes of film and television.

Shortly after, on the convention floor, when Governor Abraham Ribicoff of Connecticut put George McGovern's name in nomination, he commented that, with McGovern, "we wouldn't have Gestapo tactics on the streets of Chicago," to which the mayor of Chicago apparently responded, "Fuck you, you Jew son of a bitch, you lousy motherfucker, go home," to which the governor replied, "How hard it is to accept the truth . . . , how hard." [25] The coalition of legalist reformers put together by Franklin Roosevelt, Herbert Lehman, and innumerable judges surely had fallen apart.

The next morning, at about 5 A.M., the Chicago police attacked again—this time against the McCarthy students. After being struck with objects from above, the police invaded the hotel in which McCarthy headquarters was located and proceeded to the floor where the student volunteers were housed. They struck some students with clubs and roused others from their rooms until a campaign manager awakened the candidate himself. Only when Mc-

Carthy appeared did the police desist. Deep despair had surely descended upon those who, on the night of the New Hampshire primary, had been so hopeful that America could be changed.

The second disheartening event in the autumn of 1968, which had no connection with the presidential election, was a strike by New York City public school teachers. The genesis of the strike went back to the spring of 1968, when the community board of the experimental Ocean Hill–Brownsville district in Brooklyn, with a student body that was almost entirely African American and Latino, had demanded that thirteen teachers and six supervisors, all of whom were union members and Jewish, be removed from their positions in the district. In no instance was the community board able to document legally adequate cause for its demand; in essence, the community board perceived the nineteen as hostile to the board's effort to gain control of the educational process in its district. The union, which was defending professional control of the educational process by teachers, called a strike in the spring of 1968 in the Ocean Hill–Brownsville district. When that strike failed to resolve the issue, it escalated in the fall into a series of three city-wide strikes, which kept the schools closed through much of September, October, and November.[26]

At its core, the strike was not a labor-management dispute but a confrontation between mainly African American parents, on the one hand, and white, mostly Jewish teachers, on the other. As a special committee appointed to investigate the strike reported, "[an] appalling amount of racial prejudice—black and white—in New York City surfaced in and about the school controversy." There were "vicious anti-white attitudes on the part of some black people," including "a dangerous component of anti-Semitism," and "vicious anti-black attitudes on the part of some white people." One flyer placed in teachers' mailboxes in Ocean Hill–Brownsville demanded, for example, that "The Black Community Must Unite Itself Around The Need To Run Our Own Schools And To Control Our Own Neighborhoods Without Whitey Being Anywhere On The Scene" and that "African American History and Culture" must be taught by "African Americans who Identify With And Who Understand The Problem" and not by "The Middle East Murderers of Colored People"—"the So-Called Liberal Jewish Friend" who "is Really Our Enemy and *He* is Responsible For The Serious Educational Retardation Of Our Black Children." "Anti-black bigotry tended to be expressed in more sophisticated and subtle fashion . . . , but nonetheless [was] equally evil, corrosive, damaging, and deplorable." As one school administrator noted, African Americans had "never enjoyed the luxury of people accepting us for being competent people and responsible people," and this lack of acceptance manifested itself when many white teachers refused to yield power over schools to black parents, opposed early affirmative action programs, and even discouraged black students from applying to elite colleges that were, in fact, eager to admit them. "One of the ugliest open sores of the school strike"—"called The Black Community *vs.* The Jewish Community"—thus made it plain, as had the events in Chicago at the Democratic National Convention, that the legalist reform coalition for which Robert F. Wagner, for one, had spoken at the 1938 State Constitutional Convention had fallen apart.[27]

The third dramatic event of the autumn also had nothing to do with the presidential election, although its long-term consequences were equally significant. About two weeks after the Chicago riots, some two hundred women, mostly members of New York Radical Women, held a counterdemonstration at the annual Miss America Pageant in Atlantic City. The focus of the demonstration was a "freedom ashcan," into which "the women tossed liquid detergent, high-heeled shoes, corsets, eyelash curlers, and at least one bra."[28] As the can was filled, a new radical movement, unlike any effort from the era of legalist reform, was born.

Feminism, of course, was not new. It had been a vibrant movement through most of the nineteenth century, and one of its great legal victories had occurred at the very outset of the period under study in this book, when in 1920 the ratification of the Nineteenth Amendment gave women the right to vote. Nonetheless, throughout the decades since 1920, women had remained second-class citizens and victims of discrimination. Even in the 1960s, when the efforts of Catholic and Jewish men to assume the values of the dominant culture and thereby enter its socioeconomic mainstream had in large part succeeded and the civil rights movement, with its demand for the elimination of subordination on the basis of race, was at its height, little had been done to address the subordination of the largest underclass in American society—women.[29]

Many forms of discrimination that victimized women continued to exist as late as 1970. But a few, in particular, stand out. First, women were virtually excluded from the professions and other elite occupations. Second, women who were employed earned only 41 percent of what men earned. Third, 45 percent of households with children headed by women had incomes below the poverty line, whereas only 11 percent of all households with children had such low incomes.[30]

With the 1963 publication of Betty Friedan's *The Feminine Mystique,* the 1964 passage of Title VII of the Civil Rights Act, one of the goals of which was equal employment opportunities for women, and the 1965 founding of NOW, the National Organization for Women, a newly revived feminist movement emerged. In its earliest incarnation in the mid-1960s, the newly revived movement seemed to fit comfortably under the umbrella of legalist reform. Although "the ideological complexity of the [feminist] movement is too great to be categorized . . . simply," the early liberal feminists mostly believed that women are essentially the same as men, that gender inequality resulted from arbitrary legal distinctions, and that with the elimination of those distinctions "the human qualities of male and female will merge in a new image of the ideal person."[31]

Friedan, the author of *The Feminine Mystique* and the founder of the National Organization for Women, exemplified this liberal version of feminism. In Friedan's view, "the only way for a woman, as for a man, to find herself . . . is by creative work." Women " 'need competition just like men do,' " and "must learn to compete . . . not as . . . wom[e]n, but as . . . human being[s]." Thus the goal of NOW was " 'to bring women into full participation in the mainstream of American society . . . in truly equal partnership with men.' " Friedan never saw "women, as an oppressed class, fighting to overthrow or take power away from men as a class, the oppressors"; she hoped men would "be part of" NOW and that the movement for women's rights would "include men as equal members." She wanted to put an end to the world in which women had to " 'adjust' to prejudice and discrimination," but she did not intend to create a world in which a woman should "expect special privileges because of her sex." Many other women thinkers joined with Friedan in finding "more similarity than difference in the traits . . . [of] each sex" and in modeling gender relationships in accordance with "an image of human wholeness" involving " 'a spirit of reconciliation between the sexes' " leaving both with the "capacity for a 'full range of experience.' "[32]

As late as 1968, liberal feminists thus had not truly challenged mainstream assumptions and attitudes; their issues were not central to the agendas of key political leaders such as those campaigning for president; and their main legislative accomplishment—Title VII of the 1964 Act—remained largely unenforced. Unlike NOW and the liberal feminists, however, the activists who formed groups like New York Radical Women were not seeking the enactment and enforcement of federal legislation. Instead, their goal was to change society and culture and, above all, to change men.

The ideological fissures within radical feminism are especially complex, with disagreement over a myriad of issues ranging from the structures that should be adopted for the internal governance of women's groups, through the significance to be attached to lines of race and class, to the role of law and culture as sources of women's oppression, and even to the proper place

of lesbian sexuality in a future feminist utopia. For present purposes, however, much of the complexity can be disregarded. The important point is that
in the late 1960s new groups with different agendas than the Friedan liberals
were emerging. These more radical[33] feminists did "not believe that women
should be integrated into the male world so that they can be 'just as good as
men,'" nor did they "believe that the oppression of women" would "be ended
by giving them a bigger piece of the pie, as Betty Friedan would have it." On
the contrary, they concluded angrily that "the pie itself is rotten." Unlike the
moderates, the radicals did "not see equality as a proper, or sufficient, or moral,
or honorable final goal" for women; the ultimate goal of radical feminism was
to force "men . . . to renounce their phallocentric personalities, and the privileges and powers given to them at birth as a consequence of their anatomy,
. . . [and] to excise everything in them that they now value as distinctively
'male.'"[34]

The central fact on which radical feminists based their analysis was the fundamental "split between the two primary cultures of the world—the female
culture and the male culture." It seemed clear to the radicals that cultural
forces were "set by men, presenting only the male view," and that women were
thereby "kept from achieving an authentic picture of their reality."[35]

Thus the goal for many radicals was to "eradicate the sexual division on
which our society is based." These radicals fought vehemently for "a cultural
revolution, which, while it must necessarily involve . . . political and economic reorganization . . . must go far beyond this as well" to include "true re-
education," the elimination of "sex [a]s a status category with political implications," and the destruction of "oppressive power structures set up by Nature
and reinforced by man." The ultimate goal of radical feminists was to make
every man appreciate that every woman is "a complex human being with a self-
interest not identical with his" and to compel men to give women's interests
priority, even when they conflicted with the interests of men.[36]

A third group of women thinkers—a conservative one—also came into
existence in the 1970s. Typified by Phyllis Schlafly, this third group agreed
with the second, radical group that there were "fundamental difference[s]" between men and women both in regard to "sexual drive" and to "emotional
and psychological" matters. But the differences between man and woman, according to Schlafly, did "not in any sense make her inferior"; on the contrary,
women in America had been "'exalted'" and granted "a status . . . unknown in
the rest of the world." "It [was] on . . . women that . . . civilization depend[ed]."
For this reason, women in the third group opposed the liberation agendas of
those in the first two because liberation of women would drive them from a

position of " 'superiority to equality.' " They also opposed women's liberation as an attack on marriage, the home, and the family.[37]

With their angry divisions, their vehement attacks on tradition, and their rejection of ameliorist reforms, the feminists of the 1970s, especially the radical ones, represented a new form of politics that at least some thought would supersede the older politics of legalist reform. But before the legalist reformation could be replaced, it had to expire.

The legalist reformation surely did die as a national political force in the final dramatic event of the year, the election of 1968. Of the forty-three million Americans who had voted for the reformist candidate, Lyndon Johnson, in the 1964 election, twelve million of them, or 28 percent, repudiated him, his chosen successor, and the reform cause four years later. In place of legalist reformation, the voters chose Richard M. Nixon, who promised among other things to appoint to the federal bench judges committed to undoing much of the reform legal doctrine that had been crafted through the 1940s, the 1950s, and especially the 1960s.[38] With the election of Nixon and the subsequent elections of Ronald Reagan and George Bush, it seemed clear that the voters had tired of legalist reform, and not even the successful candidacies of Jimmy Carter and Bill Clinton could reassemble the old reform coalitions that had dominated the eras of the New Deal, World War II, and the Great Society.

With respect to the Supreme Court of the United States, President Nixon immediately translated the voters' mandate into reality by appointing first Warren E. Burger as chief justice and later Lewis F. Powell and William H. Rehnquist as associate justices. When President Reagan later raised Rehnquist to chief justice and also appointed Sandra Day O'Connor, Antonin Scalia, and Anthony M. Kennedy as associate justices, and President Bush added Clarence Thomas, the transformation of the Supreme Court was complete. The legalist reform understanding, which had come to its fullest fruition in the jurisprudence of the Warren Court, that courts should revise legal doctrine to attain liberty and justice for all, was forsaken; in contrast to the Warren Court, the Burger and Rehnquist Courts interposed "great resistance to expand[ing] the substantive reach of . . . rights deemed to be fundamental" lest "the Judiciary necessarily take . . . to itself further authority to govern the country without express constitutional authority." [39]

Not only did the Burger and Rehnquist Courts divert the jurisprudence of the legalist reformation; they also deflected the direction in which jurisprudential ideas flowed. From the era of Cardozo to the climax of the legalist reformation, ideas had moved upward from state courts, especially Cardozo's New York Court of Appeals, to the federal courts and ultimately to the Supreme

Court. Since the 1960s, in contrast, ideas have flowed downward, with the work of the Supreme Court dominating American legal thought and the work of the New York Court of Appeals and other state courts largely being ignored. Since the 1960s New York simply has not played the role of national leader that it had enjoyed during the century before the 1960s.

But the waning of New York's influence and the demise of the legalist reformation as a coherent and dynamic vehicle for judicial modification of law in the pursuit of liberty and justice did not mean that the legalist reformation disappeared completely and lost all continuing significance. In three respects, the legalist reformation remained triumphant into and even beyond the 1970s.

First, key reform concepts remained important in the postreformation era. Much as the Burger and Rehnquist Courts resisted expanding the reach of rights, they could not disavow the fundamental axiom on which the entire legalist reform movement rested—namely, that judges have a duty to protect minorities from oppression by the majority. People who had suffered defeat in the political process simply kept appearing at the judicial doorstep demanding relief, and they obtained it with sufficient frequency to encourage more demands. Nor could conservative judges renounce the corollary of this fundamental axiom—that in deciding whether and when to protect minorities, judges must choose between competing policies and implement sound visions of social justice rather than merely apply precedent. Finally, ideas of liberty, dignity, and equality remained vibrant.

Although new theories, especially the theory of efficiency, came to the fore in judicial discourse and contradictions implicit in old ideas became patent, the old ideas nonetheless endured because they served needs even of those who most passionately hated them. Radical blacks, radical students, and radical feminists may have become angry and unable to trust elites or to accept top-down reform. But as Malcolm X had noted, blacks, at least, still wanted "freedom, justice, and equality," and most of them wanted opportunities for economic advancement as well.[40] Conservatives likewise wanted their freedom and entrepreneurial opportunities, and they have striven to redefine the meaning of equality rather than abandon equality as a goal.

Whatever its failings, the ideology of the legalist reformation offers to all people the prospect of liberty, equality, and opportunity. In contrast, each of the old alternative ideologies rejects something important: Marxism rejects individual liberty, Nazism and related forms of fascism reject racial and religious equality, and populist localism undercuts the centralization of economic infrastructure needed to maximize economic opportunity. A new ideology offering freedom, equality, and opportunity thus is needed before the old ideology of the legalist reformation can be abandoned, but neither the right nor the radical left has been able to date to invent it. While they have attempted to redefine legalist reform ideas to better suit their needs, none of them has succeeded in attracting broad support for their redefinitions. Thus, as we examine cases, mostly from the 1970s, in the remaining chapters, we shall see that all economic, social, and cultural groups would, at one time or another, need to continue turning to old concepts as they demanded that the legal system ensure their liberty, treat them equally, preserve their dignity, provide them with entrepreneurial opportunity, and prevent others from exploiting them.

Second, recourse to these old concepts sometimes produced victory for those seeking doctrinal change, especially when they could demonstrate legislative backing for a proposed change or when it was plain that the change enjoyed broad electoral support. We shall observe many victories, for example, on the part of feminists and of racial minorities, as courts in the 1960s and 1970s finally recognized that women and minorities had a legal right to equal treatment. But there also were defeats. Sometimes, competing claims such as efficiency entered into judges' analysis and trumped claims for social justice. More frequently, contradictions implicit in the concepts of liberty, equality, and opportunity surfaced and thwarted reform. In any event, the gender and race cases beginning in the late 1960s do not provide the same sense of an inexorable judicial march toward a new, freer, and more just world that the jurisprudence of the mid-century New York Court of Appeals, in contrast, offers. Nor does it appear, from a vantage point three decades after 1968, that blacks and women have attained full equality, although it did appear, from a vantage point three decades after 1938, that the descendants of immigrant Catholics and Jews had done so.

Thus although feminists, African Americans, and others used the ideas of the legalist reformation and, at times, even achieved success, the legalist reformation has not brought them the liberty, equality, opportunity, and dignity that it gave white ethnics. Descendants of immigrant Catholics and Jews have entered the mainstream of New York society at the highest managerial levels, but women still face a glass ceiling and African Americans face discrimination throughout society.

The third way in which the legalist reformation continued to influence the law into the 1970s results from the march toward equality that white ethnics successfully pursued. In particular, we shall see how the presence of Catholics and Jews in business management, together with the entry of foreign firms into American markets, contributed to the breakdown of customary dispute resolution mechanisms, resulted in an increase in the filing of lawsuits, and, in turn, led to the employment of New York law firms to handle a more formalized dispute resolution process. More generally, we shall see how, as the legalist reformation fostered pluralism and pluralism eroded customary, informal processes for managing institutions, it ultimately became necessary to create new bureaucratic procedures to replace the defunct informal ones.

In the following chapters, we shall examine these often contradictory and paradoxical developments of the late 1960s and the 1970s. After focusing first on the subject of gender equity, we shall turn to other issues of equality that came before the courts. Then we shall examine the rise of bureaucracy in the wake of the legalist reformation and end with an analysis of the emergence of concerns for efficiency.

Although much doctrinal change will appear as we navigate these subjects in the chapters below, it will not point coherently in any one direction. Judges of 1980, like the legalist reformers of 1950, will understand their job to be policy choice and not the mere application of precedent, and thus legal doctrine will not be static. But it will not progress along any one, coherent path. As judges receive conflicting clues about the meaning of liberty, equality, and justice, they will reach conflicting results. In the end, some groups will attain their goals of freedom and justice some of the time, but no one will enjoy the consistent successes that the Catholic and Jewish descendants of turn-of-the-century immigrants enjoyed during the legalist reformation's height.

CHAPTER 13

GENDER EQUITY

As the last chapter suggested, one of the most important movements to emerge in the late 1960s was the resurgent movement for gender equity. In demanding an end to exploitation of women, feminists achieved considerable success. By the 1970s, few people were prepared openly to defend such exploitation, and when the path to ending exploitation was obvious, feminists typically were able to obtain the changes in legal doctrine they demanded, usually from the legislature but otherwise from the courts. Few opponents of change were prepared to argue in favor of the perpetuation of injustice. In connection with issues of gender equity, however, it often was possible to argue about the requirements of justice from more than one perspective. When such competing arguments were available — and especially when they were advanced by different subgroups of feminists — the law's susceptibility to change diminished. The significance of agreement or lack thereof among feminists and other women become especially apparent in connection with efforts during the 1970s to increase criminal liability for sexual immorality.

SEX CRIMES

Although virtually all women found rape and male violence against women and children abhorrent, disagreement emerged over prostitution and especially pornography. Liberals like Betty Friedan, who found men and women essentially the same, believed that women should have equal sexual liberty with men. At least some feminist writers came to believe that "pornography is not a homogenized discourse expressing only women's oppression"; in the view of one author, "multiple meanings coexist within pornography," including both "fantasy and rebellion," which "can be experienced as a liberating feeling" by many women. Likewise, a woman judge could object to the prosecution of women for prostitution on the ground that such prosecutions rested on "archaic notions that a woman's place is in the narrowly circumscribed, nonpublic world" and that women have no business "wander[ing] out of this protective sphere into the public" and "self-determin[ing] to whom and when they shall bestow their 'sexual favors.'" In this judge's view, a woman, whether prostitute or not, should have the same right to engage in "private consensual sexual conduct" as a man.[1]

In contrast, both the radical feminists and new right conservatives like Phyllis Schlafly adopted positions opposed to both pornography and prostitution. The opposition of many radicals grew out of their perspective on the "sexual act" itself, which, as they saw it, conferred "the feeling of power and prestige for the male, [and] of impotence and submission for the female." Sexual intercourse and violence represented "act[s] of freedom and strength" for "the male population," whereas for the "class of women," they constituted "a strange lesson" in *the objective, innate and unchanging subordination of women relative to men.* Especially "in rape, the emotions of aggression, hatred, contempt, and the desire to break or violate personality, [took] a form consummately appropriate to sexual politics."[2] Radical feminist theory thus demanded not only the reform of the law governing rape and gender-oriented violence—a reform with which virtually all women agreed—but also a thoroughgoing and much more problematic reconstitution of sexual habits and values.

For the radicals, the existence of pornography was linked closely to rape and gender violence. They began to "make the connections between media violence to women and real-life violence to them" and to recognize that while it was necessary to "deal directly with acute . . . problems like rape and wife-beating," it was equally important to "remove the images which promote a climate in which these crimes are possible." In their view, "pornography is the ideology of a culture which promotes and condones rape, woman-battering, and other crimes of violence against women," all of which " 'involve the acting out of male power over, and often hatred toward, women.' "[3]

Prostitution raised similar concerns. One connection between pornography and prostitution was the ease with which pornography models became prostitutes—by, for instance, engaging in " 'simulated sex'—even sometimes when it's not simulated." As one model argued, pornography and prostitution were "all a form of rape because the women who are involved in it don't know how to get out." As another radical argued in testimony to a committee of the New York legislature considering whether to recognize prostitution as a victimless crime, women were its victims. "Women with ambition" were victims because they had to "sell their bodies" in order to earn an independent living. As the witness continued:

There was a time when I was an unemployed actress, and working to support myself as a waitress and a file clerk. The disparity between my reality situation and my ambition for a better life was so great that I gave serious consideration to the social pressure to do a little hustling. And that is something, gentlemen, I really don't think that you comprehend. I don't think that anyone has ever asked you to sell your body, or presumed that your body was for sale. I wonder if a cab driver has ever turned around to you and remarked, "I see you're a little short of change. Perhaps we could work together. I could steer some customers your way." I wonder if a man has ever walked up to you in a hotel lobby, and muttered, "What's your price? Ten? Twenty? I'll pay it. I'll pay it." That happened to me in the Hotel Astor. I wonder if you've ever applied for work in a bar-restaurant, and the owner, or perhaps he was only the manager, looked you up and down and said, "Are you sure you're over twenty-one? Why don't you come downstairs with me and prove it?" . . . It is women who are being harassed on these streets in New York City, day and night, and they are being harassed by men and not the reverse. Yes, there is a prostitution problem, and it is expressed by . . . [men] who daydream . . . about women in clean little stalls, medically approved and at a price a workingman can afford.

The existence of prostitution thus reflected "a serious problem"—that men found "access to the female body . . . , if not a divine right, at least a monetary right"—and this serious problem would prevent women from being "equals until there's an end to prostitution."[4]

In their claims that the law of rape, sexual violence, pornography, and prostitution facilitated the exploitation of women by men, the radical feminists took a stand remarkably close to that of the new right, with its opposition to the alleged "liberation of the new morality"—a morality which the new right, like the radicals, saw as "a cheat and a thief." In speaking for the right, Phyllis Schlafly echoed many themes from the left as she urged that the new morality "rob[bed] the woman of her virtue, her youth, her beauty, and her love—for nothing, just nothing." Although the new right and the radical left differed sharply in their assessments of the institution of marriage, with the right viewing it as the ultimate protection for women, and the left, as the ultimate exploitation,[5] the two extremes were able to march toward the same ends together with virtually all women with regard to rape and family violence and with each other on the issues of pornography and prostitution. When the right and the left marched together, significant political pressure for change in the law of prostitution and pornography emerged, and when all women stood in solidarity, important changes occurred in legal doctrine making it easier to prosecute criminally male perpetrators of rape and violence.

In response to new demands from women, the story of sex crimes in the

1970s thus would be a curtailment of the trend toward decriminalization of the 1950s and 1960s. In particular, feminism would bring about fundamental doctrinal change on subjects like the law of rape, as the legislature and the courts responded to claims by women whose legitimacy went virtually unchallenged.

Rape. The most marked change would occur in what would come to be conceptualized as date rape cases, especially those in which women claimed they yielded to men who were larger and stronger out of fear of being seriously hurt. After 1975, the appellate courts, contrary to the spirit of the earlier cases, uniformly ruled that submission to larger and stronger men did not constitute consent. Indeed, in the new post-1975 world of feminist virtue, even a prostitute could complain of rape when her customer failed to pay her fee.[6]

Another dramatic change in the law of rape occurred quickly as a result of legislation enacted in 1975. Until that time, the settled rule was that evidence showing that a complainant had engaged in sexual intercourse with the defendant or other men before or after the alleged rape was admissible to prove the complainant's consent; the rule's effect, in the view of women's advocates, was to make it virtually impossible for women with histories of sexual relations outside of marriage to bring complaints in rape cases. Then, in 1975, the legislature excluded most forms of evidence of a victim's sexual activities with anyone other than the defendant. The statute was received favorably by the courts and applied routinely with statements that a "complainant's prior sexual history is not relevant and should be excluded."[7]

Perhaps the most important change occurred in the reversal of the rule, originally adopted in the *English* and *Radunovic* cases, requiring corroboration of a victim's testimony in order to obtain a conviction for rape or any lesser included offense under circumstances in which a rape had actually occurred. Within a few years of its decision in *Radunovic,* a changing majority of the Court of Appeals began to pull back from its holding in the case. Under growing objections, the court now observed that the corroboration requirement was "of minuscule practical value" and produced "disconcerting, if not mischievous consequences." The rule "frustrate[d] the prosecution of an inherently furtive act," "establishe[d] a system of false distinctions between offenses" against women, created a " 'motivation for falsehood,' " and "expresse[d] almost an irrational doubt toward the claims of women who ha[d] been victimized sexually."[8]

In response to concerns such as these, the legislature between 1972 and 1975 also enacted a series of piecemeal statutory changes that ultimately left New York with a corroboration requirement only in cases of consensual sodomy and of sex offenses against children who are too young or too incapacitated to give their consent or provide reliable testimony. The courts reacted positively to the new legislation and in appropriate instances held that corroboration was no longer required for convictions of rape and sexual abuse. Even in cases where corroboration was required, the courts required far less evidence than they had demanded before the legislation's passage. Thus, in one case, a divorced father was convicted of sexually abusing his two daughters, aged nine and seven, and their friend. The only evidence corroborating the girls' claims of sexual touching was the father's admissions that they had once seen him "exposed" and that on one occasion he had brushed urine off his daughter's friend and on another checked to see if his daughter had wet the bed, together with an earlier statement to his wife of "his intention to break 'the kids in and have intercourse with them . . . before they started menstruation."[9]

A final line of cases during the late 1970s that displayed the law's protective attitude toward women, as well as toward traditional moral values, dealt with the claim that New York's rape laws were unconstitutional because they discriminated against men. One alleged deficiency was that the laws made only men subject to conviction as principals for forcible rape; the courts, however, upheld this distinction as constitutional on the ground that only men were physiologically capable of committing the crime of rape.[10] The second claim of unconstitutionality arose in the context of the statutory rape laws, which barred men over twenty-one and eighteen respectively from engaging in sexual intercourse with women under seventeen and fourteen respectively.

People v. Whidden, which came to the same result as had earlier lower court cases, upheld the laws. One obvious justification for the legislation, found by the Court of Appeals to be "ample," was the prevention of pregnancy. A second alleged justification "was to protect the morals of young girls . . . even from their own immature indiscretions" as well as to protect them from "psychological" damage. Lower court judges had found "adolescence . . . a period of . . . emotional turbulence," when young girls were "subject to a variety of emotional and psychological wants which can often be *exploited* by an 'older man,'" and they therefore understood statutory rape laws as a protection against exploitation and victimization. The Court of Appeals, however, found this justification unconstitutional because it was "rooted" in the "stereotypical" and "unfounded assumption that underage women are more vulnerable to emotional harm than are their male counterparts."[11]

The statutory and case law developments discussed in this section completely overturned the policy direction of the law of rape in a mere ten-year period. At the beginning of the 1970s, a woman who had intercourse with a man with whom she was acquainted was presumed to have given consent, her testimony was deemed untrustworthy in the absence of corroboration, and her chastity became an issue if she made a legal complaint. In any case resting solely on the testimony of a man and woman who had engaged in intercourse, the man almost certainly would be acquitted of a rape charge, especially if the woman had had prior sexual experience. By 1980, in contrast, chastity was no longer an issue, formal legal doctrine no longer presumed consent, and a man could be convicted of rape solely on a woman's testimony; in any case of uncorroborated intercourse, the man would be without defense and would go to prison if the woman could convince a jury that he had raped her. The doctrinal inferiority of women was thus transformed into a position of theoretical legal superiority.

Of course, the social effects of this doctrinal change were far less transforming. Just as most men at the outset of the 1970s did not rape their dates even though the law did not stand in their way, so too most men who committed date rape at the decade's close were never brought to trial. Custom and social practice were at both times more determinative of sexual behavior than the law. Nonetheless, by undermining the power of men to coerce sex from women and instead giving women at least a theoretical capacity to send their lovers to jail, the doctrinal upheaval in the law of rape amounted to a powerful symbolic statement in support of new attitudes widely shared by most men and virtually all women.

Family Violence. Acting again in conjunction with tradition-minded conservatives, liberal and radical feminists won another victory when they succeeded in obtaining judicial and legislative support for the recriminalization of acts of family violence. The first steps were taken by conservative judges, when they began to halt the extension of the Family Court Act's conciliation and treatment provisions to men and women who were living together without the benefit of a formal marriage. These judges could not understand how the goal of the Family Court Act, which was the " 'restoration and preservation of marriages,' " could be accomplished by providing assistance to " 'persons who are living in a meretricious relationship.' " To assist such people would "make the court a party . . . to an immoral relationship," would "impair the . . . morals" of children, and "would not change the moral atmosphere generated by these people living together under one roof." [12]

When the issue first came before the Court of Appeals, it ruled that, if parties had contracted a common-law marriage in a state that recognized the legality of such marriages and had subsequently moved to New York, their relationship would "qualif[y] for treatment as a spousal or family relationship" under the Family Court Act. But the majority would go no further. In the leading case of *People v. Allen*, where Judges Francis Bergan and Stanley Fuld in dissent were prepared to extend decriminalization to a case of a man who had committed an act of sodomy on a woman with whom he had lived unmarried for three years, Judge Matthew Jasen writing for the majority halted the decriminalization movement in its tracks. Jasen simply thought that "making available conciliation procedures" under the Family Court Act to "informal and illicit relationships . . . would clearly be contrary to public policy."[13]

The 1970 majority opinion in *People v. Allen* marked the beginning of a sharp change in the judiciary's approach to family offense proceedings. Change continued as feminists in the next few years successfully publicized "societal concern" about brutality to women at the hands of their husbands, as well as to young children at the hands of their fathers. In particular, concern arose that police would not respond to requests for safeguarding made by or on behalf of a battered or threatened wife, apparently because they did not want to become involved in domestic disputes.[14] Thus, in one case, where a woman's husband had brandished a straight razor, torn off her blouse, and gouged her face, neck, shoulders, and hands with his nails, in full public view, the police advised her that " 'since this was a 'family' matter there was nothing they could do.' " Another woman whose arm had been sprained by her husband was told by the police that " 'there is nothing wrong with a husband hitting his wife if he does not use a weapon,' " while a third woman who had been struck by her husband with a knife heard an officer who refused her request to arrest him exclaim, " 'Maybe if I beat my wife, she'd act right too.' " As a result of the decriminalization of family offenses, the only remedy these women possessed was to go to Family Court and seek a protection order, but when they got to the court they experienced little assistance and great delay.[15] Even if a woman obtained a protection order, it often did little good.

One egregious case, *Sorichetti v. City of New York*, involved Frank Sorichetti, who prior to November 6, 1976, had been arrested six times for drunkenness and family assaults. After he had assaulted his wife, Josephine, with a knife in July 1975, she instituted a divorce action, only to be threatened by him "that he would kill her and the children if she proceeded with the divorce." In September she obtained a protection order, but on November 6, the order was amended over Josephine's objections to allow Frank weekend visitation rights with his daughter Dina. On November 8, after Josephine had delivered Dina to Frank at a police precinct, he threatened that he would kill both Josephine and Dina before the weekend was over. Josephine informed the police of the threats, showed them her protection order, and demanded that they arrest Frank, but they refused. When on the next day Frank failed to return Dina on time, Josephine again went to the police and demanded repeatedly that they arrest Frank; when she showed the protection order to a police lieutenant and demanded its enforcement, he responded, " 'So what, what have you got there—they mean nothing.' " Several hours later, when Frank's sister entered his apartment, she found that Frank had attacked Dina with a fork, a knife, and a screwdriver and had attempted to saw off her leg; Dina had been slashed from head to toe and she had sustained severe multiple internal injuries.[16]

In response to disasters such as these, the courts gave victims of serious family violence a cause of action for damages against the municipality that had negligently failed to protect them. More important, the legislature, in order "to afford more effective relief to the 'battered spouse,' " amended Article 8 of the Family Court Act to give the victim of a family assault the option of instituting criminal proceedings rather than seeking conciliation in Family Court. This 1977 amendment to the Family Court Act has been administered so as to give victims an effective choice of the court in which they want to proceed and to make it easy for them to proceed in criminal court.[17] As a result of the 1977 amendment, together with the earlier judicial narrowing of the original Article 8, the curious attempt during the 1960s to decriminalize acts of family violence in large part has come to an end.

Prostitution: Just as conservatives and radical feminists had joined forces to transform the law of rape and recriminalize family violence, the same forces struggled as well to prevent the dawn of "those halcyon days" sought by male libertines, where prostitutes were available "in clean little stalls, medically approved and at a price a workingman can afford." It seemed clear to radicals and conservatives alike that, even if "society may not be able to enforce morality, . . . it clearly can legislate it."[18]

Some judges, however, did try to enforce morality and thereby reverse the process of decriminalization. Lower court judges, for instance, continued, as they sometimes had done during the 1950s and 1960s, to distinguish both the *Gould* and *Choremi* cases in order to sustain prostitution convictions based on evidence obtained through tapping the telephones of call girls or through conversations held between defendants and undercover police, even in cases where no sexual activity had occurred or where it had not been directly observed. Lower courts also extended prostitution statutes to cover nontraditional defendants, such as the owner of an employment agency who offered jobs requiring women to submit to unlawful sexual intercourse or other lewd acts with their employers, and the owners of a massage parlor "where the female employees . . . manipulated the private parts of male customers to climax."[19]

In part, the resistance to further decriminalization of prostitution emerged out of a conservative, moralistic sense that the activity constituted "an age-old problem" for society that had to be "eradicate[d]." Solicitation by prostitutes " 'caused citizens who venture into . . . public places to be the unwilling victims of repeated harassment' " with the result that " 'such public places . . . become unsafe' " and " 'neighborhoods' " become " 'disrupted and . . . deteriorated.' " Prostitution, it was said, "spread . . . disease, lead [*sic*] . . . to ancillary criminal conduct, encourage[d] criminal organization," and thereby constituted "anti-social behavior offensive and injurious to the community."[20]

As the decade of the 1970s grew to a close, however, a new, radical feminist opposition to prostitution began to emerge as the main force behind the expansion of the criminal law. The new radical feminists saw prostitution not as an evil to society but as a harm to women; in the radical view, it was the prostitutes themselves who were victimized and exploited and needed to be protected. Prostitution became a feminist issue as women explained to the nation that the housekeeper who had sex with her employer and the teenager who left home and hitchhiked to Manhattan were not equal individuals who were voluntarily engaging in sex with the men who provided them with money. In this view, " 'men create[d] the market,' " but " 'the women who suppl[ied] the demand [paid] the penalty.' " There was, according to radical feminists, an "important state interest in proscribing" prostitution—an interest that was "emphasized," as one court noted, when the prostitute before it was, as was the case in an increasingly massive number of cases, "a fourteen year old child." The "imputation that females who engage in misconduct, sexual or otherwise, ought to be more censured . . . than males" had to be put to rest and the women, usually minors, who worked as prostitutes "protected . . . rather . . . [than] penally punished."[21]

New York had taken a step in that direction as early as 1965, when the legislature declared patronizing a prostitute to be a crime, and occasional cases had been brought under this statute against male customers. Then, in several brief experiments in New York City in the late 1970s, female undercover police officers were assigned to catch male customers and the names of the male customers were publicized, but the experiments ended in a wave of protest and law enforcement returned to a norm in which prostitutes were ten times more likely than their customers to be arrested. At the end of the decade the law of prostitution thus remained in stasis, as feminists and proponents of decriminalization fought to a standstill, with the result that moral traditionalists who found "something offensive about having women perform sex for money" continued to hold sway.[22]

Pornography. Like the law of prostitution, the law of pornography remained in stasis during the decade of the 1970s. This was true even though the two traditional "sides to the pornography issue: the conservative approach . . . and the liberal approach" were supplemented by "a third and feminist perspective: That pornography is the ideology of a culture which promotes and condones rape, woman-battering, and other crimes of violence against women."[23]

One reason for the static nature of pornography law during the decade was that New York courts and especially the New York legislature could do nothing to change it. The precise lines separating lawful pornography from illegitimate obscenity had become a matter for federal constitutional adjudication under the direction of a deeply divided United States Supreme Court. In view of the emerging contradictions in legalist reform, which led liberals to see "pornography as just one more aspect of our ever-expanding human sexuality" while conservatives found it "immoral" and feminists understood it to "promote . . . violence against women," a new consensus capable of generating a reform-oriented dynamic and of producing a complete judicial turnabout in doctrinal direction could not emerge.[24] The ultimate result was that doctrine remained incoherent and pornography cases continued to be resolved during the 1970s in the same unprincipled, ad hoc fashion that cases in other areas, like regulatory law, were resolved.

EQUAL EMPLOYMENT OPPORTUNITY

Disagreement among women was not the sole reason, however, for doctrinal incoherence in the rules addressing gender issues. A further, deeper reason was that many judges sympathetic to feminism often did not know how best to further the feminist cause. This was true especially in areas like employment law and family law.

It was sometimes easy, of course, for judges to act on behalf of equal employment opportunity. A step on behalf of equality for women had occurred as early as a 1962 case in which a policewoman had sued to invalidate a provision of the New York City Administrative Code that barred the promotion of women to the rank of sergeant. While it was, in the still sexist words of the court, "beyond dispute that women [could] not perform all the functions which male Sergeants may be called upon to perform in the Police Department," the trial judge found "it unreasonable to conceive that an organization the size of the New York City Police Department . . . would not have at least some positions of authority in which women could perform at the same level of competence as men." In the first case of its kind, the court ordered a hearing to determine whether the plaintiff could perform any of the tasks required of sergeants, on the understanding that if she could, the city's regulation would be "struck down as arbitrary and capricious."[25]

A more significant step toward ending the subordination of women was taken in the Civil Rights Act of 1964, which prohibited all employment discrimination based on sex. Like most equal rights legislation, the 1964 act was readily enforced by the courts in relatively straightforward matters like *Sontag v. Bronstein,* where the issue was whether a dumbbell lifting test, which was failed by Marilyn Sontag but passed by every male who took it, bore any relationship to the duties of audiovisual technician, the job for which Sontag had applied. As the Court of Appeals proclaimed with clarity in *Sontag,* "when a hiring standard, although neutral on its face . . . , adversely affects equal employment opportunity for a protected class of persons" such as women, the employer was required to establish that the test was "a valid predictor of employee job performance, and . . . [did] not create an arbitrary, artificial and unnecessary barrier to employment which operate[d] invidiously to discriminate on the basis of an impermissible classification" like gender.[26] The court accordingly reversed the judgment below dismissing Sontag's suit and remanded the case for a fact-finding about the job-relatedness of the dumbbell test.

Sontag and innumerable cases like it merely required clear and easy application of assimilationist equality principles requiring that women be given the same opportunities as men. But some other cases were not so simple. Consider, for example, three cases that were patently related to women's opportunities for equality of economic opportunity but could not be resolved by assuming merely that women were the same as men: *Ludtke v. Kuhn, Seidenberg v. McSorleys' Old Ale House, Inc.,* and *Scott v. Board of Education, Union Free School District #17, Hicksville.*

Ludtke was a suit by a female reporter for an injunction to compel the New York Yankees to grant her access to the team's locker room following games. The trial court made two key findings of fact. First, it found that Ludtke was denied "an equal opportunity to get a story or gather news on the same basis as her male counterparts, thus giving the latter a substantial competitive advantage." Second, the court concluded that the players could protect their privacy by "wear[ing] towels" or by "us[ing] curtains in front of th[eir] cubicle . . . to undress and hide . . . from these women." Accordingly, it found that "exclusion of women sports reporters from the locker room at Yankee Stadium [was] not substantially related to . . . privacy protection" but only "to maintaining the locker room as an all-male preserve." This, in turn, was being done for the purpose of "maintaining the status of baseball as a family sport and conforming to traditional notions of decency and propriety."[27] So understood, the effort of reporter Ludtke to crash the men's locker room, unlike the effort of the plaintiff in *Sontag,* stood in contradiction to traditional standards of manners and decency and was at war with established cultural symbols. The reporter in *Ludtke* could gain equal economic opportunity only if established norms were changed.

The issues in *Seidenberg* likewise had grave symbolic overtones. On the one hand, the continued exclusion of women from McSorley's Bar would "only serve to isolate women from the realities of everyday life, and to perpetuate, as a matter of law, economic . . . exploitation." On the other hand, there was "the occasional preference of men for a haven to which they retreat from the watchful eye of wives or womanhood in general to . . . pass a few hours in their own company." Lurking behind this urge for an all-male preserve was an "ancient chivalristic concept" of "bars as dens of coarseness and iniquity and of women as peculiarly delicate and impressionable creatures in need of protection from the rough and tumble of unvarnished humanity."[28] Equal economic opportunity for women again required a transformation of deeply held cultural assumptions.

At issue in *Scott* was whether Lori Scott, a young woman of fifteen, could wear slacks to high school. The court that decided the case made no finding that the school board's policy of requiring female students to wear traditional women's dress interfered with the opportunity of women to function as socio-economic equals, although plenty of evidence existed on which it could have based such a finding. But the court was clear about the school board's concerns: the board would not tolerate dressing that would " 'exaggerate, emphasize, or call attention to anatomical details' " or " 'provoke so widespread or constant attention as would interfere with teaching and learning . . . , espouse violence, be obscene, suggest obscenity, or call for an illegal act.' " At bottom, the board of education was seeking to impose rules of "style or taste" based on ancient chivalristic stereotypes about the behaviors and proper roles of men and women in society.[29] Again, the attainment of equality was at war with traditional cultural symbols.

Unlike *Sontag v. Bronstein,* where women, like earlier victims of exploitation, merely gained access to opportunities from which they had previously been excluded without the nature of those opportunities being changed, *Ludtke, Seidenberg,* and *Scott* sought to do more. The significance of the three cases lay in their effort to transform cultural symbols — in the rejection by the courts in all three cases of "mid-Victorian concept[s] which females [had] long since abandoned."[30] Casting Victorian culture rather than male liberty as the obstacle to change undoubtedly helped the three courts reach decisions in plaintiffs' favor. In other cases to which we must next turn, however, the feminist effort to change culture rather than merely give women access to what men already enjoyed plainly was at war not only with Victorian symbols but with the interests of many contemporary men and women as well. In these cases, the contradictions inherent in the legalist reformation vaulted to the fore and left judges with little neutral ground on which to reach decisions.

A particularly confusing line of cases dealt with gender issues in insurance, retirement, and other employee benefits cases. Some women, perhaps, obtained tangible financial gains as a result of judicial decisions outlawing gender-based discrimination in employee benefits. But most of these cases affected men as a group and women as a group in a fashion that did not improve the well-being of either. The reason was that men and women tended to be married to each other, with the result that, at least in traditional marriages, benefit payments were effectively made to the family unit, consisting of both sexes, rather than to men or women alone.

Spirt v. Teachers Insurance and Annuity Association,[31] for example, invalidated the use of sex-segregated mortality tables in determining the amount of retirement benefits payable to retirees. Since women on the average live longer than men, the consequence of using the tables was that a woman who had made the same contribution to a plan as a man would receive a lower monthly benefit upon retirement. In striking this discrimination down and requiring that women receive the same monthly benefit as men who had made the same contribution, judges did not, however, aid all women at the expense of all men. The reason is that women who were living in traditional marriages with men and were dependent on their husbands' pensions were hurt along with their husbands by the *Spirt* rule. The women who benefited from the rule were those who had supported themselves all or most of their lives and were dependent on their own retirement annuities for their current support. Perhaps annuity and insurance companies were able to gain the added funds needed to pay these independent women entirely from the pensions and annuities of single men. But if not, then the funds were obtained from the large number of workers and retirees who had entered traditional marriages. Whatever the actual distributional impact of *Spirt,* however, it seems clear that the case's newfound preference for single women of necessity represented a dramatically altered cultural assumption about the impropriety of women's dependence on men.

The same was true of the cases dealing with maternity leave policies and pregnancy benefits, cases which in New York, at least, were decided almost uniformly in favor of women plaintiffs.[32] But again, at least insofar as pregnant women were married, the conflict over pregnancy benefits typically was not between women and men but between families that would have children and those that would not. Only pregnant women who were unmarried or not otherwise financially dependent on men, which except for the uninsured poor was a relatively small group in the 1970s, enjoyed a tangible economic gain when the judiciary compelled employers to provide pregnancy benefits. Again, single women who were sufficiently well-off to carry health insurance gained at the expense of families, and the legal system arguably began propelling the culture toward a new assumption about the propriety of single women having children.

These cases, in short, suggest that one consequence of 1970s feminism, whether by inadvertence or design, was the emergence of new cultural symbols, which exalted economically independent, even single women over married women economically dependent on men. Of course, notions of individual liberty inherent in the legalist reformation legitimated a grant of freedom to women who did not wish to depend on men, but they also legitimated a grant of equal treatment to women who still sought dependence. No widely shared reform ideology authorized the preference of one group of women over the other, and thus it is not surprising that radical feminists' demands for cultural change provoked resistance that made the attainment of gender equality more difficult than the achievement of ethnic and religious equality through assimilation had been in the 1950s.

The struggle over abortion—a right essential to women if they are to achieve equality—is illustrative. Women initially obtained the right to abortion by statute in New York in 1970, and thus the right could never be questioned as it has been elsewhere on the ground that it had resulted from the Supreme Court's alleged usurpation of power in *Roe v. Wade*. Nevertheless, precisely because of the way the right to abortion conflicted with deeply held religious values and concepts of human dignity, recognition of the right provoked resistance, and when it did, New York judges cut back on the substance of the right, even though the legislature had granted it. First, the judges upheld a legislative addendum to the 1970 act which required that a doctor prepare for every abortion done in New York City a termination of pregnancy certificate including the name and address of the person obtaining the abortion. Second, they upheld requirements for the separate certification of abortion clinics along with the individual certification of every staff doctor. Third, the United States Supreme Court and the New York Court of Appeals both held that only medically indicated abortions could be funded by Medicaid reimbursements.[33]

Taken together, these restrictions tended to limit the availability of abortions, especially to poor women, thereby depriving the right to abortion of much of its substance. What remained was the cultural symbolism of the independent female, as free as a male to be sexually active without fear of the consequences. While it would be a mistake to denigrate the importance of this symbolism or to question the real freedom to control their bodies and their life destinies that women with adequate financial means gained from their right to abortion, it seems clear that on the subject of abortion as on most other subjects of gender equality, the mass of women gained less material improvement in their lives than the proponents of abortion might have hoped. Because of the difficulties of obtaining an abortion and the trauma associated with it, the grant of a formal legal right could not alone give women the sexual freedom that men had always enjoyed and continue to enjoy.

Indeed, the destruction of traditional norms and their replacement by the law of gender equality even brought tangible benefits on occasion to men. For example, cases in the 1970s flowing from the judiciary's growing concern with equal protection struck down various discriminations between the right of men and the right of women to marry, including differences in the minimal age of marriage without parental consent. A second line of cases involved issues of access to the courts by the poor. *Griffin v. Illinois* had prohibited states from discriminating against indigent criminal defendants; in response to *Griffin,* the federal courts authorized a class action suit by prisoners, who were overwhelmingly male, seeking relief from New York legislation declaring them civilly dead for purposes of matrimonial and family litigation. In a third line of cases, New York's "ancient practice of arresting only men" in civil litigation came to an end "as an unanticipated social dividend" of "the modern insistence on sex equality," even in cases where a woman was seeking to have a man arrested in the context of a marital dispute.[34]

In short, efforts to attain the goal of equality for women in employment and other contexts, which grew out of the legalist principle of equality for all, revealed the contradictions in the legalist reformation, which also called for equality for men, dignity for the unborn, and liberty for both women and men. Women did achieve some tangible gains from their drive for equality, but as of the end of the century, woman had not yet been brought into the mainstream of New York's economic and cultural life as successfully as Catholic and Jewish men had been. In this respect, legalist reform failed. Nonetheless, it remains the dominant mode of thought, as feminists continue to demand the legalist principle of equality, while their opponents argue for competing principles of human liberty and dignity, as well as equality for men.

Changes in the law dealing with marital disputes also presented a confusing, even chaotic picture, in which men paradoxically gained greater tangible benefits than women.

The doctrinal change from which women gained the clearest benefit occurred when the Court of Appeals in the 1976 case of *Echevarria v. Echevarria* held that "even one beating" could constitute cruel and inhuman treatment;[35] earlier decisions, it will be recalled, had declared that a single beating by a husband, no matter how severe, would not alone constitute cruelty.

Another change that unequivocally helped women occurred with the rejection of the old rule that a wife had to follow her husband and reside with him at the location of his choice. While one case decided in the 1970s reaffirmed the traditional view that it was "still a wife's burden to move with her husband to a location selected by him in good faith," at least when the move was related to the husband's employment, another case declared that a wife's right to remain "in a well-paying, full-time job she ha[d] held for a considerable length of time" could "not be defeated by the husband's arbitrary decision to change his domicile without some showing of necessity on his part."[36]

But every other legal change designed to end women's exploitation and render them men's equals conferred tangible benefits on men. Consider, for example, the relative rights of mothers and fathers of illegitimate children, especially in regard to custody. After mid-century, as the "harsh view of the common law that a natural child was *nullius filius*" went into decline, so too did the rule "that only the mother [could], whatever the circumstances, have custody of a child born out of wedlock." There remained a "presumption of custody in favor of the natural mother," but by the end of the 1970s, even it had been abolished by new legislation providing that no parent should have any prima facie right to custody, and judges determined "the issue of custody . . . without any artificial gender based distinctions."[37]

Changes in the law regarding custody of legitimate children likewise benefited men more than women. As one judge explained at the close of the 1970s, "outdated principles of 'maternal superiority'" could not properly "influence . . . determination[s] in awarding custody" because statute law had made it "clear that there shall be no prima facie right to the custody of a child in either parent." By recourse to these new views of gender equality, fathers appear to have been more successful in obtaining custody in the later years of the 1970s than they had been in earlier years.[38]

The law also changed in favor of men on the issue of whether the consent of fathers was required before their illegitimate children could be adopted. Throughout much of the 1970s confusion reigned on this issue as the cases addressed it only tangentially.[39] But, ultimately, those who believed that unwed fathers should have the same right as unwed mothers to block the adoption of illegitimate children won, when the Supreme Court in *Caban v. Mohammed*,[40] a case arising out of New York, so ruled on gender-equality grounds.

In contrast to the confusion that existed in regard to the rights of unwed fathers, the law was clear as to the rights of divorced fathers. Before a legitimate child could be adopted, generally by a second spouse of the divorced parent who had received custody, the noncustodial parent, usually though not necessarily the father, had to be given notice of the proposed adoption, and, if the noncustodial parent objected, the adoption could not proceed unless that parent had abandoned the child. "The natural rights of the parent to his child," it was said, were "sacred and [were] jealously guarded by the law," with the result that the "powers of the state over a child [were] not superior to the natural rights of the parent." Hence "a finding of abandonment [could] be made against a parent only after he ha[d] been given the benefit of every controverted fact." [41]

The issue on which feminist reformers most needed favorable legal change was that of support. Pressure for change had arisen early, as a result of the increasing caseload that matrimonial litigation imposed on the judiciary during the 1950s. Dealing with caseloads of seventy-five or more matrimonial matters per month in a single borough of New York City, most of which had to be "determined largely on the basis of widely conflicting affidavits manifesting a reckless inaccuracy . . . [and] perjurious absurdities," judges felt a need to "evolve modernized methods . . . introducing wholesome realism" into separation and divorce litigation. Seeking to eliminate the "stream of vituperation and recrimination" routine in matrimonial cases, some judges urged that the "element of fault should be de-emphasized" in determining whether a wife should receive an award based on her station in life or only an award designed to prevent her from becoming a public charge. And in one important case, the First Department of the Appellate Division did impose a $3,500 annual alimony payment on "a man of considerable wealth," even though his wife had abandoned him.[42]

The pressure for change was also consistent with "women's new position in our society," which rendered them "the equal of man, socially, politically and economically." It took some time, however, before women " 'advanced to a position of independence in most respects fully equal to' " that of men and to a "position of [full] equality in marriage." [43]

Not until the mid-1970s did the New York courts, in response to holdings of the federal Supreme Court,[44] declare that "sexual generalization in the law of support is the quintessence of unconstitutionality" and that "the constitutional guarantee of equal protection of the law . . . requires a uniform standard of . . . liability regardless of sex." This new approach was of some value to one "intelligent professional" woman who in the early 1970s "chose to have . . . [a] baby" out of wedlock and "live . . . by herself with the child"; in an opinion markedly different in tone from what would have been written even a few years earlier, the court treated her choice with respect and gave her a substantial support award against the child's father. The approach also assisted a young wife who had dropped out of college to finance her husband's undergraduate and law school educations, only to face a divorce when he began practice as an associate "at a prominent Wall Street law firm"; holding that the wife was "entitled to equal treatment," the court ordered her husband to pay alimony in an amount sufficient to enable her to complete college and attend medical school.[45]

But on the whole, equality was of greater financial benefit to men than to women, as courts ruled that, since women were " 'in most respects fully equal' to . . . men, they must, wherever possible, share the economic burden of a dissolved marriage." Accordingly, courts ruled that New York legislation should be read to authorize the award of alimony and counsel fees to husbands as well as wives in appropriate cases and that women with the same income as their former husbands should be required to contribute equally to the support of their children. As one judge observed in explaining these results, "a benevolent grant to women of legal rights unreasonably denied to men may help the women immediately affected but the implicit condescension and maintenance of a protective stance in the end produces the attitude that women are not equal to men." For women to become truly equal, this judge argued, it was necessary "to raise the consciousness of women to an appreciation of their true rights and their potential as functioning individuals" by treating women exactly the same as men. "The edge of sex discrimination" would thus have "two sides," making it unlawful to "discriminate against women" and equally unlawful to "discriminate against men."[46]

In light of decisions such as these, the gender revolution brought little material benefit to wives undergoing divorce or separation during the 1970s. Wives and children received as little support from their husbands and fathers during that decade as they had during the 1920s. Data from published cases throughout the half century between 1920 and 1970 shows, for example, that husbands typically were required to provide approximately one-third of their income for the support of their divorced wives and their children; husbands kept the remaining two-thirds for themselves. For the decade of the 1970s, the portion of husbands' income granted to divorced wives may have declined slightly.[47] The legislature itself gave sanction to the one-third figure in a 1975 statute allowing those involuntarily divorced on the basis of a separation agreement or decree obtained before January 21, 1970, to recover from their former spouse the amount they would have taken by intestacy if the spouse had died immediately before the divorce. The statute, it should be noted, merely preserved the economic rights that any wife in New York, except one divorced on account of her own adultery, had always possessed. In the case of a wife with children, those rights were to one-third of the husband's estate.[48]

It would again be a mistake, however, to focus on the immediately tangible consequences of the movement for gender equality rather than its long-term symbolic goals. What requires emphasis is that, beginning in the late 1960s, New York law remained committed to the legalist reform cause of ending the exploitation of women and creating gender equality. Although judges often may have been uncertain about how best to end exploitation and achieve equality, their realization that gender equality was the only legitimate goal always was clear. Despite, or perhaps because of, the inability either of the courts or of advocates for women to produce concrete results in furtherance of their goal, it seems fair to assert both that developments in the law of gender equity remained tightly cabined within the paradigm of the legalist reformation and that, on the issue of gender equality, the reformation enjoyed less than complete success.

CHAPTER 14

EQUALITY FOR UNDERDOGS
Race, Religion, Sexuality, and Poverty

Women were not alone during the 1960s and 1970s in demanding recognition of legal rights to equality. As we shall see in this chapter, racial and religious minorities, gays, and the poor made similar demands and, like women, met with mixed success.

RACIAL EQUALITY

Until the 1960s, as we saw in Chapter 6, New York judges had not been in the forefront of the movement to grant racial minorities a legal right against discrimination. Although the judges had remained sympathetic to the goal of equality and usually enforced legislation designed to bring that goal about, they proved unwilling to grant a specific, enforceable right to equality.

New York judges began to change their approach and become more rights conscious only in the aftermath of *Brown v. Board of Education*.[1] Ultimately *Brown* would have a profound impact not only on race relations law but on issues far beyond race by introducing into New York's law the concept of a judicially enforceable right to which subordinated individuals could turn in their effort to obtain equality. Regrettably, though, as we shall see, the proclamation of the right did not always result in attainment of the goal.

Brown's progeny were the first cases in which New York judges proclaimed a right to racial equality as the appropriate means to attain the goal of equality. The initial case occurred four years after the Supreme Court's 1954 decision, when a New York judge made an explicit finding of the existence of racial discrimination and granted a remedy in response. This first case was an unusual one, in which parents were brought to court for neglect of their children because they had refused to send them to their assigned public junior high schools. The parents, in turn, justified their refusal on the ground that the schools in question, "all of whose pupils [were] either Negro or Puerto Rican," offered "educationally inferior opportunities as compared to the opportunities offered in schools . . . whose pupil population [was] largely white." The court agreed. It held that, as a result of patterns of teacher assignment, "inferior educational opportunities" existed in schools with a predominantly minority student body, thereby depriving students of "the constitutional guarantee of equal protection of the laws." It followed that "the Board of Education ha[d] no moral or legal right to ask that this Court shall punish parents, or deprive them of custody of their children, for refusal to accept an unconstitutional condition."[2]

For the next six years, however, no follow-up occurred in state courts. Three years later, a federal district court did find upon a detailed examination of the facts "that the Board of Education of New Rochelle, prior to 1949, [had] intentionally created . . . a racially segregated school, . . . and that the conduct of the Board of Education even since 1949 ha[d] been motivated by the purposeful desire of maintaining the . . . racially segregated school." Accordingly, the court directed the board to develop and present a plan for desegregation. During the rest of the 1960s and into the 1970s, analogous cases in federal court arrived at the same result.[3]

But it was not until the mid-1960s that the State Education Department and local boards of education began redrawing school zone boundaries and reassigning students to improve racial balance in schools. Once this occurred, the courts routinely upheld the administrative action, and when the legislature sought to limit the authority of nonelected administrators to order racial balance, the legislative effort was held unconstitutional. In a clear statement of the right to racial equality, the three-judge court that invalidated the New York legislation observed that the statute "recognize[d] and accede[d] to local racial hostility" in a way that would "make it more difficult for racial minorities to achieve goals that are in their interest. The statute thus operate[d] to disadvantage a minority, a racial minority," and thereby constituted a "political" decision for which there could "be no sufficient justification."[4]

It appears that, once they fully accepted equal protection in the mid-1960s as a judicially enforceable right, New York judges adhered to it faithfully and vigorously. For example, the equal protection principle came to govern the New York judiciary's response to affirmative action efforts to recruit minority students for the state's colleges and universities. Thus, in one case, a trial judge rejected an argument by city authorities that he should revoke the tax exemption of Syracuse University because it was teaching a series of "race relations courses" that were "not open . . . on an equal basis" but were available only to "a closed group" composed primarily of local residents of minority background, many of whom "were undoubtedly unqualified for admission to the university's undergraduate schools." The judge found these facts to be a "virtue, not

. . . [a] defect" and concluded that the city's arguments were "irrelevant" to the university's tax-exempt status because the challenged program "fill[ed] a need in the adult's life or career." [5]

In a more important case, *Alevy v. Downstate Medical Center,* decided two years before the Supreme Court confronted essentially the same issue in *University of California v. Bakke,* the Court of Appeals also upheld affirmative action as a remedy for past discrimination. In its unanimous opinion the court observed that the Fourteenth Amendment had "been interpreted as permitting, if in fact not requiring, the correction of historical invidious discriminations" and that it "would cut against the very grain of the amendment, were the equal protection clause used to strike down measures designed to achieve real equality for persons whom it was intended to aid." At the same time, however, the court expressed doubt about merely "granting preferential treatment to some racial groups," which in its judgment "encourage[d] polarization of the races, . . . perpetuate[d] thinking in racial terms and require[d] extremely difficult racial determinations." Federal judges in New York also struck down affirmative action programs extending beyond remediation, and the federal courts made it otherwise clear that "a private organization of blacks" could not use "a public facility to carry out its discriminatory practices" in connection with improving education for minority students.[6]

Whatever difficulties they may have had in determining the remedies that equal protection required, New York judges nonetheless remained overwhelmingly committed in racial discrimination cases to judicial protection of equal rights. Thus they were prepared to hear and potentially remedy constitutional claims of racial discrimination on the part of child adoption agencies and claims alleging discriminatory denials of membership in volunteer fire departments and in clubs operating on municipal property. There was also a case that invalidated an airline antihijacking system that relied on a profile of individual characteristics, including ethnicity. Far more numerous were suits granting enforcement of civil rights legislation, especially fair housing laws designed to provide relief against discriminatory housing and zoning policies and equal employment laws prohibiting racial discrimination.[7]

It seems fair to conclude that, on the subject of race relations, federal and state judges in New York not only faithfully enforced but after the mid-1960s even welcomed the Supreme Court's mandate in *Brown,* as well as various specific legislative initiatives designed to remedy discrimination. The judges were even prepared to extend their rights-centered, equal protection jurisprudence beyond the race relations area. They extended it to one case, for example, in which a white attorney "of Italian ancestry and a Catholic" sued Cravath,

Swaine & Moore for employment discrimination when it refused to make him a partner.[8]

The reconceptualization of equality as a judicially enforceable right led, however, to an important change in the meaning of equality. Whereas early egalitarians had pursued the goal of enabling the urban, immigrant underclass to adopt elite, WASP cultural norms and thereby become assimilated and integrated into the mainstream of society, newer rights egalitarians ceased to show respect for traditional norms and instead demanded that subordinated groups receive the right to develop their own culture and to live by their own lights on a level playing field with others. While *Brown* itself did not contemplate this shift to multiculturalism but merely sought to integrate African Americans into the mainstream in the same way that Catholics and Jews were being assimilated, the shift was implicit in *Brown*. The court in *Brown* demanded that African American equality be achieved with "all deliberate speed," not as a long-term goal over an extended period of time. Assimilation, however, can be achieved only over an extended period, at least if assimilation is understood, as it had been by Catholic and Jewish immigrants and their descendants at mid-century, as the abandonment of distinctive minority lifestyles and the assumption of the lifestyle of the majority.[9] No group can undergo such a transformation overnight or probably over a period of less than several decades. Thus if blacks were to gain equality quickly, they could do so only by gaining equal recognition for what they already were rather than by striving successfully over time to become something else.

EQUALITY FOR THE UNCONVENTIONAL

None of this was apparent, however, when the Supreme Court handed down the *Brown* opinions. Multiculturalism was a gradual development that did not bloom in full until the end of the 1960s. And factors in addition to teasing out the implications of *Brown* contributed to its emergence. The emergence of multiculturalism was also connected to the efflorescence of concepts of liberty that authorized individuals to make their own value choices and to protesters' angry rejection in the late 1960s of customary cultural norms.

The anger of the late 1960s, the consequent rejection of tradition, and the connection of these attitudes to contemporary political events could all be seen in the objects that were displayed in 1966 in Stephen Radich's Madison Avenue art gallery, which was at least partly visible from the street. The objects were obviously intended to shock. Among them was "a seven-foot 'cross with a bishop's mitre on the head-piece, the arms wrapped in ecclesiastical flags and an erect penis wrapped in an American flag protruding from the vertical standard,' " the purpose of which was "to express protest against the American involvement in Vietnam."[10]

After Radich had been convicted of casting contempt on the American flag and his conviction had been affirmed both by the Court of Appeals and by an equally divided Supreme Court,[11] his case came before a federal district court on habeas corpus. In overturning Radich's conviction, the district court ruled that Radich's display "did not rape the flag of its universal symbolism" but "simply transferred the symbol from traditional surroundings to the realm of protest and dissent." In language strikingly different from that used in the many previous cases which had sanctioned repression of dissent, the court declared that the First Amendment afforded citizens "the right . . . , even, to deprecate those symbols which others hold dear." It was the "birthright of Americans" that "the free dissemination of ideas, the thoughts of all free-thinking men, even the smallest dissenting voice, might be heard without fear of prosecution." This " 'freedom to differ,' " moreover, was " 'not limited to things that do not matter much' " but included " 'things that touch[ed] the heart of the existing order' " and "ideas" that were "defiant, contemptuous or unacceptable to most Americans."[12]

As the *Radich* case shows, the African American and antiwar protest movements totally transformed the character of political discourse within a few short years. As a result of cases arising out of radical 1960s protest, it became "firmly settled that under our Constitution the public expression of ideas may not be prohibited merely because the ideas themselves are offensive."[13] In addition to cases involving disrespect for the flag, other antiwar protest cases in which First Amendment rights were judicially protected involved a teacher's wearing of a black armband, a group of eighty-six students holding an antiwar meeting in an apartment, and individuals who gave antiwar speeches or distributed antiwar literature on streets, in parks, or in public transportation facilities. Likewise, the State Athletic Commission was ordered to give Muhammad Ali a boxing license even though he had been convicted of draft evasion, a local school district was directed to allow Pete Seeger to use a high school auditorium for a concert despite his "controversial" views, and the New York City commissioner of parks was denied power to condition a permit for a poetry reading upon advance disclosure of the contents of the poetry.[14] Other controversial cases in which First Amendment rights were protected involved an authorization to black activists to picket southern state pavilions at the New York World's Fair, an order allowing an antiabortion group to march in a Memorial Day parade, and directions to reinstate a corrections officer and a schoolteacher who had been dismissed from jobs for membership in the Ku Klux Klan and for criticizing the school administration respectively. Draft boards were also prohibited from punitively reclassifying registrants who participated in antiwar protests, and a civil rights action brought on behalf of a speaker and a member of the audience at a birth control lecture was sustained.[15]

As the precedents upholding freedom of speech accumulated in cases that gave offense to many members of the community, the scope of free speech rights also grew in cases involving ordinary political speech and even potential subversive activity. Commercial speech also gained constitutional protection. As a result, the nature of public dialogue changed. In four short years in the middle of the 1960s, the right to free speech changed from " 'freedom to speak, write, print or distribute information or opinion' " that would engage governing elites in discourse affecting policy to the right to be an individual whose behavior was "non-conforming, whose dress [was] bizarre, and whose conduct [was] unconventional." It became legitimate, for example, for protesters to use words such as " 'murder' " and " 'kill' " on placards outside an abortion clinic, even though the words were "provocative and controversial." In parallel fashion, equal protection changed from a concept that allowed underclasses who assumed elite values to move upward into the social and economic mainstream to a doctrine that prohibited "exclusive use" of public space by "any one group to the exclusion of others," even when an established group "resented the invasion by . . . [a] new group" that was "unwashed, unshod, unkempt, and uninhibited."[16]

These shifts in free speech doctrine were part of a more general judicial recognition of a decline in public manners, public decency, and public civility —a recognition that was reflected, for instance, in a decision by the Court of Appeals holding the crime of vagrancy unconstitutional. As the court observed, the "only persons arrested and prosecuted as common-law vagrants" were people "whose main offense usually consist[ed] in their leaving the environs of skid row and disturbing *by their presence* the sensibilities of residents of nicer parts of the community." Another Court of Appeals decision of similar effect was one refusing to enjoin a new policy in the 1970s of releasing most patients confined in state mental hospitals. Also under challenge during the early 1970s were grooming standards for public officials and prisoners—standards that were designed "to present a favorable image" or "to inspir[e] public confidence" and "a sense of pride and self-discipline." Traditional proprieties were finally challenged in cases brought by adoptees asking to have their adoption records unsealed and by transsexuals demanding new birth certificates that would reflect their new gender.[17]

With these changes in law, the vision of America changed from a melting pot, in which all people aspired to live with each other ultimately as one, to a vision of a divided, multifarious culture, in which groups with distinctive and even irreconcilable backgrounds and lifestyles competed for their share of public space and the public good. New York was transformed from a city of opportunity, where the lowliest man through hard work and abidance by the values of his community could rise to the top, to an international marketplace, where even foreigners could enter into its public life as participants in fields as diverse as taxicab driving, civil service, law, and employment on state government contracts. Cases also granted aliens and recent arrivals from other American states quick access to public housing, while resident aliens were given equal rights to receive public educational funding.[18] These decisions made New York far more readily accessible to widely diverse people from all corners of the globe who had little need to learn its ways before participating in broad aspects of its life.

Judicial approval of enhanced competition, the extension of equal benefits to all, and a more open style of public debate did not, however, mean that judges were ready to sanction subversion of the polity itself, to cease enforcing laws in which elites had any substantial stake or to encourage even minimal redistribution of wealth. In *People v. Epton*,[19] for instance, the judges of the Court of Appeals over only one dissent had no difficulty upholding the defendant's conviction for violating the same criminal anarchy statute under which Benjamin Gitlow had been convicted some four decades earlier.

Indeed, the two cases involved remarkably similar efforts to arouse underclasses to revolution through speech. Like Gitlow, Epton was "a self-acknowledged Marxist and president of the Harlem 'club' of the Progressive Labor Movement." In the spring of 1964, he had engaged in "formation of a small cadre of followers, who, presumably, would play leadership roles in the eventual revolution toward which their movement was directed." When an off-duty police lieutenant killed an African American youth in the summer of 1964 and there was a "spontaneous build-up of pressures within the Negro ghettoes of New York," Epton immediately "took to the streets of Harlem preaching his gospel of revolution," and the "Harlem headquarters of the Progressive Labor Movement became a beehive of activity with the defendant exhorting those in attendance to organize . . . to combat the police." Undercover plainclothes agents infiltrated the movement, however, and recorded much of what was spoken, including the following:

They [the cops] declared war on us and we should declare war on them and every time they kill one of us damn it, we'll kill one of them and we should start thinking that way right now. . . . If we're going to be free, and we will not be fully free until we smash this state completely and totally. Destroy and set up a new state of our own choosing and of our own liking. And in that process of making this state, we're going to have to kill a lot of these cops, *a lot of these judges.* . . . Think about it because no people in this world have ever achieved independence and freedom through the ballot or having it legislated to them. All people in this world who are free have got their freedom through struggle and through revolution.

On the basis of his speeches alone—without any evidence that there was "any direct, causal connection between Epton's activities and the Harlem riots of the Summer of 1964" or, indeed, that anyone other than police investigators was paying attention to what he was doing—Epton was convicted of the crime of advocating criminal anarchy.[20]

In an opinion joined even by as committed a legalist reformer and as strong a civil libertarian as Stanley Fuld, the Court of Appeals concluded that the criminal anarchy statute upheld by the Supreme Court in Gitlow's case over the now honored dissents of Judges Cardozo and Pound and Justices Holmes and Brandeis was still constitutional. It recognized that "mere advocacy of the violent overthrow of the Government" would no longer be constitutional, but it reinterpreted the statute to require two additional elements for a criminal conviction: "an intent to accomplish the overthrow" and "a 'clear and present danger' that the advocated overthrow [might] be attempted."[21] Despite the absence of any evidence that anyone had acted in response to Epton's speeches or had even paid attention to them, the court found both elements present.

In the end, *Epton* needs to be seen as an unprincipled opinion. The *Epton* case shows that the clear and present danger standard does not focus, as it purports, on the existence of a connection between advocacy and conduct; proof or lack of proof about the events that transpired or might have been about to transpire at the scene of a speech is irrelevant. What matters is whether judges feel threatened. When, as in *Gitlow, Dennis, Feiner,* and *Epton,* they do, they will authorize the use of raw force to preserve the existing power structure and repress those who are threatening it.

The new tolerance in the late 1960s of unconventional, nonconforming, and even shocking speech thus did not reflect any willingness on the part of judges to authorize political action that threatened destabilization of the legal, economic, or social order. The new tolerance accordingly represented much less change than had at first appeared to be the case. It represented change from a world in which elites could expect their underlings to emulate them to a world in which they could expect insult and offense. The new world was much less pleasant and comfortable than the old, but it was also much more secure. Unlike emulation, insult and offense would not produce upward mobility. Insult and offense could be tolerated precisely because of their irrelevance and because, the moment an official felt threatened by advocacy of forcible social change, the full coercive power of government would be brought to bear upon the advocate.[22]

RELIGION

A parallel decline of reverence for traditional symbols and the substitution, in their stead, of a raucous, competitive marketplace also occurred in several religious liberty cases in the late 1960s and early 1970s. For example, the Sunday blue laws requiring the closing of commercial establishments fell under immense pressure as the courts first carved a variety of exceptions into them, then interposed procedural obstacles in the path of their enforcement, and finally declared them unconstitutional. Another line of cases sanctioned the unconventional by upholding the right of members of the Reverend Moon's Unification Church and of the Society for Krishna Consciousness to proselytize and perform religious ceremonies in public places and even door-to-door in residential neighborhoods. Finally, the allowance of religious garb in courtrooms, if it did not devalue religious symbolism, at the very least reflected judges' understanding that the symbols had lost much of their sacerdotal force.[23]

Of course, the line between the merely unconventional and shocking, on the one hand, and the threatening and dangerous, on the other, was not always clear. Thus when African American prison inmates sought to hold Muslim services in prison under the direction of the soon-to-be famous Malcolm X, who had " 'a previous criminal record,' " the corrections commissioner denied the request as contrary to the " 'interests of safety and security of the institution ... [and to a] longstanding policy ... [of not] allowing ... inmates to communicate with or to be ministered to by a person with a criminal background.' " In the face of this denial, the Court of Appeals in *Brown v. McGinnis* fractured. Three judges were prepared to sustain the commissioner's action, while three were prepared to honor the prisoners' religious rights, bizarre as they may then have seemed. The chief judge cast the deciding vote, observing in a two-sentence concurrence that the state "must extend to petitioner and his co-religionists all the rights guaranteed" by the Correction Law and the Constitution, "subject to necessary security and disciplinary measures." The Black Muslims, whom many whites in the 1960s feared as crossing the line from the unconventional to the threatening, would still be litigating their right to religious freedom for several years to come.[24] And they would receive that right only when it became clear that, however much they might upset some whites, the Muslims posed no threat to the polity's stability or to elite interests dependent thereon. They merely wanted to live by themselves, separate from the mainstream, on the basis of their own values.

Brown v. McGinnis brings us full circle back to the demands of Malcolm X for "freedom, justice, and equality."[25] The case shows both how radical demands had undermined the legalist reformation and how legalism nonetheless remained essentially the same. It shows how new groups were making new demands that failed to respect customary norms, that proved discomforting to established elites, and that thereby fractured the fragile consensus that had facilitated assimilationist equality. As a result, a centerpiece of the legalist reform agenda was undercut. Nonetheless, the legalist reformation endured. The Black Muslims, like Catholics and Jews before them, demanded "freedom, justice, and equality," and they argued for their demands in legalist reform language before judges who could respond only within a legalist reform conceptual framework. Radicals, in short, were still demanding what progressives had been demanding throughout the century, and judges were still striving as they had since the 1920s to accommodate those demands consistently with the preservation of order, as they could best understand it.

GAY RIGHTS

Homosexuals were another radical group making novel demands in the 1970s that appeared to threaten established mores. But in this connection too, as we shall see, the demands were cast in the language of the legalist reformation, and the courts responded in typical fashion. There remained judges, for example, who supported claims for the decriminalization of private, consensual sodomy, and in the late 1970s they began to write opinions proclaiming the existence of a constitutional right of privacy or an equal protection right to engage privately in oral and anal sex. Other judges, in contrast, continued to find homosexuality criminal, even if they believed that unmarried heterosexuals had a constitutional right to engage in anal and oral sex. In the face of this division of lower court opinion, the Court of Appeals in 1977 initially refused to pass on the issue of the legislature's power to prohibit private, consensual homosexual activity.[26]

But then three years later, in *People v. Onofre,* the court did decide the question, holding unconstitutional the state's legislation criminalizing private, consensual homosexual relations. The majority opinion by Hugh R. Jones, an upstate Republican elected to the court in 1972, held that the legislation violated the right to privacy, which was itself derived from several textual sources, including the federal due process clause.[27]

Jones began by observing that the right of privacy "is not, as a literal reading of the phrase might suggest, the right to maintain secrecy with respect to one's affairs or personal behavior; rather it is a right of independence in making certain kinds of important decisions." Given that courts had extended the right of privacy to cover "individual decisions as to indulgence in acts of sexual intimacy by unmarried persons" and the "satisfaction of sexual desires by resort to material condemned as obscene . . . when done in a cloistered setting," Jones could see no reason for not extending the right further to people seeking "sexual gratification from what at least once was commonly regarded as 'deviant' conduct."[28]

Nor did three justifications put forward by the state in support of its legislation carry any credence with Jones. He rejected out of hand the first claim that sodomy led to physical injury, finding no supporting evidence. Since courts sustaining privacy rights in other contexts had given no weight to the "moral indignation among broad segments of our community" arising from the private viewing of pornography or the use of contraceptives by unmarried people, Jones rejected the second justification that "disapproval [of sodomy] by a majority of the populace" could constitute "a valid basis for intrusion by the State in an area of important personal decision." Finally, he rejected the argument that prohibiting sodomy would protect "the institution of marriage, venerable and worthy as is that estate." As he observed, there was "no suggestion that the one is a substitute or alternative for the other nor is any empirical data submitted which demonstrates that marriage is nothing more than a refuge for persons deprived by legislative fiat of the option of consensual sodomy outside the marital bond."[29]

With its decision in *Onofre,* the Court of Appeals carried to ultimate fruition, but only for gay men and gay women, the legalist reform program of sexual freedom that had developed after 1940. In the cases involving homosexuals, the Court of Appeals was prepared, when only consenting adults were involved and sex acts between them took place in private, initially in cases like

Doyle to manipulate procedural rules and construe statutes, and ultimately in cases like *Onofre* to create a constitutional right under the rubric of privacy so as to give people freedom to engage with each other in private in whatever sexual behavior they enjoyed.

The recognition of a constitutional right to engage privately in homosexual acts did not, however, put an end to all legal efforts to outlaw homosexual behavior. Courts continued throughout the 1960s and 1970s to face cases involving oral and anal sex acts in public rest rooms and solicitations for such sex made to police officers, to other men, and to children as young as eight, and in these cases conservative concerns for the "rights" of "the 'public'" continued to surface. In particular, the courts worried that "infants of tender years" might witness sex acts. Worst of all in the eyes of conservatives, the courts continued to confront instances in which men had sex with boys "of vulnerable early adolescence, 13 and 14 years of age."[30]

In situations such as these, which involved something more than private behavior between consenting adults, the courts even toughened the enforcement of anti-gay laws. Judges began, for example, to perceive teens involved in homosexual acts as "child victims" rather than the "half-witted youth[s]" they had once appeared to be, and in an effort to protect such victims, the Court of Appeals *sub silentio* even overruled *People v. Doyle*. Accordingly, the court held that a boy under the age of consent was incapable of consenting to a sodomitical act, was thereby incapable of being an accomplice in such an act, and could accordingly provide all the testimony that was needed, without corroboration, to convict an adult defendant of the act.[31] And finally, as the courts began to perceive children participating in homosexual acts as victims, they began to see the men of "economic status" and "good positions" who appeared before them charged as defendants not as upstanding citizens of education and culture but as exhibitionists hoping to be "observed by an innocent member of the public."[32]

In short, the pattern of judicial behavior during the 1970s in cases regulating homosexuality was analogous to the pattern set by judges on subjects as diverse as race relations, religion, and unconventional protest activities. Judges, that is, gave recognition to expansive constitutional rights and allowed recipients of the rights to deploy them to advance their interests and increase their freedom. But the recipients remained culturally subordinated and, unlike the mid-century descendants of earlier Catholic and Jewish immigrants, never found their lifestyles fully accepted by those at the top of New York's power structure. Neither did they fully escape from a role as scapegoats for those positioned at the top.

Welfare recipients were a final group that obtained legal but not full symbolic legitimacy, as legislators and judges in the 1970s rejected, in considerable part, the classical, conservative, welfare paradigm of the 1920s. Under the conservative paradigm, society had regarded itself as stratified into social classes, with an upper class of morally respectable individuals who had earned the wealth they possessed and a lower class composed of people " 'without property, without habits of industry or thrift, improvident, usually physically or mentally deficient, who [were] unable through efforts of their own to gain a livelihood.' " [33] The poor had to look to receive support mainly from relatives, who as citizens had the obligation to save public funds from welfare liabilities. Public relief was available only as a last resort and then only as matter of grace and not right. Moreover, a recipient of public relief had to accept it humbly and thankfully on the terms on which it was offered; no matter how inconvenient or restrictive of a recipient's freedom, the recipient ought not complain.

Under a newer paradigm that legalist reformers put into place in the late 1960s and 1970s, in contrast, welfare became a right. Judges recognized the obligation of government to support the poor and put in place procedural protections to ensure that eligibility for welfare was determined fairly. In response to demands of radical welfare rights advocates, [34] judges also recognized the dignity of welfare recipients by permitting them to control their own affairs; they also strove to make the process of applying for welfare less demeaning and cumbersome.

With the enactment of the Great Society programs in the mid-1960s, a wide variety of welfare programs came into existence. Among them were rent subsidies, educational assistance, school lunches, clothing and personal needs, day care services, restaurant allowances, emergency rental and utility assistance, special payments to female public assistance recipients in their fourth or subsequent month of pregnancy, and duplication of lost or stolen welfare payments. Welfare was also extended when the Court of Appeals made it available to labor union members who were out of work because of a strike. [35]

At the same time that Congress through these various programs recognized the responsibility of government to support the poor, the courts, responding to the demands of welfare recipients, also declared that the recipients had "a substantial privilege, if not a right, to such benefit[s] based solely upon . . . establishing financial need." By recognizing welfare as a right, judges, of course, subjected welfare denials to constitutional standards such as that of equal protection. Although most equal protection challenges to welfare practices were rejected, occasional challenges were upheld on gender and, at the trial level, on age discrimination grounds. The most important equality cases were those that eliminated residence requirements for people seeking welfare who had migrated to New York from other states and even from foreign countries.[36]

A more substantial body of case law developed around due process concerns that welfare cases be adjudicated in a procedurally fair manner. The seminal case was *Goldberg v. Kelly,*[37] which held that due process required an evidentiary hearing before a recipient's right to continued receipt of welfare could be reduced or terminated. According to *Goldberg,* due process also demanded that the recipient receive adequate notice of a right to a hearing detailing the reasons for termination, the right to retain counsel, and the opportunity to present evidence and confront adverse witnesses. Moreover, decision makers, who had to be impartial, had to identify substantial evidence on which they had relied and the reasons for their determination.

In addition to elaborating procedural rules to safeguard welfare recipients' rights, judges took steps "to uphold the dignity of individual recipients by permitting them to control their own affairs." In one case, for example, a court declared that a mother could not be denied welfare benefits for an illegitimate child because of a "refusal to testify about one's intimate sex life" when such testimony might "tend to degrade her" for, perhaps, "having sex with a married man, being raped, being involved in a sordid sexual act, or even in the revelation of intimate details about the act itself that allegedly led to conception." In a second case, a court held that a welfare recipient had not forfeited public assistance by refusal to accept employment in a neighboring community when he had lacked the bus fare to reach that community, while in a third case a court declared that "lack of management skills [did] not disqualify" a person in need from receiving welfare funds.[38] Meanwhile, judges outlawed warrantless home visits executed by force or under false pretenses and sought otherwise to make the process of applying for welfare less demeaning and cumbersome. In two unusual cases, federal judges held that parents whose sincere religious beliefs precluded their obtaining social security numbers for their children should be exempted from the standard requirement that such numbers be furnished in every welfare application and that an exhibitionist, whose misconduct prevented him from holding a job, could receive welfare. Finally, the courts strove to enhance the dignity of welfare by upholding a "legislative policy which reflect[ed] a humane concern for developing meaningful work experience for relief recipients."[39]

In granting radical groups, including racial and religious minorities, gays, the unconventional, and the poor, a legal right to reject traditional cultural norms and to live by their own lights, judges were extending the values of the legalist reformation and also were empowering the various groups. But it is vital to focus on the nature of this empowerment. The egalitarian constitutional decisions of the late 1960s and 1970s encouraged radicals to withdraw from society rather than to reform society, and, as a result, the established social order may have been more solidly entrenched at the end of the 1970s than ever before. Three factors suggest this possibility.

The first was the nation's experience with rioting by black and student protesters in the decade of the 1960s. The police and the military had won every battle, often at severe cost, even death, to the rioters. Moreover, violence and rioting had never spread to sites in most of America; police and soldiers had always been able to contain it largely on the university campuses, in the ghettos, and in the occasional downtown localities where it had begun. Insofar as pure coercive force measures a social order's entrenchment, the 1960s had demonstrated that government and its instrumentalities held the overwhelming balance of power.

The second factor was the reaction of the majority of the American electorate to rioting, to other forms of violence by members of underclasses, and to the rejection of traditional cultural norms. The "forgotten Americans," as Richard Nixon called them, voted for repression. As Americans watched on television the "unrestrained and indiscriminate police violence" occurring in connection with the 1968 Democratic Convention in Chicago—violence that "was often inflicted upon persons who had broken no law, disobeyed no order, made no threat," including "peaceful demonstrators, onlookers, . . . large numbers of residents," and upon "newsmen and photographers [who] were singled out for assault"—they did not sympathize with the victims; on the contrary, they voted for the candidates of "law and order," Richard Nixon and George Wallace.[40] When demonstrators provoked police violence, they were, in short, beaten down both physically and politically.

The third factor is somewhat more subtle. It addresses issues about the moral and rhetorical strategies available to minorities seeking to persuade majorities to behave beneficently toward them. The legalist reform approach of assimilationist equality, used, for example, by Thurgood Marshall in his argument in *Brown v. Board of Education,* points out moral values shared by minorities and the majority as members of a common culture and asks the majority to abide by its values. Thus as Marshall observed in his oral argument, segregation could be upheld only by finding "that for some reason Negroes are inferior to all other human beings," and the time had come for the Supreme

Court in *Brown* to "make it clear that that is not what our Constitution stands for."[41]

In the late 1960s, in contrast, minorities began to deny their participation in a common culture with the majority and instead emphasized their cultural differences. But this approach, as minorities quickly learned, merely reified the majority's power because, when conflict occurred between the majority and a minority and one or the other had to exert power in order to resolve the conflict, no shared moral value existed to restrain the stronger party from using its power as it wished. Multiculturalism removed the mask from power and thereby strengthened the hands of those who possessed it.

Perhaps the point emerges most clearly from examination of the early 1960s agenda of attaining equality through "good-will and an appeal to conscience" and otherwise "wrench[ing] from white guilt or supposed white cowardice by violence what it could not get by law."[42] In the early 1960s, when protesters initially turned to strategies of confrontation, the white power structure feared violence and felt guilt about its causes. But as protesters rejected traditional mainstream values and police repeatedly suppressed protests, the majority's guilt and fear disappeared. By the late 1960s, confrontational protest was a familiar happening, which people who supported the established power structure could not understand but which, they were equally certain, could be suppressed by calling out the police and, if necessary, the military to do their usual job, the outcome of which was never in doubt. By the end of the 1960s, earlier uncertainties about whether repressive tactics should be used and whether those tactics would succeed had disappeared. The power of coercive government thereby was strengthened.

Faced with this strengthening of coercive governmental power, even radical minorities had little choice but to turn back to the legalist reform concepts that judges had incorporated into the law between the end of the 1930s and the 1960s. Thus women demanded an end to exploitation; blacks demanded equality; gays demanded liberty; and the poor demanded dignity. All groups sought economic opportunity. Dissatisfied as these minorities may have been with the failure of the legalist reform state to deliver fully on its promises, they still had no other concepts or language, as the twentieth century drew to a close, in which to cast their demands for social justice.

Thus it seems clear that the legalist reformation, although less than fully successful, remained firmly embedded in the nation's constitutional and political culture in several respects even in the aftermath of the late 1960s. First, it appears that litigants continued to rely on legalist reform concepts such as liberty, equality, opportunity, and dignity in presenting cases to judges. Second, we can conclude that this reliance was well placed, in that judges often gave weight to those legalist concepts in their decision of cases and routinely recognized that individuals possessed rights derived from the concepts. Third, this judicial recognition of rights led to some change in social reality. None-theless, a final observation must be that, during the 1970s, racial and religious minorities, gays, the unconventional, and the poor did not gain entry into the upper echelons of New York's power structure to the same extent that the descendants of Catholic and Jewish immigrants had done in the decades before.

CHAPTER 15

BUREAUCRACY

In addition to its persisting effect on doctrines of constitutional law, the legalist reformation also continued to influence the structure of government after its 1968 repudiation by the electorate. In particular, it continued to promote bureaucratization, albeit to the consternation of many.

Connections between legalist reform and bureaucracy went back to the 1920s, when early legislative efforts to prevent exploitation of underdogs had led to the creation of regulatory agencies to police various segments of the market. The 1930s and 1940s saw the proliferation and expansion of such agencies, along with the initial creation of welfare agencies, such as the Social Security Administration, to distribute government largess. Still a third affinity between legalist reform and bureaucracy, which is the subject of this chapter, emerged in the late 1960s and 1970s. In these decades, bureaucracies became important devices, mainly in nongovernmental institutions but also in the judiciary, for regulating interactions among the diverse peoples who had come to work or reside in New York and had even entered into the upper echelons of its economy and society.

BUREAUCRACY AND BUSINESS LITIGATION

Nowhere do the complex connections between bureaucratization and the legalist reformation emerge more clearly than in the development during the 1970s of new mechanisms for dealing with business and other commercial disputes. On the surface, the story is one of a substantial increase during the 1970s in breach of contract and other sorts of business litigation, especially in federal court in the Southern District of New York, which includes Manhattan and some adjoining counties. During the 1960s, contract cases had constituted a mere 8.6 percent of the total filings, or approximately 400 cases per year. Then, in the 1970s, the quantity of breach of contract litigation began to rise. In 1970, contract filings increased to 10.4 percent of the total, in 1971, to almost 15 percent, and in 1972, to 15.2 percent. During the period from 1973 to 1979, contract cases constituted an estimated 20.5 percent of total filings, or an average of 1,273 cases per year.[1]

Breach of contract cases were not only more numerous but also bigger and more complex. One measure of size is the amount of money either claimed or recovered in a suit: in the cases for which information exists in the 1960–70 period, the average amount was $165,000, whereas the 1971–79 average was $887,000. This is a large increase. Another gauge of size and complexity is the presence of major New York City law firms in cases. During the 1960–70 period, the major firms appeared in 17.5 percent of all contract cases or about 73 cases per year, on the average. From 1971 to 1979, in contrast, the large firms were present in almost 24.8 percent of all contract cases, an increase of some seven percentage points. Put another way, with contract cases increasing from 416 per year between 1960 and 1970 to 1,175 per year from 1971 to 1979, large firms' involvement went from an estimated 73 cases per year to over 290, a substantial increase.[2]

This rise in business litigation was a consequence of two societal changes that grew out of a half-century of legalist reform. The first change, which occurred in response to the growth of the regulatory state and to growth in the size of business enterprise, was an initial bureaucratization of business management—a bureaucratization that began to destroy traditional, informal mechanisms of dispute resolution and to encourage managers seeking advancement within business bureaucracies to adopt strategies that promoted litigation. The second fundamental change was the entry of upstarts into positions of management that had been occupied as late as the 1950s by members of the establishment—upstarts who turned to the law to protect their interests when old-line establishments failed to do so. These two changes, in turn, propagated further bureaucratization, which completed the destruction of old, informal mechanisms and imposed large numbers of business disputes on the legal system.[3]

The Bureaucratization of Management. The bureaucratization of business enterprise arguably began as a result of the growth of the regulatory state starting in the late 1930s. The rise in regulation led to greater policing of management decisions, initially by regulatory agencies and later by those agencies as well as by shareholders' derivative actions. As a result of the development of such outside policing mechanisms, business managers were no longer completely free to decide for themselves whether to settle a contract dispute or to turn it over to litigation. Outsiders could question their judgment, and although such questioning was unlikely to lead to the reversal of management decisions, its prospect tended to induce managers to create bureaucratic mechanisms for turning disputes over to lawyers, if not for full-scale litigation, at least to create a record that would bar second-guessing of whatever settlement was reached.

One means of policing management decisions was the shareholders' derivative suit, which by the late 1960s and 1970s lay whenever the directors or managers of a corporation breached their fiduciary duty to safeguard the corporation's rights and assets. If either management or the board had improperly failed to enforce contract rights, the possibility of a derivative suit existed. Pro-plaintiff decisions by some prominent courts such as the Second Circuit Court of Appeals, together with several other "highly publicized suits (or threats of suits) against directors," some charging "nothing worse than negligence, bad judgment, or even misplaced altruism on the part of the defendant directors," in fact gave rise in the late 1960s to "a vast pother . . . in corporate circles over the dreadful plight of officers and directors."[4] Business leaders, as a result, often felt constrained to consult counsel, and the lawyers sometimes commenced litigation, not because they ever expected to go to trial but because they wanted to take advantage of discovery procedures to obtain information or because they wanted the ultimate settlement to take place under the prodding of a judge, to whom the client could then shift the responsibility of settlement.

Similarly, the possibility that a regulatory agency might question a contractual arrangement between a regulated business and an independent firm sometimes involved the two enterprises in a dispute and ultimately in litigation for breach of contract. Alternatively, one of the firms might sue the agency, as occurred in one effort to enjoin the Federal Trade Commission from reaching a decision that a plaintiff feared would involve it in breach of contract suits at the hands of its distributors.[5]

The basic principle, as codified in the Restatement of Contracts, is that, "if supervening governmental action prohibits a [contractual] performance or imposes requirements that make it impracticable, the duty to render that performance is discharged," and the promisor can be neither enjoined to perform nor sued for damages for breach.[6] Although this principle is clear on its face, ambiguity can often arise in its application, and then litigation becomes likely. A problem arises whenever a general regulatory decree fails to specify whether the regulated enterprise may perform a particular contractual duty. The managers of the regulated enterprise and of the business with which they had contracted are not free, as they would be in the absence of regulation, to resolve the ambiguity by themselves through negotiation because, if they decide wrongly, the regulated business will be subject to administrative sanctions. Only the agency, or a court in a breach of contract suit, can decide whether a given regulation discharges a contractual duty.[7]

The existence of regulation and the consequent impetus toward litigation was not, of course, new in the 1970s; the regulatory state had existed for a long time. But the late 1960s and early 1970s witnessed a "trend toward greater governmental regulation,"[8] fueled largely by the organization of new public interest and consumer protection groups on both the national and state levels,[9] and the trend toward greater regulation led, in turn, to increased breach of contract litigation. The 1970s energy crisis also increased regulatory interference in contractual relations and thus led to more breach of contract suits.[10]

The growth of the regulatory state was not, however, the sole or arguably even the main factor contributing to the bureaucratization of dispute settlement processes on the part of business enterprises. Another, and probably more important, factor was the enormous expansion of American business that occurred between the 1950s and the 1970s.

Even after inflation is taken into account, the gross national product doubled between 1950 and 1970. At the same time, business concentration increased significantly. More mergers occurred in 1967 than in any previous year in American history; the total was 1,496. In 1968, there were 2,407 mergers; in 1969, 2,307; and in 1970, 1,351 — which, although a decline from the previous three years, was a larger number than in any year up to 1967. In combination, the growth of business enterprise and of business concentration produced a nearly fourfold increase in the number of firms with assets over $100 million: from 688 firms in 1950 to 2,635 firms in 1970.[11]

With the increase in firm size came an increase in the amount of money involved in contracts. As we have already seen, the amount at stake in contract cases in the Southern District increased more than fivefold between the 1960s and the 1970s. In contrast, the income of lawyers increased between three and four times in the years between the beginning of the 1960s and the end of the 1970s.[12] The fact that the amount at stake in contract cases increased almost twice as rapidly as attorneys' fees, together with some important changes in interest rates, altered the profitability of litigation.

Consider, for example, the case of a litigant who delayed settlement of a $1 million case in a year such as 1968, when the prime rate was 6 percent and the statutory prejudgment interest rate was 7.5 percent. Assume also that the litigant had to pay legal fees of $20,000 to prevent the entry of a default judgment and thus to obtain the delay. On these facts, the cost of delay to the litigant would have totaled $35,000 — $20,000 to the lawyers plus $15,000 in added interest fees resulting from paying the one year's interest at the legal prejudgment rate rather than at the market rate that could have been obtained if the $1 million had been borrowed to settle the case. In contrast, a litigant in the 1970s, when amounts in controversy averaged six times what they had been in the 1960s, with a $6 million suit in a year such as 1973, when the prime rate had risen to 10 percent and the prejudgment rate had been lowered to 6 percent,[13] would have netted a $240,000 profit on interest by paying at the prejudgment rather than the market rate. While it might have paid $80,000 for the same legal services that the 1960s litigant received for $20,000, it would still have netted $160,000 per year by bringing its case to court instead of settling it.

There is little doubt that at least some matters were brought into litigation in the 1970s to avoid paying out as damages sums of money that could be profitably invested elsewhere. Even when the savings from litigation were not so great, however, their existence reduced litigation costs and therefore made litigation a more appropriate alternative for a business if other factors favored a lawsuit over a settlement.

One such factor was a transformation in the structure of business management occurring mainly during the 1960s. Before that decade, most American firms were broken down into functional departments, such as obtaining raw materials, manufacturing, sales, finance, and the like, and coordination between departments was achieved through an executive committee, whose members had personal knowledge of the workings of each of the departments. But as firms became larger by the end of the decade, a new divisional structure became popular. Under such a structure, each division is a self-contained, quasi-autonomous unit that manages procurement, production, and sales for itself and requires little day-to-day coordination with other divisions. Only long-term planning and strategic coordination, such as the distribution of investment capital, the promotion of managers, and other major decisions such as whether to bring litigation, need to be provided by a central management committee. The important point is that such management committees typically consist entirely of people with no direct responsibilities in individual divisions and hence little personal knowledge of those divisions. The committees learn the facts on which to base decisions about whether, for example, to litigate rather than settle a dispute largely by examining bureaucratically maintained records and bureaucratically required reports,[14] and thus, if information reporting practices contain biases in favor of litigation, litigation will be more likely than if the recordkeeping methods contain contrary biases.

Biases that encourage the litigation rather than the settlement of contract disputes did, indeed, come during the 1960s and 1970s to underlie recordkeeping and accounting practices, especially the latter. This is clearly true for practices of public accounting, which are governed by Standard Number Five of the Financial Accounting Standards Board. Standard Five provides for accrual of a negative charge in a balance sheet to account for a future adverse judgment or settlement in pending or threatened litigation only if two conditions are met: first, it is "probable" that the ultimate judgment or other outcome of the litigation will be adverse, and second, the amount of the adverse judgment or settlement can be reasonably estimated. Rarely are both conditions met. Since lawyers are almost always unwilling either to give an opinion that an adverse judgment against their client is "probable" or to estimate the amount of such a judgment,[15] accountants rarely will have the information about the probability and the amount of a potential loss needed to enter the loss on a balance sheet.

Standard Five does require that, even when "no accrual is made for a loss contingency, . . . disclosure of the contingency shall be made when there is at least a reasonable possibility" of one. But even this minimal disclosure in a note appended to a financial statement will not always occur, and, even if it does, the accountant probably will state that "an estimate [of the amount of the loss] cannot be made" since lawyers will normally refuse to make such estimates.[16]

In sum, it appears that pending litigation need almost never appear as an accrued loss on a balance sheet intended for public disclosure. At most, its existence must be disclosed as a note appended to the financial report without any estimate as to amount of any likely judgment, and attorneys will often have plausible reasons for not permitting even this small degree of disclosure. Disputes that raise a prospect of litigation but have not yet matured into lawsuits will almost never be disclosed even as notes.

This treatment of pending or potential litigation contrasts with the quite different treatment that any amount paid in settlement of a dispute will receive: that amount will appear as an accrued loss on the balance sheet and will therefore result in a decreased profit or an increased overall loss for the enterprise or division involved. To the extent that executive committees make decisions about promotion and compensation of managers or about allocation of resources within a firm on the basis of the balances contained in their publicly disclosed financial statements, managers thus have every incentive not to settle disputes but instead to remit them to litigation—a strategy that will buy delay in reporting information adverse to their career interests, often for several years. Although it is not clear to what extent enterprises during the 1970s abided by FAS Standard No. 5 for purposes of internal management, calculated guesswork suggests that many internal auditors accounted for contract breaches in a fashion that helped promote litigation.[17]

Nor were the accounting practices we have been examining alone in encouraging managers to take business disputes to litigation. Lawyers also promoted litigation by providing managers who wanted them with opinion letters or other advice that nonperformance of a contract followed by litigation was a legally appropriate course. Reported cases suggest how the advice of lawyers worked to foment additional lawsuits.[18]

One revealing case arose out of a reorganization into a corporation of a limited partnership in failing financial condition. A condition precedent for the reorganization was the transfer of the partnership's assets to the corporation—a transfer to which the limited partners would not consent. Accordingly, advice of counsel was sought as to whether the general partners alone could authorize the transfer. Two lawyers, including a partner in the firm of Rosenman, Colin, Kaye, Petschek, Freund & Emil, which represented the partnership, advised that the limited partners must approve the transfer, which was the position ultimately adopted by the court. But, with the deal about to collapse, Robert S. Persky, of Finley, Kumble, Underberg, Persky & Roth, provided the required opinion, which the court subsequently found to be contrary to the plain language of the New York Partnership Law, that the assets could be transferred without the limited partner's consent. The deal was then consummated.[19]

Facts more directly parallel to the situation in which lawyers find themselves when they advise corporations and their managers about nonperformance of contracts were reported in a case in which a defendant attorney advised Howard Hughes that his corporations should not perform a contract to purchase Los Angeles Airways. The plaintiff airline alleged that the goal of the advice was to undermine the position in the Hughes empire of one Robert Maheu and to enhance the position of defendant and presumably his friends, although the advice was also clearly intended to benefit the Hughes entities. Recognizing the attorney's privilege to respond to a client's request for advice whether to perform a contract, the court expressed its belief that "advice by an agent to a principal is rarely, if ever, motivated purely by a desire to benefit only the principal" and held that advice is privileged as long as benefit to the corporation is part of the motivation. And although it did not reach the question, the court in dictum approved the giving of advice designed "to advance one's own career with an employer (even at the expense of a fellow employee's)."[20]

Taken together, the cases display a judicial willingness to countenance the giving of legal advice that a corporate entity need not perform a contract, even when the purpose and effect of the advice is to benefit a lawyer and his friends at the expense of their adversaries within the entity, at least as long as the advice was not knowingly contrary to law. This judicial willingness suggests a judicial awareness that such advice was frequently sought and given, and this frequency, in turn, affirms the fact that existing management structures encouraged corporate executives to take contract disputes to litigation when it would advance their careers. Thus the connection between changing forms of management structure and the increased litigation of contract disputes seems clear.

Upstarts in Management. As late as the early 1950s, an assumption prevailed that gentlemen controlled American business and that, when their enterprises became involved in disputes, these gentlemen would resolve matters reasonably, without recourse to lawyers and litigation. Beneath this assumption lay an important social reality—namely, that the gentlemen who controlled business had come from the same socioeconomic groups, had attended the same schools, and mingled with each other at the same clubs. This homogeneity, however, had broken down by the late 1960s, and with its breakdown the possibility that gentlemen could work out their problems without recourse to litigation also was shattered.

The persistence of ethnic and religious distrust and bias exacerbated the difficulty of informal dispute resolution. Bias continued to reveal itself in the late 1960s, for instance, in the views of the executive vice president of a major bank, who believed that "a majority of Jews today are dishonest" and, in addition, "overly aggressive, overly clever, excessively scheming and often dishonorable . . . influence wielders and responsibility avoiders." In a similar vein, one Jewish executive reported that "there are some clients that I literally cannot go near because they hate Jews," while a prominent Jewish investment banker described the opposition that existed to his 1968 election to the board of directors of International Telephone and Telegraph from those who believed "more elegant people should go on.' Another executive reported having heard use of the expression, "Catholic bastard," while yet another told of a customer who was "not too happy about the Italian" who worked on his account.[21] Although the corporate establishment was increasingly prepared in the late 1960s and 1970s to admit Catholics and Jews to its ranks, some Protestant members, at least, did not appear to believe that the new entrants would abide by the same code of gentlemanly conduct that the Protestants did. This is not to say that the new entrants abided by a different code that made them more aggressive or less gentlemanly; the only assertion here made is that some members of the establishment, no longer free to ignore Catholics and Jews, continued to deal with them through the same biased eyes that had long perceived them as different.

The persistence of even some anti-Catholic and anti-Semitic bias at a time when Catholics and Jews were beginning to enter the business mainstream created opportunities for conflict and dispute that could not be resolved by recourse to traditional, informal modes of settlement. As long as people such as a professor at the Harvard Business School could without embarrassment publish a finding that non-WASP's did "not fit into the job [as] easily" as Protestants and were more likely to possess character traits that he labeled "troublesomeness" and "aggressiveness,"[22] the mutual respect and trust that are usually essential to negotiating the settlement of disputes would not exist. If even some members of the Protestant corporate establishment continued to believe that Protestants, Catholics, and Jews conducted business by different ethical codes, they would be likely to become embroiled in disputes which they themselves could not resolve and with which only lawyers could deal when the realities of the economy forced them to engage in economic transactions with each other.

One such problem came to the courts in 1970. After "all avenues of friendly persuasion . . . had been traveled" over a period of some two years, the U.S. Department of Justice filed a civil rights suit seeking to enjoin the Palm Beach Realty Listing Bureau from pursuing its policy of not accepting multiple listings from Jewish realtors within its geographic area. Ultimately, the court entered a consent decree. But even after that decree, the WASP realtors of Palm Beach continued the stubborn refusal to deal with Jewish counterparts that had made negotiation impossible and litigation inevitable: rather than accept the decree, the Palm Beach Listing Bureau dissolved itself, perhaps in the hope that new vehicles could be found for continuing old discriminations.[23]

Another revealing incident occurred in 1969 and 1970, when a New York–based corporation was seeking to take over a midwestern railroad. The New York corporation possessed an entirely Jewish management, whereas the railroad's managers were overwhelmingly white Anglo-Saxon Protestants. In litigation growing out of the takeover attempt, the railroad's attorney was taking the deposition of a principal officer of the New York firm. The officer, who had become exasperated with the railroad's unyielding resistance to the takeover, blurted out an exclamation, the substance or effect of which was, "Why do you dislike Jews so much!"[24] Here was a case where the reality or at the very least the perception of anti-Semitism helped produce mistrust between businessmen which, in turn, led to litigation that, at any earlier time, might have been resolved informally by a WASP, old-boy network.

Another piece of litigation that continued into the 1970s involved a confrontation between an upstart shipping line and most of the major American ocean shipping firms. The major lines, in which "knowledgeable sources ha[d] frequently noted what appeared to be a marked absence of Jews from the executive and directorial ranks," had organized a series of conferences in order to control shipping rates along specified routes—in this instance, between New

York and Hong Kong and New York and Japan. The upstart firm, which, with a Catholic and a Jew as its two chief officials, was described by a spokesman for the conference lines as a "sail-by-night, hit-and-run outsider," had refused to abide by the conference rate structure because it could profitably ship goods at a lower rate and could not obtain a share of the market at the prevailing rate. The result was a rate war, in which the conference lines shipped goods at rates below their costs and drove the upstart out of the market and into bankruptcy. The upstart then brought an antitrust action alleging a conspiracy to monopolize commerce on the designated routes.[25] Here was another instance in which the refusal of established corporate elites to bargain with an upstart firm that, according to one of their spokesmen, failed to abide by sound business ethics, produced conflict that only lawyers and the courts could resolve.

In short, the entrance of Catholics and Jews into the corporate mainstream created a perception in the early 1970s that the old gentlemanly code of business had dissolved and that the new diverse groups of businessmen who had emerged in place of the old gentlemanly elite could not trust each other as the older gentlemen once had. Whatever the realities of the marketplace, the perception itself sufficed to make nonlegal dispute settlement, which depends to an immense extent on mutual trust, more difficult. •

The next great business transformation—the growth of foreign trade and the entrance into the American marketplace of entrepreneurs from around the world—completed the destruction of the old gentlemanly code and the clubby homogeneity that had nurtured it. Much of the story can be told statistically. Between 1950 and 1970, American exports and imports of goods and services each increased nearly fivefold, and between 1970 and 1980 they again increased more than five times. Between 1950 and 1970, American investments overseas grew by 307 percent, and foreign investments in the United States grew by 555 percent. Between 1970 and 1980, American assets abroad increased 367 percent, and foreign investment in America increased 468 percent. Overseas markets, investors, and managers, in short, became a very important element of business during the 1960s and 1970s.

Even more striking was the growing significance of Japan and the Third World. One measure of this significance is data regarding foreign investments in the United States, which until 1970 were broken down in the standard government publication into categories of Canada, Europe, and the rest of the world. In 1950, the rest of the world had $134 million invested in the United States, or 4 percent of all foreign investments. By 1960 that figure had grown to $269 million, or only 3.9 percent of all investments. But by 1970 change had begun. In that year Japan had $229 million and Third World countries $370 million invested in the United States, for a total of $599 million, or 4.5 percent of all foreign investments. By 1975, Japanese investment had nearly doubled and Third World investment had increased tenfold, to a total of 13.5 percent of all foreign investment. By 1980, Japanese investment amounted to nearly $5 billion, or 5.6 percent of foreign investment, and Third World investment exceeded $11 billion, or 13.8 percent of the total.[26] Another way of analyzing the data is to report that Japanese and Third World investment in America grew by 201 percent from 1950 to 1960, by 223 percent from 1960 to 1970, and by 2,704 percent from 1970 to 1980.

Business executives from throughout the world thus became important players during the 1970s in the American marketplace, bringing with them radically different business ethics that precluded settlement of contract disputes by recourse to old gentlemanly norms. These foreign executives became important clients for many New York City law firms and appeared with increasing frequency in litigation. Between 1960 and 1964, overseas corporations had appeared as parties in only 3 percent of all cases, primarily as owners of foreign vessels that had come to the port of New York. In the next decade, 1965–74, the appearance rate of foreign corporations increased only slightly to 4 percent, but in the final period, 1975–79, the appearance rate nearly doubled, to 7 percent, and in this period most of the foreign entities in question appeared not as shipowners but in virtue of more complex business dealings. By the 1980s, the provision of legal services to overseas clients had become New York City's largest export commodity measured by the amount of money it generated.[27]

Reported cases confirm how American and foreign business leaders, with their often poor understanding and sometimes contempt for each others' business norms, inevitably ended up in disputes with each other that frequently culminated in litigation in the Southern District of New York. One decision stemming from the overthrow of the Shah of Iran disposed of ninety-six separate civil actions brought for breach, repudiation, or tortious interference with contract. In the opinion of the court, all of the actions, which accounted for nearly 5 percent of contract cases filed in 1979, were "commercial in nature" and arose because of "an unequivocal intention" on the part of the defendants of "avoiding their just debts." Another case, described by the court as involving "one of the most enormous commercial disputes in history," arose when the government of Nigeria breached some one hundred contracts for the sale of nearly $1 billion of cement. Nigeria, on the one hand, and its suppliers, on the other, had quite divergent notions of contract. On its part, Nigeria ordered five times as much cement as it actually wanted so as to be sure of delivery of the required amount and then, when cement-laden vessels began to clog its port facilities, it canceled contracts by engaging in "unilateral alteration of letters of credit . . . on a scale previously unknown to international commerce." Meanwhile, its Western suppliers, believing in the sanctity of written contracts, continued to ship their cement. Although a majority of suppliers worked matters out without litigation, suits proliferated throughout the world, and New York became a center for the litigation, in part because Nigeria had authorized payment of its letters of credit through the Morgan Guaranty Trust Company of New York.[28]

These were probably the two most notable Southern District examples of breaches of contract by foreigners, but they were not the only ones. There were also other cases of contract breaches by Iranians, as well as a case that arose because of different methods of weighing grain in India and the United States and a case that turned on the meaning of the custom of the port of Bombay.[29] Business practices thus had been transformed by the 1980s from what they had been a mere three decades earlier: no longer did a homogeneous group of white, Anglo-Saxon, Protestant businessmen from the northeastern United States resolve their problems in often face-to-face settings; on the contrary, executives around the world conducted their affairs in accordance with the myriad ways of the world. This transformation led to a marked increase in business litigation and hence to a marked change in the docket of the Southern District of New York.

Lawyers as Settlement Bureaucrats. This increase in litigation, which induced law firms to develop large litigation departments to service clients, generated its own pressures toward further bureaucratization. Having put their litigation departments in place, the firms had powerful reasons to use them.

When breach of contract litigation increased suddenly in the early 1970s, the dominant partners in the elite New York City law firms proved themselves to be remarkably sophisticated businessmen. They seized the opportunity to provide new service to their clients and rapidly assembled the pools of talent necessary for carrying on a vast litigation enterprise. Both old-line and newer firms proved ready to take on new business through expansion. Sullivan and Cromwell, for example, grew from 85 lawyers in 1949 to 154 lawyers at the beginning of 1972. By 1988 it employed 345 lawyers. A new firm, Skadden, Arps, Slate, Meagher & Flom, had only 23 lawyers in 1968, but had doubled in size by 1975 and had grown to more than 850 attorneys by the end of the 1980s. Other firms experienced comparable growth.[30]

Along with growth came a second important change. Until the 1960s corporate enterprises typically used only a single outside law firm for all of their legal work that was not performed in-house by the office of general counsel. After 1970, however, a new pattern of representation emerged: instead of relying only on one law firm for all its outside work, businesses began to spread work among several firms, and the firms began to compete in providing superior legal services.

The simultaneous appearance of growth in the law firms and competition for clients among them had a synergic effect that intensified both developments and, in turn, fueled increased litigation. When a client began to bring legal work to other law firms, the firm with which it had a long-standing relationship would grow concerned about losing the client entirely. To forestall such losses, many firms decided in the 1970s to develop new capabilities so they would be ready to satisfy clients' needs. Once a few firms began expanding their litigation departments in the early 1970s to handle the rising amount of business litigation, other firms felt constrained to do the same. And once the litigation departments had been built up to serve the needs of clients, those departments had to be used if they were to remain in existence.

It is essential, however, not to overemphasize the change that the 1970s brought. The increase occurring in breach of contract litigation appears much smaller when statistics based on adversary, nonsettlement dispositions of lawsuits rather than mere filings of complaints are examined. During the twenty years from 1960 to 1980, 74.7 percent of all breach of contract actions commenced in the Southern District were terminated by settlement rather than in an adversary fashion. Even more striking is the fact that, as the number of cases increased, so too did the settlement rate. Thus during the 1960s, it appears that only 68.8 percent of all contract suits were settled, while during the 1970s, 77.6 percent were settled. Contract cases disposed of by trial or some other adversarial process rose from 2.4 percent of all filings in the 1960s to only 3.6 percent of all 1970s filings — a far slower rate of increase than the rise in contract filings as a whole, which grew from about 8 percent to 18 percent of the docket. What increased most rapidly were cases settled by lawyers after litigation was commenced. This figure rose from 5.4 percent of all actions filed during the 1960s to 12.7 percent of all cases in the 1970s.[31]

These statistics provide an important perspective on how lawyers and New York City law firms contributed to the litigation increase we have been analyzing. They suggest that the principal change in the 1970s was not an enormous increase in litigation but rather in the identity of the people who negotiated settlements to business disputes that inevitably arose. Until the 1960s, those involved in disputes worked them out for themselves, but beginning in the 1970s they called upon lawyers to solve their problems for them. When they were brought into the process, the lawyers, of course, filed complaints and used the weapons of litigation to attain their ends. Occasionally they even brought cases to trial. But on the whole, the work of the lawyers was to settle cases business executives had once settled for themselves, albeit in a more structured, formal fashion.

Seen from this perspective, the role played by lawyers in the increase of contract litigation is little more than a footnote to a larger story about the transformation of business management. Forms and methods of business management changed, in turn, largely in response to deeper changes wrought by the legalist reformation in American society and to changes in the world economy. By the end of the 1970s, business possessed both an international scope and a vast size. American business leaders could no longer preside over their firms with an air of exclusivity: they learned during the course of the 1970s to heed the wishes, first, of former social outcasts whom the legalist reformation had brought into the economic mainstream; then, of foreign businessmen; and finally, of organized nonbusiness groups at home such as bureaucrats and consumers. With the internationalization of business, the flowering of the regulatory state, the burgeoning of the scope of enterprise, and the entry of outcasts into the marketplace, the traditional and informal methods of management that had worked well for the homogenous, regionally centered American economy of the 1950s collapsed. These methods were replaced by more structured and bureaucratized styles of management that functioned on the basis of written communications, professional expertise, and fixed formalistic standards. The delegation of disputes to lawyers for formal settlement following the institution of litigation was merely one facet of this larger process of management bureaucratization.

THE BUREAUCRATIZATION OF THE CRIMINAL AND FAMILY LAW PROCESSES

Other increases in litigation occurring during the late 1960s and 1970s similarly reflected a bureaucratization of the litigation process more than a true growth of social disputation. Although some feared that increases in litigation reflected growing social chaos, those increases in fact represented, on the contrary, a growing capacity on the part of the judiciary and related bureaucracies to process cases and thereby govern effectively.

The increase in litigation that seemed most menacing occurred in criminal cases.[32] In the calendar year 1960, trial courts throughout the state had disposed of a total of 17,510 felony and misdemeanor cases. By 1968, that number had risen slightly to 19,688, but then in 1969, it rose to 23,941. The climb continued to 26,675 in 1970, to 29,272 in 1971, and to 32,574 in 1972. That is, after rising only 12.4 percent over a nine-year period from 1960 to 1968, criminal cases increased 65.5 percent over the next five years. Over the course of the next several years, the methods of reporting criminal statistics kept changing, but there do not appear to have been further striking increases in felony and misdemeanor dispositions. Indeed, dispositions in 1977 appear to have totaled only 35,465 — a mere 9 percent increase over six years.

The number of criminal cases also increased in the four federal district courts in New York.[33] During the 1960s, there was an average of 2,192 cases per year. In fiscal year 1970, that number rose to 2,449 — an 11.8 percent increase. Then there was a huge 56.8 percent increase to 3,839 cases in 1971; for the remaining years of the decade down through 1979, criminal cases in the four districts averaged 3,829 per year, which was 74.7 percent higher than the 1960s rate.

The increase in criminal dispositions did not, however, necessarily mean that criminals were menacing a weak legal order. Crime undoubtedly rose in the late 1960s and early 1970s, but government's ability to apprehend and prosecute criminals did as well. Because of the unreliability of crime statistics, it is impossible to be certain whether the power of criminals or the power of government to punish them was growing more rapidly. But the rise of criminal dispositions makes it clear that the police, prison, and criminal justice bureaucracies were growing along with crime itself.

The incarceration of larger numbers of criminals also produced a second wave of bureaucratization in federal courts in the Northern and Western Districts of New York, which constitute all of upstate New York and contain most of the state's prison population. This second wave took the form of an increase in civil filings in the two districts.

An increase in the early 1970s in suits by prisoners accounted for all the rise in civil filings in the districts during the early part of the decade. During the 1960–69 period, there had been an average of 248 prisoner suits per year out of an average for both districts of 973 civil filings. In 1970 those numbers rose to 381 prisoner suits out of 1,075 filings; in 1971, to 499 out of 1,187; and in 1972, to 568 out of 1,242.[34] Between 1969 and 1972, in short, the growth in prisoner suits was greater than the total number of additional suits. Confronted with this flood of new prisoner cases, federal judges in upstate New York were forced to become more efficient in processing them, and their efficiency resulted in the development of new, essentially bureaucratic mechanisms for disposing of nearly all the cases without ever giving full consideration to their merits.

A final rise in litigation that reflected the emergence of added bureaucracy rather than a genuine increase in litigiousness occurred in civil filings in state trial courts. In the sixty-two counties of New York State, a total of 58,633 civil cases were filed in Supreme Court, the basic trial court, for the court year 1960–61. Seven years later, in 1967–68, this number had increased only slightly to 62,683, an annual increase of approximately 1 percent. Then a litigation explosion began. In 1968–69, total filings equaled 69,783; in 1969–70, 75,809; in 1970–71, 86,026; and in 1971–72, 94,425. In 1975, a total 115,514 civil actions were filed. In less than eight years, that is, the number of civil actions filed in state court nearly doubled.

Although this litigation increase appears chaotic, it is, in fact, readily explainable as a result of the legislature's adoption of no-fault divorce, which became effective on September 1, 1967.[35] After several years of unexplained litigation increases, the state's Office of Court Administration began to divide civil cases into two categories—uncontested matrimonial actions and cases other than uncontested matrimonials. Once this new method of reporting took hold, it became apparent that little, if any, real rise in litigation had occurred during the 1970s. In 1978, for example, there were 61,800 nonmatrimonial civil actions throughout the state—essentially the same number of civil actions as in 1967–68. In 1979, there were 62,697 such actions, and in 1980, 64,212.[36]

Thus it appears that the litigation explosion which New Yorkers witnessed, whether it be in civil rights cases in the 1960s or in business dispute cases, criminal prosecutions, or matrimonial actions in the 1970s, resulted, in the end, from the admission of new social groups into positions of power from which they could make claims upon the legal system. When outcasts ranging from criminals to spouses seeking divorce, who had been shunned by traditional social institutions, sought to actualize their equal rights, the law was the only institution capable of helping them. On the whole, however, the law did not adjudicate the cases outcasts brought but merely facilitated settlement. Heavy as this burden of increased settlement facilitation may have been on the judiciary, the burden was worth bearing in return for the access to economic opportunity, the openness of decision making, and the resulting hope and equality that it brought to all New Yorkers.

TOWARD A BUREAUCRATIC VISION OF JUDGING

At the same time that judges were being forced to process larger caseloads in an increasingly bureaucratic fashion, the nineteenth-century conception of the judge as a neutral arbiter who resolved disputes on the basis of preexisting, objective rules of law was collapsing. In its place, a new conception of the judge as merely another variety of bureaucrat slowly started to emerge.

The collapse had begun as early as the 1920s, when Cardozo and other judges of his era insisted on their duty to achieve social justice rather than to decide cases pursuant to preexisting, objective rules of law. The disintegration of nineteenth-century attitudes accelerated when judges in the decades after 1950 came to understand their role, like that of other government officials, to be the making of social policy. In making policy, judges, of course, typically abandoned or reversed the preexisting, objective rules that once had constituted the foundation of the legal system.

As lawyers watched this revision and expansion of doctrine, they were inspired to file novel claims and raise novel defenses that, when accepted by the courts, further destroyed established doctrinal limitations, stretched rules into outlandish shapes, and otherwise transformed law from the fixed, categorical concepts that had traditionally given law its substance into newer fluid forms that resounded more readily to their clients' needs. And as judges responded to their perceptions of society's needs and sometimes legitimated the novel claims and defenses, they only inspired lawyers to even greater novelty. The end result was that classical doctrines were extended and applied to situations beyond the wildest imagination of the early twentieth-century profession, and law grasped at a new reach broader than what any plaintiff could have wildly dreamed or any social policy legitimately support.

Some of the new sorts of claims can be aggregated into categories. In one such category were the cases alleging misconduct by creditors in efforts to collect debts. A second group was brought by contestants on rigged television quiz shows, while a third group consisted of suits by patrons wrongfully refused service at restaurants. A final group involved allegations of intimidation and harassment, such as the case sustaining a complaint that charged a defendant with inviting a plaintiff to have sexual intercourse with him and with sending her a picture of himself with his private parts exposed.[37]

But the extraordinary breadth of the new uses to which law was put in the 1960s and 1970s can best be appreciated by closely examining two unusual cases—*Samek v. Rey* and *Corso v. Crawford Dog & Cat Hospital, Inc.*

In the former case, actress Sieglide Samek had left her wig at "an established coiffeur within the theatrical district, for cleaning, styling and setting, a not uncommon modern day practice," and the defendant had " 'teased' " it, with the result that hair fell out and holes appeared. Noting that "modern day beauty concepts defy the imagination" and could "even produce changed personalities," the court granted plaintiff damages equal to the value of the wig.[38]

In *Corso* the plaintiff had made elaborate funeral arrangements for the burial of her dog in a pet cemetery only to have the defendant place in the casket she had provided the remains of a cat. The court held that, "as in the case where a human body is withheld, the wrongfully withholding or, as here, destruction of the dog's body gives rise to an actionable tort," in which a plaintiff may recover "damages beyond the market value of the dog" for emotional distress and mental anguish. The court concluded:

> This decision is not to be construed to include an award for the loss of a family heirloom which would also cause great mental anguish. An heirloom while it might be the source of good feelings is merely an inanimate object and is not capable of returning love and affection. It does not respond to human stimulation; it has no brain capable of displaying emotion which in turn causes a human response. Losing the right to memorialize a pet rock, or a pet tree or losing a family picture album is not actionable. But a dog — that is something else. To say it is a piece of personal property and no more is a repudiation of our humaneness. This I cannot accept.[39]

Reported cases about the styling of wigs and the funerals of dogs show the enormous distance that law had traveled from the brilliant attempts of Cardozo and other judges of his era to fashion coherent, reform-oriented doctrine in cases like *MacPherson, Allegheny College,* and *Palsgraf.* The newer cases made it evident that the judiciary was implicated " 'in the politics of the people,' " especially when judges reached decisions merely by " 'champion[ing] the cause of a particular constituency.' " This new understanding that law reflected individual judges' divergent visions of social policy rather than accepted standards of authority, rationality, and justice, in turn, created "a potential for jurisprudential scandal" as courts "decide[d] one way one day and another way the next."[40]

The demise of precedent and of shared conceptions of sound policy, while confirming that judges had much in common with other sorts of bureaucrats, also made more manifest than ever the need to confer on judges some special character that elevated the judiciary as an institution. If it was no longer possible to compel every judge "to distinguish between his views as an individual and his function as a judge,"[41] then some other approach was needed to raise the judiciary to a high plane and thereby legitimate its power to coerce fellow citizens. Two approaches emerged during the course of the 1960s and 1970s.

The first approach, which materialized in the 1960s, entailed an effort to articulate a body of case law holding judges to especially high standards of judicial ethics. Before 1960 almost no reported cases on the subject of judicial ethics had existed. In fact, after only two cases in the 1920s, there was a long hiatus in which there was only one reported disciplinary case — against a judge who had permitted improper publicizing of court proceedings in violation of rules against the taking of photographs or broadcasting in a courtroom.[42] But suddenly, in the 1960s, as the disintegration of shared values and the collapse of the doctrine of precedent became increasingly apparent, cases disciplining judges for ethical misconduct became frequent.

The emergence of these disciplinary cases during the 1960s calls for explanation. Perhaps an increase occurred in actual judicial corruption after 1960, but that seems unlikely. New York has had a long and fulsome history of judicial corruption, including that under Boss William Marcy Tweed and Mayor Jimmy Walker,[43] and there is no reason to think that judicial corruption was greater after 1960 than it had been before. It seems more likely that New York witnessed an increase after 1960 in reported cases involving judicial corruption, not in corruption itself.

It further appears that increased concern about judicial integrity somehow was linked to the growing awareness that neither precedent nor broadly shared values controlled judicial decision making and hence that judges routinely needed to choose between evenly balanced, competing claims presented by the litigants. The disintegration of shared values and the collapse of the doctrine of precedent, in short, made it necessary to discern something new with which to convince the public, and perhaps even the judges themselves, of the special dignity and integrity of the bench.

At least one judge on the Court of Appeals was explicit. At a time when "many sound judicial decisions [were] unpopular" or "rest[ed] upon reasoning so evenly balanced that" it was difficult to persuade "the public to accept the result," something had to be done, he asserted, given that "courts [had] little else to enforce compliance with their judgments other than the acceptability of them borne of public respect." If the public could "not always be convinced of the correctness of the court's decisions," at least it had to be made to "believe in the integrity of the decision-making process." Otherwise, the public might not obey judicial rulings, and chaos would result. Judges therefore had to abide by "standards of conduct on a plane much higher than [those] for . . . society as a whole" in order to preserve "the integrity and independence of the judiciary."[44] Judges' ethics, in short, had to be made pure.

Nonetheless, this essentially formalist effort to impose strict canons of discipline on judges while the doctrine of precedent was collapsing and shared values were disintegrating failed. It failed for the same reasons as did the classical and kindred, formalist approaches to judging. These reasons, along with a second, alternative approach for legitimating the power of judges, will emerge in the post-1960 cases that we must now examine.

Some of the cases imposing discipline on judges were easy. For example, those involving financial or similar misdealings by judges, either while on the bench or before ascending the bench, invariably and properly led to sanctions once the facts were established.[45] But four other main categories of cases also arose, and no clear pattern of disposition appeared in any of the four.

The first category of cases involved behavior on the part of judges as disturbing as financial misdealing. One judge was removed from the bench, for example, following an incident in which, "without any justification, [he] ordered three law enforcement officers to bring a coffee vendor before him, authorized the use of handcuffs and thereafter excoriated the handcuffed vendor for the quality of his product." Another removal occurred on the basis of an episode in which a judge detained four youths he suspected of breaking glass in a parking lot—an "episode . . . marked by two frenzied displays of overt physical violence, as well as repeated outbursts involving outrageous verbal abuse and virulent racism." A third removal was of a judge who, in seeking a permit for a charity for which he was a trustee, "became angry and screamed . . . loudly into the telephone" and also stated "that he had more political clout than Dr. Beck, and in vulgar language told Dr. Beck he should stop impeding" the permit application. He also became involved in a "courthouse corridor confrontation," in which he identified himself as a judge and threatened "to use political influence to obtain the ends he sought . . . in intemperate tones and with the use of vulgarity."[46]

In contrast, a judge who became involved in open court "in an angry physical confrontation with" a criminal defendant, "expressing his intention and willingness to engage in a fight with him," received only a censure. So too did judges such as one "who persistently abuse[d] litigants, witnesses and attorneys who appear[ed] before him and who conduct[ed] his court in such a manner that counsel [could] not present their cases without obstructive interference by the court," one who met ex parte with counsel in pending cases, and one who got into an argument with an assistant prosecutor who was conducting an investigation. The Court of Appeals also erred on the side of leniency when it refused to suspend a judge pending trial on his federal indictment for suborning perjury while he had been an assistant district attorney.[47]

A second category of cases involved judges who failed to do administrative work properly. One upstate city court judge who failed to render timely decisions on 44 motions or to conduct timely arraignments in 89 cases and who had 477 undecided cases pending before him was removed from office. But two others, one of whom dismissed prosecutions prematurely, failed to impose mandatory minimum sentences, and signed papers incorrectly, and another of whom filed late reports because of "the time required for [dairy] farming," which was his principal occupation, were merely censured.[48]

The third category involved restrictions on political activities. The clear precept was that "no incumbent judge should engage in partisan political activity unrelated to his own campaign for judicial office," and thus, when one town justice ran for the state senate without resigning, contrary to a written directive from the presiding justice of the Appellate Division, he lost his judgeship and became ineligible for any future judicial position. It is impossible to square this result with the campaign one year earlier of a federal district judge, who still sits on the federal bench today, to be chief judge of the New York Court of Appeals. Even more difficult were the issues arising out of the solicitation of campaign contributions for the successful 1977 effort of Marie Lambert to become New York County surrogate, an office with more patronage attached to it than any other office in the state.[49]

Most disturbing is the final category of cases, which involved judges who displayed favoritism or sought favorable treatment of an individual by some other judge. Three cases will offer examples of the conduct that occurred. In the first, a female court employee informed a male judge of the Criminal Court of New York City that her son had been arrested for possession of marijuana. The judge assured her that in the normal course of events her son would be released without bail. Later that evening, the employee accompanied the judge to chambers, from which she went out to the adjoining balcony. "On her return, there was a personal contact, variously described as an embrace and an endeavor to soothe the complainant's condition, upset by her son's arrest." After the son's release, the judge made several telephone calls to the employee "ostensibly to discuss her son's case, in the course of the last of which . . . [he] agreed to meet her for further discussion and possibly to have a drink."[50]

The second case, which like the first resulted in censure, involved a justice of an upstate town court who urged other judges to give special treatment to two traffic offenders. In one instance, the justice sent a letter about an individual charged with unlicensed driving, in which he described the offender as " 'a nice fellow who has a great many personal problems at the moment, therefore I truly appreciate your kind consideration in the disposition of this matter.' " On another occasion, the justice intervened orally on behalf of an alleged speeder, who " 'was unemployed at the time and also recovering from a lengthy illness, and he approached me and asked me if I could help him. I felt compassion for this individual and did talk to [the town court judge] about the case.' "[51]

The third case involved a close friend of a Queens County Supreme Court justice, who was having difficulty obtaining a taxi license. The justice contacted two people on his friend's behalf. First, he arranged a meeting between his friend and a city council member, of whom his friend was a constituent. The Court of Appeals saw nothing improper in this contact. But it did find impropriety in the second contact, when the justice requested the deputy counsel of the Taxi and Limousine Commission to expedite the processing of the license application, and therefore the court, over a dissent by one of its judges, again imposed a sanction of admonishment. Indeed, in only one case, involving not only favoritism and but also interference with State Police investigations, was a judge removed from office.[52]

In several respects the results in these disciplinary cases were unsatisfactory. First, there was the triviality of the penalty of censure—the penalty most frequently imposed. The point of censure is to diminish the reputation of the person censured, but one wonders whether censure does not, in fact, often result in sympathy for the individual who was censured.

A second problem was the chaotic pattern of the results. Puzzlingly, the Court of Appeals held that a judge should be permitted to introduce a friend to a city council member who will thereupon direct a city bureaucrat to do the friend a favor but not be permitted to introduce the friend directly to the bureaucrat's counsel. Nor is it easy understand why a judge who, in a courtroom, challenged a defendant to a fight should only be censured while another judge who sought to discipline rowdy youths in a parking lot was removed from the bench.[53] Worst of all, it seems outrageous that a judge who sought clemency for a defendant plagued by illness should be censured while a judge accused of suborning perjury in order to railroad an innocent defendant into jail should be allowed to continue hearing cases while the proceedings against him went forward.

These two problems reflect the third and deeper problem that censure, or sometimes even removal of a judge from the bench, constitutes a penalty only because it publicizes wrongdoing and exposes the wrongdoer to the obloquy of the community. However, if the community is divided over whether particular conduct is wrong or understands that, even if wrong, it may be conduct in which the duties of office require an actor to engage, obloquy will not attach. Thus division within the legal community was corrosive of judicial ethical standards in the 1970s for the same reason that it had corroded first the doctrine of precedent and then the post–World War II hope that by ignoring precedent judges could make the law adhere to sound concepts of social policy.

One judge in the 1970s—Jacob D. Fuchsberg—understood why this attempt to hold judges to high ethical standards would fail. He spelled out his understanding and also adumbrated a second approach for legitimating judicial power—an approach identifying judges as benevolent bureaucrats—first, in his response to a case censuring him for his own misdeeds, and later, in a dissent in the case of the Queens justice who had tried to assist his friend with his taxi permit application.

The incoherence of New York's contemporary standards of judicial ethics emerged with unmistakable lucidity in *Matter of Fuchsberg*,[54] the leading 1978 case censuring Jacob Fuchsberg. Before ascending the bench, Fuchsberg had been an unusually successful plaintiff's personal injury lawyer. He had won election to the Court of Appeals in November 1974 and had begun his tenure on the court on January 1, 1975. As befitted his success, Fuchsberg was a wealthy man at the time; among his assets were $3.4 million in New York City municipal bonds. Arguably, his failure to divest himself of these bonds upon his ascension to the bench constituted a violation of the canons of judicial ethics.

Moreover, during Fuchsberg's early months on the Court of Appeals, New York City came close to bankruptcy and was saved only as a result of special legislation, the constitutionality of which came before the Court of Appeals in a series of " 'fiscal crisis cases.' " Fuchsberg recused himself from two of the six cases, voted against his apparent financial interest in one, and offered to recuse himself in another. Although the possible effect of the last two cases on his holdings was "indirect and insubstantial,"[55] his failure to recuse himself was nonetheless another arguable ethical violation. Finally, he continued during the course of the six cases to buy and sell city securities—a third possible ethical violation.

Inquiry into Fuchsberg's financial affairs also disclosed another differing sort of violation. In twelve cases during his brief tenure on the Court of Appeals before the investigation of his affairs, Fuchsberg had asked for the confidential advice of law professors regarding the proper disposition of the cases. In several of the cases, Fuchsberg sent the briefs to the professors, and in three, he sought and obtained draft opinions. In at least one and possibly two cases, he forwarded an unpublished draft opinion of another judge on the Court of Appeals to a professor. Fuchsberg informed neither the parties nor his colleagues of his actions.

The majority of the special Court on the Judiciary concluded that Fuchsberg's behavior merited censure, even though there was no evidence that he profited in his bond dealings as a consequence of his membership on the Court of Appeals and though he consulted professors only "because he wanted to turn out work of the 'finest judicial craftsmanship.'"[56] The majority concluded that its published opinion expressing censure constituted sufficient punishment, and hence it voted not to commence removal proceedings against the judge. Only one of the five judges on the court dissented. That judge would have directed the commencement of formal proceedings to determine, among other things, whether Fuchsberg should be removed from office.

Most significant, perhaps, was Fuchsberg's response to the proceedings. He "admit[ted] to no error in his financial dealings or his participation in the financial crisis cases. On the contrary, he insist[ed] that this conduct was at all times unimpeachable." Furthermore, even after he had received notice of the allegations concerning his consultation with law professors, "the violations continued" as he "participated in at least two appeals in which he had sought advice from professors" without giving "the required notice to the parties" or withdrawing from the cases. In the lone dissenter's view, Fuchsberg's "conduct . . . manifest[ed] a complete lack of understanding of proper judicial behavior."[57]

Judge Fuchsberg, however, had a different understanding of propriety. Like other New Yorkers in the 1970s, he lived in a pluralist culture with divergent views about where ultimate truths would be found. He sensed that as long as he possessed rhetorical skill and material resources, his view of truth was as good as that of anyone else. With money and persuasive power, he could be confident that his stature could not be diminished by critics who attacked him for failing to pay sufficient heed to values, such as the appearance of neutrality and objectivity, that he found absurd. Thus he could announce that he had been vindicated when, instead of being removed from the bench for profiteering from his insider position, he was merely "chide[d] . . . for not having been sufficiently attentive to the appearance of things which in and of themselves were perfectly innocent." As he declared, "in essence, my integrity and my good intentions remain unblemished."[58]

Two years later, in a dissent in the case of the Queens justice who had tried to assist his friend in applying for a taxicab permit, Fuchsberg not only made arguments that cast doubt on the entire disciplinary process in cases of minor favoritism but also advanced an alternative view of the proper role for judges in a pluralist society. After observing that "no substantive benefit was sought or received by the friend," who requested only that "administrative inertia with regard to a ministerial bureaucratic matter" be ended, Fuchsberg added that "in this day, when, unfortunately, the moorings the teacher, the preacher and the pater once provided no longer hold sway, a Judge at times may find himself the Nestor to whom community friends will turn."[59] Fuchsberg thereby seemed to suggest that judges could provide the community with valuable service by intervening compassionately in matters in which they had personal knowledge or contacts that could help in the attainment of socially worthwhile results in individual cases.

Fuchsberg's jurisprudence of compassion arguably is the analogue of Cardozo's jurisprudence of social justice through charity and thus represents the continuation into the 1980s of the reform movement that had its earliest roots in the 1920s. Fuchsberg's jurisprudence differed from Cardozo's, however, in two profound respects. The first difference was that Cardozo's adversaries advanced a competing substantive conception of justice; their opposition to his vision of social reform was grounded in a call for protection of the existing distribution of wealth and adherence to traditional moral values. In contrast, Fuchsberg's call for justice through compassion was resisted, at least on the face of his adversaries' opinions, by a call for procedural justice—by a demand for transparency in the decision-making process plus a full opportunity for litigants to present their cases.

The second difference was deeper. Cardozo hoped to achieve social justice through common-law adjudication. His thinking began and ended with the judicial process, and his main concern was how judges should decide cases when precedent did not point clearly in a single, unitary direction. Fuchsberg, on the other hand, had moved beyond the common law. His judge did not possess power to act compassionately because of her special jurisdiction as judge but only because she was a government official, with the same power to help people as any other government official. Fuchsberg understood that the judiciary was merely one cog in the massive bureaucracy of government and that a judge's job as an official in that bureaucracy was not only to better the lives of those who needed her help but also to push other bureaucrats to do the same. Above all else, Fuchsberg appears to have grasped how society and government had changed between Cardozo's time and his own. Whereas Cardozo assumed, perhaps rightly, that the Court of Appeals could change the law and that legal change could lead, in turn, to social change, Fuchsberg seemed to understand that, in the pluralistic culture he inhabited and the massive, bureaucratic government he served, countless individuals would continue living and doing their jobs according to their own lights with little regard to the law's requirements. Hence he appreciated that society and government had become less susceptible to judicially induced legal change. He further understood that he could make the world better only by helping the individuals who happened to seek his help and by doing his job in an exemplary fashion that would provide inspiration to others.

Unlike Cardozo's vision of judges promoting social justice—a vision that rose to dominance by the end of his own life—Fuchsberg's vision of judges and bureaucratic officials as Nestors to whom community friends can turn has not become dominant. Instead, it continues to exist in uneasy tension along with other ideas about judging. First, there is a formalist body of ethics insisting that judges and other government servants must live by a higher moral code than other citizens. Second, there remains an approach to bureaucracy, which we examined in Chapter 5, that sees officialdom, including judges, as an instrument for social control of, rather than service to, underclasses. Third, there is the perspective of the underclasses themselves, who understandably resent both the manipulative controls and the charitable ministrations of bureaucrats.

Derived as each of these approaches is from diverse and ultimately contradictory strands in legalist reform thinking, there exists no reason to expect any one of them to become dominant in the years to come. In this sense, the legalist reformation has disintegrated. Yet the majority opinion in the *Fuchsberg* case, Fuchsberg's own response to the case, and his dissent in the Queens case all illustrate the impossibility of escaping from the concepts and language of the old, legalist ways of thought. The majority opinion, the response, and the dissent all traded on those concepts and that language. And so the legalist reformation endures, but in a fragmented jurisprudence that imposes contradictory demands—that judges treat all citizens as formally equal while at the same time extending special privileges to less favored citizens in an effort to make them more equal, and that judges control underclasses while at the same time helping them and leaving them alone. The legalist reformation also endures in a paradoxical social reality—one that gives individuals extraordinary personal freedoms and unique opportunities for upward mobility while at the same time ensnaring them in a bureaucratic state that ensures political stability and makes any fundamental redistribution of wealth and power unimaginable.

CHAPTER 16

ENTERPRISE AND EFFICIENCY

As New York law entered the closing decades of the twentieth century, the legalist reformation had become an amalgam of competing concerns. Early reformers had sought to prevent the exploitation of the weak and needy and to provide all citizens with opportunity. In pursuit of these objectives, they had been prepared to deploy the regulatory powers of government. Later, they came to believe as well in individual liberty, equality, and dignity. These latter goals, in turn, led them to distrust the regulatory powers of the state.

These varied goals of the legalist reformation plainly were inconsistent with each other. Distrust of regulation was inconsistent, for example, with maximum use of regulatory power, and entrepreneurial liberty could be inconsistent with the promotion of equality. Pursuit of the goals of legalist reform thus entailed a certain incoherence. Yet it was precisely Americans' tenacious adherence to these goals that gave the legalist reformation its enduring power. Americans simply were unwilling to give any of them up. All they could do was give greater or lesser emphasis to each.

By the century's closing decades, this shifting emphasis had combined to produce at least some bias toward encouraging entrepreneurial opportunity. One means of providing opportunity was to encourage business enterprise, which, in turn, seemed to require courts to create legal rules enhancing business efficiency. In this fashion, a new concept of efficiency sprang from the root legalist concept of opportunity. And, as we shall see, once this new concept of efficiency entered the law it spread across a variety of doctrines and became a favored response to those striving to achieve competing goals of social justice.

FIDUCIARY DUTY AND THE LAW OF TRUSTS

One of the earliest manifestations of the judiciary's concern for business efficiency occurred in mid-century, when the New York courts, in a key line of cases, refused to explicate the concept of fiduciary duty in a fashion that would further regulatory policies the legislature had enacted to promote social justice. Instead, the courts construed fiduciary law in a fashion that encouraged entrepreneurs to operate their businesses efficiently even at the cost of noncompliance with regulatory laws and policies.

The first case in the line was *Hornstein v. Paramount Pictures, Inc.*,[1] in which shareholders brought a derivative suit against Paramount's directors to compel them to restore to the corporation a $100,000 payment out of corporate funds made to two labor union officials to induce them not to call a strike. Plaintiffs claimed that the payment violated section 380 of the Penal Law, which provided that anyone "who gives . . . any money . . . to any duly appointed representative of a labor organization . . . to induce him to prevent or cause a strike . . . is guilty of a misdemeanor," and the court agreed that, if the $100,000 had been given freely as a bribe, it would have been an unlawful expenditure of corporate funds, and the directors would have been required to restore it to the corporation.

The court, however, had "no difficulty or hesitancy" in finding that the board "was not the giver of a bribe but a submitter to extortion."[2] Read broadly, *Hornstein,* the result and reasoning of which were affirmed both by the Appellate Division and the Court of Appeals, held that fiduciaries who acted in good faith and received no personal benefit from their actions were not guilty of a breach of duty merely because they had breached a regulatory statute.

Five months later, *Simon v. Socony-Vacuum Oil Co.* addressed the issue of directors' liability for an adjudicated violation of the federal antitrust laws for which they had voted. Again, a court held that they were not liable because the directors had "acted honestly and reasonably and for what they believed to be the best interests of the company" and not "fraudulently, negligently, corruptly or in bad faith." The evidence also failed to show that the directors "knew, or had reason to believe," that their activities "violated the Sherman Act" or "that they made any personal profit or gained any personal advantage at the expense of the corporation or otherwise."[3] Thus *Simon* reaffirmed the broad reading of *Hornstein* that fiduciaries who acted in good faith and received no personal benefit from their actions were not guilty of a breach of duty when they had breached a regulatory statute.

Early the next year, the Court of Appeals in *Kalmanash v. Smith* removed all remaining doubts when it again addressed the issue of directors' liability for an adjudicated violation of the federal antitrust laws—in this instance, the Clayton Act, and declared succinctly that it has "been held consistently that a stockholder's derivative action does not lie for violation of the Clayton Act." Subsequent cases adhered to the rule that fiduciaries who violated a regulatory statute but otherwise acted in good faith on behalf of their beneficiary and received no personal benefit from their actions were not guilty of a breach of duty.[4]

This refusal to extend doctrine so as to make fiduciaries liable for regulatory breaches committed in a good faith belief that they were furthering the interests of their beneficiaries was not preordained. Indeed, one old case, decided by a trial court in Buffalo, had reached the opposite result when it required a man who was the manager of a business, as well as a member of its board of directors, to reimburse the business for $800 in bribes paid to local officials to overlook violations of the Sunday closing laws. More recently, another trial judge had declared that bank directors were duty-bound to abide by state banking regulations, although he had declined to allow a shareholder to maintain a suit for damages in a context in which the corporation had suffered no damages and had come into compliance with the law.[5] On the other hand, the refusal to hold fiduciaries liable for regulatory breaches was consistent with the efforts of judges after 1940 to promote entrepreneurial freedom and their tendency to recede from regulatory activities as legislatures entered the field and established complex regulatory structures. Whether they were acting out of a growing distrust of the emerging regulatory state or out of an antiprogressive desire to limit the impact of the New Deal's often redistributive legislation, the refusal of New York's judges to bring the weight of fiduciary duty to bear in support of regulatory enforcement weakened that enforcement significantly.

To appreciate the weakness, one need only focus on the weighing of risks in which a corporate officer or director had to engage in evaluating corporate behavior that might later be found to violate a regulatory statute. Typical regulatory sanctions consist of orders granting prospective relief, fines imposed on the corporate business entity, and occasionally fines or minor criminal penalties imposed on corporate fiduciaries. Often, the heaviest burden on a business subject to possible regulation will be the legal expenses and similar costs incurred in fending it off. Making fiduciaries personally liable for these costs, as the plaintiffs in *Hornstein, Simon,* and *Kalmanash* proposed, while leaving profits spread among all shareholders, would have made fiduciaries much more concerned with avoiding costs than with earning profits, would have forced them more frequently to obey regulatory legislation, and ultimately would have increased regulatory compliance at the cost of entrepreneurial activity. In the world created by the *Hornstein, Simon,* and *Kalmanash* decisions, in contrast, fiduciaries could decide how to respond to prospective regulation without fear of suffering serious personal liability. They were freed thereby to make an entrepreneurial judgment weighing possible corporate profits against possible corporate regulatory losses, with knowledge that both profits and losses would be spread among all shareholders. Thus fiduciaries could opt against regulatory compliance if prospective profits seemed sufficiently high.

The judiciary's concern for practicality and efficiency also manifested itself in the law of trusts. Thus when Congress in 1969 altered the terms on which trusts could accumulate and distribute money to charities, the New York courts promptly amended the terms of trusts created under the old Internal Revenue Code so they could continue to operate with all available federal tax benefits under the new law. Similarly, when changes in conditions relating to real estate financing made it impossible to comply with a trust settlor's investment restrictions, the trustees were "freed from the obligation imposed by" the trust and directed "to invest the funds of the trust estate in any of the investments authorized under . . . existing law." The courts also upheld investments in common trust funds against various objections in order "to provide small investors with the safety of diversified investment through a single medium." Finally, judges in the 1970s, partly in response to legislation, modified ancient strictures against invasion of principal in favor of income beneficiaries and recognized that "public policy" on occasion justified the transfer to those beneficiaries of "the principal of spendthrift trusts." Taken together, these doctrinal changes undercut the traditional assumption that an investment should at some date in the future return principal intact, with periodic interest payments during the interim.[6]

THE LAW OF NEGLIGENCE

Another subject on which ideas of efficiency emerged in mid-century and ultimately became an obstacle to the achievement of social justice was the law of negligence. As had been true in regard to the law of fiduciary duty, efficiency norms had begun to appear in tort theory as early as the 1940s, when Cardozo's valiant *Palsgraf* synthesis of negligence and proximate cause under the single rubric of foreseeability began to come apart with the adoption of Learned Hand's utilitarian calculus of risk. But efficiency concerns came to full fruition only in the 1970s.

As we have already seen, the first oblique announcement of the utilitarian calculus had occurred in Hand's opinion for the Second Circuit in the 1932 case of *Sinram v. Pennsylvania R.R.* For a decade thereafter, Hand was ignored. But then, Hand decided to proclaim the calculus of risk test in two mid-1940s cases. In the first, a 1943 case involving the loss of a shipment of cotton aboard a railroad car float in New York Harbor in the midst of a hurricane, Hand held that "in all actions for negligence the decision depends upon the risk imposed on the person who eventually suffers, matched against the prejudice or expense necessary to avoid it." He continued that the "prejudice and . . . expense were no more than the delay of a few hours; on the other hand the risk was most substantial," and he therefore reversed the judgment that the tug operator was not negligent.[7]

Finally, in 1947, Hand published his now famous opinion in *United States v. Carroll Towing Co.,* where he described a tug owner's duty to provide against injuries as "a function of three variables: (1) The probability that she will break away; (2) the gravity of the resulting injury, if she does; (3) the burden of adequate precautions." "Liability depend[ed] upon" an efficiency calculation of whether the cost of preventing the injury was greater or lesser than its gravity multiplied by the probability that it would occur; if the cost of prevention was less, a defendant would be negligent for not bearing that cost and would be liable for injuries occurring as a result, but if the cost of prevention were greater, a defendant would not be negligent and would have no liabilities.[8]

The Second Circuit continued to follow this efficiency approach, when Chief Judge Thomas Swan, citing *Carroll Towing,* dismissed a claim of negligence after observing that "negligence may be measured as a product of the gravity of the injury, if it occurs, multiplied by the factor of its probability." Similarly, Judge Henry Friendly observed in 1966 that " 'as the gravity of the possible harm increases, the apparent likelihood of its occurrence need be correspondingly less' " for a defendant to be negligent, and Judge Irving Kaufman wrote in 1968 that "in determining whether a course of conduct is reasonable, the probability and gravity of injury must be balanced against the ease of taking effective preventive measures." The calculus of risk standard was also held applicable on the issue of contributory negligence.[9]

Despite continued dicta that " 'one who collects a large number of people for gain or profit must be vigilant to protect them' " and that, whenever an individual recognizes that he or she is "caus[ing] danger of injury to the person or property of . . . [an]other, a duty arises to use ordinary care and skill to avoid such injury,"[10] New York's state appellate courts joined the federal bench in accepting Judge Hand's utilitarian calculus. Thus in a 1945 case, the Court of Appeals declared that the "protective measures" required of a defendant "were proportioned to the danger" which its activity "created." This language was taken to require courts and juries in negligence cases to balance the gravity and probability of harm against the cost of preventing the harm. Likewise, the Appellate Division declared that negligence "involves a foreseeable risk, a threatened danger of injury, and conduct unreasonable in proportion to the danger." It also ruled in product liability design defect cases, where "there is almost no difference between a prima facie case in negligence and one in strict liability," that a judge's task is one of "balancing of the alternative designs available against the existing risk while taking into account the cost of the proposed alternative."[11]

An especially telling case in the Court of Appeals, *Pulka v. Edelman,* involved the issue of whether parking garage owners should be liable to pedestrians struck by drivers carelessly exiting from garages. The answer given by a majority on the court was that liability should not be imposed "where the realities of every day experience show us that, regardless of the measures taken, there is little expectation that the one made responsible could prevent the negligent conduct." What requires attention is the mind-set of the *Pulka* majority, which was focused on the efficiency question of whether the cost to garage owners of trying to stop drivers from exiting their garages negligently would exceed whatever safety benefits their efforts might bring. The majority did not, however, pay attention to the fairness argument noted by the dissent in reliance on "the classic language of *Palsgraf*" that "the nature of . . . [being in] business as a public garage operator attracted the flow of automobile traffic across the public sidewalk" for profit and thereby imposed a duty on the operator not to "close his eyes to . . . pedestrians who are thereby imperiled."[12]

With Cardozo's *Palsgraf* synthesis undermined and Hand's utilitarian calculus of risk entrenched as the definition of negligence, judges again had to struggle with the issue of how to make sense of the requirement of foreseeability and the concept of proximate cause. Some simply reiterated without thought the old language of *Palsgraf* that "the risk reasonably to be perceived defines the duty to be obeyed" and hence the liability for injuries that a wrongdoer would incur. Others, wishing to use proximate cause as a "concept stem-[ming] from policy considerations . . . [in order] to place manageable limits upon the liability that flows from negligent conduct," took the view that "negligence and proximate cause," although they "frequently overlap[ped]," were "not the same conceptually."[13] And if they were not the same, then simple foreseeability could not be the test for proximate cause, since foreseeability was already an element of the negligence calculus of risk.

For this reason, many judges turned back to a classic definition of proximate cause as one "which, in a natural sequence, unbroken by any new cause, produces . . . [an] event, and without which that event would not have occurred." This definition, however, merely raised a new issue: when would a "new cause" be deemed to have broken a "natural sequence?"[14] Other judges, like Henry Friendly, focused not on breaks in the chain of causation but more directly on foreseeability. In doing so, however, they defined foreseeability for purposes of proximate cause differently than they defined it for negligence, suggesting that, while an ability to foresee harm of any type might render an actor negligent, the proximate cause requirement would be met only if harm of the same general sort resulted to the same general class of persons from the same general type of physical forces that required an actor, in the first place, to take care. The appellate courts did nothing to eliminate this confusion on the subject of proximate cause when they held that "no particular formula [was] required" when trial judges gave "instructions on the subject of causation."[15]

All of this was good calculation of efficiency, which entailed the interpolation of three doctrinal requirements into personal injury law. The first was the Hand calculus with its call for cost-benefit analysis that would encourage action when the benefits exceeded the costs but deter it when the costs were greater. The second was the demand for manageable limits on negligence liability so that the law would not interfere with business productivity. The third, at least for the best of judges like Henry Friendly, was the sense that the limits had to grow out of a concept of foreseeability defined in a fashion that would enable business to engage in rational planning—the only sort of planning consistent with the achievement of efficiency.

The most striking quality, however, in the calculus of risk cases and related ones like *Pulka v. Edelman* was a shift in emphasis that brought negligence doctrine into conflict with legalist reform values. *Palsgraf* ultimately had been about fairness defined as nonexploitation: it directed juries to apply a word with moral connotations—negligence—to people who, foreseeing that a particular action on their part would exploit others by threatening them with physical injury, nonetheless went forward with the action in an effort to benefit themselves. Moreover, *Palsgraf* empowered juries to make fairness judgments and declare people morally blameworthy without inquiry into the efficiency of the conduct that was foreseeably harmful. *Pulka,* on the other hand, was not about moral blame but about deterrence. The *Pulka* majority reached its decision on the premise that garage owners could do little, if anything, to reduce accidents when cars were being driven out of their garages and accordingly, without engaging in any fairness analysis, refused to impose any duty on the garage owners.

No case, however, better illustrates the efficiency concerns of the late twentieth-century Court of Appeals than *Boomer v. Atlantic Cement Co.* The case arose when plaintiffs sought to enjoin the operation of a cement plant in the vicinity of Albany owned by the Atlantic Cement Co., which sought to operate the plant even though it exploited the plaintiffs and other neighboring landowners by imposing dirt, smoke, and vibrations on them. *Boomer* presented a clear case of an industrial firm that, "at the time the plant commenced production . . . was well aware of . . . the probable consequences of its contemplated operation," yet "still chose to build and operate the plant." Nevertheless, the court denied an injunction because of "the large disparity in economic consequences" that an injunction would create: the defendant's investment in the plant, which employed some three hundred workers, exceeded $45 million, whereas the injury to plaintiffs amounted to only $185,000. Under such circumstances, the result of granting an injunction "would be to close down the plant at once" at great cost to the area's economy. Instead, the court granted a damage remedy, at least in part on an efficiency rationale that damages would provide "a reasonable effective spur to research for improved techniques to minimize" the cement plant's adverse effects on its neighbors.[16]

In so focusing on economic consequences rather than fairness and non-exploitation, the judges in *Boomer,* like other post–World War II judges, were acting consistently with the central policy goal underlying the era's tendency toward doctrinal reform in the interests of efficiency. Like other postwar Americans, the judges had internalized the wartime lesson that calm and intelligent human effort could reduce injury, illness, and premature death because accidents were a product not of fate but of human carelessness and error. They saw that accidents could be reduced to the point of elimination if people ceased to act in the ways that produced them. But as they pursued the goal of reducing accidents, they arrived at a point at which accidents could not be further reduced without ceasing activity that was socially valuable. At that point, they concluded that the goal of tort law should be the deterrence not of all accidents but only of those accidents whose cost outweighed the benefits of the conduct that had produced them. With that conclusion, they modified the postwar emphasis on efficiency from one that counseled increased compensation for injuries to one that put the brakes on compensation.

Thus, in personal injury law, the prewar struggle over whether compensatory justice demanded protection of property or compensation for injuries was transformed after World War II into an analogous efficiency debate over whether to promote injury deterrence by imposing costs on victims or alternatively on others involved, perhaps only peripherally or distantly, in causing the injuries. This shift from a vision of personal injury law grounded in fairness to one grounded in efficiency was not, however, linear. Initially, the concern for efficiency seemed to be a pro-plaintiff development. In the years immediately following World War II, the concern induced victims of injury to search out and sue those who had wronged them, and over the next thirty years it led to a significant number of doctrinal developments that imposed increased liability on defendants. But, as an analytical matter, efficiency is neither a pro-plaintiff nor a pro-defendant concept.

A further complexity concerns the relationship between the concepts of efficiency and fairness. The conception of fairness propounded by the judiciary around 1900 severely curtailed the tort liability of entrepreneurs and other potential defendants. Under this pro-defendant judicial conception, victims of injury were required to bear their own burdens far more often than would have been the case under any scheme of efficiency designed to deter the occurrence of accidents. In contrast, the conception of fairness favored by early twentieth-century tort reformers authorized recovery of damages in a greater number of cases than a scheme designed to reduce accidents to some optimal level would have done.

At the outset of World War II, tort doctrine reflected some balance between the older conception of limited entrepreneurial liability and the newer reform conception that Cardozo and the Court of Appeals had begun to incorporate into the law through *Palsgraf*. Assuming, however, that the balance continued to tilt strongly in the direction of the older conception, then the concept of efficiency appeared congruent in the aftermath of the war with the reformers' conception of fairness. Proponents of continuing tort reform along the lines begun by *Palsgraf* could, that is, add an argument about efficiency to their existing argument about fairness without any sense of inconsistency. In cases like *Carroll Towing* decided in the context of the 1940s, Hand's articulation of the calculus of risk could appear as yet another pro-plaintiff progressive development toward increased fairness.

But as tort doctrine moved increasingly in the direction urged by early twentieth-century reformers, the concept of efficiency simultaneously became less congruent with the reform conception of fairness and began instead to act as a conservative brake on further pro-plaintiff doctrinal development. Scholars such as Richard Posner began to appreciate the restraining implications of the Hand calculus, and cases like *Pulka v. Edelman* began to codify them.[17] Conflict between fairness and efficiency thus emerged in cases where the cost of foreseeable injury discounted by its probability was lower than the profit obtainable from entrepreneurial activity, as advocates like Posner argued against the award of those damages which the reform conception of fairness demanded in such cases.

With the development of efficiency as a concept for restraining further expansion of tort liability, the late nineteenth-century conception of fairness as nonredistribution, which had severely limited the tort liability of entrepreneurs and other potential defendants, largely disappeared from discussion. In part, its disappearance resulted from the fact that lawyers arguing against expansion of tort liability could turn to efficiency arguments to halt liability's ever widening scope. The disappearance was also related to a larger phenomenon that we also have already examined—the final demise under the pressures of World War II and the postwar world of the nineteenth-century precepts against redistribution of wealth which had underlain so much of the common law. Thus as the end of the twentieth century approached, all arguments addressing issues of the scope of tort liability had a pedigree in the legalist reform thought of the middle of the century. But one group of arguments—those about efficiency—was beginning to be employed for other than progressive ends.

EFFICIENCY IN THE PROCESSING OF LITIGATION

A third doctrinal area in which efficiency developed into a compelling concept during the 1960s and 1970s was the law of civil procedure. At least as long as efficiency is defined in Paretian terms, it is easy to see why it was such an attractive value. In a situation in which precedent was no longer binding, judges needed some other value to guide their decision-making process, and a precept directing them to help one litigant without doing any harm to others was attractive. For a Nestor like Jacob Fuchsberg striving from his seat on the high bench to assist those whom he could help, using judicial decisions as opportunities to create Pareto improvements would seem a noble aim. Indeed, people like Fuchsberg could look back on the great egalitarian event of the 1940s, 1950s, and 1960s—the inclusion of Catholics and Jews into the New York mainstream—as one giant Pareto improvement, in which Catholics and Jews had gained power, wealth, and status without diminishing the well-being of their former WASP oppressors.

No wonder that efficiency became an attractive goal and a powerful legal argument in the late 1960s and 1970s, as recourse to precedent declined and other legalist reform values, like liberty and equality, began to assume uncertain meanings at their margin. But as we shall see, efficiency did not always translate directly into Pareto improvement. Indeed, efficiency developed a variety of meanings as judges and lawyers deployed it in the 1960s and 1970s to deal with a wide variety of different problems.

Efficiency became the new basis, for instance, of the law of civil procedure when judges, in response to the litigation explosion of the late 1960s and 1970s, reacted entirely predictably. They became anxious about procedural rules that placed an "unnecessary burden upon the courts of this State," with their "already overladen calendar[s]," and sought to develop procedures that would be "dispositive of disputes in a more simple, direct and time saving manner" without "wast[ing] judicial resources which, through ever increasing demands, daily become more precious."[18]

In fact, judges had always shown at least some concern for the efficient processing of litigation. One area of procedural law in which concerns for judicial efficiency had early affected doctrine was the law of joinder of parties and joinder of claims. Apart from questions of who constituted a real party in interest, without the presence of which no lawsuit could be maintained, the goal of judges in the reported cases was "to avoid circuitry and multiplicity of actions, and to facilitate the dispatch of business in the courts." For this reason it was said that a court should bring "all parties before it whose presence [was] necessary to the decision of the controversy." Litigants could also join several causes of action when they presented "common questions" or grew "out of the same transaction . . . [and] present[ed] a common point of litigation, the decision of which will affect the whole subject-matter and will settle the rights of all the parties to the suit."[19]

The same "modern legal . . . policy . . . to compel litigants, whenever consistent with logic and justice to dispose of their controversy in a single action" induced courts to be, in the words of one judge, even "more liberal in the allowance and joinder of counterclaims than in the joinder of causes of action."[20] Efficiency concerns also manifested themselves at an early date—in this case, the mid-1950s—in the law of *res judicata*. Driven by those concerns, the Court of Appeals began a process of transforming some narrow exceptions in the basic principles of *res judicata* into a new statement of the general rule and thereby "greatly expand[ing] the application of collateral estoppel" and *res judicata*.[21]

In a key case, *Israel v. Wood Dolson Co.*,[22] the plaintiff had sued two defendants—one for breach of contract and another for inducement of the breach. After losing the breach of contract trial, the plaintiff sought to proceed against the second defendant, who had not been a party at the trial, on the inducement claim. The Court of Appeals held that the doctrine of *res judicata* precluded him from doing so.

The *Israel* case was important for two reasons. The first was that the Court of Appeals declared that it was "not to be treated as adding another general class of cases to the list of 'exceptions' to the rule requiring mutuality of estoppel," but "merely" as "the announcement of the underlying principle which is found in the cases classed as 'exceptions.' " The second lay in the court's understanding of the underlying efficiency concern: "that it is to the interest of the State that there should be an end to litigation."[23]

A case decided three months after *Israel* went even further in preventing litigants from "harassing the other parties involved and clogging the court's calendar" and in thereby promoting "judicial efficiency" as "a goal which should be striven for and attained by . . . the courts." The case in point was a suit by a car maintainer in the New York City Transit System complaining about his civil service classification and his resulting salary. The issue had previously been before the Court of Appeals in litigation to which the plaintiff had not been a party. Since the issue had not then "escape[d] the attention of the court" and the court was unwilling to expend time reconsidering the issue anew, it ruled that the plaintiff, who had never had the opportunity to present his claim, could not relitigate the issue.[24] Although the court's theory was *stare decisis* rather than *res judicata,* its decision nonetheless represented a significant extension of the binding effect of previous judgments.

In the next year, *Statter v. Statter,* which barred a wife from bringing an action to annul a marriage after a husband's prior successful action for separation, extended *res judicata* in another direction. Under old law, the binding effect of *res judicata* depended on "a determination" whether two "causes of action [were] the 'same' . . . [or] 'different,' " with an eye to "a comparison of the evidence needed to establish" the contentions of the parties as the "appropriate criterion" of similarity or difference. Since the Statters had not made the existence of their marriage an issue in the separation proceedings, old law arguably permitted the maintenance of a new action to litigate the question. The Court of Appeals, however, adopted a new approach that focused not on justice to the parties but on efficiency for the courts. Under the new standard, the "essence" of *res judicata* was "the fact that a court ha[d] already been presented with the *subject* sought to be litigated and ha[d] rendered a judicial determination thereon."[25] Since the subject of marriage had been before the courts once, it was not necessary for them to waste time on it again.

Hinchey v. Sellers, which continued the trend in *Statter* toward minimizing burdens on the judiciary, was a suit against an automobile owner for injuries caused by his vehicle while it was being driven by a third party. The issue was whether a New Hampshire judgment declaring that the insurer had no obligation to defend because the third party had been driving without permission within the meaning of the policy was *res judicata* on the New York tort issue of whether the third party had been driving without permission. While the Court of Appeals agreed "that the ultimate legal issue involved in the instant case [was] not the same as the ultimate legal issue involved in the New Hampshire action," it nonetheless held the New Hampshire action a bar. Citing *Israel v. Wood Dolson Co.,* which, it will be recalled, involved the identity of parties rather than the identity of issues, the court held that "since plaintiffs had a full and complete opportunity to be heard on these facts in New Hampshire, they should not be permitted to relitigate them in New York simply because the legal issue of permission here appears in the context of a New York statute rather than in . . . [an] insurance policy."²⁶

Although some cases continued to extend the logic of the *Israel* case, the trend was not uniform. In another leading case, *Commissioners of State Insurance Fund v. Low,* the court had set loose a counter trend. Clarity emerged to this process of "evolution for many years" only when the Court of Appeals announced first, "that the 'doctrine of mutuality" [was] a dead letter," and second, that New York had adopted in its place "the full and fair opportunity test," which made a finding in a prior action preclusive of relitigation as long as there was "an identity of issue" and "a full and fair opportunity" in the prior action "to contest the decision now said to be controlling." As a result of these announcements, it became clear that concepts of *res judicata* and collateral estoppel did "not have a technical and well-defined meaning" and were "not to be rigidly or mechanically applied." On the contrary, their applicability was "most often an issue of fact," in which "no single fact [was] determinative but all the circumstances must be considered."²⁷

In light of this new flexibility, the Court of Appeals reached a number of new results. It held, for example, that criminal convictions should be given collateral estoppel effect in subsequent civil cases involving the same issues. It also declared doctrines of *res judicata* applicable to suits against the government, although in a relaxed form in civil rights cases. Following the *Restatement of Judgments (Second),* the courts finally adopted new conceptual categories, such as " 'claim preclusion' " and " 'issue preclusion' " and "offensive" and "defensive" use.²⁸

No subject was as completely transformed by efficiency concerns as the law of *res judicata,* but efficiency did have an impact on other areas of civil procedure, such as the law of discovery. With the expanded use of discovery that occurred after the enactment of the Civil Practice Law and Rules, judges began to appreciate how the "wide scope of disclosure" could become an "oppressive and burdensome . . . [,] improper wholesale fishing expedition of the files and records . . . , including every scrap of paper," of opposing litigants. Discovery, in short, could become inefficient. Judges developed such concerns because they were, after all, confronting demands for the production of 36,000 pages of documents; interrogatories containing 80 main questions and some 270 subquestions over a space of 36 pages; and cases on issues such as foster child placement involving a "risk that extensive pre-trial discovery proceedings [would] delay" decisions that needed to be made promptly.²⁹

Courts would "not tolerate abuses of the disclosure process" and permitted those threatened by such abuse to seek relief by applying for protective orders. The court to which an application was made had plenary discretion to regulate the terms and provisions of discovery, subject to appellate reversal if that discretion was abused. By these means, judges strove to regulate efficiently the time, place, conditions, and manner of discovery.[30]

Summary judgment was another procedure affected by efficiency concerns. Although some state court judges began to express occasional hesitation about summary judgment, calling it a "harsh" and "drastic remedy which should only be employed when there is no doubt as to the absence of triable issues," they nonetheless recognized that summary judgment procedures were "intended to be dispositive of disputes in a more simple, direct and time saving manner" and that "an unfounded reluctance to employ the remedy" would "waste judicial resources which, through ever increasing demands, daily become more precious." Accordingly, they continued at the margins to expand the summary judgment remedy through such devices as holding that the interpretation of written documents such as contracts and treaties raised issues of law that could be resolved on a summary judgment motion rather than issues of fact that could not be so resolved.[31]

Ultimately New York's judges wrought no major change in the law of summary judgment, however, when they continued during the 1960s and 1970s to grant the remedy only in cases where they found no genuine issue of material fact and otherwise to deny it. They thus remained committed to the principle, which the Appellate Division had first formulated in the 1920s, that "summary judgment is concerned with 'issue-finding, rather than issue-determination.' "[32]

In connection with the law of summary judgment and discovery, efficiency concerns did not come into conflict with concerns for social justice. Justice and efficiency did conflict, however, in connection with the right to jury trial. Thus, just as judges were beginning to become comfortable with allowing juries a redistributive function in the pursuit of justice, their growing concern for judicial efficiency increased their willingness to take cases away from juries or otherwise intervene in traditional, common-law jury processes. By the 1950s, "calendar congestion ha[d] reached such proportions that it ha[d] become a subject of concern not only to the bench and bar, but to the public generally who in the last analysis are the primary victims of court delay." It had become apparent that the "judicial system would totally collapse if every case were required to be tried to completion." Since "a jury trial consume[d] at least 25% over the time of a trial without a jury," courts found it appropriate routinely to inquire "as to the possibility of an agreement to waive the right of trial by jury." They had also come to rely on such devices as expert panels in medical malpractice cases and "'blockbuster' part[s]" in all types of cases "to facilitate settlements." In addition to these devices for circumventing juries, they condoned interventionist techniques for greater jury efficiency, such as the bifurcation of trials into separate liability and damage segments. Finally, federal judges adopted the view that, in litigation involving lengthy and "complex issues . . . beyond the normal comprehension of the jury," they could conclude that "no jury could be expected to render a rational verdict" and thus "that there was no adequate remedy at law and [that] the case should be tried in equity without a jury."[33]

EFFICIENCY AND WEALTH MAXIMIZATION

In the end, the judiciary's deemphasis of the power of juries to redistribute wealth in the pursuit of social justice demonstrated the growing power of the concept of efficiency. So too did changes in the law of fiduciary duty, which made that body of law more pragmatic and sensitive to the business and financial needs of both fiduciaries and beneficiaries and more tolerant of entrepreneurial activities designed to increase income or grow principal. Even more important were changes in other areas of law. A growing distrust of regulation and a consequent hesitancy to enforce regulatory decrees also meant greater tolerance of entrepreneurial activities designed to produce wealth. The Uniform Commercial Code's codification, which became effective in 1964, of pro-enterprise contract doctrines and the decline in enforcement of the equitable concept of unconscionability[34] had a similar effect, as did the demise during the 1970s of the doctrine of prima facie tort as a mechanism for the enforcement of business ethics. The restructuring of business along divisional rather than central managerial lines, together with the judiciary's willingness to assume additional burdens in resolving the contract disputes arising therewith, also freed business managers to strive for increased profits. Finally, changes in welfare law in the closing years of the century, designed to force welfare recipients to work, removed fiscal burdens from business and other taxpayers and redistributed wealth from the needy to the enterprising.

New York's legislators and judges rarely proclaimed openly their biases toward promoting enterprise and business profitability, but they moved doctrine in those directions with some frequency. Of course, countervailing pressures sometimes retarded the law's move toward the political right. Feminist claims for equality, especially in employment contexts, often created compelling pressures toward the restriction of entrepreneurial freedom, as did at least some claims by African Americans for racial equality. But over the closing decades of the century, equality became a weaker countervailing force. In particular, the ideal of equality ceased to be an argument, as it had been during the middle of the century, for protecting the weak and the poor or promoting their upward social mobility.

Concerns for human dignity, which had played a major role in legal development during the World War II era, also began by the century's end to have more ambiguous effects on doctrine. With welfare reform, the return of capital punishment, and an apparent increase in police brutality, the dignity of the poor, the downtrodden, and the outcast seems to be losing significance to mainstream America. In contrast, the ideal of liberty and individual freedom has become rampantly triumphant. Except for the relatively occasional instances in which statutory and judge-made law has protected women from sexual misconduct or violence at the hands of men, everyone has been made free by the law to pursue their happiness or their other self-chosen ends. Liberty and happiness, however, are not attainable by all; only those who possess the wealth or other resources needed to pursue happiness are free to do so. The ideals of liberty and individual freedom have been deployed at the end of the century to promote enterprise and wealth maximization, not to provide opportunity to those who otherwise lack it.

In short, most of the policy values that had underlain legalist reform in mid-twentieth century New York—equality, human dignity, liberty, and enterprise and efficiency—still remained in place at the century's end, albeit in a different mix. The main difference was that the values were no longer deployed to promote progressive ends like opportunity for the downtrodden, assimilation into the mainstream, and redistribution of wealth. The legalist reformation still endured, however, to make life unimaginably better for the descendants of those who had created it than the creators themselves had ever dared to dream.

A Golden Anniversary

In October 1995, the United Nations marked the fiftieth anniversary of its birth with a gala celebration at its New York City headquarters. More than 140 heads of state or heads of government observed the event. Among those who attended were the presidents of the United States, Russia, and China, the prime ministers of Great Britain, India, and Israel, the secretary of state of the Vatican, and some particularly notable individuals — namely, Yasir Arafat, Fidel Castro, and Nelson Mandela.[1]

From the outset a half-century earlier, New York had been a contender to be the site of the United Nations. The government of Switzerland was not willing to permit the Security Council to impose military sanctions if it sat on Swiss territory, and for this and other reasons, the UN could not simply move into the former League of Nations buildings in Geneva. Nor was any other site in Europe appropriate. Meanwhile, the United States was eager to become the UN's home, and its role as leader of the World War II victory and its economic capacity as the major provider of the UN's funds induced the General Assembly to accept the American offer. But Boston, Philadelphia, and San Francisco competed with New York to be the world's capital, until a telephone call to Nelson Rockefeller, the future governor of New York, led to discussions in the Rockefeller family and ultimately to John D. Rockefeller Jr.'s donation of an $8.5 million tract of slum land along the East River for a headquarters site.[2]

New York's selection was entirely appropriate. The legalist reformation, then in its youthful exuberance, was building a consensus in support of the ideals of liberty, equality, and dignity for which Americans, under the banner of the United Nations, had fought World War II. Among the former conservatives who had accepted the consensus was the Rockefeller family — in particular, Nelson A. Rockefeller, who, although he retained the Republican Party affiliation of his maternal grandfather, Senate majority leader Nelson Aldrich, had joined the Roosevelt administration during the war and become a liberal Democrat in all but name.[3] It also was appropriate, though ironic, that a slum neighborhood, whose residents were departing in large numbers for a freer, more equal, and more dignified life in the suburbs, would become the site of an organization devoted to "a new approach to human liberty and freedom born of the experience of the Second World War and the years immediately preceding it."[4]

Over the course of the next several decades, the legalist reformation and the United Nations matured together. This book has shown how the ideals of liberty, equality, and dignity inspired profound changes in the law of New York, which, in turn, brought real liberty, equality, and dignity to increasing numbers of New Yorkers. Meanwhile, in the aftermath of World War II, the legalist reformation also became an inspiration for other peoples of the world.

The reformation's influence began to spread when, not surprisingly, Americans imposed it on the defeated Axis powers. Thus General Douglas MacArthur, the Supreme Allied Commander in Japan, sought to "build the structure of representative government. Modernize the constitution. Hold free elections. Enfranchise the women. Release the political prisoners. Liberate the farmers. Establish a free labor movement. Encourage a free economy. Abolish police oppression. Develop a free and responsible press. Liberalize education. Decentralize the political power. Separate church from state." Similarly, the Potsdam Declaration on Germany announced plans to reform the German legal system "in accordance with the principles of democracy, of justice under law, and of equal rights for all citizens without distinction of race, nationality, or religion."[5] Except for the style, words such as these on Japan and Germany could easily have come from the pens of Harlan Fiske Stone, Robert F. Wagner, or Franklin D. Roosevelt.

Especially after its role in the successful rebuilding of Japan and the Federal Republic of Germany, the legalist reformation became attractive to many citizens of the world in its own right. Europeans, in particular, often choose to speak in legalist reform language. During the 1991 battle against the Soviet state on the streets of Moscow, for example, the vice president of Russia called on "the young people . . . [to] make the right choice in favour of freedom," while the prime minister spoke out "in defence of the human rights" and the Presidium of the Moscow Soviet spoke of "the right to live as befits human beings." Giovanni Sartori, the Italian theorist, similarly has spoken of "the theory and practice of the juridical defense, through the constitutional state, . . . of individual liberty," while the former British prime minister Margaret Thatcher lectured at the 1996 Conference of Prague about shared Western values, including a "commitment to human rights, the rule of law, representative democracy, limited government, private property and tolerance." Eastern Europeans likewise have persisted in their demands for human rights, and the United States has continued pursuing a "mission . . . to organize the world along lines that would mirror American values and aspirations."[6]

As the reform ideology spread around the world, the United Nations, stymied by the Cold War and the Security Council veto, devoted its energies less to maintaining international peace and security and more to protecting individuals from the ravages of tyranny, poverty, and dependency. Like New York City, the United Nations became a vehicle to help people "of all colors, skins, faiths and tongues to live together in community."[7] The UN, in short, adopted the legalist reformation as its reigning ideology.

In his remarks at the UN birthday party, Secretary General Boutros Boutros-Ghali emphasized this "symbiotic relationship between the United Nations and New York City":

> "Let me put it more directly," he said. "The U.N. and New York have had a love affair."
>
> "Why?" he said. "We have so much in common. The people of New York represent as many nationalities as are represented in the United Nations."[8]

Boutros-Ghali might have added that New York and the United Nations have something else in common: not only do they face a common problem of getting people of different races, religions, backgrounds, and nationalities to live together, but they also agree on a common solution—that all people are obligated to recognize each others' equality, liberty, and dignity and thereby live together in tranquillity and peace.

Speakers at the UN's fiftieth birthday celebration kept reiterating this theme. President Clinton, for one, noted that "Americans should not forget that our values" are "served by working with the U.N." and especially by the faith on which the UN is based "that different people can work together for tolerance, decency, and peace." Yasir Arafat agreed that the job of the United Nations is to "ensure justice and equality among all," while the prime minister of Norway spoke of the need to "build the civilized world on law and contracts." A speech to the General Assembly by Franjo Tudjman, the president of Croatia, sounded remarkably like that of Robert F. Wagner to the 1938 New York Constitutional Convention. Tudjman spoke of the need for

> a creative vision of tomorrow's world—no longer a world of the large and small, the powerful and weak.
>
> The boundaries of our freedoms are set by the boundaries of the freedom of others. The affirmation of human dignity and the universal rights of the individual upheld by the charter of the United Nations can be achieved only through the respect for different ethnic, cultural and political identities[,] . . . through respect for a law governed state[,] . . . [and] through

respect for civilization's differences, for creative blending and dialogue on an equal footing.

In promoting the export of the legalist reformation to the world at large, President Clinton perhaps made the ideology clearest when he asserted a few years later that "successful modern states make a virtue, not a blood feud, out of ethnic and religious diversity" and that opposing "organized ethnic hatred is a moral imperative."[9]

With the 1991 collapse of the Soviet Union and the demise of Marxist-Leninism as a paradigm for revolutionary socioeconomic change that would redistribute wealth from the rich to the poor, President Clinton was accurate in seeing the ideals of the legalist reformation, on the one hand, and organized ethnic hatred, on the other, as the new axis of world conflict. Especially after Marxism's demise, many people around the world look upon the liberty, equality, dignity, and entrepreneurial opportunity that the legalist reformation has given Americans as their only hope for a brighter future. "Throughout the world America's influence has been profound, particularly upon the young," who "equate exports of American culture . . . with the very concept of modernization." Indeed, "for the young," America and "the West [are] the dream itself."[10]

Thus, however much Americans had begun to doubt its worth and question its meaning, the legalist reform ideology of liberty, equality, dignity, and entrepreneurial opportunity became the hope of the world as the twentieth century drew to a close. But even after the demise of Marxism, it is not the only available ideology. There remains an earlier progressive[11] "notion that every nationality and ethnic group should have its own independent territory." But "this . . . principle," which is a hybrid of Populist ideas of local self-rule and Nazi and similar fascist ideas, is, according to another author, "flawed . . . in principle. . . . Its central premise is that peoples of different faiths and ethnicities cannot live together in harmony." This earlier progressivism is "based on tribal loyalties, suppression of cultural differences, and often intolerance. It encourages prejudice and is prone to violence. . . . It invites majorities to be intransigent, furnishes pretexts for repression, and leads to the atomization of human societies."[12]

As we have seen, this progressive principle of self-determination was never available as a political option in mid-twentieth century New York City, where people of different religions and ethnicities were so intermixed that they had no choice but to create a society in which they could live together in harmony. This book has shown how New Yorkers after 1920 therefore moved beyond early progressivism toward a somewhat different legalist reform ideology. Although neither hostile to nor necessarily inconsistent with democracy, legalist reform emphasizes the professional elaboration of organic legal rules enabling diverse people to live together in liberty, justice, and self-fulfillment as well as democratic self-determination.

Whatever its ambiguities and imperfections, the legalist reformation epitomizes the path which New Yorkers blazed and to which they have adhered during the past six decades. With the demise of Marxism, it is the path that America and the world must follow in order to avoid further Bosnias, Chechnias, Kosovos, Rwandas, and even worse catastrophes in the new millennium.

NOTES

INTRODUCTION

1. Theodore H. White, *The Making of the President, 1968* (New York: Atheneum, 1969), 214.

2. My research covered 179 N.Y.S. through 148 N.Y.S.2d, together with the Court of Appeals cases appended thereto, and 149 N.Y.S.2d through 435 N.Y.S.2d, in which Court of Appeals cases are included; and cases with a New York venue from 261 F. to 671 F.2d and from 1 F. Supp. to 540 F. Supp.

3. Nor does it study doctrine for the purpose of understanding how today's rules came into existence. Cf. Morton J. Horwitz, "The Conservative Tradition in the Writing of American Legal History," *American Journal of Legal History* 17 (1973): 275, although a reader interested in understanding the roots of contemporary law will find much useful material in the pages that follow.

4. As I examine the relationship between law and society, however, I will not inquire systematically whether law is either a creature of society or constitutive of society, or both; such an inquiry would be foolhardy in a book that ranges as broadly over time and doctrine as this one does. My understanding of the relationship between law and society, which is more mundane, is grounded in a basic law professor's insight—that every case simultaneously involves a unique quarrel between two or more litigants, a narrow dispute over the substance of legal doctrine, and a broad contest about social justice and policy. It is always appropriate to move among these various levels of analysis, and it is often illuminating.

5. See Paula Baker, *The Moral Frameworks of Public Life: Gender, Politics, and the State in Rural New York, 1870–1930* (New York: Oxford University Press, 1991), 20–23, 43–45, 50–55, 90–118; Whitney R. Cross, *The Burned-over District: The Social and Intellectual History of Enthusiastic Religion in Western New York, 1800–1850* (New York: Harper & Row, 1965), 116–21; Robert F. Wesser, *A Response to Progressivism: The Democratic Party and New York Politics, 1902–1918* (New York: New York University Press, 1986), 7–8.

6. *Time,* April 17, 1933, p. 17, cols. 1–2. See generally Mark S. Weiner, "Race, Citizenship and Culture in American Law: Ethno-Juridical Discourse from *Crow Dog* to *Brown v. Board of Education*" (Ph.D dissertation, Yale University, 1998).

7. See David M. Ellis, James A. Frost, Harold C. Syrett, and Harry J. Carman, *A History of New York State* (Ithaca: Cornell University Press, 1967), 461, 471–72. For analogous data, see also Harold F. Gosness, *Boss Platt and His New York Machine: A Study of the Political Leadership of Thomas C. Platt, Theodore Roosevelt, and Others* (New York: Russell & Russell, 1924), 1–2; Wesser, *Response to Progressivism,* 3.

8. Of course, demographic patterns in which majorities dwelled in close proximity with minorities had long prevailed in America. Whites and blacks had always lived near each other in the South, as had native New Englanders and Irish immigrants since the 1830s in Boston. In each instance, though, only two distinct groups rather than a plurality of groups had interacted. It is equally true that some European empires, in particular Austria-Hungary, contained subjects of diverse linguistic groups, such as Germans, Hungarians, Czechs, Slovaks, Poles, Serbs, Croats, and Italians. But diverse groups like these typically lived in their own defined geographic region and had only limited interaction with each other.

9. Holzer v. Deutsche Reichsbsahn-Gesellschaft, 277 N.Y. 474 (1938).

10. See Allan Nevins, *Herbert H. Lehman and His Era* (New York: Scribner, 1963), 13–14, 19–23, 48–51; Matthew Josephson and Hannah Josephson, *Al Smith: Hero of the Cities* (Boston: Houghton Mifflin, 1969), 418–19, 452–54; Isaac Deutscher, *The Prophet Armed: Trotsky, 1879–1921* (New York: Oxford University Press, 1954), 8–9.

11. See Nevins, *Herbert H. Lehman,* 30–31, 68–76; Kenneth S. Davis, *FDR: The New York Years, 1928–1933* (New York: Random House, 1979), 201; Frank Friedel, *Franklin D. Roosevelt: The Triumph* (Boston: Little, Brown, 1956), 158–59, 322; Josephson and Josephson, *Al Smith,* 355–58, 371–72; Warren Moscow, *Politics in the Empire State* (New York: Knopf, 1948), 19; Arthur M. Schlesinger Jr., *The Crisis of the Old Order, 1919–1933* (Boston: Houghton Mifflin, 1957), 280.

12. See Davis, *FDR,* 222–23, 252–56, 265; Friedel, *Franklin D. Roosevelt,* 35–37, 143–44; Albert U. Romasco, *The Politics of Recovery: Roosevelt's New Deal* (New York: Oxford University Press, 1983), 5–6; Arthur M. Schlesinger Jr., *The Crisis of the Old Order, 1919–1933* (Boston: Houghton Mifflin, 1957), 420–28; Josephson and Josephson, *Al Smith,* 171–76, 210–16; Richard O'Connor, *The First Hurrah: A Biography of Alfred E. Smith* (New York: Putnam, 1970), 35–49; Friedel, *Franklin D. Roosevelt,* 371; Schlesinger, *Crisis of the Old Order,* 290–91; Robert P. Ingalls, *Herbert H. Lehman and New York's Little New Deal* (New York: New York University Press, 1975), 8–9, 17–18; Moscow, *Politics in the Empire State,* 20–23. On support for Smith, Roosevelt, and Lehman, see O'Connor, *First Hurrah,* 223–25; Josephson and Josephson, *Al Smith,* 395–97; Davis, *FDR,* 295; Arthur M. Schlesinger Jr., *The Coming of the New Deal* (Boston: Houghton Mifflin, 1959), 588; Ingalls, *Herbert H. Lehman,* 22–24, 254–55; Nevins, *Herbert H. Lehman,* 404–7. On hatred of Smith and Roosevelt, see O'Connor, *First Hurrah,* 207–15; Josephson and Josephson, *Al Smith,* 380–89; Davis, *FDR,* 295; Schlesinger, *Crisis of the Old Order,* 8, 434–35; Schlesinger, *Coming of the New Deal,* 476–88.

13. On the quest of late nineteenth-century intellectual elites for an alternative to democratic majoritarianism and evangelical Protestantism, see William E. Nelson, *The Roots of American Bureaucracy, 1830–1900* (Cambridge, Mass.: Harvard University Press, 1982), 82–112.

14. The most convenient recent summaries of the vast historical literature on the New Deal and its aftermath are contained in David M. Kennedy, *Freedom from Fear: The American People in Depression and War, 1929–1945* (New York: Oxford University Press, 1999), 859–71, and James T. Patterson, *Grand Expectations: The United States, 1945–1974* (New York: Oxford University Press, 1996), 791–802. Virtually all the literature sees the years 1937–38 as a watershed. One view is that those years marked the end of New Deal reform; see, e.g., Alan Brinkley, *The End of Reform: New Deal Liberalism in Recession and War* (New York: Knopf, 1995); Kennedy, *Freedom from Fear,* 363; Michael E. Parrish, *Anxious Decades: America in Prosperity and Depression, 1920–1941* (New York: Norton, 1992), 382–85. Another view is that the years marked a transformation of the reform impulse; see, e.g., Barry D. Karl, *The Uneasy State: The United States from 1915 to 1945* (Chicago: University of Chicago Press, 1983), 155–81. A particularly interesting article by Thomas Ferguson, "Industrial Conflict and the Coming of the New Deal: The Triumph of Multinational Liberalism in America," in *The Rise and Fall of the New Deal Order, 1930–1980,* ed. Steve Fraser and Gary Gerstle (Princeton: Princeton University Press, 1989), 3–31, suggests that the years 1936–38 witnessed a realignment of the parties, when leaders of capital-intensive industries like oil abandoned the Republican Party because of its protectionism and joined the Democrats in support of their internationalism. The most important work in legal theory has been done in two books by Bruce Ackerman, *We the People: Foundations* (Cambridge, Mass.: Harvard University Press, 1991), and *We the People: Transformations* (Cambridge, Mass.: Harvard University Press, 1998), which argue that 1937 saw a metamorphosis in the Supreme Court's jurisprudence of constitutional moment in response to popular pressures and pressures from the other branches of government. Barry Cushman, *Rethinking the New Deal Court: The Structure of a Constitutional Revolution* (New York: Oxford University Press, 1998), maintains, in contrast, that

the change in the Supreme Court's jurisprudence occurred gradually over a twenty-year period from the early 1920s into the 1940s.

This book agrees with scholars who find 1937–38 to be transformative years marking a new direction rather than the end of reform. It urges, however, that the transformation occurred more at a deep cultural level than at the level of high politics and Supreme Court case law. Cf. Colin Gordon, "Rethinking the New Deal," *Columbia Law Review* 98 (1998): 2029–53. The book also agrees with the many historians who have found 1968 to be another watershed year—the year that marked the dissolution of the New Deal coalition. See, e.g., Allen J. Matusow, *The Unraveling of America: A History of Liberalism in the 1960s* (New York: Harper & Row, 1984), 395–440; Patterson, *Grand Expectations,* 708–9. But see Robert M. Collins, "Growth Liberalism in the Sixties," in *The Sixties: From Memory to History,* ed. David Farber (Chapel Hill: University of North Carolina Press, 1994), 11–44, which suggests that the liberal impetus endured into the 1970s.

CHAPTER ONE

1. See Arch C. Gerlach, ed., *The National Atlas of the United States of America* (Washington, D.C.: U.S. Department of the Interior Geological Survey, 1970), 241; Allon Schoener, ed., *Portal to America: The Lower East Side, 1870–1925* (New York: Holt, Rinehart, 1967), 210–11. See generally David C. Hammack, *Power and Society: Greater New York at the Turn of the Century* (New York: Columbia University Press, 1987), 60–65.

2. Jacob A. Riis, *How the Other Half Lives: Studies among the Tenements of New York* (New York: Dover, 1971), 27, 131, 145. This 1971 edition was an unabridged republication of the text of the 1901 edition of the work originally published by Charles Scribner's Sons, New York, in 1890.

3. Jeff Kisseloff, ed., *You Must Remember This: An Oral History of Manhattan from the 1890s to World War II* (New York: Harcourt, Brace, 1989), 6, 54 (comments of Larry Schneider, who was born in 1922, about his father), 23 (comments of Samuel Pogensky, born in 1895), 29 (comments of Blanche Lasky, born in 1923).

4. Ibid., 19 (comments of Robert Leslie, born in 1885), 40 (comments of Rose Halpern, born in 1917), 41 (comments of Selma Hannish, born in 1920), 72 (comments of Larry Schneider).

5. Kate Simon, *Fifth Avenue: A Very Social History* (New York: Harcourt, Brace, 1978), 187; Kisseloff, ed., *You Must Remember,* 139–40, 95. For the late nineteenth-century origins of "Chateaux Society," see Edwin G. Burrows and Mike Wallace, *Gotham: A History of New York City to 1898* (New York: Oxford University Press, 1999), 1071–80.

6. Simon, *Fifth Avenue,* 85.

7. Riis, *How the Other Half Lives,* 229; Stephen Fox, *The Mirror Makers: A History of American Advertising and Its Creators* (New York: William Morrow, 1984), 100; Town of Manlius v. Town of Pompey, 250 N.Y.S. 690, 692 (Sup. Ct. 1930).

8. Charles N. Fay, *Business in Politics: Suggestions for Leaders in American Business* (Cambridge, Mass.: Riverside Press, 1926) (emphasis in original), 103, 164; Elbert Hubbard, *A Message to Garcia and Thirteen Other Things* (East Aurora, N.Y.: Roycrofters, 1901), quoted in Peter Baida, *Poor Richard's Legacy: American Business Values from Benjamin Franklin to Donald Trump* (New York: William Morrow, 1990), 241; James W. Prothro, *The Dollar Decade: Business Ideas in the 1920's* (Baton Rouge: Louisiana State University Press, 1954), 210.

9. Richard M. Huber, *The American Idea of Success* (New York: McGraw-Hill, 1971), 99; Baida, *Poor Richard's Legacy,* 241; Hubbard, *Message to Garcia,* quoted in Baida, *Poor Richard's Legacy,* 241; Julius H. Barnes, *The Genius of American Business* (Garden City, N.Y.: Doubleday, 1924) (emphasis in original), 6–7. See generally Prothro, *Dollar Decade,* 77–107.

10. Fox, *Mirror Makers,* 101; Howard M. Sachar, *The Course of Modern Jewish History* (Cleveland: World, 1958), 339, 341; Baida, *Poor Richard's Legacy,* 205. See generally ibid., 203–6. On the late nineteenth-century origins of prejudice against immigrants, especially Jews and Italian Catholics, see Burrows and Wallace, *Gotham,* 1087–88, 1114–26.

11. See Jewish Mental Health Soc. v. Village of Hastings, 268 N.Y. 458 (1935), *appeal dism., 297* U.S. 592 (1936); Marburg v. Cole, 286 N.Y. 202 (1941). On the existence of anti-Semitism, see Richard Polenberg, *One Nation Divisible: Class, Race, and Ethnicity in the United States* (New York: Penguin, 1980), 41–42. See also Allan Nevins, *Herbert H. Lehman and His Era* (New York: Scribner, 1963), 199–200.

12. Oscar Handlin, "Race and Nationality in American Life," quoted in Melvin Steinfeld, ed., *Cracks in the Melting Pot: Racism and Discrimination in American History,* 2d ed. (New York: Glencoe Press, 1973), 186; David M. Chalmers, *Hooded Americanism: The First Century of the Ku Klux Klan* (Garden City, N.Y.: Doubleday, 1965), 260. On the connection of Jews to socialist movements, see also Nathan Glazer and Daniel Patrick Moynihan, *Beyond the Melting Pot: The Negroes, Puerto Ricans, Jews, Italians, and Irish of New York* (Cambridge, Mass.: MIT Press, 1963), 169.

13. "Klan Urges Pastors to War on Catholics," *New York Times,* July 1, 1923, p. 14, cols. 6–7; "Ku Klux Klan Organized," *Nassau Daily Review,* Sept. 8, 1922, p. 1, col. 8; "Long Island Sees Biggest Klan Crowd," *New York Times,* June 22, 1923, p. 1, col. 2. See also Robert A. Caro, *The Power Broker: Robert Moses and the Fall of New York* (New York: Knopf, 1974), 148; Chalmers, *Hooded Americanism,* 256; Edward J. Smits, *Nassau, Suburbia, U.S.A.: The First Seventy-Five Years of Nassau County, New York, 1899 to 1974* (Garden City, N.Y.: Doubleday, 1974), 147; Laura Durkin, "Illuminating Darker Side of LI's Past," *Newsday,* Nov. 7, 1982 (on file at Long Island Studies Institute, Hofstra University, Hempstead, N.Y.); Patricia M. Roniger, "The Women's Klan of L.I., Sisters of the Klansmen," *Long Island Heritage* 5 (May 1983) (on file at Long Island Studies Institute, Hofstra University, Hempstead, N.Y.).

14. Transcript of Interview Tapes of Miss Katherine Reif for the Merrick Historical Society (1976), 9 (on file at Merrick Public Library, Merrick, N.Y.); Caro, *Power Broker,* 148; "Klan on Long Island," *New York Times,* Oct. 28, 1923, sec. 2, p. 1, col. 5; "Pastor Defends Klan," *New York Times,* Oct. 15, 1923, p. 17, col. 6. Some Protestant pastors may have seen it in the best interest of the church not to antagonize the Klan. Several Protestant churches in Nassau County received silk American flags and purses of gold from local Klans. See "K.K.K. Gives Church Flags and Purse," *Nassau Daily Review,* Mar. 9, 1925 (on file at Long Island Studies Institute, Hofstra University, Hempstead, N.Y.); "Crowd Sees Klan Give Gold Purse and Flag," *Nassau Daily Review,* Jan. 12, 1925 (on file at Long Island Studies Institute, Hofstra University, Hempstead, N.Y.).

15. Transcript of Interview of Reif, 9; "Klan Celebration Scares Residents of Valley Stream," *Nassau Daily Review,* Feb. 23, 1928 (on file at Long Island Studies Institute, Hofstra University, Hempstead, N.Y.); "Fiery Klan Crosses Light Long Island," *New York Times,* Oct. 14, 1923, p. 14, cols. 4–5; "3 Flaming Crosses Fired by the Ku Klux to Frighten Negroes in Long Island Towns," *New York Times,* Feb. 13, 1923, p. 1, cols. 5–6; William Peirce Randel, *The Ku Klux Klan: A Century of Infamy* (Philadelphia: Chilton Books, 1965), 224. See also "Klansman Parade on Merrick Road," *New York Times,* July 12, 1925, sec. 1, p. 4, cols. 1–5; "10,000 Klansmen Burn Cross at Oceanside," *New York Times,* July 26, 1925, sec. 2, p. 16, col. 5; "Long Island Klan Initiates 1,000 at Holiday Fete," *New York Herald Tribune,* July 5, 1927 (on file at Long Island Studies Institute, Hofstra University, Hempstead, N.Y.); Val Duncan, "The Good Old, Bad Old Days on LI: The Arrival of the Hate Groups," *Newsday,* May 6, 1965 (on file at Long Island Studies Institute, Hofstra University, Hempstead, N.Y.).

16. Duncan, "Good Old, Bad Old Days"; "Menaced by Klan, Druggist to Move," *New York Times,* Sept. 5, 1924, p. 36, col. 2; Heidi Fried, "Early Jewish Settlement in Nassau County: The Communities, the People, the Synagogues," 3 (on file at Long Island Studies Institute, Hofstra University, Hempstead, N.Y.).

17. See Chalmers, *Hooded Americanism,* 255; People ex rel. Bryant v. Sheriff of Erie County, 206 N.Y.S. 533 (Sup. Ct. 1924), *aff'd sub nom.* People ex rel. Bryant v. Zimmerman, 210 N.Y.S. 269 (App. Div. 1925), *aff'd,* 150 N.E. 497 (1926), *aff'd,* 278 U.S. 63 (1928).

18. "Klan Meets at Freeport," *New York Times,* Sept. 3, 1933, sec. 2, p. 4, col. 3; Duncan, "Good Old, Bad Old Days"; Lem Coley, "Bigotry on L.I. Then and Now . . . ," *New York Times,* Dec. 2, 1979, sec. 21, p. 26, cols. 2–6.

19. See David M. Ellis, James A. Frost, Harold C. Syrett, and Henry J. Carman, *A History of New York State* (Ithaca: Cornell University Press, 1967), 380–92.

20. Vivien Hart, *Bound by Our Constitution: Women, Workers, and the Minimum Wage* (Princeton: Princeton University Press, 1994), 80–83; John E. Edgerton, "Annual Address of John E. Edgerton, President of the National Association of Manufactureres, 1930," *Proceedings of the Annual Convention of the National Association of Manufacturers of the United States of America,* 15.

21. See "Justice Cardozo, A Noted Liberal: He Identified Himself More Precisely as a 'Judicial Evolutionist,' " *New York Times,* July 10, 1938, p. 30, cols. 1–5; "In Memoriam—John W. Hogan," 242 N.Y. 607 (1926); Francis Bergan, *The History of the New York Court of Appeals, 1847–1932* (New York: Columbia University Press, 1985), 234; "Ex-Judge Hogan Dies in Boston," *New York Times,* Jan. 31, 1926, sec. 2, p. 8, cols. 5. For the political affiliation, religion, and geographic locus of each of the five Republicans, see "W. S. Andrews Dies in Fall from Bed: Retired Appellate Judge, Distinguished for Rulings, Found Dead in Syracuse Home," *New York Times,* Aug. 6, 1936, p. 20, col. 1 (Andrews); "F. E. Crane, 78, Dies: Led State Jurists," *New York Times,* Nov. 22, 1947, p. 15, col. 1 (Crane); *Who Was Who in America* (Chicago: Marquis–Who's Who, 1950), 2:255 (Hiscock); "C. B. M'Laughlin, Ex-Jurist, Dead: Former Associate Judge of the Court of Appeals Succumbs in 74th Year," *New York Times,* May 13, 1929, p. 23, col. 3 (M'Laughlin); *Who Was Who in America* (Chicago: Marquis-Who's Who, Inc., 1943), 1:988 (Pound). The list of the seven judges who served on the court throughout 1920 and 1921 is derived from the page following the title page in the *New York Reports,* vols. 227 and 232, which were respectively the first volume for 1920 and the final volume for 1921.

22. Quoted in Matthew Josephson and Hannah Josephson, *Al Smith: Hero of the Cities* (Boston: Houghton Mifflin, 1969), 471.

23. See Glazer and Moynihan, *Beyond the Melting Pot,* 169; Josephson and Josephson, *Al Smith,* 399.

24. Franklin D. Roosevelt, National Radio Address, April 7, 1932, quoted in Frank Freidel, *Franklin D. Roosevelt: The Triumph* (Boston: Little, Brown, 1956), 261; Franklin D. Roosevelt, Message to the Legislature, August 28, 1931, quoted ibid., 217; Herbert H. Lehman, Speech at St. Bonaventure College (1934), quoted in Nevins, *Herbert H. Lehman,* 155; George Meany, "Foreword," in Robert P. Ingalls, *Herbert H. Lehman and New York's Little New Deal* (New York: New York University Press, 1975), vii.

25. Clinton Rossiter, *Conservatism in America* (New York: Knopf, 1956), 12, 15; Franklin D. Roosevelt, Campaign Address, Chicago, Ill., October 14, 1936, in B. D. Zevin, ed., *Nothing to Fear: The Selected Addresses of Franklin Delano Roosevelt, 1932–1945* (Boston: Houghton Mifflin, 1946), 60, 61; Franklin D. Roosevelt, Second Inaugural Address, January 20, 1937, ibid., 87, 92; Franklin D. Roosevelt, Radio Address on Brotherhood Day, February 23, 1936, ibid., 58, 59; Roosevelt, Campaign Address, October 14, 1936, ibid., 64; Franklin D. Roosevelt, First Inaugural Address, ibid., 12, 14; Franklin D. Roosevelt, Fireside Chat Reviewing the Achievements of the Seventy-Third Congress, June 38, 1934, ibid., 34, 38; Roosevelt, Campaign Address, October 14, 1936, ibid., 63, 69.

26. Franklin D. Roosevelt, Fireside Chat on the Plan for the Reorganization of the Judiciary, March 9, 1937, in Zevin, *Nothing to Fear,* 92, 96; Roosevelt, Campaign Address, October 14, 1936, ibid., 63, quoting Theodore Roosevelt; Franklin D. Roosevelt, Fireside Chat on the Plan for the Reorganization of the Judiciary, ibid., 92, 94.

27. "The Difference between the Republican and Democratic Parties in New York State," in

Alfred E. Smith, *Progressive Democracy: Addresses and State Papers of Alfred E. Smith* (New York: Harcourt, Brace, 1928), 43, 51; Richard O'Connor, *The First Hurrah: A Biography of Alfred E. Smith* (New York: Putnam, 1970), 168; Josephson and Josephson, *Al Smith,* 214, 329–31; O'Connor, *First Hurrah,* 160; Freidel, *Franklin D. Roosevelt,* 41–46, 100–119, 217–27; Ingalls, *Herbert H. Lehman* 249–55; Nevins, *Herbert H. Lehman,* 141–42, 167–68.

28. See *Who Was Who in America* (Chicago: Marquis, 1950), 2:318. On the family relationship, see Nevins, *Herbert H. Lehman,* 3–4, 15–18. The percentages for each judge's agreement with Cardozo were obtained by tabulating the votes in all nonunanimous cases in which Cardozo voted during the years he served as chief justice.

29. See *Who Was Who in America,* 2:293; "Will Advise on Men for Appeals Court: Bar Association's Committee to Confer with Heads of Big Political Parties Named," *New York Times,* July 7, 1926, p. 27, col. 1.

30. See "Judge J. F. O'Brien Dies at Home Here," *New York Times,* December 29, 1939, p. 19, col. 1; Andrew L. Kaufman, *Cardozo* (Cambridge, Mass.: Harvard University Press, 1998), 130.

31. Quoted in Richard Polenberg, *The World of Benjamin Cardozo: Personal Values and the Judicial Process* (Cambridge, Mass.: Harvard University Press, 1997), 2. Arguably, Cardozo's thought to some extent overlapped the earlier thinking of Roscoe Pound. See N. E. H. Hull, *Roscoe Pound and Karl Llewellyn: Searching for an American Jurisprudence* (Chicago: University of Chicago Press, 1997), 90 n. 47, 126. Careful analysis of the degree of overlap is beyond the scope of this book, but even assuming that their thinking was identical, Cardozo added two elements to what Pound had begun. First, Cardozo was a judge who put his ideas into practice and tested them and articulated them in the context of real-world judging. Second, Cardozo in the 1920s persuaded a majority of his court—one of the most important in the nation—to follow his approach.

32. Benjamin N. Cardozo, *The Nature of the Judicial Process* (New Haven: Yale University Press, 1921), 20, 112, 149; Benjamin N. Cardozo, *The Growth of the Law* (New Haven: Yale University Press, 1924), 4–6; Benjamin N. Cardozo to Learned Hand, July 31, 1936, in Learned Hand Manuscripts, Harvard Law Library, Cambridge, Mass.; Cardozo, *Growth of the Law,* 6.

33. Cardozo, *Nature of the Judicial Process,* 159, 136; Sternliev v. Normandie National Securities Corp., 263 N.Y. 245, 251 (1934); Brown v. Rosenbaum, 23 N.Y.S.2d 161, 171–72 (Sup. Ct. 1940), *rev'd on other grounds,* 28 N.Y.S.2d 345 (App. Div. 1941), *aff'd,* 287 N.Y. 510, *cert. denied,* 316 U.S. 689 (1942). The classic work on early nineteenth-century instrumentalism is Morton J. Horwitz, *The Transformation of American Law, 1780–1860* (Cambridge, Mass.: Harvard University Press, 1977), 1–30.

34. See Cardozo, *Growth of the Law,* 6–11.

35. For an interpretation of the jurisprudence of the 1870s and 1880s, see William E. Nelson, *The Roots of American Bureaucracy, 1830–1900* (Cambridge, Mass.: Harvard University Press, 1982), 101, 141–42. Cardozo never rejected Holmes and, in fact, acknowledged his indebtedness to him. See Kaufman, *Cardozo,* 200–203. In my view, however, Cardozo differed both from the Holmes of Oliver Wendell Holmes Jr., *The Common Law* (Boston: Little Brown, 1881), who was committed to constructing categories through historical analysis, and from the Holmes of "The Path of the Law," *Harvard Law Review* 10 (1897): 457, who argued that judges should "weigh . . . considerations of social advantage" (ibid., 467). Cardozo, as will be explained below, did not think that judges should weigh competing social values; he thought they should decide cases in order to advance the cause of social justice, which he believed was readily apparent.

36. Cardozo, *Growth of the Law,* 61–63, 65, 78–79; Cardozo, *Nature of the Judicial Process,* 136–37.

37. Cardozo, *Growth of the Law,* 94–95; Cardozo, *Nature of the Judicial Process,* 138; Cardozo, *Growth of the Law,* 240.

38. Cardozo thereby rejected the skepticism and robust positivism of the later Holmes. On Holmes's skepticism and positivism, see G. Edward White, *Justice Oliver Wendell Holmes: Law and the Inner Self* (New York: Oxford University Press, 1993), 218–24, 253–55, 378–80, 386–401, 481–82,

487. This disagreement was obscured, however, probably even from Cardozo himself, by the many matters on which he and Holmes agreed. See Kaufman, *Cardozo,* 152–53, 384–85; Polenberg, *World of Benjamin Cardozo,* 173.

39. People v. Nixson, 248 N.Y. 182, 192 (1928); "Proceedings in the Court of Appeals in Reference to the Death of Honorable Irving Lehman, Chief Judge of the Court of Appeals," 294 N.Y. vii, viii (1945); Henry W. Edgerton, "A Liberal Judge: Cuthbert W. Pound," *Cornell Law Quarterly* 21 (1935): 7, 10, 12. For similar views, see Cardozo, *Nature of the Judicial Process,* 20, 25, 149.

40. In re Miller's Will, 257 N.Y. 349, 357–58 (1931); Madfes v. Beverly Development Corp., 251 N.Y. 12, 18 (1929); Application of Gilchrist, 224 N.Y.S. 210, 240 (Sup. Ct. 1927); Welinsky v. Hillman, 185 N.Y.S. 257 (Sup. Ct. 1920); Application of Gilchrist, *supra* at 240.

41. Edgerton, "Liberal Judge," 8.

42. Cardozo, *Growth of the Law,* 87; Cardozo, *Nature of the Judicial Process,* 12.

43. Cardozo, *Nature of the Judicial Process,* 25.

CHAPTER TWO

1. 231 N.Y. 465 (1921).

2. Ibid., 479–80 (emphasis added).

3. Ibid., 484–89 (emphasis added).

4. New York Steam Corp. v. City of New York, 276 N.Y.S. 99, 109 (Sup. Ct. 1934), *aff'd,* 278 N.Y.S. 539 (App. Div.), *aff'd,* 268 N.Y. 137 (1935).

5. See, e.g., People ex rel. Trustees of Masonic Hall and Asylum Fund v. Miller, 279 N.Y. 137 (1938).

6. Little Falls Fibre Co. v. Henry Ford & Son, Inc., 229 N.Y.S. 445, 449 (App. Div.). *aff'd,* 249 N.Y. 495 (1928), *aff'd,* 280 U.S. 369 (1930); Jefferson County v. Horbiger, 243 N.Y.S. 30 (App. Div. 1930); In re Inwood Hill Park, In Borough of Manhattan, City of New York, 220 N.Y.S. 298 (App. Div. 1927); New York Cent. R.R. v. People, 186 N.Y.S. 352, 353–54 (Sup. Ct. 1920), *aff'd,* 188 N.Y.S. 939 (App. Div. 1921), *aff'd,* 233 N.Y. 638 (1922); Thompson v. Orange & Rockland Electric Co., 254 N.Y. 366, 369 (1930); Golde Clothes Shop, Inc. v. Loew's Buffalo Theatres, Inc., 236 N.Y. 465, 470 (1923).

7. 268 U.S. 652 (1925).

8. People v. Gitlow, 187 N.Y.S. 783, 786, 788–90 (App. Div. 1921).

9. People v. Gitlow, 234 N.Y. 132, 149 (1922) (concurring opinion); People v. Gitlow, 187 N.Y.S. 783, 791–793 (App. Div. 1921); Thomas C. Mackey, " 'They Are Positively Dangerous Men': The Lost Court Documents of Benjamin Gitlow and James Larkin before the New York City Magistrates' Court, 1919," *New York University Law Review* 69 (1994): 421, 433.

10. Oscar Handlin, "Race and Nationality in American Life," quoted in Melvin Steinfeld, ed., *Cracks in the Melting Pot: Racism and Discrimination in American History,* 2d ed. (New York: Glencoe Press, 1973), 186; People v. Gitlow, 187 N.Y.S. 783, 791–93 (App. Div. 1921).

11. Gitlow v. New York, 268 U.S. 652, 669 (1925). For Justice Stone's two subsequent opinions, see United States v. Carolene Products Co., 304 U.S. 144 (1938); Minersville School Dist. v. Gobitis, 310 U.S. 586, 601 (1940).

12. Two earlier cases circumscribing radical speech during the World War I era were Fraina v. United States, 255 F. 28 (2d Cir. 1918), and Masses Pub. Co. v. Patten, 246 F. 24 (2d Cir. 1917), which reversed the now classic, speech-protective opinion of Learned Hand at the District Court level in Masses Pub. Co. v. Patten, 244 F. 535 (S.D.N.Y. 1917).

13. Lorich v. State, 184 N.Y.S. 818–19 (Ct. Claims 1920), *appeal dism.,* 187 N.Y.S. 942 (App. Div. 1921); People v. Makvirta, 231 N.Y.S. 279, 280–84 (App. Div. 1928).

14. People on Complaint of O'Connor v. Smith, 263 N.Y. 255, 257 (1934); People ex rel. Doyle v. Atwell, 232 N.Y. 96, 102 (1921), *appeal dism.*, 261 U.S. 590 (1923); City of Buffalo v. Till, 182 N.Y.S. 418, 424 (App. Div. 1920); People v. Kopezak, 274 N.Y.S. 629 (Special Sess. 1934), *aff'd*, 266 N.Y. 565 (1935). In fairness to the judges, it should be noted that they stood steadfastly against the threat of street violence whether it originated from the radical left or the radical right. In particular, they were as ready to help suppress the Ku Klux Klan as socialist labor groups. Thus they reversed a conviction against a woman who was distributing an NAACP pamphlet titled " 'Stop the Ku Klux Klan Propaganda in New York' " on the ground that the Klan was "stirring up . . . prejudices and animosities against certain races and religions in this country" and that it "would be a dangerous and un-American thing to sustain an interpretation of a city ordinance which would prohibit the free distribution by a body of citizens of a pamphlet setting forth their views against what they believed to be a movement subversive of their rights as citizens." People v. Johnson, 191 N.Y.S. 750 (General Sess. 1921). Even more important, the state courts and ultimately the United States Supreme Court upheld the constitutionality of a state statute requiring secret societies such as the Klan to provide the secretary of state with a list of their members and officers. People ex rel. Bryant v. Sheriff of Erie County, 206 N.Y.S. 533 (Sup. Ct. 1924), *aff'd*, 210 N.Y.S. 269 (App. Div. 1925), *aff'd*, 241 N.Y. 405 (1926), *aff'd*, 278 U.S. 63 (1928). Observing that the Klan "was conducting a crusade against Catholics, Jews and Negroes and stimulating hurtful religious and race prejudices," 278 U.S. at 76, the judges held that the legislature had "to protect . . . its citizens from malicious discrimination and wanton intimidation." 210 N.Y.S. at 273. It was "not required to await active violations before enacting legislation" but could "anticipate them." 206 N.Y.S. at 535.

15. In re Lithuanian Workers' Literature Soc., 187 N.Y.S. 612, 615, 617 (App. Div. 1921); People v. American Socialist Soc., 195 N.Y.S. 801, 806 (App. Div. 1922); Gitlow v. Kiely, 44 F.2d 227 (S.D.N.Y. 1930), *aff'd*, 49 F.2d 1077 (2d Cir.), *cert. denied*, 284 U.S. 648 (1931); Pathe Exch., Inc. v. Cobb, 195 N.Y.S. 661 (App. Div. 1922), *aff'd*, 236 N.Y. 539 (1923).

16. American Woolen Co. v. State, 180 N.Y.S. 759, 765 (Ct. Claims 1920), *rev'd on other grounds*, 187 N.Y.S. 341 (App. Div. 1921); Van Alstyne v. Rochester Telephone Corp., 296 N.Y.S. 726, 731 (City Ct. Rochester 1937).

17. Meyer v. Price, 250 N.Y. 370, 381 (1929); Employers' Fire Ins. Co. v. Cotten, 245 N.Y. 102, 105 (1927); Meisel Tire Co. v. Ralph, 1 N.Y.S.2d 143, 147 (City Ct. Rochester 1937).

18. Thorn v. Austin Silver Mining Co., 12 N.Y.S.2d 675, 678 (Sup. Ct. 1939); In re Gellis' Estate, 252 N.Y.S. 725, 733 (Surr. Ct. 1931); In re DiCrocco's Estate, 12 N.Y.S.2d 276, 278 (Surr. Ct. 1939).

19. See Kimmerle v. New York Evening Journal, Inc., 262 N.Y. 99, 102 (1933).

20. Laws of 1912 c. 393, *as amended*, Laws of 1913 c. 713; Laws of 1920, c. 902, as amended, Laws of 1921, c. 370. The board had been created by Laws of 1904, c. 664.

21. See "Preliminary Statement," in *Report of the Board of Statutory Consolidation on the Simplification of the Civil Practice in the Courts of New York containing the Civil Practice Act* (Albany: J. B. Lyon, 1915), 1:3; 253 N.Y.S. at v (1932), the last volume in which Rodenbeck's name is listed as a judge; *Who Was Who in America* (Chicago: Marquis, 1943), 1:862; Francis M. Ellis and Edward F. Clark Jr., *A Brief History of Carter, Ledyard & Milburn from 1854 to 1988* (New York: Peter E. Randall, 1988), 27–31; Mitchell C. Harrison, *New York State's Prominent and Progressive Men: An Encyclopaedia of Contemporaneous Biography* (New York: Tribune, 1900), 2:66–67.

22. See Wood v. Sutton, 12 Wend. 235 (N.Y. Sup. Ct. 1834); Broome County Bank v. Lewis, 18 Wend. 565 (N.Y. Sup. Ct. 1836); Code of Procedure sec. 152; People v. McCumber, 18 N.Y. 315 (1858); Wayland v. Tysen, 45 N.Y. 281 (1871).

23. Applebaum v. Gross, 191 N.Y.S. 710, 715 (Sup. Ct. 1921), *aff'd*, 192 N.Y.S. 913 (App. Div. 1922); Rogan v. Consolidated Coppermines Co., 193 N.Y.S. 163, 164 (Sup. Ct. 1922); Morris v. Dorfmann, 233 N.Y.S. 460 (App. Div. 1929); 103 Park Ave. Cop. v. Exchange Buffet Corp., 197 N.Y.S. 422 (App.

Div. 1922); Curry v. Mackenzie, 239 N.Y. 267 (1925); Schwed v. E. N. Kennedy, Inc., 221 N.Y.S. 179 (App. Div. 1927); Joseph Mogul, Inc. v. C. Lewis Lavine, Inc., 247 N.Y. 20 (1928).

24. Montgomery v. Lans, 194 N.Y.S. 96, 97 (App. Term 1922); Hanna v. Mitchell, 196 N.Y.S. 43, 55–56 (App. Div. 1922), aff'd, 235 N.Y. 534 (1923); Title Guarantee & Trust Co. v. Smith, 213 N.Y.S. 730 (App. Div. 1926); Waxman v. Williamson, 256 N.Y. 117 (1931).

25. See Notes of Advisory Committee to Fed. R. Civ. Proc. 56; Levine v. Behn, 282 N.Y. 120, 123 (1940) (dictum); Cooper v. Greyhound Bus Corp., 215 N.Y.S.2d 281, 283 (App. Div. 1961); Vaudable v. Montmartre, Inc., 193 N.Y.S.2d 332, 334 (Sup. Ct. 1959). For a general discussion of the 1932 amendment, see Louis C. Ritter and Evert H. Magnuson, "The Motion for Summary Judgment and Its Extension to All Classes of Actions," *Marquette Law Review* 21 (1936): 33, 34–37.

26. Town Board of Town of Greece v. Murray, 223 N.Y.S. 606, 608 (Sup. Ct. 1927); Loesch v. Manhattan Life Insurance Co., 218 N.Y.S. 412, 414 (Sup. Ct. 1926), aff'd, 222 N.Y.S. 845 (App. Div. 1927); Brownell v. Board of Education of Inside Tax District of City of Saratoga Springs, 239 N.Y. 369 (1925); Grainger v. Engel, 265 N.Y. 118 (1934); Leibowitz v. Bickford's Lunch System, 241 N.Y. 489 (1926); Town Board of Town of Greece v. Murray, *supra* at 608. The one constitutional case was Board of Education of City of Rochester v. Van Zandt, 195 N.Y.S. 297 (Sup. Ct. 1922), aff'd, 197 N.Y.S. 899 (App. Div. 1922), aff'd, 234 N.Y. 644 (1923).

27. See Baumann v. Baumann, 250 N.Y. 382 (1929); Morecroft v. Taylor, 234 N.Y.S. 2 (App. Div. 1929); Pratter v. Lascoff, 249 N.Y.S. 211 (Sup. Ct. 1931), aff'd, 258 N.Y.S. 1002 (App. Div. 1932), aff'd, 261 N.Y. 509, *cert. denied*, 289 U.S. 754 (1933); Howard v. Town of Brighton, 257 N.Y.S. 41 (Sup. Ct. 1931); Town of Cortland v. Village of Peekskill, 281 N.Y. 490 (1939); Dun & Bradstreet, Inc. v. City of New York, 276 N.Y. 198 (1937); City of New York v. Maltbie, 274 N.Y. 90, 100 (1937); Reed v. Littleton, 275 N.Y. 150 (1937).

28. Laws of 1920, ch. 925; Brand v. Butts, 273 N.Y.S. 181, 183 (App. Div. 1934); Columbus Trust Co. v. Upper Hudson Electric & R.R. Co., 190 N.Y.S. 737, 739 (Sup. Ct. 1921).

29. Eagle-Picher Lead Co. v. Mansfield Paint Co., 196 N.Y.S. 447, 449 (App. Div. 1922); Newman v. Potter, 194 N.Y.S. 207, 208 (App. Div. 1922); Fulton v. National Aniline & Chemical Co., 211 N.Y.S.2d 769, 770 (App. Div. 1925); E. L. Parker & Nimme Co. v. Enterprise Tinware Co., 182 N.Y.S. 909 (App. Term 1920).

30. See Shaw v. Samley Realty Co., 194 N.Y.S. 531, 532 (App. Div. 1922); Educational Films Corp. v. Lincoln & Parker Co., 183 N.Y.S. 113 (App. Div. 1920).

31. Love v. Charles H. Brown Paint Co., 185 N.Y.S. 428, 429 (App. Div. 1920); Klink v. Hershon, 181 N.Y.S. 459, 460 (App. Div. 1920).

32. Harmon v. Alfred Peats Co., 243 N.Y. 473, 476 (1926); Elman v. Ziegfeld, 193 N.Y.S. 133, 136 (App. Div. 1922).

33. Feingold v. Walworth Bros., 238 N.Y. 446, 455 (1924); People v. George Henriques & Co., 267 N.Y. 398, 402 (1935); Levine v. Moskowitz, 200 N.Y.S. 597 (App. Div. 1923); Island Supply Co. v. Steitz, 217 N.Y.S. 154 (App. Term 1926).

34. Adelson v. Sacred Associates Realty Corp., 183 N.Y.S. 265, 269 (App. Div. 1920). *Accord,* Waterman v. Title Guarantee & Trust Co., 293 N.Y.S. 168, 169 (Sup. Ct. 1936); Cavanagh v. Hutcheson, 250 N.Y.S. 127, 133 (Sup. Ct. 1931).

35. Bouton v. Van Buren, 229 N.Y. 17, 22 (1920); Harrigan v. Pounds, 265 N.Y.S. 676, 685 (App. Div. 1933); Brenner v. Title Guarantee & Trust Co., 276 N.Y. 230, 238 (1937); Brown (Advance-Rumely Co.) v. Werblin, 244 N.Y.S. 209 (Sup. Ct. 1930).

36. Bergheim v. Hofstatter, 276 N.Y.S. 188 (App. Div. 1934); United Cloak & Suit Designers' Mut. Aid Ass'n v. Sigman, 218 N.Y.S. 483, 485 (App. Div. 1926); Berle v. Dawkins, 271 N.Y.S. 579, 580 (Sup. Ct. 1934).

37. See Akely v. Kinnicutt, 203 N.Y.S. 741 (App. Div.), aff'd, 238 N.Y. 466 (1924).

38. 95 U.S. 714 (1877).

39. Tort cases, according to standard black-letter law, were governed by the law of the place where the tort occurred. See M. Salimoff & Co. v. Standard Oil Co., 262 N.Y. 220, 226 (1933). Cases involving contracts and other written instruments, in contrast, were governed by the law chosen by the parties, if they had expressed a clear choice, see Westchester Mortgage Co. v. Grand Rapids & I.R.R., 246 N.Y. 194, 197–99 (1927), or by the law of the place where the contract had been made and was to be performed if the parties had made no choice. See Compania de Inversiones Internationales v. Industrial Mortgage Bank of Finland, 269 N.Y. 22, 26 (1935), *cert. denied,* 297 U.S. 705 (1936).

40. Holzer v. Deutsche Reichsbahn-Gesellschaft, 277 N.Y. 474, 478–479 (1938). A sign of the court's knowledge of the likely unpopularity of its opinion was its issuance of a fairly lengthy opinion as an unsigned *per curiam,* for which no judge would have had to take responsibility.

41. Kleve v. Basler Lebens-Versicherungs-Gesellschaft, 45 N.Y.S.2d 882, 887–88 (Sup. Ct. 1943).

42. Moscow Fire Insurance Co. v. Bank of New York & Trust Co., 294 N.Y.S. 648, 673 (Sup. Ct. 1937), *aff'd,* 3 N.Y.S.2d 653 (App. Div. 1938), *aff'd,* 280 N.Y. 286 (1939), *aff'd sub nom.* United States v. Moscow Fire Ins. Co., 309 U.S. 624 (1940); Vladikavkazsky Ry. v. New York Trust Co., 263 N.Y. 369, 377–79 (1934); P. V. Baranowsky Co. v. Guaranty Trust Co., 280 N.Y.S. 427, 434–35 (Sup. Ct. 1934). Cf. Frenkel & Co. v. L'Urbaine Fire Insurance Co., 251 N.Y. 243, 249 (1929) (French statute confiscating German assets during World War I not enforced).

43. Blackwell v. Glidden Co., 203 N.Y.S. 380 (App. Div.), *aff'd,* 239 N.Y. 545 (1924); Nocero v. Denitto, 208 N.Y.S. 601, 602–603 (App. Div. 1925); Clark v. Foreign Products Co., 185 N.Y.S. 99, 100 (App. Div. 1920).

44. Jarvis v. Stoddart, 213 N.Y.S. 829 (App. Div. 1926); Poplawski v. Cook, 208 N.Y.S. 803 (App. Term 1925); Drena v. Travelers' Insurance Co., 183 N.Y.S. 439 (App. Div. 1920); Capitula v. New York Central R.R., 192 N.Y.S. 745 (App. Div. 1922).

45. Travelers' Insurance Co. v. Pomerantz, 246 N.Y. 63, 69 (1927).

46. Veihelmann v. Manufacturers Safe Deposit Co., 303 N.Y. 526, 530 (1952); Frechette v. Special Magazines, Inc., 136 N.Y.S.2d 448, 453 (App. Div. 1954); O'Connor v. Papertsian, 309 N.Y. 465 (1956).

47. See People ex rel. Hilton v. Fahrenkopf, 279 N.Y. 49 (1938); Schindler v. Royal Insurance Co., 258 N.Y. 310 (1932).

48. For example, a determination in a suit would be binding in a subsequent suit only for or against those who had been parties to the first suit and, even then, only if both parties were mutually bound. See St. John v. Fowler, 229 N.Y. 270, 274 (1920). A second principle was that a prior judgment would be binding in a subsequent suit only if "identity of cause of action" and of subject matter and issues existed between the two suits, Loomis v. Loomis, 288 N.Y. 222, 224–225 (1942), and, even then, would be binding only as to issues " 'which were or might have been litigated' " in the first action, Jasper v. Rozinski, 228 N.Y. 349, 357 (1920); if identity of cause of action and subject matter did not exist, findings in the suit would constitute an estoppel in the second "only as to those matters [actually] litigated, and not as to matters which might have been litigated." Luce v. New York, C. & St.L. R.R., 211 N.Y.S. 184, 187 (App. Div. 1925), *aff'd,* 242 N.Y. 519 (1926). A third principle was that a prior judgment would be binding if it was a final one entered on the merits, but not otherwise. See Caruthers v. Bankers' Trust Cop., 242 N.Y. 554 (1926).

49. Elder v. New York & Pennsylvania Motor Express, Inc., 284 N.Y. 350, 352 (1940); DeCoss v. Turner & Blanchard, Inc., 267 N.Y. 207 (1935).

50. On the late nineteenth-century origins of the war on sin, see Edwin G. Burrows and Mike Wallace, *Gotham: A History of New York City to 1898* (New York: Oxford University Press, 1999), 1162–69.

51. See Joseph R. Gusfield, *Symbolic Crusade: Status Politics and the American Temperance Movement* (Urbana: University of Illinois Press, 1963); James H. Timberlake, *Prohibition and the Progressive Movement, 1900–1920* (Cambridge, Mass.: Harvard University Press, 1963); Michael A. Lerner, "Dry

Manhattan: Class, Culture, and Politics in Prohibition-Era New York City, 1919–1933" (Ph.D. diss., New York University, 1999). Norman H. Clark, *Deliver Us from Evil: An Interpretation of American Prohibition* (New York: Norton, 1976), 134–35, accepts the basic premises of the earlier work but argues that the main thrust of Prohibition was symbolic rather than coercive. K. Austin Kerr, *Organized for Prohibition: A New History of the Anti-Saloon League* (New Haven: Yale University Press, 1985), 212–13, argues that some advocates of Prohibition sought to reform the lower classes through coercion, while others strove to achieve their goal through education.

52. Harry G. Levine, "Preface," in John J. Rumbarger, *Profits, Power, and Prohibition: Alcohol Reform and the Industrializing of America, 1800–1930* (Albany: State University of New York Press, 1989), xiii–xiv. Rumbarger's book fully argues the points made by Levine. Another author who takes essentially the same position is George Chauncey, *Gay New York: Gender, Urban Culture, and the Making of the Gay Male World, 1890–1940* (New York: Basic Books, 1994), 335. On the conflict in the context of Prohibition between nineteenth-century New England Protestant culture and a newly emerging culture in 1920s New York, see Ann Douglas, *Terrible Honesty: Mongrel Manhattan in the 1920s* (New York: Farrar, Straus and Giroux, 1995), 24–26.

53. See Chauncey, *Gay New York,* 233, 305–10, 327–28; Clark, *Deliver Us from Evil,* 140–80; Kerr, *Organized for Prohibition,* 242–83.

54. People v. Defore, 242 N.Y. 13, 21–24, *cert. denied,* 270 U.S. 657 (1926).

55. See Matthew Josephson and Hannah Josephson, *Al Smith: Hero of the Cities* (Boston: Houghton Mifflin, 1969), 291–96.

56. Quoted in Paul S. Boyer, *Purity in Print: The Vice-Society Movement and Book Censorship in America* (New York: Scribner, 1968), 4. On the class aspects of the law's repressive policies during the 1920s and 1930s, see generally ibid., 3–10; Barbara Meil Hobson, *Uneasy Virtue: The Politics of Prostitution and the American Reform Tradition* (New York: Basic Books, 1987), 163. One exception to the repressive tendencies of the two decades was People on Complaint of Savory v. Gotham Book Mart, 285 N.Y.S. 563, 567 (Magis. Ct. 1936), in which a magistrate found "unwelcome" the idea of "a judge-made list of what people should or should not read." One other case made a passing reference to the belief of some individuals, other than the judge, that prostitution should be decriminalized. See People v. Anonymous, 292 N.Y.S. 282, 286 (Magis. Ct. 1936).

57. John D'Emilio and Estelle B. Freedman, *Intimate Matters: A History of Sexuality in America* (New York: Harper & Row, 1988), 222–48, 256–60; Kevin F. White, "The Flapper's Boyfriend: The Revolution in Morals and the Emergence of Modern American Male Sexuality, 1910–1930" (Ph.D. diss., Ohio State University, 1990), 318–91; Linda Gordon, *Heroes of Their Own Lives: The Politics and History of Family Violence, Boston, 1880–1960* (New York: Viking, 1988), 141–46; Robert A. Woods, "Prohibition and Social Hygiene," *Social Hygiene* 5 (1919): 137, 144; Thomas C. Mackey, *Hammer at Vice: The Use of Law for Moral Reform and the Changing Business of Prostitution in New York City, 1900–1932* (forthcoming).

58. See John D'Emilio, *Sexual Politics, Sexual Communities: The Making of a Homosexual Minority in the United States, 1940–1970* (Chicago: University of Chicago Press, 1983), 10–20, 22; George Chauncey Jr., "Christian Brotherhood or Sexual Perversion? Homosexual Identities and the Construction of Sexual Boundaries in the World War I Era," in *Hidden from History: Reclaiming the Gay and Lesbian Past,* ed. Martin B. Duberman, Martha Vicinus, and George Chauncey Jr. (New York: NAL Books, 1989), 294; Chauncey, *Gay New York,* 331–61.

59. Boyer, *Purity in Print,* illustration 7; Felice Flanery Lewis, *Literature, Obscenity, and Law* (Carbondale: Southern Illinois University Press, 1976), 102, 135–36; Ultem Publications, Inc. v. Arrow Publications, Inc., 2 N.Y.S.2d 933, 937 (Sup. Ct. 1938).

60. People v. Seltzer, 203 N.Y.S. 809, 813 (Sup. Ct. 1924); People v. Friede, 233 N.Y.S. 565, 568–69 (Magis. Ct. 1929).

61. People v. Clark, 2 N.Y.S.2d 433, 434 (App. Div. 1937).

62. People v. Hall, 16 N.Y.S.2d 328, 329–30 (County Ct. 1939); Halsey v. New York Society for the Suppression of Vice, 234 N.Y. 1, 12 (1922) (dissenting opinion); People v. Berg, 272 N.Y.S. 586, 587 (App. Div. 1934), *aff'd,* 269 N.Y. 514 (1935).

63. Eureka Productions, Inc. v. Byrne, 300 N.Y.S. 218 (App. Div. 1937), *leave to appeal denied,* 276 N.Y. 688 (1938); Public Welfare Pictures Corp. v. Lord, 230 N.Y.S. 137–38 (App. Div. 1928); Foy Productions, Ltd. v. Graves, 3 N.Y.S.2d 573, 574–75, 577–78 (App. Div.), *aff'd,* 278 N.Y. 498 (1938).

64. People v. Wendling, 258 N.Y. 451, 455 (1932); Bonserk Theatre Corp. v. Moss, 34 N.Y.S.2d 541, 548 (Sup. Ct. 1942).

65. United States v. One Book Entitled Ulysses by James Joyce, 72 F.2d 705, 707–708 (2d Cir. 1934). In People v. Miller, 279 N.Y.S. 583 (Magis. Ct. 1935), another judge allowed circulation of an allegedly obscene book on the ground that "the public concept of decency has changed" and "the task of the judge is to record the tides of public opinion, not to emulate King Canute in an effort to turn back the tide." Ibid., 584–85.

66. 72 F.2d at 711; People ex rel. Kahan v. Jaffe, 35 N.Y.S.2d 104, 106–7 (Magis. Ct. 1942).

67. People v. Smith, 300 N.Y.S. 651, 652 (App. Div. 1937); People v. Burke, 276 N.Y.S. 402, 411–12 (App. Div. 1934) (dissenting opinion), *aff'd,* 267 N.Y. 571 (1935).

68. People v. Swasey, 180 N.Y.S. 629, 630–31 (Gen. Sess. 1920); People v. Morris, 18 N.Y.S.2d 448 (App. Div. 1940); People v. Vickers, 19 N.Y.S.2d 165 (App. Div. 1940).

69. Such as the sufficiency of the evidence that the defendant had prostituted herself, compare People v. Lorraine, 196 N.Y.S. 323 (App. Term 1922), with People v. Wachtel, 244 N.Y.S. 462 (App. Part 1930), that the defendant had procured a woman for prostitution, see People v. Silverman, 245 N.Y.S. 568 (App. Part 1930), *aff'd,* 258 N.Y.S. 1049 (App. Div. 1932), or that the defendant's premises had knowingly been used for the purpose of prostitution. Compare People v. Royall, 281 N.Y.S. 875 (App. Part 1935), with People v. Botto, 237 N.Y.S. 513 (App. Part 1929).

70. People v. Anonymous, 292 N.Y.S. 282, 286 (Magis. Ct. 1936); People v. Edwards, 180 N.Y.S. 631, 635 (Gen. Sess. 1920); Mackey, *Hammer at Vice.*

71. People v. Odierno, 2 N.Y.S.2d 99, 102–3 (County Ct. 1938); People v. Kramer, 203 N.Y.S. 156, 159 (App. Div. 1924). On the conditions of inequality that induced many women to choose lives of prostitution, see Ruth Rosen, *The Lost Sisterhood: Prostitution in America, 1900–1918* (Baltimore: Johns Hopkins University Press, 1982), 137–68.

72. People v. Anonymous, 292 N.Y.S. 282, 286 (Magis. Ct. 1936); People v. Odierno, 2 N.Y.S.2d 99, 101, 103 (County Ct. 1938) (emphasis in original); People v. VanWhy, 32 N.Y.S.2d 379 (County Ct. 1941), *rev'd on other grounds,* 288 N.Y. 659 (1942). The quoted language in *Odierno,* which had its origin in substance in People v. Draper, 154 N.Y.S. 1034, 1038 (App. Div. 1915), was also used as late as People v. Jelke, 152 N.Y.S.2d 479, 483 (Ct. App. 1956).

73. Halsey v. New York Society for the Suppression of Vice, 234 N.Y. 1, 13–14 (1922) (dissenting opinion); Foy Productions, Ltd. v. Graves, 3 N.Y.S.2d 573, 577 (App. Div.), *aff'd,* 278 N.Y. 498 (1938); Ultem Publications, Inc. v. Arrow Publications, Inc., 2 N.Y.S.2d 933, 937 (Sup. Ct. 1938).

74. Rosenstiel v. Rosenstiel, 262 N.Y.S.2d 86, 101 (Ct. App. 1965), *cert. denied,* 384 U.S. 971 (1966) (Scileppi, J., dissenting); Hubbard v. Hubbard, 228 N.Y. 81, 85 (1920).

75. Hubbard v. Hubbard, 228 N.Y. 81, 85 (1920). On the position of the Catholic hierarchy, see Norma Basch, *Framing American Divorce: From the Revolutionary Generation to the Victorians* (Berkeley: University of California Press, 1999), 88–89.

76. Grillo v. Sherman-Stalter Co., 186 N.Y.S. 810, 812 (App. Div.), *aff'd,* 231 N.Y. 621 (1921). One way to encourage legitimation was for the judges themselves to declare children legitimate in borderline cases where evidence of their status was indeterminate. This result was achieved through what the Court of Appeals labeled "an established legal presumption that every person is born legitimate," Matter of Estate of Fay, 404 N.Y.S.2d 554, 556 (Ct. App. 1978), which was "described as 'one of the strongest and most persuasive [presumptions] known to the law.' " Ibid.

77. Their present agreement to marry could be oral or in writing and could be proved by circumstantial evidence, such as cohabitation and repute. See Fisher v. Fisher, 227 N.Y.S. 345, 349 (App. Div. 1928), *aff'd*, 250 N.Y. 313 (1929).

78. Thus a common-law marriage that was void in one state would become valid if the parties traveled as husband and wife to another state, where no bar existed to common law marriage in general or their marriage in particular. See In re Sokoloff's Estate, 2 N.Y.S.2d 602, 605–6 (Surr. Ct. 1938).

79. In re Seymour, 185 N.Y.S. 373 (Surr. Ct. 1920).

80. Anonymous v. Anonymous, 21 N.Y.S.2d 71, 75 (Dom. Rel. Ct. 1940); Cavanaugh v. Valentine, 41 N.Y.S.2d 896, 898 (Sup. Ct. 1943); Estate of Watts, 341 N.Y.S.2d 609, 612 (Ct. App. 1973); In re Schneider's Will, 131 N.Y.S.2d 215, 219 (Surr. Ct. 1954).

81. In re Goode's Estate, 188 N.Y.S. 188 (Surr. Ct. 1921), *aff'd*, 197 N.Y.S. 916 (App. Div. 1922); Cohen v. Cohen, 103 N.Y.S.2d 426, 428 (Sup. Ct. 1951).

82. Messing v. Messing, 76 N.Y.S.2d 375, 378 (Sup. Ct. 1947); Crowley v. Crowley, 186 N.Y.S.2d 60, 61 (Sup. Ct. 1959); Messing v. Messing, *supra* at 378; Nottingham v. Nottingham, 204 N.Y.S. 750 (App. Div. 1924).

83. Gelbman v. Gelbman, 184 N.Y.S. 902, 903 (App. Div. 1920).

84. Hubbard v. Hubbard, 228 N.Y. 81, 84–85 (1920).

85. See Butler v. Butler, 198 N.Y.S.2d 391, 395–396 (App. Div. 1923).

86. Fratello v. Fratello, 193 N.Y.S. 865, 867 (Sup. Ct. 1922).

87. Shonfeld v. Shonfeld, 260 N.Y. 477, 479 (1933); Woronzoff-Daschkoff v. Woronzoff-Daschkoff, 303 N.Y. 506, 511–12 (1952).

88. Vanden Berg v. Vanden Berg, 197 N.Y.S. 641, 642 (Sup. Ct. 1923); Steinberger v. Steinberger, 33 N.Y.S.2d 596, 597 (Sup. Ct. 1940); Hiebink v. Hiebink, 56 N.Y.S.2d 394 (Sup. Ct.), *aff'd*, 56 N.Y.S.2d 397 (App. Div. 1945); Vanden Berg v. Vanden Berg, *supra* at 642. Cf. B. v. B., 355 N.Y.S.2d 712 (Sup. Ct. 1974) (granting annulment to wife whose husband was a female transsexual who had not yet developed male sexual organs); Anonymous v. Anonymous, 325 N.Y.S.2d 499 (Sup. Ct. 1971) (granting annulment to husband who discovered on wedding night that his "wife" had male sexual organs, even though "she" promised to have them removed). But see Anonymous v. Anonymous, 74 N.Y.S.2d 899 (Sup. Ct. 1947), which refused to grant an annulment to "a woman past middle life" who had married "a man much her senior" obviously "in feeble health" with "*a tremor*" and "*difficulty walking*." In the court's view "her expectations of sexual enjoyment should not [have] be[en] judged by the standards of youth but proportioned to their years." Ibid., 901 (emphasis in original).

89. Kershner v. Kershner, 278 N.Y.S. 501 (App. Div. 1935), *aff'd*, 269 N.Y. 655 (1936); Sophian v. Von Linde, 253 N.Y.S.2d 496, 499 (App. Div. 1964), *aff'd*, 262 N.Y.S.2d 505 (Ct. App. 1965); Becher v. Becher, 74 N.Y.S.2d 44, 48 (Dom. Rel. Ct. 1947); DeBaillet-Latour v. DeBaillet-Latour, 301 N.Y. 428 (1950).

90. Gordon v. Gordon, 232 N.Y.S. 541 (App. Div. 1929); Donovan v. Donovan, 263 N.Y.S. 336 (Sup. Ct. 1933); Iati v. Iati, 272 N.Y.S. 32 (Sup. Ct. 1934); Smith v. Smith, 221 N.Y.S. 672 (Sup. Ct. 1927).

91. Keegan v. Keegan, 204 N.Y.S. 405 (App. Div. 1924); Audley v. Audley, 187 N.Y.S. 652 (App. Div. 1921); Johnson v. Johnson, 295 N.Y. 477 (1946).

92. Chayka v. Chayka, 41 N.Y.S.2d 487 (Sup. Ct. 1943). For the location of Dubra, see Gary Mokotoff and Sallyann Amdur Sack, *Where Once We Walked: A Guide to the Jewish Communities Destroyed in the Holocaust* (Teaneck, N.J.: Avotaynu, 1991), 78; Leon E. Seltzer, ed., *The Columbia Lippincott Gazetteer of the World* (New York: Columbia University Press, 1952), 537.

93. Hayden v. Hayden, 215 N.Y.S. 326, 327–28 (Sup. Ct. 1926).

94. See Babington v. Yellow Taxi Corp., 220 N.Y.S. 420 (App. Div. 1927); Laws of 1922, c. 279; In re Santos, 230 N.Y.S. 395 (Sup. Ct. 1928) (applying statute); Application of Magaraci, 215 N.Y.S.2d 546 (App. Div. 1961). Another area of confusion surrounding annulment doctrine involved promises

of a religious nature. One issue was whether an annulment was appropriate when before a civil marriage ceremony a spouse fraudulently agreed to be married again in a subsequent religious ceremony and then failed to honor the agreement. Until the 1950s, some cases granted annulments, see, e.g., Rutstein v. Rutstein, 222 N.Y.S.2d 688 (App. Div. 1927), while others did not. See, e.g., McHale v. McHale, 67 N.Y.S.2d 794 (Sup. Ct. 1947). Then, in 1958, the Court of Appeals declared it "settled" that such annulments were appropriate. See Brillis v. Brillis, 173 N.Y.S.2d 3, 5 (Ct. App. 1958). The courts also split on whether to grant annulments for one spouse's failure to honor a commitment to adopt the other spouse's religion, compare Williams v. Williams, 86 N.Y.S.2d 490 (Sup. Ct. 1947) (annulment granted), with Nilsen v. Nilsen, 66 N.Y.S.2d 204 (Sup. Ct. 1946) (annulment denied), and they declared that similar promises to raise children in a particular religion "cannot be treated lightly"; Ross v. Ross, 149 N.Y.S.2d 585, 589 (Sup. Ct. 1956), even when they were declining to enforce them. See ibid. Accord, Martin v. Martin, 68 N.Y.S.2d 41 (Sup. Ct. 1947). Another religious issue that began to come before the courts in the 1970s was whether Orthodox Jewish men could be compelled to provide their wives with a "Get," or Jewish religious divorce, upon their obtaining a secular divorce. See Waxstein v. Waxstein, 395 N.Y.S.2d 877 (Sup. Ct. 1976), aff'd, 394 N.Y.S.2d 253 (App. Div. 1977).

95. Lapides v. Lapides, 254 N.Y. 73, 80 (1930); Woronzoff-Daschkoff v. Woronzoff-Dashkoff, 303 N.Y. 506, 511–12 (1952); Chaddock v. Chaddock, 226 N.Y.S. 152, 157 (Sup. Ct. 1927).

96. Darling v. Darling, 105 N.Y.S.2d 475, 478 (Sup. Ct. 1951); McLean v. McLean, 143 N.Y.S.2d 129, 130 (Sup. Ct. 1955); Smelzer v. Smelzer, 265 N.Y.S. 220 (Sup. Ct. 1933); Pawloski v. Pawloski, 65 N.Y.S.2d 413 (Sup. Ct. 1946) (defendant claimed to be of German rather than Polish descent). But there were exceptional cases, such as one where the husband after promising not to keep secrets secretly placed a chattel mortgage on the couple's wedding presents, see Madden v. Madden, 125 N.Y.S.2d 384 (Sup. Ct. 1953); one where a man married a woman without ever intending to live with her in order to obtain her support of his medical education, see Feynman v. Feynman, 4 N.Y.S.2d 787 (Sup. Ct. 1938); and one where an American, "unaccustomed to dealing with the workings of a shrewd and cunning European mind" and unmindful "of the fact that his own country is firmly grounded on principles opposed to divine rights of titled personages," had married a European noble woman bent on seizing his wealth. Ryan v. Ryan, 281 N.Y.S. 709, 710–11 (Sup. Ct. 1935). See also Tuchsher v. Tuchsher, 184 N.Y.S.2d 131 (Sup. Ct. 1959) (defendant told specific lies about his income and wealth). Judges also tended to be sympathetic to suits seeking annulment when a defendant had lied about love in order to marry an American citizen and thereby gain entry into the United States in circumvention of the immigration laws. See, e.g., Rubman v. Rubman, 251 N.Y.S. 474 (Sup. Ct. 1931). See also Fusco v. Fusco, 107 N.Y.S.2d 286 (Sup. Ct. 1951) (American citizen living in Italy in 1942 who married Italian to avoid internment as enemy alien entitled to annulment). Marriages would also be annulled when one spouse falsely claimed American citizenship. See, e.g., Truiano v. Truiano, 201 N.Y.S. 573 (Sup. Ct. 1923).

97. Darling v. Darling, 105 N.Y.S.2d 475, 478 (Sup. Ct. 1951).

98. Haskell v. Haskell, 194 N.Y.S. 28, 30 (App. Div. 1922), aff'd, 236 N.Y. 635 (1923); Cariola v. Cariola, 225 N.Y.S. 692, 694–95 (Sup. Ct. 1927).

99. People ex rel. Jones v. Johnson, 199 N.Y.S. 695, 697 (App. Div. 1923); Darlington v. Cobb, 239 N.Y.S.2d 301 (Sup. Ct. 1930).

100. Jackson v. Jackson, 290 N.Y. 512, 516 (1943); Seitz v. Seitz, 183 N.Y.S. 79 (App. Div. 1920); Prindle v. Dearborn, 291 N.Y.S. 295, 297–98 (Dom. Rel. Ct. 1936); Sternheim v. Sternheim, 20 N.Y.S.2d 823 (Dom. Rel. Ct. 1940); Kommel v. Karron, 273 N.Y.S. 226, 227 (App. Term 1934).

101. People ex rel. Roberts v. Kidder, 242 N.Y.S. 108, 109–10 (Sup.Ct. 1929).

102. In re Davis' Adoption, 255 N.Y.S. 416, 418–22 (Surr. Ct. 1932).

103. People ex rel. Lentino v. Feser, 186 N.Y.S. 443, 444–48 (App. Div. 1921).

104. In re Miller, 197 N.Y.S. 880–81 (County Ct. 1922).

105. In re Cohen's Adoption, 279 N.Y.S. 427, 429–30, 434–35 (Surr. Ct. 1935); People ex rel. Walters v. Davies, 257 N.Y.S.2d 118, 120–21 (Sup. Ct. 1932).

106. See Wainman v. Richardson, 196 N.Y.S. 262 (Sup. Ct. 1922). Adoption by relatives, at least, for the purpose of raising and supporting destitute children did not necessarily entail the complete termination of the rights of natural parents or their total supplanting by adoptive parents. Nor did it require the termination of all emotional bonds between the child and its natural parents. As noted in the *Wainman* case, *supra,* adoption resulted in "no hardship to the parent," since he could "visit this child as often as he desire[d] . . . , but all the time it will be under the protection of a close relative." 196 N.Y.S. at 264. Adoption also did not destroy an adopted child's right to inherit from its natural kindred, see In re Monroe's Executors, 229 N.Y.S. 476, 478 (Surr. Ct. 1928), nor did an adopted child become next of kin so as to be entitled to inherit from the adoptive parents' collateral relatives. See In re Powell's Estate, 183 N.Y.S. 939 (Surr. Ct.), *aff'd,* 184 N.Y.S. 945 (App. Div. 1920). Finally, adoption was not final: an adoption could "be abrogated" if a child was "ill-behaved and . . . violated her duty toward her foster parents." In re Anonymous, 285 N.Y.S. 827, 829 (Surr. Ct. 1936).

107. In re Bistany, 201 N.Y.S. 684, 688 (County Ct. 1923), *rev'd,* 204 N.Y.S. 599 (App. Div.), *rev'd,* 239 N.Y. 19 (1924); 239 N.Y. at 24.

108. In re Duffy, 202 N.Y.S. 323–24 (Sup. Ct. 1923).

109. The quoted language is from In re Davis' Adoption, 255 N.Y.S. 416, 418 (Surr. Ct. 1932). For a discussion of other devices created in the early decades of the twentieth century to put children in as homelike a situation as possible, see Michael B. Katz, *In the Shadow of the Poorhouse: A Social History of Welfare in America* (New York: Basic Books, 1986), 124–29, 145.

110. Wilkie v. O'Connor, 25 N.Y.S.2d 617, 618–20 (App. Div. 1941).

111. In re Kinney, 272 N.Y.S. 520, 521, 523 (Children's Ct. 1934).

112. Elco Shoe Manufacturers, Inc. v. Sisk, 260 N.Y. 100, 103 (1932); McCauley v. Georgia Railroad Bank, 245 N.Y. 245, 250 (1927). See Herbert Hovenkamp, *Enterprise and American Law, 1836–1937* (Cambridge, Mass.: Harvard University Press, 1991), 62, who so defines the New York standard.

113. Brown v. Cleveland Trust Co., 233 N.Y. 399, 405 (1922). Although officers, directors, and other employees of corporations did not "technically fall . . . within any of the defined fiduciary categories," the law similarly imposed on them a duty "analogous to" that "of a trustee towards his cestui que trust." Levy v. Pacific Eastern Corp., 275 N.Y.S. 291, 297 (Sup. Ct. 1934). With "this concept," according to the leading text of the 1930's, "corporation law bec[a]me in substance a branch of the law of trusts," although the application of fiduciary principles in the corporate context was "less rigorous, since the business situation demand[ed] greater flexibility than the trust situation." But the basic fiduciary principle was the same for the corporation as for the trust—that "powers [were] conceded to the management . . . to act for the corporation as a whole . . . not . . . for the purpose of benefitting one set of participants as against another." Adolf A. Berle Jr. and Gardiner C. Means, *The Modern Corporation and Privte Property* (New York: Macmillan, 1933), 274–275. Going back to a debate between Adolf A. Berle Jr., "For Whom Corporate Managers Are Trustees," *Harvard Law Review* 45 (1932): 1365, and E. Merrick Dodd, "For Whom Are Corporate Managers Trustees?," *Harvard Law Review* 45 (1932): 1145, scholars have disagreed about the precise extent to which corporate fiduciary doctrine does and should mirror trust doctrine. The two leading recent articles are Norwood P. Beveridge Jr., "The Corporate Director's Fiduciary Duty of Loyalty: Understanding the Self-Interested Director Transaction," *DePaul Law Review* 41 (1992): 655, and Harold Marsh Jr., "Are Directors Trustees? Conflict of Interest and Corporate Morality," *Business Lawyer* 22 (1966): 35. This book takes no position in regard to this disagreement; it recognizes that the scope of fiduciary duty in corporate and trust law were never identical in this century and argues only that both bodies of law changed in the same direction, though not necessarily at the same rate, as the century progressed.

114. Meinhard v. Salmon, 249 N.Y. 458, 464 (1928).

115. Although *Meinhard* was a partnership rather than a corporate or trust case, it was also cited

in the corporate and trust contexts. See, e.g., Parker v. Rogerson, 307 N.Y.S.2d 986, 991 (4th Dept.), *appeal dism.,* 311 N.Y.S.2d 7 (Ct. App. 1970). Nevertheless, its impact on corporate fiduciary law is unclear, since states such as Delaware and New Jersey had already begun a process of inducing corporations to incorporate in their jurisdictions by providing them with favorable law. This "race to the bottom" has been the subject of immense scholarly literature. An outstanding analysis is Roberta Romano, *The Genius of American Corporate Law* (Washington, D.C.: AEI Press, 1993). Important legislative changes limiting the ability of judges to protect noncontrolling shareholders from management self-favoritism were enacted in Delaware in 1927 and 1929, see Joel Seligman, *The Transformation of Wall Street: A History of the Securities and Exchange Commission and Modern Corporate Finance,* rev. ed. (Boston: Northeastern University Press, 1995), 43–44, thereby making *Meinhard's* impact uncertain at best.

116. 48 Stat. 74 (1933); 48 Stat. 881 (1934); quoted in Seligman, *Transformation of Wall Street,* 29–30, 100, which develops fully the history of the statutes, see ibid., 6–100, and of the case law elaborating them—subjects beyond the scope of this book.

117. Penato v. George, 383 N.Y.S.2d 900, 904–5 (App. Div. 1976), *aff'd,* 397 N.Y.S.2d 1004 (Ct. App. 1977); State by Lefkowitz v. ITM, Inc., 275 N.Y.S.2d 303, 316 (Sup. Ct. 1966).

CHAPTER THREE

1. *Public Papers of Alfred E. Smith, Forty-Seventh Governor of the State of New York, Fourth Term, 1928* (Albany: J. B. Lyon, 1938), 66; *Public Papers of Alfred E. Smith, Forty-Seventh Governor of the State of New York, 1924* (Albany: J. B. Lyon, 1926), 60, 629, 633.

2. See, e.g., Lawton v. Steele, 119 N.Y. 226 (1890), *aff'd,* 152 U.S. 133 (1894); Metropolitan Board of Health v. Heister, 37 N.Y. 661 (1868); Radcliff's Executors v. Mayor of Brooklyn, 4 N.Y. 195 (1850).

3. People v. Perretta, 253 N.Y. 305, 309 (1930); People v. Cunard White Star, Ltd., 280 N.Y. 413, 418 (1939); Hafner v. Erdreich Realty Corp., 11 N.Y.S.2d 142, 144 (Mun. Ct. 1939).

4. Adamec v. Post, 273 N.Y. 250, 255, 260 (1937).

5. Munn v. Illinois, 94 U.S. 113, 126 (1877); Coty, Inc. of New York v. Hearn Department Stores, 284 N.Y.S. 909 (Sup. Ct. 1935); J. Aron & Co. v. Panama R.R., 255 N.Y. 513, 516, *cert. denied,* 284 U.S. 635 (1931); Niagara, Lockport & Ontario Power Co. v. Seneca Iron & Steel Co., 219 N.Y.S. 418 (Sup. Ct. 1926), *aff'd,* 221 N.Y.S. 869 (App. Div. 1927); Delaware & H.R.R. v. Public Service Commission of State of New York, 281 N.Y.S. 155, 157 (App. Div. 1935), *aff'd,* 270 N.Y. 519 (1936).

6. People v. Federated Radio Corp., 214 N.Y.S. 670, 671 (App. Div.), *aff'd,* 244 N.Y. 33 (1926); People on the Complaint of Spencer v. Capitol Fuels of Queens, Inc., 11 N.Y.S.2d 26, 28 (App. Part 1939); Rueffer v. Department of Agriculture and Markets, 279 N.Y. 16 (1938); People v. Gordon, 14 N.Y.S.2d 333 (Special Sess. 1939), *rev'd on other grounds,* 16 N.Y.S.2d 833 (App. Div.), *aff'd,* 283 N.Y. 705 (1940); People v. Levitt, 260 N.Y.S. 458 (Magis. Ct. 1932); Biddles, Inc. v. Enright, 239 N.Y. 354 (1925); Dunham v. Ottinger, 243 N.Y. 423 (1926), *appeal dism.,* 276 U.S. 592 (1928); Roman v. Lobe, 243 N.Y. 51 (1926).

7. People v. Weller, 237 N.Y. 316, 326, 328 (1924), *aff'd,* 268 U.S. 319 (1925).

8. People v. Sterling, 220 N.Y.S. 315, 317 (Sup. Ct. 1927), *aff'd,* 226 N.Y.S. 881 (App. Div. 1928); Morrison v. Gentler, 273 N.Y.S. 952, 953–54 (Mun. Ct. 1934); Coty, Inc. of New York v. Hearn Department Stores, 284 N.Y.S. 909, 916 (Sup. Ct. 1935); People v. Moynihan, 200 N.Y.S. 434, 437 (County Ct. 1923); Gould v. Bennett, 276 N.Y.S. 113, 116 (Sup. Ct. 1934).

9. People ex rel. Durham Realty Corp. v. LaFetra, 230 N.Y. 429, 438, 443–45 (1921), *appeal dism.,* 257 U.S. 665 (1921). See also Laws of 1921, chs. 942–53.

10. The concurring opinion of Judge Crane was published in Guttag v. Shatzkin, 230 N.Y. 647, 648–49 (1921).

11. The dissent of Judge McLaughlin was published in Edgar A. Levy Leasing Co. v. Siegel, 230 N.Y. 634, 635 (1921).

12. Ullmann Realty Co. v. Tamur, 185 N.Y.S. 612, 620 (Sup. Ct. 1920).

13. See Laws of 1933, chs. 745, 793; Laws of 1935, ch. 19.

14. McCarty v. Prudence-Bonds Corp., 266 N.Y.S. 629, 631–33 (Sup. Ct. 1933).

15. Klinke v. Samuels, 264 N.Y. 144, 149 (1934); People by VanSchaick v. Title & Mortgage Guarantee Co. of Buffalo, 284 N.Y. 69, 94 (1934); Mooney v. Miller, 195 N.Y.S. 437 (Sup. Ct. 1922).

16. People v. Teuscher, 248 N.Y. 454, 460 (1928).

17. People v. Perretta, 253 N.Y. 305, 309–10 (1930).

18. Ibid., 311; Barns v. Dairymen's League Co-op Ass'n., 222 N.Y.S. 294, 305 (App. Div. 1927).

19. Mayflower Farms, Inc. v. Baldwin, 267 N.Y. 9, 16 (1935), *rev'd on other grounds sub nom.* Mayflower Farms, Inc. v. TenEyck, 295 U.S. 266 (1936); People v. Nebbia, 262 N.Y. 259, 268 (1933). See also Laws of 1933, ch. 158; Laws of 1934, ch. 126.

20. Nebbia v. New York, 291 U.S. 502, 515–16, 521, 530, 537 (1934).

21. Ibid., 515, 537.

22. People v. Sterling, 6 N.Y.S.2d 479, 480 (Sup. Ct. 1938), *aff'd,* 13 N.Y.S.2d 574 (App. Div. 1939). The word "revolutionary" was used in connection with the Nebbia case by Barry Cushman, *Rethinking the New Deal Court: The Structure of a Constitutional Revolution* (New York: Oxford University Press, 1998), 79.

23. People v. Sterling, 220 N.Y.S. 315, 318 (Sup. Ct. 1927), *aff'd,* 226 N.Y.S. 881 (App. Div. 1928); Corron v. State, 10 N.Y.S.2d 960 (Ct. Claims 1939); Briegel v. Day, 195 N.Y.S. 295 (App. Div. 1922), *appeal dism.,* 236 N.Y. 646 (1923); Mid-State Advertising Corp. v. Bond, 274 N.Y. 82 (1937).

24. People v. Sterling, *supra* note 23, at 317; Cowan v. City of Buffalo, 288 N.Y.S. 239, 242 (App. Div. 1936); People v. Cunard White Star, Ltd., 280 N.Y. 413, 418 (1939).

25. 261 U.S. 525 (1923).

26. People ex rel. Tipaldo v. Morehead, 270 N.Y. 233, 237–38, *aff'd sub nom.* Morehead v. New York ex rel. Tipaldo, 298 U.S. 587 (1936).

27. Sausser v. Department of Health of City of New York, 242 N.Y. 66, 69–70 (1926); New York Dugan Bros., Inc. v. City of New York, 7 N.Y.S.2d 162, 164 (Sup. Ct. 1938). *Accord,* Good Humor Corp. v. City of New York, 290 N.Y. 312 (1943).

28. Lyons v. Prince, 281 N.Y. 557 (1939); Elite Dairy Products, Inc. v. TenEyck, 288 N.Y.S. 162, 166 (App. Div.), *modified on other grounds,* 271 N.Y.S. 488 (1936).

29. Central Sav. Bank in City of New York v. City of New York, 279 N.Y. 266, 277 (1938), *cert. denied,* 306 U.S. 661 (1939).

30. Felix Frankfurter and Nathan Green, *The Labor Injunction* (New York: Macmillan, 1930), 249–52 (Appendix III); A. L. Reed Co. v. Whiteman, 238 N.Y. 545, 547 (1924); Berg Auto Trunk & Specialty Co. v. Wiener, 200 N.Y.S. 745, 746 (Sup. Ct. 1923); Pre'Catelan, Inc. v. International Federation of Workers in the Hotel, Restaurant, Lunch Room, Club, and Catering Industry, 188 N.Y.S. 29, 33 (Sup. Ct. 1921); Yablonowitz v. Korn, 199 N.Y.S. 769, 770 (App. Div. 1923).

31. Gottlieb v. Matckin, 191 N.Y.S. 777 (Sup. Ct. 1921); L. Daitch & Co. v. Cohen, 217 N.Y.S. 817 (App. Div. 1926); Edelman, Edelman & Berrie Inc. v. Retail Grocery and Dairy Clerks' Union of Greater New York, 198 N.Y.S. 17, 18 (Sup. Ct. 1922); Welinsky v. Hillman, 185 N.Y.S. 257 (Sup. Ct. 1920).

32. Exchange Bakery & Restaurant, Inc. v. Rifkin, 245 N.Y. 260, 268 (1927).

33. Ibid., 266–67.

34. Interborough Rapid Transit Co. v. Lavin, 247 N.Y. 65, 75, 79, 82 (1928). On remand, the trial court found that no "violence, threats, fraud, or overreaching conduct" on the part of defendants had been proved, and it accordingly refused to grant injunctive relief to the IRT. See Interborough Rapid Transit Co. v. Green, 227 N.Y.S. 258, 263 (Sup. Ct. 1928).

35. Nann v. Raimist, 255 N.Y. 307, 319 (1931) (emphasis added).

36. Stillwell Theatre, Inc. v. Kaplan, 259 N.Y. 405, 409–12 (1932), *cert. denied sub nom.* Windsor Circuit Corp. v. Kaplan, 288 U.S. 606 (1933) (emphasis added); Wise Shoe Co. v. Lowenthal, 266 N.Y. 264 (1935); J. H. & S. Theatres, Inc. v. Fay, 260 N.Y. 315 (1932); J. T. Cousins Co. v. Shoe & Leather Workers' Industrial Union of New York, 268 N.Y.S. 547 (Sup. Ct. 1933), *aff'd,* 270 N.Y.S. 973 (App. Div. 1934); Schwartz & Benjamin, Inc. v. Alexanderson, 246 N.Y.S. 422, 423 (Sup. Ct. 1930).

37. Goldfinger v. Feintuch, 276 N.Y. 281 (1937). See Laws of 1935, ch. 477. Indeed, the growing judicial tolerance for picketing became evident in other cases in which, for example, judges refused to enjoin picketing by African Americans seeking to compel retail stores in Harlem to hire black workers, see A. S. Beck Shoe Co. v. Johnson, 274 N.Y.S. 946 (Sup. Ct. 1934), or by patrons objecting to high prices. See Julie Baking Co. v. Graymond, 274 N.Y.S. 250 (Sup. Ct. 1934).

38. O'Keefe v. Local 463 of United Ass'n of Plumbers and Gasfitters of the United States and Canada, 277 N.Y. 300, 309 (1938); Miller v. Ruehl, 2 N.Y.S.2d 394 (Sup. Ct. 1938); O'Keefe v. Local 462, *supra* at 309 (emphasis in original); Kaplan v. Elliot, 261 N.Y.S. 112, 118 (Sup. Ct. 1932), *modified,* 261 N.Y.S. 975 (App. Div. 1933).

39. Mortimer v. Natapow, 14 N.Y.S.2d 971, 974 (City Ct. 1939), *rev'd on other grounds,* 31 N.Y.S.2d 844 (App. Div. 1941); Labor Law secs. 27–29; Red Hook Cold Storage Co. v. Department of Labor, 291 N.Y. 1 (1945); Laws of 1921, ch. 50; People ex inf. Hertzberger v. John R. Thompson Co., 243 N.Y.S. 618 (App. Div.), *aff'd,* 255 N.Y. 530 (1930); Laws of 1933, ch. 584; Mary Lincoln Candies, Inc. v. Department of Labor, 289 N.Y. 262 (1942); Labor Law secs. 172, 174, 182; People v. Kent Stores, Inc., 288 N.Y.S. 1008 (App. Div.), *aff'd,* 272 N.Y. 371 (1936); First American Natural Ferns Co. v. Picard, 23 N.Y.S.2d 39 (Sup. Ct. 1940); General Business Law sec. 186; Acorn Employment Service, Inc. v. Moss, 292 N.Y. 147 (1944); Labor Law secs. 196–97; People v. Grass, 11 N.Y.S.2d 803 (App. Div. 1939); Austin v. National Employment Exchange, 266 N.Y.S. 306 (Mun. Ct. 1933); People on Complaint of Falzia v. Meyer, 3 N.Y.S.2d 870, 873 (Magis. Ct. 1938).

40. 201 N.Y. 271 (1911).

41. New York Central R.R. v. White, 243 U.S. 188 (1916); Helfrick v. Dahlstrom Metallic Door Co., 256 N.Y. 199, 205 (1931), *aff'd,* 284 U.S. 594 (1932).

42. Devitt v. Haglin, 289 N.Y.S. 626, 629 (App. Div. 1936), *aff'd sub nom.* Dewitt v. Schottin, 274 N.Y. 188 (1937); Laws of 1921, ch. 50; Campbell v. City of New York, 244 N.Y. 317 (1927); Gaston v. Taylor, 274 N.Y. 359 (1937); Watson v. McGoldrick, 286 N.Y. 47 (1941).

43. W. H. H. Chamberlain, Inc. v. Andrews, 271 N.Y. 1, 8–10, *aff'd,* 299 U.S. 515 (1936). See Laws of 1935, ch. 468.

44. Busch Jewelry Co. v. United Retail Employees Union, Local 830, 281 N.Y. 150 (1939); People v. Bellows, 281 N.Y. 67 (1939); Canepa v. Doe, 277 N.Y. 55 (1938); The Nevins, Inc. v. Kasmach, 279 N.Y. 323 (1938); Thompson v. Boekhout, 273 N.Y. 390 (1937); Hoffman's Vegetarian Restaurant, Inc. v. Lee, 10 N.Y.S.2d 287 (Sup. Ct. 1939); Paul v. Mencher, 7 N.Y.S.2d 821 (Sup. Ct. 1937), *aff'd,* 6 N.Y.S.2d 379 (App. Div.), *appeal denied,* 279 N.Y. 813 (1938). See also Florsheim Shoe Store Co. v. Retail Shoe Salesmen's Union of Brooklyn and Queens, Local 287, 288 N.Y. 188 (1942).

45. See State Street Trust Co. v. Ernst, 278 N.Y. 104 (1938); Union Exchange National Bank v. Joseph, 231 N.Y. 250 (1921); Mirizio v. Mirizio, 242 N.Y. 74, 84 (1926).

46. In re Gallagher's Estate, 241 N.Y.S. 759, 763 (Surr. Ct. 1930).

47. Cushing v. Hughes, 195 N.Y.S. 200, 202 (Sup. Ct. 1922).

48. See Criterion Holding Co. v. Cerussi, 250 N.Y.S. 735, 737 (Sup. Ct. N.Y. Co. 1931) (dictum).

49. 223 N.Y.S. 796 (Sup. Ct. 1927), *rev'd,* 231 N.Y.S. 435 (App. Div. 1928).

50. Ibid., 808, 810–11.

51. Graf v. Hope Building Corp., 254 N.Y. 1, 4, 7, 8–10 (1930).

52. Criterion Holding Co. v. Cerussi, 250 N.Y.S. 735, 737 (Sup. Ct. 1931); Westchester Laborato-

ries Sales Corp. v. Westchester Laboratories, Inc., 3 N.Y.S.2d 224, 225 (Sup. Ct. 1938); Woodworth v. Prudential Insurance Co., 13 N.Y.S.2d 145, 151 (Sup. Ct.), *rev'd on other grounds,* 15 N.Y.S.2d 541 (App. Div. 1939), *aff'd,* 282 N.Y. 704 (1940).

53. Lumbrazo v. Woodruff, 256 N.Y. 92, 97–98 (1931). *Accord, e.g.,* Alaska Pacific Salmon Co. v. Reynolds Metals Co., 163 F.2d 643, 656–57 (2d Cir. 1947).

54. Moore v. Schlossman's, Inc., 161 N.Y.S.2d 213, 216 (Mun. Ct. 1957); Lynn v. Radio Center Delicatessen, Inc., 9 N.Y.S.2d 110, 112 (Mun. Ct. 1939).

55. 101 N.Y.S.2d 20 (App. Div. 1950).

56. Ibid., 21; Mandel v. Liebman, 303 N.Y. 88, 94 (1951).

57. Graf v. Hope Building Corp., 254 N.Y. 1, 8 (1930) (dissenting opinion); New York Annotations to section 2-302; Comment 1 to section 2-302; New York Annotations to section 2-302; Matter of Friedman, 407 N.Y.S.2d 999, 1007–8 (App. Div. 1978). For the drafting of section 302, see Arthur Allen Leff, "Unconscionability and the Code—The Emperor's New Clause," *University of Pennsylvania Law Review* 115 (1967): 485, 489–527, 541–43.

58. 274 N.Y.S.2d 757 (Dist. Ct. 1966), *rev'd on other grounds,* 281 N.Y.S.2d 964 (App. Term 1967).

59. 298 N.Y.S.2d 264 (Sup. Ct. 1969). For the effective date of the code, see Laws of 1962, ch. 553.

60. Brooklyn Union Gas Co. v. Jimeniz, 371 N.Y.S.2d 289, 291 (Civil Ct. 1975); Federal Deposit Insurance Corp. v. Frank L. Marino Corp., 425 N.Y.S.2d 34 (App. Div. 1980); Colonial Roofing Corp. v. John Mee, Inc., 431 N.Y.S.2d 931, 935 (Sup. Ct. 1980).

61. Austin Instrument, Inc. v. Loral Corp., 324 N.Y.S.2d 22, 25 (Ct. App. 1971); Fair Pavilions, Inc. v. First National City Bank, 281 N.Y.S.2d 23, 27 (Ct. App. 1967) (dictum); Rowe v. Great Atlantic & Pacific Tea Co., 412 N.Y.S.2d 827, 830 (Ct. App. 1978); Gordon v. Bialystoker Center & Bikur Cholim, Inc., 412 N.Y.S.2d 593 (Ct. App. 1978); Christian v. Christian, 396 N.Y.S.2d 817, 824 (Ct. App. 1977).

62. 379 Madison Avenue, Inc. v. Stuyvesant Co., 275 N.Y.S. 953, 956 (App. Div. 1934), *aff'd,* 268 N.Y. 576 (1935); Harwood v. Lincoln Square Apartments Section 5 Inc., 359 N.Y.S.2d 387, 390 (Civil Ct. 1974); People v. Berger, 254 N.Y.S. 136, 139 (Gen. Sess. 1931); Texaco Inc. v. A. A. Gold Inc., 357 N.Y.S.2d 951, 956 (Sup. Ct.), *aff'd,* 358 N.Y.S.2d 973 (App. Div. 1974). *Accord,* Soule v. Bon Ami Co., 195 N.Y.S. 574, 577 (App. Div. 1922), *aff'd,* 235 N.Y. 609 (1923) (dictum). Related to freedom of contract in a manner never fully specified by the courts were the concepts of consideration and mutuality of obligation. The core principle of freedom of contract also dictated the core principle of contract interpretation—namely, that "in construing contracts the courts endeavor[ed] to arrive at the meaning intended by the parties." Fox Film Corp. v. Springer, 273 N.Y. 434, 436 (1937).

63. See Leff, "Unconsionability and the Code," 489–527, 541–43.

64. See Saratoga State Waters Corp. v. Pratt, 227 N.Y. 429, 441 (1920).

65. Laws of 1920, ch. 275; Berkovitz v. Arbib & Houlberg, Inc., 230 N.Y. 261, 269 (1921); River Brand Rice Mills, Inc. v. Latrobe Brewing Co., 305 N.Y. 36, 41 (1953); Amtorg Trading Corp. v. Camden Fibre Mills, Inc., 304 N.Y. 519 (1952); Cored Panels, Inc. v. Meinhard Commercial Corp., 420 N.Y.S.2d 731 (App. Div. 1979).

66. Stern v. Premier Shirt Corp., 260 N.Y. 201 (1932); A. B. Murray Co. v. Lidgerwood Mfg. Co., 241 N.Y. 455, 457 (1926); Foster v. Stewart, 188 N.Y.S. 151, 153 (App. Div. 1921) (dictum); Spielvogel v. Veit, 189 N.Y.S. 899, 901 (App. Div. 1921) (dictum); Heyman Cohen & Sons, Inc. v. M. Lurie Woolen Co., 232 N.Y. 112, 113–14 (1921); Kleinschmidt Division of SCM Corp. v. Futuronics Corp., 395 N.Y.S.2d 151, 152 (Ct. App. 1977).

67. Compare e.g., Sun Printing & Publishing Ass'n v. Remington Paper & Power Co., 235 N.Y. 338 (1923), with, e.g., Franklin Sugar Refining Co. v. Lipowicz, 247 N.Y. 465, 473 (1928). See Uniform Commercial Code section 2-305.

68. Distillers Factors Corp. v. Country Distillers Products, Inc., 71 N.Y.S.2d 654, 658 (Sup. Ct. 1947); Mesibov, Glinert & Levy, Inc. v. Cohen Bros. Mfg. Co., 245 N.Y. 305, 312–13 (1927); Brooklyn

Public Library v. City of New York, 250 N.Y. 495, 501 (1929); Kirke LaShelle Co. v. Paul Armstrong Co., 263 N.Y. 79, 87 (1933).

69. See, e.g., Johnson Brothers v. American Union Line, 185 N.Y.S. 390 (App. Term 1920).

70. Jacob & Youngs, Inc. v. Kent, 230 N.Y. 239, 240–41 (1921).

71. Ibid., 242–44.

72. Ibid., 247.

73. Ibid., 243; Jacob & Youngs, Inc. v. Kent, 230 N.Y. 656 (1921).

74. Dearstine v. Dunckel, 228 N.Y.S. 191 (App. Div. 1928), *reversing* 223 N.Y.S. 234 (Sup. Ct. 1926); Nieman-Irving & Co. v. Lazanby, 263 N.Y. 91 (1933); American Steel & Iron Co. v. L. B. Foster Co., 266 N.Y.S. 800 (Sup. Ct. 1932), *aff'd,* 262 N.Y.S. 1008 (App. Div.), *aff'd,* 262 N.Y. 623 (1933) (allowing a party that had only substantially performed a contract to recover damages for the other party's breach); Hadden v. Consolidated Edison Co., 356 N.Y.S.2d 249, 255 (Ct. App. 1974), *modified,* 410 N.Y.S.2d 274 (Ct. App. 1978); Witherell v. Lasky, 145 N.Y.S.2d 624, 627 (App. Div. 1955); Barney's Clothes, Inc. v. W. B. O. Broadcasting Corp., 1 N.Y.S.2d 42, 44 (Sup. Ct. 1937), *aff'd,* 3 N.Y.S.2d 206 (App. Div. 1938). See Uniform Commercial Code sec. 2-508, which granted the opportunity to cure to all sellers except those who had no reasonable ground to believe their performance would be aceptable to their buyers.

75. 246 N.Y. 369 (1927).

76. Ibid., 373–75.

77. 221 N.Y. 431 (1917).

78. 234 N.Y. 479 (1923).

79. Lieberman v. Templar Motor Co., 236 N.Y. 139, 147, 149 (1923).

80. Russian Symphony Society v. Holstein, 192 N.Y.S. 64, 65 (App. Div. 1922).

81. 246 N.Y. at 374.

82. I. & I. Holding Corp. v. Gainsburg, 276 N.Y. 427, 433–34 (1938); In re Cooke's Estate, 264 N.Y.S. 336, 344 (Surr. Ct. 1933); Washington Heights Methodist Episcopal Church v. Comfort, 246 N.Y.S. 450, 452 (Mun. Ct. 1930); In re Estate of Lipsky, 256 N.Y.S.2d 429, 431 (Surr. Ct. 1965); Comfort v. McCorkle, 268 N.Y.S. 192, 197 (Sup. Ct. 1933).

83. In re Brunswick's Estate, 256 N.Y.S. 879, 886 (Surr. Ct. 1932); Rubin v. Dairymen's League Co-Op. Ass'n, 284 N.Y. 32, 39 (1940).

84. Arden v. Freydberg, 214 N.Y.S.2d 400, 401, 403 (Ct. App. 1961).

85. Rose v. SPA Realty Associates, 397 N.Y.S.2d 922, 926–27 (Ct. App. 1977); Huggins v. Castle Estates, Inc., 369 N.Y.S.2d 80, 87 (Ct. App. 1975).

86. V. Valente, Inc. v. Mascitti, 295 N.Y.S. 330, 335 (City Ct. 1937); Ricketts v. Pennsylvania R.R., 153 F.2d 757 (2d Cir. 1946).

87. Sabo v. Delman, 3 N.Y.2d 155, 161 (1957); Danann Realty Corp. v. Harris, 5 N.Y.2d 317, 323 (1959); Stryker v. Rusch, 187 N.Y.S.2d 663 (App. Div. 1959).

88. Swift v. Hale Pontiac Sales, Inc., 34 N.Y.S.2d 888, 891 (Mun. Ct. 1942); 119 Fifth Avenue, Inc. v. Taiyo Trading Co., 73 N.Y.S.2d 774, 776 (Sup. Ct. 1947), *aff'd,* 87 N.Y.S.2d 430 (App. Div. 1949).

89. Uniform Commercial Code sec. 1-102(2)(a); Comment 1 to Uniform Commercial Code sec. 1-102.

CHAPTER FOUR

1. Frederick Lewis Allen, *The Big Change: America Transforms Itself, 1900–1950* (New York: Harper, 1952), 202, quoted in Otto L. Bettmann, *The Good Old Days— They Were Terrible* (New York: Random House, 1974), 136.

2. Yair Aharoni, *The No-Risk Society* (Chatham, N.J.: Chatham House, 1981), 47; Allen, *Big*

Change, 56; Bettmen, *Good Old Days,* 71, quoted in William W. Lowrance, *Of Acceptable Risk: Science in the Determination of Safety* (Los Altos, Calif.: W. Kaufmann, 1976), 5; Aharoni, *No-Risk Society,* 47.

3. The No. 1 of New York, 61 F.2d 783, 784 (2d Cir. 1932); Bolivar v. Monnat, 248 N.Y.S. 722, 729 (App. Div. 1931); The No. 1 of New York, *supra* at 784; Rozell v. Rozell, 8 N.Y.S.2d 901, 904 (App. Div.), *aff'd,* 281 N.Y. 106 (1939).

4. Morison v. Broadway & Seventh Ave. R.R., Sup. Ct. 1890, quoted in Randolph E. Bergstrom, *Courting Danger: Injury and Law in New York City, 1870–1910* (Ithaca: Cornell University Press, 1992), 60; Laidlaw v. Sage, 158 N.Y. 73, 104 (1899); Ryan v. New York Central R.R., 35 N.Y. 210, 217 (1866). *Accord,* Bergstrom, *Courting Danger,* 172.

5. Laidlaw v. Sage, 158 N.Y. 73, 102 (1899).

6. Pardington v. Abraham, 87 N.Y.S. 670, 671 (App. Div. 1904), *aff'd on opinion below,* 183 N.Y. 553 (1906).

7. Bergstrom, *Courting Danger,* 142–43, 166, 171–78; M. Bruce Linn, *The Lawyer an Officer of the Court: A Lecture before the Students of the Albany Law School* (Albany: Albany Law School, 1912), 15, quoted in Bergstrom, *Courting Danger,* 173; William B. Hornblower, "New York State Bar Association Minutes," *American Lawyer* 1 (1893), 49, quoted in Bergstrom, *Courting Danger,* 171.

8. Bergstrom, *Courting Danger,* 172, quoted in Bergstrom, *Courting Danger,* 171 n. 12; Elihu Root, *Judicial Decisions and Public Feeling: Address as President of the New York Bar Association at the Annual Meeting in New York City, January 19, 1912* (Washington, D.C.: U.S. Government Printing Office, 1912), 5, quoted in Bergstrom, *Courting Danger,* 172–73; H. T. Smith, "Liability Investigations and Adjustments," in *Liability and Compensation Insurance* (Hartford: Insurance Institute of Hartford, 1913), 67.

9. Lawrence M. Friedman, *Total Justice* (New York: Russell Sage Foundation, 1985), 57–59; Bergstrom, *Courting Danger,* 175.

10. Bolivar v. Monnat, 248 N.Y.S. 722, 729 (App. Div. 1931); Rozell v. Rozell, 8 N.Y.S.2d 901, 904 (App. Div.), *aff'd,* 281 N.Y. 106 (1939); Gould v. Flato, 10 N.Y.S.2d 361, 368 (Sup. Ct. 1938); M. L. Stewart & Co. v. Marcus, 207 N.Y.S. 685, 691 (Sup. Ct. 1924).

11. 248 N.Y. 339 (1928).

12. Pease v. Sinclair Refining Co., 104 F.2d 183, 185 (2d Cir. 1939).

13. 248 N.Y. at 341.

14. Ibid., 350; International Products Co. v. Erie R.R., 244 N.Y. 331, 337, *cert. denied,* 275 U.S. 527 (1927).

15. 248 N.Y. at 350–52, 354–55.

16. See Morton J. Horwitz, *The Transformation of American Law, 1870–1960: The Crisis of Legal Orthodoxy* (New York: Oxford University Press, 1992), 61; G. Edward White, *Tort Law in America: An Intellectual History* (New York: Oxford University Press, 1980), 98–99.

17. Salsedo v. Palmer, 278 F. 92, 99–100 (2d Cir. 1921).

18. Miller v. City of Rochester, 188 N.Y.S. 334, 336 (App. Div. 1921); Glanzer v. Shepard, 233 N.Y. 236, 240–42 (1922). *Glanzer* was later read as support for a far-reaching rule that "a negligent statement may be the basis for a recovery of damages," International Products Co. v. Erie R.R., 244 N.Y. 331, 337 (1927), and that rule, in turn, was held to permit a damage suit by an African American who purchased a bus ticket from Buffalo, New York, to Montgomery, Alabama, on an oral assurance of the ticket agent that he would not be discriminated against on the basis of his race. See Battle v. Central Greyhound Lines, Inc., 13 N.Y.S.2d 357 (Sup. Ct. 1939).

19. Palsgraf v. Long Island R.R., 248 N.Y. 339, 346 (1928). Note should be taken of the parallelism between Cardozo's rulings in *Glanzer* and *Palsgraf,* on the one hand, and MacPherson v. Buick Motor Co., 217 N.Y. 382 (1916), on the other.

20. 248 N.Y. at 341–42, 345.

21. Payne v. City of New York, 277 N.Y. 393, 396 (1938); McGlone v. William Angus, Inc., 248 N.Y.

197, 199 (1928); Storm v. New York Telephone Co., 270 N.Y. 103, 108–9 (1936); Saugerties Bank v. Delaware & Hudson Co., 236 N.Y. 425, 430 (1923).

22. Wagner v. International Ry., 232 N.Y. 176, 180 (1921).

23. Comstock v. Wilson, 257 N.Y. 231, 235 (1931); Gambon v. City of New York, 271 N.Y.S. 244, 248 (Sup. Ct. 1934); Comstock v. Wilson, *supra* at 234–35.

24. Zelenko v. Gimbel Bros., Inc., 287 N.Y.S. 134 (Sup. Ct. 1935), *aff'd*, 287 N.Y.S. 136 (App. Div. 1936); Franklin Fire Ins. Co. v. Weinberg, 181 N.Y.S. 15 (App. Term 1920), *aff'd*, 188 N.Y.S. 610 (App. Div. 1921); Harriman v. New York, C. & St.L.R.R., 253 N.Y. 398 (1930).

25. H. R. Moch Co. v. Rensselaer Water Co., 247 N.Y. 160, 164 (1928); Ultramares Corp. v. Touche, 255 N.Y. 170, 180 (1931); H. R. Moch Co. v. Rensselaer Water Co., *supra* at 168; Ultramares Corp. v. Touche, *supra* at 179–80.

26. H. R. Moch Co. v. Rensselaer Water Co., *supra* at 169; Ultramares Corp. v. Touche, *supra* at 190; State Street Trust Co. v. Ernst, 278 N.Y. 104 (1938).

27. Palsgraf v. Long Island Railroad, 248 N.Y. 339, 350–55 (1928); Pease v. Sinclair Refining Co., 104 F.2d 183, 186 (2d Cir. 1939). Of course, difficult issues could arise at the edges when it became necessary to determine whether a plaintiff was a member of the class on which risk was imposed or whether the injury was of the nature which the defendant should have anticipated. See, e.g., Petition of Kinsman Transit Co., 338 F.2d 708 (2d Cir. 1964), *cert. denied,* 380 U.S. 944 (1965).

28. United States v. Carroll Towing Co., 159 F.2d 169 (2d Cir. 1947); Laidlaw v. Sage, 158 N.Y. 73, 104 (1899); Schubert v. Hotel Astor, Inc., 5 N.Y.S.2d 203, 207 (Sup. Ct. 1938), *aff'd,* 8 N.Y.S.2d 567 (App. Div. 1938), *aff'd,* 281 N.Y. 597 (1939).

29. The No. 1 of New York, 61 F.2d 783, 784 (2d Cir. 1932).

30. Sinram v. Pennsylvania R.R., 61 F.2d 767, 771 (2d Cir. 1932).

31. American Law Institute, Torts Conference Minutes, 1:39–43, quoted in Andrew L. Kaufman, *Cardozo* (Cambridge, Mass.: Harvard University Press, 1998), 290–91. Balancing the utility of conduct against the risk of harm to which it might lead was not novel in contributory negligence cases; in New York, it dated back at least to the nineteenth century case of *Eckert v. Long Island R.R.,* 43 N.Y. 502 (1871). Moreover, reasons of policy called for cost-benefit analysis in contributory negligence while prohibiting it in negligence. Declaring people contributorily negligent for taking risks warranted by self-interest would have interfered excessively with individual freedom of choice, but holding them negligent for profiting from risks they imposed on others merely made them pay for their callousness. For these reasons, the use of cost-benefit analysis in contributory negligence cases was easily reconcilable with the general tendency of New York law during the 1920s and 1930s to impose tort liability on those who intended to impose or foresaw that they would impose harm on another.

32. 217 N.Y. 382 (1916).

33. Genesee County Patrons Fire Relief Ass'n v. Sonneborn Sons, Inc., 263 N.Y. 463 (1934); Smith v. Peerless Glass Co., 259 N.Y. 292 (1932).

34. Creedon v. Automatic Voting Machine Corp., 276 N.Y.S. 609, 611 (App. Div. 1935), *aff'd,* 268 N.Y. 583 (1935); Cook v. A. Garside & Sons, Inc., 259 N.Y.S. 947, 948 (Sup. Ct. 1932); Boyd v. American Can Co., 291 N.Y.S. 205 (App. Div. 1936), *aff'd,* 274 N.Y. 526 (1937).

35. A. J. P. Contracting Corp. v. Brooklyn Builders Supply Co., 15 N.Y.S.2d 424 (App. Div. 1939), *aff'd,* 283 N.Y. 692 (1940); Chysky v. Drake Bros. Co., 235 N.Y. 468 (1923); H. R. Moch Co. v. Rensselaer Water Co., 247 N.Y. 160, 164, 168 (1928); Ultramares Corp. v. Touche, 255 N.Y. 170, 179–80 (1931).

36. Lane v. City of Buffalo, 250 N.Y.S. 579, 582 (App. Div. 1931); Warner v. New York, O.& W.R.R., 204 N.Y.S. 607, 609 (App. Div. 1924), *aff'd,* 239 N.Y. 507 (1924); Loesberg v. Fraad, 197 N.Y.S. 229, 232 (Mun. Ct. 1922); Rochester Gas & Electric Co. v. Dunlop, 266 N.Y.S. 469, 473 (County Ct. 1933).

37. Martin v. Herzog, 228 N.Y. 164, 168 (1920) (emphasis in original). For one reiteration, see Tedla v. Ellman, 280 N.Y. 124, 131 (1939) (dictum).

38. On assumption of risk and contributory negligence, see Dougherty v. Pratt Institute, 244 N.Y. 111 (1926); Camardo v. New York State Ry., 247 N.Y. 111 (1928). There were occasional ameliorations of the rule that contributory negligence totally barred a plaintiff's recovery, such as the doctrine of last clear chance, see Dino v. Eastern Glass Co., 246 N.Y.S. 306 (App. Div. 1930), and the statutory rule transforming contributory negligence into comparative negligence in FELA cases. See Caldine v. Unadilla Valley Ry., 246 N.Y. 365 (1927), *rev'd on other grounds,* 278 U.S. 139 (1928).

39. On liability of landowners, see Miller v. Gimbel Bros, Inc., 262 N.Y. 107 (1933). On joint liability, the basic starting rule was that "a person [was] responsible only for his own torts." Hennessy v. Walker, 279 N.Y. 94, 98 (1938). There were exceptions to this general rule, however, although they were construed narrowly during the 1920s and 1930s. The first exception arose in "the case of master and servant," where "the negligence of the servant, while acting within the scope of his employment, [was] imputable to the master." Dunne v. Contenti, 4 N.Y.S.2d 148, 150 (Sup. Ct. 1938), *aff'd,* 9 N.Y.S.2d 248 (App. Div. 1939). The second exception occurred when two or more people had control over an instrumentality and both acted negligently in operating it or when the negligence of two or more people otherwise "concurred in contributing to the accident." Murphy v. Rochester Telephone Co., 203 N.Y.S. 669, 672 (App. Div. 1924), *aff'd,* 240 N.Y. 629 (1925). Then all or both might be liable.

40. Second Natl. Bank of Toledo v. M. Samuel & Sons, Inc., 12 F.2d 963, 967 (2d Cir.), *cert. denied,* 273 U.S. 720 (1926).

41. Union Car Advertising Co. v. Collier, 263 N.Y. 386 (1934); VanWyck v. Mannino, 9 N.Y.S.2d 684 (App. Div. 1939).

42. Michaels v. Hillman, 183 N.Y.S. 195, 197–200, 202 (Sup. Ct. 1920). Evidence of the importance of the case to the union was its representation by Felix Frankfurter.

43. Grand Shoe Co. v. Children's Shoe Workers' Union, 187 N.Y.S. 886, 888–89 (Sup. Ct. 1920); United Traction Co. v. Droogan, 189 N.Y.S. 39, 41–42 (Sup. Ct. 1921).

44. Schlesinger v. Quinto, 194 N.Y.S. 401, 409 (App. Div. 1922).

45. Harley & Lund Corp. v. Murray Rubber Co., 31 F.2d 932, 934 (2d Cir.), *cert. denied,* 279 U.S. 872 (1929).

46. Stiffler v. Boehm, 206 N.Y.S. 187 (Sup. Ct. 1924); Ryther v. Lefferts, 250 N.Y.S. 699, 701 (App. Div. 1931); Stiffler v. Boehm, *supra* at 188; Morrow v. Yannantuono, 273 N.Y.S. 912, 913 (Sup. Ct. 1934).

47. Knapp v. Penfield, 256 N.Y.S. 41, 42–44 (Sup. Ct. 1932).

48. Beardsley v. Kilmer, 193 N.Y.S. 285, 286, 288–90 (App. Div. 1922), *aff'd,* 236 N.Y. 80 (1923).

49. In re Spencer Kellogg & Sons, Inc., 52 F.2d 129, 135 (2d Cir. 1931), *rev'd on other grounds sub nom.* The Linseed King, 285 U.S. 502 (1932); Carroll Bldg. Corp. v. Louis Greenberg Plumbing Supplies, Inc., 214 N.Y.S. 42, 44 (App. Div. 1926), *aff'd,* 244 N.Y. 543 (1926); Al Raschid v. News Syndicate Co., 267 N.Y.S. 221 (App. Div. 1933), *modified,* 265 N.Y. 1, 4 (1934).

50. 265 N.Y. at 4.

51. Du-Art Film Labs, Inc. v. Consolidated Film Industries, Inc., 15 F. Supp. 689, 690 (S.D.N.Y. 1936).

52. Benton v. Kennedy-Van Saun Mfg. & Eng. Co., 145 N.Y.S.2d 703, 706 (Sup. Ct. 1955), *aff'd,* 152 N.Y.S.2d 955 (App. Div. 1956); Rager v. McCloskey, 305 N.Y. 75, 80 (1953); Advance Music Corp. v. American Tobacco Co., 50 N.Y.S.2d 287, 292 (Sup. Ct. 1944); Herbert Products, Inc. v. Oxy-Dry Sprayer Corp., 145 N.Y.S.2d 168, 171 (Sup. Ct. 1955); Advance Music Corp. v. American Tobacco Co., 296 N.Y. 79 (1946); Ruiz v. Bertolotti, 236 N.Y.S.2d 854, 855 (Sup. Ct. 1962); Wilson v. Hacker, 101 N.Y.S.2d 461 (Sup. Ct. 1950).

53. Lincoln Trust Co. v. Williams Building Corp., 229 N.Y. 313 (1920); Village of Great Neck Estates v. Bemak & Lehman, Inc., 218 N.Y.S. 359, 361 (Sup. Ct. 1926), *rev'd on other grounds,* 228 N.Y.S.

917 (App. Div.), *aff'd*, 248 N.Y. 651 (1928); Cohen v. Rosedale Realty Co., 199 N.Y.S. 4, 7 (Sup. Ct. 1923), *aff'd*, 206 N.Y.S. 893 (App. Div. 1924); Joyce v. Dobson, 4 N.Y.S.2d 648 (Sup. Ct.), *rev'd on other grounds*, 8 N.Y.S.2d 768 (App. Div. 1938); Keenly v. McCarthy, 244 N.Y.S. 63, 66 (Sup. Ct. 1930).

54. Wulfsohn v. Burden, 241 N.Y. 288, 300–301 (1925); Westchester Housing Corp. v. Bunnell, 224 N.Y.S. 326, *modified on other grounds*, 227 N.Y.S. 358 (Sup. Ct. 1927); 14th Street Warehouse Corp. v. Murdock, 297 N.Y.S. 420, 423 (Sup. Ct. 1937). Among the uses excluded from business districts were a wholesale and retail coal business, see Welch v. City of Niagara Falls, 205 N.Y.S. 454 (App. Div. 1924); multicar garages and parking fields, see Best & Co. v. Incorporated Village of Garden City, 286 N.Y.S. 980 (App. Div. 1936), *aff'd*, 273 N.Y. 564 (1937); and gasoline filling stations, especially if they posed a danger of fire or increased traffic congestion. See Larkin Co. v. Schwab, 242 N.Y. 330 (1926). Industrial uses could also be excluded from business zones, at least when they bordered on residential zones. See Hamlett v. Snedeker, 283 N.Y.S. 906 (App. Div. 1935).

55. 444 East Fifty-Seventh St. Corp. v. Deegan, 235 N.Y.S. 11 (App. Div. 1929); People ex rel. Helvetia Realty Co. v. Leo, 183 N.Y.S. 37 (Sup. Ct. 1920), *aff'd*, 185 N.Y.S. 949 (App. Div.), *aff'd*, 231 N.Y. 619 (1921); Town of Islip v. F. E. Summers Coal & Lumber Co., 257 N.Y. 167 (1931).

56. Monument Garage Corp. v. Levy, 266 N.Y. 339, 344 (1935); In re Kensington-Davis Corp., 239 N.Y. 54, 58 (1924); Dowsey v. Village of Kensington, 257 N.Y. 221, 230–31 (1931); Ficaro v. Walsh, 235 N.Y.S. 254 (App. Div. 1929); People ex rel. Bruckner v. Walsh, 205 N.Y.S. 396 (App. Div. 1924).

57. Beckmann v. Talbot, 278 N.Y. 146 (1938); City of New Rochelle v. Beckwith, 278 N.Y. 315, 318–19 (1938).

58. 278 N.Y. 222 (1938).

59. See People ex rel. Arverne Bay Const. Co. v. Murdocik, 286 N.Y.S. 785, 786 (App. Div. 1936), *aff'd*, 271 N.Y. 631 (1936).

60. Arverne Bay Const. Co. v. Thatcher, 2 N.Y.S.2d 112, 114 (App. Div. 1938).

61. Arverne Bay Const. Co. v. Thatcher, 278 N.Y. 222, 229 (1938).

62. 260 U.S. 393 (1922).

63. 278 N.Y. 231–32 (emphasis in original).

CHAPTER FIVE

1. Stephen Fox, *The Mirror Makers: A History of American Advertising and Its Creators* (New York: William Morrow, 1984), 101.

2. Alan Brinkley, *The End of Reform: New Deal Liberalism in Recession and War* (New York: Knopf, 1995), 5.

3. Walter Lippmann, *The Method of Freedom* (New York: Macmillan, 1934), 41–42.

4. Ibid., 45–46, 57–58; quoted in Arthur M. Schlesinger Jr., *The Politics of Upheaval* (Boston: Houghton Mifflin, 1960), 407.

5. "Nazis Smash, Loot and Burn Jewish Shops and Temples Until Goebbels Calls Halt," *New York Times,* Nov. 11, 1938, p. 1, cols. 6–8.

6. "Austria Disappears," *New York Times,* Mar. 14, 1938, p. 14, col. 1; "Austria Absorbed into Hitler Reich," *New York Times,* Mar. 14, 1938, p. 2, col. 3.

7. Quoted in Anthony Read and David Fisher, *Kristallnacht: The Nazi Night of Terror* (New York: Random House, 1989), 151; "'Great Germany,'" *New York Times,* Nov. 11, 1938, p. 24, col. 1; "War on Anti-Semitism Held Universal Cause," *New York Times,* Mar. 13, 1938, p. 35, col. 1; "Sees Menace to Freedom: Dr. R. C. Knox Warns of Danger in Totalitarian State," *New York Times,* Mar. 14, 1938, p. 10, col. 5. On the background of Dewey, see Lawrence Fleischer, "Thomas E. Dewey and Earl

Warren: The Rise of the Twentieth Century Urban Prosecutor," *California Western Law Review* 28 (1991): 1.

8. "Rallies Jews to Defense," *New York Times*, Mar. 14, 1938, p. 3, col. 8; "War on Anti-Semitism Held Universal Cause," *New York Times,* Mar. 13, 1938, p. 35, col. 1; quoted in Read and Fisher, *Kristallnacht,* 154.

9. Quoted in Arthur M. Schlesinger Jr., *The Politics of Upheaval* (Boston: Houghton Mifflin, 1960), 407; quoted in Brinkley, *End of Reform,* 146; Reinhold Niebuhr, "The Collectivist Bogy," *Nation,* Oct. 21, 1944, 478.

10. Harlan Fiske Stone to Irving Lehman, Apr. 26, 1938, quoted in Alpheus T. Mason, *Harland Fiske Stone: Pillar of the Law* (New York: Viking, 1956), 515; *United States v. Carolene Products Co.,* 304 U.S. 144, 152 n.4 (1938).

11. For an eloquent statement of the received wisdom, see Robert M. Cover, "The Origins of Judicial Activism in the Protection of Minorities," *Yale Law Journal* 91 (1982): 1287–89.

12. Quoted in Dorothy Thompson, *Let the Record Speak* (Boston: Houghton Mifflin, 1939), 256–60; quoted in Read and Fisher, *Kristallnacht,* 155.

13. See *Record of the Constitutional Convention of the State of New York, 1938* (Albany: J. B. Lyon, 1938), 395, 404, 879. On an earlier tentative vote, the margin had been sixty-seven in favor and eighty-four opposed. See ibid., 616. See also ibid., 513–14.

14. Ibid., 612, 606–7, 522, 468, 405, 407, 468, 606–7, 612. On Dewey, see Fleischer, "Thomas E. Dewey and Earl Warren." On conservative fears of immigrants, especially Italians, see generally Nathan Glazer and Daniel Patrick Moynihan, *Beyond the Melting Pot: The Negroes, Puerto Ricans, Jews, Italians, and Irish of New York City* (Cambridge, Mass.: MIT Press, 1963), 196–97, 210–12.

15. *Record of Constitutional Convention,* 461–63, 514, 577.

16. Ibid., 514–15.

17. Ibid., 546–47.

18. Interview with John Sargent, quoted in Lizabeth Cohen, *Making a New Deal: Industrial Workers in Chicago, 1919–1939* (Cambridge: Cambridge University Press, 1990), 293. See generally ibid., 251–360; Philip Taft, *Organized Labor in American History* (New York: Harper & Row, 1964), 492–522. See also Sidney Lens, *The Labor Wars from the Molly Maguires to the Sitdowns* (Garden City, N.Y.: Doubleday, 1973), 291–321. For a contemporaneous account, see Benjamin Stolberg, *The Story of the CIO* (New York: Viking, 1938), 156–86.

19. *Record of Constitutional Convention,* 487–88.

20. *The Complete Report of Mayor LaGuardia's Commission on the Harlem Riot of March 19, 1935* (New York: Arno, 1969), 116, 120–21.

21. *Record of Constitutional Convention,* 1120–21, 1123 (emphasis added).

22. For an example of the judiciary's growing sensitivity to issues of religious prejudice, see Bowen v. Mahoney Coal Corp., 10 N.Y.S.2d 454 (App. Div. 1939) (mention of possibly prejudicial reference to opposing co-counsel being Jewish).

23. For general studies of the home front during World War II, see John Morton Blum, *V Was for Victory: Politics and American Culture during World War II* (New York: Harcourt, Brace, 1976); William O'Neill, *A Democracy at War: America's Fight at Home and Abroad in World War II* (New York: Free Press, 1993); Richard Polenberg, *War and Society: The United States, 1941–1945* (Philadelphia: Lippincott, 1972). An unusual and noteworthy book is William M. Tuttle Jr., *Daddy's Gone to War: The Second World War in the Lives of America's Children* (New York: Oxford University Press, 1993).

24. "On Plans for 1941" [Mar. 12, 1941], in folder titled "Program and Policy, 1940–42," Box 34, Morris Waldman Papers, YIVO Institute for Jewish Research, New York, N.Y., quoted in David B. Truman, "A Report on Common Council for American Unity and Recommendations," August 1946,

Records of the American Council for Nationalities Service, Immigration History Research Center, St. Paul, Minn.; Council for Democracy, "First Annual Report," October 1941, Box 10, Lowell Mellett Papers, Franklin D. Roosevelt Library, Hyde Park, N.Y.; Read Lewis to Frederick Keppel, Feb. 3, 1939, folder titled "Foreign Language Information Service—Division of Intercultural Interpretation, 1939," Records of American Council for Nationalities Service, Immigration History Research Center, St. Paul, Minn. See generally Richard W. Steele, "The War on Intolerance: The Reformulation of American Nationalism, 1939–1941," *Journal of American Ethnic History* 9 (1989): 9, 14.

25. Ulric Bell and William B. Lewis to Archibald MacLeish, Feb. 3, 1942, quoted in Richard Polenberg, *One Nation Divisible: Class, Race, and Ethnicity in the United States since 1938* (New York: Viking, 1980), 47; Ashley Montagu, *Man's Most Dangerous Myth: The Fallacy of Race* (New York: Columbia University Press, 1942), 179–80; Wilman v. Miller, 35 N.Y.S.2d 352, 353–54 (Sup. Ct. 1942), aff'd, 36 N.Y.S.2d 187 (App. Div. 1942); "Let Our Hearts Be Stout: A Prayer by the President of the United States," *New York Times*, June 7, 1944, p. 1, cols. 2–3, quoted in Frances Perkins, *The Roosevelt I Knew* (New York: Viking, 1946), 113.

26. John Hersey, *A Bell for Adano* (New York: Knopf, 1944), vi; Ernie Pyle, *Here Is Your War* (New York: Military Heritage Press, 1943), 126; Polenberg, *One Nation Divisible*, 50; Tuttle, *Daddy's Gone to War*, 231–35.

27. See Kenneth T. Jackson, *Crabgrass Frontier: The Suburbanization of the United States* (New York: Oxford University Press, 1985), 234–38, 278–82; Polenberg, *One Nation Divisible*, 145; Bureau of the Census, *Fourteenth Census of the United States: 1920, State Compendium: New York. Statistics of Population, Occupation, Agriculture, Manufacture and Mines and Quarries for the State, Counties, and Cities* (Washington, D.C.: U.S. Government Printing Office, 1924), 38 (Table 9); Bureau of the Census, *Fifteenth Census of the United States: 1930, Population, Volume 3: Reports by States, Showing the Composition and Characteristics of the Population for Counties, Cities, and Townships or Other Minor Civil Divisions* (Washington, D.C.: U.S. Government Printing Office, 1932), 298–99 (Table 18); Bureau of the Census, *Sixteenth Census of the United States: 1940, Population, Volume 2: Characteristics of the Population, Part 5: New York–Oregon* (Washington, D.C.: U.S. Government Printing Office, 1943), 39 (Table 21); Bureau of the Census, *Eighteenth Census of the United States: 1960, Population, Volume 1: Characteristics of the Population, Part 34: New York* (Washington, D.C.: U.S. Government Printing Office, 1963), 355 (Table 82). In 1920, immigrants from Italy constituted the largest proportion of the foreign-born group with 4,290, slightly outnumbering the 4,073 German immigrants. Poles with 3,644 and the Irish with 3,499 followed. See *1920 Census*, 53–54 (Table 12). By 1930, the foreign-born white population grew to 63,437, or 21 percent of the county population. Interestingly, most of these immigrants came from northern Europe, not central or southern Europe. German immigrants (11,588) outnumbered those from the United Kingdom (England, Scotland, Wales, and Northern Ireland) with 10,168, from Italy with 9,145, and from Poland with 5,923. See *1930 Census*, 298–99 (Table 18). In 1940, Germans still constituted the largest part of the foreign-born group with 12,050. Immigrants from Italy (9,973), the United Kingdom (9,458), and Ireland (5,013) followed. See *1940 Census*, 63 (Table 24).

Since census data do not report religion, the best measure of this influx is the founding of new houses of worship—a phenomenon that is also a precondition of suburban migration, since without parishes and synagogues Catholics and Jews would have had to give up their faiths when they moved into the suburbs. The numbers, in fact, are striking: more than half of all synagogues in Nassau County and approximately one-fourth of all Roman Catholic parishes were founded between the end of World War II and the end of the 1950s. See Tobie Newman and Sylvia Landow, *"That I May Dwell among Them": A Synagogue History of Nassau County* (New York: Conference of Jewish Organizations of Nassau County, 1991); *1992–93 Blue Book: Official Directory and Buyers Guide to Catholic Institutions* (Brooklyn: Tablet Publishing, 1992), 269–89; Joan deL. Leonard, *Richly Blessed:*

The Diocese of Rockville Centre, 1957–1990 (Rockville Centre, N.Y.: Diocese of Rockville Centre, 1991), 331–48.

28. This information is compiled from *1992–93 Blue Book,* 269–89; Leonard, *Richly Blessed,* 331–48.

29. See Robert Reed Coles and Peter Luyster Van Santvoord, *A History of Glen Cove* (Glen Cove, N.Y.: Privately published, 1967), 26; Newman and Landow, *"That I May Dwell among Them,",* 13, 128; Jay Schulman, "The Jews of Great Neck: A Heritage Affirmed," in *Ethnicity in Suburbia: The Long Island Experience,* ed. Salvatore J. LaGumina (N.p.: Privately published, 1980), 71; American Jewish Committee, *American Jewish Year Book, 1961* (1961), 59 (Table 1).

30. See Heidi Fried, "Early Jewish Settlement in Nassau County: The Communities, the People, and the Synagogues," 21 (manuscript on file at Long Island Studies Institute, Hofstra University, Hempstead, N.Y.); Newman and Landow, *"That I May Dwell among Them,",* 13, 119. Whereas Temple Gates of Zion in Valley Stream, founded by twenty-five families in 1929, possessed a membership of only forty families in 1932 and eighty in 1939, see ibid., 156, Temple Beth-El in Great Neck, one of the largest in the county, counted more than fifteen hundred families among its membership in the postwar decades. See ibid., 59.

31. Henry Wallace, "The Century of the Common Man," in *America at War: The Home Front, 1941–1945,* ed. Richard Polenberg (Englewood Cliffs, N.J.: Prentice-Hall, 1968);, 158, 159; "An Economic Bill of Rights," Jan. 11, 1944, in Henry Steele Commager, ed., *Documents of American History,* 8th ed. (New York: Appleton-Century-Crofts, 1968), 2:483, 484–85; Ulric Bell and William B. Lewis to Archibald MacLeish, Feb. 3, 1942, quoted in Polenberg, *One Nation Divisible,* 47; Archibald MacLeish to Franklin D. Roosevelt, May 16, 1942, quoted in Blum, *V Was for Victory,* 29.

32. See U.S. Department of Commerce, Bureau of the Census, *Historical Statistics of the United States: Colonial Times to 1970, Part 1* (Washington, D.C.: U.S. Government Printing Office, 1976), 224; U.S. Department of Commerce, Bureau of the Census, *Statistical Abstract of the United States,* 116th ed. (Washington, D.C.: U.S. Government Printing Office, 1996), 443. The increases in the text have been adjusted for inflation and measure growth rates in constant dollars. Changes in the government's statistical categories made it necessary to move from GNP to GDP in making the calculation for 1980. Both GNP and GDP are readily available for 1960, and thus the 930 percent figure in the text reflects percentage increase in GNP to 1960 and percentage increase in GDP after that date. In comparison with these post-1940 growth rates, the growth rate from 1920 to 1929 was a mere 12.7 percent, and in the Great Depression, gross national product fell below its 1920 amount, which it did not again attain until 1940. The 1929 GNP was not reached and surpassed until 1941, by which time the phenomenal growth of the new era had begun. See U.S. Department of Commerce, Bureau of the Census, *Historical Statistics, Part 1,* 224.

33. Statement of James Covert, in Mark J. Harris, Franklin D. Mitchell, and Steven J. Schechter, eds., *The Homefront: America during World War II* (New York: Putnam, 1984), 240; Statement of Henry Fiering, ibid., 242; Sherman H. Dryer, *Radio in Wartime* (New York: Greenberg, 1942), quoted in Blum, *V Was for Victory,* 26. *Accord,* Statement of Laura Briggs, in Harris, Mitchell, and Schechter, eds., *The Homefront,* 255. See also Blum, *V Was for Victory,* 12–13.

34. See Jackson, *Crabgrass Frontier,* 234–38, 278–82.

35. John D'Emilio, *Sexual Politics, Sexual Communities: The Making of a Homosexual Minority in the United States* (Chicago: University of Chicago Press, 1983), 24; John D'Emilio and Estelle B. Freedman, *Intimate Matters: A History of Sexuality in America* (New York: Harper & Row, 1988), 260; Allan Berube, "Marching to a Different Drummer: Lesbian and Gay GIs in World War II," in *Hidden from History: Reclaiming the Gay and Lesbian Past,* ed. Martin B. Duberman, Martha Vicinus, and George Chauncey (New York: New American Library, 1989), 383–85; Winston W. Ehrmann, *Premarital Dating Behavior* (New York: Holt, 1959), 70.

36. Statement of Virginia Rasmussen, in Harris, Mitchell, and Schechter, eds., *The Homefront,* 172, 174–75; Statement of Frances Veeder, ibid., 175, 177; quoted in Ehrmann, *Premarital Dating,* 74; Statement of Roger Montgomery, in Harris, Mitchell, and Schechter, eds., *The Homefront,* 185, 186; quoted in Ehrmann, *Premarital Dating,* 73.

37. Quoted in Allan Berube, *Coming Out under Fire: The History of Gay Men and Women in World War Two* (New York: Free Press, 1990), 98, 102, 119; D'Emilio, *Sexual Politics,* 27–30; quoted ibid., 30 (emphasis in original).

38. See John D'Emilio, "Gay Politics and Community in San Francisco since World War II," in *Hidden from History,* ed. Duberman, Vicinus, and Chauncey, 456, 458; Ehrmann, *Premarital Dating,* 75; quoted in Berube, *Coming Out under Fire,* 244–45; Beth L. Bailey, *From Front Porch to Back Seat: Courtship in Twentieth-Century America* (Baltimore: Johns Hopkins University Press, 1988), 49, 51.

39. Linda Gordon, *Heroes of Their Own Lives: The Politics and History of Family Violence* (New York: Viking, 1988), 269–70.

40. "An Economic Bill of Rights," Jan. 11, 1944, in Commager, ed., *Documents of American History,* 2:483–85; Daniel T. Rodgers, *Contested Truths: Keywords in American Politics since Independence* (New York: Basic Books, 1987), 217–22; Berube, *Coming Out under Fire,* 228–54; John Stuart Mill, ed. Currin V. Shields, *On Liberty* (New York: Bobbs, Merrill, 1956), 13; "The Law: Sin and Criminality," *Time,* May 30, 1955, p. 13, col. 1, quoting an unspecified ALI source; James Burnham, "Rhetoric and Peace," *Partisan Review* 17 (1950), 861, 870.

41. Wuebker v. James, 58 N.Y.S.2d 671, 677–78 (County Ct. 1944); Emergency Price Control Act of 1942, sec. 1(a), 56 Stat. 23 (1942).

42. People on Complaint of Cooper v. Roth, 44 N.Y.S.2d 193, 197 (Magis. Ct. 1943). For the relevant legislation, see Laws of 1942, ch. 544.

43. 321 U.S. 414 (1944).

44. See Wuebker v. James, 58 N.Y.S.2d 671 (County Ct. 1944).

45. See, e.g., Butter & Egg Merchants Ass'n v. LaGuardia, 47 N.Y.S.2d 913 (Sup. Ct. 1944).

46. People v. Brongofsky, 50 N.Y.S.2d 32, 35, 39 (Magis. Ct. 1943); Yakus v. United States, 321 U.S. 414, 461 (1944) (Rutledge, J., dissenting); ibid., 424, 432.

47. Bowles v. Willingham, 321 U.S. 503 (1944); Schwartz v. Trajer Realty Corp., 56 F. Supp. 930, 932 (S.D.N.Y. 1944); Twentieth Century Assocs., Inc. v. Waldman, 294 N.Y. 571 (1945), *appeal dism.,* 326 U.S. 696 (1946). For the legislation controlling commercial rents, see Laws of 1945, ch. 3, sec. 1 (1945) (emphasis added). The initial statute was enacted as emergency legislation in January 1945 but was extended on a more permanent basis later in the same year. See Laws of 1945, chs. 314 and 315.

48. See Revenue Act of 1942, secs. 102–3, 56 Stat. 798, 802–3 (1942); Individual Income Tax Act of 1944, secs. 3–4, 58 Stat. 231–32 (1944).

49. But some were reinstated temporarily after their initial expiration. See United States v. Porhownik, 182 F.2d 829 (2d Cir.), *cert. denied,* 340 U.S. 825 (1950).

50. For cases decided under the Trading with the Enemy Act, 40 Stat. 411 (1917), see United States v. Broverman, 180 F. Supp. 631 (S.D.N.Y. 1959); United States v. Weishaupt, 167 F. Supp. 211 (E.D.N.Y. 1958). For cases decided under the Defense Production Act, 64 Stat. 798 (1950), see United States v. Edwin P. Stimpson Co., 155 F. Supp. 289 (E.D.N.Y. 1957); United States v. S. Rosengarten & Co., 106 F. Supp. 436 (S.D.N.Y. 1952); United States v. K. & F. Packing & Food Corp., 102 F. Supp. 26 (W.D.N.Y. 1951). See Revenue Act of 1964, sec. 111, 78 Stat. 19–23 (1964).

51. See George Chauncey, *Gay New York: Gender, Urban Culture, and the Making of the Gay Male World, 1890–1940* (New York: Basic Books, 1994), 131–40, 151–267.

52. See ibid., 305–29, 335 (emphasis in original).

53. See Leonard V. Harrison and Elizabeth Laine, *After Repeal: A Study of Liquor Control Administration* (New York: Harper & Bros., 1936), 93, 215–16. See also Chauncey, *Gay New York,* 335–47.

54. Maurice A. Fitzgerald, Sheriff of Queens County, to Fiorello H. Guardia, Mayor of the City of New York, May 31, 1939, in Mayors' Papers, New York City Municipal Archives.

55. *Record of Constitutional Convention,* 1121; William P. LaPiana, "Book Review," *New York Law School Law Review* 39 (1994) 607, 632.

56. LaPiana, "Book Review," 632.

57. Of course, the political consensus of the 1950s resulted, at least in part, from the political marginalization during that decade of certain groups of people, such as Communists, immigrants, and homosexuals. For some of the vast literature on this marginalization, see, e.g., James MacGregor Burns, *The Crosswinds of Freedom* (New York: Knopf, 1989), 230–32, 238–46, 251–59; Chauncey, *Gay New York,* 8–11; Richard M. Fried, *Nightmare in Red: The McCarthy Era in Perspective* (New York: Oxford University Press, 1990); Robert Goldston, *The American Nightmare: Senator Joseph R. McCarthy and the Politics of Hate* (Indianapolis: Bobbs-Merrill, 1973); Paul L. Murphy, *The Constitution in Crisis Times, 1918–1969* (New York: Harper & Row, 1972), 279–309.

58. Woods v. Lancet, 303 N.Y. 349, 354–55 (emphasis added).

59. Bing v. Thunig, 163 N.Y.S.2d 3, 11 (Ct. App. 1957); Heyert v. Orange & Rockland Utilities, Inc., 271 N.Y.S.2d 201, 207 (Ct. App. 1966); Board of Education of Central School District No. 1 v. Allen, 281 N.Y.S.2d 799, 804 (Ct. App. 1967), *aff'd,* 392 U.S. 236 (1968); Letendre v. Hartford Accident & Indemnity Co., 289 N.Y.S.2d 183, 189 (Ct. App. 1968).

60. Fortunato v. Craft, 250 N.Y.S.2d 746, 747 (App. Div. 1964); Killip v. Rochester General Hospital, 146 N.Y.S.2d 164, 167 (Sup. Ct. 1955); People v. Morton, 132 N.Y.S.2d 302, 307 (App. Div.), *aff'd,* 308 N.Y. 96 (1954); In re Hahn, 149 N.Y.S.2d 140, 145 (Sup. Ct,), *rev'd sub nom.* People ex rel. Hahn v. Haines, 149 N.Y.S.2d 407 (App. Div. 1956).

61. Heyert v. Orange & Rockland Utilities, Inc., 271 N.Y.S.2d 201, 206 (Ct. App. 1966) (dictum); Isadore Rosen & Sons, Inc. v. Cerussi, 144 N.Y.S.2d 602, 604 (Sup. Ct. 1955); Higby v. Mahoney, 421 N.Y.S.2d 35, 36 (Ct. App. 1979); Simonson v. Cahn, 313 N.Y.S.2d 97, 98–99 (Ct. App. 1970).

62. Klein v. Klein, 87 N.Y.S.2d 293, 294 (Domestic Relations Ct. 1949) (italics omitted); Powell v. Columbian Presbyterian Medical Center, 267 N.Y.S.2d 450, 452 (Sup. Ct. 1965); Bator v. Hungarian Commercial Bank, 87 N.Y.S.2d 700, 703 (Sup. Ct.), *modified on other grounds,* 90 N.Y.S.2d 35 (App. Div. 1949); Davies v. Davies, 62 N.Y.S.2d 790, 793 (Dom. Rel. Ct. 1946); State Tax Commission v. Shor, 400 N.Y.S.2d 805, 808 (Ct. App. 1977); Astor v. Watson, 71 N.Y.S.2d 332, 335 (Sup. Ct.), *aff'd,* 71 N.Y.S.2d 296 (App. Div. 1947); In re Verly Building Corp., 35 N.Y.s.2d 891, 892 (App. Div. 1942).

63. People v. Velez, 388 N.Y.S.2d 519, 530 (Sup. Ct. 1976); Simon v. City of New York, 279 N.Y.S.2d 223, 228 (Civil Ct. 1967); Donawitz v. Danek, 397 N.Y.S.2d 592, 595 (Ct. App. 1977); Jones v. Beame, 408 N.Y.S.2d 449, 452 (Ct. App. 1978); Endresz v. Friedberg, 301 N.Y.S.2d 65, 73 (Ct. App. 1969).

64. See Henry M. Hart Jr. and Albert M. Sacks, *The Legal Process: Basic Problems in the Making and Application of Law,* ed. William N. Eskridge and Philip Frickey (Westbury, N.Y.: Foundation Press, 1994); "In Memoriam: Henry J. Friendly," *Harvard Law Review* 99 (1986): 1709–27; Paul Gewirtz, "A Lawyer's Death," *Harvard Law Review* 100 (1987): 2053–56; William E. Nelson, "Judge Weinfeld and the Adjudicatory Process: A Law Finder in an Age of Judicial Lawmakers," *New York University Law Review* 50 (1975): 980–1007.

65. A book that recapitulates this approach is Ronald Dworkin, *Law's Empire* (Cambridge, Mass.: Harvard University Press, 1986), which criticizes the earlier realist view of Llewellyn and others that policy entered the law only in occasional hard cases, not in all cases. See ibid., 31–46.

66. The history of twentieth-century academic jurisprudence in America has been a subject of intense scholarly debate, but all writers agree on the main outlines of the received wisdom as stated in the text. The two most prominent recent books are Neil Duxbury, *Patterns of American Jurisprudence* (Oxford: Clarendon Press, 1995), and Morton J. Horwitz, *The Transformation of American Law, 1870–1960: The Crisis of Legal Orthodoxy* (New York: Oxford University Press, 1992). Two influential

seminal articles are by G. Edward White, "From Sociological Jurisprudence to Realism: Jurisprudence and Social Change in Early Twentieth-Century America," *Virginia Law Review* 58 (1972): 999–1028, and "The Evolution of Reasoned Elaboration: Jurisprudential Criticism and Social Change," *Virginia Law Review* 59 (1972): 279–302.

CHAPTER SIX

1. People on Complaint of Grahl v. Vogt, 34 N.Y.S.2d 968, 969–70 (Magis. Ct. 1942).

2. Ibid., 971. See Chaplinsky v. New Hampshire, 315 U.S. 568 (1942).

3. Dennis v. United States, 341 U.S. 494, 501, 551 (Frankfurter, J.), 570 (Jackson, J.).

4. Claim of Albertson, 202 N.Y.S.2d 5 (Ct. App. 1960), *rev'd in part sub nom.* Communist Party, U.S.A. v. Catherwood, 367 U.S. 389 (1961).

5. See, e.g., Lerner v. Casey, 357 U.S. 468 (1958); Harisiades v. Shaughnessy, 342 U.S. 580 (1952); Adler v. Board of Education of City of New York, 342 U.S. 485 (1952); Daniman v. Board of Higher Education of City of New York, 306 N.Y. 532 (1954), *rev'd in part sub nom.* Slochower v. Board of Higher Education of City of New York, 350 U.S. 551 (1956); United States v. Hauck, 155 F.2d 141 (2d Cir. 1946); Long v. Somervell, 22 N.Y.S.2d 931 (Sup. Ct. 1940), *aff'd,* 27 N.Y.S.2d 445 (App. Div. 1941).

6. People v. Nahman, 298 N.Y. 95, 100 (1948); People v. Carcel, 150 N.Y.S.2d 436, 437 (Magis. Ct. 1956), *rev'd,* 165 N.Y.S.2d 113 (Ct. App. 1957); Ellis v. Dixon, 118 N.Y.S.2d 815 (Sup. Ct.), *aff'd,* 120 N.Y.S.2d 854 (App. Div. 1953), *cert. dismissed,* 349 U.S. 458 (1955).

7. People v. Feiner, 300 N.Y. 391, 401 (1950), *aff'd,* 340 U.S. 315 (1951).

8. People v. Kunz, 300 N.Y. 273, 277 (1949), *rev'd,* 340 U.S. 290 (1951); People v. Feiner, 300 N.Y. 391, 396 (1950). I fully appreciate the inconsistency of my interpretation with the central canon of today's First Amendment jurisprudence. Judges during the 1940s and 1950s did, however, exclude broad categories of speech, such as commercial speech, from First Amendment protection—an exclusion that has since come to be seen as content-based discrimination. See Linmark Associates, Inc. v. Willingboro, 431 U.S. 85 (1977). For New York cases denying constitutional protection to commercial speech, see, e.g., Gold Sound, Inc. v. City of New York, 89 N.Y.S.2d 860 (Sup. Ct. 1949).

9. See Railway Mail Association v. Corsi, 293 N.Y. 315 (1944), *aff'd,* 326 U.S. 88 (1945), where the Court of Appeals held that legislation prohibiting discrimination by labor unions on grounds of race, color, or creed invalidated the provision in the association's constitution limiting membership to whites and native Americans, and American Jewish Congress v. Carter, 190 N.Y.S.2d 218 (Sup. Ct. 1959), *aff'd,* 213 N.Y.S.2d 60 (Ct. App. 1961), which upheld the priority of New York's antidiscrimination legislation over Saudi Arabian anti-Semitism in hirings by the Arabian-American Oil Company.

10. Ridgway v. Cockburn, 296 N.Y.S. 936, 943 (Sup. Ct. 1937); Kemp v. Rubin, 69 N.Y.S.2d 680, 683, 685 (Sup. Ct.), *aff'd,* 75 N.Y.S.2d 768 (App. Div. 1947), quoting Hirabayashi v. United States, 320 U.S. 81, 110 (1943) (Murphy, J., dissenting); Dury v. Neely, 69 N.Y.S.2d 677 (Sup. Ct. 1942). Kemp v. Rubin was reversed only when the Supreme Court reached the opposite result in Shelley v. Kraemer, 334 U.S. 1 (1948). See 298 N.Y. 590 (1948). On the increasing use of restrictive covenants, see John P. Dean, "Only Caucasian: A Study of Race Covenants," *Journal of Land Public Utility Economics* 23 (1947): 428.

11. Dorsey v. Stuyvesant Town Corp., 299 N.Y. 512, 531, 535 (1949), *cert. denied,* 339 U.S. 981 (1950); Dorsey v. Stuyvesant Town Corp., 74 N.Y.S.2d 220, 226 (Sup. Ct. 1947).

12. 299 N.Y. at 536, 545, quoting Hirabayashi v. United States, 320 U.S. 81, 110 (1943) (Murphy, J., dissenting).

13. Goldstein v. Mills, 57 N.Y.S.2d 810 (Sup. Ct. 1945), *aff'd,* 62 N.Y.S.2d 619 (App. Div. 1946).

See Tax Law sec. 4. Paradoxically, discrimination on ethnic and religious grounds had increased between the mid-1930s and the late 1940s. See Harry Schneiderman and Morris Fine, eds., *American Jewish Yearbook: Volume 50 (5709) 1948–1949* (1949), 768; Commission on Law and Social Action of the American Jewish Congress, "Dr. Howard E. Wilson's Report to the New York State Board of Regents on the Admissions Practices of the Nine New York State Medical Schools," 18 (ms. in Blaustein Library, American Jewish Committee, New York, N.Y., 1953).

14. See E. Digby Baltzell, *The Protestant Establishment: Aristocracy and Caste in America* (New York: Random House, 1964), 211; "A.D.A. Head Assails Report by Horner," *New York Times,* Feb. 9, 1945, p. 32, col. 5; "Dentists Protest Columbia Merger," *New York Times,* Feb. 8, 1945, p. 21, col. 8; "Columbia Merger Is Linked to Fund," *New York Times,* Feb. 13, 1945, p. 19, col. 4; Naomi W. Cohen, *Not Free to Desist: The American Jewish Committee, 1906–1966* (Philadelphia: Jewish Publication Society of America, 1972), 409–11; "Educators Fight College Quotas," *New York Times,* Feb. 9, 1945, p. 32, col. 4.

15. People v. Bell, 125 N.Y.S.2d 117, 118–19 (Co. Ct.), *aff'd,* 306 N.Y. 110 (1953).

16. People v. Bell, 306 N.Y. 110, 113–14 (1953).

17. For two cases indicative of the special status granted even to very small religious organizations, see O'Neill v. Hubbard, 40 N.Y.S.2d 202 (Sup. Ct. 1943), and In re Saunders (Hubbard), 37 N.Y.S.2d 341 (Sup. Ct. 1942), both of which struck down as unconstitutional recent legislation that had permitted only clergymen affiliated with a religion listed in the last federal census to perform marriages.

18. People ex rel. Fish v. Sandstrom, 279 N.Y. 523, 527–28 (1939).

19. Ibid., 534, 536, 538–39 (concurring opinion).

20. Ibid., 532–33.

21. People ex rel. Unity Congregational Society of City of New York v. Mills, 71 N.Y.S.2d 873, 875 (Sup. Ct. 1947); Christian Camps, Inc. v. Village of Speculator, 88 N.Y.S.2d 377 (App. Div. 1949); Silver Bay Ass'n for Christian Conferences & Training v. Braisted, 80 N.Y.S.2d 548 (Sup. Ct. 1920); Hunter College Student Social, Community & Religious Clubs Ass'n v. City of New York, 63 N.Y.S.2d 337, 338–39 (Sup. Ct. 1946).

22. Williams Institutional Colored Methodist Episcopal Church v. City of New York, 89 N.Y.S.2d 300, 302 (App. Div. 1949), *aff'd,* 300 N.Y. 716 (1950); People ex rel. Near East Foundation v. Boyland, 106 N.Y.S.2d 736, 740–41 (Sup. Ct. 1951).

23. Holy Sepulchre Cemetery v. Board of Appeals of Town of Greece, 60 N.Y.S.2d 750 (App. Div. 1946); North Shore Unitarian Soc. v. Village of Plandome, 109 N.Y.S.2d 803 (Sup. Ct. 1951); Concordia Collegiate Institute v. Miller, 301 N.Y. 189, 192–93 (1950); Hoelzer v. Incorporated Village of New Hyde Park, 150 N.Y.S.2d 765, 767 (Sup. Ct. 1956) (sustaining amendment to village ordinance that permitted erection of parochial schools). *Accord,* Application of LaPorte, 152 N.Y.S.2d 916 (App. Div. 1956), *aff'd,* 161 N.Y.S.2d 886 (Ct. App. 1957).

24. 154 N.Y.S.2d 15 (Ct. App. 1956).

25. 154 N.Y.S.2d 849 (Ct. App. 1956).

26. 154 N.Y.S.2d at 852.

27. "Synagogue Loses L.I. Zoning Plea," *New York Times,* July 15, 1956, p. 33, col. 3; Tobie Newman and Sylvia Landow, *"That I May Dwell among Them": A Synagogue History of Nassau County* (New York: Confrence of Jewish Organizations, 1991), 11, 20, 54, 134–35; "Policy of Neglect Charged to GOP," *New York Times,* Oct. 3, 1954, p. 37, col. 1.

28. Brief of Petitioners-Appellants, Diocese of Rochester v. Planning Board of Town of Brighton, p. 48; Brief of American Jewish Congress, *Amicus Curiae,* in Diocese of Rochester v. Planning Board of Town of Brighton, p. 25.

29. 154 N.Y.S.2d at 858–59 (emphasis added).

30. 154 N.Y.S.2d at 26.

31. Walz v. Tax Commission of City of New York, 298 N.Y.S.2d 711 (Ct. App. 1969), *aff'd*, 397 U.S. 664 (1970); Westchester Reform Temple v. Brown, 293 N.Y.S.2d 297 (Ct. App. 1968); People ex rel. Watchtower Bible and Tract Society, Inc. v. Haring, 207 N.Y.S.2d 673 (Ct. App. 1960); Application of Garden City Jewish Center, 155 N.Y.S.2d 523, 528 (Sup. Ct. 1956) (also reported at 157 N.Y.S.2d 435 [Sup. Ct. 1956]); Greater New York Corp. of Seventh Day Adventists v. Miller, 290 N.Y.S.2d 673, 676 (Sup. Ct. 1967), *aff'd*, 296 N.Y.S.2d 1021 (App. Div. 1968), *appeal denied*, 303 N.Y.S.2d 1025 (Ct. App. 1969) (also reported at 282 N.Y.S.2d 390 [Sup. Ct. 1967]); Mikveh of South Shore Congregation, Inc. v. Granito, 432 N.Y.S.2d 638 (App. Div. 1980).

32. Unitarian Universalist Church of Central Nassau v. Shorten, 314 N.Y.S.2d 66, 70 (Sup. Ct. 1970); Slevin v. Long Island Jewish Medical Center, 319 N.Y.S.2d 937, 948 (Sup. Ct. 1971); American Friends of Society of St. Pius, Inc. v. Schwab, 417 N.Y.S.2d 991, 994 (App. Div. 1979), *appeal denied*, 425 N.Y.S.2d 1027 (Ct. App. 1980); Jewish Reconstructionist Synagogue of North Shore, Inc. v. Incorporated Village of Roslyn Harbor, 379 N.Y.S.2d 747, 756 (Ct. App. 1975), *cert. denied*, 426 U.S. 950 (1976) (concurring opinion).

33. See Congregation Beth El of Rochester v. Crowley, 217 N.Y.S.2d 937, 940 (Sup. Ct. 1961); YM & YWHA of Mid-Westchester, Inc. v. Town of Eastchester, 201 N.Y.S.2d 622 (Sup. Ct. 1960); Weiss v. Willow Tree Civic Association, 467 F. Supp. 803 (S.D.N.Y. 1979); Congregation Kollel Horabonim, Inc. v. Williams, 422 N.Y.S.2d 909 (Ct. App. 1979); Congregation Beth Mayer, Inc. v. Board of Assessors of Ramapo, 417 N.Y.S.2d 754 (App. Div. 1979); Congregation K'hai Torath Chaim, Inc. v. Town of Ramapo, 421 N.Y.S.2d 923 (App. Div. 1979); Loder v. Goodday, 268 N.Y.S.2d 507 (App. Div. 1966), *aff'd*, 279 N.Y.S.2d 182 (Ct. App. 1967). Even while denying relief to the Hasidim, one court conceded that community groups were lobbying to keep a Hasidic housing development out of Ramapo. See Weiss v. Willow Tree Civic Association, *supra*.

34. See Zorach v. Clauson, 343 U.S. 306 (1952); Cohen, *Not Free to Desist*, 440–41, 447.

35. See Board of Education of Central School District No. 1 v. Allen, 192 N.Y.S.2d 186 (Sup. Ct. 1959); Board of Education of Central School District No. 1 v. Allen, 392 U.S. 236 (1968); Committee for Public Education and Religious Liberty v. Regan, 444 U.S. 646 (1980). Earlier and less carefully tailored legislation for the same purpose had been struck down in New York v. Cathedral Academy, 434 U.S. 125 (1977), and Levitt v. Committee for Public Education and Religious Liberty, 413 U.S. 472 (1973).

36. Scales v. Board of Education of Union Free School District No. 12, Town of Hempstead, 245 N.Y.S.2d 449 (Sup. Ct. 1963); College of New Rochelle v. Nyquist, 326 N.Y.S.2d 765, 770 (App. Div. 1971); Canisius College of Buffalo v. Nyquist, 320 N.Y.S.2d 652, 655 (App. Div. 1971), *rev'd on other grounds*, 329 N.Y.S.2d 105 (Ct. App. 1972); Committee for Public Education & Religious Liberty v. Nyquist, 413 U.S. 756 (1973).

37. See Toomey v. Farley, 156 N.Y.S.2d 840, 848 (Ct. App. 1956) (praising "all churches in America" for being "opposed to communism"); Brasich v. Port Authority of New York and New Jersey, 484 F. Supp. 697 (S.D.N.Y. 1979), *aff'd*, 791 F.2d 224 (2d Cir. 1980); Lewis v. Allen, 207 N.Y.S.2d 862 (App. Div. 1960), *aff'd*, 252 N.Y.S.2d 80 (Ct. App.), *cert. denied*, 379 U.S. 923 (1964); Dickens v. Ernesto, 330 N.Y.S.2d 346 (Ct. App.), *appeal dism.*, 407 U.S. 917 (1972); Baer v. Kolmorgen, 181 N.Y.S.2d 230 (Sup. Ct. 1958); People v. Friedman, 302 N.Y. 75 (1950), *appeal dism.*, 341 U.S. 907 (1951); Engel v. Vitale, 218 N.Y.S.2d 659 (Ct. App. 1961), *rev'd*, 370 U.S. 421 (1962); Kreshik v. St. Nicholas Cathedral of the Russian Orthodox Church of North America, 363 U.S. 190 (1960); Kedroff v. St. Nicholas Cathedral, 344 U.S. 94 (1950).

38. Richard W. Steele, "The War on Intolerance: The Reformulation of American Nationalism, 1939–1941," *Journal of American Ethnic History* 9 (1989): 9; Brief Submitted on Behalf of the American Jewish Committee as Friend of the Court in Kemp v. Rubin, p. 3 (ms. in Library of American Jewish Committee, New York, N.Y.); Gino Speranza, *Race or Nation: A Conflict of Divided Loyalties*

(Indianapolis: Bobbs-Merrill, 1923), 243, 259, 268 (emphasis in original); Lewis Allen, "The House I Live In," with lyrics by Earl Robinson. See also Cohen, *Not Free to Desist*, 333–41.

39. People on Complaint of Shapiro v. Dorin, 99 N.Y.S.2d 830, 834–37 (Dom. Rel. Ct. 1950), *aff'd sub nom.* People v. Donner, 103 N.Y.S.2d 757 (App. Div.), *aff'd*, 302 N.Y. 857, *cert. denied*, 342 U.S. 884 (1951).

40. 92 N.Y.S.2d 344 (Sup. Ct. 1949).

41. Ibid., 345–46; Hazelton Spencer, *The Art and Life of William Shakespeare* (New York: Harcourt, Brace, 1940), 240, quoted in Trenton Committee for Unity, "Memorandum on *The Merchant of Venice*," May 2, 1945, p. 2 (ms. in Library of American Jewish Committee, New York, N.Y.).

42. 92 N.Y.S.2d at 346.

43. Three decades later, in Pico v. Board of Education, Island Trees Union Free School District No. 26, 638 F.2d 404 (2d Cir. 1980), *aff'd*, 457 U.S. 853 (1982), a school district would explicitly "emphasize the inculcative function of secondary education, and argue that . . . [it] must be allowed *unfettered* discretion to 'transmit community values.' " 457 U.S. at 869 (emphasis in original). Even in 1982, the plurality opinion of Justice Brennan did not reject that argument in a *Rosenberg* context, where a school board was merely seeking " 'to establish . . . curriculum in such a way as to transmit community values' " and to promote " 'respect for authority and traditional values be they social, moral, or political.' " Ibid., 864. But though *Pico* did leave school officials free to establish a hegemonic curriculum, it did deny them the power to "remove books [from a school library] for the *purpose* of restricting access to the political ideas or social perspectives discussed in them, when that action [was] motivated simply by the officials' disapproval of the ideas involved." 457 U.S. at 879–80 (Blackmun, J., concurring) (emphasis in original). Accord, Presidents Council, District 25 v. Community School Board No. 25, 457 F.2d 289 (2d Cir.), *cert. denied*, 409 U.S. 998 (1972).

44. In other cases, state judges were more willing than in *Rosenberg* to provide legal protection against hate speech, although the U.S. Supreme Court was not. Consider, for example, People v. Kunz, 300 N.Y. 273 (1949), *rev'd*, 340 U.S. 290 (1951), where the defendant had engaged in "scurrilous attacks on Catholics and Jews," 340 U.S. at 296 (dissenting opinion), and Joseph Burstyn, Inc. v. Wilson, 303 N.Y. 242, 250 (1951), *rev'd*, 343 U.S. 495 (1952), where the Court of Appeals was willing to uphold censorship of a "sacrilegious" movie.

45. In re Whitmore, 47 N.Y.S.2d 143, 146 (Dom. Rel. Ct. 1944); Matter of Sampson, 317 N.Y.S.2d 641 (Family Ct. 1970), *aff'd*, 323 N.Y.S.2d 253 (App. Div. 1971), *aff'd*, 328 N.Y.S.2d 686 (Ct. App. 1972); In re Seiferth, 309 N.Y. 80, 86–87 (1955) (dissenting opinion); ibid., 85; Stark v. Wyman, 299 N.Y.S.2d 686 (Sup. Ct. 1969).

46. People v. Stover, 240 N.Y.S. 734, 735–36 (Ct. App.), *appeal dism.*, 375 U.S. 42 (1963).

47. Ibid., 741 (dissenting opinion). It is impossible to be certain, but the Stovers probably constituted a mere political rather than an ethnic or religious minority.

48. Ibid., 738–40.

49. Mark Yudof, "Equal Protection, Class Legislation, and Sex Discrimination: One Small Cheer for Mr. Herbert Spencer's Social Statics," *Michigan Law Review* 88 (1990): 1366, 1372 (reviewing William E. Nelson, *The Fourteenth Amendment: From Political Principle to Judicial Doctrine* (Cambridge, Mass.: Harvard University Press, 1988). See also Melissa Saunders, "Equal Protection, Class Legislation, and Colorblindness," *Michigan Law Review* 96 (1997): 245–68.

CHAPTER SEVEN

1. See Michael J. Bennett, *When Dreams Came True: The GI Bill and the Making of Modern America* (Washington, D.C.: Brassey's, 1996), 122–31, 237–76; John Morton Blum, *V Was for Victory: Politics*

and American Culture during World War II (New York: Harcourt Brace Jovanovich, 1976), 248–50; Milton Greenberg, *The GI Bill: The Law That Changed America* (New York: Lickle, 1997), 35–62. On the relative exclusion of African Americans from the educational programs funded by the GI Bill, see Bennett, *When Dreams Came True,* 260–263.

2. On the effective exclusion of most African Americans from federal programs, see Bennett, *When Dreams Came True,* 296–99.

3. See John P. Herzog and James S. Earley, *Home Mortgage Delinquency and Foreclosure* (New York: Columbia University Press, 1970), 7–9, 12; Saul B. Klaman, *The Postwar Residential Mortgage Market* (Princeton: Princeton University Press, 1961), 78, 287.

4. See 58 Stat. 284 (1944); 59 Stat. 623, 626–27 (1945); Klaman, *Postwar Residential Mortgage Market,* 158.

5. Ibid., 53–55, 285–87.

6. 64 Stat. 48 (1950). See Klaman, *Postwar Residential Mortgage Market,* 54–55, 285–87; Herzog and Earley, *Home Mortgage Delinquency and Foreclosure,* 7–8. The 1950 act also expanded the FHA's authority by creating two new, liberal mortgage insurance programs, one for housing in rural communities and another for cooperative housing projects. See Klaman, *Postwar Residential Mortgage Market,* 55. In an especially intrusive involvement in the residential mortgage market, Congress authorized the Veterans Administration to participate directly in the private mortgage market by granting mortgage loans on terms equal to those on its guaranteed loans in areas where private lenders refused to grant VA loans. Ibid.

7. See Klaman, *Postwar Residential Mortgage Market,* 8.

8. See ibid., 33.

9. See An Act to Increase the Revenue, Title I, Part I, secs. 1(b), 5(a), 39 Stat. 756, 759 (1916). See Individual Income Tax Act of 1944, secs. 3–4, 58 Stat. 231–32 (1944). The mortgage interest deduction is currently codified in modified form at 26 U.S.C. sec. 163 (h) (1994). Some types of interest payments were deductible as early as 1864, and by 1870 all interest payments became deductible. See Act of July 14, 1870, ch. 255, sec. 9, 16 Stat. 256, 258 (1870).

10. Peter W. Salsich Jr., "A Decent Home for Every American: Can the 1949 Goal Be Met?," *North Carolina Law Review* 71 (1993): 1619, 1627 (quoting James R. Follain and David C. Ling, "The Federal Tax Subsidy to Housing and the Reduced Value of the Mortgage Interest Deduction," *National Tax Journal* 44 [1991]: 147, 148). On the property tax deduction and treatment of capital gains, see 26 U.S.C. sec. 164(a)(1) (1994); Taxpayer Relief Act of 1997, sec. 312(a), 111 Stat. 836 (1997). On the cost to the treasury, see Salsich, "A Decent Home," 1627–28. This figure is referred to by economists as a "tax expenditure" since it represents the loss of tax revenue due to a deduction or tax credit. See Stanley S. Surrey and Paul R. McDaniel, *Tax Expenditures* (Cambridge, Mass.: Harvard University Press, 1985), 3.

11. See Bennett, *When Dreams Came True,* 295; Geoffrey Mohan, "Suburban Pioneers," *Newsday,* Sept. 28, 1997, sec. H, pp. 10, 13. This monthly payment is based on a thirty-year mortgage at a 5 percent rate of interest. Of course, a homeowner also had to pay real estate taxes after making the monthly mortgage payments, but according to a Levittown advertisement the taxes brought total monthly payments to a tax-deductible sum of $58. See Mohan, "Suburban Pioneers," 10.

12. N.Y. Laws of 1945, ch. 292, sec. 10 (1945); Kemp v. Rubin, 298 N.Y. 590 (1948); Shelley v. Kraemer, 334 U.S. 1 (1948).

13. Uniform Commercial Code sec. 2-103(1)(b); ibid., sec. 2-609, comment 1; ibid., sec. 2-101, comment; ibid., sec. 2-306, comment 1.

14. Beardsley v. Kilmer, 193 N.Y.S. 285, 290 (App. Div. 1922), *aff'd,* 236 N.Y. 80 (1923) (dissenting opinion).

15. Kline v. Robert M. McBride & Co., 11 N.Y.S.2d 674, 679 (Sup. Ct. 1939); Damron v. Doubleday, Doran & Co., 231 N.Y.S. 444, 445–446 (Sup. Ct. 1928), *aff'd,* 234 N.Y.S. 774 (App. Div. 1929).

16. Clarke v. Public Nat. Bank & Trust Co., 259 N.Y. 285, 290 (1932).

17. Ashare v. Mirkin, Barre, Saltzstein & Gordon, P.C., 435 N.Y.S.2d 438 (Sup. Ct. 1980), *aff'd as modified,* 441 N.Y.S.2d 408 (App. Div.), *aff'd,* 444 N.Y.S.2d 918 (Ct. App. 1981); Health Delivery Systems, Inc. v. Scheinman, 344 N.Y.S.2d 190 (App. Div. 1973); Merrick v. Four Star Stage Lighting, Inc., 400 N.Y.S.2d 543, 544 (App. Div. 1978); Four Star Stage Lighting, Inc. v. Merrick, 392 N.Y.S.2d 297 (App. Div. 1977); Merrick v. Four Star Stage Lighting, Inc., 378 N.Y.S.2d 65, 66 (App. Div. 1975); Federal Insurance Co. v. Fries, 355 N.Y.S.2d 741 (Civil Ct. 1974).

18. Brandt v. Winchell, 170 N.Y.S.2d 828, 833–34 (Ct. App. 1958) (emphasis in original).

19. Sloan v. Clark, 277 N.Y.S.2d 411, 415 (Ct. App. 1966).

20. Ryan v. Brooklyn Eye & Ear Hospital, 360 N.Y.S.2d 912, 916 (App. Div. 1974); Frank v. 903 Park Avenue Co., 354 N.Y.S.2d 329, 331n. (Civil Ct. 1974); Belsky v. Lowenthal, 405 N.Y.S.2d 63, 65 (App. Div. 1978), *aff'd on opinion below,* 418 N.Y.S.2d 573 (Ct. App. 1979).

21. See, e.g., Lynn v. Cohen, 359 F. Supp. 565 (S.D.N.Y. 1973); Livoti v. Elston, 384 N.Y.S.2d 484 (App. Div. 2d Dept. 1976); Penn-Ohio Steel Corp. v. Allis-Chalmers Manufacturing Co., 280 N.Y.S.2d 679 (App. Div. 1967), *aff'd,* 289 N.Y.S.2d 752 (Ct. App. 1968); Stevens v. Siegel, 239 N.Y.S.2d 827 (App. Div. 2d Dept. 1963).

22. Robbins v. Ogden Corp., 490 F. Supp. 801, 811 (S.D.N.Y. 1980); Royal Farms, Inc. v. Minute Maid Co., 236 N.Y.S.2d 368 (Sup. Ct. 1962); Williamson, Picket, Gross, Inc. v. 400 Park Avenue Co., 405 N.Y.S.2d 709, 711 (App. Div. 1978), *aff'd,* 417 N.Y.S.2d 460 (Ct. App. 1979); Luxonomy Cars, Inc. v. Citibank, N.A., 408 N.Y.S.2d 951, 954 (App. Div. 1978); Stillman v. Ford, 290 N.Y.S.2d 893, 897 (Ct. App. 1968); Shaitelman v. Phoenix Mutual Life Ins. Co., 517 F. Supp. 21, 25 (S.D.N.Y. 1980).

23. Guard-Life Corp. v. S. Parker Hardware Manufacturing Corp., 428 N.Y.S.2d 628, 638 (Ct. App. 1980).

24. Ibid., 631, 633–34.

25. Weintraub v. Weintraub, 302 N.Y. 104, 108 (1951); Cohen v. Cabo, 61 N.Y.S.2d 145, 146 (Sup. Ct. 1946).

26. Gerstle v. Gamble-Skogmo, Inc., 478 F.2d 1281, 1300 (2d Cir. 1973); Gaines Service Leasing Corp. v. Carmel Plastic Corp., 432 N.Y.S.2d 760, 763 (Civil Ct. 1980), *aff'd,* 453 N.Y.S.2d 391 (App. Term 1981); United States v. Garcia & Diaz, Inc., 291 F.2d 242, 245–46 (2d Cir. 1961).

27. Chiarella v. United States, 445 U.S. 222, 233 (1980); Hartford Accident & Indemnity Co. v. Kranz, 184 N.Y.S.2d 918, 921 (App. Div. 1959).

28. Dolgow v. Anderson, 53 F.R.D. 664, 686 (E.D.N.Y. 1971), *aff'd,* 464 F.2d 437 (2d Cir. 1972).

29. Washer v. Seager, 71 N.Y.S.2d 46, 54 (App. Div. 1947), *aff'd,* 297 N.Y. 918 (1948).

30. Commonwealth Sanitation Co. of New York, Inc. v. Fox, 107 N.Y.S.2d 935, 938 (Sup. Ct. 1951); Burg v. Horn, 380 F.2d 897 (2d Cir. 1967); Heyman v. Heyman, 33 N.Y.S.2d 235, 241 (Sup. Ct. 1942); Broderick v. Blanton, 59 N.Y.S.2d 136 (Sup. Ct. 1945); Feiger v. Iral Jewelry, Ltd., 382 N.Y.S.2d 216, 220 (Sup. Ct. N.Y. Co. 1975), *aff'd,* 382 N.Y.S.2d 221 (App. Div. 1976), *aff'd,* 394 N.Y.S.2d 626 (Ct. App. 1977).

31. Blaustein v. Pan American Petroleum & Oil Transport Co.,21 N.Y.S.2d 651, 722, 731 (Sup. Ct. 1940), *rev'd,* 31 N.Y.S.2d 934 (App. Div. 1941), *aff'd,* 293 N.Y. 281 (1944), *relying on* Meinhard v. Salmon, 249 N.Y. 458 (1928).

32. 31 N.Y.S.2d at 951; 293 N.Y. at 303.

33. Turner v. American Metal Co., 50 N.Y.S.2d 800, 829–30 (App. Div. 1944), *reversing* 36 N.Y.S.2d 356 (Sup. Ct. 1942), *appeal dism.,* 295 N.Y. 822 (1946).

34. See William E. Leuchtenburg, *Franklin D. Roosevelt and the New Deal, 1932–1940* (New York: Harper & Row, 1963), 32.

35. Nilan v. Colleran, 283 N.Y. 84, 91 (1940).

36. Matter of Miglietta, 287 N.Y. 246, 254–255 (1942).

37. Rous v. Carlisle, 26 N.Y.S.2d 197, 200 (App. Div. 1941), *aff'd,* 290 N.Y. 869 (1943); Dumont v.

Raymond, 49 N.Y.S.2d 865, 868 (Sup. Ct. 1944), aff'd, 56 N.Y.S.2d 592 (App. Div. 1945); November v. National Exhibition Co., 173 N.Y.S.2d 490, 496 (Sup. Ct. 1958); Cullen v. Governor Clinton Co., 110 N.Y.S.2d 614, 616 (App. Div. 1952).

38. Kalmanash v. Smith, 291 N.Y. 142, 155 (1943); Greenebaum v. Felix Lilienthal & Co., 111 N.Y.S.2d 835, 837 (App. Div. 1952); Auerbach v. Bennett, 419 N.Y.S.2d 920, 926 (Ct. App. 1979); In re Peoples Nat. Bank & Trust Co. of White Plains, 90 N.Y.S.2d 384 (Surr. Ct. 1949); Gordon v. Elliman, 306 N.Y. 456, 464 (1954).

39. See Woodard v. Southampton Federal Savings & Loan Ass'n, 161 N.Y.S.2d 522 (Sup. Ct. 1957); Box v. Northrop Corp., 459 F. Supp. 540 (S.D.N.Y. 1978), aff'd, 598 F.2d 609 (2d Cir. 1979); Lawrence v. Decca Records, Inc., 195 N.Y.S.2d 431 (Sup. Ct. 1959); Semensohn v. Weisblum, 118 N.Y.S.2d 57 (Sup. Ct. 1952); Mandel v. Liebman, 303 N.Y. 88 (1951).

40. Herzfeld v. Laventhol, Krekstein, Horwath & Horwath, 378 F.2d 112, 122 (S.D.N.Y. 1974), aff'd in part and rev'd in part on other grounds, 540 F.2d 27 (2d Cir. 1976). The Southern District of New York and the Court of Appeals for the Second Circuit were, not surprisingly, the center of this rigorous development of federal securities law during the 1960s and 1970s. See, e.g., List v. Fashion Park, Inc., 340 F.2d 457 (2d Cir.), cert. denied, 382 U.S. 811 (1965). The best history of federal securities regulation is Joel Seligman, The Transformation of Wall Street: A History of the Securities and Exchange Commission and Modern Corporate Finance, rev. ed. (Boston: Northeastern University Press, 1995). This history is outside the scope of this book.

CHAPTER EIGHT

1. Robert R. Palmer, Bell I. Wiley, and William R. Keast, The Procurement and Training of Ground Combat Troops (Washington, D.C.: U.S. Government Printing Office, 1947), 4; U.S. Bureau of the Census, Historical Statistics of the United States: Colonial Times to 1970 (Washington, D.C.: U.S. Government Printing Office, 1975), 2:1140.

2. Major John D. Kenderdine, Your Year in the Army: What Every New Soldier Should Know (New York: Simon & Schuster, 1940), 3, 134, 178.

3. Morris Janowitz and Roger Little, Sociology and the Military Establishment (New York: Russell Sage Foundation, 1965), 93; quoted in Bell I. Wiley, "The Building and Training of Infantry Divisions," in The United States Army in World War II: The Army Ground Forces, the Procurement and Training of Ground Combat Troops, ed. Robert R. Palmer et al. (Washington, D.C.: Department of the Army, 1948), 429, 449; William R. Keast, "The Training of Enlisted Replacements," ibid., 365, 387, 389; U.S. Infantry Association, Our Armed Forces: A Source Book on the Army and Navy for High School Students (Washington, D.C.: U.S. Office of Education, 1943), 14–15; Alan Gregg, Challenges to Contemporary Medicine (New York: Columbia University Press, 1956), 68; Lt. Gen. Jacob L. Devers to Lt. Gen. Lesley J. McNair, February 4, 1944, quoted in United States Army in World War II, ed. Palmer et al., 227. See also Janowitz and Little, Sociology and the Military Establishment, 91.

4. Albert Q. Maisel, Miracles of Military Medicine (New York: Duell, Sloan and Peace, 1943), x; Joseph R. Darnall, What the Citizen Should Know about Wartime Medicine (New York: Norton, 1942); William H. Taliaferro, ed., Medicine and the War (Chicago: University of Chicago Press, 1944); Gerald Wendt, "What Happened in Science," in While You Were Gone: A Report on Wartime Life in the United States, ed. Jack Goodman (New York: Simon & Schuster, 1946), 249, 264–70; Max Lerner, America as a Civilization: Life and Thought in the United States Today (New York: Simon & Schuster, 1957), 124; Gregg, Challenges to Contemporary Medicine, 4, 36.

5. Data from Erie County are not included in the statistics that follow because the Erie County records did not adequately describe the nature of the cause of action in civil cases in the relevant years under study. Total populations were created by aggregating samples in each of the seven remain-

ing jurisdictions and thereby creating a fraction consisting of total sample personal injury cases in the numerator and total sample cases in the denominator. Using standard statistical methods, it can be stated at a 95 percent level of confidence that the tort population for the ten-year interval 1936–45 ranged between 11.79 percent and 13.63 percent. In the following ten-year period, 1946–55, tort population ranged between 17.24 percent and 19.36 percent at the same level of confidence. At the 95 percent confidence level, tort cases in 1945 ranged between 6.21 percent and 11.17 percent of all cases, while in 1946 tort cases ranged from 11.39 percent to 17.53 percent.

6. Unfortunately, the random sample produced only sixty-five cases in which the amount of the jury verdict was stated, out of a total population of over eight hundred thousand filings. Thus the sample is too small to perform any year-by-year calculations, and the statistical reliability of the numbers stated in the text cannot be guaranteed.

7. Bureau of the Census, *Historical Statistics,* 2, 720. Statistics on the percentage of plaintiff success stated in the text are derived from a total of only 111 cases, which is too small to make the percentages statistically reliable. On insurance requirements, see Motor Vehicle Financial Security Act, Laws of 1956, ch. 655.

8. David Sarnoff, "The Fabulous Future," in *The Fabulous Future: America in 1980,* ed. Fortune (New York: Dutton, 1955), 13–14.

9. John Kenneth Galbraith, *The Affluent Society* (Boston: Houghton Mifflin, 1958), 98; Lerner, *America as Civilization,* 129; Yair Aharoni, *The No-Risk Society* (Chatham: Chatham House, 1981), 47–50.

10. Geoffrey Perrett, *Days of Sadness, Years of Triumph: The American People, 1939–1945* (New York: Penguin, 1973), 408, 442–43; Eric F. Goldman, *The Crucial Decade—And After: America, 1945–1960* (New York: Knopf, 1973), 13; quoted ibid., 14; quoted in John Morton Blum, *V Was for Victory: Politics and American Culture during World War II* (New York: Harcourt Brace Jovanovich, 1976), 326–27.

11. Philpot v. Brooklyn National League Baseball Club, Inc., 303 N.Y. 116, 121 (1951); Abbott v. Page Airways, Inc., 297 N.Y.S.2d 713, 716 (Ct. App. 1969); Havas v. Victory Paper Stock Co., 426 N.Y.S.2d 233, 236 (Ct. App. 1980).

12. See Bernardine v. City of New York, 294 N.Y. 361 (1945); Dillon v. Rockaway Beach Hospital & Dispensary, 284 N.Y. 176 (1940); Spano v. Perini Corp., 302 N.Y.S.2d 527 (Ct. App. 1969); Doundoulakis v. Town of Hempstead, 398 N.Y.S.2d 401 (Ct. App. 1977); Millington v. Southeastern Elevator Co., 293 N.Y.S.2d 305 (Ct. App. 1968); Thrasher v. United States Liability Insurance Co., 278 N.Y.S.2d 793 (Ct. App. 1967). One consequence of the end of municipal immunity was that a series of cases came up to the Court of Appeals in which municipalities were held liable for police insensitivity and brutality. See, e.g., McCrink v. City of New York, 296 N.Y. 99 (1947).

13. MacPherson v. Buick Motor Co., 217 N.Y. 382 (1916); Hyams v. King Kullen Grocery Co., 223 N.Y.S.2d 263, 269 (Mun. Ct. 1961), *aff'd in part and rev'd in part on other grounds,* 230 N.Y.S.2d 962 (App. Term 1962), *aff'd,* 246 N.Y.S.2d 575 (App. Div. 1964).

14. Campo v. Scofield, 301 N.Y. 468, 471, 474–75 (1950).

15. Inman v. Binghamton Housing Authority, 164 N.Y.S.2d 699, 703 (Ct. App. 1957).

16. Mueller v. Teichner, 190 N.Y.S.2d 709, 712 (Ct. App. 1959).

17. 167 N.Y.S.2d 996 (App. Div. 1957).

18. Greenberg v. Lorenz, 213 N.Y.S.2d 39, 41–42, 43 (Ct. App. 1961) (concurring opinion).

19. Langer v. Jessup Holding Co., 216 N.Y.S.2d 692 (Ct. App. 1961); McLaughlin v. Mine Safety Appliances Co., 226 N.Y.S.2d 407 (Ct. App. 1962); Randy Knitwear, Inc. v. American Cyanamid Co., 226 N.Y.S.2d 363, 368, 370 (Ct. App. 1962).

20. Goldberg v. Kollsman Instrument Corp., 240 N.Y.S.2d 592, 593–95 (Ct. App. 1963).

21. Ibid., 599–600.

22. Guarino v. Mine Safety Appliance Co., 306 N.Y.S.2d 942, 946 (Ct. App. 1969).

23. Schwartz v. Macrose Lumber & Trim Co., 270 N.Y.S.2d 875, 885 (Sup. Ct. 1966), *rev'd on*

other grounds, 287 N.Y.S.2d 706 (App. Div. 1968), *aff'd,* 301 N.Y.S.2d 91 (Ct. App. 1969); Bolm v. Triumph Corp., 341 N.Y.S.2d 846 (App. Div. 1973), *aff'd,* 350 N.Y.S.2d 644 (Ct. App. 1973). Accord, Delaney v. Towmotor Corp., 339 F.2d 4, 5–6 (2d Cir. 1964).

24. DiPerna v. Roman Catholic Diocese of Albany, 292 N.Y.S.2d 177 (App. Div. 1968); Stief v. J. A. Sexauer Mfg. Co., 380 F.2d 453, 460 (2d Cir. 1967), *cert. denied,* 389 U.S. 897 (1967). Accord, Brownstone v. Times Square Stage Lighting Co., 333 N.Y.S.2d 781 (App. Div. 1972).

25. 345 N.Y.S.2d 461 (Ct. App. 1973).

26. Ibid., 474 (concurring opinion).

27. Ibid., 466–68.

28. Rogers v. Dorchester Associates, 347 N.Y.S.2d 22 (Ct. App. 1973); Velez v. Craine & Clark Lumber Corp., 350 N.Y.S.2d 617 (Ct App. 1973); Victorson v. Bock Laundry Machine Co., 373 N.Y.S.2d 39, 43 (Ct. App. 1975).

29. Micallef v. Miehle Co., 384 N.Y.S.2d 115, 121 (Ct. App. 1976), *overruling* Campo v. Scofield, 301 N.Y. 468 (1950).

30. Halloran v. Virginia Chemicals, Inc., 393 N.Y.S.2d 341, 343 (Ct. App. 1977); Milau Associates, Inc. v. North Avenue Development Corp., 398 N.Y.S.2d 882, 886 (Ct. App. 1977). For a Court of Appeals case upholding a jury verdict in favor of a manufacturer, see Torrogrossa v. Towmotor Co., 405 N.Y.S.2d 448 (Ct. App. 1978).

31. See Wilder v. Ayers, 156 N.Y.S.2d 85, 88 (App. Div. 1956), *aff'd,* 163 N.Y.S.2d 966 (Ct. App. 1957); LoCasto v. Long Island R.R., 190 N.Y.S.2d 366 (Ct. App. 1959).

32. Jenkins v. 313–321 W. 37th Street Corp., 284 N.Y. 397, 402 (1940); Rashid v. Weill, 46 N.Y.S.2d 711, 713–14 (Sup. Ct. 1944); Klein v. Herlim Realty Corp., 54 N.Y.S.2d 144, 146 (Sup. Ct.), *aff'd,* 58 N.Y.S.2d 344 (App. Div. 1945).

33. Miller v. Roman Catholic Church of St. Stephen, 262 N.Y.S.2d 361, 363 (App. Div. 1965), *rev'd on other grounds,* 278 N.Y.S.2d 212 (Ct. App. 1966); Skupeen v. City of New York, 287 N.Y.S.2d 596, 598 (App. Div. 1968) (dictum); McCarthy v. Port of New York Authority, 290 N.Y.S.2d 255, 257 (App. Div. 1968) (dictum); Glassbrook v. Mahni Realty Corp., 108 N.Y.S.2d 652 (App. Div. 1951); Koenig v. Patrick Const. Corp., 298 N.Y. 313 (1948); Rufo v. Orlando, 309 N.Y. 345, 351 (1955); DeCasiano v. Morgan, 308 N.Y. 526 (1955). See Labor Law secs. 240, 272.

34. Gallagher v. St. Raymond's Roman Catholic Church, 289 N.Y.S.2d 401, 404 (Ct. App. 1968), overruling Boyce v. 228th & Carpenter Ave. Holding Co., 295 N.Y. 575 (1945) (by implication).

35. Carney v. Buyea, 65 N.Y.S.2d 902, 905 (App. Div. 1946); Friedman v. Berkowitz, 136 N.Y.S.2d 81, 82 (City Ct. 1954).

36. Clifton v. Patroon Operating Corp., 63 N.Y.S.2d 597, 601–2 (App. Div. 1946).

37. Mayer v. Temple Properties, 307 N.Y. 559, 565 (1954); Patterson v. Proctor Paint & Varnish Co., 288 N.Y.S.2d 622, 624 (Ct. App. 1968); Hirsch v. Hade, 304 N.Y.S.2d 40, 42, 46 (Civil Ct. 1969), *rev'd on other grounds,* 310 N.Y.S.2d 14 (App. Term), *aff'd,* 318 N.Y.S.2d 445 (App. Div. 1970) (emphasis in original).

38. Basso v. Miller, 386 N.Y.S.2d 564, 567–68 (Ct. App. 1976); Quinlan v. Cecchini, 394 N.Y.S.2d 872 (Ct. App. 1977); Goodman v. Vizsla Club of America, Inc., 422 N.Y.S.2d 755 (App. Div. 1979).

39. Monacelli v. State, 295 N.Y. 332 (1946); Porter v. Alvis Contracting Corp., 394 N.Y.S.2d 226, 229 (App. Div. 1977).

40. Van Gaasbeck v. Webatuck Central School District, 287 N.Y.S.2d 77 (Ct. App. 1967); Verni v. Johnson, 295 N.Y. 436 (1946); Padula v. State, 422 N.Y.S.2d 943 (Ct. App. 1979); Broderick v. Cauldwell-Wingate Co., 301 N.Y. 182, 188 (1950).

41. Wartels v. County Asphalt, Inc., 328 N.Y.S.2d 410, 416 (Ct. App. 1972); Condon v. Epstein, 168 N.Y.S.2d 189, 191 (Civil Ct. 1957); Sorrentino v. United States, 344 F. Supp. 1308, 1310 (E.D.N.Y. 1972); Long v. Zientowski, 340 N.Y.S.2d 652, 654 (City Ct. 1973); Binder v. Supermarkets General Corp., 370 N.Y.S.2d 184, 186 (App. Div. 1975).

42. Laws of 1975, ch. 69 (1975), codified in CPLR 1411–13; Knieriemen v. Bache Halsey Stuart Shields, Inc., 427 N.Y.S.2d 10, 14 (App. Div.), *appeal dism.,* 435 N.Y.S.2d 720 (Ct. App. 1980); Lippes v. Atlantic Bank of New York, 419 N.Y.S.2d 505, 510–13 (App. Div. 1979); Akins v. Glens Falls City School District, 429 N.Y.S.2d 467, 468 (App. Div. 1980), *rev'd on other grounds,* 441 N.Y.S.2d 644 (Ct. App. 1981).

43. See Bush Terminal Buildings Co. v. Luckenbach S.S. Co., 214 N.Y.S.2d 428 (Ct. App. 1961); Baidach v. Togut, 196 N.Y.S.2d 67 (Ct. App. 1959).

44. Dole v. Dow Chemical Co., 331 N.Y.S.2d 382, 387 (Ct. App. 1972); Kelly v. Long Island Lighting Co., 334 N.Y.S.2d 851 (Ct. App. 1972); Hall v. E. I. Du Pont de Nemours & Co., 345 F. Supp. 353, 376 (E.D.N.Y. 1972). Joint liability would not be imposed on parties who were merely engaged in an activity together, such as playing in a touch football game, if their activity was not inherently dangerous. See Beaver v. Batrouny, 419 N.Y.S.2d 391 (App. Div. 1979).

45. Ingersoll v. Liberty Bank of Buffalo, 278 N.Y. 1, 7 (1938); Popper v. City of New York, 117 N.Y.S.2d 335, 341 (App. Div. 1952); Chisholm v. Mobil Oil Corp., 356 N.Y.S.2d 699, 702 (App. Div. 1974); Gerard v. American Airlines, 272 F.2d 35, 37 (2d Cir. 1959).

46. Compare Zaninovich v. American Airlines, 271 N.Y.S.2d 866, 869 (App. Div. 1966), with Citrola v. Eastern Air Lines, 264 F.2d 815, 818 (2d Cir. 1959). See Abbott v. Page Airways, Inc., 297 N.Y.S.2d 713 (Ct. App. 1969).

47. Panico v. American Export Lines, 213 F. Supp. 116, 118 (S.D.N.Y. 1962); Wartels v. County Asphalt, Inc., 328 N.Y.S.2d 410 (Ct. App. 1972).

48. Lipton v. Lockheed Aircraft Corp., 307 N.Y. 775 (1954); Coster v. Coster, 289 N.Y. 438, 442 (1943); Kilberg v. Northeast Airlines, Inc., 211 N.Y.S.2d 133, 135 (Ct. App. 1961); Babcock v. Jackson, 240 N.Y.S.2d 743, 749–750 (Ct. App. 1963).

49. McLean v. Triboro Coach Corp., 302 N.Y. 49, 51 (1950); Becker v. Schwartz, 413 N.Y.S.2d 895 (Ct. App. 1978); Howard v. Lecher, 397 N.Y.S.2d 363 (Ct. App. 1977); White v. Guarente, 401 N.Y.S.2d 474 (Ct. App. 1977); Olsen v. Chase Manhattan Bank, 215 N.Y.S.2d 773 (Ct. App. 1961); R. H. Bowman Associates, Inc. v. Danskin, 338 N.Y.S.2d 224 (Sup. Ct.), *aff'd,* 338 N.Y.S.2d 224 (App. Div. 1972); A & R Construction Co. v. New York State Electric & Gas Corp., 261 N.Y.S.2d 482 (App. Div. 1965); Cavallo v. Metropolitan Life Insurance Co., 262 N.Y.S.2d 618 (Sup. Ct. 1965) (*overruling,* by implication, Thorne v. Deas, 4 Johns. Cas. 84 [N.Y. Sup. Ct. 1809]); Brodsky v. Nerud, 414 N.Y.S.2d 38 (App. Div. 1979); Santoro v. DiMarco, 320 N.Y.S.2d 132 (Dist. Ct. 1971).

CHAPTER NINE

1. Bonserk Theatre Corp. v. Moss, 34 N.Y.S.2d 541, 545–46 (Sup. Ct. 1942); People on Complaint of Arcuri v. Finkelstein, 114 N.Y.S.2d 810, 813 (Magis. Ct. 1952); People v. Eagle, 117 N.Y.S.2d 380, 383 (Magis. Ct. 1952).

2. People v. Stevens, 74 N.Y.S.2d 346, 347 (County Ct. 1947) (conviction set aside); People ex rel. Prudhomme v. Superintendent of New York State Reformatory for Women, 21 N.Y.S.2d 563, 565 (Sup. Ct. 1940) (conviction set aside); People v. Reese, 212 N.Y.S.2d 696 (Dist. Ct. 1960) (information dismissed); People v. Radaha, 69 N.Y.S.2d 722, 724 (County Ct.), *rev'd sub nom.* People ex rel. Radaha v. Mock, 69 N.Y.S.2d 725 (Sup. Ct. 1947) (conviction reversed) (parenthetical in original).

3. People on Complaint of Arcuri v. Finkelstein, 114 N.Y.S.2d 810, 812–13 (Magis. Ct. 1952) (information sustained); People v. Casey, 67 N.Y.S.2d 9, 11–12 (City Ct. 1946) (conviction upheld); People v. Reilly, 124 N.Y.S.2d 746 (App. Div. 1953) (conviction reversed).

4. Edwin M. Schur, *Crimes without Victims: Deviant Behavior and Public Policy, Abortion, Homosexuality, Drug Addiction* (Englewood Cliffs, N.J.: Prentice-Hall, 1965), 79–80, 114. On enforcement of the laws against homosexuality, see "Note: The Consenting Adult Homosexual and the Law: An

Empirical Study of Enforcement and Administration in Los Angeles County," *U.C.L.A. Law Review* 13 (1966): 647, 686–792.

5. People v. Doyle, 304 N.Y. 120 (1952). On the oppression of the 1950s, see John D'Emilio, *Sexual Politics, Sexual Communities: The Making of a Homosexual Minority in the United States, 1940–1970* (Chicago: University of Chicago Press, 1983), 40–53.

6. 304 N.Y. at 123–24 (dissenting opinion).

7. People v. Deschessere, 74 N.Y.S. 761 (App. Div. 1902); People v. LaCasse, 42 N.Y.S.2d 730 (App. Div. 1943); Griswold v. Connecticut, 381 U.S. 479 (1965).

8. People v. Randall, 214 N.Y.S.2d 417, 421–22 (Ct. App. 1961), quoting statutory language (emphasis in original).

9. People v. Maggio, 228 N.Y.S.2d 791, 794 (App. Div. 1962) (dissenting opinion), *rev'd*, 235 N.Y.S.2d 377 (Ct. App. 1962); People v. Crocker, 74 N.Y.S.2d 593 (App. Div. 1947); People v. Dalrymple, 112 N.Y.S.2d 390, 392 (App. Div. 1952) (involving sodomy on a young woman of fourteen); People v. Deschessere, 74 N.Y. Supp. 761, 762, 764 (App. Div. 1902).

10. The cases are set out and analyzed in William N. Eskridge, "Privacy Jurisprudence and the Apartheid of the Closet, 1946–1961," *Florida State University Law Review* 24 (1997): 703, 779–80.

11. Herbert L. Packer, *The Limits of the Criminal Sanction* (Stanford, Calif.: Stanford University Press, 1968), 328–31. Of course, much old doctrine also endured, such as that defining an accomplice whose testimony would not provide sufficient corroboration for a conviction, see People v. Guardino, 30 N.Y.S.2d 729 (County Ct. 1941), *aff'd*, 37 N.Y.S.2d 981 (App. Div. 1942), *aff'd*, 290 N.Y. 749 (1943), or that dealing with the sufficiency of evidence. See People v. Lynn, 307 N.Y. 683 (1954).

12. People ex rel. Colletti v. Morehead, 50 N.Y.S.2d 78, 79 (Sup. Ct. 1944).

13. Ibid., 81; People v. Costello, 395 N.Y.S.2d 139, 142 (Sup. Ct. 1977); People v. Catalano, 205 N.Y.S.2d 618, 621 (Magis. Ct. 1960). In *Catalano*, defendant ran an employment agency where "the only employment which the defendant offered these girls (two of whom were seventeen) were jobs for which they would have to submit to unlawful sexual intercourse, or other lewd acts, etc., with their employers" (ibid., 620). On those facts, defendant was found guilty of violating the same statute which the *Colletti* defendant was acquitted of violating.

14. People v. Choremi, 301 N.Y. 417, 421 (1950) (dissenting opinion).

15. People v. Gould, 306 N.Y. 352, 355 (1954) (dissenting opinion).

16. Ibid., 354.

17. People v. Choremi, 301 N.Y. 417, 423 (1950) (dissenting opinion).

18. Ibid., 419–20.

19. People v. Feiner, 300 N.Y. 391 (1950), *aff'd*, 340 U.S. 315 (1951); People v. Choremi, 301 N.Y. 417, 421–22 (1950).

20. People v. Jelke, 152 N.Y.S.2d 479, 483 (Ct. App. 1956); People v. Moss, 309 N.Y. 429, 431 (1956).

21. People v. Moss, 309 N.Y. 429, 432 (1956); People on Complaint of Harrington v. Marcial, 110 N.Y.S.2d 361, 364 (Magis. Ct. 1952); People v. Moss, *supra* at 432.

22. People v. Costello, 395 N.Y.S.2d 139, 142 (Sup. Ct. 1977) (emphasis added); In re P., 400 N.Y.S.2d 455, 468 (Family Ct. 1977), *rev'd*, 418 N.Y.S.2d 597 (App. Div. 1979).

23. People v. Moss, 309 N.Y. 429, 432–33 (1956); People v. Jelke, 152 N.Y.S.2d 479, 484, 492 (Ct. App. 1956). On the issue of economic necessity, see Ruth Rosen, *The Lost Sisterhood: Prostitution in America, 1900–1918* (Baltimore: Johns Hopkins University Press, 1982), xvii.

24. See "Note: Jurisdiction over Family Offenses in New York: A Reconsideration of the Provisions for Choice of Forum," *Syracuse Law Review* 31 (1980): 601.

25. Linda Gordon, *Heroes of Their Own Lives: The Politics and History of Family Violence, Boston, 1880–1960* (New York: Viking, 1988), 250–88; "Report of Joint Legislative Committee on Court Reorganization, The Family Court Act," 1962 McKinney's Session Laws (vol. 2), 3428, 3444.

26. M. v. M., 336 N.Y.S.2d 304, 305, 309 (Family Ct. 1972). See An Act to Establish a Family Court

secs. 813–23, N.Y. Laws of 1962, ch. 686; Douglas J. Besharov, "Introductory Practice Commentary" to Article 8 of Family Court Act.

27. People v. Johnson, 282 N.Y.S.2d 481, 484 (Ct. App. 1967); People v. DeJesus, 250 N.Y.S.2d 317 (App. Div. 1964); People v. Davis, 278 N.Y.S.2d 750, 756 (App. Div. 1967); S. v. S., 311 N.Y.S.2d 169, 179 (Family Ct. 1970).

28. People v. Harkins, 268 N.Y.S.2d 482, 484 (County Ct. 1966); People v. Dugar, 235 N.Y.S.2d 152, 153 (Dist. Ct. 1962).

29. People v. Richmond County News, 179 N.Y.S.2d 76, 81 (Spec. Sess. 1958), rev'd, 205 N.Y.S.2d 94 (App. Div. 1960), aff'd, 216 N.Y.S.2d 369 (Ct. App. 1961).

30. Sunshine Book Co. v. McCaffrey, 112 N.Y.S.2d 476, 483 (Sup. Ct. 1952), modified, 168 N.Y.S.2d 268 (App. Div. 1957); People v. Eagle, 117 N.Y.S.2d 380 (Magis. Ct. 1952); People v. Gonzales, 107 N.Y.S.2d 968, 971 (Magis. Ct. 1951).

31. Joseph Burstyn, Inc. v. Wilson, 303 N.Y. 242, 257, 259–60 (1951) (emphasis added).

32. Ibid., 268, 276.

33. Joseph Burstyn, Inc. v. Wilson, 343 U.S. 495 (1952).

34. Commercial Pictures Corp. v. Board of Regents, 305 N.Y. 336, 339, 342, 347 (1953).

35. Ibid., 358–59; Superior Films, Inc. v. Department of Education, 346 U.S. 587 (1954).

36. Kingsley International Pictures Corp. v. Regents, 175 N.Y.S.2d 39, 41–42, 52, 59 (Ct. App. 1958), rev'd, 360 U.S. 684 (1959). See John M. Blum, V Was for Victory: Politics and American Culture during World War II (New York: Harcourt Brace Jovanovich, 1976), 297, quoting the statement of vice presidential candidate John Bricker, "Insidious and ominous are the forces of communism linked with irreligion that are worming their way into national life."

37. People v. Fritch, 243 N.Y.S.2d 1, 3–4, 6, 8, 10 (Ct. App. 1963).

38. Excelsior Pictures Corp. v. Regents, 165 N.Y.S.2d 42, 43, 51 (Ct. App. 1957).

39. People v. Urban, 222 N.Y.S.2d 461 (App. Div. 1961); Connection Co. v. Regents, 230 N.Y.S.2d 103 (App. Div.), aff'd, 234 N.Y.S.2d 722 (Ct. App. 1962); Broadway Angels, Inc. v. Wilson, 125 N.Y.S.2d 546, 549 (App. Div. 1953); Capitol Enterprises, Inc. v. Regents, 149 N.Y.S.2d 920, 921 (App. Div. 1956).

40. People v. Richmond County News, Inc., 216 N.Y.S.2d 369, 376, 378 (Ct. App. 1961); People v. Abronovitz, 335 N.Y.S.2d 279 (Ct. App. 1972); People v. Hartman, 297 N.Y.S.2d 143 (Ct. App. 1968); People v. Tannenbaum, 274 N.Y.S.2d 131 (Ct. App. 1966), appeal dism., 388 U.S. 439 (1967), conviction vacated, 296 N.Y.S.2d 798 (Ct. App. 1968); People v. Buckley, 320 N.Y.S.2d 91, 96–97 (Crim. Ct. 1971) (dictum), aff'd, 340 N.Y.S.2d 191 (App. Term 1972), aff'd sub nom. People v. Heller, 352 N.Y.S.2d 601 (Ct. App. 1973), cert. denied sub nom. Buckley v. New York, 418 U.S. 944 (1974); People v. G. I. Distributors, Inc., 281 N.Y.S.2d 795, 796–797 (Ct. App.), cert. denied, 389 U.S. 905 (1967); People v. Buckley, supra at 94; People v. Bercowitz, 308 N.Y.S.2d 1, 6 (Crim. Ct. 1970).

41. Brandon Shores, Inc. v. Incorporated Village of Greenwood Lake, 325 N.Y.S.2d 957 (Sup. Ct. 1971); People v. Nixon, 390 N.Y.S.2d 518 (App. Term 1976); Lucifer's Gate, Inc. v. Town of VanBuren, 373 N.Y.S.2d 304 (Sup. Ct. 1975); TJPC Restaurant Corp. v. State Liquor Authority, 402 N.Y.S.2d 483, 485 (App. Div. 1978) (statement of facts from dissenting opinion), aff'd, 424 N.Y.S.2d 896 (Ct. App. 1979); People v. Wilhelm, 330 N.Y.S.2d 279 (City Ct. 1972); Carr v. Hoy, 158 N.Y.S.2d 572, 574 (Ct. App. 1957).

42. Louis Henkin, "Morals and the Constitution: The Sin of Obscenity," Columbia Law Review 63 (1963): 391, 414.

43. Susan Estrich, "Rape," Yale Law Journal 95 (1986): 1087, 1088; People v. Florio, 301 N.Y. 46, 53 (1950).

44. Seymour L. Halleck, "Emotional Effects of Victimization," in Sexual Behavior and the Law, ed. Ralph Slovenko (Springfield, Ill.: Thomas, 1965), 673, 675.

45. People v. Pandeline, 251 N.Y. Supp. 384 (Gen. Sess. 1931); Eric R. v. Ploskitt, 312 N.Y.S.2d 447, 449 (App. Div. 1970); People v. Yannucci, 15 N.Y.S.2d 865, 866 (App. Div. 1939) (dictum), rev'd on

other grounds, 283 N.Y. 546 (1940); People v. Anthony, 293 N.Y. 649 (1944); People on Complaint of Lore v. Smith, 256 N.Y.S.2d 422, 425 (City Ct. 1965).

46. People v. Porcaro, 189 N.Y.S.2d 194, 195–97 (Ct. App. 1959).

47. People v. Oyola, 189 N.Y.S.2d 203, 204–5, 208, 211 (Ct. App. 1959).

48. People v. LoVerde, 195 N.Y.S.2d 835, 836 (Ct. App. 1959).

49. People v. English, 262 N.Y.S.2d 104 (Ct. App. 1965); People v. Reynolds, 307 N.Y.S.2d 201, 204 (Ct. App. 1969).

50. People v. Radunovic, 287 N.Y.S.2d 33, 38–39 (Ct. App. 1967); Kingsley International Pictures Corp. v. Regents, 175 N.Y.S.2d 39, 50 (Ct. App. 1958), *rev'd,* 360 U.S. 684 (1959); People v. Radunovic, *supra* at 39–40.

51. People v. J. T. Nixon, 374 N.Y.S.2d 491 (App. Div. 1975); People v. Butt, 313 N.Y.S.2d 461 (App. Div. 1970); People v. L. B. Nixon, 374 N.Y.S.2d 491 (App. Div. 1975); People v. Mills, 298 N.Y.S.2d 549, 551–52 (App. Div. 1969), *aff'd,* 309 N.Y.S.2d 603 (Ct. App. 1970).

52. People v. Liller, 275 N.Y.S.2d 69, 71–72 (App. Div. 1966), *rev'd on other grounds,* 283 N.Y.S.2d 51 (Ct. App. 1967).

53. People v. Evans, 379 N.Y.S.2d 912, 917 (Sup. Ct. 1975), *aff'd,* 390 N.Y.S.2d 768 (App. Div. 1976).

54. Ibid., 922.

55. People v. Hughes, 343 N.Y.S.2d 240, 241–44 (App. Div. 1973), *appeal dism.,* 374 N.Y.S.2d 601 (Ct. App. 1975) (majority and dissenting opinion).

56. Halleck, "Emotional Effects of Victimization," 675; Cliff Friend, "There's Yes! Yes! in Your Eyes," in *Sing Along with Mitch: The Mitch Miller Family Songfest, A Treasury of Funtime Favorites,* ed. Mitch Miller (New York: Random House, 1961), 67; People v. Evans, 379 N.Y.S.2d 912, 922 (Sup. Ct. 1975), *aff'd,* 390 N.Y.S.2d 768 (App. Div. 1976). For a sharp critique of the *Evans* case, see Estrich, "Rape," 1116–21.

57. See Gallagher v. City of New York, 292 N.Y.S.2d 139 (App. Div. 1968); Foster v. State, 292 N.Y.S.2d 269 (Ct. Claims 1968); People v. Meli, 193 N.Y.S. 365, 366–367 (Sup. Ct. 1922).

58. Ira Reiss, *Premarital Sexual Standards in America* (Glencoe, Ill.: Free Press, 1960), 245. Accord, Winston Ehrmann, *Premarital Dating Behavior* (New York: Holt, 1959), 268.

59. John D'Emilio and Estelle B. Freedman, *Intimate Matters: A History of Sexuality in America* (New York: Harper & Row, 1988), 179 (emphasis in original). See also ibid., 267, 274.

60. Barbara Sichtermann, *Femininity: The Politics of the Personal,* trans. John Whitlam, ed. Helga Geyer-Ryan (Minneapolis: University of Minnesota Press, 1986), 32–33, 39.

CHAPTER TEN

1. See, e.g., Bunim v. Bunim, 298 N.Y. 391, 394 (1949).

2. Clair v. Clair, 64 N.Y.S.2d 889, 890–91 (Sup. Ct. 1946); People ex rel. Geismar v. Geismar, 54 N.Y.S.2d 747, 756 (Sup. Ct. 1945).

3. Oraf v. Oraf, 47 N.Y.S.2d 45, 46 (Dom. Rel. Ct. 1944); People ex rel. Geismar v. Geismar, 54 N.Y.S.2d 747, 755 (Sup. Ct. 1945).

4. See Michael S. Sherry, *In the Shadow of War: The United States since the 1930's* (New Haven: Yale University Press, 1995), 88–90.

5. People ex rel. Foussier v. Uzielli, 260 N.Y.S.2d 329, 333 (App. Div.), *aff'd,* 266 N.Y.S.2d 131 (Ct. App. 1965); People ex rel. Ragona v. DeSaint-Cyr, 137 N.Y.S.2d 275 (Sup. Ct. 1955); People ex rel. Choolokian v. Mission of Immaculate Virgin, 76 N.Y.S.2d 509 (Sup. Ct. 1947), *aff'd,* 86 N.Y.S.2d 462 (App. Div.), *modified on other grounds,* 300 N.Y.S.2d 43 (Ct. App. 1949), *cert. denied,* 339 U.S. 912 (1950).

6. 130 N.Y.S.2d 389 (Sup. Ct.), *aff'd*, 131 N.Y.S.2d 888 (App. Div. 1954).

7. Seley v. Seley, 178 N.Y.S.2d 988, 989 (Sup. Ct. 1958).

8. Michael Grossberg, *Governing the Hearth: Law and the Family in Nineteenth-Century America* (Chapel Hill: University of North Carolina Press, 1985), 238–53; Application of Feigin, 163 N.Y.S.2d 812, 813 (Sup. Ct. 1957); People ex rel. Himber v. Himber, 136 N.Y.S.2d 456, 458 (Sup. Ct. 1954); Hechemy v. Hechemy, 368 N.Y.S.2d 709, 713 (Sup. Ct. 1975) (dictum).

9. Application of Kades, 202 N.Y.S.2d 362 (Sup. Ct. 1960); Application of Richman, 227 N.Y.S.2d 42, 50, 52 (Sup. Ct. 1962); In re Dubin, 112 N.Y.S.2d 267, 269 (Dom. Rel. Ct. 1952); People ex rel. Newitt v. Newitt, 117 N.Y.S.2d 711, 712 (Sup. Ct. 1952) (dictum) (emphasis in original); Feldman v. Feldman, 358 N.Y.S.2d 507, 511 (App. Div. 1974); Matter of Mara, 150 N.Y.S.2d 524, 525 (Dom. Rel. Ct. 1956). Of course, fathers, in response to the specific facts of cases, often received custody. See, e.g., Toni FF v. James FF, 325 N.Y.S.2d 291 (App. Div. 1971).

10. See In re Souers, 238 N.Y.S. 738, 745 (Surr. Ct. 1930); Linda Gordon, *Pitied but Not Entitled: Single Mothers and the History of Welfare, 1890–1935* (New York: Free Press, 1994), 253–306.

11. Betz v. Horr, 294 N.Y.S. 546, 547–48 (App. Div. 1937), *affirming* 290 N.Y.S. 500 (Dom. Rel. Ct. 1936), *rev'd*, 276 N.Y. 83 (1937).

12. 294 N.Y.S. at 549; 276 N.Y. at 87–88. *Accord,* In re Silberman's Will, 295 N.Y.S.2d 478, 485 (Ct. App. 1968).

13. People ex rel. McGaffin v. Family and Children's Service of Albany, 153 N.Y.S.2d 701, 703 (Sup. Ct.) (emphasis in original), *modified,* 158 N.Y.S.2d 45 (App. Div. 1956); People ex rel. Swasing v. Rebecca Talbot Perkins Adoption Society, Inc., 296 N.Y.S. 778, 780 (Sup. Ct.), *aff'd,* 298 N.Y.S. 500 (App. Div. 1937); Matter of Linda F. M., 409 N.Y.S.2d 638 (Surr. Ct. 1978), *aff'd,* 442 N.Y.S.2d 963 (App. Div. 1979), *aff'd,* 437 N.Y.S.2d 283 (Ct. App.), *cert. denied,* 454 U.S. 806 (1981).

14. Adoption of Anonymous, 137 N.Y.S.2d 720, 722 (County Ct. 1955).

15. In re Upjohn's Will, 304 N.Y. 366, 376–77 (1952) (including taking by descent from collateral relatives); Matter of Linda F. M., 409 N.Y.S.2d 638, 643 (Surr. Ct. 1978), *aff'd,* 442 N.Y.S.2d 963 (App. Div. 1979), *aff'd,* 437 N.Y.S.2d 283 (Ct. App.), *cert. denied,* 454 U.S. 806 (1981) (dictum). Thus, once adoptable infants became scarce in the United States, procedures were developed to allow childless couples to find infants overseas and to facilitate the adoption in and immigration to the United States. See Matter of Adoption of Pyung B., 371 N.Y.S.2d 993 (Family Ct. 1975). On the hesitancy of courts before 1980 to allow adoptions by single parents, see Adoption of H., 330 N.Y.S.2d 235 (Family Ct.), *rev'd and remanded for further hearing sub nom.* Matter of Hipps, 333 N.Y.S.2d 846 (App. Div. 1972).

16. In re Adoption of Anonymous, 143 N.Y.S.2d 90, 93–94 (App. Div. 1955); People ex rel. Anonymous v. Anonymous, 222 N.Y.S.2d 945, 946 (Ct. App. 1961); People ex rel. Anonymous v. Rebecca Talbot Perkins Adoption Society, Inc., 68 N.Y.S.2d 238, 241 (App. Div.), *aff'd,* 297 N.Y. 559 (1947); In re Selover, 106 N.Y.S.2d 758, 759–60 (Sup. Ct. 1951); In re Marino's Adoption, 5 N.Y.S.2d 328, 329–30 (Surr. Ct. 1938).

17. In re Adoption of Anonymous, 88 N.Y.S.2d 829, 831–32 (Surr. Ct. 1949).

18. See People ex rel. Anonymous v. Anonymous, 91 N.Y.S.2d 591, 592–94 (Sup. Ct. 1949).

19. 303 N.Y. 539 (1952).

20. Ibid., 541, 543–44; 105 N.Y.S.2d 905 (App. Div. 1951).

21. Hobson v. York Studios, Inc., 145 N.Y.S.2d 162, 167 (Mun. Ct. 1955) (refusing so to frown and awarding plaintiffs, an interracial couple, a remedy of $100 each against a hotel that had refused in violation of the state's civil rights law to provide them with accommodations); 303 N.Y. at 542, 544 (emphasis added). A later case that similarly strove to sidestep racial conflict was Raysor v. Gabbey, 395 N.Y.S.2d 290 (App. Div. 1977), where an African American who had fathered a child out of wedlock with a white mother sought after the mother's death to recovery custody of the child from its maternal grandparents, who had seized the child without informing the father. Noting the presence

of an issue about the ability of white parents in general and of these grandparents in particular to raise "an obviously black young lady . . . matur[ing] in an all-white environment," ibid., 294, the Appellate Division remanded to the trial court for "background investigations by appropriate social agencies into the homelife and neighborhood environment of both petitioner and respondent" and private interviews of the child, her teachers, and "others who might have pertinent information helpful to the court" (ibid., 295). See also Naim v. Naim, 350 U.S. 891 (1955), where the Supreme Court refused to pass on the constitutionality of southern miscegenation statutes. The Court could not bring itself to invalidate such laws and thereby state its approval of interracial marriage until Loving v. Virginia, 388 U.S. 1 (1967). See Meyer v. Nebraska, 262 U.S. 390 (1923).

22. People ex rel. Kropp v. Shepsky, 305 N.Y. 465, 466–467 (1953), *reversing* 117 N.Y.S.2d 695 (App. Div. 1952).

23. People ex rel. Gill v. Lapidus, 120 N.Y.S.2d 766, 769 (Sup. Ct. 1953) (rejecting the quoted assumption); 305 N.Y. at 468. *Accord,* People ex rel. Johnson v. Michael, 240 N.Y.S.2d 779, 780 (Sup. Ct. 1963).

24. Application of Anonymous, 170 N.Y.S.2d 178, 183 (Sup. Ct. 1958); Matter of Jewish Child Care Association of New York, 183 N.Y.S.2d 65, 70–71 (Ct. App. 1959); Spence-Chapin Adoption Service v. Polk, 324 N.Y.S.2d 937, 939 (Ct. App. 1971). For an example of the judiciary's preference for agency adoptions over private placements, see People ex rel. Anonymous v. Talbot Perkins Adoption Service, 259 N.Y.S.2d 440 (Sup. Ct. 1965).

25. Laws of 1972, ch. 639 (Domestic Rel Law sec. 115-b); Matter of Adoption of T.W.C., 379 N.Y.S.2d 1 (Ct. App. 1975); Matter of Sanjivini, 418 N.Y.S.2d 339, 344 (Ct. App. 1979); Spence-Chapin Adoption Service v. Polk, 324 N.Y.S.2d 238, 241–42 (App. Div.), *aff'd,* 324 N.Y.S.2d 937 (Ct. App. 1971); Matter of Anonymous (G.), 393 N.Y.S.2d 900, 903 (Surr. Ct. 1977).

26. Glaser v. Glaser, 276 N.Y. 296, 301 (1938); Williams v. North Carolina, 317 U.S. 287 (1942) and 325 U.S. 226 (1944); Matter of Holmes, 291 N.Y. 261, 268 (1943); Caldwell v. Caldwell, 298 N.Y. 146 (1948); Querze v. Querze, 290 N.Y. 13 (1943).

27. Baker v. Baker, 40 N.Y.S.2d 445 (Sup. Ct. 1943); Matter of Lindgren, 293 N.Y. 18 (1944); Rose v. Rose, 101 N.Y.S.2d 172 (App. Div. 1950); Hubbard v. Hubbard, 228 N.Y. 81 (1920); Ruderman v. Ruderman, 82 N.Y.S.2d 479, 481 (Sup. Ct. 1948), *aff'd,* 89 N.Y.S.2d 894 (App. Div. 1949).

28. Johnson v. Muelberger, 340 U.S. 581, 584 (1951), *reversing* In re Johnson's Estate, 301 N.Y. 13 (1950); Edelman v. Edelman, 161 N.Y.S.2d 717 (App. Div. 1957); Guibord v. Guibord, 153 N.Y.S.2d 457, 459 (App. Div. 1956).

29. Compare Maltese v. Maltese, 224 N.Y.S.2d 946 (Sup. Ct. 1962), with Busk v. Busk, 236 N.Y.S.2d 336 (App. Div.), *modifying* 229 N.Y.S.2d 904 (Sup. Ct. 1962), and Deshler v. Rivas, 108 N.Y.S.2d 837 (Sup. Ct. 1951), *aff'd,* 113 N.Y.S.2d 673 (App. Div. 1952).

30. Rosenstiel v. Rosenstiel, 262 N.Y.S.2d 86, 93, 101 (Ct. App. 1965), *cert. denied,* 383 U.S. 943 (1966) (concurring and dissenting opinions). By upholding Mr. Rosenstiel's Mexican divorce from his first wife, the Court of Appeals legitimated his marriage to his second wife, from whom he was then seeking to escape. Litigation over this second marriage continued for many years. See Rosenstiel v. Rosenstiel, 368 F. Supp. 51 (S.D.N.Y. 1973), *aff'd,* 503 F.2d 1397 (2d Cir. 1974).

31. Application of Sood, 142 N.Y.S.2d 591 (Sup. Ct. 1955); In re Levy's Estate, 6 N.Y.S.2d 544 (Surr. Ct. 1938).

32. Siecht v. Siecht, 41 N.Y.S.2d 393, 394 (Sup. Ct. 1943).

33. Kober v. Kober, 264 N.Y.S.2d 364 (Ct. App.), *rev'g,* 256 N.Y.S.2d 615 (App. Div. 1965); Opinion of Trial Court, quoted at 256 N.Y.S.2d 615, 620 (dissenting opinion).

34. 256 N.Y.S.2d at 618; Darling v. Darling, 105 N.Y.S.2d 475, 478 (Sup. Ct. 1951).

35. 264 N.Y.S.2d at 369–70.

36. Laws of 1966, ch. 254, which took effect on September 1, 1967; Yoli v. Yoli, 285 N.Y.S.2d 470,

474 (Sup. Ct. 1967). Judges Bergan, Dye, Fuld, and Van Voorhis constituted the majority of the seven-member court in both *Rosenstiel* and *Kober.*

37. Echevarria v. Echevarria, 386 N.Y.S.2d 653, 654 (Ct. App. 1976); Wolfson v. Wolfson, 331 N.Y.S.2d 844, 846 (App. Div.), *appeal dism.,* 336 N.Y.S.2d 907 (Ct. App. 1972) (by implication); Schlachet v. Schlachet, 378 N.Y.S.2d 308 (Sup. Ct. 1976).

38. See Christian v. Christian, 396 N.Y.S.2d 817, 821 (Ct. App. 1977); Gleason v. Gleason, 308 N.Y.S.2d 347 (Ct. App. 1970); Christian v. Christian, *supra* at 822; Timmins v. Timmins, 375 N.Y.S.2d 71 (App. Div. 1975), *appeal denied,* 382 N.Y.S.2d 1027 (Ct. App. 1976). Colascione v. Colascione, 291 N.Y.S.2d 559 (Sup. Ct. 1968). Prior law had given a spouse a right to terminate a marriage when the other spouse was sentenced to life imprisonment. See Zizzo v. Zizzo, 247 N.Y.S.2d 38 (Sup. Ct. 1964).

39. As a result of the institution of no-fault divorce, the number of civil filings in state courts nearly doubled between 1967 and 1975. Nearly all of the increase consisted of uncontested matrimonial actions. See Chapter 15, second section, "The Bureaucratization of the Criminal and Family Law Processes," below.

40. Bruno v. Bruno, 334 N.Y.S.2d 242, 248 (Sup. Ct. 1972), *modified on other grounds,* 355 N.Y.S.2d 817 (App. Div. 1974); Shamsee v. Shamsee, 381 N.Y.S.2d 127 (App. Div. 1976). Such issues continued to arise, however, in regard to old marriages which at least one spouse had sought to terminate before the 1967 legislation; there was then a question whether the attempt at termination had succeeded. See, e.g., Matter of Estate of Joseph, 317 N.Y.S.2d 338 (Ct. App. 1970). Occasional cases also arose when New Yorkers turned to foreign courts for a speedier divorce than they could obtain at home. See, e.g., Greschler v. Greschler, 434 N.Y.S.2d 194 (Ct. App. 1980).

41. Grillo v. Sherman-Stalter Co., 186 N.Y.S. 810, 812 (App. Div.), *aff'd,* 231 N.Y. 621 (1921); In re Vincent's Estate, 71 N.Y.S.2d 165, 168 (Surr. Ct. 1947).

42. In re Jones, 98 N.Y.S.2d 524, 525–27 (Children's Ct. 1950).

43. Thurber v. Thurber, 63 N.Y.S.2d 401, 402–3 (Sup. Ct. 1946).

44. See Yucabezky v. Yucabezky, 111 N.Y.S.2d 441 (Sup. Ct. 1952); Smith v. Smith, 77 N.Y.S.2d 902 (App. Div. 1948); Burdes v. Burdes, 90 N.Y.S.2d 97 (Dom. Rel. Ct. 1949); Musso v. Musso, 143 N.Y.S.2d 331 (Sup. Ct. 1955); Pankiw v. Pankiw, 256 N.Y.S.2d 448 (Sup. Ct. 1965).

45. Roger v. Roger, 203 N.Y.S.2d 576, 577 (Sup. Ct. 1960) (quoting language from West Publishing Co. headnote); Florio v. Florio, 143 N.Y.S.2d 105, 107 (Sup. Ct. 1955); Ehrlich v. Ehrlich, 112 N.Y.S.2d 244 (Sup. Ct. 1952); Schulman v. Schulman, 46 N.Y.S.2d 158 (Sup. Ct. 1943).

46. Blessing v. Blessing, 215 N.Y.S.2d 284 (App. Div. 1961); Nilsen v. Nilsen, 183 N.Y.S.2d 210 (Sup. Ct. 1959); Becker v. Becker, 260 N.Y.S.2d 879, 880 (Sup. Ct. 1965) (emphasis added); Axelrod v. Axelrod, 150 N.Y.S.2d 633, 639 (Sup. Ct. 1956).

47. McCarthy v. McCarthy, 103 N.Y.S.2d 808, 811 (Dom. Rel. Ct. 1951); Traylor v. Traylor, 159 N.Y.S.2d 818, 819 (App. Div. 1957); Pearson v. Pearson, 230 N.Y. 141, 148 (1920); Smith v. Smith, 200 N.Y.S.2d 542 (App. Div. 1960); Reese v. Reese, 185 N.Y.S. 110, 111 (App. Div. 1920); Baker v. Baker, 228 N.Y.S.2d 470, 472 (App. Div. 1962); McClinton v. McClinton, 200 N.Y.S.2d 987, 989–990 (Sup. Ct. 1960); In re Smith's Will, 72 N.Y.S.2d 609, 612 (Surr. Ct. 1947); Straub v. Straub, 204 N.Y.S. 61, 62 (App. Div. 1924); Brown v. Brown, 208 N.Y.S. 17, 19 (Sup. Ct. 1924).

48. DiCroce v. DiCroce, 209 N.Y.S.2d 624, 627 (Sup. Ct. 1961); Barretta v. Barretta, 46 N.Y.S.2d 261, 263 (Sup. Ct. 1944); McClinton v. McClinton, 200 N.Y.S.2d 987 (Sup. Ct. 1960); Shepetin v. Shepetin, 229 N.Y.S.2d 457 (App. Div. 1962). But male conduct described by a court as "sexual raids," "unreasonable exercise of marital rights," and "excessive and unreasonable sexual indulgence" would be held cruel. Harnish v. Harnish, 60 N.Y.S.2d 153, 154 (App. Div. 1946).

49. Petrella v. Petrella, 255 N.Y.S.2d 962, 963 (App. Div. 1965); Rosner v. Rosner, 108 N.Y.S.2d 196, 200 (Dom. Rel. Ct. 1951).

50. Sengstack v. Sengstack, 176 N.Y.S.2d 337 (Ct. App. 1958); Diemer v. Diemer, 203 N.Y.S.2d

829, 833 (Ct. App. 1960); Vetrano v. Vetrano, 54 N.Y.S.2d 537 (Sup. Ct. 1945); Palese v. Palese, 267 N.Y.S.2d 542 (App. Div. 1966); Cavallo v. Cavallo, 359 N.Y.S.2d 628, 629 (Sup. Ct. 1974); Vetrano v. Vetrano, *supra* at 538.

51. Anastasiadis v. Anastasiadis, 279 N.Y.S.2d 936, 937 (Sup. Ct. 1967).

52. Brandt v. Brandt, 233 N.Y.S.2d 993, 995 (Sup. Ct. 1962); Brownstein v. Brownstein, 268 N.Y.S.2d 115, 122–23 (App. Div. 1966); Doyle v. Doyle, 158 N.Y.S.2d 909, 912 (Sup. Ct. 1957).

CHAPTER ELEVEN

1. Reinhold Niebuhr, "The Collectivist Bogy," *Nation,* October 21, 1944, 478.

2. Baddour v. City of Long Beach, 279 N.Y. 167 (1938), *affirming* 297 N.Y.S. 796 (App. Div. 1937), *appeal dism.,* 308 U.S. 503 (1939).

3. Moore v. City of East Cleveland, 431 U.S. 494 (1977); 279 N.Y. at 174–75, 179.

4. Learned Hand, "Is There a Common Will," *Michigan Law Review* 28 (1929): 46, 50; John Dickinson, "Democratic Realities and Democratic Dogma," *American Political Science Review* 24 (1930): 283, 291–92.

5. Ellis W. Hawley, *The New Deal and the Problem of Monopoly: A Study in Economic Ambivalence* (Princeton: Princeton University Press, 1966), 276; John Chamberlain, *The American Stakes* (New York: Carrick & Evans, 1940), 31–32; V. O. Key, *Politics, Parties, and Pressure Groups,* 5th ed. (New York: Crowell, 1964), iv; Douglass Adair, "The Tenth Federalist Revisited," *William and Mary Quarterly* 3d ser., 8 (1951): 48; Theodore J. Lowi, *The End of Liberalism: Ideology, Policy, and the Crisis of Public Authority* (New York: Norton, 1969), 71 (emphasis in original).

6. 4 Hill 140 (N.Y. Sup. Ct. 1843).

7. Nalore v. Baker, 279 N.Y.S. 944, 948 (App. Div. 1935); People ex rel. Hirschberg v. Board of Supervisors of Orange County, 251 N.Y. 156 (1929).

8. Hacker v. State Liquor Authority, 278 N.Y.S.2d 806, 811 (Ct. App. 1967).

9. Cummings v. Regan, 350 N.Y.S.2d 119, 127 (Sup. Ct. 1973), *aff'd,* 357 N.Y.S.2d 260 (App. Div. 1974), *rev'd on other grounds,* 373 N.Y.S.2d 563 (Ct. App. 1975); Swalbach v. State Liquor Authority, 200 N.Y.S.2d 1, 4 (Ct. App. 1960); Weiss v. Herman, 216 N.Y.S.2d 829, 833 (Sup. Ct. 1961), *aff'd,* 229 N.Y.S.2d 152 (App. Div. 1962), *rev'd on other grounds,* 241 N.Y.S.2d 167 (Ct. App. 1963); Rochester Colony, Inc. v. Hostetter, 241 N.Y.S.2d 210, 215 (App. Div. 1963); Kilgus v. Board of Estimate of City of New York, 308 N.Y. 620, 627 (1955); Guardian Life Insurance Co. v. Bohlinger, 308 N.Y. 174, 183 (1954).

10. Hecht v. Monaghan, 307 N.Y. 461, 470 (1954); Costello v. New York State Liquor Authority, 236 N.Y.S.2d 453, 455 (App. Div. 1963); Simpson v. Wolansky, 380 N.Y.S.2d 630, 634 (Ct. App. 1975); Murray v. Murphy, 299 N.Y.S.2d 175, 181 (Ct. App. 1969); Rivera v. Blum, 420 N.Y.S.2d 304, 310 (Sup. Ct. 1978); Henegar v. Wyman, 313 N.Y.S.2d 318, 320 (Sup. Ct. 1970); New York State Commission for Human Rights v. E. Landau Industries, Inc., 293 N.Y.S.2d 917, 920 (Sup. Ct. 1968).

11. For a rare case in which a pro bono attorney was able to rescue a case that had been lost at an informal hearing, see Williams v. White Plains Housing Authority, 309 N.Y.S.2d 454 (Sup. Ct.), *aff'd,* 317 N.Y.S.2d 935 (App. Div. 1970).

12. Bates v. Toia, 410 N.Y.S.2d 265, 267 (Ct. App. 1978); Jones v. Berman, 371 N.Y.S.2d 422, 429 (Ct. App. 1975).

13. Sabot v. Lavine, 399 N.Y.S.2d 640 (Ct. App. 1977); Suffolk County Builders Association, Inc. v. County of Suffolk, 415 N.Y.S.2d 821, 824 (Ct. App. 1979); Bethlehem Steel Co. v. Joseph, 130 N.Y.S.2d 178, 181 (App. Div. 1954); Green v. Lang, 276 N.Y.S.2d 604 (Ct. App. 1966); Harbolic v. Berger, 400 N.Y.S.2d 780, 784 (Ct. App. 1977) (dictum).

14. 307 N.Y. 493, 499 (1954).

15. See Scarsdale Supply Co. v. Village of Scarsdale, 206 N.Y.S.2d 773, 776 (Ct. App. 1960) (dictum); Summers v. City of Glen Cove, 270 N.Y.S.2d 611, 612 (Ct. App. 1966); Mary Chess, Inc. v. City of Glen Cove, 273 N.Y.S.2d 46, 49 (Ct. App. 1966); Golden v. Planning Board of Town of Ramapo, 334 N.Y.S.2d 138, 155 (Ct. App.), *appeal dism.,* 409 U.S. 1003 (1972) (dictum); Williams v. Town of Oyster Bay, 343 N.Y.S.2d 118, 123 (Ct. App. 1973) (dictum); Ilasi v. City of Long Beach, 379 N.Y.S.2d 831, 835 (Ct. App. 1976) (dictum); Fred F. French Investing Co. v. City of New York, 385 N.Y.S.2d 5, 7 (Ct. App.), *cert denied,* 429 U.S. 990 (1976); National Merritt, Inc. v. Weist, 393 N.Y.S.2d 379, 385–86 (Ct. App. 1977) (dictum); Marcus Associates, Inc. v. Town of Huntington, 410 N.Y.S.2d 546, 547–48 (Ct. App. 1978) (dictum); Megin Realty Corp. v. Baron, 414 N.Y.S.2d 687, 688 (Ct. App. 1979) (dictum).

16. Megin Realty Corp. v. Baron, 414 N.Y.S.2d 687, 688 (Ct. App. 1979) (dictum); Town of Bedford v. Village of Mount Kisco, 351 N.Y.S.2d 129, 136 (Ct. App. 1973) (dictum); Tarrant v. Incorporated Village of Roslyn, 197 N.Y.S.2d 317 (2d Dept.), *aff'd,* 209 N.Y.S.2d 813 (Ct. App. 1960); Rammar Associates Inc. v. Incorporated Village of Westbury, 300 N.Y.S.2d 698, 699–700 (Sup. Ct. 1969).

17. Udell v. Haas, 288 N.Y.S.2d 888, 893 (Ct. App. 1968); Westchester County Society for the Prevention of Cruelty to Animals v. Mengel, 292 N.Y. 121, 126 (1944); Aknin v. Phillips, 404 F. Supp. 1150, 1153 (S.D.N.Y. 1975), *aff'd,* 538 F.2d 307 (2d Cir. 1976); Gardner v. Downer, 305 N.Y.S.2d 252, 256 (Sup. Ct. 1969), *aff'd,* 317 N.Y.S.2d 1013 (App. Div. 1970), *aff'd,* 323 N.Y.S.2d 1025 (Ct. App. 1971); Village of Belle Terre v. Boraas, 416 U.S. 1, 9 (1974).

18. Levitt v. Incorporated Village of Sands Point, 189 N.Y.S.2d 212 (Ct. App. 1959); Voelcker v. City of Glen Cove, 212 N.Y.S.2d 835 (Sup. Ct. 1961); Berenson v. Town of New Castle, 378 N.Y.S.2d 672, 679, 681–82 (Ct. App. 1975); Robert E. Kurzius, Inc. v. Incorporated Village of Upper Brookville, 434 N.Y.S.2d 180 (Ct. App.), *cert. denied,* 450 U.S. 1042 (1980). A parallel device was the "regulation of trailer camps," which, it was said, bore "a substantial relation to public health, safety, morals and general welfare." Stevens v. Smolka, 202 N.Y.S.2d 783, 785 (App. Div. 1960).

19. Pforzheimer v. Seidman, 99 N.Y.S.2d 87, 90 (Sup. Ct. 1950), *rev'd on other grounds,* 103 N.Y.S.2d 886 (App. Div. 1951); Brous v. Smith, 304 N.Y. 164 (1952).

20. 304 N.Y. at 170–71.

21. Gulino Construction Corp. v. Hilleboe, 167 N.Y.S.2d 787 (Sup. Ct. 1956); Oakwood Island Yacht Club, Inc. v. Board of Appeals of City of New Rochelle, 223 N.Y.S.2d 907 (Sup. Ct. 1961); Gulest Associates, Inc. v. Town of Newburgh, 209 N.Y.S.2d 729 (Sup. Ct. 1960), *aff'd,* 225 N.Y.S.2d 538 (App. Div. 1961); Jenad, Inc. v. Village of Scarsdale, 271 N.Y.S.2d 955, 957, 960–61 (Ct. App. 1966).

22. See Slavin v. Ingraham, 376 N.Y.S.2d 463 (Ct. App. 1975); Peckham Industries v. Ross, 306 N.Y.S.2d 1006 (Sup. Ct.), *aff'd,* 312 N.Y.S.2d 627 (App. Div. 1970).

23. Golden v. Planning Board of Town of Ramapo, 334 N.Y.S.2d 138, 155–156 (Ct. App.), *appeal dism.,* 409 U.S. 1003 (1972) (dictum).

24. Presnell v. Leslie, 165 N.Y.S.2d 488, 492 (Ct. App. 1957) (dictum); Mid-State Advertising Corp. v. Bond, 274 N.Y. 82 (1937); Presnell v. Leslie, *supra* at 492 (dictum).

25. People v. Stover, 240 N.Y.S.2d 734, 738 (Ct. App.), *appeal dism.,* 375 U.S. 42 (1963).

26. Ibid., 742–43.

27. See Wambat Realty Corp. v. State, 393 N.Y.S.2d 949 (Ct. App. 1977); New York State Water Resources Commission v. Liberman, 326 N.Y.S.2d 284 (App. Div. 1971), *appeal dism.,* 330 N.Y.S.2d 63 (Ct. App. 1972); Incorporated Village of Westbury v. Samuels, 260 N.Y.S.2d 369 (Sup. Ct. 1965).

28. See Old Farm Road, Inc. v. Town of New Castle, 311 N.Y.S.2d 500 (Ct. App. 1970); Penn Central Transportation Co. v. New York City, 438 U.S. 104 (1978); Lutheran Church in America v. City of New York, 359 N.Y.S.2d 7 (Ct. App. 1974).

29. People v. Grant, 306 N.Y. 258, 260 (1954); Wiggins v. Town of Somers, 173 N.Y.S.2d 579, 581 (Ct. App. 1958); Atlantic Beach Property Owners' Ass'n v. Town of Hempstead, 165 N.Y.S.2d 737, 740 (Ct. App. 1957).

30. See People v. Chodorov, 237 N.Y.S.2d 689 (Ct. App. 1962), *cert. denied,* 375 U.S. 46 (1963); Laws of 1950, ch. 1 and ch. 250 (1950).

31. Parrino v. Lindsay, 323 N.Y.S.2d 689 (Ct. App. 1971); Teeval Co. v. McGoldrick, 304 N.Y. 981 (1953); Bucho Holding Co. v. Temporary State Housing Rent Commission, 230 N.Y.S.2d 977, 982–83 (Ct. App. 1962).

32. See, e.g., Windsor Park Tenants' Association v. New York City Conciliation and Appeals Board, 397 N.Y.S.2d 828 (App. Div. 1977), *appeal dism.,* 416 N.Y.S.2d 1027 (Ct. App. 1979); Jaffe v. McGoldrick, 137 N.Y.S.2d 519 (App. Div. 1955).

33. 9 NYCRR 2204.6(d).

34. Hudson View Properties v. Weiss, 431 N.Y.S.2d 632, 634 (Civil Ct. 1980).

35. Hudson View Properties v. Weiss, 442 N.Y.S.2d 367 (App. Term 1981), *rev'd,* 448 N.Y.S.2d 649 (App. Div. 1982).

36. Hudson View Properties v. Weiss, 463 N.Y.S.2d 428, 429 (Ct. App. 1983).

37. Laws of 1983, ch. 403 (1983). See Braschi v. Stahl Associates Co., 544 N.Y.S.2d 784 (Ct. App. 1989), for a case allowing a gay life partner of a deceased tenant to continue living in the decedent's apartment.

38. See Rochester Gas & Electric Corp. v. Maltbie, 76 N.Y.S.2d 671 (App. Div. 1948), *aff'd,* 298 N.Y. 867 (1949); Cherlob, Inc. v. Barrett, 293 N.Y. 442 (1944); International Railway Co. v. Public Service Commission, 36 N.Y.S.2d 125 (App. Div. 1942), *aff'd,* 289 N.Y. 830 (1943); Brooklyn Union Gas Co. v. Public Service Commission, 187 N.Y.S.2d 207 (App. Div. 1959), *aff'd,* 202 N.Y.S.2d 322 (Ct. App. 1960); New York Telephone Co. v. Public Service Commission, 410 N.Y.S.2d 124, 133 (App. Div. 1978), *appeal denied,* 414 N.Y.S.2d 1028 (Ct. App. 1979); Public Service Commission v. Jamaica Water Supply Co., 397 N.Y.S.2d 784 (Ct. App. 1977).

39. See Consolidated Edison Co. v. Public Service Commission, 402 N.Y.S.2d 551 (Sup. Ct.), *rev'd,* 407 N.Y.S.2d 735 (App. Div. 1978), *aff'd,* 417 N.Y.S.2d 30 (Ct. App. 1979), *rev'd,* 447 U.S. 530 (1980); *on remand sub nom.* Rochester Gas and Electric Corp. v. Public Service Commission, 433 N.Y.S.2d 420 (Ct. App. 1980), *appeal dism.,* 450 U.S. 961 (1981). See also Central Hudson Gas & Electric Corp. v. Public Service Commission, 447 U.S. 557 (1980).

40. City of New Rochelle v. Westchester Electric R. Co., 29 N.Y.S.2d 805, 807 (Sup. Ct. 1940), *aff'd,* 29 N.Y.S.2d 719 (App Div. 1941), *aff'd,* 288 N.Y. 571 (1942); Eighth Avenue Coach Corp. v. City of New York, 286 N.Y. 84 (1941).

41. Defiance Milk Products Co. v. DuMond, 309 N.Y. 537, 541–42 (1956).

42. 309 N.Y. at 541.

43. Trio Distributor Corp. v. City of Albany, 163 N.Y.S.2d 585, 589 (Ct. App. 1957).

44. Swalbach v. State Liquor Authority, 200 N.Y.S.2d 1, 3, 5, 7, 10 (Ct. App. 1960).

45. Circus Disco Ltd. v. New York State Liquor Authority, 431 N.Y.S.2d 491, 498–99 (Ct. App. 1980).

46. Bologno v. O'Connell, 196 N.Y.S.2d 90 (Ct. App. 1959).

47. People v. Holbrook Transportation Corp., 378 N.Y.S.2d 939, 945 (Dist. Ct. 1976), *appeal dism.,* 389 N.Y.S.2d 514 (App. Term 1976).

48. Wignall v. Fletcher, 303 N.Y. 435, 441–42 (1952).

49. New York City Housing Authority v. Muller, 270 N.Y. 333, 339–40, 342 (1936).

50. Weitzner v. Stichman, 64 N.Y.S.2d 40 (Sup. Ct.), *aff'd in part and rev'd in part,* 64 N.Y.S.2d 50 (App. Div. 1946), *aff'd,* 296 N.Y. 907 (1947); Cannata v. City of New York, 227 N.Y.S.2d 903 (Ct. App. 1962); Kaskel v. Impellitteri, 306 N.Y. 73 (1953), *cert. denied,* 347 U.S. 934 (1953); Murray v. La-Guardia, 291 N.Y. 320 (1943), *cert. denied,* 321 U.S. 771 (1944); Yonkers Community Development Agency v. Morris, 373 N.Y.S.2d 112, 117–18 (Ct. App.), *appeal dism.,* 423 U.S. 1010 (1975).

51. See Deniham Enterprises, Inc. v. O'Dwyer, 302 N.Y. 451 (1951); Fifth Avenue Coach Lines, Inc. v. City of New York, 229 N.Y.S.2d 400 (Ct. App. 1962); In re United Nations Development

District, 339 N.Y.S.2d 292 (Sup. Ct. 1972); Hotel Dorset Co. v. Trust for Cultural Resources of City of New York, 413 N.Y.S.2d 357 (Ct. App. 1978); New York State Urban Development Corp. v. Vanderlex Merchandise Co., 413 N.Y.S.2d 982 (Sup. Ct. 1979). The ultimately successful effort to save Carnegie Hall resulted in complex litigation that came before the Court of Appeals on three separate occasions. See Keystone Associates v. State, 411 N.Y.S.2d 8 (Ct. App. 1978), *reversing* 389 N.Y.S.2d 895 (App. Div. 3d Dept. 1976); Keystone Associates v. State, 352 N.Y.S.2d 194 (Ct. App. 1973); Keystone Associates v. Moerdler, 278 N.Y.S.2d 185 (Ct. App. 1966).

52. 240 N.Y.S.2d 1 (Ct. App.), *appeal dism.,* 375 U.S. 78 (1963).

53. Ibid., 396–98 (dissenting opinion).

54. Cities Service Oil Co. v. City of New York, 180 N.Y.S.2d 769, 774 (Ct. App. 1958), *cert. denied,* 360 U.S. 934 (1959); Mercury Aircraft, Inc. v. State, 264 N.Y.S.2d 7, 8 (App. Div. 1965). Although they continued to adhere formally to the old rule that consequential damages for a change in grade of a highway were compensable when a statute authorized compensation, see Williams v. State, 309 N.Y.S.2d 795 (App. Div. 1970), courts in at least some cases found diverse, often technical reasons to avoid granting damages to plaintiffs to whom a statute made damages available. See, e.g., In re Brooklyn-Queens Connecting Highway & Parks, 300 N.Y. 265 (1949).

55. Nature Conservancy, Inc. v. State, 325 N.Y.S.2d 540, 544 (Ct. Claims 1971), *rev'd on other grounds,* 341 N.Y.S.2d 38 (App. Div. 1973). For rules limiting full compensation, see, e.g., City of New York v. Allied Stores of New York, Inc., 408 N.Y.S.2d 327 (Ct. App. 1978); Rochester Carting Co. v. Levitt, 367 N.Y.S.2d 242 (Ct. App. 1975); Great Atlantic & Pacific Tea Co. v. State, 291 N.Y.S.2d 299, 310–11 (Ct. App. 1968); Tarrant Manufacturing Co. v. State, 390 N.Y.S.2d 658 (App. Div. 1977); Application of Westchester County, 127 N.Y.S.2d 24, 32 (Sup. Ct. 1953).

56. N.Y. Laws of 1920, ch. 949 (1920); Hermitage Co. v. Goldfogle, 236 N.Y. 554 (1923); People ex rel. Waitt Operating Co. v. Goldfogle, 201 N.Y.S. 262, 264 (Sup. Ct. 1923), *aff'd,* 203 N.Y.S. 947 (App. Div.), *aff'd,* 239 N.Y. 522 (1924).

57. People ex rel. 1170 Fifth Avenue Corp. v. Goldfogle, 254 N.Y. 476 (1930); Webster Apartments v. City of New York, 193 N.Y.S. 650, 651 (Sup. Ct. 1922), *aff'd,* 200 N.Y.S. 956 (App. Div. 1923).

58. People v. Westchester County National Bank of Peekskill, 231 N.Y. 465 (1921); Williams v. Walsh, 289 N.Y. 1, 8–9 (1942); August v. Bronstein, 369 F. Supp. 190 (S.D.N.Y.), *aff'd,* 417 U.S. 901 (1974).

59. Garlin v. Murphy, 273 N.Y.S.2d 374, 376 (Sup. Ct. 1966).

60. Grace v. New York State Tax Commission, 371 N.Y.S.2d 715, 718 (Ct. App. 1975); Board of Cooperative Educational Services v. Buckley, 259 N.Y.S.2d 858 (Ct. App. 1965); Town of Harrison v. County of Westchester, 246 N.Y.S.2d 593 (Ct. App. 1963); AFC Industries, Inc. v. Board of Assessors of City of Buffalo, 214 N.Y.S.2d 915 (App. Div. 1961), *aff'd,* 248 N.Y.S.2d 397 (Ct. App. 1964); Fort Hamilton Manor, Inc. v. Boyland, 173 N.Y.S.2d 560 (Ct. App. 1958); Application of S. S. Silberblatt, Inc., 180 N.Y.S.2d 210, 215 (App. Div. 1958), *aff'd,* 186 N.Y.S.2d 646 (Ct. App.), *cert denied,* 361 U.S. 912 (1959); Simonelli v. City of New York, 95 N.Y.S.2d 316 (App. Div.), *aff'd,* 301 N.Y. 752 (1950); Liberty National Bank and Trust Co. v. Buscaglia, 288 N.Y.S.2d 33, 34 (Ct. App. 1967), *cert. denied,* 396 U.S. 941 (1969); Dime Savings Bank of Brooklyn v. Beecher, 260 N.Y.S.2d 500, 505 (App. Div. 1965), *aff'd,* 274 N.Y.S.2d 901 (Ct. App. 1966).

61. Application of Thomas S. Clarkson Memorial College of Technology, 87 N.Y.S.2d 491, 492–93 (App. Div.), *aff'd,* 300 N.Y. 595 (1949); Pratt Institute v. Boyland, 174 N.Y.S.2d 112 (Sup. Ct. 1958), *aff'd,* 185 N.Y.S.2d 753 (App. Div. 1959); University of Rochester v. Wagner, 408 N.Y.S.2d 157 (App. Div. 1978), *aff'd,* 418 N.Y.S.2d 583 (Ct. App. 1979); Faculty-Student Association of Harpur College, Inc. v. Dawson, 292 N.Y.S.2d 216, 228 (Sup. Ct. 1967). Schools conducted for profit were not tax exempt. See Semple School for Girls v. Boyland, 308 N.Y. 382 (1955).

62. See St. Luke's Hospital v. Boyland, 237 N.Y.S.2d 308 (Ct. App. 1962); People ex rel. Unter-

myer v. McGregor, 295 N.Y. 237 (1946); Hotel Dorset Co. v. Trust for Cultural Resources of City of New York, 413 N.Y.S.2d 357 (Ct. App. 1978).

63. See Diehm v. City of New York, 143 N.Y.S.2d 298 (Sup. Ct. 1955); Nicolette v. Village of Clyde, 310 N.Y.S.2d 896 (App. Div. 1970); Engle v. Talarico, 351 N.Y.S.2d 677 (Ct. App. 1973).

64. Newsday, Inc. v. Town of Huntington, 426 N.Y.S.2d 409, 413 (Sup. Ct. 1980), *aff'd,* 441 N.Y.S.2d 689 (App. Div. 1981), *aff'd,* 449 N.Y.S.2d 157 (Ct. App. 1982); R. P. Adams Co. v. Nist, 411 N.Y.S.2d 504, 506 (Sup. Ct. 1978), *rev'd on other grounds,* 422 N.Y.S.2d 184 (App. Div. 1979); United Artists Theatre Circuit, Inc. v. State Tax Commission, 438 N.Y.S.2d 295, 296 (Ct. App. 1981), *reversing* 429 N.Y.S.2d 299 (App. Div. 1980); Boston Stock Exchange v. State Tax Commission, 375 N.Y.S.2d 308, 311 (Ct. App. 1975). The New York scheme favoring transactions conducted entirely on the New York Stock Exchange was held to be an unconstitutional restraint on commerce, however, in Boston Stock Exchange v. State Tax Commission, 429 U.S. 318 (1977), which reversed the judgment of the Court of Appeals. The original imposition of a tax on out-of-state stock transfers having only a tangential relationship to New York had been sustained in O'Kane v. State, 283 N.Y. 439 (1940).

65. Erie County Agricultural Society v. Cluchey, 386 N.Y.S.2d 366, 370 (Ct. App. 1976).

66. 356 N.Y.S.2d 555 (Ct. App. 1974).

67. 356 N.Y.S.2d at 563. For the legislation terminating exemptions, see N.Y. Laws of 1971, ch. 414.

68. People ex rel. The Frick Collection v. Chambers, 91 N.Y.S.2d 525 (Sup. Ct. 1949), *aff'd,* 94 N.Y.S.2d 819 (App. Div. 1950); Petition of Union Free School District No. 3 of Town of Huntington, 225 N.Y.S.2d 430, 433 (Sup. Ct. 1962), *aff'd,* 245 N.Y.S.2d 993 (App. Div. 1963), *appeal denied,* 247 N.Y.S.2d 1027 (Ct. App. 1964).

69. 371 N.Y.S.2d 388 (Ct. App. 1975). See Real Property Tax Law sec. 306. Its history was discussed in *Hellerstein* at 371 N.Y.S.2d at 389–93.

70. 700 Shore Road Associates v. Board of Assessment Review of County of Nassau, 335 N.Y.S.2d 114, 117 (Sup. Ct. 1972); Rokowsky v. Finance Administrator of City of New York, 394 N.Y.S.2d 176, 178 (Ct. App. 1977); Hoffman v. Assessor of Town of Stephentown, 406 N.Y.S.2d 373 (App. Div. 1978); Laws of 1978, ch. 163, sec. 1; Colt Industries, Inc. v. Finance Administrator of City of New York, 446 N.Y.S.2d 237, 240 (Ct. App.), *appeal dism. sub nom.* Equitable Life Assurance Soc'y v. Finance Administrator of City of New York, 459 U.S. 983 (1982).

71. Slewett & Farber v. Board of Assessors, 412 N.Y.S.2d 292, 295–96 (Sup. Ct. 1978), *modified and vacated,* 438 N.Y.S.2d 544 (App. Div. 1981), *modified and aff'd,* 446 N.Y.S.2d 241 (Ct. App. 1982).

72. State Tax Commission v. Barnes, 178 N.Y.S.2d 932 (County Ct. 1958); New York Mobile Homes Association v. Steckel, 215 N.Y.S.2d 487 (Ct. App. 1961); Ames Volkswagen, Ltd. v. State Tax Commission, 418 N.Y.S.2d 324, 326 (Ct. App. 1979); Federated Department Stores, Inc. v. Gerosa, 266 N.Y.S.2d 378, 381 (Ct. App. 1965), *appeal dism.,* 385 U.S. 454 (1967); Long Island Lighting Co. v. State Tax Commission, 410 N.Y.S.2d 561, 563–64 (Ct. App. 1978).

73. See First National City Bank v. City of New York Finance Administration, 365 N.Y.S.2d 493 (Ct. App. 1975); People ex rel. Empire State Building Corp. v. Boyland, 135 N.Y.S.2d 764 (Sup. Ct. 1954), *aff'd,* 149 N.Y.S.2d 214 (App. Div. 1956), *aff'd,* 177 N.Y.S.2d 705 (Ct. App. 1958).

CHAPTER TWELVE

1. United States v. Freeman, 357 F.2d 606, 618 n.35 (2d Cir. 1966).

2. Quoted in E. Digby Baltzell, *The Protestant Establishment: Aristocracy and Caste in America* (New York: Random House, 1964), 321, 324; Osborn Elliott, *Men at the Top* (New York: Harper, 1959), 167; Baltzell, *Protestant Establishment,* 321, 364; F. W. Gregory and I. D. Neu, "The Ameri-

can Industrial Elite in the 1870s: Their Social Origins," in *Men in Business: Essays in the History of Entrepreneurship,* ed. William Miller (Cambridge, Mass.: Harvard University Press, 1952), 200; Mabel Newcomer, *The Big Business Executive; The Factors That Made Him, 1900–1950* (New York: Columbia University Press, 1955), 48; F. Sturdivant and R. Adler, "Executive Origins: Still a Gray Flannel World?" *Harvard Business Review* 54 (November–December 1976): 125; G. William Domhoff, *Fat Cats and Democrats* (Englewood Cliffs, N.J.: Prentice-Hall, 1972), 54.

3. The Protestant proportion remained at 85 percent, but the study's approach of counting the religion only of executives who chose to state it in their *Who's Who* biographies makes this figure suspect. See Richard L. Zweigenhaft and G. William Domhoff, *Jews in the Protestant Establishment* (New York: Praeger, 1982), 20–21.

4. See *Korn/Ferry International's Executive Profile: A Survey of Corporate Leaders in the Eighties* (New York: Korn/Ferry International, 1986), 23, 45; "No Longer a WASP Preserve," *New York Times,* June 29, 1986, sec. 3, p. 1, col. 3.

5. See Zweigenhaft and Dumhoff, *Jews in the Protestant Establishment,* 25–29; Bernard Sarachek, "American Jewish Entrepreneurs," *Journal of Economic History* 40 (1980): 359, 370–72.

6. "U.S. Catholics Find Prejudices Waning," *New York Times,* Oct. 2, 1979, p. 9, col. 5; "Jews in the Thousands Join Migration to Sun Belt," *New York Times,* Mar. 31, 1980, p. 1, col. 4; "Jews in the Corporate Establishment," *New York Times,* Apr. 24, 1983, sec. 3, p. 2, col. 3; "No Longer a WASP Preserve," *New York Times,* June 29, 1986, sec. 3, p. 1, col. 3. See also "New Names in the Board Room: Ethnic Groups Receiving Recognition," *New York Times,* Oct. 31, 1971, sec. 3, p. 3, col. 1.

7. See Andrew M. Greeley, *Ethnicity in the United States: A Preliminary Reconnaissance* (New York: Wiley, 1974), 65–67; Wade Clark Roof, "Socioeconomic Differentials among White Socioreligious Groups in the United States," *Social Forces* 58 (1979): 280–89.

8. Kates v. Lefkowitz, 216 N.Y.S.2d 1014, 1016 (Sup. Ct. N.Y. Co. 1961).

9. Charles DeBenedetti and Charles Chatfield, *An American Ordeal: The Antiwar Movement of the Vietnam Era* (Syracuse: Syracuse University Press, 1990), 206–8; quoted in Peter Braestrup, *Big Story: How the American Press and Television Reported and Interpreted the Crisis of Tet 1968 in Vietnam and Washington* (New Haven: Yale University Press, 1983), 68; quoted in Walter Isaacson and Evan Thomas, *The Wise Men: Six Friends and the World They Made* (New York: Simon & Schuster, 1986), 643; Theodore H. White, *The Making of the President, 1968* (New York: Atheneum, 1969), 5.

10. Quoted in Charles Kaiser, *1968 in America: Music, Politics, Chaos, Counterculture and the Shaping of a Generation* (New York: Weidenfeld & Nicolson, 1988), 64.

11. Robert Goralski and Joseph C. Harsch, quoted in Irwin Unger and Debi Unger, *Turning Point: 1968* (New York: Charles Scribner's Sons, 1988), 103; Harry McPherson, quoted ibid., 104.

12. Quoted in White, *Making of the President,* 103.

13. Ibid., 107, 143.

14. Hubert Humphrey, quoted in Robert V. Daniels, *Year of the Heroic Guerrilla: World Revolution and Counterrevolution in 1968* (New York: Basic Books, 1989), 227; White, *Making of the President,* 100; quoted ibid., 100; Todd Gitlin, *The Sixties: Years of Hope, Days of Rage* (New York: Bantam Books, 1987), 256–57, 286.

15. Malcolm X and James Farmer, "Separation or Integration: A Debate," in *Negro Protest in the Twentieth Century,* ed. Francis L. Broderick and August Meier (Indianapolis: Bobbs-Merrill, 1965), 357, 361–63.

16. John O. Killens, "Explanation of the 'Black Psyche,'" *New York Times (Magazine),* June 7, 1964, p. 37; quoted in J. David Bowen, *The Struggle Within: Race Relations in the United States,* rev. ed. (New York: Grosset & Dunlap, 1972), 158. See generally Bowen, *Struggle Within,* 149–74; William H. Grier and Price M. Cobbs, *Black Rage* (New York: Basic Books, 1968), 200–213. For two now classic statements, see Eldridge Cleaver, *Soul on Ice* (New York: Dell, 1968); Malcolm X., *The Autobiography of Malcolm X.* (New York: Grove, 1965).

17. Ralph Abernathy, Hosea Williams, Cesar Chavez, and Anonymous, quoted in Arthur M. Schlesinger Jr., *Robert Kennedy and His Times* (Boston: Houghton Mifflin, 1978), 799, 879.

18. Robert Kennedy and Dolores Huerta, quoted ibid., 791, 800, 909.

19. See Kaiser, *1968 in America*, 146–49; Schlesinger, *Robert Kennedy*, 877; Unger and Unger, *Turning Point*, 192–98; White, *Making of the President*, 243–44.

20. See Daniels, *Year of the Heroic Guerrilla*, 127–31; Kaiser, *1968 in America*, 155–60; Unger and Unger, *Turning Point*, 254–64.

21. Quoted in Kaiser, *1968 in America*, 161; quoted in Unger and Unger, *Turning Point*, 265–66.

22. Kaiser, *1968 in America*, 163–65; Unger and Unger, *Turning Point*, 270–74.

23. Richard Hofstadter, quoted in Kaiser, *1968 in America*, 165.

24. White, *Making of the President*, 214; Kaiser, *1968 in America*, 185; White, *Making of the President*, 214; David Hollander, quoted in Kaiser, *1968 in America*, 189.

25. *Rights in Conflict: Convention Week in Chicago, August 25–29, 1968, a Report Submitted by Daniel Walker, Director of the Chicago Study Team, to the National Commission on the Causes and Prevention of Violence* (New York: E. P. Dutton, 1968), 5; White, *Making of the President*, 347–49; Abraham Ribicoff and Richard Daley, quoted in Unger and Unger, *Turning Point*, 496–97; Abraham Ribicoff, quoted in Kaiser, *1968 in America*, 241.

26. See generally, Robert Rossner, *The Year without an Autumn: Portrait of a School in Crisis* (New York: Richard W. Baron, 1969); Martin Mayer, *The Teachers Strike: New York, 1968* (New York: Harper & Row, 1969).

27. "Excerpts from the Botein Report," in *Confrontation at Ocean Hill–Brownsville: The New York School Strikes of 1968*, ed. Maurice R. Berube and Marilyn Gittell (New York: Frederick A. Praeger, 1969), 174; quoted in ibid., 168; "Botein Report," 174; Interview with Rhody A. McCoy, in Melvin Urofsky ed., *Why Teachers Strike: Teachers' Rights and Community Control* (Garden City, N.Y.: Anchor Books, 1970), 111, 128; Rossner, *Year without an Autumn*, 225–29, 242–49, 256–57.

28. Unger and Unger, *Turning Point*, 444.

29. See Elaine Tyler May, *Homeward Bound: American Families in the Cold War Era* (New York: Basic Books, 1988), for the best study of post–World War II "domesticity that rested on distinct roles for women and men." Ibid., 9. For a study of government's contribution to that domesticity, see Maureen Honey, *Creating Rosie the Riveter: Class, Gender, and Propaganda during World War II* (Amherst, Mass.: University of Massachusetts Press, 1984). For work that places this "domestic stereotype in historical context" and argues that in the postwar era "most American women lived, in one way or more, outside the boundaries of the middle-class suburban home," see Joanne Meyerowitz, "Introduction: Women and Gender in Postwar America, 1945–1960," in *Not June Cleaver: Women and Gender in Postwar America, 1945–1960*, ed. Joanne Meyerowitz (Philadelphia: Temple University Press, 1994), 2; see D'Ann Campbell, *Women at War with America: Private Lives in a Patriotic Era* (Cambridge, Mass.: Harvard University Press, 1984); Susan M. Hartmann, *The Home Front and Beyond: American Women in the 1940s* (Boston: Twayne, 1982); Eugenia Kaledin, *Mothers and More: American Women in the 1950s* (Boston: Twayne, 1984); Susan Lynn, *Progressive Women in Conservative Times: Racial Justice, Peace, and Feminism, 1945 to the 1960s* (New Brunswick: Rutgers University Press, 1992). An important early work was William Chafe, *The American Woman: Her Changing Social, Economic, and Political Roles, 1920–1970* (New York: Oxford University Press, 1972).

30. See U.S. Department of Commerce, *Statistical Abstract of the United States, 1989* (Washington, D.C.: U.S. Government Printing Office, 1989), 449, 456.

31. Betty Friedan, *The Feminine Mystique* (New York: Norton, 1963); Sarah M. Evans, *Personal Politics: The Roots of Women's Liberation in the Civil Rights Movement and the New Left* (New York: Knopf, 1979), 18–19; Jo Freeman, *The Politics of Women's Liberation: A Case Study of an Emerging Social Movement and Its Relation to the Policy Process* (New York: McKay, 1975), 51; Janet Z. Giele, *Women and the Future: Changing Sex Roles in Modern America* (New York: Free Press, 1978), 360.

32. Betty Friedan, *The Feminine Mystique,* 10th Anniversary ed. (New York: Norton, 1973), 344, 374, 384; Giele, *Women and the Future,* 327, 351. For a survey of the literature written before 1978 in support of this assimilationist view, see ibid., 325–28, 350–60.

33. See Freeman, *Politics of Women's Liberation,* 51. In using the word "radical" to describe feminists who eschewed liberal reform through the political and legal process, I follow Winifred D. Wandersee, *On the Move: American Women in the 1970s* (Boston: Twayne, 1988), xiii–xv, 55–101. Of course, many divergent viewpoints existed within the radical camp, and in some senses, the radicals—"who emphasized life-style rather than politics—were actually more conservative than the political activists who challenged the system on its own terms." Ibid., 55. For a detailed analysis of the divisions in feminism in the years around 1970, see generally Alice Echols, *Daring to Be Bad: Radical Feminism in America, 1967–1979* (Minneapolis: University of Minnesota Press, 1989).

34. Bonnie Kreps, "Radical Feminism 1," in *Radical Feminism,* ed. Anne Koedt, Ellen Levine, and Anita Rapone (New York: Quadrangle, 1973), 234, 239; Andrea Dworkin, *Our Blood: Prophecies and Discourses on Sexual Politics* (New York: Harper & Row, 1976), 11, 13.

35. Barbara Burris, "The Fourth World Manifesto," in *Radical Feminism,* ed. Koedt, Levine, and Rapone, 322, 341; Shulamith Firestone, *The Dialectic of Sex: The Case for Feminist Revolution* (New York: Morrow, 1970), 178. See also Kate Millett, *Sexual Politics* (Garden City, N.Y.: Doubleday, 1970), 232.

36. Kreps, "Radical Feminism 1," 239; Millett, *Sexual Politics,* 24, 362–63; Firestone, *Dialectic of Sex,* 16, 184. On the opposition of Friedan and other feminists who saw men and women as essentially the same to the "manhating sex/class warfare" radicals, see Friedan, *The Feminine Mystique* 10th anniversary ed. (1973), 388–89.

37. Phyllis Schlafly, *The Power of the Positive Woman* (New Rochelle, N.Y.: Arlington House, 1977), 16–17, 30, 33, 54, 139, 159–63. See also Rayna Rapp and Ellen Ross, "The 1920s: Feminism, Consumerism, and Political Backlash in the United States," in *Women in Culture and Politics: A Century of Change,* ed. Judith Friedlander et al. (Bloomington: University of Indiana Press, 1986), 52.

38. See White, *Making of the President,* 462; Stephen E. Ambrose, *Nixon: The Triumph of a Politician, 1962–1972* (New York: Simon & Schuster, 1989), 159, 201.

39. Bowers v. Hardwick, 478 U.S. 186, 195 (1986).

40. Malcolm X and James Farmer, "Separation or Integration: A Debate," in *Negro Protest,* ed. Broderick and Meier, 357, 361.

CHAPTER THIRTEEN

1. Zillah R. Eisenstein, *The Female Body and the Law* (Berkeley: University of California Press, 1988), 163–64; In re P., 400 N.Y.S.2d 455, 461 n.11, 468 (Family Ct. 1977) (opinion of Margaret Taylor, J.), *rev'd,* 418 N.Y.S.2d 597 (App. Div. 1979).

2. Barbara Mehrof and Pamela Kearon, "Rape: An Act of Terror," in *Radical Feminism,* ed. Anne Koedt, Ellen Levine, and Anita Rapone (New York: Quadrangle, 1973), 228, 229–30, 233 (emphasis in original); Kate Millett, *Sexual Politics* (Garden City, N.Y.: Doubleday, 1970), 44.

3. Laura Lederer, "Introduction," in *Take Back the Night: Women on Pornography,* ed. Lederer (New York: Morrow, 1980), 16, 17, 19–20. For further radical critiques of pornography, see Andrea Dworkin, *Woman Hating* (New York: Dutton, 1974), 51–90; Catharine A. MacKinnon, *Feminism Unmodified: Discourses on Life and Law* (Cambridge, Mass.: Harvard University Press, 1987), 127–213.

4. Laura Lederer, "Then and Now: An Interview with a Former Pornography Model," in *Take Back the Night,* ed. Lederer, 57, 64; Susan Brownmiller, "Speaking Out on Prostitution," in *Radical Feminism,* ed. Koedt, Levine, and Rapone, 72, 74, 76.

5. Phyllis Schlafly, *The Power of the Positive Woman* (New Rochelle, N.Y.: Arlington House, 1977), 16; Eisenstein, *Female Body,* 4, 70–73, 164.

6. See People v. Vicaretti, 388 N.Y.S.2d 410, 414–15 (App. Div. 1976); People v. Gonzalez, 409 N.Y.S.2d 497 (Crim. Ct. 1978).

7. People v. Thompson, 212 N.Y. 249 (1914); Woods v. People, 55 N.Y. 515 (1874); N.Y. Criminal Procedure Law sec. 60.42; People v. Bronson, 419 N.Y.S.2d 329, 330 (App. Div. 1979).

8. People v. English, 262 N.Y.S.2d 104 (Ct. App. 1965); People v. Radunovic, 287 N.Y.S.2d 33, 38–39 (Ct. App. 1967); People v. Linzy, 335 N.Y.S.2d 45, 47–48 (Ct. App. 1972).

9. Penal Law sec. 130.16; William C. Donnino, "Practice Commentaries" to N.Y. Penal Law sec. 130.16; People v. Weyant, 419 N.Y.S.2d 200 (App. Div. 1979); People v. St. John, 426 N.Y.S.2d 863, 864–65 (App. Div. 1980).

10. See People v. Reilly, 381 N.Y.S.2d 732, 738 (County Ct. 1976).

11. People v. Whidden, 434 N.Y.S.2d 936 (Ct. App. 1980), appeal dism., 454 U.S. 803 (1981); People v. Dozier, 424 N.Y.S.2d 1010 (App. Div. 1st Dept.), aff'd, 436 N.Y.S.2d 620 (Ct. App. 1980) (emphasis added); People v. Whidden, *supra* at 938; People v. Weidiger, 410 N.Y.S.2d 209, 211 (County Ct. 1978); People v. Mndange-Pfupfu, 411 N.Y.S.2d 1000, 1005 (County Ct. 1978); People v. Dozier, *supra* at 1014–15; People v. Whidden, *supra* at 938.

12. People v. Ostrander, 295 N.Y.S.2d 293, 297 (County Ct. 1968), aff'd, 302 N.Y.S.2d 998 (App. Div. 1969); Best v. Macklin, 260 N.Y.S.2d 219, 221 (Family Ct. 1965).

13. People v. Haynes, 308 N.Y.S.2d 391, 392 (Ct. App. 1970); People v. Allen, 313 N.Y.S.2d 719, 723 (Ct. App. 1970).

14. Bruno v. Codd, 419 N.Y.S.2d 901, 905–6 (Ct. App. 1979).

15. Bruno v. Codd, 396 N.Y.S.2d 974, 976–77 (Sup. Ct. 1977), rev'd, 407 N.Y.S.2d 165 (App. Div.), aff'd, 419 N.Y.S.2d 901 (Ct. App. 1979).

16. Sorichetti v. City of New York, 408 N.Y.S.2d 219, 221–22 (Sup. Ct. 1978), aff'd, 417 N.Y.S.2d 202 (App. Div. 1979), aff'd, 492 N.Y.S.2d 591 (Ct. App. 1985).

17. Ibid.; Baker v. City of New York, 269 N.Y.S.2d 515 (App. Div. 1966); 1977 McKinney's Sess. Laws 2501 (Governor's memorandum of approval of N.Y. Laws of 1977, ch. 449); N.Y. Laws of 1977, ch. 449; People v. Daniel T., 408 N.Y.S.2d 214 (Crim. Ct. 1978). See also N.Y. Laws of 1978, chs. 628, 629.

18. People v. Costello, 395 N.Y.S.2d 139, 142 (Sup. Ct. 1977); Brownmiller, "Speaking Out on Prostitution," 76; People v. Costello, *supra* at 142.

19. People on Complaint of Cirile v. Catalano, 205 N.Y.S.2d 618, 620 (Magis. Ct. 1960) (distinguishing People v. Gould, 306 N.Y. 352 [1954]); People v. Hansuld, 114 N.Y.S.2d 243, 246 (Magis. Ct. 1952) (distinguishing People v. Choremi, 301 N.Y. 417 [1954]); People v. Hansuld, 114 N.Y.S.2d 243 (Magis. Ct. 1952); People on Complaint of Cirile v. Catalano, 205 N.Y.S.2d 618, 620 (Magis. Ct. 1960); People v. Block, 337 N.Y.S.2d 153, 155 (County Ct. 1972).

20. People v. Bronski, 351 N.Y.S.2d 73, 75 (Crim. Ct. 1973); People v. Smith, 407 N.Y.S.2d 462, 464 (Ct. App. 1978); In re P., 400 N.Y.S.2d 455, 466 (Family Ct. 1977) (dictum), rev'd, 418 N.Y.S.2d 597 (App. Div. 1979).

21. In re P., 400 N.Y.S.2d 455, 461 (Family Ct. 1977); In re Dora P., 418 N.Y.S.2d 597, 604 (App. Div. 1979); A. v. City of New York, 335 N.Y.S.2d 33, 37 (Ct. App. 1972) (dictum); In re P., *supra* at 468.

22. N.Y. Penal Law sec. 230.02; People v. Bronski, 351 N.Y.S.2d 73 (Crim. Ct. 1973); "Female Officers Arrest Men Searching for Prostitutes," *New York Times,* July 4, 1978, p. 8, col. 1; "First 'John Hour' on WNYC Names Clients of Prostitutes," *New York Times,* Oct. 24, 1979, p. B3, col. 5; "Jail Terms Planned for Vice Customers," *New York Times,* Nov. 16, 1977, p. D17, col. 5; "The 'John' Minute," *New York Times,* Oct. 26, 1979, p. 30, col. 1; "WNYC May Discontinue Broadcasts of 'John Hour,'"

New York Times, Nov. 9, 1979, p. B3, col. 5; In re P., 400 N.Y.S.2d 455, 460, 468 (Family Ct. 1977), *rev'd*, 418 N.Y.S.2d 597 (App. Div. 1979).

23. Lederer, "Introduction," 19–20.

24. Ibid.

25. Shpritzer v. Lang, 224 N.Y.S.2d 105 (Sup. Ct.), *modified and aff'd*, 234 N.Y.S.2d 285 (App. Div. 1962), *aff'd*, 241 N.Y.S.2d 869 (Ct. App. 1963).

26. Sontag v. Bronstein, 351 N.Y.S.2d 389, 392 (Ct. App. 1973).

27. Ludtke v. Kuhn, 461 F. Supp. 86, 97–98 (S.D.N.Y. 1978).

28. Seidenberg v. McSorley's Old Ale House, Inc., 308 F. Supp. 1253, 1260 (S.D.N.Y. 1969), and 317 F. Supp. 593, 605–6 (S.D.N.Y. 1970).

29. Scott v. Board of Education, Union Free School District #17, Hicksville, 305 N.Y.S.2d 601, 606–7 (Sup. Ct. 1969).

30. Calzadilla v. Dooley, 286 N.Y.S.2d 510, 516 (App. Div. 1968) (dictum).

31. 475 F. Supp. 1298 (S.D.N.Y. 1979), *modified and aff'd*, 691 F.2d 1054 (2d Cir. 1982), *vacated and remanded*, 463 U.S. 1223 (1983), *modified on other grounds*, 735 F.2d 23 (2d Cir.), *cert. denied*, 469 U.S. 881 (1984).

32. See, e.g., Monell v. Department of Social Services of City of New York, 436 U.S. 658 (1978); Health Insurance Association of America v. Harnett, 405 N.Y.S.2d 634 (Ct. App. 1978).

33. N.Y. Laws of 1970, ch. 127; Roe v. Wade, 410 U.S. 113 (1973); Schulman v. New York City Health and Hospitals Corporation, 379 N.Y.S.2d 702 (Ct. App. 1975); State v. Mitchell, 321 N.Y.S.2d 756 (Sup. Ct. 1971); Poelker v. Doe, 432 U.S. 519 (1977); Maher v. Roe, 432 U.S. 464 (1977); Beal v. Doe, 432 U.S. 438 (1977); City of New York v. Wyman, 330 N.Y.S.2d 385 (Ct. App. 1972).

34. Berger v. Adornato, 350 N.Y.S.2d 520 (Sup. Ct. 1973); Griffin v. Illinois, 351 U.S. 12 (1956); Johnson v. Rockefeller, 58 F.R.D. 42, 51–52 (S.D.N.Y. 1972); Repetti v. Gil, 372 N.Y.S.2d 840, 842 (Sup. Ct. 1975); Gould v. Gould, 371 N.Y.S.2d 267 (Sup. Ct. 1975).

35. Echevarria v. Echevarria, 386 N.Y.S.2d 653, 654 (Ct. App. 1976).

36. Cavallo v. Cavallo, 359 N.Y.S.2d 628, 629 (Sup. Ct. 1974); Weintraub v. Weintraub, 356 N.Y.S.2d 450, 453 (Family Ct. 1974).

37. Application of "Virginia Norman," 205 N.Y.S.2d 260, 262, 264 (Sup. Ct. 1960); Godinez v. Russo, 266 N.Y.S.2d 636, 639 (Family Ct. 1966); In re Anonymous, 416 N.Y.S.2d 729, 731–32 (Family Ct. 1979).

38. Andrews v. Andrews, 425 N.Y.S.2d 120 (App. Div. 1980), *aff'd*, 439 N.Y.S.2d 918 (Ct. App. 1981); Bergson v. Bergson, 414 N.Y.S.2d 593, 594 (App. Div. 1979).

39. Compare, e.g., Matter of Adoption of Malpica-Orsini, 370 N.Y.S.2d 511 (Ct. App. 1975), *appeal dism.*, 423 U.S. 1042 (1976), with, e.g., Matter of Gerald G.G., 403 N.Y.S.2d 57, 60 (App. Div. 1978), *appeal dism.*, 416 N.Y.S.2d 586 (Ct. App. 1979).

40. 441 U.S. 380 (1979).

41. Matter of Adoption of Anonymous, 323 N.Y.S.2d 358 (Surr. Ct. 1971); Matter of Adoption of Goldman, 393 N.Y.S.2d 989 (Ct. App. 1977); In re Metzger, 186 N.Y.S. 269, 270 (Surr. Ct. 1921); Cocozza v. Antidormi, 316 N.Y.S.2d 471, 473 (App. Div. 1970).

42. Palmieri v. Palmieri, 168 N.Y.S.2d 48, 49, 51–52 (Sup. Ct. 1957); Doyle v. Doyle, 158 N.Y.S.2d 909, 911 (Sup. Ct. 1957); Brownstein v. Brownstein, 268 N.Y.S.2d 115, 123 (App. Div. 1966).

43. Doyle v. Doyle, 158 N.Y.S.2d 909, 912 (Sup. Ct. 1957); Dulber v. Dulber, 311 N.Y.S.2d 604, 606 (Sup. Ct. 1970), *modified on other grounds*, 322 N.Y.S.2d 862 (App. Div. 1971), *aff'd sub nom.* Kover v. Kover, 328 N.Y.S.2d 641 (Ct. App. 1972).

44. See Orr v. Orr, 440 U.S. 268 (1979); Craig v. Boren, 429 U.S. 190 (1976); Frontiero v. Richardson, 411 U.S. 677 (1973); Reed v. Reed, 404 U.S. 71 (1971).

45. Carole K. v. Arnold K., 380 N.Y.S.2d 593, 596–97 (Family Ct. 1976); S. v. K., 335 N.Y.S.2d

124, 126 (Family Ct. 1972); Morgan v. Morgan, 366 N.Y.S.2d 977, 979, 981 (Sup. Ct. 1975), *modified and aff'd*, 383 N.Y.S.2d 343 (App. Div.), *aff'd*, 387 N.Y.S.2d 839 (Ct. App. 1976).

46. Dulber v. Dulber, 311 N.Y.S.2d 604, 606 (Sup. Ct. 1970), *modified on other grounds,* 322 N.Y.S.2d 862 (App. Div. 1971), *aff'd sub nom.* Kover v. Kover, 328 N.Y.S.2d 641 (Ct. App. 1972); Thaler v. Thaler, 391 N.Y.S.2d 331 (Sup. Ct.), *rev'd on other grounds,* 396 N.Y.S.2d 815 (App. Div. 1977); Kapuscinski v. Kapuscinski, 426 N.Y.S.2d 582 (App. Div. 1980); Thaler v. Thaler, *supra* at 333.

47. Between 1920 and 1970, alimony as a percentage of net income of the husband had a mean value of 35.92 percent. Between 1970 and 1980, alimony as a percentage of net income of the husband had a mean value of 29.37 percent. But this decline is too small and the data were not collected with sufficient randomness to give the decline statistical significance as a barometer of alimony paid in all cases.

48. See Domestic Relations Law sec. 170-a; Pearson v. Pearson, 429 N.Y.S.2d 851 (Sup. Ct. 1980), *aff'd,* 440 N.Y.S.2d 345 (App. Div. 1981). This book does not consider the impact of New York's equitable distribution law, which took effect in July 1980, at the end of the period under study. For one early case under the new law, see Mercier v. Mercier, 432 N.Y.S.2d 123 (Sup. Ct. 1980).

CHAPTER FOURTEEN

1. 347 U.S. 483 (1954).

2. Matter of Skipwith, 180 N.Y.S.2d 852, 855, 872–73 (Dom. Rel. Ct. 1958).

3. Taylor v. Board of Education of City School District of City of New Rochelle, 191 F. Supp. 181, 183 (S.D.N.Y.), aff'd, 294 F.2d 36 (2d Cir.), *cert. denied,* 368 U.S. 940 (1961); Hart v. Community School Board of Education, New York School District #21, 512 F.2d 37 (2d Cir. 1975).

4. See Offermann v. Nitkowski, 248 F. Supp. 129 (W.D.N.Y. 1965), *aff'd,* 378 F.2d 22 (2d Cir. 1967); Lee v. Nyquist, 318 F. Supp. 710, 720 (W.D.N.Y. 1970), *aff'd,* 402 U.S. 935 (1971).

5. Application of Syracuse University, 300 N.Y.S.2d 129, 135–36 (Sup. Ct. 1969).

6. Regents of University of California v. Bakke, 438 U.S. 265 (1978); Alevy v. Downstate Medical Center, 384 N.Y.S.2d 82, 89–90 (Ct. App. 1976); Hupart v. Board of Higher Education of City of New York, 420 F. Supp. 1087 (S.D.N.Y. 1976); Auerbach v. African American Teachers Association, 356 F. Supp. 1046, 1048 (E.D.N.Y. 1973).

7. See Child v. Beame, 412 F. Supp. 593, 608–9 (S.D.N.Y. 1976); Everett v. Riverside Hose Co. No. 4, 261 F. Supp. 463 (S.D.N.Y. 1966); Citizens Council on Human Relations v. Buffalo Yacht Club, 438 F. Supp. 316, 321 (W.D.N.Y. 1977); United States v. Lopez, 328 F. Supp. 1077 (E.D.N.Y. 1971); Kennedy Park Homes Association v. City of Lackawanna, 318 F. Supp. 669 (W.D.N.Y.), *aff'd,* 436 F.2d 108 (2d Cir. 1970), *cert. denied,* 401 U.S. 1010 (1971); Kirkland v. New York State Department of Correctional Services, 520 F.2d 420 (2d Cir. 1975), *cert. denied,* 429 U.S. 823 (1976).

8. Lucido v. Cravath, Swaine & Moore, 425 F. Supp. 123, 125 (S.D.N.Y. 1977).

9. See Brown v. Board of Education, 349 U.S. 294, 301 (1955); Gino Speranza, *Race or Nation: A Conflict of Divided Loyalties* (Indianapolis: Bobbs-Merrill, 1925), 31–33, 257–59, 262–67.

10. United States ex rel. Radich v. Criminal Court of City of New York, 385 F. Supp. 165, 168–69 (S.D.N.Y. 1974).

11. See People v. Radich, 279 N.Y.S.2d 680 (Criminal Ct. N.Y. Co. 1967), *aff'd,* 294 N.Y.S.2d 285 (App. Term 1968), *aff'd,* 308 N.Y.S.2d 846 (Ct. App. 1970), *aff'd by equally divided Court,* 401 U.S. 531 (1971). See also United States Flag Foundation, Inc. v. Radich, 279 N.Y.S.2d 233 (Sup. Ct. 1967) (denying motion to dismiss civil action for damages against Radich).

12. United States ex rel. Radich v. Criminal Court of City of New York, 385 F. Supp. 165, 178, 183–84 (S.D.N.Y. 1974).

13. Street v. New York, 394 U.S. 576, 592 (1969), *reversing* 282 N.Y.S.2d 491 (Ct. App. 1967) (over-

turning conviction of African American who, on learning of the shooting of James Meredith, declared while burning a flag, "We don't need no damn flag," and, "If they let that happen to Meredith, we don't need an American flag.").

14. See Russo v. Central School District No. 1, Town of Rush, 469 F.2d 623 (2d Cir. 1972), *cert. denied*, 411 U.S. 932 (1973) (teacher cannot be dismissed for refusing to pledge allegiance to flag); Long Island Vietnam Moratorium Committee v. Cahn, 437 F.2d 344 (2d Cir. 1970), *aff'd*, 418 U.S. 906 (1974) (enjoining prosecution for affixing peace symbol to flag); James v. Board of Education of Central District No. 1 of Towns of Addison, 461 F.2d 566 (2d Cir.), *cert. denied*, 409 U.S. 1042 (1972); Bilick v. Dudley, 356 F. Supp. 945 (S.D.N.Y. 1973); Wolin v. Port of New York Authority, 268 F. Supp. 855 (S.D.N.Y. 1967), *aff'd*, 392 F.2d 83 (2d Cir.), *cert. denied*, 393 U.S. 940 (1968); Muhammad Ali v. Division of State Athletic Commission of Department of State of State of New York, 316 F. Supp. 1246 (S.D.N.Y. 1970); East Meadow Community Concerts Ass'n v. Board of Education of Union Free School District No. 3, County of Nassau, 278 N.Y.S.2d 393 (Ct. App. 1967), and 272 N.Y.S.2d 341 (Ct. App. 1966).

15. See Percikow v. Morris, 263 N.Y.S.2d 673 (App. Div. 1965); Farmer v. Moses, 232 F. Supp. 154 (S.D.N.Y. 1964); North Shore Right to Life Committee v. Manhasset American Legion Post No. 304, 452 F. Supp. 834 (E.D.N.Y. 1978); Curle v. Ward, 399 N.Y.S.2d 308 (App. Div. 1977), *modified*, 416 N.Y.S.2d 549 (Ct. App. 1979); Puentes v. Board of Education of Union Free School District No. 21 of Town of Bethpage, 302 N.Y.S.2d 824 (Ct. App. 1969); Wolff v. Selective Service Local Board No. 16, 372 F.2d 817 (2d Cir. 1967); Manfredonia v. Barry, 401 F. Supp. 762 (E.D.N.Y. 1975).

16. People v. Taub, 375 N.Y.S.2d 303 (Ct. App. 1975); Keyishian v. Board of Regents of University of State of New York, 385 U.S. 589 (1967); Wright v. Chief of Transit Police, 558 F.2d 67 (2d Cir. 1977); People v. Stover, 240 N.Y.S.2d 734, 740 (Ct. App.), *appeal dism.*, 375 U.S. 42 (1963); People v. Wise, 281 N.Y.S.2d 539, 543 (Crim. Ct. 1967); O.B.G.Y.N. Associations v. Birthright of Brooklyn and Queens, Inc., 407 N.Y.S.2d 903, 906 (App. Div. 1978); People v. Wise, *supra* at 543.

17. Fenster v. Leary, 282 N.Y.S.2d 739, 744 (Ct. App. 1967) (emphasis in original); Jones v. Beame, 408 N.Y.S.2d 449 (Ct. App. 1978); Romano v. Kirwan, 391 F. Supp. 643 (W.D.N.Y. 1975), *vacated and remanded*, 425 U.S. 929 (1976) (invalidating grooming regulations of New York State Police); Alma Society Inc. v. Mellon, 601 F.2d 1225 (2d Cir.), *cert. denied*, 444 U.S. 995 (1979); Hartin v. Director of Bureau of Records and Statistics, Department of Health of City of New York, 347 N.Y.S.2d 515 (Sup. Ct. 1973).

18. See Sundram v. City of Niagara Falls, 357 N.Y.S.2d 943 (Sup. Ct. 1973), *aff'd*, 356 N.Y.S.2d 1023 (App. Div. 1974); Sugarman v. Dougall, 413 U.S. 634 (1973); In re Griffiths, 413 U.S. 717 (1973); Salla v. County of Monroe, 423 N.Y.S.2d 878 (Ct. App. 1979), *cert. denied sub nom.* Abrams v. Salla, 446 U.S. 909 (1980); Lopez v. White Plains Housing Authority, 355 F. Supp. 1016, 1025–26 (S.D.N.Y. 1972); Nyquist v. Mauclet, 432 U.S. 1 (1977).

19. 281 N.Y.S.2d 9 (Ct. App. 1967), *cert. denied*, 390 U.S. 29 (1968).

20. Ibid., 12–14.

21. Ibid., 17.

22. See Boikess v. Aspland, 299 N.Y.S.2d 163 (Ct. App. 1969) (requiring public advocates of drug use to appear before a grand jury to testify about actual use of which they knew).

23. See Haroche v. Levy, 314 N.Y.S.2d 553 (Sup. Ct. 1970), *aff'd*, 331 N.Y.S.2d 1005 (App. Div. 1972); People v. L. A. Witherill, Inc., 328 N.Y.S.2d 668 (Ct. App. 1972); People v. Abrahams, 386 N.Y.S.2d 661 (Ct. App. 1976); Troyer v. Town of Babylon, 483 F. Supp. 1135 (E.D.N.Y.), *aff'd*, 628 F.2d 1346 (2d Cir.), *cert. denied*, 449 U.S. 988 (1980); International Society for Krishna Consciousness, Inc. v. Barber, 650 F.2d 430 (2d Cir. 1981), *reversing* 506 F. Supp. 147 (N.D.N.Y. 1980); People v. Rodriguez, 424 N.Y.S.2d 600 (Sup. Ct. 1979) (lawyer who was also Roman Catholic priest could wear clerical collar while representing criminal defendant).

24. Brown v. McGinnis, 225 N.Y.S.2d 497, 498, 501 (Ct. App. 1962); Bryant v. Wilkins, 258

N.Y.S.2d 455 (Sup. Ct.), *aff'd,* 265 N.Y.S.2d 995 (App. Div. 1965), *appeal denied,* 268 N.Y.S.2d 1025 (Ct. App.), *cert. denied,* 383 U.S. 972 (1966).

25. Malcolm X and James Farmer, "Separation or Integration: A Debate," in *Negro Protest in the Twentieth Century,* ed. Francis L. Broderick and August Meier (Indianapolis: Bobbs-Merrill, 1965), 357, 361.

26. See In re P., 400 N.Y.S.2d 455, 464–66 (Family Ct. 1977), *rev'd,* 418 N.Y.S.2d 597 (App. Div. 1979); People v. Mehr, 383 N.Y.S.2d 798 (App. Term 1976), *aff'd sub nom.* People v. Rice, 395 N.Y.S.2d 626 (Ct. App. 1977); People v. Johnson, 355 N.Y.S.2d 266 (City Ct. 1974); People v. Rice, 395 N.Y.S.2d 626 (Ct. App. 1977).

27. People v. Onofre, 434 N.Y.S.2d 947 (Ct. App. 1980), cert. denied, 451 U.S. 987 (1981). On Jones, see "Republicans' Appeals Court Victories Not Likely to Signal a Veering to Right," *New York Times,* Nov. 9, 1972, p. 26, cols. 6–8.

28. 434 N.Y.S.2d at 949, 951.

29. Ibid., 951 n.3, 952.

30. People v. Sanabria, 249 N.Y.S.2d 66 (App. Term 1964); People v. Anonymous, 415 N.Y.S.2d 921 (Justice Ct. 1979); People v. Hale, 203 N.Y.S.2d 71 (Ct. App. 1960); People v. Willmott, 324 N.Y.S.2d 616 (Justice Ct. 1971); People v. Spencer, 322 N.Y.S.2d 266 (Crim. Ct. 1971); People v. Anonymous, 415 N.Y.S.2d 921, 923–924 (Justice Ct. 1979); People v. Fielding, 385 N.Y.S.2d 17 (Ct. App. 1976).

31. People v. Fielding, 385 N.Y.S.2d 17 (Ct. App. 1976); People v. Deschessere, 74 N.Y.S. 761, 764 (App. Div. 1902); People v. Fielding, *supra. Fielding* was decided after the statutory changes in the law of corroboration of sex crimes discussed above, and like the rape cases discussed above, *Fielding* should be read as a response to the new legislative policy. As late as 1972, the court was applying the old rule requiring corroboration in the case of consensual but not forcible sodomy. See People v. Thompson, 335 N.Y.S.2d 832 (Ct. App. 1972).

32. People v. Anonymous, 415 N.Y.S.2d 921, 924 (Justice Ct. 1979).

33. Town of Manlius v. Town of Pompey, 250 N.Y.S. 690, 692 (Sup. Ct. 1930).

34. See generally Martha Davis, *Brutal Need: Law, Lawyers, and the Welfare Rights Movement, 1960–1973* (New Haven: Yale University Press, 1993).

35. See Kahn v. Smith, 401 N.Y.S.2d 264 (App. Div. 1978); Matter of Charilyn N., 361 N.Y.S.2d 215 (App. Div. 1974); Justice v. Board of Education, 351 F. Supp. 1252 (S.D.N.Y. 1972); Matter of Hall, 410 N.Y.S.2d 496 (Family Ct. 1978); Kiley v. Lavine, 358 N.Y.S.2d 331 (Sup. Ct. 1974), *aff'd,* 378 N.Y.S.2d 479 (App. Div. 1976); Delgado v. Sipprell, 388 N.Y.S.2d 807 (App. Div. 1976); Guiles v. Toia, 400 N.Y.S.2d 650 (App. Div. 1977); Burroughs v. Nassau County Department of Social Services, 329 N.Y.S.2d 958 (Sup. Ct. 1971); Rankin v. Lavine, 394 N.Y.S.2d 618 (Ct. App. 1977); Jones v. Berman, 371 N.Y.S.2d 422 (Ct. App. 1975); Lascaris v. Wyman, 340 N.Y.S.2d 397 (Ct. App. 1972), *cert. denied,* 414 U.S. 832 (1973).

36. People v. Soto, 352 N.Y.S.2d 144, 147 (Criminal Ct. 1974); Termini v. Califano, 611 F.2d 367 (2d Cir. 1979); Novak v. Harris, 504 F. Supp. 101 (E.D.N.Y. 1980); Montoroula v. Parry, 373 N.Y.S.2d 980 (Sup. Ct. 1975), *rev'd,* 388 N.Y.S.2d 916 (App. Div. 1976); Gaddis v. Wyman, 304 F. Supp. 717 (N.D.N.Y. 1969), *aff'd sub nom.* Wyman v. Bowens, 397 U.S. 49 (1970); Holley v. Lavine, 553 F.2d 845 (2d Cir. 1977), and 605 F.2d 638 (2d Cir. 1979), *cert. denied sub nom.* Blum v. Holley, 446 U.S. 913 (1980).

37. 397 U.S. 254 (1970). *Accord,* Damiano v. Shuart, 343 N.Y.S.2d 723 (Sup. Ct. 1973).

38. Adkin v. Berger, 378 N.Y.S.2d 135, 138 (App. Div. 1976), *aff'd,* 395 N.Y.S.2d 640 (Ct. App. 1977); Commissioner of Social Services v. C.C., 411 N.Y.S.2d 809, 810 (Family Ct. 1978); Pringle v. Nassau County Department of Social Services, 342 N.Y.S.2d 497 (Sup. Ct. 1973); Rivera v. Berger, 390 N.Y.S.2d 537, 543 (Sup. Ct. 1976).

39. James v. Goldberg, 303 F. Supp. 935 (S.D.N.Y. 1969), *rev'd on other grounds sub nom.* Wyman v. James, 400 U.S. 309 (1971); Seidel v. D'Elia, 428 N.Y.S.2d 321 (App. Div. 1980); Perez v. Lavine,

412 F. Supp. 1340 (S.D.N.Y. 1976), *as amended,* 422 F. Supp. 1259 (S.D.N.Y. 1977); Stevens v. Berger, 428 F. Supp. 896 (E.D.N.Y. 1977); Flam v. Califano, 469 F. Supp. 793 (E.D.N.Y. 1979); Gotbaum v. Sugarman, 358 N.Y.S.2d 635, 640 (Sup. Ct. 1974).

40. Richard M. Nixon, "Speech Accepting Republican Presidential Nomination, August 9, 1968," quoted in Theodore H. White, *The Making of the President, 1968* (New York: Atheneum, 1969), 297; *Rights in Conflict, Convention Week in Chicago, August 25–29, 1968: A Report Submitted by Daniel Walker, Director of the Chicago Study Team, to the National Commission on the Causes and Prevention of Violence* (New York: E. P. Dutton, 1968), 1; White, *Making of the President,* 219–60, 465–68.

41. Quoted in Richard Kluger, *Simple Justice: The History of* Brown v. Board of Education *and Black America's Struggle for Equality* (New York: Knopf, 1976), 674.

42. White, *Making of the President,* 238.

CHAPTER FIFTEEN

1. These percentages are based on a random survey of cases in the Southern District. The percentage for the 1960s is accurate within a range of 6.7 to 10.5 percent, given a 95 percent level of confidence. With a confidence level of 90 percent, contract litigation ranged between 5.3 and 15.6 percent of total filings for 1970; between 7.6 and 21.9 percent, at a confidence level of 95 percent, for 1971; between 7.9 and 22.6 percent, at a confidence level of 95 percent, for 1972; and between 17.1 and 23.9 percent at a 95 percent confidence level for 1973–79. The comparatively low rate of contract litigation in the 1960s and its increase in the 1970s has been observed and commented on in Stewart Macaulay, "Non-Contractual Relations in Business: A Preliminary Study," *American Sociological Review* 28 (1963): 55; Stewart Macaulay, "An Empirical View of Contract," *Wisconsin Law Review* 1985 (1985): 465, 466–70; Marc Galanter, "Reading the Landscapes of Disputes: What We Know and Don't Know (and Think We Know) about Our Allegedly Contentious and Litigious Society," *U.C.L.A. Law Review* 31 (1983): 4, 22.

2. The figures in the text for the amount of money involved in contract suits are based on too small a sample to be statistically reliable. But at a confidence level of 80 percent, the proportion of large firms involved in contract cases is accurate within +/- 5.4 percentage points for 1960–70 and within +/- 4.7 points for 1971–79. Generally, more money must be at stake to induce a major firm to undertake litigation than would be necessary to induce a small firm to do so.

For the purposes of this study, the following were counted as large firms: Breed, Abbot & Morgan; Burlingham Underwood, Lord; Cahill Gordon & Reindel; Carter, Ledyard & Milburn; Chadbourne & Parke; Cleary, Gottlieb, Steen & Hamilton; Conboy Hewitt O'Brien & Boardman; Cravath, Swaine & Moore; Curtis, Mallet-Prevost, Colt & Mosle; Davis Polk & Wardwell; Debevoise & Plimpton; Dewey, Ballantine, Bushby, Palmer & Wood; Donovan Maloof Walsh & Repetto; Fried, Frank, Harris, Shriver & Jacobson; Hill, Betts & Nash; Hughes Hubbard & Reed; Kirklan & Ellis; Lord Day & Lord, Barret Smith; Marshall, Bratter, Greene, Allison & Tucker; Millbank, Tweed, Hadley & McCloy; Mudge Rose Guthrie Alexander & Ferdon; Parker Chapin Flattau & Klimpl; Paul, Weiss, Rifkind, Wharton & Garrison; Phillips, Nizer, Benjamin, Krim & Ballon; Poletti, Friedin, Prashker, Feldman & Gartner; Proskauer Rose Goetz & Mendelsohn; Reid & Priest; Rogers & Wells; Rosenman & Colin; Royall, Koegel & Rogers; Shea & Gould; Shearman & Sterling; Simpson Thacher & Bartlett; Skadden, Arps, Slate, Meagher & Flom; Stroock & Stroock & Lavan; Sullivan & Cromwell; Tenzer, Greenblatt, Fallon & Kaplan; Townley & Updike; Wachtell, Lipton, Rosen & Katz; Weil, Gotshal & Manges; Whitman & Ransom; Wilkie Farr & Gallagher. Firm names are given as listed in *The Martindale-Hubbell Law Directory* (Summit, N.J.: Reed Reference, 1988).

3. Of course, the major transformations just mentioned were gradual ones taking place over the entire period under study in this book. Hence they cannot explain why the amount of breach of con-

tract litigation began to rise suddenly in the early 1970s. The immediate impetus appears, instead, to have been a series of short-term economic swings and changes in interest rates that began to occur in 1970, a year in which the American economy performed poorly. But these temporary developments cannot account for the persistence of increased contract litigation throughout the 1970s. To account for the long-term, nationwide increase, it is necessary to search for equally long-term transformations in the business corporations that large law firms serve and in the elite legal profession itself. See William E. Nelson, "Contract Litigation and the Elite Bar in New York City, 1960–1980," *Emory Law Journal* 39 (1990): 413, 419–24.

4. E.g., Lasker v. Burks, 567 F.2d 1208 (2d Cir. 1978), *rev'd*, 441 U.S. 471 (1979); Joseph W. Bishop Jr., "Sitting Ducks and Decoy Ducks: New Trends in the Indemnification of Corporate Directors and Officers," *Yale Law Journal* 77 (1968): 1078, 1099.

5. Pepsico, Inc. v. Federal Trade Commission, 472 F.2d 179 (2d Cir. 1972), *cert. denied*, 414 U.S. 876 (1973)

6. *Restatement of Contracts, Second*, sec. 264, comment (a) (1981).

7. Typically, once the court has rendered a decision, the agency will recognize its concurrent jurisdiction and "defer to the court" by treating its judgment as res judicata of the matter in dispute. See Arkansas Louisiana Gas Co. v. Hall, 30 Pub. Util. Rep.4th 224, 226 (Fed. Energy Reg. Comm'n 1979).

8. *Restatement, Second, of Contracts,* sec. 264, comment a (1981).

9. On the national level, for example, Ralph Nader published his first book, *Unsafe at Any Speed* (New York: Grossman, 1965), in 1965 and organized the Center for the Study of Responsive Law in 1968. See Charles McCarry, *Citizen Nader* (New York: Saturday Review Press, 1972), xii–xiii. That year also saw the founding of the Consumer Federation of America, which enjoyed a significant political presence during most of the 1970s. See Michael Pertschuk, *Revolt against Regulation: The Rise and Pause of the Consumer Movement* (Berkeley: University of California Press, 1982), 29–30. Between 1967 and 1973, Congress enacted more than twenty-five consumer, environmental, and other social regulatory laws. See ibid., 5. On the state level, in turn, Richard M. Kessel, who as executive director of the New York Consumer Protection Board now receives editorial support for his positions, see *New York Times,* Oct. 18, 1985, pt. I, p. 30, col. 1, led a consumer protest in 1974, while a young candidate for the state assembly, against rate increases requested by the Long Island Lighting Company. See ibid., Aug. 11, 1974, pt. I, p. 85, col. 1. By the next year, Kessel, described as a "consumer activist," had organized Long Island Consumer Action. See ibid., Nov. 16, 1975, pt. I, p. 121, col. 1. Another group organized at about the same time was the Consumer Watchdog Committee. See ibid., Nov. 16, 1975, pt. I, p. 123, col. 1.

10. See Nelson, "Contract Litigation," 454–55. Another change in legal rules that may have resulted in increased litigation was the adoption of the Uniform Commercial Code throughout the United States. Surely the aim of the UCC was not to increase litigation; on the contrary, the aim was to encourage businesses to solve for themselves problems that under prior law had demanded the institution of a lawsuit. See Uniform Commercial Code sec. 2-302, Comment 1. But the changes in legal doctrine wrought by the code may not have had the desired effect: the doctrinal changes of the code, instead of reducing litigation, may have introduced uncertainty into the law and thereby had the effect of promoting litigation. It is not intuitively obvious which of these two effects the UCC had, and, since the code's changes in substantive law occurred in the context of so many other variables, systematic study of its effects is probably impossible. As a result, it is difficult to know what the Uniform Commercial Code's impact, if any, has been.

11. See U.S. Bureau of the Census, *Statistical Abstract of the United States: 1971* (Washington, D.C.: U.S. Government Printing Office, 1971), 306; U.S. Bureau of the Census, *Historical Statistics of the United States: Colonial Times to 1970* (Washington, D.C.: U.S. Government Printing Office, 1975), 2:914. As a result, the largest firms controlled a larger portion of the nation's business: whereas in 1947,

the largest 100 manufacturing firms had accounted for 23 percent of the total value added to goods through manufacturing and the largest 200 had accounted for 30 percent, in 1970 those percentages were 33 and 43 percent respectively (ibid., 686).

12. The only run of statistics for the entire twenty-year period appears in a series of articles, "Economic Facts for Lawyers," published in the periodical *Law Office Economics and Management.* These statistics are less than ideal for purposes of comparison over time since the data gathered at the beginning of the period were somewhat different from those gathered at the end. Nonetheless, two sorts of data do emerge. The first is information on the income of partners in law firms. In 1960, that income averaged about $16,400 per year. See "Economic Facts for Lawyers: Part I: Earnings of Lawyers, 1955 to 1960," *Law Office Economics and Management* 3 (1963): 403, 405. By 1966, that figure had risen to $24,500. See "Income of Lawyers, 1966 and 1965," *Law Office Economics and Management* 10 (1969): 207, 208. In 1978, the median compensation of partners was $69,100. See "The 1979 Survey of Law Firm Economics," *Law Office Economics and Management* 20 (1979): 256. This was slightly more than a fourfold increase since 1960 and less than a threefold increase since 1966, assuming that there were no significant differences between median and average incomes for the years in question.

The second set of data deals with salaries of recent law school graduates. In 1962, these salaries averaged $6,600 per year. See "Economic Facts for Lawyers," *Law Office Economics and Management* 4 (1963): 97, 98. By 1979, the median starting salary for law firms was $22,000, while the median rate in firms with twelve to nineteen lawyers was $18,500. See "The 1979 Survey of Law Firm Economics," *Law Office Economics and Management* 20 (1979): 256. Again, with all the caveats that must be dropped as a result of the imperfect nature of the data, the starting salaries of young lawyers appear to have increased between three and four times during the years in question.

13. See Nelson, "Contract Litigation," 421–22.

14. Alfred D. Chandler, *Strategy and Structure: Chapters in the History of the Industrial Enterprise* (Cambridge, Mass.: MIT Press, 1962).

15. See Financial Accounting Standards Board (FASB), Statement of Financial Accounting Standards No. 5, paragraph 8; American Bar Association, "Statement of Policy Regarding Lawyers' Responses to Auditors' Requests for Information," *Business Lawyer* 31 (1976): 1709, 1713. See also "ABA Statement of Policy Regarding Lawyers' Responses to Auditors' Request for Information," *Business Lawyer* 32 (1976): 177; American Bar Association, "Statement of Policy Regarding Lawyers' Responses to Auditors' Requests for Information," 1714.

16. FASB Standard No. 5, paragraph 10.

17. See Nelson, "Contract Litigation," 431–36.

18. See, e.g., Parksville Mobile Modular, Inc. v. Estate of Goodstein, 422 N.Y.S.2d 710 (App. Div. 1979), *appeal dism.,* 49 N.Y.2d 801 (1980).

19. Newburger, Loeb & Co., Inc. v. Gross, 563 F.2d 1057 (2d Cir. 1977), *cert. denied,* 434 U.S. 1035 (1978).

20. Los Angeles Airways, Inc. v. Davis, 687 F.2d 321, 324 n.2, 328 (9th Cir. 1982). On the privilege to respond to a request for advice, see D. & C. Textile Corp. v. Rudin, 246 N.Y.S.2d 813 (Sup. Ct. 1964).

21. Quoted in Edwin Kiester Jr., *The Case of the Missing Executive: How Religious Bias Wastes Management Talent . . . and What Is Being Done about It* (New York: American Jewish Committee, 1973), 11; quoted in Ruth Ziff, "Ethnic Penetration into Top Managerial Positions in Advertising Agencies," (Ph.D. diss., City University of New York, 1975), 484; Ralph Nader and William Taylor, *The Big Boys: Power and Position in American Business* (New York, 1986), 221 (describing the career of Felix Rohatyn); quoted ibid., 484, 489. See also Robert P. Quinn et al., *The Chosen Few: A Study of Discrimination in Executive Selection* (Ann Arbor: Institute for Social Research, 1968), 36–38.

22. Quoted in E. Digby Baltzell, *Protestant Establishment: Aristocracy and Caste in America* (New York: Random House, 1964), 324–25.

23. Memorandum of Samuel Rabinove to Area Directors, "AJC Utilization of Federal Fair Housing Law," April 2, 1970 (ms. on file at Blaustein Library, American Jewish Committee, New York, N.Y.). See also Complaint, United States v. Palm Beach Realty Listing Bureau, Inc., Civil Action No. 70–379, Southern District of Florida, Mar. 23, 1970 (ms. on file at Blaustein Library, American Jewish Committee, New York, N.Y.); Memorandum from Walter Zand to Sam Rabinove, Apr. 9, 1970 (ms. on file in Blaustein Library, American Jewish Committee, New York, N.Y.); Transcript of Trial, United States v. Palm Beach Realty Listing Bureau, Civil Action No. 70–379, Southern District of Florida, Nov. 9, 1970.

24. Conversation with Eleanor Fox, Professor of Law, New York University, Aug. 4, 1988.

25. "Employment Discrimination in Big Business," *Rights: Reports on Social, Employment, Educational and Housing Discrimination* 7 (1968): 121, 123; "Ship Lines' Rates Called Too Low," *New York Times,* Apr. 22, 1967, p. 62, col. 5; Sabre Shipping Corp. v. American President Lines, 298 F. Supp. 1339 (S.D.N.Y. 1969); Sabre Shipping Corp. v. American President Lines, 285 F. Supp. 949 (S.D.N.Y. 1968), *cert. denied sub nom.* Japan Line, Ltd. v. Sabre Shipping Corp., 407 F.2d 173 (2d Cir. 1969), *cert. denied,* 395 U.S. 922 (1969).

26. See U.S. Bureau of the Census, *Statistical Abstract of the United States: 1987* (Washington, D.C.: U.S. Government Printing Office, 1986), 776, 779–780; U.S. Bureau of Census, *Historical Statistics,* 2, 864, 868–69, 871–72.

27. See "Pervasive Problems Threaten New York's Economic Base," *New York Times,* June 26, 1988, sec. 1, p. 1, col. 5.

28. New England Merchants' National Bank v. Iran Power Generation and Transmission Co., 502 F. Supp. 120, 122 n.1, 123 (S.D.N.Y. 1980), *rev'd sub nom.* Marschalk Co. v. Iran National Airlines Corp., 657 F.2d 3 (2d Cir.), *certified question answered,* 453 U.S. 919 (1981); Texas Trading & Milling Corp. v. Federal Republic of Nigeria, 647 F.2d 300, 305 (2d Cir. 1981), *cert. denied,* 454 U.S. 1148 (1982). Sixty-five of the ninety-six cases in the *Iran Power* case were filed in 1979, when a total of 1,280 breach of contract cases were filed in the Southern District.

29. See Marschalk Co. v. Iran National Airlines Corp., 518 F. Supp. 69 (S.D.N.Y. 1981), *rev'd,* 657 F.2d 3 (2d Cir.), *certified question answered,* 453 U.S. 919 (1981); United Technologies Corp. v. Citibank, N.A., 469 F. Supp. 473 (S.D.N.Y. 1979); Government of India v. Cargill, Inc., 445 F. Supp. 714 (S.D.N.Y. 1978); Hellenic Lines, Ltd. v. Director General of the India Supply Mission, 452 F.2d 810 (S.D.N.Y. 1971).

30. See Nancy Lisagor and Frank Lipsius, *A Law Unto Itself: The Untold Story of the Law Firm Sullivan and Cromwell* (New York: Morrow, 1988), 236, 279; *Skadden Arps Slate Meagher & Flom: The First 40 Years* (New York: Privately published, 1988), 1, 8–9; "Growth of 20 Law Firms, 1963–1981" (New York City), *New York Law Journal,* Mar. 16, 1981, p. 3, col. 1.

31. The number of cases in the sample from which these percentages are derived is too small to be confident of its statistical reliability.

32. The following statistics in the text are derived from a series of publications by the New York State Judicial Conference, variously entitled *Annual Report of the Judicial Conference of the State of New York, Report of the Administrative Board of the Judicial Conference of the State of New York for the Judicial Year,* and *Report of the Administrative Board of the Judicial Conference and the Office of Court Administration for the Calendar Year,* which cover the years between 1960 and 1980.

33. The following statistics in the text, for total dispositions, are derived from the series entitled *Federal Offenders in the United States District Courts,* published annually by the Administrative Office of the U.S. Courts, beginning in 1962.

34. Using standard statistical methods, the number of habeas filings is accurate for 1960–69 at a 95 percent level of confidence within a range of 245 to 271 cases; for 1970, within a range of 292 to 470 cases; for 1971, within a range of 397 to 601 cases; and for 1972, within a range of 461 to 675 cases. The number of prisoner suits declined after 1972, while the total number of filings grew slightly: during

the entire 1971–79 period, prisoner suits declined to 367 per year (which is accurate within a range of 334 to 400 cases)—about the same number as in 1970—while total filings rose to an average of 1,309—a 5.3 percent increase over the 1972 rate.

No ready explanation is apparent. We might, however, speculate. The basis for speculation is a postulate that, once courts have developed a capacity to process a certain amount of litigation, lawyers will not allow that judicial time to go to waste; they will file additional lawsuits to use up the available judicial time. Thus when the number of cases by prisoners declined after 1972, lawyers stepped in with random other cases to fill the void. Told in this fashion, the story of the litigation rise in upstate New York is not one of chaos but one of more effective government and of citizens taking advantage of government's efficiency and making use of its services.

Increased litigation also occurred in the Eastern District of New York, which consists of Long Island and Staten Island. These are the areas where most of the state's population increase occurred during the second half of the century. In the Eastern District, the rise in litigation appears to have tracked population growth, although the rise in litigation was somewhat greater than and lagged somewhat behind the increase in population. Between 1950 and 1970, population in the district increased from 5.34 million people to 7.44 million—an increase of 39.3 percent. See *1997 New York State Statistical Yearbook,* 22d ed. (Albany: Nelson A. Rockefeller Institute of Government, 1997), 6. Meanwhile, litigation increased from an average of 1,293 cases per year for the 1960s to an average of 2,202 cases per year for the 1970s—an increase of 70.3 percent. Population growth thus appears to have accounted for about half of litigation growth.

35. See Laws of 1966, ch. 254, which took effect on September 1, 1967.

36. Unfortunately, consistent data are not readily available for the intervening years; nonetheless, it does appear that the litigation explosion in state courts in the late 1960s and early 1970s reflects not a growth of litigiousness among the people of the state as a whole but only unhappy couples taking advantage of a new legislatively sanctioned procedure to break the chains of matrimony.

37. See Lincoln First Bank v. Barstro & Associates Contracting, Inc., 374 N.Y.S.2d 485 (App. Div. 1975); Morrison v. National Broadcasting Co., 266 N.Y.S.2d 406 (App. Div. 1965), *rev'd on other grounds,* 280 N.Y.S.2d 641 (Ct. App. 1967); Harder v. Augerge des Fougeres, Inc., 338 N.Y.S.2d 356 (App. Div. 1972); ATI, Inc. v. Ruder & Finn, Inc., 398 N.Y.S.2d 864 (Ct. App. 1977); Mitran v. Williamson, 197 N.Y.S.2d 689 (Sup. Ct. 1960).

38. Samek v. Rey, 261 N.Y.S.2d 548, 549–50 (Civil Ct. 1965).

39. Corso v. Crawford Dog & Cat Hospital, Inc., 415 N.Y.S.2d 182, 183 (Civil Ct. 1979).

40. People v. Smith, 331 N.Y.S.2d 81, 85 (County Ct. 1972); People v. Hobson, 384 N.Y.S.2d 419, 425 (Ct. App. 1976). The anti-democratic tendencies of the judiciary were most troubling to those who saw the courts as the weakest and least dangerous branch of government and who urged that judges practice self-restraint. See generally Alexander M. Bickel, *The Least Dangerous Branch* (Indianapolis: Bobbs-Merrill, 1962).

41. Kates v. Lefkowitz, 216 N.Y.S.2d 1014, 1016 (Sup. Ct. 1961).

42. See Application of Reigi, 225 N.Y.S.2d 226, 227 (App. Div. 1927); In re Strahl, 195 N.Y.S. 385 (App. Div. 1922); Matter of Diserio, 140 N.Y.S.2d 478, 479 (App. Div. 1955).

43. See Alexander B. Callow Jr., *The Tweed Ring* (New York: Oxford University Press, 1966), 135–51; Denis T. Lynch, *"Boss" Tweed* (New York: Boni and Liveright, 1927), 357, 373, 389; Seymour J. Mandelbaum, *Boss Tweed's New York* (New York: Wiley, 1965), 73, 83; Herbert Mitgang, *The Man Who Rode the Tiger: The Life and Times of Judge Samuel Seabury* (Philadelphia: Lippincott, 1963), 178–96. But see Leo Hershkowitz, *Tweed's New York: Another Look* (Garden City, N.Y.: Anchor Press, 1977), 225–32.

44. Matter of Fuchsberg, 426 N.Y.S.2d 639, 666–67 (Judiciary Ct. 1978) (dissenting opinion); Kuehnel v. State Commission on Judicial Conduct, 426 N.Y.S.2d 461, 463 (Ct. App. 1980).

45. See, e.g., Spector v. State Commission on Judicial Conduct, 418 N.Y.S.2d 565 (Ct. App. 1979).

46. Matter of Perry, 385 N.Y.S.2d 589, 590 (App. Div. 1976); Keuhnel v. State Commission on Judicial Conduct, 426 N.Y.S.2d 461, 463 (Ct. App. 1980); Shilling v. State Commission on Judicial Conduct, 434 N.Y.S.2d 909, 910, 912 (Ct. App. 1980), *appeal dism.,* 451 U.S. 978 (1981).

47. Matter of Richter, 409 N.Y.S.2d 1013, 1015 (Judiciary Ct. 1977); Matter of Waltemade, 409 N.Y.S.2d 989, 995 (Judiciary Ct. 1975); Matter of Filipowicz, 388 N.Y.S.2d 920 (App. Div. 1976); In re DiLorenzo, 330 N.Y.S.2d 394 (App. Div. 1972); Matter of Cornelius, 425 N.Y.S.2d 552 (Ct. App. 1980).

48. Matter of MacDowell, 393 N.Y.S.2d 748 (App. Div. 1977); In re Schmidt, 296 N.Y.S.2d 49 (App. Div. 1968); Rogers v. State Commission on Judicial Conduct, 433 N.Y.S.2d 1001 (Ct. App. 1980).

49. Elias v. Ellenville Chapter of National Association for the Advancement of Colored People, 325 N.Y.S.2d 302 (App. Div. 1971); In re Schamel, 362 N.Y.S.2d 39 (App. Div. 1974), *appeal dism.,* 366 N.Y.S.2d 1029 (Ct. App. 1975); In re Schamel, 372 N.Y.S.2d 742 (App. Div. 1975), *appeal dism.,* 382 N.Y.S.2d 1033 (Ct. App. 1975); Nicholson v. State Commission on Judicial Conduct, 431 N.Y.S.2d 348 (Ct. App. 1980), in which the Court of Appeals authorized an inquiry into the campaign despite claims that the inquiry would violate First Amendment rights of political expression. The judge who ran for the Court of Appeals was Jack B. Weinstein, senior district judge in the Eastern District of New York. On his campaign for the Court of Appeals in 1973, see "For the Court of Appeals," *New York Times,* May 29, 1973, p. 34, col. 2.

50. In re Suglia, 320 N.Y.S.2d 352, 353–54 (App. Div. 1971).

51. Dixon v. State Commission on Judicial Conduct, 419 N.Y.S.2d 445 (Ct. App. 1979).

52. See Lonschein v. State Commission on Judicial Conduct, 430 N.Y.S.2d 571 (Ct. App. 1980); Bartlett v. Enea, 359 N.Y.S.2d 364 (App. Div. 1974).

53. Perhaps this judge was removed because of his racist comments. But if so, one then wonders why George Bush could be permitted to use his barely disguised, racist Willie Horton ads to smooth his path to the White House. See "Foes Accuse Bush Campaign of Inflaming Racial Tension," *New York Times,* Oct. 24, 1988, p. 1, cols. 5–6.

54. 426 N.Y.S.2d 639 (Judiciary Ct. 1978).

55. Ibid., 642–43.

56. Ibid., 666 (dissenting opinion).

57. Ibid., 665–66 (dissenting opinion).

58. "Fuchsberg Censured for Trading in New York Notes during Appeals," *New York Times,* Mar. 17, 1978, p. A1, col. 4, and p. 19, col. 1.

59. Lonschein v. State Commission on Judicial Conduct, 430 N.Y.S.2d 571, 573–74 (Ct. App. 1980) (dissenting opinion).

CHAPTER SIXTEEN

1. 37 N.Y.S.2d 404 (Sup. Ct. 1942), *aff'd,* 41 N.Y.S.2d 210 (App. Div. 1943), *aff'd,* 292 N.Y. 468 (1944).

2. 37 N.Y.S.2d at 412.

3. Simon v. Socony-Vacuum Oil Co., 38 N.Y.S.2d 270, 273 (Sup. Ct. 1942), *aff'd,* 47 N.Y.S.2d 589 (App. Div. 1944).

4. Kalmanash v. Smith, 291 N.Y. 142, 157 (1943); Borden v. Cohen, 231 N.Y.S.2d 902 (Sup. Ct. 1962).

5. Roth v. Robertson, 118 N.Y.S. 351 (Sup. Ct. 1909); Runcie v. Corn Exchange Bank Trust Co., 6 N.Y.S.2d 616 (Sup. Ct. 1938).

6. In re Estate of Klosk, 319 N.Y.S.3d 685 (Surr. Ct. 1971); In re Estate of Simons, 182 N.Y.S.2d

1005, 1008 (Surr. Ct. 1958); In re Dugmore's Will, 199 N.Y.S.2d 630 (Surr. Ct. 1960); In re Chusid's Estate, 301 N.Y.S.2d 766, 770 (Surr. Ct. 1969). The traditional assumption about return of principal grew out of the fact that the purchasing power of the dollar in 1930 was identical to what it had been in 1801. Between 1930 and 1933, a further decline in prices meant that only 78 cents was required to buy what had cost $1.00 in 1801; this figure had risen only to 84 cents by 1940. See U.S. Department of Commerce: Bureau of the Census, *Historical Statistics of the United States: Colonial Times to 1970*, Bicentennial ed. (Washington, D.C.: U.S. Government Printing Office, 1976), 1:210–11. By 1980, however, the dollar had declined to merely 16.98 percent of its 1940 value, with the result that a fixed-value investment of $1,000 in 1940, with interest paid out annually, would return a principal in 1980 with a purchasing power of only $170 in 1940 dollars. See U.S. Department of Commerce, Bureau of the Census, *Statistical Abstract of the United States, 1996*, 116th ed. (Washington, D.C.: U.S. Government Printing Office, 1996), 483. In the face of this inflation, the traditional assumption made no sense.

7. Sinram v. Pennsylvania R.R., 61 F.2d 767 (2d Cir. 1932); Sidney Blumenthal & Co. v. Atlantic Coast Line R.R., 139 F.2d 288, 291 (2d Cir. 1943), *cert denied*, 321 U.S. 795 (1944).

8. United States v. Carroll Towing Co., 159 F.2d 169, 173 (2d Cir. 1947).

9. Rosenquist v. Isthmian S.S. Co., 205 F.2d 486, 489 (2d Cir. 1953); Mamiye Bros. v. Barber S.S. Lines, Inc., 360 F.2d 774, 777 (2d Cir. 1966), *cert. denied,* 385 U.S. 835 (1966); Eaton v. Long Island R.R., 398 F.2d 738, 742 (2d Cir. 1968); Richards v. New York, New Haven & Hartford R.R., 250 F.2d 609, 610 (2d Cir. 1957).

10. Antinucci v. Hellman, 174 N.Y.S.2d 343, 345 (App. Div. 1958); Havas v. Victory Paper Stock Co., 426 N.Y.S.2d 233, 236 (Ct. App. 1980).

11. Bennett v. New York & Queens Electric Light & Power Co., 294 N.Y. 334, 337–338 (1945); Central Greyhound Lines, Inc. v. Bonded Freightways, Inc., 82 N.Y.S.2d 671, 676 (Sup. Ct. 1948); Morris v. Troy Savings Bank, 302 N.Y.S.2d 51, 53 (App. Div. 1969), *aff'd,* 320 N.Y.S.2d 78 (Ct. App. 1971); Lancaster Silo & Block Co. v. Northern Propane Gas Co., 427 N.Y.S.2d 1009, 1013–14 (App. Div. 1980).

12. Pulka v. Edelman, 390 N.Y.S.2d 393, 396–97 (Ct. App. 1976).

13. Cole v. New York Racing Ass'n, 266 N.Y.S.2d 267, 270 (App. Div. 1965), *aff'd,* 270 N.Y.S.2d 421 (Ct. App. 1966); Derdiarian v. Felix Contracting Corp., 434 N.Y.S.2d 166, 169 (Ct. App. 1980); Sheehan v. City of New York, 387 N.Y.S.2d 92, 95 (Ct. App. 1976).

14. Hallenbeck v. Lone Star Cement Corp., 77 N.Y.S.2d 807, 811 (App. Div. 1948), *aff'd,* 299 N.Y. 777 (1949). The courts answered that when "harmful consequences" were brought about by "forces, the operation of which might have been reasonably foreseen," then there was not a sufficient break in the chain of causation to relieve the initial actor from liability. See Kingsland v. Erie County Agr. Soc., 298 N.Y. 409, 424 (1949). In contrast, "'if the consequences were only made possible by the intervening act of a third party which could not have reasonably been anticipated then the sequential relation between act and results would not . . . come within the rule of proximate cause.'" See Gralton v. Oliver, 101 N.Y.S.2d 198, 114 (App. Div. 1950).

15. Mull v. Colt Co., 31 F.R.D. 154, 168 (S.D.N.Y. 1962); Petition of Kinsman Transit Co., 338 F.2d 708, 722–25 (2d Cir. 1964), *cert. denied,* 380 U.S. 944 (1965) (Friendly, J.); Karlson v. 305 East 43rd Street Corp., 370 F.2d 467, 472 (2d Cir.), *cert. denied,* 387 U.S. 905 (1967).

16. Boomer v. Atlantic Cement Co., 309 N.Y.S.2d 312, 315–17, 322 (1970).

17. See Richard A. Posner, "A Theory of Negligence," *Journal of Legal Studies* 1 (1972): 29, 32–33; Pulka v. Edelman, 390 N.Y.S.2d 393 (Ct. App. 1976).

18. Bader & Bader v. Ford, 414 N.Y.S.2d 132, 136 (App. Div.), *appeal dism.,* 421 N.Y.S.2d 199 (Ct. App. 1979); Interstate Steel Co. v. Manchester Liners, Ltd., 145 N.Y.S.2d 754, 755 (Mun. Ct. 1955); Flushing National Bank v. Brightside Manufacturing Inc., 298 N.Y.S.2d 197, 199 (Sup. Ct. 1969); Kule Resources, Ltd. v. Reliance Group, Inc., 427 N.Y.S.2d 612, 613 (Ct. App. 1980).

19. Rosenfeld v. Hotel Corp. of America, 281 N.Y.S.2d 308, 310 (Ct. App. 1967); Greenhouse v. Rochester Taxicab Co., 218 N.Y.S. 167, 170 (App. Div. 1926), *appeal dism.*, 244 N.Y. 559 (1927); Luitwieler v. Luitwieler Pumping Engine Co., 191 N.Y.S. 111, 112 (Sup. Ct. 1921); Akely v. Kinnicutt, 238 N.Y. 466, 472 (1924); Village of Mt. Morris v. Pavilion Natural Gas Co., 183 N.Y.S. 792, 795 (Sup. Ct. 1920).

20. Harrolds Motorcar Co. v. Gordon, 221 N.Y.S. 486, 487 (Sup. Ct. 1927); Schechner v. Wittner, 224 N.Y.S. 66, 71 (City Ct. 1927).

21. S. T. Grand, Inc. v. City of New York, 344 N.Y.S.2d 938, 941 (Ct. App. 1973).

22. 151 N.Y.S.2d 1 (Ct. App. 1956).

23. Ibid., 3, 5.

24. Headley v. Noto, 290 N.Y.S.2d 726, 729 (Ct. App. 1968); Offner v. Rothschild, 386 N.Y.S.2d 188 (Sup. Ct. 1976); Foy v. Schechter, 154 N.Y.S.2d 927, 934 (Ct. App. 1956).

25. Statter v. Statter, 163 N.Y.S.2d 13, 16–17 (Ct. App. 1957) (emphasis added).

26. Hinchey v. Sellers, 197 N.Y.S.2d 129, 133–34 (Ct. App. 1959), *citing* Israel v. Wood Dolson Co., 151 N.Y.S.2d 1 (Ct. App. 1956).

27. Bronxville Palmer, Ltd. v. State, 277 N.Y.S.2d 402 (Ct. App. 1966); Cummings v. Dresher, 271 N.Y.S.2d 976 (Ct. App. 1966); Commissioners of State Insurance Fund v. Low, 170 N.Y.S.2d 795 (Ct. App. 1958); Schwartz v. Public Administrator of County of Bronx, 298 N.Y.S.2d 955, 964 (Ct. App. 1969); B. R. DeWitt, Inc. v. Hall, 278 N.Y.S.2d 596, 601 (Ct. App. 1967); Schwartz v. Public Administrator of County of Bronx, *supra* at 959–960; Watts v. Swiss Bank Corp., 317 N.Y.S.2d 315, 320 (Ct. App. 1970); People v. Plevy, 436 N.Y.S.2d 224, 227 (Ct. App. 1980) (dictum); Watts v. Swiss Bank Corp., *supra* at 320.

28. Vavolizza v. Krieger, 352 N.Y.S.2d 919, 923 (Ct. App. 1974); Murphy v. Erie County, 320 N.Y.S.2d 29, 32 (Ct. App. 1971); Williams v. Codd, 459 F. Supp. 804, 812 (S.D.N.Y. 1978); American Insurance Co. v. Messinger, 401 N.Y.S.2d 36, 39 n.2 (Ct. App. 1977); Parklane Hosiery Co. v. Shore, 439 U.S. 322, 329–31 (1979).

29. Curea v. Romonel Knitting Mills, Inc., 358 N.Y.S.2d 446, 447 (App. Div. 1974); Butler v. District Council 37, American Federation of State, County and Municipal Employees, AFL-CIO, 422 N.Y.S.2d 74, 76 (App. Div. 1979); Snyder v. Parke, Davis & Co., 391 N.Y.S.2d 579 (App. Div. 1977); Horn Construction Co. v. ICOS Corp. of America, 406 N.Y.S.2d 78 (App. Div. 1978); L. v. Sugarman, 357 N.Y.S.2d 987, 999 (App. Div. 1974).

30. Barouh Eaton Allen Corp. v. International Business Machines Corp., 429 N.Y.S.2d 33, 36 (App. Div. 1980); In re Welch's Estate, 265 N.Y.S.2d 198, 200 (App. Div. 1965); U.S. Pioneer Electronics Corp. v. Nikko Electric Corp. of America, 419 N.Y.S.2d 484 (Ct. App. 1979); Quarto v. Westchester Premier Theatre, Inc., 382 N.Y.S.2d 353 (App. Div. 1976); Spatz v. Wide World Travel Service, Inc., 418 N.Y.S.2d 19 (App. Div. 1979).

31. Bakerian v. Horn, 249 N.Y.S.2d 646, 648 (App. Div. 1964); Andre v. Pomeroy, 362 N.Y.S.2d 131, 133 (Ct. App. 1974); Flushing National Bank v. Brightside Manufacturing Inc., 298 N.Y.S.2d 197, 199 (Sup. Ct. 1969); Kule Resources, Ltd. v. Reliance Group, Inc., 427 N.Y.S.2d 612, 613 (Ct. App. 1980); Oppenheimer v. Dresdener Bank A.G., 394 N.Y.S.2d 634 (Ct. App. 1977); Rosman v. Trans World Airlines, Inc., 358 N.Y.S.2d 97, 103 (Ct. App. 1974).

32. Rinaldi v. Holt, Rinehart & Winston, Inc., 397 N.Y.S.2d 943 (Ct. App.), *cert. denied,* 434 U.S. 969 (1977); Ilasi v. City of Long Beach, 379 N.Y.S.2d 831 (Ct. App. 1976); Kuniholm v. Kuniholm, 222 N.Y.S.2d 509, 512 (App. Div. 1961), *rev'd on other grounds,* 229 N.Y.s.2d 412 (Ct. App. 1962).

33. Schollmeyer v. Sutter, 151 N.Y.S.2d 795 (Sup. Ct. 1956), *appeal dism.,* 158 N.Y.S.2d 354 (App. Div. 1957); Maxie v. Gimbel Bros., Inc., 423 N.Y.S.2d 802, 808–9 (Sup. Ct. 1979); Halpern v. Gozan, 381 N.Y.S.2d 744 (Sup. Ct. 1976); Weiser v. City of New York, 268 N.Y.S.2d 457, 458, 460 (Civil Ct. 1965), *aff'd,* 268 N.Y.S.2d 460 (App. Term 1966); Jack Parker Construction Corp. v. Williams, 317

N.Y.S.2d 911 (App. Div. 1970); Rosen v. Dick, 83 F.R.D. 540, 543–44 (S.D.N.Y. 1979), *modified on other grounds,* 639 F.2d 82 (2d Cir. 1980).

34. See "Note: Reviving the Law of Substantive Unconscionability: Applying the Implied Covenant of Good Faith and Fair Dealing to Excessively Priced Consumer Credit Contracts," *U.C.L.A. Law Review* 33 (1986): 940, 942.

EPILOGUE

1. See "The U.N. at 50: Facing the Task of Reinventing Itself," *New York Times,* Oct. 22, 1995, p. 1, cols. 3–6; "In Oratory and Fanfare, U.N. Celebrates 50 Years," *New York Times,* Oct. 22, 1995, p. 11, cols. 1–2.

2. See "U.S. Bids U.N. Delay on Site till Late '47," *New York Times,* Dec. 10, 1946, p. 1, col. 7; Clark M. Eichelberger, *Organizing for Peace: A Personal History of the Founding of the United Nations* (New York: Harper & Row, 1977), 284–87; Shirley Hazzard, *Defeat of an Ideal: A Study of the Self-Destruction of the United Nations* (Boston: Little, Brown, 1973), 6–7.

3. See Cary Reich, *The Life of Nelson A. Rockefeller: Worlds to Conquer, 1908–1958* (New York: Doubleday, 1996), 3–7, 174–373, 493–501, 728–31.

4. Leland M. Goodrich, *The United Nations* (New York: Crowell, 1959), 242.

5. Douglas MacArthur, quoted in Tony Smith, *America's Mission: The United States and the World-wide Struggle for Democracy in the Twentieth Century* (Princeton: Princeton University Press, 1994), 146; U.S. Department of State, *Foreign Relations of the United States: The Conference of Berlin (the Potsdam Conference), 1945* (Washington, D.C.: U.S. Government Printing Office, 1960), 2:1503.

6. *Putsch, The Diary: Three Days That Collapsed the Empire,* trans. from Russian (Oakville, Ontario: Mosaic Press, 1992), 45, 66, 79; Giovanni Sartori, *The Theory of Democracy Revisited* (Chatham, N.J.: Chatham House, 1987), 380; quoted in Walter A. McDougall, *Promised Land, Crusader State: The American Encounter with the World since 1776* (Boston: Houghton Mifflin, 1997), 220; Zbigniew Brzezinski, "The Cold War and Its Aftermath," in *The American Encounter: The United States and the Making of the Modern World,* ed. James F. Hoge Jr. and Fareet Zakaria (New York: Basic Books, 1997), 482, 491–92; James Chace, *The Consequences of the Peace: The New Internationalism and American Foreign Policy* (New York: Oxford University Press, 1992), 7. See also ibid., 169–70, 178–79; Joshua Muravchik, *The Imperative of American Literature: A Challenge to Neo-Isolationism* (Washington, D.C.: AEI Press, 1996), 181; Smith, *America's Mission,* 239–307; Ronald Steel, *Temptations of a Superpower* (Cambridge, Mass.: Harvard University Press, 1995), 14–15, 19, 36.

7. Goodrich, *United Nations,* 164–168, 242–291; Theodore H. White, *The Making of the President, 1968* (New York: Atheneum, 1969), 214.

8. "In Oratory and Fanfare, U.N. Celebrates 50 Years," *New York Times,* Oct. 22, 1995, p. 11, cols. 1–2.

9. "And Now for the Next 50 Years: New Promises, Familiar Demands," *New York Times,* Oct. 23, 1995, p. A8, cols. 1–5; "Clinton's View of U.S. Goal: 'Peaceful Time for Europe,'" *New York Times,* Apr. 16, 1999, p. A11, cols. 5–6.

10. Steel, *Temptations of a Superpower,* 14; David Remnick, *Lenin's Tomb: The Last Days of the Soviet Empire* (New York: Random House, 1993), 337. See also Donald W. White, *The American Century: The Rise and Decline of the United States as a World Power* (New Haven: Yale University Press, 1996), 417–18.

11. See Smith, *America's Mission,* 7, 13–19, 312–18, which labels the concept of democratic self-determination Wilsonian and argues that it remains the key contribution of the United States to the global political order.

12. Steel, *Temptations of a Superpower,* 96–97.

ACKNOWLEDGMENTS

My work on this book over the course of some fifteen years has resulted in the accumulation of innumerable debts. I can only acknowledge the major ones here.

Let me begin by discussing the acquisition of source materials. First are the nearly fifty thousand cases randomly gathered by a small army of research assistants from records of state and federal trial courts in New York. The two student research assistants who did the most valuable work in setting up the sampling procedures, in gathering sample cases, and then in analyzing them were Steven Biener and David Montoya. The most outstanding student research assistant who worked with the sample was Norman Williams, who wrote the first draft of an article derived from the sample, which we ultimately published under both our names; I am grateful both for the work he did and for his permission to publish solely under my name excerpts from that article. I also am grateful for the yeoman editorial help he provided on yet another article from which this book has been in part derived.

The book is also based on a second body of sources: published cases in the *New York Supplement* and various federal reporters. The late Diana Vincent-Daviss, then librarian of the New York University Law Library, obtained for me a complete set of the *New York Supplement,* both first and second series; I could never have completed the book without round-the-clock access to the New York case materials in my office at home. Merely owning the *Supplement,* however, did not put me in possession of all the legal source material I required, and every summer for a decade the staff of the Law School's duplicating room copied mountains of additional material that I needed. I am especially grateful to Joel Mohammed, the manager of the Law School's Duplicating Services.

Obtaining possession of New York and federal cases and statutes was only the beginning of my library needs. I also needed hundreds of books and articles. The New York University Law Library fulfilled every request for materials that I presented to it, including requests that were often vaguely and imprecisely articulated. I am deeply indebted to the library's entire research staff, but especially to Ronald Brown and Elizabeth Evans. I also made extensive use of the Hofstra University Law Library, for which I am grateful.

The Nassau County Public Library System, which has an excellent American history collection, was another source of many books. I am especially indebted to Jeffrey Mason, the reference librarian at the Hewlett-Woodmere Public Library, who responded far beyond the call of duty to many research requests, obtained books on interlibrary loan, and, above all, taught me how to access the Internet for materials, including Westlaw materials, that I needed. I also found the Axinn Library at Hofstra University helpful and accommodating, and I used it a great deal. Finally, I wish to express my appreciation for the courtesies extended by the Blaustein Library of the American Jewish Committee and by the YIVO Institute for Jewish Research.

Nearly all of this book has been published previously in a series of articles, which are longer, more detailed, and far more extensively documented than this book. Scholars needing the detail and more extensive documentation should consult the following articles:

William E. Nelson, "Contract Litigation and the Elite Bar in New York City, 1960–1980," *Emory Law Journal* 39 (1990): 413.

William E. Nelson, "Criminality and Sexual Morality in New York, 1920–1980," *Yale Journal of Law and the Humanities* 5 (1993): 265.

William E. Nelson, "The Changing Meaning of Equality in Twentieth-Century Constitutional Law," *Washington and Lee Law Review* 52 (1995): 3.

William E. Nelson, "Patriarchy or Equality: Family Values or Individuality," *St. John's Law Review* 70 (1996): 435.

William E. Nelson, "The Growth of Distrust: The Emergence of Hostility toward Government Regulation of the Economy," *Hofstra Law Review* 25 (1996): 1.

William E. Nelson, "Civil Procedure in Twentieth-Century New York," *Saint Louis University Law Journal* 41 (1997): 1157.

William E. Nelson, "Two Models of Welfare: Private Charity versus Public Duty," *Southern California Interdisciplinary Law Journal* 7 (1998): 295.

William E. Nelson, "The Integrity of the Judiciary in Twentieth-Century New York," *Rutgers Law Review* 51 (1998): 1.

William E. Nelson, "A Man's Word and Making Money: Contract Law in New York, 1920–1960," *Mississippi College Law Review* 19 (1998): 1.

William E. Nelson, "From Fairness to Efficiency: The Transformation of Tort Law in New York, 1920–1980," *Buffalo Law Review* 47 (1999): 117.

William E. Nelson and Norman R. Williams, "Suburbanization and Market Failure: An Analysis of Government Policies Promoting Suburban Growth and Ethnic Assimilation," *Fordham Urban Law Journal* 27 (1999): 197.

William E. Nelson, "From Morality to Equality: Judicial Regulation of

Business Ethics in New York, 1920–1980," *New York Law School Law Review* 43 (1999): 223.

William E. Nelson, "Government Power as a Tool for Redistributing Wealth in Twentieth-Century New York," in *Law as Culture and Culture as Law: Essays in Honor of John Phillip Reid,* ed. Hendrick Hartog and William E. Nelson (Madison, Wis.: Madison House, 2000), 322.

William E. Nelson, "The Law of Fiduciary Duty in New York, 1920–1980," *Southern Methodist Law Review* 53 (2000): 283.

I am indebted to the holders of the copyright on the above articles for permission to reprint portions of the articles herein.

Each of these articles, as well as a draft of this entire book, were presented to the Legal History Colloquium at New York University School of Law. I am indebted to all the participants in the colloquium over the decade-long period during which I inflicted various drafts on the group, but especially to (in alphabetical order) Louis Anthes, Christopher Eisgruber, Martin Flaherty, Sarah Gordon, Larry Kramer, William LaPiana, Gregory Mark, Howard Venable, and Mark Weiner. I also presented a summary of the book and excerpts from it at faculty workshops at Fordham Law School, Ohio State University Law School, and Western New England Law School, and I delivered individual chapters at the Constitutional Theory Colloquium at New York University and as lectures or at workshops at Mississippi College School of Law, Saint Louis University School of Law, and Southern Methodist University Law School. I am grateful to the many faculty members of these schools who offered me useful guidance and ideas, but especially to John Attanasio and Michael Les Benedict.

I owe an unredeemable debt to John Sexton, who has made New York University School of Law the best place in the world for the scholarly study of law in general and of legal history in particular. It is impossible to thank him enough for all the support he has given to the Legal History Colloquium, to my career in general, and to this book in particular. Extremely generous financial support was provided by the Filomen D'Agostino and Max E. Greenberg Faculty Research Fund of New York University School of Law.

The American Society for Legal History and the University of North Carolina Press entered the picture late, when I submitted the book for publication in their legal history series. The editors selected the perfect reader for the book, Laura Kalman, whose detailed comments based on her unparalleled knowledge of twentieth-century American history gave me months of work, resulting in vast improvement of the manuscript. Most helpful of all were the two editors of the series, Thomas Green and Hendrik Hartog. With his accustomed aplomb and tact, Green prevailed upon me to temper my more extreme contentions, while Hartog proposed a restructuring of the book that clarified and strengthened its overall argument. The editors at the Press exhibited extraordinary patience and, in the end I hope, wisdom in agreeing to go forward with this massive project and in seeing it to final fruition.

Then there are the most important people in my life—teachers, friends, and family. I have dedicated this book to Bernard Bailyn, into whose seminar I plunged fortuitously because Mark DeWolfe Howe was not offering a seminar during the semester I began my graduate studies. Bailyn's seminar remains the most important and exciting intellectual experience of my life; I learned from him that fallible mortals like me can think about the past in a principled, organized, and systematic fashion that will contribute usefully to the ideas of others. Shirley Gray, my secretary for more than a decade, provided administrative and diplomatic support that kept the various people whose help I needed for the project on board my team; thanks to her efforts, I was able to concentrate on ideas and on expressing those ideas. Lisa Mihajlovic has capably taken up where Gray left off. Thomas Mackey, a former Golieb Fellow in the Legal History Colloquium who has spent most summers during the past decade with me, provided a constant sounding board amidst interludes of gardening, baseball, and running errands.

Finally, my family lived with this project for fifteen years and, as a result, must have concluded at times that I was at least eccentric, if not certifiably insane. When my personal set of the *New York Supplement* arrived at my home, my late father said as much as he expressed his concerns that the house would collapse under the weight. My wife, Elaine, quietly and patiently endured the project, and my son, Greg, also endured it, if not always quietly and patiently. My daughter, Leila, involved herself in the book and contributed not only ideas and support, but also an early design for the book's jacket.

Woodmere, New York
January 2000

INDEX

Hong Kong, 336
Hornblower, William, 96
Hornstein v. Paramount Pictures, Inc., 354–55
Housing: public, 21, 63; fair, 312
Housing Act of 1948, 169
Housing Act of 1950, 169–70
How the Other Half Lives, 13
H. R. Moch Co. v. Rensselaer Water Co., 101–2, 106
Hubbard v. Hubbard, 50, 230
Hubbs, Irving G., 21
Hudson View Properties v. Weiss, 251–52
Hue (Vietnam), 276
Huerta, Dolores, 279
Hughes, Howard, 333
Hull, N. E. H., 98n
Human Rights Law, 252
Humphrey, Hubert, 277–79
Hunter College, 155
Huntley, Chet, 276

Illegality, 77
Illegitimacy, 48–49, 234–35, 306–7, 323
Il Miracolo, 211–12
Immigrants, 3–4, 16, 18–19, 41–42, 115, 271, 275, 313
Immunity, of charities and municipalities, 188
Imperfect tender, cure of, 85
Impossibility, as defense, 88–90
Incapacity, as basis for annulment, 52–53
Indefiniteness, of contract terms, 83–84
Industrial Development Agency Act, 263–64
Injunctions, 34; in labor disputes, 72–76
Injuries, personal, 34; law of, 93–107, 112, 184–99
Instrumentalism, 24
Insurance, 86, 186, 303–4
Interborough Rapid Transit Co. v. Lavin, 73–74
Interest: conflicts of, 60; public, 64, 66
Interest groups, 242–43, 256, 260, 266–67
Internal Revenue Code, 139, 356
Internal Revenue Service, 139
International Ladies' Garment Workers' Union, 37
Invitees, 194–96
Iran, 337–38
Irish, 4
Israel v. Wood Dolson Co., 363–65
Italians, 4, 125

Italy, 124
Ives v. South Buffalo Ry., 75–76

Jackson, Robert H., 149
Jacob & Youngs, Inc. v. Kent, 84–85
James, Henry, 15
Japan, 336–37, 370
Jefferson, Thomas, 7
Jehovah's Witnesses, 154–55
Jenad, Inc. v. Village of Scarsdale, 248
Jews and Judaism, 19, 21, 42, 48, 82, 232, 283–84; as victims of discrimination, 3–4, 14, 16, 26, 119, 128–29, 150, 152, 282, 313, 334–36; as Nazi victims, 38, 121–24; equality demanded by, 128, 154–64, 319; upward mobility of, 131–32, 166–67, 168, 171–73, 178, 183, 271–74, 289–90, 321, 326, 362; Hasidic, 159; Orthodox, 159
Johnson, Lyndon B., 276–78, 287
Joinder, of claims and parties, 363
Jones, Hugh R., 320
Jones v. Star Credit Corp., 80
Joseph Burstyn, Inc. v. Wilson, 211–12
Judgment, summary, 33–34, 62, 366; declaratory, 34–35, 37
Judiciary: legislation by, 54, 151, 188–90, 192; ethics of, 344–52
Jurisdiction, 37
Jurisprudence: sociological, 98; legal process, 146
Jury, trial by, 38–40, 102–3, 366–67

Kalman, Laura, 98
Kalmanash v. Smith, 181, 354–55
Kaufman, Irving, 357
Kellogg, Henry T., 22
Kelly v. Long Island Lighting Co., 197
Kennedy, Anthony M., 287
Kennedy, Robert F., 276–77, 279–81
Kennedy International Airport, 160
Kent, James, 23
Key, V. O., 242
Keynes, John Maynard, 121
Khe Sanh, 276
King, Martin Luther, Jr., 279–80
King, William A., 14
Kingsley International Pictures Corp. v. Regents, 213